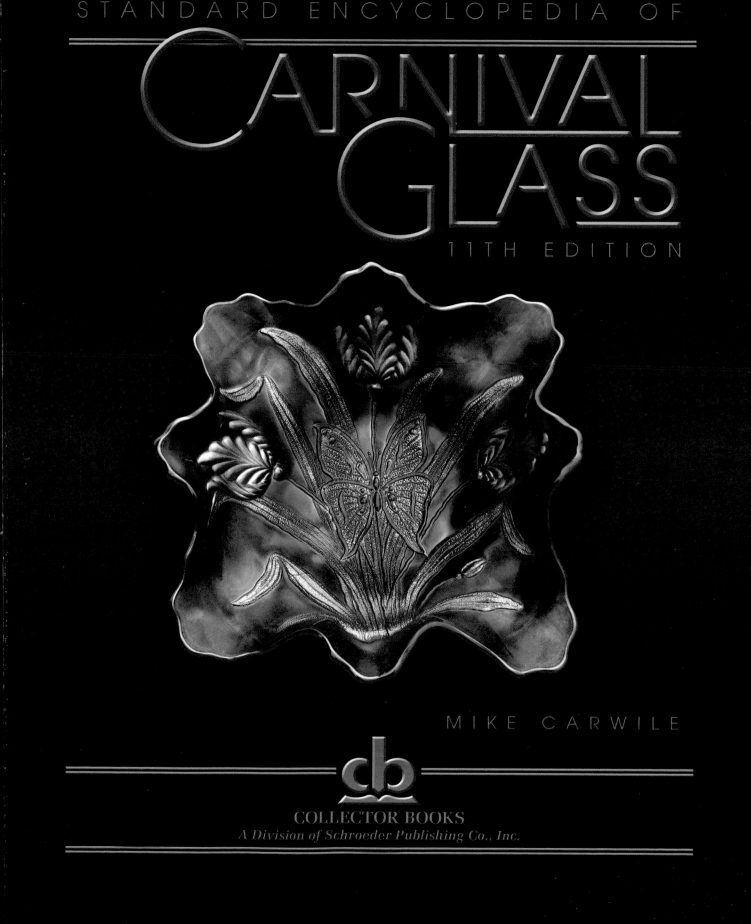

STANDARD ENCYCLOPEDIA OF

CARNIVAL GLASS

11TH EDITION

MIKE CARWILE

COLLECTOR BOOKS
A Division of Schroeder Publishing Co., Inc.

On the Front Cover
Dragon and Lotus bowl, blue, $100.00.
Butterfly and Tulip bowl, amethyst, $2,500.00.
Peacocks (On the Fence) bowl, blue, $600.00.

On the Back Cover
Horses' Heads bowl, green, $275.00.
Lion bowl, marigold, $115.00.
Dragon and Strawberry bowl, blue, $1,200.00.
Peter Rabbit ruffled bowl, marigold, $1,250.00.

Cover design ❖ *Beth Summers*   *Book design* ❖ *Terri Hunter*
Book layout ❖ *Barry Buchanan*

COLLECTOR BOOKS

P.O. Box 3009
Paducah, Kentucky 42002-3009

www.collectorbooks.com

Copyright © 2008 Mike Carwile

Mike Carwile
email: mcarwile@jetbroadband.com
180 Cheyenne Dr.
Lynchburg, VA 24502
Phone: 434-237-4247
If you would like a reply, please include a self addressed stamped envelope.

The current values in this book should be used only as a guide. They are not intended to set prices, which vary from one section of the country to another. Auction prices as well as dealer prices vary greatly and are affected by condition as well as demand. Neither the author nor the publisher assumes responsibility for any losses that might be incurred as a result of consulting this guide.

Searching for a Publisher?

We are always looking for people knowledgeable within their fields. If you feel that there is a real need for a book on your collectible subject and have a large comprehensive collection, contact Collector Books.

Proudly printed and bound in the
United States of America

Contents

Dedication

To Samantha Prince for providing me with many beautiful photographs for this book and especially the wonderful cover photos.

Acknowledgments

Many of the fine photos for this and previous books come from the generous auctioneers who specialize in carnival glass. I want to give a very special thanks to all of them; they allow me to use their photos, really making this book possible. They include Debra Jo and Kris Remmen, Mickey Reichel, Jan and Jim Seeck, David and Amy Ayers, Jim and Laurie Wroda, Tom Burns, and Bill Richards, father and son, Gateway Auctions, J & J Auctions and PA. Onsite Auction Co. Bless all of you.

In addition, I'd like to thank all the individuals who contribute information, photos, or other services. Thank you: Clint Arsenault, Karen and Allan Rath, Ray Rogers, George Webb, Peter Dahlin, Bob Smith, Carolyn Gregg, Robert Brown, Edgar Burney, Cindy Mackley, Irene Tyler, Gene Keefover, Dave Cotton, Roger Lane, Gary Roach, Darrell Long, Christine and Dennis Golden, Jenny Lowe, Kathy Mayfield, Darryl and Jolene Field, Jackie Peay, Josh Wilson, Rick Kojis, Dick Betker, Casy Rich, Ron Britt, Tom and Sharon Mordini, Bruce and Darcy Hill, Jerry and Cleo Kudlac, Bill and Sharon Mizell, Wayne Anderson, Doug Siska, Dustin Siska, Allen Bossoli, Alan Sedgwick, John and Rae Ann Calai, Mr. and Mrs. Bill Layne, Ray and Lynne Nagy, Joe DiRienzo, Marty Hoenig, J. P. and Melbalene Harbin, Cindy and Tom Joneson, Kristina Plomgren, Bob Smigal, Connie Wilson, Dorothy Harding, Candy Brockmeyer, Gerald Welsh, Patricia Caron, Connie Cook, Lawrence Vanderwerff, Fred Stubbe, Kenny and Connie Reynolds, Dee and Gary Perras, Charles Kmucha, Roger Barnes, Sharon Witcher, Rene Bettis, Gary and Sharon Vandevander, Lance Hilkene, Mary P. Hare, Margaret Yvonne Iley, Peter Baerwald, Chuck and Dianna Hollenbach, Samantha Prince, Mitchell Stewart, josh_eagle, forsale.org, Lucas Bidart "Gardelboys" from Argentina, Adriana Sanchez from la*tienda*loka Argentina, Luciano Dutari and Hernan Otranto in Argentina, a special thanks to Wayne Delahoy from Australia for providing the additions and corrections to some of the pattern names commonly used in Australia, and to anyone I may have overlooked.

Also, I'd like to express my gratitude to the carnival glass clubs and organizations that keep the information flowing and help so much in advancing the interest of collectors. These include, but are not limited to, the American Carnival Glass Association, the International Carnival Glass Association, Lincoln Land Carnival Glass Club, the Heart of America Carnival Glass Association, as well as all the state and district clubs, and Woodsland (www.cga).

A special thanks goes out to Jetbroadband.com in Rustburg, Virginia, for keeping me in touch with the world.

Finally, I'd like to give a huge thanks to Siegmar Geiselberger from Germany who has provided his vast knowledge of, and his research material pertaining to, non-American glass. Without it, much of the information on this wonderful glass from around the world would not be known.

Photos, catalog information, and other information used in this book, including any information obtained from the Internet is used with the permission of those who own the glass and/or the data.

Introduction

For the benefit of the novice, carnival glass is that pressed and iridized glass manufactured between 1905 and 1940. It was made by companies in the United States, England, France, Germany, Australia, Czechoslovakia, Sweden, Finland, Argentina, and various other parts of the world.

The iridization, unlike the costly art glass produced by Tiffany and his competitors, was achieved by a spray process on the surface of the glass before firing, thus, producing a very beautiful product at a greatly reduced cost, giving the housewife a quality product well within her budget. In addition, carnival glass was the last hand-shaped glass mass produced in America and remains as a beautiful reminder of the glassmaker's skill.

In this volume, I will show the variety of shapes and colors of carnival glass and will also attempt to define the patterns by manufacturer and put the entire field of carnival glass into one reference book for the collector. It is my hope that this effort will bring new interest to this truly beautiful glass and stimulate its growth as a collectible; and my only regret is a lack of space to show every known pattern.

The Basics of Carnival Glass Collecting

This section is primarily for those just starting a carnival glass collection but may also be of help to the intermediate collector as well.

First comes color. To tell the true color of a piece of carnival glass, hold the piece to a strong light; the base color you see is the color of the piece. The colors given off by the iridescence have little or nothing to do with the true color of the glass. Many have asked me to provide a color chart to aid beginners, but capturing glass colors on paper is nearly impossible. The best advice I can offer on color is to handle as much of this glass as you can, holding it to the light and observing; soon, colors will come naturally, at least the basic colors.

Next, perhaps I should discuss shapes. Bowls and plates are usually easy to understand, as are pitchers, tumblers, and vases; but even these have variations: bowls can be ruffled, unruffled (shallow unruffled bowls are called ice cream shape), deep, or shallow. Pitchers can be standard, smaller (milk pitcher), taller (tankard), or squat. Tumblers can be standard size, tall (lemonade), or small (juice), even as small as shot glasses. Vases can range from tiny 4" bud vases to monster 22" sizes called funeral vases. Vases may be straight topped, flared, or JIP (jack-in-the-pulpit) shaped with one side down and one side up. In addition there are table sets, consisting of a creamer, a sugar, a covered butter dish, and a spooner (this piece has no lid). There are decanters and stemmed goblets of several sizes; there are rose bowls, evident by the lips being pulled in equally around the top of the piece; candy dishes that have the rims flared out; and nut bowls that have the rim standing straight up. There are banana bowls that are pulled up on two sides, baskets that have handles, bonbons that have handles on opposite sides, and nappies with only one handle. In addition we have berry sets (small and large bowls that are deep and usually come with one large bowl and six small ones), orange bowls (large footed bowls that held fruit), handled mugs, and plates (these are shallow without any bowl effect, coming straight out from the base and no higher from base to rim than 2"). Specialized shapes include candlesticks, hatpins, hatpin holders (footed pieces with the rim turned in to hold hatpins), epergnes (pieces that hold flower lilies), card trays (flattened bonbons or nappies), toothpick holders, cracker and cookie jars with lids, stemmed compotes (or comports as they were originally called), hair receivers, powder jars with lids, as well as many novelties that include paperweights, animal novelties, and wall pocket vases. Finally we have punch sets, which consist of a punch bowl, standard or base, and matching cups. These are all the general shapes of carnival glass. In addition we have many specialty shapes that include light shades, beads, beaded purses, odd whimsey shapes of all sorts that have been fashioned from standard pieces, pintrays, dresser trays, pickle casters in metal frames, and bride's baskets likewise. The list of shapes is almost endless and the beginner should study these and ask other collectors about odd pieces they can't identify.

Now, let's talk briefly about the iridescence itself. By far the major portion of carnival glass items will be found with a satiny finish that has many colored highlights across the surface, like oil on water, but another very popular finish was developed by the Millersburg Company and used by all other makers in limited amounts. This is called "radium" finish and can be recognized by its shiny, mirror-like lustre on the surface. Often, with radium finish, the exterior of the piece has no iridization and the piece has a light, watery shine. Beyond that, some colors, especially pastels such as white, ice blue, and ice green, have a frosty look. This treatment is always satin, never radium. Finally, there is the addition of milky edge treatments that are called opalescent. Added to the marigold finish, this is called "peach opalescent" and with an aqua base color, it becomes "aqua opalescent." Other opalescent treatments with carnival glass are blue opalescent, amethyst opalescent, lime green opalescent, ice green opalescent, vaseline opalescent, and red opalescent.

Also of consideration are the many new color labels that have come about over the last few years. These are mostly shadings of primary or secondary colors; they are often hard to understand and even harder to describe. Here are a few: moonstone (opaque glass, not as dense as milk glass); clambroth (pale ginger ale color); black amethyst (nearly black glass iridized); horehound (a shade darker than amber); Persian blue (opaque, like moonstone but blue); smoke (grayish, with blue and gold highlights); teal (a mixture of blue and green); vaseline (a yellow/green); lavender (a pale amethyst); and lime (green with a yellow mix). Lastly, there are a handful of colors, now in vogue, that nobody seems to agree on a definition: colors such as Renniger blue, a smoky/teal/sapphirish blue, according to some! Have we carried all this too far? Of course, but it isn't in my hands to stop this proliferation of colors. I can only hope the above information proves helpful in some way. Remember, we are all learning and knowledge comes in time and with patience. The trip is worth the effort.

Carnival or Stretch Glass?

While the techniques used for carnival glass and stretch glass are very similar, the results have a very different appearance. Both are molded or pressed. Both are sprayed with a metallic salt solution to achieve the surface iridescence. Both were generally made at the same factories.

The main differences that set stretch glass apart from its carnival cousin is the lack of pattern, the obvious onion-skin look, and the time frame of production (stretch glass began about a decade after carnival glass and continued a few years after production of carnival glass ended). In addition, stretch glass was usually sprayed with the salts or "dope" and then shaped, while carnival glass was usually shaped before iridizing.

But despite all that has been said above, certain carnival patterns are known with a stretch appearance and many pieces of plain or patternless glass are found with no stretching whatsoever. It is for this reason we make only a token effort to separate patterns into either stretch or carnival absolutes in this book. In point of fact, it would be impossible since carnival collectors have been claiming stretch pieces as their own for decades and I have no intention of beginning a collectors' war with this book.

For those who are purists, I recommend they read *American Iridescent Stretch Glass* by John Madeley and Dave Shetlar. It is, by far, the best reference on stretch glass. Personally, I like both types of glass and have no qualms mixing them together on my shelves.

The Dugan and Diamond Story

When Harry Northwood sold his Indiana, Pennsylvania, glass business to the National Glass Combine, in 1899, returning to England as a National manager, Thomas E. Dugan became manager of the old Indiana plant. Two years later, Northwood had abandoned National, purchased the Hobbs, Brockunier factory in Wheeling, West Virginia, and established H. Northwood & Company.

In Indiana, the Dugans (Thomas and Alfred) operated the glass plant until 1904 when they purchased the factory and all assets (including old Northwood moulds) and the Indiana, Pennsylvania, plant became the Dugan Glass Company. They added several lines, experimented with formulae, and even started their own production of iridized glass. The Indiana plant continued in this manner until 1913, when for some unknown reason, both of the Dugans left the plant. The plant name was changed to the Diamond Glass Company, with John P. Elkin as president, H.W. Thomas as secretary, D.B. Taylor as treasurer, and Ed Rowland as plant manager. Many of the patterns continued, but others were soon added along with a host of new colors in iridized glass (some collectors feel the design quality of the Diamond production was in many ways inferior to the earlier lines, and I agree). The Diamond factory operated until 1931 when the plant was destroyed by fire.

The Fenton Story

First organized in April 1905, the Fenton Art Glass company didn't really materialize until the following July. At that time the glass decorating shop was opened in Martins Ferry, Ohio, in an abandoned factory rented by Frank L. Fenton and his brother, John (who was later to found the famous Millersburg Glass Company).

The next few months were occupied in obtaining financial backers and glassworkers, buying land to be plotted into lots as a money-raising venture, and constructing their own plant in Williamstown, West Virginia. At times, everything seemed to go wrong, and it wasn't until 1907 that the company was "on its way."

From the first, the design abilities of Frank Fenton were obvious, and each pattern seemed to bear his own special flair. He (along with Jacob Rosenthal who had come to the Fenton factory after fire had destroyed the renowned Indiana Tumbler and Goblet Company in Greentown, Indiana) was greatly responsible for sensing what the public admired in glass ornamentation.

In 1908 friction arose between the two brothers, and John exited to pursue his dreams in Millersburg, Ohio. By this time, the Fenton process of iridization had taken the mass-scale art glass field by storm and carnival glass was on its way.

For the next 15 years, the Fenton company would produce the largest number of patterns ever in this beautiful product, and huge amounts of iridized glass would be sent to the four corners of the world to brighten homes. While the company made other decorative wares in custard, chocolate glass, mosaic inlaid glass, opalescent glass, and stretch glass, nothing surpassed the quality and quantity of their iridized glass. Almost 150 patterns are credited to the company in carnival glass alone, and many more probably credited to others may be of Fenton origin.

All this is truly a remarkable feat, and certainly Frank L. Fenton's genius must stand along side Harry Northwood's as inspiring.

The Imperial Story

While the Imperial Glass Company of Bellaire, Ohio, was first organized in 1901 by a group of area investors, it wasn't until January 13, 1904, that the first glass was made; and not until nearly five years later the beautiful iridized glass we've come to call carnival glass was produced.

In the years between these dates, the mass market was sought with a steady production of pressed glass water sets, single tumblers, jelly jars, lamp shades, chimneys, and a full assortment of table items such as salt dips, pickle trays, condiment bottles, and oil cruets.

All of this was a prelude, of course, to the art glass field which swept the country, and in 1909, Imperial introduced their iridescent line of blown lead lustre articles as well as the Nuruby, Sapphire, and Peacock colors of carnival glass.

Quite evident then, as now, this proved to be the hallmark of their production. Huge quantities of the iridized glass were designed, manufactured, and sold to the mass marketplace across America and Europe for the next decade in strong competition with the other art glass factories. Especially sought was the market in England early in 1911.

In quality Imperial must be ranked second only to the fine glass produced by the Millersburg Company and certainly in design, it is equal to the great Northwood Company. Only the Fenton Company produced more recognized patterns and has outlasted them in longevity (the Imperial Glass Company became a subsidiary of the Lenox Company in 1973).

Along the way came the fabulous art glass line in 1916. This was an iridescent product often in freehand worked with a stretch effect. This is so popular today that many glass collectors have large collections of this alone.

In 1929 Imperial entered the machine glass era and produced its share of what has come to be called Depression glass. In the early 1960s, the company revived their old moulds and reproduced many of the old iridized patterns as well as creating a few new ones for the market that was once again invaded by "carnival glass fever." While many collectors purchased these items, purists in carnival glass collecting have remained loyal to the original and without question, the early years of carnival glass production at the Imperial Company will always be their golden years.duction at the Imperial Company will always be their golden years.

The Millersburg Story

While the techniques used for carnival glass and stretch glass are very similar, the results have a very different appearance. Both Interestingly enough, if John and Frank Fenton hadn't had such adverse personalities, there would have been no Millersburg Glass Company. Both brothers had come to the Martins Ferry, Ohio, area in 1903, to begin a glass business in partnership, but Frank was conservative and level-headed while John was brash and eager — a constant dreamer and the pitchman of the family. Each wanted to make a name in the business, and each wanted to do it his way.

By 1908 with the Fenton Art Glass Factory going strong, the clashes multiplied, and John went in search of a location for a plant of his own. He was 38, a huge strapping man with a shock of heavy brown hair and a pair of steely eyes that could almost hypnotize. He would sire five children.

After weeks of travel and inquiry, he came to Holmes County, Ohio, and was immediately impressed with the land and the people. Here were the heartland Americans whose families had come from Germany and Switzerland. They were hard workers like the Amish that lived among them, good businessmen who led simple lives.

Word soon spread that John Fenton wanted to build a glass plant, and the people welcomed him. By selling his interest in the Fenton plant and borrowing, John secured an option on a 54.7 acre site on the north edge of Millersburg. Lots were plotted and sold, and ground was broken on September 14, 1908. And like John Fenton's dreams, the plant was to be the grandest ever. The main building was 300' x 100', spanned by steel framing with no center support. A second building, 50' x 300', was built as a packing and shipping area as well as a tool shop. The main building housed a 14-pot furnace, a mix room, an office area, a lehr area, and a display area for samples of their production.

During construction, gas wells were drilled to supply a source of power, and stocks were sold in the company, totaling $125,000. On May 20, 1909, the first glass was poured. The initial moulds were designed by John Fenton and were Ohio Star and Hobstar and Feather. While at the Fenton factory, he had designed others, including the famous "Goddess of Harvest" bowl, a tribute to his wife. The glass that now came from the Millersburg factory was the highest quality of crystal and sample toothpick holders in the Ohio Star pattern were given to all visitors that first week.

In addition to the crystal, iridized glass in the Fenton process was put into production the first month in amethyst, green, and soft marigold. A third pattern — a design of cherry clusters and leaves — was added and soon sold well enough to warrant new moulds, bringing the Multi-Fruit and Flowers design into being as a follow-up pattern.

Early in January 1910 the celebrated radium process was born. It featured a softer shade of color and a watery, mirror-like finish on the front side of the glass only; it soon took the glass world by storm and became a brisk seller. Noted glassworker, Oliver Phillips, was the father of the process, and it was soon copied by the Imperial Company and others in the area.

In June of that same year, the famous Courthouse bowl was produced as a tribute to the town and to the workers who had laid the gas lines to the factory. These bowls were made in lettered, unlettered, radium, and satin finish and were given away by the hundreds at the factory, just as the crystal Ohio Star punch sets had been given to all the town's churches and social organizations, and the famous People's Vase was to be made as a tribute to the area's Amish.

During the next year the Millersburg plant was at its zenith, and dozens of new patterns were added to the line from moulds produced by the Hipkins Mold Company. They included the noted Peacock patterns as well as the Berry Wreath, Country Kitchen, Poppy, Diamond, Pipe Humidor, and Rosalind patterns. By late March 1911 Hipkins wanted pay for their work, as did other creditors, and John Fenton found his finances a disaster. The plant kept producing, but bankruptcy was filed, and Samuel Fair finally bought the works in October, renaming it the Radium Glass Company. In the next few months, only iridized glass in the radium process was produced while John Fenton tried to find a way to begin again.

But time soon proved Fair couldn't bring the factory back to its former glory, and he closed the doors, selling the factory and its contents to Frank Sinclair and the Jefferson Glass Company in 1913. Sinclair shipped many of the crystal and carnival moulds to the Jefferson plant in Canada for a production run there, which included Ohio Star, Hobstar and Feather, and Millersburg Flute. The rest of the moulds were sold for scrap despite the success of the patterns with the Canadians who bought the graceful crystal designs for several years. Jefferson's production at the Millersburg plant itself was brief. The known pieces include a 6" Flute compote just like the famous Millersburg Wildflower, marked "Crys-tal" with no interior pattern.

In 1919 the empty plant was again sold to the Forrester Tire and Rubber Company; the great stack was leveled and the furnace gutted. The Millersburg Glass factory was no more. But as long as one single piece of its beautiful glass is collected, its purpose will stand, and the lovers of this beautiful creation will forgive John Fenton his faults in business and praise his creative genius.

8

Word soon spread that John Fenton wanted to build a glass plant, and the people welcomed him. By selling his interest in the Fenton plant and borrowing, John secured an option on a 54.7 acre site on the north edge of Millersburg. Lots were plotted and sold, and ground was broken on September 14, 1908. And like John Fenton's dreams, the plant was to be the grandest ever. The main building was 300' x 100', spanned by steel framing with no center support. A second building, 50' x 300', was built as a packing and shipping area as well as a tool shop. The main building housed a 14-pot furnace, a mix room, an office area, a lehr area, and a display area for samples of their production.

During construction, gas wells were drilled to supply a source of power, and stocks were sold in the company, totaling $125,000. On May 20, 1909, the first glass was poured. The initial moulds were designed by John Fenton and were Ohio Star and Hobstar and Feather. While at the Fenton factory, he had designed others, including the famous "Goddess of Harvest" bowl as a tribute to his wife. The glass that now came from the Millersburg factory was the highest quality of crystal and sample toothpick holders in the Ohio Star pattern were given to all visitors that first week.

In addition to the crystal, iridized glass in the Fenton process was put into production the first month in amethyst, green, and soft marigold. A third pattern — a design of cherry clusters and leaves — was added and soon sold well enough to warrant new moulds, bringing the Multi-Fruit and Flowers design into being as a follow-up pattern.

Early in January 1910 the celebrated radium process was born. It featured a softer shade of color and a watery, mirror-like finish on the front side of the glass only; it soon took the glass world by storm and became a brisk seller. Noted glassworker, Oliver Phillips, was the father of the process, and it was soon copied by the Imperial Company and others in the area.

In June of that same year, the famous Courthouse bowl was produced as a tribute to the town and to the workers who had laid the gas lines to the factory. These bowls were made in lettered, unlettered, radium, and satin finish and were given away by the hundreds at the factory, just as the crystal Ohio Star punch sets had been given to all the town's churches and social organizations, and the famous People's Vase was to be made as a tribute to the area's Amish.

During the next year the Millersburg plant was at its zenith, and dozens of new patterns were added to the line from moulds produced by the Hipkins Mold Company. They included the noted Peacock patterns as well as the Berry Wreath, Country Kitchen, Poppy, Diamond, Pipe Humidor, and Rosalind patterns. By late March 1911 Hipkins wanted pay for their work, as did other creditors, and John Fenton found his finances a disaster. The plant kept producing, but bankruptcy was filed, and Samuel Fair finally bought the works in October, renaming it the Radium Glass Company. In the next few months, only iridized glass in the radium process was produced while John Fenton tried to find a way to begin again.

But time soon proved Fair couldn't bring the factory back to its former glory, and he closed the doors, selling the factory and its contents to Frank Sinclair and the Jefferson Glass Company in 1913. Sinclair shipped many of the crystal and carnival moulds to the Jefferson plant in Canada for a production run there which included Ohio Star, Hobstar and Feather, and Millersburg Flute. The rest of the moulds were sold for scrap despite the success of the patterns with the Canadians who bought the graceful crystal designs for several years. Jefferson's production at the Millersburg plant itself was brief. The known pieces include a 6" Flute compote just like the famous Millersburg Wildflower, marked "Crys-tal" with no interior pattern.

In 1919 the empty plant was again sold to the Forrester Tire and Rubber Company; the great stack was leveled and the furnace gutted. The Millersburg Glass factory was no more. But as long as one single piece of its beautiful glass is collected, its purpose will stand, and the lovers of this beautiful creation will forgive John Fenton his faults in business and praise his creative genius.

The Northwood Story

An entire book could be written about Harry Northwood, using every superlative the mind could summon and still fail to do justice to the man, a genius in his field. Of course, Harry had an advantage in the glass industry since his father, John Northwood, was a renowned English glassmaker.

Harry Northwood came to America in 1880 and first worked for Hobbs, Brockunier and Company of Wheeling, West Virginia, an old and established glass-producing firm. For five years, Harry remained in Wheeling, learning his craft and dreaming his dreams.

In 1886 he left Hobbs, Brockunier and was employed by the La Belle Glass Company of Bridgeport, Ohio, where he advanced to the position of manager in 1887. A few months later, a devastating fire destroyed much of the La Belle factory, and it was sold in 1888. Harry next went to work for the Buckeye Glass Company of Martin's Ferry, Ohio. Here he remained until 1896 when he formed the Northwood Company at Indiana, Pennsylvania. Much of the genius was now being evidenced, and such products as the famous Northwood custard glass date from this period.

In 1899 Northwood entered the National Glass Combine only to become unhappy with its financial problems, and in 1901 he broke away to become an independent manufacturer once again. A year later, he bought the long-idle Hobbs, Brockunier plant, and for the next couple of years, there were two Northwood plants.

Finally in 1904, Northwood leased the Indiana, Pennsylvania, plant to its managers, Thomas E. Dugan and W.G. Minnemeyer, who changed the name of the plant to the Dugan Glass Company. In 1913 the plant officially became known as the Diamond Glass Company and existed as such until it burned to the ground in 1931.

In 1908 Harry Northwood, following the success of his student, Frank L. Fenton, in the iridized glass field, marketed his first Northwood iridescent glass, and Northwood carnival glass was born. For a 10-year period carnival glass was the great American craze, and even at the time of Harry Northwood's death in 1919, small quantities were still being manufactured. It had proved to be Northwood's most popular glass, the jewel in the crown of a genius, much of it marked with the well-known trademark.

Other American Companies

Besides the five major producers of carnival glass in America, several additional companies produced amounts of iridized glass.

These companies include Cambridge Glass Company of Cambridge, Ohio; Jenkins Glass Company of Kokomo, Indiana; Westmoreland Glass Company of Grapeville, Pennsylvania; Fostoria Glass Company of Moundsville, West Virginia; Heisey Glass Company of Newark, Ohio; McKee-Jeannette Glass Company of Jeannette, Pennsylvania; and U.S. Glass Company of Pittsburgh, Pennsylvania.

The Cambridge Glass Company had a long and productive life (1901 – 1958), making many types of glass that included production of carnival glass beginning in 1908 with their "Near-Cut" lines. Patterns that were iridized include:

Horn of Plenty	Buzz Saw Cruet	Toy Punch Set
Double Star (Buzz Saw)	Inverted Feather	Near Cut Decanter
Tomahawk	Sweetheart (Marjorie)	Number 2351
Inverted Strawberry	Near-Cut Souvenir	Number 2635 (Snowflake)
Inverted Thistle		

The Jenkins Glass Company made only a handful of carnival glass patterns, mostly in the marigold color, and nearly all patterns in intaglio with a combination of flower and near-cut design. Their patterns include:

Cane and Daisy Cut	Stork Vase	Cut Flowers
Diamond and Daisy Cut	Oval Star and Fan	Stippled Strawberry

In the past few years, Westmoreland's contribution to carnival glass has been more widely recognized and many of their patterns that were once attributed to others have now been placed where they should be. These include:

Checkerboard	Orange Peel	Pearly Dots
Pillow and Sunburst	Shell and Jewel	Scales
Basketweave and Cable	Carolina Dogwood	Daisy Wreath
Corinth	Estate (Filigree)	Smooth Rays

Fruit Salad	Leaf Swirl	Louisa
Strutting Peacock	#294 or #295 (plain	Keystone Colonial
Footed Shell	breakfast sets, compotes)	

The Fostoria Company had two types of iridized glass. The first was their Taffeta Lustre line which included console sets, bowls, and candlesticks; the second was their Brocaded patterns which consisted of an acid cutback design, iridized and decorated with gold. These patterns include:

Brocaded Acorns	Brocaded Palms	Brocaded Daffodils
Brocaded Rose	Brocaded Summer Garden	

Heisey sold very few iridized items and those found have a light, airy lustre. Patterns include:

Heisey #357	Heisey Flute	Heisey Colonial
Heisey Tray Set	Paneled Heisey	

The McKee-Jeannette Company had a few carnival glass patterns as follows:

Aztec	Rock Crystal	Heart Band Souvenir
Hobnail Panels	Lutz	Plutec

The U.S. Glass Company was a combine headquartered in Pittsburgh. Their plants were usually designated by letters, making it nearly impossible to say which pattern came from which factory. Some patterns known to be from U.S. Glass include:

Beads & Bars	Cosmos and Cane	Feather Swirl
Golden Harvest	Shoshone (Diamond Sparkler)	Butterfly Tumbler
Palm Beach	Field Thistle	Daisy in Oval Panels

In addition to all the glass produced by these minor concerns, specialty glasshouses contributed their share of iridized glass in the large Gone with the Wind lamps, shades, chimneys, etc.; as well as minute amounts of iridized glass from Libby, Anchor-Hocking, Tiffin, DeVilbiss, Riverside, Hig-Bee, and Jeannette.

Non-American Carnival Glassmakers

Factories in Sweden, Finland, Denmark, Czechoslovakia, Holland, Mexico, France, Germany, and Argentina are now known to have produced some amount of iridized glass. While it would be impossible for us to catalog all these companies, I will list a few of the more prolific and their currently known patterns.

Germany

Since the appearance of the 62-page Brockwitz catalog that was unearthed by Bob Smith, I've been able to piece together a better picture of the carnival glass from Germany. Brockwitz opened in 1903 and the factory was indeed a huge concern with a veritable army of workers. By the late 1920s the factory was largest in Europe. In addition, I've learned that patterns shown in the Brockwitz catalog were also made by Riihimaki and Karhula of Finland and Eda of Sweden so it is possible Brockwitz sold or transferred some of their moulds to other concerns in Europe. Patterns shown in the Brockwitz catalog include Rose Garden, Curved Star (Cathedral), Moonprint (also thought to have been made in England), Lattice and Leaves, Footed Prism Panels, Sunflower and Diamond, Superstar, Daisy and Cane (Tartan), Diamond Cut Shields, Christ and Maria candlesticks (Saint), Draped Arcs, and Rose Band, as well as the Triple Alliance biscuit jar I show. Colors are primarily marigold or cobalt blue with the glass of a fine quality.

Finland

Carnival glass from Finland has been traced to two factories: Riihimaki Glass and the Karhula-Iittala factory. Riihimaki was established about 1911 or 1912 and began their production of iridized glass in the late 1920s. Patterns include Western Thistle, Grand Thistle, Drapery Variant, Moth (Firefly), Four Flowers, Tiger Lily Variant, Lustre Rose, Garland and Bows, Tulip and Cord, Starburst, Flashing Stars, Fir Cones, and Column Flower (Square Diamond). Colors are mostly marigold, blue, or amber. The Karhula-Iittala factory began their iridized production about 1932. Their patterns include Diamond Ovals (once believed to be from England), the Britt tumbler, Quilted Fans, and another version of the Curved Star pattern. In addition there appear to be some pieces of Fleur de Lis that are very close to the Inwald pieces. Colors are mostly marigold or cobalt blue.

Non-American Carnival Glassmakers

Czechoslovakia

As collectors, we all continue to learn more each year about iridized glass vase production in this region of Europe. The discovery of catalogs by Bob Smith and more recently by Siegmar Geiselberger in Germany have given me at least a partial list of items produced by Inwald, Rindskopf, and factories around the Gablonz area that made beads, hatpins, buttons, and jewelry. Production was greater than I ever suspected and continued from the early 1900s to the beginning of WWII (in some areas production resumed after the war and continues today).

Sweden

In 1920 five Swedish glassmakers came to America to learn the American process of glassmaking, spending two years at Durand Glass, then moving to Imperial, and later to Fenton. When they returned to Sweden they took the knowledge of iridized glassmaking and shared this knowledge throughout Sweden and Finland. Swedish and Finnish companies had a close relationship, and mould swapping between the two countries was fairly common. In addition, both areas bought and traded moulds with Brockwitz, and iridized glass became a production item well into the 1930s. Colors seem to be marigold or cobalt blue but amber is known in Finnish glass. Swedish patterns include Asters, Northern Lights (Star and Hobs), Sunflower and Diamond, Rose Garden, Curved Star (Lasse), Sunk Daisy (Amerika), and Kulor.

Holland (The Netherlands)

Some minor production of iridized glass seems to have occurred in the Netherlands by the Leerdam Glass Works. Production is said to date to the 1930s with much of the glass made for export. Patterns include the Meydam design, which I show in a covered butter dish. The coloring of the known pieces is soft marigold, similar in many respects to glass made in England.

France

Little information about iridized glass from France is known but I do know of pieces that are marked "Made in France" or just "France." I show a small bowl called French Grape and the beautiful Fircone vase is from France. The bowl is a clear iridized piece with a vaseline flashing while the rare vase is in marigold. Future research is bound to turn up more patterns from France and only time will tell the complete story.

Argentina

Three glass companies produced iridized glass in Argentina. These were the Cristalerias Rigolleau S.A. (a company founded by Leon Rigolleau in Buenos Aires and maker of both the Beetle ashtray and the CR ashtray); Cristalerias Papini of Buenos Aires; and Cristalerias Piccardo. The companies were all nationalized in the 1940s and only the Rigolleau and Papini companies are still in business. (The latter is now called Cristalux, and it no longer produces iridized glass.) In addition, Argentina imported glass from the U.S., Finland, Sweden, Czechoslovakia, and England. Cristalerias Papini patterns include the Goodyear ashtray, the Industria Argentina Star pattern, as well as some European patterns that include Jacobean, Princeton, and Curved Star. Cristalerias Piccardo patterns include Graceful (aka Fantasia), Band of Roses, and a rare pitcher called Imperial (it has matching goblets and resembles the Octagon pattern). Finally, many patterns of U.S. Glass (The States, Ominbus, and Rising Sun) have shown up in Mexico and South America and are suspect.

Mexico

Glass production in Mexico began in the early 1900s with the Vitro Company of Vidriera, Monterrey, producing glass for beer bottles and continuing with an expansion when American companies began supplying natural gas for glass production in the 1920s. Other companies arose, one of which was Cristales Mexicanos, a producer of household glass and dinnerware. Here, iridized glass seems to have been concentrated and production continued for several years. Patterns include Oklahoma, Ranger, and the Votive Light piece.

Peru

While there has been little documentation of glass from Peru, I know the 9½" bottle called Inca was made there (it bears the lettering: "Huaco de Oro Peruano") and another bottle of the same design is imprinted on the base: "Vina Santa Josefa... Imitation Moderna. SEH...2171." All of the Inca bottles reported to date were produced by Hartinger Peru and the number of variations is estimated to be between six and ten. See the section later in this edition, Inca Bottle Variations, for additional information and lettering.

China

When I first showed the Shanghai tumbler two years ago, I thought it was perhaps just a one-shot move toward iridized glass from China but since then I've found other tumblers including one called Golden Triangle and another called Snow Chrysanthemum, as well as the Etched Vine tumbler. Markings may say, "Shanghai," "China," or "Made in China." Most have a #4 on the base. I believe these were all made in the 1930s prior to WWII. In addition, I've been told that some items in iridized glass may have been made in Indonesia including versions of an iridized Buddha (probably made for export). Obviously I have no proof of this but hope future research will give me the facts. Rumors also persist about glass from the Philippines but I have no evidence of any at this time.

India

When I first learned about the products of the Jain Glass Works, I felt I'd covered the subject, but through long correspondence with Vikram Bachhawat, I've learned there were indeed more than 20 glassmakers in India following World War II. Jain was simply one of the prominent ones. Others include Paliwal Glass Works and Agarwal Glass Works. Since I see pieces that are signed AVM and CB, I still have much to learn. Jain was founded in 1928 and at one time employed some 2,500 workers. It closed in 1986.

English Carnival Glass

Once iridized pressed glass became a success in the United States and American makers began to export this product, glassmakers in Britain soon began to look at this product as something they could produce. Sowerby had been in the business of making fine glass since the 1850s and soon rose to the task producing such patterns as the Sowerby Drape vase, the Diving Dolphin footed bowls, the Daisy Block Rowboat, the Covered Swan and Covered Chick (Hen), Pineapple (Pineapple and Bows), Pinwheel, Derby, Wickerwork, Flora, African Shield, Cane and Scroll (Sea Thistle), English Hob and Button (aka Chunky), Lea and the variants, and Royal Swans. Sowerby also copied the Imperial Scroll Embossed pattern and used it in several ways including the interior of their Diving Dolphins pieces.

In addition, other smaller glass firms made some limited carnival glass. These include Molineux, Webb of Manchester, Crystal Glass in Knottingley, Yorkshire, the Canning Town Glass Works Ltd., and Walsh of Birmingham. English carnival glass began in the 1920s and continued throughout the 1930s with many pieces that equal or exceed U.S. quality. Colors were primarily marigold or cobalt blue, but amethyst, amber, aqua, and scarce green are known.

Australian Carnival Glass

The Australian Crystal Glass Company Limited was established in 1914 and was making carnival glass by 1922. Most of the well-known patterns from this company began in 1924 in bowls, compotes, salvers, and vases. The product was mostly pressed moulded and the main colors were marigold or purple, however a bottle green treatment with amber iridescence is known in an Emu bowl and an ice blue with flashed marigold is reported. Patterns known from Australia are:

Swan	Feathered Flowers	Petals and Cane
Heavy Banded Diamonds	Flannel Berry	Rose Panels
Blocks and Arches	Flannel Flower	S Band (Broken Chain)
Bull Rush and Orchids	Hobnail and Cane	Star and Drape
Butterflies and Bells	Kangaroo & variants	Style
Butterflies and Waratah	Kingfisher & variants	Threads
Butterfly Bower	Kiwi	Shrike (Thunderbird, Piping Shrike)
Butterfly Bush	Kookaburra & variants	Water Lily & Dragonfly
Crystal Diamonds	Magpie & variants	Wild Fern
Emu (also called Ostrich)	Pin Ups	

Old Trademarks

Over the years there have been many requests for information about carnival glass trademarks and while this section will be old news to seasoned collectors, it may just help beginners avoid costly purchases they will regret. If it saves just one from mistaking reproductions for old carnival, the effort is well worth it. Northwood, Imperial, Cambridge, Dugan-Diamond, McKee, Higbee, Jeannette, Sowerby (England), and Cristales de Mexico (Mexico) are the trademarks on old glass that collectors will see. All these companies marked at least a part of their production. The dates for marking vary and range from 1904 to 1939, depending on the company's lifespan and when they first started marking glass.

On the other hand, many well-known glassmakers never marked old glass. These include Fenton, Millersburg, U.S. Glass, Fostoria, Indiana, and others. Fostoria and Fenton used paper labels on their products and over the years these have been washed off. Others depended on advertising to identify their product and marked the packaging. Now let's take a look at the most often seen old glass markings.

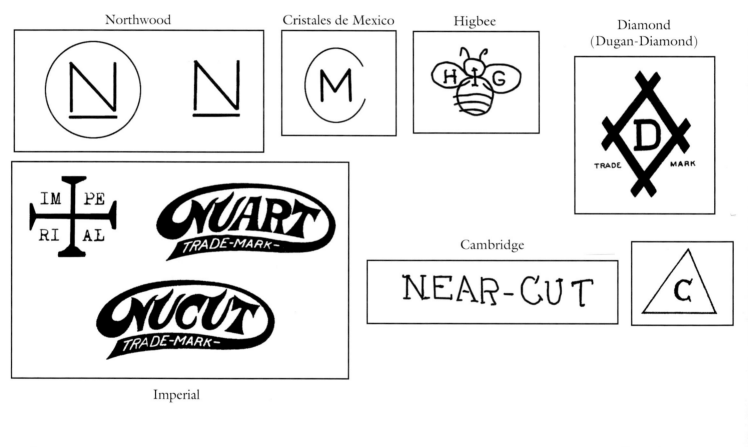

Northwood

Cristales de Mexico

Higbee

Diamond
(Dugan-Diamond)

Imperial

Cambridge

NEAR-CUT

Jeannette

On some pieces of Aurora Pearls, there is a trademark.

Sowerby

Jain Glass Works of Firozabad, India

JAIN

McKee

PRES-CUT

14

New glass trademarks generally fall into two categories: marks intended to appear close enough to old, well-known trademarks to fool buyers; or completely new trademarks that bear no resemblance to old markings. Here are some of each, all familiar to many carnival glass collectors and dealers. Remember, the old Northwood trademark is owned by the American Carnival Glass Association; the purchasing of this trademark was done to keep it from being copied and the hard work of this organization has stopped many dishonest attempts at copying. The A.C.G.A. has to be commended for their efforts but as you can see from the first two modern markings, clever attempts to deceive weren't completely stopped. Here are the most often found new marks:

L.G. Wright

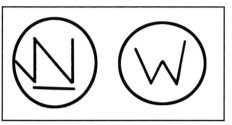

This trademark, often found on many patterns that were made in old carnival, is an obvious attempt to fool the buyer into believing the product is old Northwood and has caused great confusion over the years.

Boyd

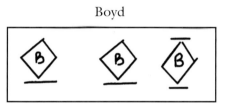

Boyd is currently using this mark on many types of glass including carnival as well as making some items that are not marked.

Smith Glass Company   Summit Glass Company

Mosser

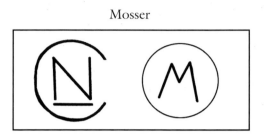

Once again, an attempt to deceive the buyer into thinking the product was Northwood. This mark is even more deceptive than the Wright mark and can be found on Northwood patterns that were also made in old glass. *Beware!* In addition, Mosser has a third mark, consisting of an "M" inside the outline of the state of Ohio. All three marks can be found on new carnival glass as well as other types of glass.

Fenton

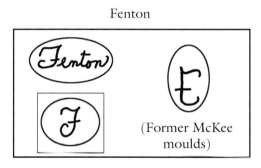

(Former McKee moulds)

The Fenton Company has been the most responsible glasshouse as far as marking their new glass reproductions. Beginning in 1971 virtually every piece of glass from the Fenton factory has been marked and they are to be complimented.

Imperial (1951 – 1972) Imperial Glass Liquidation Corp (1973 – 1981) Imperial Glass (Lorch Ownership) (1981 – 1982)

The Imperial Company began using their "IG" logo on reissue patterns in 1951. They marked most of their products until the liquidation in 1973 when a large "L" was added to the trademark. In 1981 Arthur Lorch bought the company and added an "A" to the mark. In 1982 Lorch sold the firm to Robert Stahl who declared bankruptcy in 1984 and closed the plant in 1985. Moulds were sold off. Some came to Summit Glass and are still in production. In addition other firms bought moulds including Rosso. Their trademark is an "R" in a keystone shape.

Many companies are making new carnival from old moulds or creating new moulds never found in old glass production. The Indiana Glass Company of Dunkirk, Indiana, has revived some of their old patterns and created new ones. Their large production of geometric patterns in red carnival and the copycat version of the Imperial 474 vase in red have caused unexperienced collectors concern. Hardly a week goes by I don't hear from someone who bought these as old glass. Another small concern is the copying old patterns in carnival and opalescent glass without marking them in any way. So please be cautious; buy only what you know is authentic. If a pattern shape or color not listed in this book shows up in a mall booth, it is probably not old. Toothpick holders, table set pieces, and water set pieces seem to be the most copied shapes but there are bowl copies flooding the stands from the east, especially Taiwan and Hong Kong. Many Northwood, Fenton, and other company patterns are among these, so beware!

Grading Carnival Glass

A frequent question is "What is my carnival glass item worth?" On the other side of the coin is "My piece is worth $75 because that is the book price." In this section I will attempt to deal with both of these issues to give readers (especially beginners) a better understanding of how to judge a piece of carnival glass and to determine a reasonable value. In doing this, I've chosen a simple and plentiful pattern called Windflower to make the points. It is often said a piece of carnival glass is only worth what someone is willing to pay for it and this is true. However, the beginning collector as well as the majority of shop and mall dealers rely on book prices and this can be a disaster unless they use a process of grading the glass before they buy (collectors) or sell (dealers). Experience is always the best teacher. You must handle as much glass as possible, read all the books, attend auctions and glass conventions, and join as many glass clubs as your budget will allow. If possible, talk with seasoned collectors before you invest. You will soon learn that the quality of iridescence, base color, shape, desirability, and rarity of a piece of glass are the keys to its value. Of course, the condition is equally important. Does it have a small chip, a flea bite, a medium or large chip, are there carbon streaks, heat separations, a hairline crack, or a major crack? The list of damages goes on, and damage always lowers price, regardless of how rare an item is. It is nearly impossible to cover prices for damaged glass but as a general rule damaged glass will bring about 10 – 30% of mint condition glass. For example, a Windflower bowl in marigold with 10 ruffles with average iridescence in mint condition will bring about $30 while the same bowl with a small chip may sell in the $10 – 20 range or with a crack will usually bring $5 – 10. On the other hand, the same bowl with superb iridescence with no damage may go as high as $50.

On the following pages the Windflower pattern is shown in several shapes, colors, quality of iridescence, and various edge treatments to help you understand a bit more about grading. The most common shapes shown are the 8- and 10-ruffled bowls. I also show the less common 6-ruffled examples, the ice cream shape bowls, the rare deep round bowl, and the rare plate shape. Colors most often found are marigold, amethyst, or blue. Colors like lavender, horehound, amber, black amethyst, smoke, and smokey-blue are scarce and demand a higher price regardless of shape. Considering this, the following examples may help.

A Windflower bowl with 10 ruffles in average iridescence in marigold will probably bring $30 on a good day. The same bowl with poor iridescence can go for about $15, and with superb iridescence, about $50. A Windflower bowl in ice cream shape or 6 ruffles with average iridescence will bring a bit more or about $35, while the same bowl with poor iridescence will bring $15 – 20, and one with superb iridescence about $60 – 65. A 10-ruffle bowl in amber, a rare color, will bring about $100 with average iridescence, about $60 – 70 with poor iridescence, and about $125 with superb iridescence. Just remember that a price guide is only a guide and every bowl in that color doesn't fit the price listed. To publish a price guide with complete value grading would take untold hours to do and would be so large the average person wouldn't be able to lift it. Experience is the key to pricing.

I hope these explanations will help clear up some of the questions, especially for beginners, as far as grading carnival glass, and will make you more comfortable when buying carnival glass, whether for your own collection or for resale in a shop or mall. Just remember prices are not etched in stone whether they come from a book with a price for each item or from books that give price ranges. Following are a few examples of the Windflower pattern in all its various shapes, colors, and gradings. I'd like to thank Mr. and Mrs. Jerry Kudlac for sharing a portion of their Windflower collection to illustrate these points.

deep round bowl marigold (rare shape)

10 ruffle marigold (average iridescence)

10 ruffle amethyst (superb)

ice cream bowl light marigold (poor)

6 ruffle marigold (superb)

ice cream shape amethyst (superb)

ice cream shape "pink" (rare color)

10 ruffle pastel lavendar (poor) rare color

10 ruffle ox blood (a rare purple-red color)

10 ruffle smoky blue (very rare color)

10 ruffle smoke with satin finish (rare color)

10 ruffle blue (superb finish)

flat plate cobalt blue
(rare with superb iridescence)

Feet and Base Identification

After being asked by beginners; what is meant by collar base, dome base, and many other base types of various distinctions, I have decided to add a photo illustrated section on identifying different types of bases and feet found on carnival glass pieces. The following illustrations should clear up many of these questions. Thanks again to Samantha Prince for the photo illustrations.

collar base

collar base, eight sided

dome base, footed

ball footed

scroll footed

spatula footed

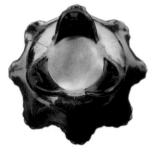

bracket footed

bracket footed, decorative

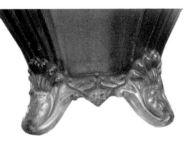

twig footed

stemmed compote

stemmed vase

ball and claw footed

Inca Bottle Variations

I decided to include this short section concerning the various Inca bottles that have come on the scene in recent years, specifically because I felt a need to explain the reason behind their chosen names as well as to allow readers to get a look at some of the varieties in a group photo.

You will notice in this edition that I only show four variations and all have their own names, as opposed to being Variant #1 and Variant #2, etc. This was done at the request of the owners of the three that came in after the first Inca bottle was shown, who wanted to name the patterns, and I have honored their request. The main reason being, I can't see having six to ten variants in future editions and ending up with ten different variant names. Somehow, Inca bottle variant #10 doesn't sound too pleasing to me, and besides, where would it all end if other variants showed up in the future.

The following is what I have found out to date concerning these interesting bottles; the regular Inca bottle pattern I show can be found with various labels and embossing. Some will have "Huaco De Oro Peruano" on a paper label, some will have a second label with "Industria Peruano," some will have "Imitacion Moderna," and others might have "Industria Argentina" on the label. Then, if that's not confusing enough, some will be embossed on the bottom with "Vina Santa Josefa, Ind. Peruana, Reg. IND-8067, SHE-2171, Imitacion Moderna," which is what is embossed on the second bottle I show called Inca Sun bottle. Then we move to the third example sent to me, the Huaco De Oro bottle which has a paper label with "Huaco De Oro – Peruano" on it.

Are you with me so far? Well, lets complicate this a bit more. We now come to the fourth bottle I'm showing in this book, and the newest edition, the Peruvian Pisco Inca bottle. This particular variation has two paper labels. The front label says, "Pisco Peruano Anejo" while the back label has "Huaco Peruano." Next is the embossing on the bottom which reads "Vina Santa Josefa // Ind. Peruana."

One collector has told me that some of these bottles contained grape juice and another collector has said that they contained wine, which from the looks of the bottles, the latter sounds correct to me.

They were all made by Hartinger Peru and can be found throughout Peru, Argentina, and Brazil, and also they have filtered through to other countries as well.

Most of the information contained here is courtesy of Clint Arsenault, Adriana Sanchez in Argentina, and Wayne Delahoy of Australia. The photo is from the collection of Clint Arsenault. Also, in memory of a special Inca bottle collector, Christa Karas. You will be sadly missed.

From the collection of Clint Arsenault.

Millersburg "Peacock" Variations

Many collectors, especially beginners, are often puzzled by all the variations in the peacock designs from Millersburg. Why so many is certainly a mystery and I'd have to get into John Fenton's psyche to understand his reasoning; but beyond that I feel these variations need discussing again from time to time.

First is Millersburg Peacock. It is the easiest to remember since it has no bee and no beading on the urn. The top of the urn is flared with scalloping rather than banding. Shapes are large and small bowls and a small plate (made from the small bowl). A small proof bowl is also known with part of the feet missing, but these are scarce. In addition, shapes include tri-cornered bowls, rose bowls, banana bowls, and a spittoon whimsey shape. Bowls can also be ice cream shaped, evenly flared, or ruffled.

Next is the Millersburg Peacock and Urn pattern. It is found in both large and small bowls (ice cream shaped, ruffled, three-in-one edged), a large stemmed compote, and a chop plate. Pieces have a small bee by the beak of the bird, and examples are found with beading at the top of the column and the top of the urn, or with no beading at all.

The third example is the Mystery Peacock pattern. It is found with a larger bee and beads at the top of the urn and at the top of the column. It has been found in large bowls, but a rare small bowl has been reported but not confirmed. The key to the design is the saucer-like plate the urn rests on before it flares out to join the column. Shapes are ruffled, three-in-one, or ice cream.

The bowl shown here is known as the "Shotgun" bowl or Millersburg's Peacock Variant. It is distinguished by the absence of a true urn with only the suggestion of a flat bowl. These bowls are normally about 7½" in diameter and are mostly found with a three-in-one crimping but here is a six-ruffled bowl and I've seen an ice cream shaped 5½" bowl in green.

Finally, here is the Peacock and Urn Variant pattern. It is found (so far) only on amethyst sauce bowls measuring about 6". It has a bee, three rows of beads, and four tail feathers. It is rare like so many of the Millersburg Peacock pieces, with less than a dozen reported.

Remember, all Millersburg Peacock pieces have a wide panel exterior with some sort of rayed base (there are variations), and all have gently arced or scalloped edges rather than the sawtooth edge found on Fenton Peacock and Urn pieces. Finishes are both satin and radium, depending on the pattern.

Patterns

Abalone Shade

This shell shade with a nice pearl iridescent finish looks like it may have just been picked up at the beach. The reverse rim has the lettering, "Pat. Pend." "Conneaut." It is a real beauty of a shade indeed. Thanks to Ron Britt for sharing it.

Absentee Dragon

If you take a close look at this very rare 9" plate, you will see it is very different from the Dragon and Berry pattern it resembles. It is a top rarity in Fenton glass. It has a Bearded Berry reverse pattern, and the color is excellent. It was, no doubt, an experimental piece. Two examples are known.

Absentee Fern (Plume)

This rare, one-of-a-kind piece, showing only the butterflies before the ferns were added, is apparently the prototype for the Butterfly and Fern pitcher. Thanks to Jim and Jan Seeck for sharing this rarity.

Absentee Miniature Blackberry Variant

Marion Hartung called this the "Miniature Wide Panel compote" but most collectors know it by the Absentee Variant title. It is simply the Miniature Blackberry piece without the interior design. Hartung also said the examples she had seen all had twisted stems. But as you can see the one shown has the regular stem, so two types must exist. At any rate, this piece is about 2½" tall with a top diameter of 4½". Besides marigold, amethyst and green are known and I certainly wouldn't rule out white.

Acanthus (Imperial)

First advertised in 1911 as Imperial's #465, this very fluid pattern can be found on both bowls and plates. The bowls are either round or ruffled and measure 8" – 9". They are found in marigold, green, purple, aqua, clambroth, and cobalt blue. Plates are from the same mould and measure 10". They are known in marigold, clambroth, or smoke. Shown is an amethyst bowl with fantastic finish.

Acorn (Fenton)

This realistic design was originally Fenton's #835 pattern and is found mostly in bowls of all shapes and a few very rare plates. Colors are marigold, green, cobalt blue, amethyst, red, vaseline, ice blue, amber, amber opalescent, lime, teal, celeste blue, moonstone, peach opalescent, amberina, and a few others in bowls. Amethyst, marigold, cobalt blue, and white plates have been reported, some with damage. You can probably count the total number of plates on two hands with room to spare. The white plate shown is the only reported example to date.

Acorn (Millersburg)

What a shame the Millersburg company didn't make this realistic design in other shapes. The compote is one of the best designed in all of carnival glass with realistic acorns and leaves, an exterior of flute, and the typical Millersburg clover base. Colors are marigold, amethyst, green, and a rare vaseline.

Acorn Burrs

Acorn Burrs, one of Northwood's premier patterns from around 1911, is found in a berry set, water set, table set, whimsey vase (from the tumbler), and a punch set. Colors are many and include marigold, amethyst, and green in all pieces except the vase, white, ice blue, ice green, lime green, aqua opalescent, and cobalt blue in the punch set. Thanks to Bruce Hill I am happy to show a superb tumbler in wisteria.

Acorn Vase

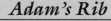

While some collectors believe this is a U.S. Glass pattern, others feel it may well be from Millersburg. At any rate, it is a rare item, standing 5⅜" tall. Colors known are marigold, amethyst, green, and the vaseline shown, but only one vase in each color has been confirmed.

Adam's Rib

Adam's Rib was made by the Diamond Glass Company (their #900 pattern) in the mid-1920s. It can be found in ice green, celeste blue, and marigold (the console bowl is also known in marigold-over-milk glass). Shapes include a lemonade pitcher and mug, covered candy jar, 10" vase (shown), candlesticks, a large footed console, a fan vase, a compote, open sugar, a large bowl, and probably a creamer.

African Shield

This small vase shape originally had a wire flower holder that held the stems of freshly cut blossoms in a neat arrangement. It is 2⅞" tall and 3¼" wide at the top. It is made by Sowerby. Marigold is the only color reported so far.

Age Herald

This famous advertising pattern, known to have come from the Fenton factory, is found only in amethyst. Both bowls and plates are known. The pattern was designed as a give-away item from the well-known Birmingham, Alabama, newspaper. The exterior pattern is a wide panel.

Allan's Rings

This neat little cracker jar is courtesy of Karen and Allan Rath who tell me it comes from Germany. It has a Depression era look about it, so I suspect it was from the 30s or possibly early 40s, but can't be sure without additional information. The iridescence is very good and the hardware suits the piece quite well. Anyone who can shed light on this item is urged to contact me.

Alternating Dimples

This squat vase is eight sided and every other side is dimpled. The coloring is a fine clambroth. The neck is crimped then flared out at the top with dimples all around and the bowl has fine enameled flowers between the dimpled sections. Anyone with more information on this piece is requested to contact me.

Aman (India)

Aman is from India, and was named by Vikram Bachhawat who has so generously shared photos of so much of his Indian glass. Shown are a 6½" pitcher and the matching 3¾" tumbler in marigold.

Amaryllis

Amaryllis was once firmly thought to be by Northwood, now some questions have been raised and it is thought to more than likely be by Diamond. It is found on a small compote (ruffled, triangular, or deep round) and a plate shape from the same mould. Production seems to be from 1912, in marigold, amethyst, cobalt blue, and white. The exterior is a pattern carnival collectors call Poppy Wreath and opalescent glass collectors call Thistle Patch. Despite all the controversy, Marion Hartung long ago reported seeing a crystal version of this compote with the Northwood mark.

American

The American pattern was one of Fostoria's most important crystal patterns, and it is no surprise to also find it among their iridized items. The footed tumbler shown is slightly taller than most tumblers.

AMV Hand Vase (India)

If you compare this Indian hand vase to the others shown, you will see there are differences in style and pattern. This one is marked "AMV," and according to Vikram Bachhawat, this was one of several competitors of Jain Glass Works. Other competitors included Paliwal Glass Works, Agarwal Glass, and CB Works.

Andean Cherries

This well designed tumbler named by Bob Smith can be found in a Rindskopf catalog as their #2201 and certainly is a must for tumbler collectors.It has rich marigold iridescence and no other colors have been reported to date. Thanks to the Rath's for sharing the photo.

Angoori (India)

This Indian tumbler from Vikram Bachhawat is marked "AGW." Vikram tells me this probably stands for Agarwal Glass Works. The beautiful marigold tumbler is 5¾" tall.

Apple and Pear Intaglio

Like its cousin Strawberry Intaglio, this rather rare bowl is a product of the Northwood Company and is seen mostly in crystal or goofus glass. The example shown measures 9¾" in diameter and is 2¾" high. The glass is ½" thick!

Apple Blossom (Diamond)

Made late in the Diamond Glass production (1928 – 1930), this design is well known by collectors. It is quite available in 6" – 7" diameter marigold bowls. It can also be found in bowls in amethyst, white, green, cobalt blue, and the rare marigold over Afterglow (Diamond's pink glass) shown. In addition, the rose bowl shape is known in marigold. Plates have long been reported but most turn out to be a low ruffled bowl.

Apple Blossom (Enameled) (Northwood)

This rather scarce Northwood enameled water set has large enameled flowers in shades of yellow and orange on a stem with three pale green leaves above and two larger leaves below. The glass color is cobalt blue and the iridescence is usually quite good. There is also a little known berry set in the same pattern and color that is quite rare.

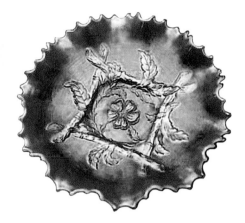

Apple Blossom Twigs

This is a simple design of a central apple blossom.
with four overlapping twigs that form a square around it. It is found on bowls that can be ruffled or ice cream shape and plates with either a smooth or serrated edge. The plate may also be whimsied into a banana bowl shape. Colors are marigold, purple, amethyst, lavender, peach opalescent, blue, celeste blue, green, smokey lavender, or white. Apple Blossom Twigs is a Dugan pattern and has the Big Basket-weave exterior.

Apple Panels

Apple Panels is an intaglio pattern found only in the breakfast set shown so far. The design consists of two panels with an apple, stem, and leaves; these are separated by panels of hob-stars and fans. Colors are marigold and green but others may someday surface.

Apple Tree (Fenton)

First made in 1912 (Fenton's #1561), this well-known design is found in crystal, milk glass, and carnival glass. Only water sets are found in the latter (the pitcher turns up in several treatments as a vase whimsey). Carnival colors are marigold, cobalt blue, white, and a rare marigold over milk glass that was made in a limited 1915 run.

April Showers (Fenton)

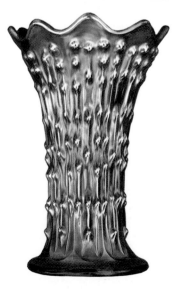

This was Fenton's #412 pattern, made first in 1911. The vase has many similarities to their Rustic design but the hobs are in bunches on April Showers and patterned evenly on Rustic. April Showers sometimes has an interior pattern of Peacock Tail, as in the one shown. Colors are marigold, amethyst, green, cobalt blue, and white. The green example shown is a desirable 7" squat size.

A-Q Perfume

This perfume stands 4" tall and has enameling as shown. On the bottom, lettering reads "WARRANTED-UNBREAKABLE COVERED THREAD." In the center is a circle that reads "A-Q." Any additional information readers may have would be appreciated. Thanks to the Hamlets for this interesting item.

Aramis (Dunbar)

This unusual water set was made in 1936 by the Dunbar Glass Company in marigold, smoky blue, pastel marigold, and flashed cranberry. There are two different pitchers known. One is a squatty pitcher; the other, a tankard, is shown. Tumblers are known in at least three sizes.

Aramis Variant

Since I showed the Aramis water set by Dunbar Glass, I felt it would be a good idea to show the variant shape in the pitcher (the tumblers are the same for both sets and are found in three sizes). Colors for the variant are primarily marigold but examples in smoky blue or flashed cranberry are also known. Date of production was 1936.

Arched Flute (Fenton)

Produced in the early 1920s, these scarce toothpick holders stand 2¾" tall and have a stem, dome base, and six fluted panels. Colors are Wisteria (lavender), Florentine green (ice green), and celeste blue, with other colors possible such as topaz, Velva rose (pink), and Persian pearl (white). Fenton called these "pen holders" but most collectors feel they really are toothpick holders.

Arched Panels

Similar to both Portland and Long Buttress, this pattern is shown in the last Hartung book in a tumbler shape where she speculates there must be a pitcher to match. Here it is and the Arched Panels name is confirmed by Kamm in the second *Pattern Glass Pitchers* book. The coloring is a soft marigold but Hartung says there is also a pastel blue known in tumblers.

Arcs (Imperial)

The Arcs pattern was first advertised in 1910, and is found as the exterior pattern on some Imperial bowls like Pansy, Star of David, and Cobblestones. Colors are those of the primary patterns and include marigold, purple, green, clambroth, smoke, blue, amber, powder blue, and emerald green. Arcs is often confused with Scroll Embossed by beginning collectors because it is a similar design and was also made by Imperial.

Argentina Blossom

This beautiful inkwell is marked "Cristolerias Rigolleau," so it was certainly made by that company in Argentina. It has unopened blossoms and leaves with a very rich iridescence. Thanks to Gary Vandevander for sharing it with me.

Argentina Ribbed Barrel

These tumblers were found in Argentina and are marked "NCP" on the base. They are not the same as the #660 Barrel tumblers shown in the Christalerias Papini catalog, however, so they may well be from a glassmaker outside Argentina. Any information readers have would be appreciated.

Argentine Honey Pot

This 6" tall jar or pot holds 1½ pints and has a very interesting design with a honeycomb on the lower portion and "dripping honey" above. It was purchased in Argentina and I have no other information about it. The coloring is rich and dark and the mould work excellent.

Asters

Found on a rose bowl shape, a 12" chop plate (shown), and a 7" compote, this very nice exterior now has been traced to the Brockwitz Glass Works of Germany. The interesting design of asters in arched panels of nailhead is certainly not easy to forget. Colors are marigold in all shapes with the rose bowl found in cobalt blue.

Atlantic City Elks Bell (Fenton)

This is one of the three bells made by Fenton for various Elks gatherings (the others are Portland and Parkersburg). All the bells are cobalt blue and very collectible. The Portland bell is the rarest by far.

Auckland

Since I first showed this vase, I've received copies of various catalogs from glasshouses in Germany, Finland, and Czechoslovakia, and while this vase isn't shown in any of them, there are other shapes that closely resemble the design elements in glass from the Karhula-Iittala plant, so this may well be from that concern. It was found in Auckland, New Zealand, and stands 7¼" tall.

August Flowers

This beautifully patterned Imperial Glass light shade, #486C, is shown in ads for both electric and gas lamps. So far, though, I've only seen the electric size (shown). Colors reported are marigold or helios green but they were also made in uniridized versions in crystal. The mould work is very good, as is the design and this shade would grace any collection.

Aurora Daisies

Like the other Aurora patterns, this one comes from Europe and is marked "Austria." It is a bride's basket with beautiful daisies enameled on white carnival. Thanks to the Remmens for sharing it.

Aurora Pearls

This beautiful bowl was made in Austria (examples with paper labels have been reported) in iridized custard as well as iridized ruby, cobalt blue, and green. It is known in both 10" and 12½" sizes. The decoration on these bowls is hand applied and may be gold or other enamels.

Aurora Primrose Scroll

The Austrian Aurora pattern is delicate enameled flowers on a dark blue iridized glass. It is found in both 10" and 12" sizes.

Aurora Rubina Verde

This Austrian piece is on rubina verde glass with trailing flowers and gold vining. The color of the glass runs from red to topaz and is striking. Thanks to the Remmens for sharing it with me.

Australian Daisy (Jain)

This tumbler was first found in Australia, but in fact it is a product of the Jain Glass Works of India. Robert Smith indicated that the tops of these tumblers, which shown here are clear, were originally colored frosty white and this process wears away with use. The tumblers (two reported) stand 4¼" tall, are 2¾" across the lip, and have a base diameter of 1⅛". The bottom is depressed and contains a raised six-petaled flower.

Australian Daisy & Shield

Similar to Australian Daisy, this pattern has the same shape but a different design on the base and the body. And despite its title, it is a product of India. The marigold can be very strong or a bit weak.

Australian File Band

This exterior pattern is found on *some* Butterfly Bower bowls and may well have another name in Australia. The piece shown is on black amethyst glass and has a bullet edging.

Australian Holly (Crystal)

It is a privilege to show this very scarce Australian pattern from the Crown Crystal Glass Company, seen only on marigold to date. Please notice how thick the glass is. The bowl is 7½" in diameter and sits on three slender feet. The exterior pattern is one called Panels and Diamonds. Australian Holly and Fenton's Holly show a very close similarity.

Australian Kookaburra (Lettered)

It is believed this very rare bowl is the first of this design and it was then altered for production. This one has lettering that reads "AUSTRALIAN KOOKA-BURRA." The bowl is marigold and only the center has any pattern with the lettering in an outer ring. Only marigold has been reported and I thank Wayne Delahoy for sharing the photo.

Austral Jug

Since Austral is a university in Argentina, it seems to place this 7¼" jug in aqua glass with amber iridescence as a product of South America. Nothing definite is known about the maker and I'd certainly like to hear from anyone who can pin down this jug.

Autumn Acorns

Fenton's Autumn Acorns is similar to their Acorn pattern. This version, though, has a grape leaf rather than the oak leaves on the Acorn. Although found mostly on bowls, there are rare plates such as the one shown here. The pattern is a good one and colors for bowls include marigold, blue, green, amethyst, vaseline, and red.

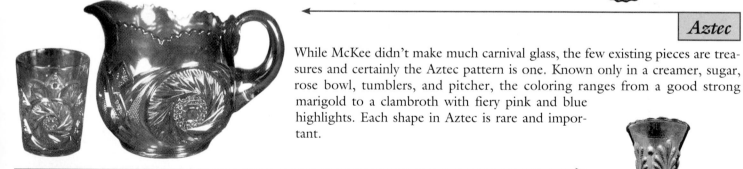

Aztec

While McKee didn't make much carnival glass, the few existing pieces are treasures and certainly the Aztec pattern is one. Known only in a creamer, sugar, rose bowl, tumblers, and pitcher, the coloring ranges from a good strong marigold to a clambroth with fiery pink and blue highlights. Each shape in Aztec is rare and important.

Aztec Headdress

This vase is a real beauty with a row of stairs leading up to a center band of circled medallions, then topped off by a group of plumes surrounding the top. Marigold is the only reported color so far. It is likely a product of Argentina. Thanks to the Raths for providing it.

Ballard-Merced

This advertising piece has the basketweave exterior pattern so you can safely say that Northwood is the established maker. The lettering says "Ballard, Merced, Cal." Bowls and plates are found in amethyst only. It is nice advertising piece to choose from out of the many available.

29

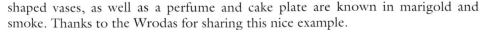

Balloons

This Imperial pattern is blown rather than press molded and most examples are found with various wheel cut designs, with exception of the blank vase. The name likely came from the first examples found which have a cut design resembling a series of hot air balloons circling the center of the vase. Several sizes and shaped vases, as well as a perfume and cake plate are known in marigold and smoke. Thanks to the Wrodas for sharing this nice example.

Bamboo Spike

This pale 4¼" marigold tumbler is another of the patterns from China. It has 12 spikes or spears around the base (unlike the Golden Triangle tumbler which has eight spikes). There have been five documented tumbler patterns from China and I feel there are probably more out there. All have the same pale frosty marigold coloring and rather poor iridescence and were made in the 1930s.

Band

Like most of the violet basket inserts, this one relies on a metal handle and holder for any decoration it might have. It was made by Diamond and came in marigold as well as the amethyst shown.

Banded Diamonds and Bars

This Inwald pattern is found in a squat pitcher, tumbler, juice glass, shot glass, a stemmed sherbet, and the bowl shape shown. Marigold is the only color reported at this time.

Banded Drape

The #1016 pitcher was made by the Fenton Company in 1912, and is also known as Iris and Ribbon (enameled version), Ribbon and Drape, and Diagonal Band. It stands 11½" tall and is found in marigold, blue, green, or white. Thanks the Wrodas for sharing this fine example.

Banded Flute

Thanks to Art and Barbara True who contacted me to say this pattern is shown in a 1910 Butler Brothers ad for Imperial, I can now list a definite maker. I appreciate the help they gave. A copy of this ad also appeared in Presznick's Book Four. No other colors besides the marigold are mentioned but certainly others may exist.

Banded Grape and Leaf

Once thought to be a pattern made in Australia, this pattern is now known to be from the Jain Glass Works in India. Only marigold has been reported, and both the tumbler shown as well as the matching pitcher are considered on the rare side. The pitcher is flared at the top in an unusual shape.

Banded Laurel Wreath

This Rindskopf pattern is shown in their catalog(s) in several shapes including a bowl, compote, and a tall stemmed goblet shown in the eighth edition. Here is the compote which shows the design to a better advantage. It is also known as just Laurel Wreath by some collectors.

Banded Moon and Stars (Jain)

This attractive tumbler from the Jain Glass Works in India has floral stocks separated by pyramids of dots that are topped with a star. The most prominent feature is the ribbed band that contains stars and half-moons and the clear top that was often frosted. The color is quite good below this band with fine iridescence.

Banded Rib

Banded Rib is now known to be from Jeannette. This nicely done pattern is found on water sets only in various hues of marigold, ranging from nearly amber to a dark marigold. Many items seem to have a radium finish.

Banded Rib Neck Vase

This vase has a black banded base as well as the banding at the neck, and is very similar to the Belted Rib vase shown elsewhere. The rest of the piece is ribbed and on the base is a paper label that reads "Made in Czechoslovakia." The color is a good strong marigold.

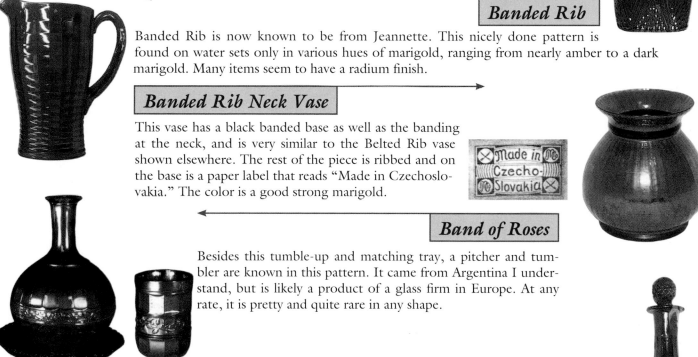

Band of Roses

Besides this tumble-up and matching tray, a pitcher and tumbler are known in this pattern. It came from Argentina I understand, but is likely a product of a glass firm in Europe. At any rate, it is pretty and quite rare in any shape.

Band of Stars

Band of Stars, a rare non-American pattern, found on a wine set that consists of a 12½" decanter and 4" stemmed wines, is a treasure. The coloring is a strong marigold with very good iridescence and the design is exactly what the name implies, a band of stars that runs around the piece over fluting. On the decanter, a second incised band of stars fills an incised band of diamonds.

Barbella

This rather plain Northwood pattern, similar to so many Flute, Wide Panel, and Colonial designs, often goes unnoticed except by tumbler collectors. Shapes include a scarce tumbler, bowls, compotes, covered candy jars, and plates. Colors are vaseline, jade blue, emerald green, russet, and ivory. Note that the tumbler has a collar base and is marked with the Northwood "N."

Baroque

What a beautiful and rare tumbler this is (only one example reported). It stands 3⅞" tall and is marked "Germany." The enameling is of Richard Wagner, the German composer, with sheet music on either side of the portrait framed with heavily raised gilt and flowers. If you find one of these splendid tumblers consider yourself lucky. I'd certainly like to know anything readers can tell me about this superb tumbler. Thanks to Bill and Sharon Mizell for sharing it.

31

Basket of Roses

This rare Fenton pattern is sometimes confused with the common Wreath of Roses bonbon made by Fenton. It comes in both stippled or plain versions in marigold, amethyst, and cobalt blue. Please note that there are fewer roses and no center design of roses, buds, and leaves. The exterior is the familiar Basketweave pattern and the Northwood trademark is usually found on the exterior's base. Shown is a very rich marigold that has the stippling; please notice the Basketweave can be seen through the coloring.

Basketweave (Northwood)

This very pretty overall design was made in Northwood's earlier years at Wheeling. It is found on many bowls and plates as an exterior pattern as well as on compotes, The example shown is a bit of a rarity since it is on a previously unreported aqua glass. As you can see, the interior pattern on this piece is Northwood's Stippled Rays.

Basketweave and Cable

Westmoreland's Basketweave and Cable is a seldom-found pattern that must have been made in limited amounts. The mould work is excellent and the lustre is satisfactory. Colors are marigold (often pale), amethyst, green, and rarely white.

Basketweave/Vintage Variation

This oddity is always found as an exterior pattern of dome-base bowls and was originally a Jefferson Glass pattern called #245. Northwood bought this mould from Jefferson and used it with some of their interior patterns, but somewhere along the line, they tooled the mould, adding a basketweave pattern. So on some patterns like Three Fruits, the exterior shows both a basketweave with the remains of grapes and vine from the original Vintage design.

Bavarian Berry

This tankard pitcher with the nice enameling has sprays of berries and leaves and a message written in German. The maker hasn't been identified but I suspect it is European. I welcome any information about its origin.

Beaded Acanthus

It's hard to believe this outstanding pattern was made in this one shape only. This milk pitcher measures 7" high and has a base diameter of 3¾". It is found mostly on marigold or smoke glass, but a very outstanding green exists, and I suspect amethyst is also a possibility. The color is usually quite good, and the iridescence is what one might expect from the Imperial Company.

Beaded Band and Octagon Lamp

This lamp has been found in clear glass marked "AQUILA HECH OPOR LOX MTVMEX," so it is felt that the carnival examples may also be of Mexican origin. The lamp is found in both 7½" and 9¾" sizes in marigold.

Beaded Basket

This Diamond pattern was made at Indiana, Pennsylvania, after the Dugans departed. It is well known in the two-handled basket shape. Colors are marigold, amethyst, cobalt blue, lime green with marigold luster, white, aqua, and pink with marigold luster. Production began about 1914 or 1915 and lasted until at least 1928, the date of pink production. Green examples have been reported but not confirmed.

Beaded Bull's Eye

This well-designed Imperial item comes in the vase shape only (6" – 15" tall). Colors include marigold, purple, green, smoke, amber, lime green, cobalt blue, and the beautiful teal. Some of these vases, especially the squat ones, have the tops stretched out to outrageous sizes, like the one shown.

Beaded Cable

This popular Northwood rose bowl was made in carnival glass in 1913 after a run in both Mosaic glass and opalescent glass. It stands about 4½" tall on three feet. The example shown has a broad gilt stripe around the top and gilding on the cable as an added effect. Thanks to Mickey Reichel.

Beaded Daisy Panels

This daisy design with borders of beading is often found on European glass, so chances are this glass is from there. The flared compote has a marigold bowl but the stem and base are clear. I welcome any information about this pattern. The compote is 3½" tall with a 5" diameter.

Beaded Floral Band

The tumbler in this enameled set, which was found by the author and named by John Britt, was shown in earlier editions. Here is the matching pitcher. The design features iridized bands above and below, edged by dots. The center has enameled leaves, flowers, and rows of blue dots.

Beaded Mirrors (Jain)

Beaded Panels is similar to so many designs from the Jain Glass Works of India with its overall crosshatching except for two large ovals, which are left perfectly plain and look just like a mirror with the heavy iridescence. Around the rim is the typical band that is unpatterned and lighter in color. A variant of this pattern exists with rose-like flowers in the ovals.

Beaded Panels (Dugan)

Beaded Panels is called Opal Open by opalescent glass collectors. The carnival pieces were made by the Dugan Company from the Northwood moulds. Only the compote shape is known in carnival glass in marigold, amethyst, peach opalescent, and cobalt blue (quite rare). Be aware, however, this pattern was reproduced in opalescent glass for L.G. Wright and like the current peach opal Twigs vases that are being reproduced, peach opalescent is a strong reproduction possibility down the road.

Beaded Panels and Grapes

This 4½"tumbler has beaded panels that remind one of the old Holly Amber design. Three panels feature grapes and leaves that drop from a band of vines, leaves, and grape clusters. Marigold is the only color reported to date.

Beaded Shell

This Dugan-Diamond pattern, once called New York, is found in custard glass, opalescent glass, and carnival. The shapes include table sets, water sets, berry sets, and mugs. Colors are marigold, purple, cobalt blue, green, peach opalescent, and white but not all shapes are known in all colors. Opalescent glass collectors call this pattern Shell.

Beaded Spears (Jain)

This interesting pattern is found in water sets as well as tumblers in several sizes and several variations. The main design features are the band below the rim that contains plain circles in a file design and the wedge sections that run from the base to the top. Marigold is the known color but the variant pieces are known in blue glass with marigold iridescence.

Beaded Spears Variants (Jain)

There appears to be several variations to this pattern made by Jain Glass of India. Please note that the tumbler on the right has a collar base. The color is a soft blue with marigold iridescence. And while all of these variants have similar patterning, each has some portions that are different, as evidenced by the difference in the panels down the sides, as well as the base design.

Beaded Star Medallion

Here is a Northwood shade, shown with the complete wall fixture holding both gas and electric shades. These are marked Northwood and the color is just superb. Notice there is stippling on the exterior.

Beaded Stars (Fenton)

Made by Fenton in 1905, this pattern underwent some variations in other types of glass. In opalescent glass a variant pattern called Beaded Stars and Swag exists. The carnival pattern is also made in opalescent glass and is known as Beaded Moon and Stars by opalescent glass collectors. Shapes in carnival glass are bowls, banana bowls, a 9" plate, and a rose bowl. Marigold appears only in carnival glass.

Beaded Swag Medallion

This vase is from Alan Sedgwick who owns the only two reported examples in carnival glass (it is found in malachite glass). He believes it may be from Sowerby despite having no trademark. It stands 5½" tall and has incredible color and iridescence.

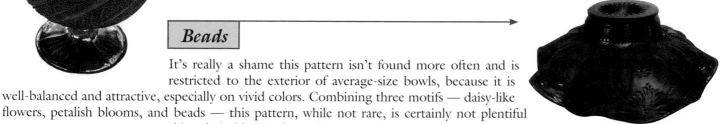

Beaded Swirl

This pattern was also called Beads and Diamonds by Marion Quintin-Baxendale. It is shown in a Leerdam of Holland catalog. In carnival glass it can be found in a compote (shown), a stemmed salver from the same mould, a covered butter dish, open stemmed sugar, creamer, and a milk pitcher.

Beads

It's really a shame this pattern isn't found more often and is restricted to the exterior of average-size bowls, because it is well-balanced and attractive, especially on vivid colors. Combining three motifs — daisy-like flowers, petalish blooms, and beads — this pattern, while not rare, is certainly not plentiful and is a desirable Northwood item.

Beads and Bars

While I've known about this pattern for years from the Hartung drawing, this is the very first example I've been able to show. She discusses her piece being a spooner but the one shown here is definitely a rose bowl shape, in a fine clambroth coloring. I can confirm both marigold and clambroth in this pattern. The rose bowl is 3¾" tall and is about the same size across.

Bearded Berry

This well-known Fenton exterior pattern dates from 1911 and is found on bowls of all shapes. The name comes from the "hairy" look of each of the berries.

Beauty Bud Vase

This Diamond pattern was a popular one, made in large runs, and is easily found today, mostly in marigold. You will notice that except for the missing limbs around the base, it is exactly like the Twigs vase from the same maker.

Bee Ornament

This tiny solid glass ornament is only about 1½" long and reminds me of the famous Butterfly ornaments that were made to attach to flower arrangements. The Bee Ornament has been found in marigold. I've been told Westmoreland is the maker.

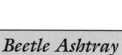

Beetle Ashtray

This Beetle ashtray was made by Christalerias Rigolleau of Buenos Aires, Argentina, and is found in cobalt blue as well as this amberish marigold color. Either color is considered rare. The mould work is outstanding with the naturalistic beetles around the rim and the lettering in the center.

Bellaire Souvenir

This deep bowl was obviously made by the Imperial Glass Company and is seldom discussed. It measures 7" in diameter and has lettering that says "Bellaire — Good Will Tour." Marigold is the only color reported and the date of production isn't known.

Bell Flower (Fuchsia)

This rare Fenton pattern is found in marigold or cobalt blue as shown. It was first called Bell Flower by Rose Presznick although most collectors call it Fuchsia.

Bell Flower Vase

This is truly a very rare and lovely vase, one of only two reported to date, both in blue. If you'll notice the Dragon Vase listed elsewhere in this book (one black amethyst and one blue reported) you can see the similarities. The maker has yet to be established but I'm sure the owners of these rare beauties don't mind waiting a while longer to find out. Thanks to the Remmens for sharing the photo.

Bells and Beads (Dugan)

This Dugan pattern, from about 1910, is found on small bowls, plates, hat shaped pieces, a nappy, a card tray, and a compote. Colors are marigold, peach opalescent, purple, and the bowl is found in a rare green.

Belted Rib

Much like the Black Bottom or Halloween patterns, this very attractive vase has very rich marigold color and a center band of black enameling as well as a similar band around the base to give it emphasis. The interior is ribbed and the lip flared widely with a touch of stretch appearance.

Bernheimer Bowl

This bowl from Millersburg is like the Many Stars bowls except it has a smaller center star and says "Bernheimer Brothers." Bernheimer bowls are rare and desirable and usually bring top dollar.

Berry Leaf

The owners of this mustard jar call it a maple leaf but on close inspection, it doesn't resemble a maple leaf and certainly not an acorn leaf so it was simply given the name Berry Leaf. I am indebted to Dennis and Denise Harp for this cute rarity.

Bertha

Bowls, a creamer, open sugar, and a covered butter are shown in the 1928 Brockwitz catalog. Here is one of the deeper bowls in iridized glass. The marigold is typical of European carnival glass.

Big Basketweave (Dugan)

This very nice Dugan-Diamond pattern dates from 1914 (according to company ads) and was called Wicker Weave by the company. It can be found on bowl exteriors, on small handled baskets in two sizes, as a stand for fruit bowls, and on vases as shown. Colors reported are marigold, amethyst, blue, white, peach opalescent, and the scarce celeste blue shown.

Although this Millersburg design is very similar to the Trout & Fly pattern, it is without a fly and has added waterlillies. It is found only on bowls. The bowls can be found in several shapes including round, oval, ruffled, a three-in-one edge, and even an ice cream shape. Colors are marigold, amethyst, green, and rarely vaseline.

Big Thistle (Millersburg)

Two of these sets (punch bowl and base) are confirmed and a third reported. All are amethyst and have a Wide Panel exterior with the Big Thistle pattern on the inside of the bowl. The example shown has a flared top while the other example has a straight top or goblet shaped top. Strangely, I recently heard rumors of a set with cups in northeast Ohio but this hasn't been verified and to my best knowledge, no cups are known to exist.

Bird and Strawberry (Bluebird)

Made by the Indiana Glass Company shortly after 1910, this pattern was made in many shapes in crystal including compotes, table sets, water sets, punch sets, cake stand, relish, and a wine. Some pieces were decorated or in colors but in carnival glass only the tumbler is known at this time. The design consists of two bands of hexagonal crosshatching that encase birds and a cluster of strawberries and leaves.

Bird Epergne

I feel sure this neat miniature epergne or bud vase is from Czechoslovakia. With its bird on a nest and the lily that is iridized, it makes a great item for people who collect the unusual or miniatures. It is the only example I've seen and is a real conversation piece.

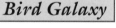

Bird Galaxy

I've shown this strange 10½" vase in white carnival and it is also known in green, but here, thanks to Lance Hilkene, is an iridized milk glass example that has a painted top. This vase is now known to be a product of Gillinder and Sons in the 1920s. Beware, as Gillinder Glass is currently reproducing this pattern in various colors and sizes. The new ones I've seen are jadite green in the 10½" size and emerald green in a 14 – 15" size and I'm told other colors are being made as well.

Bird-in-the-Bush

This tumbler is from Germany and has the same dome base as the Reindeer tumbler shown elsewhere. The bird seems to be flying among branches of check flora and leaves. Bob Smith has shared this tumbler with me and it is the first I've seen.

Birds and Cherries

Originally Fenton's #1075 pattern, Birds and Cherries can be found in bowls, compotes, rare plates, and bonbons. Colors are marigold, amethyst, green, cobalt blue, white, pastel marigold, and vaseline (or topaz). The pattern, a series of birds on branches that have leaves, blossoms, and cherries, is a good one and deserves more attention than it usually gets.

Bird with Grapes

Bird with Grapes is also known as Cockatoo. This vase dates to the goofus glass era. The carnival pieces are most prevalent however and are found in marigold (ranging from amberish to bright pumpkin) and an odd smoky shade. This vase is a wall pocket shape, hung by a hole in the back. The maker is currently in question.

Bishop's Mitre

This distinctive vase is usually found in cobalt blue, but here is shown a marigold example from Wayne Delahoy in Australia. The vase is Finnish, from Riihimaki Glass Works, and was shown in a 1939 catalog. This pattern was their #5911 and #5912.

Black Band

Here is another of those rather plain vases, 4¾" tall, imported from Czechoslovakia. Its only distinction seems to be the black enamel bands (one thin and one wide) on both the top edge and the base. The glass is quite thin but the marigold color is very strong.

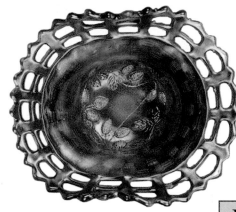

Blackberry (Fenton)

Most pieces of this Fenton basketweave exterior and open-edge treatment are ruffled hat shapes. Rarely plates, vases, banana bowls, JIP bowls, and spittoon whimsies can also be found. Colors range from the standard ones to unusual ones like teal, aqua, and vaseline.

Blackberry (Northwood)

The Northwood version of this fruit pattern from 1911 is found on compotes (with a Basketweave exterior) or as the interior of Daisy and Plume footed pieces. Colors found are marigold, amethyst, green, a rare white, and rare blue.

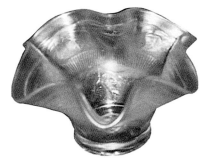

Blackberry Banded

Limited to only the hat shape, this interior pattern is similar to the Blackberry Spray pattern but with a wide ribbed band beneath the berries and leaves. The exterior is plain. This pattern dates to 1915. Colors in carnival glass are marigold, cobalt blue, green, moonstone, marigold over milk glass, and the very rare white example shown. It is the first in this color reported.

Blackberry Bark

This vase was once credited to U.S. Glass by some collectors, but shards were found at the Millersburg factory site so this vase seems to have found its home. Only two examples are known and both are amethyst. The design is very well executed and imaginative.

Blackberry Block

This is one of the better Fenton water set patterns. It can be found in marigold, blue, amethyst, green, and rarely white. The allover pattern of wire-like squares with berries and leaves vining over them is very pleasing.

Blackberry Bramble

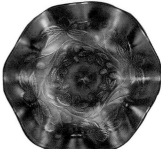

Blackberry Bramble is available on stemmed compotes of average size. It is a very close cousin to the Fenton Blackberry pattern but has more leaves, berries, and thorny branches. I decided to show a straight on shot of the compote so the pattern can be viewed fully. Colors are marigold, amethyst, green, and cobalt blue, but others may certainly exist.

Blackberry/Daisy and Plume

This Northwood piece is found mostly with the Daisy and Plume pattern on the exterior and a plain interior, but it can also be found with the Blackberry interior. Dugan made a three-footed piece nearly identical. Colors are marigold, amethyst, green, white, and the beautiful cobalt blue shown.

Blackberry Intaglio

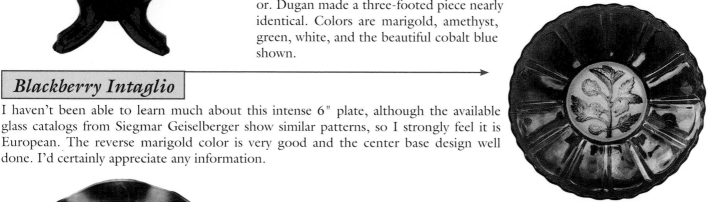

I haven't been able to learn much about this intense 6" plate, although the available glass catalogs from Siegmar Geiselberger show similar patterns, so I strongly feel it is European. The reverse marigold color is very good and the center base design well done. I'd certainly appreciate any information.

Blackberry Rays (Northwood)

Rarer than the regular Blackberry compote, this one has the sunburst lustre method of iridization that shows 40 rays of spray lustre in a pattern. In addition the exterior has no pattern. Colors known are amethyst, green, and the rare marigold shown.

Blackberry Spray

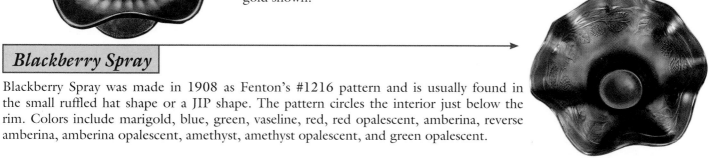

Blackberry Spray was made in 1908 as Fenton's #1216 pattern and is usually found in the small ruffled hat shape or a JIP shape. The pattern circles the interior just below the rim. Colors include marigold, blue, green, vaseline, red, red opalescent, amberina, reverse amberina, amberina opalescent, amethyst, amethyst opalescent, and green opalescent.

Blackberry Spray Absentee Variant (Fenton's #106)

This hat shape was advertised in a 1921 company ad along with many stretch items from the Fenton Company. It is the blank mould to which Fenton added several interior patterns including Holly, Blackberry Spray, and Blackberry Banded. Colors made were ruby, wisteria, Grecian gold, topaz, celeste blue, and the white carnival that Fenton called Persian Pearl shown. The line was generally known as the Florentine Line.

Blackberry Spray Variant

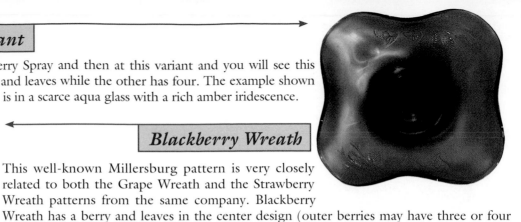

Look closely at the regular Blackberry Spray and then at this variant and you will see this piece has only two sprays of berries and leaves while the other has four. The example shown is in a scarce aqua glass with a rich amber iridescence.

Blackberry Wreath

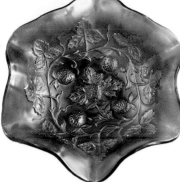

This well-known Millersburg pattern is very closely related to both the Grape Wreath and the Strawberry Wreath patterns from the same company. Blackberry Wreath has a berry and leaves in the center design (outer berries may have three or four leaves giving variation to the pattern). Colors are the usual Millersburg ones of marigold, green, or amethyst, but vaseline, clambroth, and a rare blue are also known.

Black Bottom

Shown is a hard to find decorated example made in Grecian gold in the 1920s. It is really Fenton's #735 pattern. Two shapes of this covered candy jar and can be found with or without the black enamel work on the base. Since many Grecian gold treatments also had engraved patterns, I wouldn't be surprised if the Black Bottom pieces may show up with etched designs also. Thanks again to Samantha Prince for the nice photo.

Blazing Cornucopia

Also called Paisley or Golden Jewel, this U.S. Glass pattern was first made in 1913. It is found in crystal, gilded, or stained glass but here is the first piece reported in carnival glass. It is a two-handled spooner and has to be a real rarity.

Block Band Diamond (#27)

Block Band Diamond is now known to have been made in carnival glass in a pitcher as well as the tumbler shown and the syrup. This pattern was a crystal pattern from George Duncan & Sons in the 1800s. In 1903, the company became the famous Duncan and Miller Glass Company and built a steady reputation for opalescent glass. The iridizing is on the plain portions above the banding of diamonds and most pieces have the enameled flower as well.

Blocks and Arches

Often confused with the very similar Ranger pattern, Blocks and Arches is really an Australian design found only on tumblers and pitchers like the one shown. Colors are marigold and amethyst.

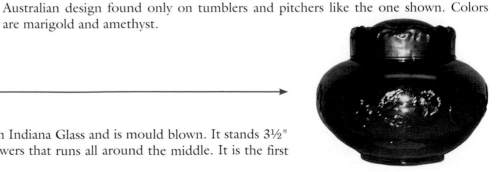

Blossom

This #480 pattern covered piece is from Indiana Glass and is mould blown. It stands 3½" tall and 4¾" wide. It has a band of flowers that runs all around the middle. It is the first example in carnival glass reported.

Blossom and Shell

While most opalescent glass collectors call this pattern Blossom and Shell, carnival glass collectors have long lumped it with the Northwood Wild Rose pattern (which it isn't). As you can see there are important differences including more petals to the flowers, more leaves, and a scrolling below the flowers that doesn't appear on Wild Rose. The color shown is called Alaskan and is an amber finish over green glass. It is also known as Blossom and Palm.

Blossoms and Band

Made late in the carnival era, this pattern is credited to Hazel-Atlas but some collectors put it in the Diamond Glass camp. Shapes include 9" and 5" bowls and the pocket vase shown. All pieces are known in marigold but the bowls can also be found in amethyst on occasion.

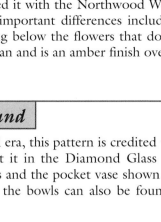

Blossomtime

This very nice pattern is from the Northwood Company and found on stemmed compotes with the Wildflower exterior (the stem is always a threaded screw-like configuration). It is found in purple, green, or marigold. Green is the most difficult to find, but the marigold isn't found every day either.

Bluebell Band and Ribs

This beautiful pitcher is similar to both Ganador and Berry Band and Ribs. It was found in Argentina so there isn't much question about its origin. It was named by Bill Edwards. I'd appreciate any additional information from readers.

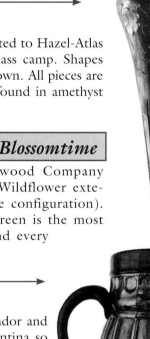

Blueberry (Fenton)

Fenton's #1562 pattern, first made in 1912, is simply one of their best designs. Colors are marigold, cobalt blue, and white. Once seen, the shape of the pitcher isn't easily mistaken for any other and that is much of the pattern's charm. Pitcher tops are scalloped and flared out and the handles are applied.

Blue Ring

Besides the decanter shown (the 3" stopper is missing), there are shot glasses that complete this set from Czechoslovakia. The glasses are 2¾" tall, the decanter 6½" tall. The surface has a nice marigold finish except for the enameled blue rings.

Blum Department Store

Despite coming late in the carnival glass era, this rather rare advertising tumbler is very collectible. It reads "Compliments of Blum Dept. Store...54th Anniversary...October 8th, 1930." The color is a good rich marigold.

Boggy Bayou

Often confused with a sister vase called Reverse Drapery, Boggy Bayou has a different base pattern consisting of geometric rays and diamonds while the former has a many rayed base. It is found in opalescent glass as well as the carnival colors of marigold, amethyst, green, blue, and lime opalescent. Boggy Bayou is known in two sizes of marie and can be found in heights of 5" to 15". There are seven arc-like rings in each section of six panels. The example shown is a dark marigold.

Bond

Shown as a tumbler design (wasserbecher) in a Brockwitz catalog, this vase shape has been called Bond by collectors in Europe and England. Factory numbers for the tumbler are 815, 816, and 817, but I do not have a designation for the vase shape. Colors seem to be the very rich blue shown and marigold. It is remarkable how much outstanding carnival glass came from the Brockwitz concern and this piece is no exception.

Booker

This cutie is in the collection of Carl and Eunice Booker, so it was appropriately named after them. It is smaller than most and has a beautiful spray of enameled flowers and an amethyst handle! It is probably European. A matching pitcher exists.

Bo Peep

This child's set is much prized by collectors. It was made only in a mug and the much harder-to-find, raised-rim plate in marigold. Examples have been seen in crystal. Westmoreland is considered the maker of this set.

Border Plants

This Dugan dome-based bowl (also found in a collar base) has a large central flower design bordered by stippling and a series of stemmed flowers that alternate with a series of three-leafed designs. Colors are amethyst, lavender, and the usual peach opalescent.

Bouquet

Bouquet is one of Fenton's better designs found only on water set pieces in marigold, cobalt blue, or white (the tumbler has been reported in Persian blue). This lovely bulbous pitcher has sections of daisy-like foliage separated by panels of scale and a flower that resembles embroidery stitching. Note the ruffled top on the pitcher that is typical of this pattern.

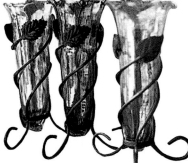

Boutonniere

This little beauty is a Millersburg product. It usually has a fine radium finish and is most often seen in amethyst. And although I haven't seen one, I've been told there is a variation sometimes found with a different stem and base. Boutonniere is also found in marigold and green.

Braziers Candies

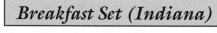

This fine Fenton advertising piece can be found in amethyst bowls, plates, or a handgrip plate.

Breakfast Set (Indiana)

Collectors have long thought this set was from the Heisey Company but I now know it was made at Indiana Glass as their #165 pattern. In carnival only the matched creamer and open sugar are known, but in crystal many shapes including a water set, a berry set, a table set, shakers, a cruet, jelly compote, celery vase, pickle dish, celery dish, and various bowls are known.

Bride's Bouquet

This Jain Glass Works tumbler stands 5¾" tall. It has a threading background and a hand holding a plant that has three branches, leaves, and flowers. The threading stops 1" from the tumbler's top where a band of alternating leaves and flowers circle the rim. Some collectors may know this pattern as Rin-roll (not a very descriptive name) but I believe Bride's Bouquet describes the pattern in a better manner. Thanks to Andres Neveu for sharing this tumbler.

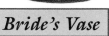

Bride's Vase

Named by Rose Presznick, this very nice vase and metal holder is reported in two sizes and several pastel flashed colors including marigold, blue, and white. The glass pieces shown are 6" tall and as you can see the metal holders are found in black or brass with slight differences in the design. I am told these vases were used primarily by florists and date from the 1920s and 1930s but can't confirm the age at this time.

Bride's Wall Vase

Like the Bride's vase shown above these are in metal holders, but instead are meant to be hung from the wall. The glass portions were approximately 4½" tall, were made in the 1920s I'm told (but have no concrete proof), and can be found in flashed marigold, blue, clear, rose, and white. The glass is very thin and clear.

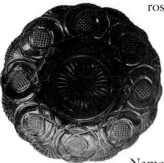

Brilliant Medallions

This 5" bowl, found in a 1914 Inwald catalog, is a little jewel. I expect other shapes will turn up and perhaps other colors. Thanks to Lance Hilkene for sharing it with me.

Britt

Named for the late John Britt, this beautiful water set is from Karhula of Finland and is shown in their catalog as pattern #4041. I'm told that the first tumbler was found in England in 1984. Tumblers can be found in marigold and blue, all of which are considered very rare. Here I am pleased to be able to show the only reported pitcher, which is in blue. Many thanks to Ron Britt for sharing this extremely rare beauty. I'd certainly appreciate any further information on this beautiful pattern.

Brocaded Acorns

This is one of Fostoria's well-known "brocaded" patterns. It can be found in pastel colors including pink, ice blue, lavender, white, ice green, vaseline, and clear. Shapes include bonbons, vase, plates, ice bucket, console set (candlesticks and bowl), divided bowl, and a very rare water set.

Brocaded Base Vase

Like so many of the other vases that were used in Arkansas for advertising, this one says "Hale Bath House." Apparently bathhouses were very popular in the early part of this century in the Hot Springs area. The color of this piece is a very good marigold, but aside from the pattern around the base, there is little design to notice. Riverside Glass called this their Winsome pattern.

Brocaded Daffodils

This is one of the "brocaded" patterns not credited to Fostoria. I am told it was made by Imperial (unconfirmed to date) and the pattern is less distinctive. Colors for this acid-cut pattern are pink, ice blue, ice green, white, and vaseline, and shapes include handled bowls, bon-bons, a cake plate, tray, center bowl, creamer and sugar with matching tray, and a divided bowl.

Brocaded Palms

Brocaded Palm is part of Fostoria's acid etched iridized series. These palm trees and can be found on several shapes including a bonbon, centerpiece bowl, covered dish, nappy, large footed bowl, stemmed relish, vase, candlesticks, and the planter shown. Colors are ice green, ice blue, pink, white, rose, and vaseline.

Brocaded Summer Gardens

As another of Fostoria's "brocaded" patterns, this has all the beauty of a garden in full bloom. It is found on an array of shapes, primarily in white. This would make a wonderful addition to the other "brocaded" patterns in any collection.

Brockwitz Hens

These are believed to be the same covered hen pieces that are shown in a 1928 catalog from the Brockwitz Company. They appear beside other covered pieces that include a rabbit and a duck, and are listed in two sizes. Thanks to Alan Sedgwick for sharing these.

Broeker's Flour

This Northwood piece is found in amethyst glass and is a bit hard to find. The lettering says, "We use Broeker's Flour." I've heard of only the plate shape at this time.

Broken Arches, one of Imperial's more distinctive patterns, is found only in a punch set of good size. Colors are marigold or amethyst and the latter sometimes has silvery iridescence. The bowl interior sometimes carries a distinctive pattern but may have plain interiors. Large bowls have been reported but I haven't seen any.

Broken Chain

This Australian exterior pattern was made by Crystal Glass. It is known as S-Band in America. It can be found with several primary Australian patterns, in both marigold and purple, and no matter which name you call it, the pattern is a good one. Thanks to Wayne Delahoy for the photo.

Brooklyn Bottle

I suspect this beautiful 9⅝" cruet may be of European origin. The glass is very thin, and the non-iridized handle and stopper are very attractive amethyst glass.

Brooklyn Bridge

Brooklyn Bridge is one of the easily recognized lettered bowl patterns. It is found only in marigold and credited to the Diamond Glass Company around 1930. Rare examples are missing the lettering usually found just under the blimp and one known example has gold lettering. Bowls can have six ruffles, eight ruffles, or ten ruffles. In addition, there are examples of pink glass with marigold iridescence.

Bubble Waves

This rare 3¼" x 5¼" compote is a soft peach opalescent color with clear stem and base. The stem has a center finial and the design inside the bowl consists of six rows of bubbles separated by thin ridging. I suspect this to be a Dugan-Diamond piece but have no proof. Thanks to Tom Dryden for sharing this rarity.

Buckingham

This pattern was previously listed as Feathered Lotus, but it is without question a U.S. Glass pattern known as Buckingham. I suspect there may have been a lid at one time, but have no proof. The design is quite strong as is the color. Thanks to the Ayers family for sharing it.

Buddha

Buddha can be found in both 6" and 10" sizes and four colors (marigold, white, blue, and green). There is also a "reclining" example reported in marigold. I can't vouch for age or maker. Thanks to Connie Wilson for sharing this green example.

Bull Rush and Orchids

From Crystal in Australia, this rarely discussed but well-done pattern can be found on 8" – 9" bowls and plates, primarily in marigold carnival glass. This may be the only pattern where the name is composed from both the interior and the exterior design, as opposed to most patterns that get their name from the interior pattern only. If the interior is plain, then the pattern name is derived from the exterior design. It is also known as Bull Rushes and Bush Orchids. Thanks again to Wayne Delahoy.

Bull's Eye and Beads

This very elusive pattern, described and named by Marion Hartung, has been confused with Rustic, April Showers, and Millersburg's Swirl Hobnail, and in many ways has features of all these with rows of beads or hobnails, swirls, and bull's eyes. The example shown is 13" tall in marigold. It is also known in amethyst and blue, and I suspect green and possibly other colors were made. Thanks to Roger Lane for sharing it.

Bull's Eye and Diamonds

This pattern was found in the Cristalerias catalog from Bob Smith, so it is now known to be from Argentina. While other shapes are shown in the catalog, only this mug has shown up in carnival glass.

Bull's Eye and Leaves

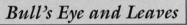

Confined to the exterior of bowls and found mostly in green or marigold, this pattern is a trifle too busy to be very effective and is certainly not one of Northwood's better efforts. All in all, there are five motifs, including leaves, beads, circles, fishnet, and a petal grouping. Each appears on other Northwood products, but not in this combination. This pattern is also known as Netted Roses.

Bull's Eye and Loop (Millersburg)

This very scarce Millersburg vase is found in the usual colors: marigold (rare), amethyst (most often seen), and green. They can be found as tall as 11½" and as short as 7". All have a 3⅝" base diameter and are usually found with a radium finish.

Bushel Basket (Northwood)

Bushel Basket is found in a wide array of colors in carnival, as well as in other treatments (opalescent, crystal, ebony), with some shape and handle variations (some are eight-sided, some have a plain handle mount). Colors include amethyst, black amethyst, marigold, green, blue, electric blue, smoky blue, Persian blue, lavender, Celeste blue, horehound, white, ice blue, ice green, lime green, lime green opalescent, sapphire blue, smoke, vaseline, and violet.

Bushel Basket Variant

If you look closely at the handle of this variant, you will see it has no design below the top of the basket. Just why Northwood made this mould variation is a mystery. It is much harder to find than the regular one and is found in green and amethyst only. These baskets were made during the 1910 – 1913 era.

Butterflies

This Fenton pattern is found only on bonbons often flattened into a card tray shape. It has eight butterflies around the edges and one in the center. The exterior carries a typical wide panel pattern and often is found with advertising on the base. Colors are marigold, cobalt blue, green, amethyst, and white. At least these are the ones about which I've heard.

Butterfly (Northwood)

This popular Northwood bonbon pattern shows a well-designed butterfly with rays emanating from the center. The usual exterior is plain but a "threaded" exterior can sometimes be found. Colors are marigold, amethyst, blue, purple, green, electric blue, ice blue, lavender, and smoke.

Butterfly (with Threaded Exterior)

This is just like the Northwood bonbon shown elsewhere, except this one has the threaded exterior instead of a plain exterior. The threaded back examples are much rarer and are found in marigold, blue, green, amethyst, and the ice blue shown.

Butterfly and Berry (Fenton)

This is one of Fenton's best-known and most prolific patterns in production from 1911 to 1926 in carnival glass. Shapes include a table set, water set, berry set, orange bowl, sauce, hatpin holder (shown), and several whimsies. Most pieces are footed and colors include marigold, amethyst, blue, green, red, white (rare), Nile green (rare), red slag, amber, electric blue, and vaseline.

Butterfly and Corn Vase

Evidence (shards) points to the Millersburg Glass Company as the maker of this very rare vase. There are marigold, vaseline, green, and amethyst examples known (one of each has been verified). The vases are 5⅞" tall with a 2¾" dome base. The design shows an ear of corn with a flying shuck and a butterfly that more nearly resembles a moth. Shown is the recently discovered amethyst example and it is a rare and beautiful thing.

Butterfly and Fern (Plume)

This nicely designed water set is Fenton's #910 pattern and is known as both Butterfly and Fern and Butterfly and Plume. In addition a rare variant exists with only butterflies and no fern that was probably a prototype piece. Colors are marigold, amethyst, green, and cobalt blue (the variant is marigold). I am happy to show a blue example with electric iridescence from J. & J. Auctions. Thanks, guys.

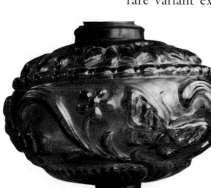

Butterfly and Single Flower

This oil lamp with a carnival glass font is pink and shows a butterfly between blossoms and leaves with a swirled rib design below and a butterfly banding above. These have been reported in Australia but I do not know the maker. In color it resembles the Chrysanthemum Drape lamp shown elsewhere in this edition. Courtesy of Dr. Jack Adams.

Butterfly and Tulip

Make no mistake about it, this is a very impressive Dugan pattern. The bowl is large, the glass heavy, and the mould work exceptional. Found in either marigold or purple, this footed jewel has the famous Feather Scroll for an exterior pattern. Typically, the shallower the bowl, the more money it brings with the purple bringing many times the price of the underrated marigold. A rare peach opalescent bowl is known.

Butterfly Bower (Crystal)

This Australian pattern has a center butterfly flanked by trellis work and some flora. Colors are usually marigold or purple but here is a stunning piece on black amethyst glass.

Butterfly Bush

This Australian pattern is known by several names, depending on where you are and who you are, such as Butterfly and Waratah, Waratah and Butterfly, Butterfly Bower and Butterfly Bells, as well as Christmas Bells by some collectors. Confused? You should be. (I'll be happy when everyone agrees on one name for this and other patterns.) This beautiful compote can be found in purple or marigold and is a standout in any collection. Shaping can be ruffled as shown or flattened into a salver or cake stand. The exterior carries a pattern called Petals in Australia that is similar to the American Rays design.

Butterfly Bush and Christmas Bells

This was also called Butterflies and Bells by Marion Hartung. There are at least three variations to the design. This pattern is found on compotes and salver shapes with either smooth or ruffled edges and is known in marigold or purple. Thanks again to Wayne Delahoy.

Butterfly Bush and Flannel Flower

This large stunning compote is called just Flannel Flower by Australians and can be found in marigold or purple. It measures 9" across the top and shows the usual Australian ruffling. The iridescence is rich and multicolored.

Butterfly Bush and Waratah

This pattern is also known by some as Butterflies and Waratah or Waratah and Butterflies. Here, there is no butterfly center but a floral one. It is found on large compotes like the example shown that measure about 9½" in diameter. They are seen in marigold or purple and on a decorative metal base in purple only.

Butterfly Lamp

Named for the wing-like projections of the metal base, this very unusual lamp stands approximately 13" tall to the burner. The very rich marigold font has a series of stylized designs around the curving that resemble the Art Deco bowl shown elsewhere in this book. I suspect the lamp may well be from England also, but have no proof to date.

Butterfly Ornament

I'm told this interesting bit of glass was made as a giveaway item and attached to bon-bons, baskets, and compotes by a bit of putty when purchasers visited the Fenton factory. This would certainly explain the scarcity of the Butterfly ornament, for few are around today. Colors reported are marigold, amethyst, cobalt blue, ice blue, white, and green.

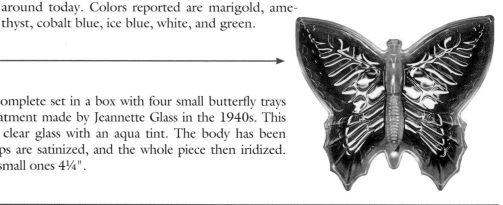

Butterfly Party Set

In the seventh edition I showed the complete set in a box with four small butterfly trays and one large one. Here I show a treatment made by Jeannette Glass in the 1940s. This piece is the large butterfly and is on clear glass with an aqua tint. The body has been stained with a pale green, the wing tips are satinized, and the whole piece then iridized. The large pieces are 8" across and the small ones 4¼".

Butterfly Tumbler

This very rare and desirable U.S. Glass tumbler is also called Big Butterfly (in crystal there is a matching pitcher but none have appeared in carnival glass). Colors are mainly a strange olive green with a smoky finish (four reported) but one marigold example is known.

Buttermilk Goblet

This goblet with the plain interior is from the same Fenton mould as the Iris goblets shown elsewhere. Colors are marigold, green, amethyst, and a scarce red but this pattern doesn't bring a large price, even in the latter color.

Buttons and Stars

Little is known about this very unusual sugar cube dish with a spring metal handle except that is was purchased in Norway. Thanks to Mary P. Hare for sharing it.

Buzz Saw and File

Here is shown a tall pitcher, a 4⅛" tumbler, a tall lemonade tumbler, and a stemmed goblet. In design, it resembles the Double Star pattern from Cambridge. All pieces of Buzz Saw and File are scarce and desirable with the goblet being the first reported. The maker is unknown at this time, although U. S. Glass is another possibility.

Buzz Saw and File Framed

Found in Malaysia by Peter Dahlin, this 5½" bowl has the same marie (base) design as the Diamond Chain piece shown elsewhere. Please note the base is clear while the rest of the piece has a rich marigold finish. I suspect this pattern is European but have no proof at this time. It isn't shown in the Brockwitz or Inwald catalogs. I'd appreciate any further information from readers.

Buzz Saw Cruet

This Cambridge pattern (their #2699) is actually the same as the Double Star shown elsewhere in this book but the collectors of carnival glass long ago separated them. The Buzz Saw cruet is found in two sizes in marigold or green in carnival glass but was also made in uniridized crystal. Shown is the large size cruet in green.

Buzz Saw Shade

This shade is shown in the Hartung series books and she assigned the name so I'm honoring it. I feel certain that it is not from the same maker as the previous Buzz Saw patterns but I haven't been able to locate it to date. If I had to wager a guess it would be Imperial, but that would be speculation only. Marigold is the only color reported. Anyone with additional information is urged to contact me. Thanks to Gail Kantz for the photo.

Cactus (Millersburg)

Found as the exterior design with Millersburg's Rays and Ribbons interior, Cactus is an interesting but seldom discussed pattern. In design, it is a series of fans with tiny outlines that resemble cactus needles. Topping each pair of these is a hobstar, and below each pair is a triangle of file. Like most Millersburg exterior geometric designs, this one is bold and well done.

Calcutta Diamonds

This Indian water set, shared with me by Vikram Bachhawat, is a good one. The pitcher measures 7½" tall and the tumbler 4". The marigold is a rich finish, typical of Jain glass.

Calcutta Rose

Vikram Bachhawat tells me this is the correct name for this beautiful Indian tumbler. It stands 5½" tall and has a rich marigold finish. The flower and leaves cover a background of fine crosshatching.

Cambridge #2351

Until recently only the punch set and a bowl shape were known in carnival glass although this pattern was made in many shapes in crystal. Now, a rare 4" bud vase in a beautiful clambroth color has appeared. In old Cambridge ads this was called a bouquet vase and it came in 7" and 4" sizes. The punch set was advertised in marigold, amethyst, and green carnival, and the single reported bowl is green. Most pieces are marked "Near-cut" but the vase shown is not.

Cambridge #2660/108 Cologne Bottle

Sometimes called a barber bottle, this Cambridge pattern is found in scarce green, and rare marigold. It stands 8½" tall to the top of the stopper. Rose Presznick calls this pattern Broken Arches Variant.

Cambridge #2760 Daisy

If you compare this pattern to the Riihimaki pattern called Sunk Daisy, you will see these two patterns are identical. Cambridge first made this design as their #2760 Daisy pattern (it is shown in their catalog in crystal in many shapes) but Riihimaki then copied the pattern in the 1930s. These shakers are Cambridge. The glass insert is marked "Pat'd June 1909." In addition the Cambridge footed rose bowl has only seven arcs at the top while the one from Finland has eight arcs.

Cambridge Colonial #2750

This pattern was made by the Cambridge Glass Company in many shapes in crystal, but this cruet with original stopper is the only iridized piece I've seen. Thanks to the Hollenbachs for sharing it. If you compare it to the other three cruets in Flute or Wide Panel shown elsewhere, you can see the distinct differences.

Cambridge Hobstar Napkin Rings

These neat miniature napkin rings are just a bit over 1¾" high and have a hobstar on each side and diamonds of file in between. The napkin ring is flat on the back to allow it to rest on a table and on this smooth section is a very fancy "N" etched into the glass, apparently to identify the owner. This pattern is listed as Fostoria #600 in Hartung but has been found by the Britts in a Cambridge Near Cut book. In the same pattern, the book shows a salt dip and toothpick holder.

Cameo

Cameo is Fenton Art Glass Company's #1531 pattern from 1928. (For some reason this design designation was later changed to #1631 when it was produced in a cameo opalescent treatment.) The vase can be found in tangerine, white, marigold, and the fine celeste blue shown. Sizes range from 11" to 17" and all pieces I've seen have the wide mouthed lip.

Cameo Medallion Basket (Westmoreland #752)

Cameo Medallion basket was shown in old catalogs as Westmoreland's #752 made in 5", 6", and 7" sizes in crystal. The example shown is a soft amber color and is iridized. The medallion was possibly meant to be etched on the crystal pieces but probably had no other use, especially on any iridized ones.

Cameo Pendant

This very attractive pendant is from Germany but I can't confirm the company who made it. The center cameo is purple carnival glass as are the 14 jewel-like stones around outer ring. The pendant measures 1" tall and is ⅞" wide. It may have come in other iridized colors.

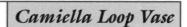

Camiella Loop Vase

This 5¾" squat vase shape was named by David Ayers for his daughter and it is the first example I've seen. It certainly looks European but I have no confirming information at this time. The color is a good marigold.

Campbell & Beesley Spring Opening

This rare and very collectible advertising plate from the Millersburg Glass Company is found on handgrip plates in amethyst. The plate says "Campbell & Beesley-Spring Opening-1911." The firm it advertised is said to be a ladies' apparel store in Nashville, Tennessee.

Canada Dry Bottle

I am happy to show the Canada Dry Sparkling Orangeade bottle, just as it was packaged in the mid-1920s. The bottle has a paper label and is marked "Canada Dry Incorporated – Gingerale #13" on the base. I've also seen these bottles in white carnival as well as the marigold shown.

Canary Tree (Jain)

This 4" tall marked Jain tumbler is from the collection of Bob Smith and the first example reported in this country. The fine design in marigold carnival and frosted crystal shows a bird on a tree limb with leaves. There are four of these patterns repeated around the piece. Around the top is a band of marigold carnival.

Can-Can

I haven't been able to pin down the maker of this oblong candy dish, but it is very similar to one made by Cambridge (their #2507). It measures approximately 8" in length. The photo and the name were supplied by Alan Sedgwick. I'd appreciate any information about this piece.

Candle Vase

The vase shown stands 9½" tall, has excellent color, and may be from the same mould as the Bud vase whimsey. I'm sure the Candle vase is a rarer shape and was probably made in the same colors of marigold, cobalt blue, and amethyst. The only way to compare these designs is to look at the pedestal base since everything else is determined by the shape.

Cane

One of the older Imperial patterns, Cane is found on wine goblets, bowls of various sizes, and pickle dishes. The coloring is nearly always a strong marigold, but the bowl has been seen in smoke, and I'm sure amethyst is a possibility. Cane is not one of the more desirable Imperial patterns and is readily available, especially on bowls; however, a rare color would improve the desirability of this pattern.

Cane and Daisy Cut

Cane and Daisy Cut is found in a rare basket and the vase shown. This pattern is better known in crystal. The vase is found in marigold, while the basket is known in marigold or smoke. Jenkins is thought to be the maker.

Cane and Panels

This is a tumble-up (the saucer is missing) in a Cristalerias Papini pattern from Argentina. There is also a short tumbler.

Cane and Scroll (Sea Thistle)

It is a pleasure to show both the creamer and the open ruffled sugar bowl in this pattern that was only seen on the creamer shape for so long. In addition, I am told there are other bowl shapes as well, including a rose bowl in cobalt blue. All other shapes are reported in only marigold at this time.

Cane and Wedge

This small, 4⅞" vase, from Finland is a rich amber and has a most unusual pattern. I welcome any information about this pattern, including the name.

Cane Open Edge Basket

Yes, even in 2007 there are still "one of a kind" pieces out there to find and this is one of them. This rare find is made by Imperial, shown in old catalogs as their #7455, and is shown here in marigold on milk glass. Several shapes are shown in the catalog in this particular pattern but this is the first example discovered to date with an iridized carnival treatment. Thanks to the Remmens for sharing the photo.

Cannonball Variant

This marigold water set has the same shape as the Cherry and Blossom set usually found in cobalt, but has a different enameled design. The tumblers have an interior wide panel design. I'm sure this is quite a scarce item.

Captive Rose

Fenton's Captive Rose is a very familiar decorative pattern found in bowls, bonbons, compotes, and occasional plates in marigold, cobalt blue, green, amethyst, amber, and smoke. The design is a combination of embroidery circles, scales, and diamond stitches, and is a tribute to the mould maker's art. The roses are like finely stitched quilt work.

Carnation Wreath

Carnation Wreath was made in the early 1900s in crystal and in goofus glass, but this is the first piece of iridized glass I've seen. The 9" bowl is shown (a 5" marigold bowl is also reported). The pattern is all exterior and a bit hard to see but there are eight stems of leaves and flowers up the sides of the bowl and a full-blown flower on the base.

Carnival Beads

I have always resisted showing strands of beads, even though they are very collectible and quite attractive, but when Lee Briix sent this very interesting photo using a Diamond Point Columns vase as a prop, I changed my mind. Most of these beads were made in smaller glass factories or in Europe.

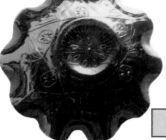

Carnival Cruets

Shown are two cruets, obviously from the same company. One has 14 interior panels and the other does not. The paneled one has the figure "12" raised on the base while the unpaneled one has the figure "5" on the base. I thank Jane Dinkins for sharing these with me. I believe this is really the cruet shown in Hartung's Book #5, which she called Panelled Cruet.

Carolina Dogwood

This well-done Westmoreland interior pattern looks a bit common in marigold but the other colors, teal on milk glass, peach opalescent, marigold on milk glass, and the blue opalescent shown, are all outstanding. Dogwood sprays with leaves and a central blossom make up the design.

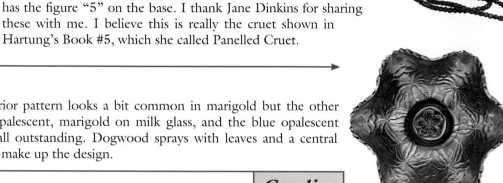

Caroline

This exterior Dugan pattern is usually found on bowls, plates, and handled baskets, and accompanies a Smooth Rays interior. Colors are primarily peach opalescent with some marigold pieces known and lavender opalescent reported. Here I am pleased to show a very hard to find bowl in amethyst.

Cartwheel (Heisey)

Besides the stemmed candy dish we've shown before, we've now seen this very scarce bonbon in the same pattern. The color is the usual pale-yellowish marigold found on most Heisey iridized items. (Heisey iridized no glass at their factory but jobbed it out for this treatment.) Other shapes probably exist in this pattern but to date we've seen only the two.

Car Vase

This automobile vase was once shown as the Benzer car vase, which is incorrect, as the Benzer vase has "Benzer" embossed on the bottom. I suspect this rather plain vase to be from Dugan as well but have not pinned it down to that factory to date. The only reported color is marigold, but others may exist. Additional information is appreciated. Thanks to Wayne Delahoy for the photo.

Castle Shade Lamp

This lamp shows examples of a very brightly painted shade that features a castle scene with water and a rocky shoreline. Two of these shades have been joined with a brass lamp of the same era and the whole piece is a very attractive item indeed. The shades are about 5" tall and have a bell diameter of 4½".

Cat Face

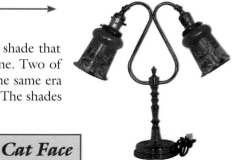

This ashtray comes from Argentina and was likely made there, although I have proof to date. It has a bit of good humor in the design. I'm told that there is a variant to this pattern as well. It is also known as Cat's Meow. Thanks to both Clint Aresnault and Gary Vandevander for sharing the information and photo.

Cathedral Arches

This is now known to be from the Brockwitz Glass Works. The one-piece punch bowl shape shown and a ruffled salver from the same mould were shown in Brockwitz's 1921 catalog. The punch bowl piece is listed as a fruit bowl in the catalog. The design is a good one, with a bold oval with a flaming star, bordered by sections of prismed stars in a column. Marigold is the only reported color in carnival glass at this time.
Thanks to Siegmar Geiselberger for his Brockwitz catalogs.

Cathedral Windows

This nice water set from India has great shape, a good design, and outstanding iridescence. In the last few years, the number of patterns from this country has become enormous.

CB Vase

Vikram Bachhawat shares this fine dark marigold vase that is clearly marked "CB." The rest of the design has leaves and flowers on stems that run from the middle of the vase to almost the collar of the neck.

CB Vase Variant

This vase which is shaped like the other Indian vases with a nearly hour-glass design has flowers and leaves set into a "V" design with butterfly-like patterns on either side. The glass is very thin and the pattern lightly done. Like Jain, CB was one of more than 20 glassworks in India.

Celebration Tumbler

This 5⅜" Jain tumbler is very unusual. It has the words "Good Luck" as well as a figure of a boy in a cap, two tall geometric designs, and other objects. Below the rim is a two-row banding of checkerboard. The color is a watery marigold, much like other Jain items. Thanks to Andres Neveu for the photo of, and information about, this rare item.

Central Shoe Store

The plate shown was also made in a handgrip plate and bowls by Fenton. The lettering says "Compliments of the Central Shoe Store – Corner of Collinsville and St. Louis Avenues – East St. Louis, Illinois."

Chain and Star

Here is the tumbler in this Fostoria pattern. Besides this shape, both a creamer and sugar are known in iridized glass (many shapes are known in crystal). The color is a soft marigold that has hints of amber in the tint. The creamer and open sugar are called a hotel set in ads of the day and apparently had no accompanying butter or spooner.

55

Channeled Flute (Northwood)

While most collectors just lump this with the regular Northwood #21 Flute, there are enough differences to consider this as a variation. First there are the endings above the base that flair much like the Imperial Flute. Then there are shallow channels running in the center of each flute, hence the name. Colors are marigold, amethyst, green, cobalt blue, white, vaseline, aqua opalescent, sapphire blue, and the Alaskan treatment shown, a marigold over green.

Chariot

Chariot is now known in the creamer and matching open sugar shown, as well as the compote shape shown in previous editions. Stems on the compote and open sugar may be iridized as on the example shown or clear as on previously shown pieces.

Charlotte (Brockwitz)

This beautiful compote from Brockwitz was named for Charlotte Eisensoe, a Danish glass collector who has done much to advance the collecting of carnival glass. The compote is known in blue (as shown) or marigold. Thanks to the Ayers family for the photo and the information.

Charlotte's Web Mirror

What an intriguing piece of glass this hand mirror is. Once thought to be from Europe, I've now been told that Imperial is the maker, although I haven't found proof of such to date. As you can see, the bulk of the glass has soft clambroth iridescence but the center web is a stronger luster. Photo courtesy of Samantha Prince.

Chatalaine

This is Imperial's #407½ pattern, made in 1909 in a crystal water set and the following year in a beautiful purple carnival glass. Crystal pieces are scarce and the iridized items are rare. The pattern is very strong and balanced.

Checkerboard (Westmoreland)

Originally called Old Quilt, this very scarce Westmoreland pattern is found on water sets, a goblet, and a punch cup (no punch bowl is currently known). The example shown is a beautiful lavender color, but most pieces are amethyst except for rare examples of marigold tumblers, goblets, and punch cups, with less than a dozen pieces in any color or shape known.

Checkerboard Bouquet

This late carnival 8" plate is seldom seen. It has an all-exterior design of checkerboard rim with an overlapping winding vine, while in the center the pattern becomes a large poinsettia with other blossoms around its edges.

Checkerboard Panels

Checkerboard Panels is also called Zipper Round in England. The interior is plain with all the pattern on the outside where it forms a series of ovals that are filled with file and it has a raised border below and above of raised file. The base has a radiating star and only the bowl shape has been reported so far.

Checkers

Now credited to Hazel-Atlas, this pattern can be found in a rose bowl, an ashtray, 4" bowl, 8" – 9" bowl, 7" plate, and two sizes of covered butter dishes. It has to be considered late carnival of course, but the rich marigold is quite good. The covered butters are not that easy to find.

Cherries and Little Flowers (Northwood)

Although exactly like the Fenton Cherry Blossoms version shown elsewhere, this set is marked Northwood. Colors are mostly cobalt blue but scarce marigold and rare amethyst examples are known. Only the water set pieces are reported. Just why both Fenton and Northwood turned out identical patterns is a mystery but this is apparently the case.

Cherry (Dugan)

This nicely done Dugan interior pattern is found on large and small bowls, a plate (usually crimped), and large footed bowls called Paneled Cherry in opalescent glass. The regular bowls and the plate all have the Jewelled Heart pattern on the exterior. The footed piece may have a plain or a Cherry interior. Colors are marigold, peach opalescent, amethyst, purple, and lavender.

Cherry (Millersburg)

Some collectors call this Millersburg pattern Hanging Cherries but it was first called by the name listed here. Shapes include a berry set, table set, water set, milk pitcher, a very rare powder jar with lid, a rare 7" compote, 7" and 10" shallow bowls, and 7" and 10" plates. In addition there is a cherry bowl with a hobnail exterior found in two sizes.

Cherry and Cable

This scarce carnival pattern is from Northwood and sometimes called Cherry and Thumbprint. (It is also known in decorated crystal.) It is found in a table set, a berry set, and a water set (only three or four pitchers are known). The color is always marigold on iridized pieces. The pattern dates from 1908. It has been widely reproduced.

Cherry Blossoms (Fenton)

Here is the Fenton version of this pattern on a cannonball pitcher with matching tumblers (the Northwood version is known as Cherries and Little Flowers and is nearly identical). It is shown in 1910 Fenton ads and was probably a copy of the Northwood version when Frank Fenton worked for Northwood. All pieces are found in cobalt blue with enameled flowers, and the tumblers are flat based without collars.

Cherry Chain (Fenton)

Here is the regular Cherry Chain pattern (three cherries in each circle). It can be found on bowls, plates, and bonbons in marigold, white, cobalt blue, green, ice green, amethyst, and clambroth. Bowls are known in 6", 8", and 9" sizes and at least two of the larger sizes are found in red slag carnival. There is also a variant with six cherries in each circle. Shown is a very rare emerald green 6½" plate. It has an Orange Tree exterior.

Cherry Chain Variant (Fenton)

While most collectors make no effort to separate the regular design (it has three cherries and less leaves in each circle) from this variant with more cherries and leaves, there really are enough differences to become a variant. It is found on plates, bonbons, and bowls with some of the bonbons being flattened into banana bowl shapes. Cherry Chain Variant can be found with either Orange Tree or Bearded Berry as the exterior pattern.

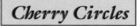

Cherry Circles

This large bonbon was Fenton's #1426 pattern, made around 1920. It is found in round, square, or banana bowl shaped pieces. It resembles Fenton's Cherry Chain pattern in design except for the scale band edging and the scale circle center. Colors are marigold, amethyst, green, blue, aqua, red, and white, with ice blue reported.

Cherry/Hobnail (Millersburg)

The interior cherry design varies enough from the regular Millersburg Cherry to show this separate example with the Hobnail exterior. These bowls are quite rare and are found in marigold, amethyst, and blue, and measure roughly 9" in diameter. A 5" bowl can also be found, both with and without the Hobnail exterior.

Cherry Smash

This U.S. Glass pattern, called Cherryberry by Depression glass collectors, was first made in 1928. Besides the Depression colors of pink and green, some pieces were iridized (marigold). It was available in a tumbler, berry bowls, table set, plate, and the pitcher shown.

Shown is a very rare plate, thought to be a Millersburg product by most experts. It measures some 10¾" in diameter and has three clusters of fruit and leaves that match other Millersburg Cherry designs, but the exterior is plain except for a rayed star on the marie. Color is a strong amethyst and the outer edges have fluting.

Chesterfield

This was Imperial's #600 pattern, found in candlesticks, creamer and sugar, a rose bowl, a toothpick holder, tankard pitcher, tumblers, an open salt, lemonade mug, compotes in several sizes, a covered candy dish, a stemmed sherbet, and a champagne glass. Colors are marigold, clambroth, smoke, celeste blue, white, red, and teal. Not all shapes are found in all colors of course, and some pieces have the Iron Cross marking.

Chevrons

The owners of this beautiful vase tell me this is the correct name and that it was made by Josef Rindskopf. It has six rows of chevrons and part of a seventh at the base. The color is a rich marigold with good iridescence. I've heard of no other colors at this time.

Chippendale Kry-stol

Shown are two sizes of Jefferson's Chippendale Kry-stol pattern. The larger stemmed bonbon is marked "Chippendale Kry-stol," while the smaller version has no marking. In design they resemble two Westmoreland designs (Keystone Colonial and #1700 Colonial) both shown elsewhere in this book. The color is a soft watery marigold.

Christmas Compote

This beautiful, large compote from Dugan is both rare and desirable. It is found in either marigold or amethyst and has a well-designed pattern of holly and berries on the exterior and the same pattern grouped with rays on the interior. The compote was reproduced in 1998 from the original mould. Photo courtesy of Seeck Auction.

Chrysanthemum

Chrysanthemum from 1914 is one of Fenton's fine large bowl patterns. It can be found with a collar base and ball or spatula footed. Colors include marigold, amethyst, green, blue, red, teal, white, and a rare vaseline.

Chrysanthemum Drape Lamp

This beauty would grace any glass collection. As you can see, the font is beautifully iridized. It has been found in pink glass as well as white. Strangely, most of these lamps have been found in Australia, but the maker is, thus far, unknown.

Chrysanthemum Drape Variant

Although similar to the regular Chrysanthemum Drape lamp, this pattern shown has more design and the flowers are more pronounced. The color is white carnival glass. Thanks to Mary and Jack Adams for sharing this beauty.

Circled Rose

Circled Rose is much like the Golden Cupid design. It is on clear glass with a base design that has been glided and then iridized. Here I show a 7" plate with a single handle from the collection of Wayne Delahoy of Australia. Other shapes probably exist.

Circled Star and Vines

Marked "PGW" (Vikram Bachhawat tells me this means Paliwal Glass Works), this 4¾" tall tumbler has a strange plant that has thorns, a circled star in the middle of the stem, and an unusual flower that joins a vine around the top. The color is a good marigold.

Circle Scroll

I'm pleased to show this hard-to-find bowl shape. This Dugan pattern is best known in a hat shape (from the tumbler). Other shapes include a water set, berry set, compote, table set, and a vase whimsey. Colors include marigold and purple.

Classic Arts

This pattern and its sister pattern, Egyptian Queen (shown elsewhere in this edition), were made by Josef Rindskopf in the 1920s. Classic Arts pieces include a vase shape, a rose bowl, and the powder jar with lid shown. The decoration is green stain on the band. Thanks to Siegmar Geiselberger for the information.

Cleveland Memorial

Made to celebrate Cleveland's centennial, this ashtray from Millersburg has scenes that depict the Garfield statue, his tomb at Lake View cemetery, the Soldiers and Sailors monument, the Superior Street viaduct, and Cleveland's Chamber of Commerce building. These rare ashtrays can be found in amethyst or marigold.

Cobblestone (Imperial)

This Imperial pattern has Arcs as an exterior pattern. It is found mostly in 8½" – 10" ruffled bowls (one plate is reported in purple). Purple is most often seen, with marigold a bit scarce, helios green less scarce, amber rare, and cobalt blue even rarer. In addition, a similar pattern by Fenton is found on a bonbon with a honeycomb exterior.

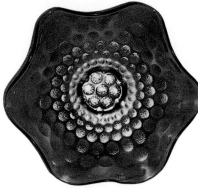

Coin Dot Variant (Fenton)

This pattern is much like the regular Coin Dot, but has added dots at the edges of the center grouping at 12, 2, 4, 6, 8, and 10 clockwise. It is believed this mould was later retooled into the Feather Stitch pattern. Colors are marigold, green, amethyst, and blue. Thanks to Mr. and Mrs. A.T. McClelland for sharing this scarce green example.

Coin Spot

This well-known pattern was made by the Dugan Company and continued by Diamond Glass. It is found on the compote shown or a goblet shape, all from the same mould. (In opalescent glass a vase was also pulled from this mould.) Colors in carnival glass include marigold, amethyst, cobalt blue, peach opalescent, ice green, and celeste blue. (Green has long been rumored.) Peach opalescent examples are the easiest to find.

Colonial (Imperial)

Colonial is often mistaken for the Chesterfield pattern or even Wide Panel, all by Imperial. It is found in candlesticks, a buttermilk goblet, a breakfast creamer and sugar set, a lemonade mug, and the child's mug shown. This mug was designated #593 by the factory as were all the shapes except the #41 candlesticks. Coloring is always marigold except for the candlesticks, which were made in amber, purple, and clambroth as well.

Colonial Decanter

The pattern on this very nice decanter reminds me of several pressed glass patterns as well as the Colonial Loop piece shown elsewhere in this edition. The maker and age have not been established at this time. Anyone with information is requested to contact me. Thanks to Gary Roach for sharing this.

Colonial Lady

Both very scarce and very desirable, this beautiful 5½" Imperial vase is a collectors' favorite. It is found in either marigold or purple. The purple often has an electric iridescence that rivals Tiffany glass.

Colonial Loop

The maker of this wine glass hasn't been established, but the piece is on quality glass with light marigold iridescence. I welcome any information about this piece.

Colonial Tulip (Northwood)

This very pretty 5½" stemmed compote is called by this name in a Northwood ad in a 1909 G. Sommers & Company catalog. It is found mostly in the Alaskan treatment (marigold over green glass), but in a spring 1909 Butler Brothers ad it is shown in other colors and simply called a high footed comport. It can be found with either a ribbed or plain interior and other colors are marigold, amethyst, or green. Here I show it in a rare teal color with the Starburst lustre interior.

Colorado

This well-known U.S. Glass pattern hasn't been found on carnival glass before. This piece was discovered with a primary pattern called Threaded Butterflies. It is a footed plate in aqua and must be classified as extremely rare. The current owner is Maxine Burkhardt and I appreciate her sharing this find with me.

Columbia

Mostly found in marigold, Imperial's #246 pattern is rather plain but the fantastic color often makes it a standout. Besides the marigold, it can be found in purple, smoke, clambroth, and the green shown. Shapes include a plate, compote, ruffled vase, and a rare rose bowl.

Columbia Variant

Please compare this true compote to the regular Columbia pattern and you will see the design is very similar, yet the base is a bit different. Few of these variants seem to have been made, and in old Imperial ads which show some 16 shapes from the standard Columbia design, not a single example of this variant is shown.

Columbus

Seldom discussed, but actually a very fine piece of carnival glass, this plate was first described by Marion Hartung in 1965. It measures 8¼" across and the pattern is on the exterior with an intaglio ship on the base, a ring of raised beads, and an intaglio rim design. The color is very rich marigold.

Columns and Rings

Shaped from a tumbler, this very unusual hat-shaped whimsey is like many designs from the Duncan Company in that it has 20 short concave columns around the body with nine rings above that have been stretched to form wide banding. The color is a rich marigold with strong iridescence. I suspect this piece came along rather late in the carnival glass age. Any further information on this pattern would be greatly appreciated.

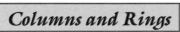

Compass

Compass is a Dugan pattern of hobstars, hexagons, and other geometric designs that manages to fill nearly all the allowed space. It is found on exteriors of Dugan Heavy Grape bowls, and the example shown demonstrates why peach opalescent is such a collected color.

Compote Vase

Approximately 6" tall, this nicely done stemmed piece is found in all the standard colors but is mostly seen in amethyst or green. Often, the stem is not iridized, but the lustre on the rest of the compote vase more than makes up for it.

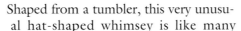

Compote Vase Variant (Fenton)

This is much like the regular Compote Vase, except the stem is quite short and the interior has a Smooth Rib pattern. The piece is approximately 4" tall and the base is not iridized. Only green has been reported but surely other colors were made. Please note the iridized finish is very much a radium one.

Concave Columns Vase

If you look closely, you will discover this is the Coin Spot pattern, usually found on compotes, turned into a vase shape. The vase was done in some quantity in opalescent glass, but here is the first reported aqua opalescent example in iridized glass. As you may know, this was a pattern that came first from Dugan and then was continued by the Diamond Company, so the aqua opalescent treatment is a real surprise. I do know some Dugan opalescent pieces have been recently iridized so I will reserve any opinion until more information comes to light.

Concave Diamond

Concave Diamond was made by Northwood in 1917 as part of their Satin Sheen line. Shapes include a water set, a tumble-up, and a pickle castor. Colors are marigold (pickle castor only), Venetian blue, topaz, or russet. The tumble-up is also found in jade blue, an opaque treatment.

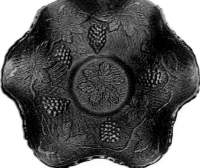

Concave Flute (Westmoreland)

Found mostly on somewhat plain looking rose bowls, this Westmoreland pattern really comes to life on the bowl shape or even the rare banana bowl. The only design is exterior, a series of nine flutes that bleed out from a sharp arch. Colors are marigold, amethyst, green, teal, and a very pretty amber with much gold.

Concord

This very collectible Fenton pattern has a background of fine netting, making it distinctive. It can be found in 8" – 9" bowls as well as 10" plates. Colors are marigold, amethyst, blue, green, or amber. Bowls can be six-ruffled, three-in-one edges, or ice cream shaped.

Cone and Tie (Imperial)

Shown in a 1909 Imperial catalog in crystal, this simply designed tumbler (no water pitcher is known), is a collectors' prize. The only iridized color is a fantastic purple. These are rare and very desirable, and bring high prices when sold. Iridized both inside and out, Cone and Tie has a concave base with a whirling star design. The base is ground. Rumors of a marigold example have long persisted but none has been confirmed.

Connie

Connie, from Northwood, was named for Connie Moore, and is one of the better enameled water sets in white. Pieces are very scarce and bring sizable prices when offered for sale. The iridescence is a frosty white and the flower branches very colorful with blue, white, and orange.

Consolidated Shade

This 16" wide shade, I'm told, comes from Consolidated Glass and was sold at auction in June 2007. No one could remember the proper name so I've given it a temporary one. In 1972 while helping catalog the Dugan shards with William Heacock, my former co-author Bill Edwards was staying in Columbus, Ohio, and noticed his room had one of these shades hanging from the ceiling. He asked the manager about it and found that each room had the same shade, which had been installed when the hotel was built in 1922. Colors found are pearl carnival and the nice marigold on milk glass shown.

Constellation

Constellation is one of the smaller compotes at 5" tall and about the same size across the rim. It has an exterior pattern called Seafoam, which is really the S-Repeat pattern. The Constellation pattern consists of a large center star with bubble-like dots over the area and a series of raised bars running out to the rim. Colors are marigold, amethyst, peach opalescent, white, and a frosty pearlized finish over vaseline glass. Thanks to Samantha Prince for the nice photo.

Cooleemee, N.C.

Tooled from Fenton's well known Heart and Vine pattern, this 9" plate served double duty as an advertising piece. It is a rare and much sought item. The lettering reads "Souvenir of Cooleemee, N.C. — J.N. Ledford Company." The Ledford Company was a textile mill in North Carolina. The only color reported in this plate is marigold.

Coral

Coral, similar in design to Fenton's rare Peter Rabbit pattern, can be found on 8¾" bowls (ice cream or ruffled shapes) and plates. 8¾". Colors include marigold, green, blue, vaseline, and white.

Corinth (Dugan)

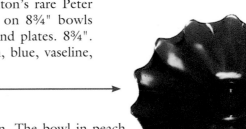

Both Westmoreland and Dugan-Diamond had a try at this pattern. The bowl in peach opalescent shown appears to be from the latter. Dugan-Diamond pieces are bowls, vases, and banana bowls in marigold, amethyst, and peach opalescent. Westmoreland made the same shapes in marigold, green, teal, amber, and blue, as well as marigold over milk glass and aqua over milk glass.

Corinth (Westmoreland)

If you will compare this vase to the one with a J.I.P. shape, you will see they really came from the same mould. This vase in amethyst stands 9" tall. These can be found as short as 6" and as tall as 21". The base has a 3⅛" diameter and is plain and slightly sunken in. All Westmoreland Corinth pieces have 12 ribs. Colors are marigold, amber, amethyst, green, teal, blue opalescent, peach opalescent, marigold on milk glass, and topaz. Lamps made from the amethyst vase have turned up as well.

Corn Bottle

This neat little bottle from Imperial is only 5" tall and usually has a superb radium finish. Colors are marigold, green, and smoke, and we've seen several with a cork stopper. I understand they might have been premium items that held some product, but can't be positive.

64

← Corn Cruet

Since I first saw this years ago, I've been able to learn little about it. The only color reported is the white. Rumor places it in the Dugan line, but I can't be sure.

Corning Insulator →

While I've never been very excited by insulators, this one has superb color and is marked "Corning – Reg. USA Pat." It is only one of several sizes that can be found.

← Corn Vase

This well-known vase from the Northwood Company is desirable, well designed, and a collectors' favorite. It can be found in a few variations and the one shown has the corn leaf base (some bases are plain). In addition there is one called a Pulled Husk vase. Colors of the Corn vase are many and include marigold, amethyst, green, white, ice blue, ice green, teal, olive green, and the very rare aqua opalescent shown.

Coronation (Victorian Crown) →

This bulbous vase shape is about 5" tall and has a diameter of 3". This unusual piece has four crowns around it with suspended coronets above them. The color is a strong marigold and the maker hasn't been determined, although both British factories and makers from India are possibilities.

← Cosmos (Millersburg)

Found only on a 6" ice cream shaped bowl, a deep ruffled sauce, and a 6¼" plate in a beautiful green radium finish, this pattern should have been made on other shapes for it is just that nice. A marigold bowl is known. The center of the flower design is well stippled and the petals have ridging nearly to their ragged edges.

Cosmos and Cane →

This is one of the better iridized patterns from U.S. Glass. It was made in berry sets, table sets, water sets, a tall compote, plates, and many different whimsey shapes. Colors are marigold, honey-amber, white, and a hard-to-find amethyst. In addition, an advertising tumbler is a popular item.

← Cosmos and Hobstar

There is something special about these fruit bowls on metal standards, and this is one of the pretty ones. The pattern is one I don't recall seeing before and is a series of diamond panels with alternating hobstars and cosmos blossoms. Above the diamonds are fans and below are half-diamonds filled with a file pattern. The marigold is very rich, but I can't say if other colors were made. It is from Brockwitz.

Cosmos Variant

Cosmos variant was made by Diamond Glass in the early 1920s. It is found in ads that feature Diamond's Double Stem Rose. Shapes known are ruffled bowls, ice cream shaped bowls, and a large plate from the same mould. Colors are marigold, amethyst, blue, and vaseline (bowl only) but since I own a green non-iridized bowl in the ice cream shape, it was possibly iridized in this color too.

Country Kitchen (Millersburg)

Country Kitchen is one of Millersburg's standard patterns that can be found in crystal as well as carnival glass. Shapes include a berry set, table set, the exterior of the Fleur-de-lis bowls, vase whimsies, and a spittoon whimsey (all from the spooner mould shown). Colors in carnival glass are marigold, amethyst, green, and a rare vaseline.

Courtesy

This deep, oddly shaped bowl is listed in marigold under this name by Rose Presznick in her fourth glass book. Here it is shown in a soft amethyst (the color Fenton called Wisteria). The bowl is 3¼" tall, has a base diameter of 3¼", and has the following inscription: "Patented June 24 – 1924." The maker has not been confirmed as far as I know.

Courthouse

This Millersburg pattern from 1910 is found on 7" – 7½" bowls (with or without the "Courthouse, Millersburg, Ohio"). They are all amethyst glass and can be either six-ruffled, three-in-one ruffled, or ice cream shaped.

Covered Frog

This novel covered dish, made by the Co-Operative Flint Glass Company of Beaver Falls, Pennsylvania, is a standout in design and color. It measures 5½" long and 4" tall and has been seen in pastel green, pastel blue, marigold, and rarely amethyst. The eyes are painted black and are very realistic. Some are marked on the bottom with an H and T joined together at the horizontal section of the H.

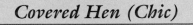

Covered Hen (Chic)

The Covered Hen is probably the best-recognized piece of English carnival glass made at the Sowerby Works. The Covered Hen is 6⅞" long and known in a good rich marigold as well as a weak cobalt blue. The mould work is very good but the color ranges from very good to poor. While reproductions have been reported, my British sources tell me this isn't true, and that no examples have been made since the 1940s.

Covered Swan

This beautiful English pattern is a companion to the Covered Hen and can be found in both marigold and amethyst. It measures 7¾" long, and the neck doesn't touch the back! What a mould maker's achievement! The base is similar to that of the Covered Hen dish. Both are butter dishes.

Crab Claw/Blaze (Imperial)

Marion Hartung called this pattern Crab Claw and Rose Presznick called it Blaze, so take your pick of names. It is Imperial's #3437 pattern, found in bowls and plates in crystal and a berry set and ice cream set in carnival glass. Iridized colors are marigold, green, purple, and clambroth (shown), and the small bowl in cobalt blue, and both sizes are now confirmed in smoke.

Crab Claw Variant (Imperial)

I'm sure that feathers will be ruffled by calling this a variant, but that is just what it has to be according to a 1906 factory catalog. Crab Claw bowls are #3437. This water set is #409. It is found in crystal and scarce pieces in marigold carnival glass. In addition, the small decanter (cruet) listed also as Crab Claw, has a catalog number of 302 and is not the same pattern as either Crab Claw or Crab Claw Variant. Thanks to Samantha Prince for sharing the photo.

Crackle

Jeannette's Crackle can be found on two sizes of pitchers, two sizes of tumblers, a goblet, bowls, covered candy jar, candlesticks, 6" – 8" plates, wall vase, two sizes and shapes of car vase, and salt shakers. Colors are mostly marigold but purple, light blue, and green exist on some items.

CR Ashtray

This interesting item is a favorite of ashtray collectors as well as collectors of South American glass. The pattern is simply a large C and R combined. The colors reported are marigold, green, blue, and amber is a strong possibility. The maker is Christalerias Rigolleau of Buenos Aires, Argentina. Many thanks to Clint Arsenault for sharing this nice group photo.

Creole Rose Bowl

So very much like the Venetian giant rose bowl in design, it has the same general geometric parts but differs in the scalloped top, has no honeycomb ring above the base, and has a hobstar rather than the diamond on each side of the primary design. The piece shown has not been cataloged before as far as I know. The rare Orleans pattern from McKee is very close also, but has some variations too. I'd like to hear from anyone who has information about this piece. The name is credited to Bill Edwards.

Crosshatch

Credited to the Sowerby Company, this pattern isn't often seen on the market and is seldom discussed. In crystal, several shapes are known but in carnival glass only the stemmed creamer and the stemmed open sugar (shown) are reported to date. All iridized pieces we've heard about are marigold but certainly other colors are possible.

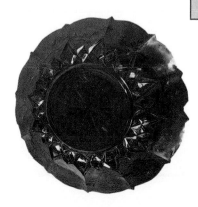

Crown of Diamonds (Crystal)

Here is the attractive exterior pattern of the Trailing Flowers bowl. As you can see the diamonds extend upward from the collar base and are two sizes that alternate. The bowl measures 7" in diameter. This is a seldom discussed pattern.

Crucifix Candlestick

These very collectible novelty candlesticks are readily found in crystal made by Imperial, Cambridge, and other companies. The carnival ones are only from Imperial, are 9½" tall, and are known only in marigold.

Curtain Optic

Made in the 1920s by the Fenton Company, this beautiful pattern is a kissin' cousin to the stretch pieces. It can be found on ice tea sets, guest sets, and possibly other shapes as well. The pastel coloring is a pleasant relief and complements the opal drapery effect.

Curved Star/Cathedral

Here is a pattern that may qualify for frequent flyer mileage! It is known to have been made in Sweden, at Brockwitz of Germany, probably by U.S. Glass, and recently acknowledged from Karhula-Iittala of Finland (their 1938 catalog). It is also called Cathedral by some collectors and can be found in a chalice (celery vase), pitcher, bowls, flower holder, large epergne, compote in two sizes, a two-piece fruit bowl, creamer, covered butter dish, open sugar, vase, and the covered cheese dish shown (some call this a large butter). Colors are marigold or cobalt blue.

Cut Arcs

While it is most often found on the exterior of 8" to 9" bowls, Fenton's Cut Arcs is occasionally seen on compotes of standard size and a vase whimsey pulled from the bowl shape. On the example shown the edging is a tight candy ribbon, and the interior carries no pattern at all.

Cut Cosmos

Hard to find and mysterious as to origin, this tumbler is a very desirable find. It is found only in marigold and has no reported matching pitcher. There are six arched panels with the pattern of leaves and flowers intaglio or cut in. The finish is usually a watery radium one, leading some to speculate Cut Cosmos may be from Millersburg but there is no proof.

Cut Flowers

Here is one of the prettiest of all the Jenkins patterns. The intaglio work is deep and sharp, and the cut petals show clear glass through the lustre, giving a beautiful effect. Most Cut Flowers vases are rather light in color, but the 10½" one shown has a rich deep marigold finish. Cut Flowers can also be found in a smoke color.

Cut Grecian Gold Lamp

Fenton made several items with similar wheel-cut designs including Engraved Grape and Engraved Zinnia, but this is the first lamp font I've seen. The coloring is very good and I suspect this item came along in the late 1920s. It would add to any collection.

Cut Ovals (Riihimaki)

Not to be confused with the candlesticks of the same name that were made by the Fenton Art Glass Company, this covered butter dish is believed to have been made by the Riihimaki Glass Works in Finland. The reason for this tentative attribution (I have no actual proof at this time) is the rich amber color of the glass, a color known to have been produced at Riihimaki.

Cut Prisms

This pattern was named by Rose Presznick. It has a mould seam above the base, circling through the prominent prism. The base has a many rayed star and the bowl is perfectly round with iridescence inside and out. The color is a rich marigold with good iridescence. Other shapes may have been made but the closest I've seen is a faceted hatpin. This pattern is now credited to Rindskopf.

Czech Flower

This very nice cruet is suspected to be from Czechoslovakia, hence the name. It has a clear applied handle and a clear stopper and the glass is thin with a soft marigold iridescence that has enameled twigs, buds, and odd blossoms of two different colored dots. In the center of the neck is a band that is also clear. Anyone who can shed more light on this piece is urged to contact me.

Czech Interior Coin Dot

There isn't much information about this vase except to say it has interior coin dots, is a thin glass with blue coloring, and is iridized. I feel this piece may well be from Czechoslovakia, thus the name. Anyone with additional or contrary information is urged to contact me.

Czech Interior Swirl

This very pretty decanter and the matching glasses are from Czechoslovakia and are so marked with a paper label. The glass is very thin and the iridescence watery. The bases, handles, and lid finial are done in blue glass while a banding of blue is found on the top of the decanter.

Czechoslovakian

Shown is the small liquor set in this pattern, but it can also be found in tankard water sets. In addition, the tumblers are known in at least two sizes, including a lemonade size. These pieces all have the mark "MADE IN CZECHOSLOVAKIA" stamped on the bottom, so there is little doubt of their origin. The decanter is 6¾" tall (8⅝" with the stopper) and the glasses are 2½" tall. All pieces seen are dark marigold and all seem to have the black enameled rings.

Czech Swirls

This tumbler has a red swirled paint design over marigold iridescence. The tumbler has five rings of melon-ribbing from the base up and then a taller ring at the top. Its age is questionable, and anyone with information on this is urged to contact me.

Dagny

Found in a 1929 Eda Glass catalog, this version of the familiar Curved Star pattern is different from the Brockwitz Curved Star vase in that it has a large mostly unpatterned area around the base, with only indented ribbing running in vertical lines. This vase is reported in both marigold and blue iridized glass and the coloring is superb.

Dahlia

This is another product of the Dugan Glass Company. It is found in water sets (reproduced), a berry set, and a table set (reproduced). Colors in old items are marigold, purple, and white that is often decorated. Beware of reproductions in purple water sets and all pieces in opalescent glass for they are new. In addition the new water sets are found in pink, red, black amethyst, white, and ice blue. They were made first by Wright and then Mosser.

Dahlia (Jenkins)

Dahlia is from the Jenkins Glass Company and is known mostly in crystal, but here is an iridized vase shape (their #286). It is the first carnival example I've heard about. The marigold is only at the top of this piece.

Dahlia Button

While I've never intended to show a parade of all the various buttons made in carnival glass, I do feel the one shown here is attractive enough to warrant attention. It is actually green but the iridescence is so very rich it looks purple. The flower-like pattern is very realistic and it appears to rest on a stippled background.

Dainty Flower

This neat little vase has an enameled design of what appears to be a dogwood blossom with leaves on each side. It is around 4 to 5 inches tall and on red base glass. It is a very nice item for the collector of enameled pieces. Thanks to the Hamlets for sharing this fine piece.

Daisies and Diamonds

Named by Dave Cotton, its owner, this 9" bowl looks European but I certainly have no proof and would like to hear from anyone who has more information. It is all exterior and the marigold is very strong and rich.

Daisy

Fenton's Daisy pattern is very scarce, found only in the bonbon shape. The pattern is a simple one of four strands of flowers and leaves around the bowl and one blossom with leaves in the center. While marigold has been reported, blue is the color most often found, and although I haven't seen amethyst or green, they may exist.

70

Daisy and Cane (Tartan)

This pattern is known to have been made at Brockwitz of Germany but is also shown in catalogs from Karhula-Iittala and Riihimaki of Finland. The Brockwitz catalog number for this pattern is 19900. Shapes include pedestal vase, bowls, cake stand, salver (several sizes), rare spittoon, decanter and wine glass, celery vase, epergne, and the pitcher shown. There is a variant with smooth buttons in existence. This pattern is also known as Tartan by some collectors.

Daisy and Drape

Northwood's Daisy and Drape from 1911 was probably copied from a U.S. Glass novelty pattern called Vermont. The vase can be found with the top flared or slightly turned in. Colors include marigold, amethyst, blue, green, white, aqua opalescent, ice blue, ice green, aqua, and the ice lavender.

Daisy and Little Flowers

This Northwood water set (mould blown pitcher and pressed tumblers) is a bulbous or cannon ball shape. The tumblers are very distinctive with a flared base and rolled sides. The only color I've heard about is cobalt blue.

Daisy and Plume

While the Northwood Company seems to be the primary user of this pattern, the Dugan Company also had a version. Most Northwood pieces are marked. They include a stemmed rose bowl, a compote with Blackberry interior, and a rose bowl or three-footed novelty bowl (very much like the Dugan one). Dugan pieces sometimes have the Dugan Cherry interior but not always. Both companies made this pattern in opalescent glass also and carnival colors are marigold, white, purple, electric blue, green, and aqua from Northwood and peach opalescent, marigold, green, and amethyst from Dugan. Shown is a rare example of the three-footed bowl in amber with Northwood's Blackberry pattern interior.

Daisy and Scroll

The maker of this distinctively modern pattern is unknown at this time. It is found in the decanter shown and small wine glasses with pedestal bases. Thanks to the Ayers family for sharing it with me.

Daisy Basket

The Daisy basket is like many other of the Imperial handled baskets in shape and size. It is a large hat-shaped basket with one center handle that is rope patterned. The basket stands 10½" tall to the handle's top and is 6" across the lip. The colors are a good rich marigold and smoke, but be advised this is one of the shapes and patterns Imperial reproduced in the 1960s.

Daisy Block Rowboat

In crystal, this Sowerby product was originally used as a pen tray with a matching stand. I've never seen the stand in carnival. Daisy Block was made in marigold, amethyst, and aqua in iridized glass. It measures 10½" in length.

Daisy Cut Bell

This was called a "tea bell" in a 1914 Fenton ad. It is 6" tall, is known only in marigold, has a scored handle that is clear, and is marked inside: "PATD APPLD." One whimsey that is ruffled around the bottom is reported and I've heard of non-iridized crystal examples.

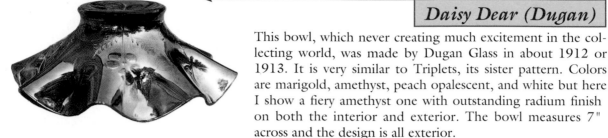

Daisy Dear (Dugan)

This bowl, which never creating much excitement in the collecting world, was made by Dugan Glass in about 1912 or 1913. It is very similar to Triplets, its sister pattern. Colors are marigold, amethyst, peach opalescent, and white but here I show a fiery amethyst one with outstanding radium finish on both the interior and exterior. The bowl measures 7" across and the design is all exterior.

Daisy Drape Vase (India)

The Daisy Drape vase is shaped like the Diamond Heart vase. It has a border around the base of diamond-in-diamonds, a large centered flower, and three bands of drapery at the top under the extended neck. The example shown is very rich marigold with a clear top, and is 6" tall.

Daisy in Oval Panels

Daisy in Oval Panels was made by U.S. Glass and is very close to their Bullseye and Fan pattern. It is advertised in Butler Brothers catalogs of 1916 – 1918 and titled their "sovereign dining set assortment." It is known in a berry set, water set, and table set in gold decorated crystal. In carnival only the creamer, sugar, and spooner in marigold have been reported. The piece shown is the sugar with its lid missing.

Daisy May

While I don't care much for the name, it is the one used in opalescent glass where the Leaf Rays compote has the pattern on the exterior rather than on the inside. On some of the carnival pieces you will find both the Leaf Rays interior and a faint outside pattern of Daisy May. In the marie there is a petaled blossom and then the leaves fan out from the base.

Daisy Rose

This 8" vase has an unusual design of roses on one side and daisies on the other, hence the name. (It is also called Lady Fingers because of the shape of the top.) The maker is unknown at this time.

Daisy Squares

This very pretty pattern has a simple design of daisies, stems, and leaves arranged to form squares. It is found in stemmed rose bowls, compotes, and goblets. Around the raised base is a row of raised beads and the inside has honeycombing. Colors are marigold, amethyst, amber, and a soft green.

Daisy Web

Daisy Web is found only on the hat shape, often turned out and heavily ruffled, or like the one shown with one edge turned up to give a JIP shape. It is found in marigold, blue, or amethyst. The exterior carries the Beaded Panels pattern, a design known to have come from Dugan.

Daisy Wreath

This 8½" Westmoreland bowl is found in marigold over milk glass, peach opalescent, marigold, blue opalescent, and blue opaque iridized glass. Occasionally a plate and a very rare vase whimsey are found. Please note on the piece shown here the stretched surface between the flower center and the wreath.

Dance of the Veils

I've heard of three of these beauties by the Fenton Company in iridized glass, and they are truly a glassmaker's dream. Marigold is the only carnival color although crystal, pink, green, custard, and opalescent ones were made.

Dandelion

The Dandelion pattern is by Northwood. The water set with tankard pitcher has a design that looks more like a sunflower, but the mug has a true dandelion design. The mug can also be found with a Knights Templar design on the base. Colors of the water set range from pastel to dark, and the Templar mug is found in marigold, ice blue, and ice green.

Dart

From the 1880s, the Dart pattern has heretofore been found only on crystal items in many shapes. This very rare and attractive oil lamp is a pleasure. The iridescence is soft with a lot of pinks and blues and the coloring is a fine pastel marigold.

Davann

This vase certainly has a European flavor, although I have yet to find it in any of the many catalogs I have from there. This particular vase is listed as being lilac with marigold iridescence and looks to be between 8 and 9 inches tall. I have no idea where the name came from but I do thank Seeck Auction for sharing the photo.

Davidson's Society Chocolates

This fine advertising piece is credited to Northwood. It can be found in a handgrip plate or a double-hand-grip one (shown) that is sometimes called a card tray shape. Colors are amethyst or lavender.

Decorama

This very modern Josef Inwald water set can be found in crystal or marigold carnival glass. It was first made in the 1920s. The crystal tumblers are known with ruby staining.

Deco Vases

These two very similar vases are 9½" tall and have nicely blended marigold iridescence. Although likely to be European in origin, and similar to some vases shown in a Brockwitz catalog (especially their #8259), the maker is uncertain at this time. Regardless of maker these are very nice vases.

Deep Grape (Millersburg)

This very desirable and attractive Millersburg compote can be found in several shapes including the flared round top as shown (found in amethyst, marigold, green, or blue), a square top (marigold or amethyst), a ruffled top (amethyst), or a turned-in rose bowl shape (green). The pattern is all exterior with well-done grape clusters, leaves, and tendrils filling most of the available space.

Delta Base Candlesticks (Imperial)

Delta Base candlesticks, Imperial's #419 pattern, was made in 1920 and advertised in at least two sizes. Colors include marigold, amber, clambroth, purple, and smoke (shown). The design is simple but somehow effective, especially on the very scarce purple examples.

DeSvenska Vase

This seems to be the vase shown in one of the catalogs from a Stockholm factory called DeSvenska Kristallglasbruken. The drawing in the catalog shows a slightly different shape to the top but the rest of the vase seems to be the same. On the same page is the Sunflower and Diamond vase, which was also made by the Brockwitz Company. Apparently glass moulds moved with the speed of sound from one company to another in Europe and the surrounding area.

Dewhirst Berry Band

This stunning carafe was discovered in Argentina by the late Gerald Dewhirst from California, and so I've given it his name in remembrance. The design is much like Cristalerias Piccardo's Band of Roses pattern but it has a band of leaves that resemble grape leaves and berries that are like stylized strawberries. The color is a rich marigold. Other shapes are a tumbler, compote, and a saucer. Thanks to Alan Sedgwick for sharing this photo. The carafe is 7" tall. A tray is also known.

Diagonal Ridge

Diagonal Ridge is found in water sets with the pitcher in the same mould shape as Hex Optic, Niagara Falls, and several other late carnival sets. This particular design has very rich coloring and is a step above all the rest. The diagonal ridges are all interior and the lustre is near-radium. Tumblers are known in two sizes. This pattern is also called Wiggles by many tumbler collectors.

Diamantes Star

Diamantes Star is one of the better vase patterns from India. It is heavily patterned and can be found in both a 6½" and an 8½" size. Most vases are marigold, but the soft Indian blue can be found. Several similar patterns occur including Diamantes, Diamante Leaves, Diamond Heart, and Daisy Drape.

Diamond

This two-handled Australian sugar is similar to the Panelled pattern shown later in this edition except it has a diamond design on the top two-thirds instead of the plain panels. Both have exterior designs interrupted by banding around the waist of the piece and both are reported in marigold or amethyst carnival.

Diamond and Bows

This 4" Indian tumbler is also known as Diamond and Grapes. The design is a good one and the color very well done. I thank Vikram Bachhawat for sharing it.

Diamond and Daisy Cut

This pattern is from U. S. Glass and is also called Floral and Diamond Band. The water set has two sizes of tumblers (shown in 4" and 5"). Other shapes reported are a butter dish and 10" vases and there is a variant punch bowl I show.

Diamond and Daisy Cut Variant

While not exactly like the water set with the same name, this punch bowl is near enough to be termed a variant. It more nearly resembles the compote. It is the only reported example. I know of no base or cups, but certainly there must have been.

Diamond and Fan (Millersburg)

While it takes a back seat to the beautiful interior pattern of Nesting Swan it accompanies, this Millersburg exterior is strong enough to stand alone. It is a series of diamonds, fans, and reverse fans, arranged in a most attractive way. The diamonds are prisms and on the marie they form a star! Millersburg had no peer in exterior patterns and Diamond and Fan proves that.

Diamond and File

Many collectors lump this pattern with a similar Fenton design called Diamond Point Columns, but if you will examine the photo of the very attractive banana bowl, you will see that the columns on the Diamond and File pieces truly have lines of filing while the ones on Diamond Point Columns are plain. In addition Diamond and File has seven columns while the other pattern has only five. Both designs are believed to be Fenton and Diamond Point Columns is shown in Fenton ads in both bowl and vase shapes.

Diamond and Rib (Fenton)

Listed as their #504 in factory catalogs, this well-known vase shape can be found in a jardiniere (the large vase, unpulled), a jardiniere whimsey, standard vases, and funeral vases. Colors are marigold, green, cobalt blue, amethyst, and white. The design is one of circles with ribbing inside. When stretched, these resemble diamonds (to some). Shown is a large funeral vase in green with a helios finish.

Diamond and Sunburst

Once a questionable pattern, this interesting design is shown in the 1909 Imperial catalog so I know the maker. Carnival pieces are fewer than those found in crystal and consist of a rare oil cruet whimsey in amethyst, a stemmed goblet in marigold, a stemmed wine in marigold or amethyst, and a decanter in the same colors. Some collectors feel the cruet is not Imperial but there is no proof at this time.

Diamond Arches

This average size bowl sports a very nice ruffled, candy ribbon crimped edge and has a series of diamonds going from the outer edge of the collar base to about mid way up toward the edge. The pattern is all exterior and it carries a diamond sunburst design inside the collar base. The edge treatment is very similar to some of those seen by Brockwitz and Inwald but I can't place this pattern with either factory at this time. Thanks to Lance Hilkene for the name and photo.

Diamond Block Shade

The Diamond Block shade was made by the Imperial Glass Company as their #699C in marigold only. The design is very strong and this shade looks really great on a lamp. It is reported in the electric style only and apparently was not offered in a gas shade.

Diamond Cane

This neat covered box (it is called a sugar box in European glass catalogs) has a pattern of cane at top and bottom with a center section of diamond wedges. It is Czechoslovakian I believe. Thanks to Carol Wylds for sharing it.

Diamond Cattails

This 5½" tumbler from India is a light marigold with a bit of an amber tint. The pattern consists of small diamond-in-diamonds separated by plain diamonds filled with three raised teardrops.

Diamond Chain

Like the Buzz Saw and File Framed bowl shown earlier, this 6½" bowl was found in Malaysia by Peter Dahlin, and has the same marie design. I haven't been able to trace these Malaysian bowls but believe they are all European. The base is clear and the rest of the piece has strong marigold iridescence. Anyone with further information should contact me.

76

Diamond Collar

Diamond Collar was shown in an Indiana Glass catalog as their #7 in a line of miscellaneous items. This pattern has a swirl interior and a band of diamond file above the base. Thanks to Leo and Penny Smith for sharing this piece with me.

Diamond Cut (Crystal)

The interior of this nice bowl is plain and the base shows a 26-pointed star within a large star with the same number of points. The rose bowl shown measures 9½" in diameter and is 5" tall, but the size varies depending on shape. It is by Crystal Glass Works of Australia. Colors are marigold or purple. The rose bowl shape is rare and spectacular, the only example reported so far.

Diamond Cut Shields

Shown in Brockwitz's 1931 catalog, this very nice geometric pattern is found in marigold carnival glass in a pitcher and the matching tumbler. The design is sound, well balanced, and typically European. Pieces are hard to find.

Diamond Flower

This mini-compote is less than 4" tall and was found in Malaysia by Peter Dahlin. Please notice the base design is like that of the Pandora bowl shown later in this edition (it was also found in Malaysia). While I don't find this piece in either the Brockwitz or Josef Inwald catalogs, I strongly suspect these patterns are European.

Diamond Fountain (Higbee)

This pattern was made by Bryce, Higbee, and Company in many shapes in crystal, in 1904. It is also called Palm Leaf Fan. In carnival glass, the pickings are limited to the very scarce cruet shown, bowls, and hand-grip plates. Higbee isn't really known for iridized glass and made such a small amount, all pieces should be considered scarce and desirable.

Diamond Heart

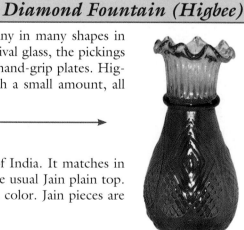

This is another rare vase from the Jain Glass Works of India. It matches in many respects the Jain Diamantes Star vase and has the usual Jain plain top. Diamond Heart stands 5" tall and has good marigold color. Jain pieces are known in blue also so that may be a possibility.

Diamond Honeycomb

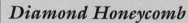

This sugar with lid comes from Argentina and this particular example doesn't have the best iridescence I've seen, but nonetheless it's a new discovery, so I've named it. The piece is referred to as a sugar pot in Argentina. I've seen these in marigold as well as the blue shown. If anyone has additional information I'd appreciate hearing from you. Thanks to Lucas Bidart (gardleboys) in Argentina for sharing it.

Diamond Lace

Diamond Lace was shown in Imperial's 1909 catalog in crystal. Carnival pieces are limited to the stunning water set, berry set, an ice cream set, and rose bowl whimsey (from the tumbler). Colors are purple for the water set (the tumbler is known in marigold); marigold, purple, or green for the berry set; marigold, green, purple, and a rare clambroth for the ice cream set.

Diamond Ovals

Besides the large stemmed compote and the perfume bottle shown in earlier editions, this Rindskopf pattern is known in a three-piece table set (open stemmed sugar), a salver, candlesticks, and large and small bowls.

Diamond Panels and Ribs

This is a well-shaped tumbler from India, with diamonds that stand out arranged in vertical rows between ribbing. The color is the usual soft marigold found on carnival from India. Thanks to the Ayers for this one.

Diamond Pinwheel

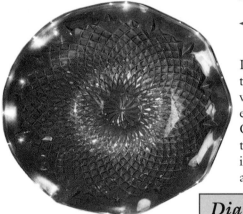

I first showed the covered butter dish in this English pattern, but this 10⅞" bowl shows the pattern better. The pinwheel forms the base (often ground down) and the other edges of the pattern are bordered by 14 larger diamonds. Only marigold has been reported. The shapes known are the bowl, the covered butter dish (where the pattern is interior), and a compote, but I suspect an open sugar was also made.

Diamond Point (Northwood)

This well-known Northwood vase pattern can be found in crystal, opalescent glass, and carnival glass. Carnival colors are purple, marigold, amethyst, green, cobalt blue, white, ice blue, ice green, teal, sapphire blue, lime green, aqua opalescent, and horehound. Sizes seem to fall in the 9" to 13" range. The example shown is purple with electric iridescence but its chief claim to fame is the intact Northwood paper label on the base. It is a real collectors' find.

Diamond Point Columns (Fenton)

This is known in bowl shapes as Diamond and File. The bowls are primarily known in marigold, but the vases are found in marigold, green, amethyst, cobalt blue, white, ice green, and (rarely) celeste blue. Although short at 6", these may be stretched to nearly twice that size.

Diamond Point Columns (Late)

Here is the powder jar in this elusive, late carnival pattern. As I've said before this piece may have been originally a U.S. Glass pattern but it is shown in some shapes in a 1938 Iittala Glass Company catalog from Finland. Shapes in carnival glass include the powder jar, a covered butter dish, creamer, bowl, plate, and a compote.

Most collectors put this footed and handled basket in the Northwood camp. In crystal I've seen many footed shapes including bowls, banana bowls, and even plates. Carnival colors are very scarce and are found only in the basket shape; these include marigold, amethyst, and cobalt blue.

Diamond Points Variant

This is similar to, but not the same pattern as, the Diamond Points. This very rare rose bowl is 3½" tall with a top opening of 2¼". Seven rows of diamonds circle the bowl; each diamond contains nine smaller diamonds. The color is a fine marigold with good iridescence. It was made by Fostoria and is known in crystal also.

Diamond Prisms

Besides the compote, this pattern is found on this rare basket shape that stands 8" tall and has a width of 9¼". The color is a soft marigold with pinks and blues in the iridescence. The maker is unknown at this time.

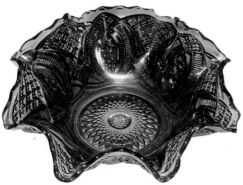

Diamond Rain

I know very little about this tumbler except its name, that it is 5" tall, and comes courtesy of Bob Smith. The glass is a bit thin but the iridescence is very good.

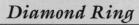

Diamond Ring

This typical geometric design of file fillers, diamonds, and scored rings is found on berry sets as well as a fruit bowl of larger dimensions. The usual colors of marigold and smoke are to be found, and in addition, the fruit bowl has been reported in a beautiful deep purple. While Diamond Ring is not an outstanding example of the glassmakers' art, it certainly deserves its share of glory. It was manufactured by Imperial.

Diamonds (Millersburg)

Found mostly in water sets, this very attractive allover pattern was also made in rare punch bowl and base pieces (no cups have been reported so far) in amethyst (three reported), green (only one bowl), and marigold (one set reported). Water sets are known in marigold, green, and amethyst with a rare aqua reported. In addition, an odd pitcher without a pouring spout is known in amethyst and green and a marigold spittoon whimsey (from a tumbler) is known.

Diamond Shield

This Sowerby pattern is a real oddball. It is found in carnival glass in creamers and stemmed open sugars, but here is a piece on a metal base, mounted with a screw through the glass. Thanks to Margaret Yvonne Illey for sharing this piece.

Diamond Sparkler

This pattern was found in a 1906 Butler Brothers ad of U.S. Glass patterns called their Triumph assortment. It is also known as Shoshone or Blazing Pinwheels by collectors of crystal, where many shapes are known in gilded or ruby stain. In carnival glass I know of only this 11½" vase with a hexagonal base.

Diamond's Royal Lustre

Made by Diamond in the 1920s, this console set (bowl and matching candlesticks), hailed the return to glass without pattern where only the quality of the iridization carried the load. Colors were many and the bowls were made in more than one size and shape.

Diamond's Soda Gold

The Diamond version of this well-known pattern, found on some Four Flowers and some Garden Path pieces, is a pale design when compared to the Imperial version. The latter is strong and sharp while Diamond's Soda Gold doesn't have the mould clarity or the boldness. Nevertheless, it does add something to the allover design of the plates and bowls, especially on the peach opalescent pieces.

Diamond Storm

Diamond Storm comes to me courtesy of Bob Smith and is similar to the Diamond Rain tumbler shown elsewhere. This pattern is shown in three sizes (3" to 5"). Please note that the two 4" tumblers have different diameters and were meant for different uses. They are, of course, late carnival patterns.

Diamond Stud

This pattern from India (so I'm told) with an allover design of raised diamonds can be found on both a pitcher and a tumbler. The coloring like most glass from India ranges from dark marigold at the bottom to nearly clear at the top. Thanks to the Ayers family for sharing it.

Diamond Studs

This interesting green spittoon whimsey was sold by Mickey Reichel. It measures 5½" wide and 2½" tall. The design is on the exterior of the piece. The maker is unknown. I suspect it may be a late production item. Anyone with additional information is urged to contact me.

Diamond Thumbprint Lamp

This 6½" tall miniature lamp may be known by another name, but I haven't been able to find one so it was given a name in a previous edition. It is a rich marigold with a 2" diameter base. The design somewhat resembles one called Quilt and Flute in clear glass. Thanks to Richard Conley for this rare item and I'd appreciate any information readers may have about this pattern.

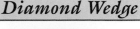

After this photo was received, I tried to learn just what this pattern was but with very little success. It is similar in design to one called Roanoke, made by Gillinder and then U.S. Glass but I don't believe they are the same. I'd appreciate any information readers can share about this tumbler.

Diamond Wheel

Here is the exterior of the Threaded Petals bowl. The diamonds are much like that found on Sowerby's Pinwheel exterior shown elsewhere and the horizontal mould seam is very evident in this view, separating the designs. Thanks to the Hilkenes for sharing this with me.

Diana, the Huntress

Long believed to be a companion bowl to the smaller Golden Cupid pieces, this 8" bowl is similar to the other "golden" patterns from overseas. Similar patterns are shown in a 1938 Finnish catalog but the Golden Cupid is known with a label from Poland so the maker (or makers) is a bit questionable. All these patterns are incised on clear glass and then gilded and iridized.

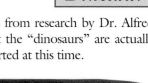

Dimples

Dimples is similar to the Diamond Hearts vase. This one is 6½" tall and has panels of bubbles with a dimple in the center of each one. The color is a good marigold with the usual clear top that is so familiar in vases from India. Thanks to the Ayres family for this one too.

Dinosaur

The owner of this bowl, Peter Baerwald, tells me he understands from research by Dr. Alfred Villaanueva-Collado that this is a product of Rindskopf, and that the "dinosaurs" are actually supposed to be peacocks. Only two of these bowls have been reported at this time.

Diving Dolphins

This well-done Sowerby pattern has three dolphin feet, an exterior design of delicate flowers, and a copied version of the Scroll Embossed pattern originally by Imperial on the inside. Colors are marigold, aqua, amethyst, and a rare green. Shapes of the top include ruffled, flared, rose bowl shape, or nut bowl shape.

Dog and Deer

This very attractive enameled miniature is 2" tall and has a base diameter of 1". The marigold finish is quite good and the enameling very fine. It depicts a dog chasing a deer over a woodsy terrain. In the background is a spider web of fine lines meant to give a crackle look to the piece. A decanter is also known and examples with a hunt scene have been reported.

Dogwood Sprays

This dome-based Dugan pattern of two large sprays of flowers, leaves, and tendrils is nicely done. It is often found on bowls that have been pulled up to become a compote shape. With a center design of one blossom and four leaves, Dogwood Sprays isn't often confused with other patterns. Colors of this design are mostly purple or peach opalescent but rare blue as well as very rare blue opalescent examples are known.

Dolphins Compote

Millersburg created many fine glass items but nothing better in design or execution than the Dolphins compote. From the Rosalind interior to the three detailed dolphins that support the bowl from the plate base, it is a thing of beauty. Colors are amethyst, green, and a rare blue.

Doria

Doria was named by Rose Presznick and shown in her third book. This sauceboat and underplate has the look of late carnival but I can't list a maker at this time. A ladle is also mentioned to go with these pieces. Thanks to Don and Barb Chamberlain for sharing it with me.

Dorsey and Funkenstein

This rather hard to find Fenton advertising pattern, found on Garden Mums bowls and plates has the following lettering: "Dorsey and Funkenstein Fine Furniture." Either shape is very scarce and amethyst is the only color reported. Thanks to Seeck Auction for the photo.

Dot

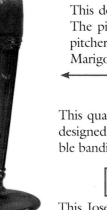

This vase is similar to the Kulor vase (from Sweden) shown elsewhere in this book, and somewhat like the Dot pattern from U.S. Glass. The vase shown is amethyst, and stands 5¼" tall with a 4½" top diameter and a 3½" smooth base. The finish is much like European glass. It may be that like other moulds from U.S. Glass, this one traveled to Europe or Scandinavia, or this vase may be a product from there. Only time and additional research will tell.

Dotted Diamonds and Daisies

This decorated water set has a diamond of dots that hangs from the flower spray. The pitcher is Fenton's Drapery pitcher that is shaped the same as the Zig-Zag pitcher. Both it and the tumbler are seldom found and should be considered rare. Marigold is the only reported color.

Double Banded Flute

This quaint bud vase never receives much attention, but it is well designed with flute panels above the stem topped by a row of double banding. It stands about 7" tall and has only fair iridescence.

Double Diamonds (Inwald)

This Josef Inwald pattern is easily recognized — two diamonds within an oval. It is known in marigold and shapes include a tumble-up, perfume bottle and atomizer, cologne bottle in two sizes, ring tray, pin tray, covered puff box, and a waste bowl. The puff box or powder jar has a six-petal flower on the lid.

Double Dolphin

This is one of the Fenton designs that bridge the gap between carnival glass and its cousin, stretch glass. The Double Dolphin pieces are found in covered stemmed candy jars, compotes, bowls, vases (shown is a fan vase in tangerine), a cake plate, and candlesticks. Colors are ice blue, ice green, white, tangerine, pink, red, topaz, marigold, and amethyst.

82

Double Dutch

While it's difficult to say whether this pattern came before or after Windmill and the NuArt plate, it is quite obvious they were all the work of the same artist. All depict various rural scenes with trees, a pond, and bridge. This Imperial pattern is featured on a 9½" footed bowl, usually in marigold but occasionally found in smoke, green, and amethyst. The color is superior and the mould work very fine. The exterior bowl shape and pattern is much like the Floral and Optic pattern.

Double Loop (Northwood)

Just why Northwood made this very nice pattern in so few shapes is a mystery, but only a creamer and a footed open sugar (sometimes called a chalice) are known. Colors are marigold, amethyst, green, cobalt blue, and aqua opalescent. On occasion, some examples like the one shown, exhibit a spectacular electric iridescence. Nearly all of the pieces I've seen are trademarked. Custard and dark blue non-iridized pieces are known.

Double Scroll

The Double Scroll pattern was originally made to be used as a three-piece console set consisting of two candlesticks and a dome-base bowl that measured 11½" across the oval top. It has a very modern look and can be found in carnival treatment or with a stretch glass look. Colors are marigold, clambroth, teal, red, smoke, amberina, and possibly green, plus the rare white examples shown that have gilt trim, enameling, and a very interesting bird decoration that appears to be a parrot. It is also known as Imperial's #320 Packard pattern.

Double Star (Cambridge)

Actually mis-named, this is really Cambridge's #2699 Buzz Saw pattern. Early on, carnival researchers failed to see they were the same pattern, so two names are standard now. Double Star is found in many shapes in crystal but in carnival glass, only the pitcher, tumbler, rare 9" bowl, and whimsies from the tumbler shape are known. Colors are mostly green, but amethyst and marigold are known on the water sets. Please note that the pitcher shown is green but the tumbler is amethyst.

Double Stem Rose

First shown in the company catalog in 1916, Double Stem Rose was made for a decade thereafter by both Dugan and then Diamond Glass. All pieces are on a dome base and may be shaped in many ways. Colors are many and include marigold, amethyst, green, blue, peach opalescent, white, lavender, aqua, celeste blue, olive green, ice green, cobalt blue opalescent, and the sapphire blue shown.

Double Stippled Rays

This Stippled Rays shallow bowl has a very distinct exterior. It is shown in amber and is the first I've heard about. The reverse also has a stippled rays pattern that ends with a large marie that has a pinwheel design. I would certainly appreciate any information about this piece from readers.

A Dozen Roses

This rare footed bowl, found in marigold, amethyst, and green, has an exterior pattern with the same ovid frames as the interior but without the roses. The maker hasn't been confirmed as far as I know but most collectors feel this pattern is from Imperial.

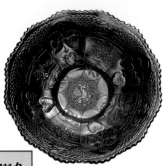

Dragon and Lotus

This collectors' favorite is from Fenton and is found in flat or footed bowls as well as scarcer plates. It can be found in many colors including marigold, blue, amethyst, green, aqua opalescent, red, peach opalescent, amber, iridized milk glass, and pastels. Shown is an outstanding green plate. Thanks to Samantha Prince for sharing it.

Dragon and Strawberry

Dragon and Strawberry is a companion pattern to, but scarcer than, Fenton's Dragon and Lotus. Pieces can be either collar based or footed. Colors are marigold, green, amethyst, or blue. The example shown is pastel marigold. Bowls can be ice cream shape or ruffled.

Dragonfly Lamp

Dragonfly Lamp is reported mostly in pink carnival, but it is also known in pearly white carnival glass. Here I show a green example. The design is a good one with dragonflies, separated by scrolls and fleur-de-lis. This lamp is also called Butterflies by some collectors. Thanks to Jack and Mary Adams for sharing this rarity.

Dragon's Tongue

This Fenton pattern is found on light shades in marigold-on-moonstone or iridized milk glass as well as these large (10" – 11") bowls. The bowls can be found in a ruffled or ice cream shape and are considered rare.

Dragon Vase

I have yet to learn anything new about this pattern, other than there are now two black examples (the latest found in June of 2007) in addition to the blue one known. There is also the discovery of its cousin the "Bellflower Vase" shown earlier in this edition. There is a large plate shape in purple that matches the six-sided vase with a many-rayed star in the base. The glass quality is good and the iridescence very well done. I suspect it isn't American but would really like to know more about this pattern. Thanks to the Remmens for the photo.

Drapery (Northwood)

Drapery was made by Northwood in a vase, rose bowl, and a candy dish. Once in a while you might find one of the oddballs that is crimped in on the ribs rather than the drapes. Most of the rib crimped ones I've seen have been in aqua opalescent. Colors include marigold, blue, purple, green, white, aqua opalescent, Renninger blue, sapphire, lime green, ice green, ice blue, lavender, and a very rare blue slag (rose bowl). Thanks to Samantha Prince for the nice photo.

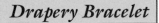

Drapery Bracelet

This very interesting water set from India has a unique corset shape. The design of drapes, star-squares, and oval rings is a good one. Thanks to the Ayers family for this one.

Drapery Rose

This 6½" vase from India is very interesting and also has great color to add to the mix. The base is unusual for Indian products because of its shape.

Drapery Variant (Finland)

Not to be confused with the Drapery Variant pattern credited to the Northwood Company, this pattern was made at the Riihimaki Glass plant of Finland, at least the tumbler was. (Other pieces are uncertain as to the maker.) Only a pitcher, tumbler, and a 1½" tall shot glass has come to my attention, but certainly other shapes may exist. The only color reported is marigold but this factory also made blue iridized glass so that is a possibility. Shown are the tumbler and the shot glass.

Drapery Variant (Northwood)

A close comparison of this variant vase and the regular Northwood one will show this has a plain banded top and the vertical ribs or pillars do not extend to the base. These variants are found in marigold, amethyst, green, lavender, and cobalt blue, and generally stand 8" – 12" tall. The base has a 2¾" diameter.

Dreibus Parfait Sweets

This Northwood advertising plate (it is also known in bowls and handgrip plates) was offered by a company in Omaha, Nebraska. All pieces are in amethyst and the exterior has the basketweave pattern.

Dresser Bottle Set

Sherman Hand first showed two bottles in this set about three decades ago, but here is the complete set in its original holder. The bottles are 2½" square and stand 4" tall. They are labeled "cotton," "toilet water," "alcohol," "astringent," "hair oil," and "witch hazel."

Duckie

I'm sure that every carnival collector has seen at least one example of either the scottie dog, poodle, or deer powder jars and now I can finally show a photo of the duckie. This is probably the least seen of the group, although none will demand very much money. Thanks to Irene Tyler for sharing this piece.

Dugan-Diamond's Rainbow

Just as the Northwood Company had a line of iridized glass advertised as their Rainbow Line, so did the Diamond Glass Company in the early 1920s. It consisted of stretch items and some patterns like the one shown that were produced with or without a stretch finish. Shown is a green covered bonbon on a short stem without stretch finish. It is 5½" tall and 4⅜" wide. The short stem has a twist. Other colors were marigold, celeste blue, pink, white, and amethyst.

Dugan's #1013R

Most people lump this vase with its sister pattern, also from Dugan-Diamond, called Wide Rib. That vase has eight ribs while the 1013R vase has only six ribs that end in a thinner configuration at the base. The example shown stands 8" tall, and as is typical of Dugan products, runs from strong marigold at the top to nearly clear near the base with residual lustre built up in the bottom. Colors are mostly marigold, amethyst, and peach opalescent.

Dugan's Flute

While unable to establish the carnival connection, this vase is shown in a Dugan-Diamond ad of 1914 in an assortment of opalescent glass including a Mary Ann vase, Windflower bowl, Stork and Rushes mug and tumbler, and a Beaded Shell sauce. The vase is 13" tall and has eight flutes or wide panels on the exterior. The color is a strong marigold at the top that dissolves to clear at the base. It was probably made in other colors including amethyst but none are reported.

Dugan's Hyacinth Vase

Produced as part of their Venetian art glass line, this vase dates to the 1909 – 1910 period of production. Believe it or not the vase shown is marigold! The lustre has such a strong shading of bronze in the mix it actually looks purple. This same vase mould was used in earlier production on different treatments (see Pompeian Hyacinth vase) and must have been one of Dugan's first tries at carnival glass.

Dugan's Many Ribs

Shown in the hat shape in peach opalescent, this seldom discussed Dugan pattern can also be found in small vases. Colors are marigold, peach opalescent, blue, and amethyst. The ribs are slightly wider than either Northwood or Fenton's Fine Rib patterns. The hat shape shown is 4½" tall and 6½" across the top and has a base diameter of 2⅝".

Dugan's Plain Jane

Found as the interior of some bowls and plates with Leaf Rosette and Beads (Flower and Beads) exteriors, these totally plain interiors are usually so very well iridized they are a riot of color all their own. The exteriors are often without any iridization at all like the one shown and add very little to the piece. Colors include marigold, purple, and peach opalescent.

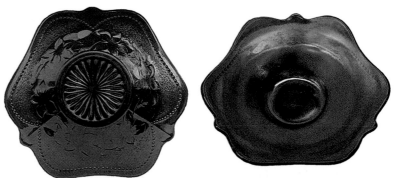

Dugan's Stippled Rays

As you can see this is a very undistinguished, little discussed pattern, confined to unimaginative bowls and an occasional hat shape like the one shown. The pattern is all on the inside, leaving a plain shiny exterior.

Dugan's Trumpet Vase

Trumpet is known in a pinch-style vase as well as this beautiful 15" tall trumpet style. This rich blue color doesn't have any stretch appearance. In one ad it is called rainbow lustre and colors listed are pearl, gold, blue, green, and amethyst. It was produced in the 1918 – 1920 period. The shape shown was used in the Diamond Butterfly and Blue Bird lines of gold decorated crystal of 1918. It is also called Zoom.

Dugan's Twist

The owner tells me this is a Dugan pattern, but I haven't been able to track it thus far. The pattern is all exterior with whirling ribs and a deep star in the base. The iridization is light and watery. Any ideas?

Dugan's Venetian

Advertised in 1906, this line of art glass from the Dugan plant was meant to imitate European glass imports. The shapes and colors are too numerous to mention. Shards of "spatter ware" from the Dugan site have been documented and some collectors lump them in with this pattern. Here is a rose bowl that is on lavender glass and is iridized. It has a hammered look and faint bubbles in the glass.

Dugan's Venetian Honeycomb

The Dugan Company introduced their iridized glass in these art glass novelties where the glass was patterned with frit and iridescence. It is also called Japanese or even Pompeian in some of their ads. Shown is the familiar Honeycomb pattern that was made in a beautiful cobalt blue with silver frit bars running down the piece. This example is iridized but most were not.

Dugan's Vintage Variant

Actually made by the Diamond Company after the Dugans were gone, this pattern is similar to the Fenton version. The Diamond version is found on bowls and plates. The bowl can be either dome based or collar based and the plate is dome based. Colors include marigold, cobalt blue, amethyst, green, white, and a rare celeste blue for the bowl while the plate is known in marigold and amethyst.

Durand Advertisement

This advertisement is found on the exterior marie of the footed orange bowl with the Grape & Cable pattern from Fenton. This rare piece is seen in cobalt blue carnival glass. The word "Durand" is raised in large lettering and the interior has the normal Persian Medallion interior.

Dutch Plate

This pattern was called this by Mrs. Hartung and Windmill and Checkerboard by Rose Presznick. The plate is of course late carnival. It is not being found that often. It measures 8" in diameter and has a pale amber look. The iridescence is only fair but it certainly does qualify as carnival glass and has a place in glass history.

Dutch Twins

This 6" ashtray has a raised pattern of a Dutch boy and a Dutch girl on the inside. It is only reported in marigold, usually with good color. The rim is raised with four cigarette or cigar rests while the center has a match holder. Most collectors place this piece in the 1920s.

Eagle Furniture Company

This advertising piece was made by Northwood in plates (shown), handgrip plates, and a double handgrip plate (called a card tray). It has a Basketweave exterior, is found in amethyst, and reads "Eagle Furniture Co., 282-284 South Main Street." The business was located in Memphis, Tennessee.

E.A. Hudson Furniture

Found in both plates and bowls, this Northwood advertising piece has an exterior pattern of Basketweave. The most often found shapes are the flat plate and the handgrip plate. The lettering says "E.A. HUDSON FURNITURE CO., 711-TRAVIS ST." This company was in Houston, Texas, I'm told.

Early American

Early American is a copy of a Sandwich glass design by the Duncan and Miller Glass Company in 1925. This pattern was advertised as their Early American pattern. It was made in ruby glass, crystal, green, rose, amber, and yellow-green. The idea was to give new colors in a lacy glass but somehow along the way this iridized example came into being. The pattern has been reproduced by Indiana Glass but I haven't seen other pieces of the iridized examples.

Eastern Star

This pattern is from Imperial and most often seen as the exterior design for the larger Scroll Embossed compotes. It is also found on water sets that are sometimes called Hobstar and File. The compote is about 4½" tall, with a short stem, and octagonal base. Colors for the compote are marigold, purple, lime green, emerald green, helios green, and a beautiful clambroth. The rare Hobstar and File water set is reported in marigold only.

Egg and Dart

These candlesticks stand 3½" tall and have a base diameter of 4½". The color is rather pale but the iridescence is quite good. The name comes from the famous decoration often used by wood workers in furniture and architects for mouldings.

Egyptian Lustre

In the early 1920s Diamond introduced their lustre lines (Golden Lustre, Royal Lustre, Rainbow Lustre, and Egyptian Lustre). Egyptian Lustre seems to have been the description of a dark, dark amethyst glass, nearly black, that has a Tiffany type of lustre. The ad for this glass in 1921 shows a rolled edge vase like I show here, as well as bowls, plates, and "flower and fruit centers." As you can see the color is very different and in some ways resembles Imperial's Jewels line.

Egyptian Queen's Vase

Known in two sizes, the Egyptian vases are similar to Classic Arts (both are from Josef Rindskopf), but have wider bands of figures. The decoration is a green stain. I thank Siegmar Geiselberger for sharing information about these patterns.

Very little additional information is known about this unusual pattern except it has now been found in two marigold bowls that measure 8¼" in diameter, one ice blue bowl, and two ice blue plates like the one now shown. The pattern is very busy but pleasing with rows of beading, triangles, stippling, floral sprays, and a center of a multi-layered flower. Elegance is very rare and desirable and I'd really like to know who made it.

Elegance

Found on a matching pitcher as well as the tumbler shown, this pattern's maker has not been identified as far as I know. The color is a soft marigold with enameled flowers in white that show much more artistic design than most decorated pieces. The name is a good one but unfortunately it is also the name of another carnival pattern and this could cause confusion to beginning collectors.

Elektra

Elektra was first called Hobstar Whirl or Whirligig in this country. It was made by both Brockwitz (shown in the 1931 company catalog) and by Riihimaki of Finland in 1939. Brockwitz called the pattern Elektra and I feel that is the name that should be used. Shapes in iridized glass include a small compote, an oval bowl, round bowl, vases, and the breakfast creamer and sugar (here I show the creamer). Most pieces are found in marigold but the compote is also known in cobalt blue.

Elephant's Foot Vase

While this piece from Northwood is from the large funeral vase mould of the Tree Trunk pattern, it is generally looked at by collectors as in a class of its own. They generally measure 7" to 9" tall and the top may be opened from 7½" to a wide 10½". Colors are marigold, amethyst, and green, and the coloring is spectacular. All are very rare, selling for thousands of dollars currently.

Elephant's Vase

Like the Hand Vase and the Fish Vase, this pattern was made in India. It has the head of the elephant with the trunk circling the vase. It is found in marigold and is reported in three sizes.

Elephant Vase Variant

If you compare these vases to the regular Elephant Vase from Jain, you will see that the bases are different. Some have trunks that wind to the right rather than the left. The variant on the left shows the Indian "swastick" symbol (a trademark of Jain) and the variant on the right is different in that the ear is blank, without the usual design. In addition, I've heard of at least two sizes in variant #2 shown on the right.

Elks (Dugan)

Three or four of these little spade-shaped nappies are reported, all in amethyst. They were made with an Elk convention in mind I'm sure, but may have been samples that weren't used, test items, or just a design that was rejected. They do not look "finished" since they have no lettering and may have been only a brief run that wasn't completed. At any rate, they are considered rare and desirable.

Elks (Fenton)

Always a collectors' favorite, the Elks pieces from Fenton are found on handled bells, bowls, or plates. In the Fenton pieces, the elk faces right while the Millersburg elk faces left. Colors for bowls are marigold, amethyst, green, and blue, but the plates are known in blue and green. The bells are known only in blue. Lettering may say Detroit, Parkersburg, Atlantic City, and one rare bell says Portland.

Elks (Millersburg)

The Millersburg example is called Two-Eyed Elk. It is larger than the Fenton Elks bowl and more detailed. It is found only in amethyst with a radium finish. Millersburg also made a rare Elks paperweight with the same design in amethyst and green.

Elks Paperweight (Millersburg)

These paperweights are equally rare companion pieces to the Elks bowls from Millersburg. They are found in both green and amethyst carnival glass. They are 4" long and 2⅝" wide and except for a rim on the underside, are solid glass. Most examples have some damage but these are still eagerly sought by collectors.

Elysian Vase

Sold by Mickey Reichel, this 9½", blown-mold vase is a very nice item. It has good marigold color and an interesting design with small blossoms placed rather randomly on the lower section. It looks Czech but I have no proof.

Embroidered Flower and Urn (Jain)

This tall tumbler is marked "Jain" in the base so I know it came from the Jain Glass Works of India but even if it weren't marked, the design is so much like other Jain items, the maker would be obvious. The color is strong at the lower portion but lightens at the top like most Jain pieces.

Embroidered Mums

Embroidered Mums, a close cousin to the Hearts and Flowers pattern also made by the Northwood company, is a busy but attractive pattern. It can be found on bowls, plates, and stemmed bonbons in a wide range of colors including marigold, pastel marigold, ice blue, ice green, purple, teal blue, electric blue, aqua opalescent, lavender, sapphire blue, lime opalescent, and the bonbons in white.

Embroidered Panels

Previously reported in two variations of tumblers, this beautiful pattern seems to be found mostly in India or Pakistan, but some pieces have shown up in Australia. This lamp base shown is 5" tall and measures 6" across the middle. The color is outstanding. The piece shown was sold to the current owner with a mismatched cover, 2½" tall and 4" wide, shown also. It is made by Jain Glass.

Emma's Vase

This beautiful 7¼" tall vase belongs to Ken and Pauline Birkett who have named it after their first grandchild. The maker appears to be unknown at this time, although it does resemble several vase patterns made in Argentina by Christalerias Papini.

Emu

Emu is from Crown Crystal Glass in Australia. (Hartung called this pattern Ostrich, which it's not.) It can be found in 5" and 10" bowls as well as a stemmed compote. The compote is actually a variant with a stand of trees replacing the wreath of flora but I've listed it along with the regular pattern by request from Australia, as I'm told they don't separate the two. Colors are marigold, amethyst, black amethyst, and a scarce aqua. The exterior may carry the Fern and Wattle pattern. Thanks to Wayne Delahoy for the information.

Enameled Blossom Spray (Dugan)

This enameled version, shown on the interior of Dugan's Single Flower bowl, is called Blossom Spray and is similar to several other designs. These added decorations date to the time of opalescent production or about 1910 – 1911, and really enhance the piece both in beauty and desirability. Thanks to W.R. Delano for this fine bowl.

Enameled Cherries (or Grape)

This Northwood pattern is sometimes called Enameled Cherries or Enameled Grape, or even Ground Cherries. The tumblers are often signed. The only color reported is cobalt blue, which seems to be the color of choice when the Northwood Company made decorated carnival glass.

Enameled Chrysanthemum

Enameled Chrysanthemum has a cannonball style water pitcher and a very well done design. The tumblers have a slight flare and the applied handle of the pitcher is clear. The set is found in marigold as shown or cobalt blue.

Enameled Chrysanthemum with Prism Band

This is found on the Prism Band water set. Most of these designs can be found on marigold, amethyst, blue, green, and pastel carnival glass.

Enameled Columbine

This beautiful water set is found on Fenton's zig zag pitcher design in marigold, amethyst, green, or cobalt blue as shown. The enameled flower doesn't resemble a columbine but few of these painted sets are that precise.

Enameled Coral

I have very little information about this well-done pitcher except to say it has an iridized crackle finish with an enameled design of coral or seaweed on each side. The handle is applied. I'd enjoy hearing from anyone with more information about this piece.

Enameled Crocus

This popular enameled design has at least two variations, which are shown. Here the Crocus design is on a green tumbler but it can also be found on marigold, blue, and white carnival glass.

Enameled Crocus Variant

Here the enameled design runs horizontally around the tumbler instead of vertically. It is shown on a beautiful ice green tumbler but examples in marigold, cobalt blue, and white are known.

Enameled Crocus with Prism Band

Here is the third variation of the Enameled Crocus tumbler. This one has the well-known Fenton Prism Band that is moulded into the design. Colors reported are marigold, cobalt blue, and white.

Enameled Diamond Point

This oddly shaped bottle seems to be another Czechoslovakian piece. The fine enameling has sprays of flowers on the neck and a diamond point pattern filled with flowers on the body. It is missing its stopper. The color is a rich dark marigold.

Enameled Dogwood

This pitcher's shape and decoration have me baffled. I examined a Dogwood tree in my yard and it certainly looks very much like blooms from that tree. The pitcher's shape is something else I can't seem to locate, although I feel that it has to be from Fenton or Northwood. It is a very pleasing design and I hope someone (a horticulturist perhaps) has information they can share with me on this. Thanks to Remmen Auction for the photo.

Enameled Double Daisy

Besides the cannonball shaped water set in this patern, there is also this bullet tankard shaped pitcher (tumblers are the same). Somehow, the design seems a step above most enameled water sets and this one is distinctive and beautiful.

Enameled Floral Spray

This very pretty water set is clear carnival glass with fine enamel decoration. It is considered rare with only one pitcher and four tumblers known so far. The iridescence is excellent, the floral design superior, and the shape of the pitcher very interesting. The handle is applied and reeded. The pitcher measures 9½" tall and has a very pretty ruffled top. The tumblers are 3⅞" tall and have a slight flare.

Enameled Forget-Me-Not

This water set with the diagonal banded center is a very nice pattern and is very popular with collectors. I consider this to be one of Fenton's best decorations of all the enameled water sets. It can be found in marigold, green, and blue. Thanks to the Remmens for sharing it.

This enameled design is a good one and resembles several others that do not have the Prism Band moulding. It can be found with the impressive tankard pitcher. Fenton made many of these decorated sets and this is one of the better ones.

Enameled Gooseberry (Northwood)

This design is much like the painted design on the Enameled Crocus tumbler shown elsewhere. It has the Northwood trademark and is in blue. Also note the scroll design is like that on the Enameled Cherries (or Grape) pieces, also from Northwood. I believe this pattern may also be known by another name so if anyone knows about this design I'd like to hear from them.

Enameled Grape Band

Like some of the other white enameled pieces I show, this tumbler came along late in the carnival era and probably dates from the late 1920s. The iridescence is well done however and the gold banding and enameled grapes all add to the look. I do not know the maker.

Enameled Honeysuckle

This tumbler is from Germany and stands 3⅝" tall. It is heavily iridized except for a panel where the honeysuckle is enameled. I'd guess these date from the 1930s but have no evidence of the age.

Enameled Lily of the Valley

This enameled decoration is shown in a 1911 Butler Brothers catalog so I know it was a factory-applied decoration. It is found on Dugan-Diamond's Stippled Flower as well as Single Flower pieces. The example shown has a Single Flower exterior and a peach opalescent treatment. This same pattern with the enameling has also been seen in bride's baskets and with an attached metal base.

Enameled Lotus (Fenton)

This very scarce Fenton design is found on their cannonball pitcher with an interior drapery pattern. I've heard of marigold and green, and here is a rare ice green example.

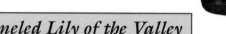

Enameled Panel

While this very pretty goblet has all sorts of designs, one matched against another such as etching, gold enameling, and mould work, it is the applied enamel panel with beautifully hand-painted roses that makes it quite elegant. The base is hollow, giving another strange twist to the whole. The marigold coloring is very rich and the look very much one of quality.

Enameled Periwinkle

Here, the enameled flower and leaves are on a stem that points downward and to the left, and is similar to another from Fenton called Enameled Lotus. The color is a very rich marigold but other colors exist.

Enameled Phlox

This beautiful pitcher is on Fenton's #628 mould, which was used more often for crystal, decorated crystal, or opalescent glass. Here it is in amethyst carnival with enameling and it is terrific. Thanks to the Seecks for sharing it.

Enameled Prism Band

This beautiful Fenton tankard water set is a standout in the series of enameled water sets. It can be found in marigold, blue, green (rarely), and a very impressive and scarce white. Also the floral work may vary slightly from one item to another.

Enameled Punty Band (Heisey)

Found mostly in custard glass, crystal, or ruby stained glass, this Heisey pattern is a rare, rare thing in iridized glass. It stands 3⅞" tall and has a 24-point star on the underside of the base. The banding at the base from which the pattern gets its name has 24 small ovals and the band is sawtoothed at both edges. The color is outstanding, as are the enameled flower, leaves, blossoms, and stem.

Enameled Rose of Paradise

This very pretty tumbler stands 4" tall with a 2¼" base. It has eight interior panels and the top flares to 3". The unusual enameling is top-notch, with a large pink rose that shades to mauve, and two buds and leaves. It covers only one side of the tumbler. The color of the glass is an unusual shade of green with a touch of blue, just short of being teal. The iridescence is rich and lustrous. No matching pieces have surfaced and to date the maker is unknown.

Enameled Stippled Petals

Enameled Stippled Petals is like the regular Dugan-Diamond pattern with the added enamel work of forget-me-nots. This bowl is a very rich pumpkin color with a peach opalescent treatment on the exterior. The bowl measures 9½" in diameter and has a 10-ruffle edge. Stippled Petal pieces are dome based and can be shaped in several ways that include a banana bowl, a handled basket, or even tricornered.

Enameled Stork

This water set has a tankard pitcher with ribbing above the base and below the neck. Its inscription is in German and reads "BROTHERS DRINK TIL YOU SINK." The enameling shows storks and cattails. If you will look at the Late Enameled Bleeding Hearts pattern shown elsewhere in this edition, you will see the tumblers are from the same mould.

Enameled Swallow

Besides the tankard pitcher I showed in the eighth book, this Czechoslovakian pattern is also known in a tankard stein and tumblers that match the pitcher (all shown here). Thanks to Don and Barb Chamberlain for sharing these pieces.

Enameled Wildflower

Enameled Wildflower is another of the many, many enameled designs. It is mostly found on stock size tumblers and pitchers. The owner of this tumbler believes it was called Enameled Wildflower so I've acquiesced. Anyone knowing differently might let me know.

Encrusted Vine

Very little information is known about this Bartlett-Collins pattern and besides supposing there was a pitcher, I'd prefer not to guess. What I do know is, I found four of these at a local flea market several years ago, and sent one to the late John Britt and he named it. The tumbler shown has very strong color, stands 5" tall, and has a very pretty design of gold frit vining with a wide gold band at the rim and a smaller band below the design. The frit was made from glass granules fired into the glass, making it permanent.

English Flute and File

This pattern is reportedly from Sowerby Glass. It is known in a stemmed open sugar (shown) as well as a matching creamer. The sugar is also called a compote and colors reported are marigold and lavender carnival.

English Hob and Button

This pattern has been reproduced in the last few years, especially on trays and bowls in an odd shade of amberish marigold on very poor glass. The English version shown is another thing, however. The glass is clear and sparkling. The shapes are bowls, mostly, in marigold, green, amethyst, and blue. It is also known as Chunky (Sowerby's #2266).

English Hobstar

This 6" by 4" boat shape was made by the Sowerby Company as their #2480. It is often found in a silver holder. English Hobstar was made in straight sided or curved pieces and was called a salad bowl by the maker in 1933.

Engraved Cornflower (Fenton)

Engraved Cornflower was one of the cut designs in Fenton's Grecian Gold line that began in 1915 and continued as part of their stretch glass line into the 1920s. The tumbler is tall and was also sold as a vase, but the entire set is called a lemonade set. Notice the applied cobalt handle that Fenton used so often.

Engraved Daisy

This wheel or copper-cut etched piece is a really beautiful example of the engravers' art. Don't confuse it with a similar pattern called Grecian Daisy that is shown elsewhere in this book. It shows a large daisy with swirls of stems and leaves on either side. The tumbler is oval in shape.

Engraved Daisy and Spears

Made by Fenton in their Grecian Cut Gold Assortment, this very interesting small goblet (4½" tall) is very much like the Engraved Daisy tumblers except for the added "spears." All the Grecian Cut Gold items date from 1916 to 1918 and are color flashed.

Engraved Grapes

This lovely etched pattern is from the Fenton factory and has been seen on many shapes including vases, candy jars, tall and squat pitchers, tumblers, juice glasses, and a tumble-up. Colors are marigold and white.

Engraved Zinnia

While the engraving of tall- and short-stemmed flowers is rather difficult to see, the tumbler has good lustre, and the shape is quite nice. Has anyone seen the pitcher?

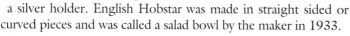

Esberard-Rio

This is a 4¼" lemon plate with the lettering: "Esberard-Rio." The finish is a soft marigold on the interior with the floral and scroll pattern on the exterior.

Estate

Carnival collectors know this pattern as Estate. It was called Filigree in Westmoreland's ads. Shapes include a small mug, vase, and breakfast set (creamer and sugar). Colors are marigold, aqua, aqua opalescent, and a rare smoke. Shown is the breakfast set in aqua and the vase with advertising in smoke.

Etched Deco

Etched Deco was shown in glass catalogs as the Trudy pattern from the Standard Glass Company of Lancaster, Ohio. It dates from the 1920s and is found in many shapes, all with the etched or wheel cut design shown. Here is a rolled rim 7½" bowl on a 3½" pedestal base. The color is a rich deep marigold on the bowl but the base is clear. Standard Glass chose women's names for all their glass patterns of that time.

Etched Garden Mums

Most advertising pieces were mould decorated, but a few like this one had either enameled writing or etched writing. After all, cost was a consideration and this had to be cheaper than making a new mould.

Etched Leaves

This 6⅞" tall oil bottle with two handles is possibly from Czechoslovakia but it isn't marked. The light iridescence is typical of Czech work, as is the etched vine and leaves pattern. I'd be happy to hear from anyone with additional information about this item.

Etched Vine

I now have some evidence that this may be an unmarked tumbler from China because the etching is just like the Etched Shanghai tumbler shown elsewhere in this book and a collector of this type of glass found examples of both with the same source. The base does have a rayed star however and this casts some doubt. Perhaps I will soon be able to learn more about this pattern but can't place it with a China maker until I do.

Etched Vine and Flowers

This etched pattern is a plain design on a rolled ring base found in both a pitcher and tumble (shown). The maker is unknown to me although it is believed to be from India.

Euro

I found this vase and named it, and I haven't heard anything different since first showing it, so I've kept the name. It stands 7¾" tall and has a unique metal filagree shield covering the top of the base. The color is a rich marigold. I am confident this piece is from Europe and may be Czechoslovakian. Anyone with further information is requested to contact me.

Euro Diamonds

At least three berry sets are known in this strange all-exterior pattern with a very fine but unusual ruffling. I can't attest to the age but have been told it may be late German glass. Additional information is welcomed. Thanks to Thelma Harmon for sharing it. All pieces reported are green.

This very plain vase (it has interior wide paneling) stands 9¾" tall and has a 4" base diameter. The color is a rich marigold at the top, fading to almost clear at the bottom. The glass is quite thin, much like from Czechoslovakia, but I cannot determine a maker at this time.

European Poppy

I once called this Poppy and Hobstar, but have since learned most collectors in Europe know this pattern as European Poppy so I've made the correction. It is found on the interior of the butter dish as shown as well on as bowls where the pattern is on the exterior. Colors are marigold, blue, or amber, and although I have no proof, I suspect this pattern to be from Riihimaki in Finland, since they are known to have made amber items.

European Vintage Grape

I'd like to thank Martin and Jan Hamilton for what little information I have on this bowl. It was shown in a 1939 Riihimaki catalog as #5391. It measures 8" across and is 3½" deep. The color is a good strong marigold, and the grapes are heavy and stand out.

Evelyn (Fostoria)

I've learned there is also a matching water tray in green, as well as the bowl shown and a punch bowl with base in crystal, so other carnival pieces may well turn up in the future. I've also heard that it has other names including Thumballa, Diamond and Fan, and Feathered Diamond and Sunburst. I now know of four green bowls and the tray in iridized glass.

Fan

Despite the fact that most collectors have credited this pattern to Northwood, it is a Dugan product. In custard glass it has been found with the well-known Diamond marking. Of course, many more shapes of the Fan pattern were made in custard. In carnival glass, the availability is limited to the sauce dish and an occasional piece that is footed and has a handle. The colors seen are marigold, peach, and purple. Peach is the most available color.

Fanciful

Dugan's Fanciful was from 1905, and can be found in bowls and plates with a Big Basketweave exterior. Colors include marigold, amethyst, peach opalescent, blue, and white. Thanks to Peter Baerwald for sharing the photo.

Fancy

Northwood used this very nice design sparingly as an interior pattern on some Finecut and Roses pieces and it is a shame it wasn't expanded to bowls, table sets, and plates. The design is a busy one, well balanced, with a blossom center, cross-stitching, a circle of file, scrolling, and leaflets! And despite all this, it is balanced, attractive, and interesting. The example shown is on aqua opalescent with a bright butterscotch finish.

Fancy Cornhusk Vase (Dugan)

This Dugan version of the corn vase is a beautiful thing. Only this single marigold piece is confirmed in carnival glass. It stands about 9" tall. This well-known pattern is often found in opalescent glass or crystal. Just why it was made in carnival glass is a mystery. Fancy Husk vases have been reproduced in non-carnival treatments since the 1980s so be aware of examples with flat tops and solid husks.

Fancy Cut

Much like the small creamers in design, Fancy Cut is actually the pitcher from a child's water set (tumblers to match are known in crystal). The color is a good rich marigold. The pitcher measures 4" tall and has a base diameter of 2¼". The design is a bit busy, combining several near-cut themes, but the rarity of the iridized version more than makes up for this.

Fancy Flowers

This Imperial pattern is found only in the shape shown in carnival glass. This large compote measures 10" across the top and is nearly 5" tall. It was Imperial's #737 pattern, shown in crystal in their 1909 catalog. Carnival examples are quite scarce. It has been reproduced in marigold.

Fan Montage

This interesting biscuit jar was found and named by Gary Vandevander and is the first I've seen. It is likely European but doesn't appear in any of my references at this time. I welcome any information about the pattern or its maker.

Fans

This is Rindskopf's #1887 pattern and can be found in the small pitcher (5" tall, 7" across the handle), a matching tumbler, and a cracker jar with metal lid. The pattern is very pretty with an allover design, and the color is usually quite rich. It has been reported in marigold only.

Fan Star (Millersburg)

Very few Millersburg pieces had plain exteriors and the one shown here has only the marie or base design to avoid being called plain. The Fan Star base can be found on the Zig Zag bowl and accompanying the Cactus exterior on Rays and Ribbons pieces. The design is just a 24-rayed star that feathers out in fan-like lines at the end of each ray.

Fan-Tail

Fan-Tail is found as an interior pattern on some Butterfly and Berry bowls and chop plates (shown). The design is a series of whirling peacock tails. Colors are marigold, cobalt blue, green, and white. Fenton has reproduced this pattern in some modern glass.

Far Eastern

This 3½" jar was probably from U.S. Glass since it is very similar to their Daisy in Oval Panels and the Bullseye and Fan pattern which was also made in other types of glass. This piece has gold trim around the top band and may have taken a lid at one time. The color is a rich marigold. Thanks to the Vandevanders for sharing it.

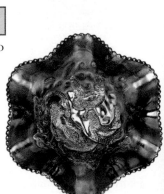

Farmyard

Farmyard is one of Dugan's best designs and is found in large bowls and a rare plate. Colors are amethyst, peach opalescent (rare), and green (rare), and all are sought. Thanks to Remmen Auction for sharing the photo.

Fashion (Imperial)

Fashion was from Imperial (their #402½) and is found in a water set, punch set, breakfast set, 9" bowls, a large compote, and a rose bowl. Colors include marigold, purple, red, smoke, and horehound. Fashion was also made in many shapes in crystal in 1910.

Feather and Heart

This fine water set, found in green, marigold, and amethyst, is typical in many ways of all the Millersburg water sets. The pitcher lip is long and pulled quite low, while the rim is scalloped quite like its cousin, the Marilyn set. The glass is quite clear, rather heavy, and has excellent iridescence. A little difficult to find, the pattern adds greatly to any collection.

Feather Columns (Aakriti)

This 4½" tumbler comes from Vikram Bachhawat. It is another pattern from India. The design is similar to others from that area.

Feathered Arrow

I've seen this in ruffled deep bowls, ice cream shaped bowls, a rose bowl, and a bowl with a retourne rim. Non-carnival colors include a strange olive green and a rose colored glass as well as crystal. In carnival glass only various hues of marigold are known. Any information on this pattern would certainly be helpful.

Feathered Flowers (Crystal)

This Australian pattern is the exterior design on Kiwi bowls. It had a factory listing as #1928. It is series of scrolls and daisy-like flowers that are repeated around the bowl. Colors are marigold or purple. Not all Kiwi pieces have this exterior design.

Feathered Rays

Every now and then a very interesting pattern comes to light to delight me and this one, owned by Carol Spurgeon, is just that. It is from Fenton and is a retooling of the Stippled Rays bowl mould with sections of fine feathering added where the plain rays once were. The color is green on this one but there may well be more colors out there. Please note that centered on the feathered rays are what appear to be tied bows.

Feathered Serpent

This Fenton pattern was available on large and small bowls as well as a rare spittoon whimsey. It has an exterior design called Honeycomb and Clover. Colors are marigold, green, blue, and amethyst. The lustre is usually heavy and the finish satin.

Feathers (Northwood)

While it doesn't cause very much excitement among collectors, this Northwood vase is found in both carnival glass and opalescent glass. Carnival colors are marigold, green, amethyst, a rare ice blue, and the even rarer white shown. The base diameter is about 3½" and the height from 7" to 11". In opalescent glass a bowl has been whimsied from the vase mould so this is a possibility in carnival glass as well. Thanks to Samantha Prince for the photo.

This pa
bowl sl

This s
patter
are fi

Forum

I finally found these candlesticks in a 1939 Riihimaki catalog as their #5861 pattern, so the rio pink glass with marigold iridization on the one shown **makes** sense. Other colors may exist, including cobalt blue or amber.

Fostoria Flemish

This nicely shaped Fostoria **vase** stands 8¾" tall and has a soft amber lustre. The base is a heavy six-sided pedestal **and** the stem rises in six wide panels to a curved top. Fostoria began making colored **glass** in 1924 and I feel this piece soon followed.

Fountain Epergne

This very attractive epergne **has** a sterling frame that is hallmarked. The lilies have a twisted swirl in the design and are **clear** except for the marigold carnival tops. There are three smaller lilies and the massive center **one**. While the whole piece is similar to the Five Lily epergne, the Fountain epergne is more **graceful** and seems to be of better quality. Due to recent information on the similar pattern Ribbed Panels, I'm simply saying that the possibly exists that this came from the Stourbridge region of **England**, but have no proof. Thanks to Dave Peterson for the information.

Four Flowers

As collectors learn **more** about this pattern and the variant, we are left with almost as many questions as answers. Four Flowers was known to be made by Dugan as well as by Riihimaki Glass of Finland **in 1939**. Apparently once the Diamond factory closed in 1931, the moulds were sold or simply copied. Dugan made this pattern in bowls and plates in peach opalescent, marigold, purple, **green**, blue, and smoke. And to complicate matters, this pattern seems to be shown in an Eda **catalog** in 1925 so they may have been the middlemen.

Four Flowers Variant

Attributed to Eda, this pattern is one of many **that** were copied from the American design (the regular Four Flowers was copied by Riihimaki of Finland). Since this variant is found in peach opalescent, it must have been **first** made at Dugan. Shapes are bowls and plates (some pieces are mounted on metal **stands**) and colors are lavender, teal, purple, emerald green, horehound, and a topaz yellow, **as** well as peach opalescent.

Four Garlands

Four Garlands **was** named by the owners, Chuck and Dianna Hollenbach. This vase has a ridge around the **inside** that may have held a flower frog. It stands 6⅞" tall **and** has a top diameter of 7½". There are **four** garlands draped around the top of the vase, eight flutes around the base, **and** four ovals between the garlands and the flutes. The color is a strong marigold. I **believe** the vase is European, but it was purchased in Canada.

I know very little about this small handled bowl or sauce except to say it is English and very much like the Scroll Embossed Variant from Sowerby. Marigold is the only color reported so far.

Four Pillars

Four Pillars is often credited to Northwood, even though examples in amber, green, and amethyst have also been seen with the Diamond-D mark. Other colors known are marigold, peach opalescent, ice blue, ice green, white, aqua opalescent, and the strange yellow-green shown called citrine. Occasionally, advertising appears on the base, and pieces with gold decoration on the lip are found. Shards have also been found at Millersburg.

Four Pillars with Drapes

Some collectors refer to this pattern as a drapery variant but we already have a variant in that pattern, so it has been given a new name. However, if you'd like to refer to it as Drapery Variant #2, that's fine. The pattern is credited to the Northwood Company and can be found in carnival glass in marigold, peach opalescent, blue, sapphire, and green (amethyst may eventually turn up). The four pillars extend down as feet with the drapes between each pillar.

Four Suits (Jain)

This tumbler from Jain Glass Works of India has ovals with a heart, diamond, club, and spade within a Maltese Cross configuration. It is 5½" tall, has a 2¼" base diameter, and measures 3⅛" across the top. The coloring is soft, like many Jain pieces.

474

This pattern, #474, was one of Imperial's best. It can be found in crystal as well as carnival glass. Shapes include a water set, milk pitcher, punch set, goblet, wine, sherbet, cordial, compote, bowls, and pedestal vases in three sizes. Colors in iridized glass are marigold, amethyst, green, olive, teal, aqua, lime green, cobalt blue, and red (vase only). Not all shapes are known in all colors of course. This pattern was reproduced in the 1960s and 1970s. New mugs are found but were not made in old carnival glass.

49er

The 49er pattern is Czechoslovakian and rarely found or discussed by collectors. It can be found on a variety of shapes, including a wine decanter, stemmed wines, a squat pitcher, tumblers, and a dresser set (shown) consisting of atomizer, perfume bottles in three sizes, a ring tray, a pin dish, a pin box, and a powder box. Only marigold has been reported at this time. There is also a variant tumbler.

Foxhunt

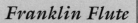

This stoppered decanter has a hunter and a dog, and in design, is much like the Dog and Deer tumblers shown elsewhere in this edition. Tumblers are also known that match this decanter. Thanks to Gary Vandevander for sharing this piece.

Franklin Flute

Franklin Flute was first made in crystal by Franklin Flint Glass, and then in iridized glass by Gillinder for U.S. Glass. This piece was shaped from a tumbler mould and turned down to form the hat vase shown. It had a flower frog that fit the grooves of the design's interior. The only color I've seen is a rich marigold that has an amberish tint. Thanks to Mary P. Hare for sharing this piece.

Freefold (Imperial)

This Imperial vase, which is also known as Interior Rays, can be found in sizes from 7" to 14" tall. Two sizes of moulds were used, one with a 2⅞" base, the other with a 3¼" one. The smaller has a 12-point star, the larger a 16-point star. Colors are pastel marigold, marigold, clambroth, smoke, green, purple, lavender, and white.

Freesia

Like so many enameled carnival pieces from the Fenton Art Glass Company, this tumbler has a matching water pitcher. The only color I've heard about is marigold but certainly other colors may well exist. The design of three buds rising from a "v" of foliage is interesting but certainly not unique, but this pattern is still very collectible.

French Grape

The photo certainly does not do justice to the design of this 5" bowl. The simple grape and leaf design is one I had not seen before. The finish is a watery flashed iridescence of vaseline color. It is marked "Made in France."

French Knots

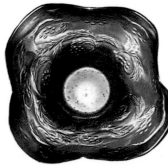

I suppose most people credit this pattern to Fenton because of the shape — a typical hat with ruffled top. The design is quite nice and gracefully covers most of the space except the base. The exterior is plain but nicely iridized. The only colors I've heard about are marigold and blue. French Knots is 4" tall and has a base diameter of 2½".

Frit Pinched Vase (Dugan)

This vase was advertised in 1905 and 1906 as part of Dugan's Japanese and Pompeian lines (this one is Venetian). This is a type of peach opalescent glass with a glass frit dusting the surface, giving it an art glass look. It is shaped like the hyacinth vases in other treatments from Dugan but has a pinched-in base.

Frolicking Bears

This is a U.S. Glass pattern. It is found in crystal and decorated crystal as well as the few rare pitchers and tumblers found in olive green carnival glass, mostly with an odd gun-metal finish. A crystal tumbler with a sterling silver overlay on the entire piece is also known.

Fronds and Arches

This very nice looking bowl was found in Argentina in June of 2007. It was picked up at a flea market in San Telmos by Mr. And Mrs. Lance Hilkene and they named it. I like the bowl and the name. This 4½" bowl is the only piece in this pattern found to date, but I wouldn't be surprised if a large bowl or other shapes existed. The color is a nice rich marigold.

Frosted Block

This is Imperial's #710 pattern, called Beaded Block in opalescent and other types of glass. In carnival glass it is known as Frosted Block. It can be found in marigold, clambroth, white, and occasionally smoke. Shapes include a round or square bowl, round or square plate, milk pitcher, open sugar, creamer, oval pickle dish, rose bowl (two sizes), pedestal vase, and a compote. Shown is an outstanding plate in marigold.

Frosted Indian

You'll notice that other than the pattern design on this vase from India it is the exact same shape and size as the Frosted Lotus pattern that follows. The design reminds me of coral floating on the ocean floor but I'll stick to the name it was given. Thanks again to Seeck Auction for sharing it.

Frosted Lotus

This vase shape from India is 6½" tall. It has the unusual platform base like the Drapery Rose vase shown elsewhere. The frosting covers much of the surface with iridescent arcs covering the rest except for the lotus blossoms.

Frosted Oxford Bobeche

Rose Presznick showed this years ago in a drawing, named it, and listed it as being made in marigold, blue, and white carnival glass. To date, I've only seen this marigold example. It measures 4½" across with a 1½" diameter opening, and is nearly 1" thick. It is a bobeche used to catch candle wax on a candlestick.

Fruit Band

This very scarce wine set (it has wine glasses rather than stemmed wines) could have been called Fruit Chain because the individual strings of fruits are hanging from a chain. The outer edges of this banding is beaded and the rest of the piece, up to the neck, has ribbing. Fruit Band is known in both marigold and the cobalt blue shown. The color is good, especially on the marigold pieces. I suspect (and it is only a suspicion) this pattern may be from South America.

Fruit Basket (Millersburg)

This pattern has an exterior design and shape exactly like the Roses and Fruit compote with an interior basketweave design and a pineapple, grapes, and fruit. It is my belief that this compote was the original pattern that had to be modified because of the difficulty in producing the intricate design and remaining in a competitive price area. With so few known, it must be classified as a top Millersburg rarity.

Fruit Bonbonniere

This very attractive covered bowl (edges are sawtoothed and mesh) is 5½" in diameter. It has a frosted fruit design in the bottom that has grapes, a pear, and apples. Thanks to Alan Sedgwick for sharing it.

Fruit Salad

This very fine punch set is credited to Westmoreland. It can be found in marigold, amethyst, and the scarce peach opalescent color shown. The prominent design shows cherries, pineapples, and grapes.

Fruits and Flowers (Northwood)

Fruits and Flowers looks much like the Three Fruits pattern, but with added blossoms and no center design, with exception of the very hard to fine stippled variant, which has three center leaves with tips nearly touching. The large bowls (such as the 10½" ice green shown) are found with four cherries instead of the usual three on the smaller bowls. Other shapes are small bowls, plates, a handgrip plate, and stemmed, handled bonbons. It can be found in a wide variety of colors. Thanks to the Remmens for sharing it.

120

Fruits and Flutes

Fruits and Flutes is similar to the Matte Fruits pattern from Brockwitz. This small bowl has the satin finished fruit in the base and a ring of fruit bands around the side of the bowl. This pattern was named by the bowl's owner. It may well be known by another name. I'd appreciate any information about this pattern from readers.

Gaelic

This was made primarily in crystal or decorated crystal by Indiana Glass and advertised in 1910. Shapes include a table set, water set, punch set, berry set, cruet, pickle dish, toothpick holder, shakers, and a relish. In carnival glass only pieces of the table set are known and all are rare finds.

Galloway

This U.S. Glass pattern is also known as Virginia and was their #15086 pattern. It is usually seen in noniridized pressed glass. I am pleased to show the first example of this pattern in iridized glass. It is an individual creamer in a nice marigold an I would consider it to be rare at this time. Thanks to Mike Sopra and Carl Booker for sharing it.

Ganador

This pattern was shown in a Cristalerias Papini (Argentina) catalog in a vase shape labeled "Ganador." This water pitcher has berry-like banding centered between convex columns. The fruit band resembles Papini's Berry Band and Ribs pattern. Tumblers as well as the vase may have been iridized but I have no proof.

Ganges Garden (India)

This 5" tumbler is similar to other designs from India. It has a ringed base and stylized flowers. This is another design furnished to me by Vikram Bachhawat and I am very grateful for his help.

Garden Arbor

Sometimes the names given to these Indian tumblers are more impressive than the patterns. The Garden Arbor 6" tumbler has beaded bands at the top and bottom. The design appears to be a series of vertical panels separated by a vine that trails from top to bottom.

121

Garden Mums

Garden Mums is found as the floral pattern on several advertising pieces, but it is a rather scarce item when found alone. Seen primarily on plates, here is the hard to find deep bowl shape. I've heard about several in this shape. It is 5" wide across the top and 2" deep. The only color reported in Garden Mums is amethyst.

Garden Path

Just why there are two nearly identical patterns as this one and the variant shown below is puzzling. The major difference is the addition of minor embellishments at the outer edge of the design. Not much reason in my opinion to call for a second mould but evidently reason enough for the makers.

Garden Path Variant

The Garden Path Variant is essentially the same as the regular Garden Path pattern except for the addition of six winged hearts and an equal number of five-petaled flora. It can be found on 9" bowls, 10" fruit bowls, 6 – 7" plates, and a rare 11" plate. The exterior pattern is Soda Gold and colors found are amethyst and peach opalescent.

Garland

This rather common pattern was made by the Fenton Art Glass Company about 1911. It is found only in the rose bowl shape. Colors are marigold, cobalt blue, a scarce amethyst, and a very rare green. There are three sets of drapery around the bowl, which is stippled, and each drape is joined by a flower. An amethyst example is shown.

Gay 90s

This very rare and desirable Millersburg water pitcher and tumbler pattern is a real collectors' favorite. The pitcher is found in amethyst (three or four known) and green (only one reported) and the tumblers are found in amethyst where several are known, marigold (two or three reported), and this first known green example. I am very grateful to Steve Maag for sharing this rare tumbler with me.

Geo. W. Getts

This Fenton advertising piece says "Geo. W. Getts, Pianos, Grand Forks (the s is backwards), N. Dak." The piece can be found on bowls, plates, and handgrip plates. A must have for collectors of advertising pieces.

Georgette

This Indian tumbler can be found with three distinct base designs: a star base, a snowflake base, or a plain base. The design is similar to other tumblers from India with opposing diamonds and a floral motif above.

Georgia Belle

This exterior pattern, from Dugan and then Diamond Glass, is always found in carnival glass with the Question Marks interior. Shapes are usually compotes but the same mould has been used to produce stemmed plates or card trays. The design is intaglio and very attractive.

German Steins

Until I received the photos of these enameled steins (one is dated Nov. 17, 1892), I had no idea carnival glass examples even existed. The sizes are 8", 10", 11", and 12". The lettering is in German (one says "PROSIT," another "ZUR EVINNERUNG," and the dated one says "STUTTGART").

Gervurtz Brothers

This ice cream shaped Fenton advertising piece has the standard Garden Mums decoration. It reads "Gervurtz Bros. – Furniture & Clothing – Union Ave. & East Burnside St." The only color I've heard about is amethyst. It can also be found in a plate shape.

Gibson Girl

This cute little toothpick holder has no pattern whatsoever! It stands 2" tall. I haven't a clue who made it and in what other colors.

Globe Vase

This pale marigold 9½" vase with a watery finish is shaped like the Thistle vase. The lower section is shaped like a globe and is divided into squares of longitude and latitude. The upper section is plain on the exterior and has an interior fluting. The maker is unknown and I somewhat question the age being pre 1940.

Goa Vase

The Goa vase is shaped like other vases from India. It has a very strange design, more like symbols than actual floral or geometric designs, with crosshatched feathering and a crown-like design with a jewel in the center.

God and Home (Diamond)

God and Home is one of my favorite water sets. It was first made in 1912. It was once regarded as one of the top sets but reproductions lessoned its popularity. The old pitchers are really hard to find and the tumblers are scarce. It was made only in cobalt blue. The design is a laurel wreath and shield with a sun and rays. The lettering on one side reads "In God We Trust" and on the other "God Bless Our Home." The reproductions from L.G. Wright are also made in cobalt blue, so be sure of what you are buying.

Goddess of Harvest

According to Nellie Fenton Glasgo, this pattern was designed by her father (John Fenton) while he was still associated with the Fenton Company and represented her mother's likeness. It is found on both rare bowls and rarer plates. Colors are marigold, amethyst, or blue. Bowls can be ruffled, ice cream shape, three-in-one, or tightly crimped.

Goddess Vase (Jain)

This scarce pattern is from the Jain Glass Works of India like the Fish, Hand, and Elephant vases. It stands 7½" tall. The complicated pattern appears to be a group of unrelated designs consisting of a mask-like section, and other parts that look like floral cones, simplified ridge rows, and other odd figural forms.

Golden Bird

The maker of this very attractive three-footed, handled nappy hasn't been determined to date. It has feet like some of their items and the detailed enamel decoration is much like their best. It measures 4" wide, 6" long, and is 2¾" tall. On one side is a very pretty blue and yellow bird on a branch and on the other a series of flowers and buds with leaves. The feet, handle, and top banding are all marigold carnival.

Golden Cupid

A recent reporting of an example of this pattern in Australia with a label that is marked "Poland" adds to the puzzle about these similar and related Golden patterns (Golden Cupid, Golden Thistle, Golden Pansies, etc.). I have catalogs from Karhula (1938) in Finland that show similar pieces so perhaps the moulds were moved from one location to another.

The Golden Flowers vase is much harder to find and usually has a richer finish than the stork vase, although both were made by Jenkins. It is 7½" tall with a top opening of 3" and a base measuring 2⅞". The background has a heavy stippling, and the flowers are both large and small.

Golden Grapes

This small Diamond bowl pattern is often lost among all the similar grape patterns. Rose bowls from the same mould are also known. The exterior is without any pattern, the marie is plain, and the interior design doesn't cover much of the available space. Shown is a pastel marigold, unusual in that most pieces in this pattern are a dark, heavy marigold.

Golden Hare

This interesting pitcher has a frosted surface, two iridized bands at the top, and an iridized hare or rabbit standing amid grass and bushes. This is one of the better frosted designs with more detailing than most. It is from India.

Golden Harvest

Golden Harvest was long felt to be a product of U.S. Glass. It is now thought that this pattern is from the Diamond factory. It was first advertised in 1916 after the Dugans departed. It is known in a wine decanter and stemmed wines in marigold or amethyst. Be advised this pattern was reproduced for L.G. Wright in amethyst, and later by Gibson in iridized ivory (custard) and a flashy electric blue.

Golden Honeycomb

Apparently this is just a part of Jeannette's Hex Optic line that happened to get another name in the past. For years it was considered a separate design and attributed to Imperial, but that has now changed. Shapes are bowls, plates, compote, creamer, and sugar, all in marigold. The design is all interior and the color can go from poor to quite good.

Golden Oxen

This mug has never been very desirable like the Heron and some others, but they are easily found if you want one. Taller than most mugs, the only color I've seen is marigold. It was made by Jeannette.

Golden Pansies

Like the Golden Thistle and the Golden Cupid pieces shown elsewhere in this edition, this very attractive tray is a real rarity. It measures 10" long and 5½" wide. There are five flowers on stems that radiate from the center with stylized leaves used as fillers. This rare and desirable piece dates back to the 1930s.

Golden Pineapple and Blackberries

The maker of Golden Pineapple and Blackberries seems to be somewhat clouded. Similar designs (Diana the Huntress, Golden Cupid, Golden Thistle, etc.) are shown in a Finnish (Karhula) catalog of 1938, but some items including the Golden Thistle and the Golden Cupid have surfaced with labels or partial labels that are marked Poland. Golden Pineapple and Blackberries is reported in a 9" bowl and the 10" tray shown.

Golden Press Wine Bottle

These wine bottles were produced by the Armstrong Cork Co. at the Whitall Tatum Glass Plant in 1939 for the New England Wine Company, Inc., Boston, Massachusetts. Left: Peach wine. Right: Blackberry wine. Greg Dillian wrote an article about these bottles in 1997. Both bottles have their original black caps, but are missing the outer shot cup. On the bottom you will find an "A" in a circle because the Armstrong Cork Co. had bought the Whitall Tatum Glass Co. (1938 – 1968). Thanks to Clint Arsenault and Greg Dillian for sharing.

Golden Thistle

Like all the rest of the similar "golden" patterns (Diana, the Huntress, Golden Cupid, etc.) there seems to be some mystery about the origin. Similar patterns are shown in a 1938 Finnish catalog from Karhula but both the Golden Cupid and the Golden Thistle have been reported with labels that are marked Poland. These moulds were possibly moved from one area to another as many European patterns did but only time will give a better understanding of all this.

Golden Wedding

Shown are five different size molds of the Golden Wedding whiskey family: half gallon, one quart, one pint, half pint, and one-tenth pint. There are three different molds for the one pints and two different molds for the half pints. They have paper labels (three different ones, on the back of the bottles) and fused labels. They held different types of whiskey. The best find was the book of matches. The bottles were produced from Nov. 28, 1924, to 1938. The half gallon bottle, which has a cork top and was produced in 1938, is missing. From the collection of Clint Arsenault.

Good Luck

This is one of Northwood's better designs, found in both bowls and plates in a wide range of colors. Bowls can be ruffled or with a piecrust edge and exteriors are either a basketweave or ribbed design. And besides the regular ones like this aqua opalescent bowl shown, there are at least three variants that have less leaves and flowers. And finally, pieces may be plain or stippled with the latter more desirable.

This third variation to Northwood's Good Luck pattern must have been the original design. It has very little foliage or leaves. The exterior has the Basketweave pattern. Bowls can be found ruffled with a piecrust edge.

Good Luck Variant

It is a real privilege to show this very rare plate shape in the rare variant. If you will take the time to compare the design to the regular one you will see this variant has less flowers, berries, leaves, and sheaves of wheat and the design doesn't extend to the edges as much as the other. The exterior shows the Basketweave pattern nicely. Only bowls and this plate in marigold are known in the variant.

Goodyear Ashtray (Industria Argentina)

This nicely done ashtray was made in Argentina (Cristalerias Papini) as an advertisement for Goodyear tires. It has a miniature rubber tire with a carnival glass ashtray insert in the center. The date inscribed on the tire is 1928. This unique novelty has a cousin in a Firestone ashtray with the same sort of tire and carnival glass center and both are collectible.

Gooseberry Spray

This seldom seen U.S. Glass pattern is found on the interior of bowls (5", 10") and compotes. The color is often a dark amber as on the piece shown but other colors have been reported. The design, a series of three arching leaf groups and stems of berries circling above and below, is well balanced and very artistic.

Gothic Arches (Imperial)

While there are still a few doubters as to this being an Imperial pattern, this rare and fine vase pattern is found in smoke so that should tell us something. It is also known in a rare marigold too. Sizes range from 9" to 17+" and I've never seen a poorly iridized one. The tops of every vase seem to be widely flared, much like the shape of the Imperial Morning Glory vase.

Grace

This Sowerby pattern was first produced in 1880 and then revived in 1927 in this iridized version. The shallow bowl is sometimes called a "float bowl." This one has the Sowerby peacock trademark. Thanks to Alan Sedgwick for the photo and information.

Graceful

This rather plain vase is attributed to the Northwood Glass Company and is very similar to the Simple Simon vase shown elsewhere. The only design is the fine horizontal threading around the stem and the ribbing on the base. Colors are marigold, amethyst, or green.

Graceful Water Set

Graceful was made by Christalerias Piccardo of Buenos Aires in 1934 and originally called Fantasia. This rare pattern has been renamed to honor Grace Rinehart. Only cobalt blue has been reported. I am very grateful to Ronald and Carolyn Chesney as well as John H. Nielsen for sharing the photo.

Grand Thistle

Grand Thistle was shown in a 1939 Riihimaki of Finland catalog. The pitcher was numbered 5167 and the tumbler 5066. The pattern is also known as Alexander Floral or Wide Paneled Thistle by some collectors. Colors are a rich amber or cobalt blue, and the pattern is angular and intaglio with a sculptured look that is hard to mistake for many other water sets.

Grankvist

This beautiful rose bowl, credited to Eda Glass, is found in both marigold and blue (shown). It is also found in flared bowl shapes. Thanks to the Ayers family for sharing this photo and information.

Grape and Cable (Fenton)

Yes, Fenton made a Grape and Cable pattern, and it is often hard to distinguish it from Northwood's. Fenton's contribution is found in bowls (both flat and footed), plates, and large orange bowls usually with the Persian Medallion interior. Colors are marigold, green, amethyst, blue, and rarely red.

Grape and Cable (Northwood)

This is Northwood's premier pattern. It is found with many mould variations because of the demand. The number of shapes and colors is staggering. Items can be found either plain or stippled. Shown is a ruffled bowl with fantastic iridescence, courtesy of the Remmens.

Grape and Cable Banded

This is one of several variations of the Grape and Cable pattern by Northwood. A large plain band often replaces the cable. Pieces include a hatpin holder (shown) in amethyst, blue, or marigold; fruit (or orange) bowl; a banana boat in marigold, blue, green, or aqua; and a dresser tray in marigold. All banded variations are in limited supply and are very desirable. Photo courtesy of Samantha Prince.

Grape and Cable Variant

This Grape and Cable Variant is found in ruffled bowls or in a rare double handgrip plate as shown. This version of the pattern is also by Northwood but has only one leaf in the center while the standard design has a clear center and four small leaves around the sides and below the grapes and larger leaves. I've seen these variants in amethyst, green, blue, ice blue, aqua opalescent, smoke, and marigold but certainly other colors may exist. The example shown has a basketweave exterior.

Grape and Cable with Thumbprint

As I've said before, this pattern is really a part of the Northwood Grape and Cable line, but some collectors, especially those of crystal or opalescent glass, call this by a different name. It can be found in berry sets, table sets, cookie jars, tobacco humidor, ruffled hat whimsey, and water sets with a standard or tankard style pitcher. Also there is a large spittoon whimsey from the tobacco jar base.

Grape and Cherry

This pattern is believed by some to be from Sowerby, by others to be from Diamond, and was reproduced by L.G. Wright in opalescent glass. The only shapes are bowls with the design all exterior. Old carnival colors are marigold or cobalt blue. The design is a series of grapes or cherries separated by a scroll and torchere design.

Grape and Gothic Arches

Made in a variety of glass including crystal, custard, gold decorated, and carnival, this pattern is certainly one of the earlier grape patterns. The arches are very effective, reminding one of a lacy arbor framing the grapes and leaves. While the berry sets often go unnoticed, the water sets are very desirable and are a must for all Northwood collectors.

Grape Arbor (Dugan)

While most collectors think of Northwood as the maker of this pattern, Dugan-Diamond had a try at it too with this very pretty large footed bowl. The pattern of lattice, grapes, and leaves covers most of the interior while the exterior has the Inverted Fan and Feather or Feather Scroll pattern, the same pattern as the Butterfly and Tulip bowls. The Dugan Grape Arbor pattern is known in marigold, amethyst, blue, and peach opalescent.

Grape Arbor (Northwood)

Northwood's Grape Arbor is better known than the Dugan version of this pattern. The shapes are the beautiful water set shown and a hat whimsey shaped from the tumbler. Colors are marigold, amethyst, cobalt blue, white, ice blue, ice green, with only the tumbler reported in pearl carnival. The hat whimsey can be found in the same colors except for the pearl. Grape Arbor was one of Northwood's early custard glass patterns, usually stained.

Grape Basket

This very attractive Imperial basket is rather scarce. Colors are marigold or smoke but a green or purple would be a great catch. Iridization is on both the inside and outside of the example shown. Measured to the top of the handle, this basket stands nearly 8" tall.

Grape Delight

This footed Dugan-Diamond rose bowl and nut bowl pattern has been highly reproduced in the last few years. Some of the new ones aren't marked and some have a fake Northwood mark so beware. Old examples are made in marigold, amethyst, cobalt blue, and white. I've seen the reproductions in a bad white, blue, ice blue, ice green, and amethyst so be careful what you buy and where.

Grape Frieze (Northwood)

Grape Frieze is found most often on Northwood's famous verre d'or line of heavily gilded ware. This rare and desirable carnival glass version is shown on a large 10" footed bowl in custard glass that has been iridized. The edge is gilded. Only a few of these pieces are known and all are highly prized.

Grape Leaves (Millersburg)

This seldom found and always costly Millersburg pattern is quite like the Blackberry, Grape, and Strawberry Wreath patterns except for its rarity. The major design difference lies in the center leaf and grapes. It is found in marigold, amethyst, green, and vaseline.

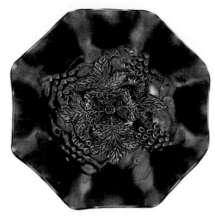

Grape Leaves (Northwood)

While it doesn't get the raves of the famous Grape and Cable pattern, this Northwood design is just as attractive. With four grape stems and leaves and four bunches of grapes, it is very balanced. Colors are marigold, amethyst, green, blue, black amethyst, ice blue, amber, and smoke. The exterior is the Blossom and Palm (sometimes called Blossom and Shell) from Northwood's opalescent glass era.

Grapes of Rath

More new patterns than ever are showing up from Argentina, and this happens to be one of them. This interesting little vase has rich marigold iridescence and a pattern design of grapes, leaves, and a banded neck with a scalloped top. The most interesting thing about this vase, in my opinion, is the name. Yes, it is spelled correctly. It was named by the owners Karen and Allan Rath. How original is that for a pattern name.

Grape Variant

Yes, even the ordinary Grape tumbler from Imperial has a variant. The example shown is a rare white and the variation comes in the tumbler's interior which has a ribboning or ribbing running from top to bottom. The exterior design is just like regular Grape tumblers. Colors for this variant, besides the white, are the usual marigold, purple, and green; but since this pattern is found in smoke, amber, lavender, clambroth, and a rare ice green, all these colors are possibilities. Three of these white examples are reported at this time.

Grapevine Lattice (Dugan)

From Dugan, then Diamond, this pattern is found on bowls, plates, a hat whimsey, and the tankard water set. Colors are the usual Dugan ones, including marigold, amethyst, peach opalescent (bowls and plates), cobalt blue, and white. I personally doubt the plate is really the same pattern as the water set known by the same name, but I will give in to tradition and list them as one and the same. Thanks to Jim Seeck for sharing this rare white tankard pitcher.

Grape Wreath (Millersburg)

This pattern is identical to the Strawberry Wreath shown elsewhere except the Grape Wreath has a center pattern. Here I show the regular Feather or Feathered Leaf center and elsewhere are the other three center patterns that make up all Grape Wreath pieces. Shapes are sauces, bowls (7" – 10"), plates (6" and 10"), and a rare spittoon whimsey.

Grape Wreath Clover and Feather Variant

Like the other variants of the Grape Wreath pattern, this one differs only in the center design, a sort of four-leaf clover like swirl with feathers or fronds that stick out from them on four sides. It can be found in 5½", 7", and 8½" bowls in the usual colors of marigold, amethyst, or green. The example shown is a 5½" sauce in amethyst with a fine radium finish.

Grape Wreath/Multi-star Variant

Here is the third example of a Millersburg variant in this pattern and as you can see, the difference lies in the center design of concentric stars. Some collectors call this the spider web center, and I can certainly see why. It can be found on the same sizes as the other Grape Wreath bowls and in the same colors.

Grape Wreath Variant (Millersburg)

Only the center design has been changed on these. On this one, as you can see, it is a stylized sunburst. I've seen several sizes of bowls with this center, but it looks best on the large 10" ice cream bowls. Colors are marigold, green, amethyst, and a beautiful clambroth with much fire in the lustre.

Grecian Daisy

Grecian Daisy is much like the copper-etched Grecian Gold pieces. This very nice water pitcher with lid has a different shape than any other I've seen. The tumbler resembles the Engraved Grape and Engraved Zinnia tumblers shown elsewhere in this book.

Grecian Urn

Perfume bottles seem to have a charm all their own and this graceful example is a prime item. It stands 6" tall and has a gilt stopper with a dauber attached. And while it isn't marked, an atomizer that is marked DeVilbiss is known that matches in size and shape. The color is a good strong marigold.

Greek Key (Northwood)

Greek Key is from Northwood (1909 – 1912) and is found in bowls, plates, a water pitcher, and tumblers. Colors are mostly marigold, amethyst, or green but bowls and plates are found in cobalt blue as well as ice green, and here is the first reported white ruffled bowl! Thanks to Don and Becky Hamlet for sharing it.

Greek Key and Scales (Northwood)

Here's a rather nice Northwood secondary pattern usually found on dome-based bowls with the Stippled Rays variant interior. The design is crisp and does a nice job.

Greengard Furniture

Greengard Furniture was one of Millersburg's very rare advertising patterns. It is known in a single ruffled bowl, a handgrip plate (one known), and three double handgrip plates (shown). The lettering reads "Greengard Furniture Co. – 11020 Mich. Ave. – Roseland, Ill." The mould is the same as the Campbell and Beesley piece shown elsewhere in this edition.

Guest Set

This popular Fenton pitcher with matching tumbler, which fits into the pitcher opening, is from the Grecian Gold line and is often called a tumble-up set. It is found in marigold only. The example shown has a cobalt blue handle. It would be very nice addition to any collection. Photo courtesy of Remmen Auction.

Gum Tips Vase

Here is the normal shape of this Australian pattern. It simply flares from the base and stands 9¼" tall, with a 5½" top and a 4¾" base diameter. The glass color is black amethyst. This vase is very collectible and a bit hard to find.

Gum Tips Vase Variant

This vase, from Australia's Crystal Glass Works, has a smaller base diameter than the regular one and 10 ribs instead of the usual eight. It is found mostly in black amethyst (shown) but is also known in marigold.

Halloween

This is a very appropriately named pattern since the bright rich marigold is contrasted nicely with narrow black banding at top and bottom. There are two sizes in both tumblers and the matching pitchers, and the pitchers have black handles.

133

Hamburg (Eda)

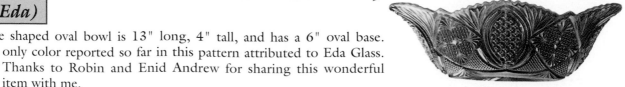

This fine jardiniere shaped oval bowl is 13" long, 4" tall, and has a 6" oval base. Cobalt blue is the only color reported so far in this pattern attributed to Eda Glass. Thanks to Robin and Enid Andrew for sharing this wonderful item with me.

Hammered Bell

This well-known light shade is a very imaginative work of art and was used in a variety of ways: as a hanging shade, suspended over lights on a chandelier, or even in pairs or alone as a shade for a sconce. The metal fittings vary from one shade to the next, and the example shown is a very pretty Art Deco hanger that matches a neat wall sconce dated 1913.

Handled Tumbler

Just who made this odd handled tumbler remains a mystery, at least to me. It has a lot of things going for it that seem to put it in either the Imperial or Dugan-Diamond camp but who can say it isn't from Fenton or one of the lesser concerns? At any rate, it comes in several colors: marigold, amethyst, and blue, and green may well be a possibility. It stands 4⅞" tall, has a top lip that flares slightly, and a flat base. Apparently these pieces are not plentiful.

Handled Vase

This Imperial pattern is also called Two-Handled. It was made in two varieties of vases and a candle bowl with a handled candlestick in the center of a serving bowl. The vase can be plain as shown or can have a swirl optic interior. Colors are the usual marigold or smoke, and vase tops may be straight, rolled, or pulled into a J.I.P. shape.

Hand Vase

This vase, from India, is found in several sizes as well as some variations (with or without beads, watches, or flowers). In addition, these vases can be either left or right handed. Here is shown a 9" and a 6" vase, both with watches on the wrist and beading.

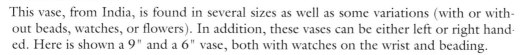

Harvard Yard

This Tarentum Glass Company pattern is usually found in crystal, ruby-stained crystal, emerald green glass, and pink opaque, but here is the first iridized piece I've heard about. It is a tall, thin cruet bottle in marigold. Thanks to Gary Vandevander for sharing it with me.

This pattern, found only in a rare water pitcher and rare tumblers, is now attributed to the Diamond Glass Company. Colors are marigold for both shapes but rare amethyst tumblers are known (shown), and a pale green one with marigold overlay has been found. Thanks to Mickey Reichel for sharing this photo.

Harvest Poppy

The verdict is still out on exactly who made this pattern. The shape and general size of the compote both suggest Fenton, but most collectors feel it is Northwood. It is 5½" tall and has three mould marks. The exterior is plain. The pattern is a series of realistic poppies, leaves, and five strands of wheat-like flora, with a stippled background. Colors are marigold, amethyst, green, cobalt blue, and amber, with peach opalescent rumored. All are rare.

Hattie

First known as Imperial's #496, Hattie is an intriguing pattern that covers the entire piece, front and back! Shapes found are 8" bowls, a rare rose bowl, and a rare 10" plate that is sometimes referred to as a chop plate. Bowls are round and found in marigold, purple, green, smoke, and amber, while the rose bowl has been reported in marigold, purple, and amber. The plate can be found in marigold, purple, green, clambroth, and the beautiful amber example here.

Havelli

This tumbler from Jain Glass Works in India reminds me a bit of Millersburg's Gay 90s design but is much simpler. It stands 5½" tall. Vikram Bachhawat provided me with the photo and the name, and his help with Indian glass has been invaluable.

Hawaiian Moon

This is a machine-enameled item with a flashed finish like the Late Waterlily tumbler shown elsewhere. It has been seen in marigold and a scarce cranberry and came along during the Depression era.

Hazel

This vase stands around 6" tall. I believe it was possibly made by the same company who produced the Davann vase because the designs are somewhat similar, although I'm not sure who made that one either. Thanks to Seeck Auction for sharing it.

Headdress

Recent findings indicate that at least some of the Headdress pieces originated at U.S. Glass. A Cosmos and Cane small bowl with Headdress interior is now known. And since there is speculation that U.S. Glass also made some of the Curved Star pieces, perhaps all Headdress items are American. Only time and additional research will clear all this up. Headdress can be found on 7", 9", and 10½" bowls with either Cosmos and Cane or Curved Star exteriors. Colors reported are marigold, green, and blue.

Headdress Variant

Despite the conflicts with this pattern's history I now suspect the bowl with the Cosmos and Cane exterior is from U.S. Glass. This can be found in marigold, honey-amber, white, or a scarce green. The pieces found with Curved Star, Nutmeg Grater, or European Poppy exteriors are made in Europe and were possibly copied from the U.S. Glass version. In addition there is a compote (probably a stemmed sugar) from Europe too.

Heart and Horseshoe (Fenton)

This is Fenton's Heart and Vine pattern with an added horseshoe and the words "Good Luck." It was, no doubt, their answer to Northwood's famous Good Luck pattern. It is found in bowls and there has been a rumor of a plate for many years. The only color seems to be marigold despite some indications a few years back that green also existed. Heart and Horseshoe is a very scarce article indeed.

Heart and Trees

This Fenton pattern was sometimes used as the interior pattern of the Butterfly and Berry footed bowls. It combines scales, hearts, and floral trees. Colors are mostly marigold, but cobalt blue, green, and one ice green are reported at this time. Shown is a green bowl with the very desirable candy ribbon edge. Photo courtesy of Remmen Auction.

Heart and Vine

This well-known Fenton design is found on both bowls and plates and can also be seen as part of the Spector advertising plate. Colors for the regular pieces are marigold, amethyst, blue, and green on ruffled, three-in-one, or crimped bowls and amethyst, blue, and green on the plates.

Heart and Vine Variant

If you compare this design to the regular Heart and Vine shown above, you will see a distinct difference. This variant has fewer vine leaves, more open area between them, and the five leaves that go toward the center are smaller. Just why the mould difference can only be explained by a mould replacement since this was a popular pattern in its day.

This readily available McKee pattern was used for more souvenir lettering than almost any other pattern. This pattern can be found in mugs of two sizes as well as a regular tumbler and a mini tumbler, or shot glass as some call it. The colors are marigold and green with most having watery silver flashed on iridescence. Thanks to the Remmens for sharing it.

Hearts and Flowers

Hearts and Flowers, with its finely stitched look, is similar in technique to the Embroidered Mums and Fenton's Captive Rose patterns. The design is an intricate one, covering the allotted space. Found in bowls (mostly with a ribbed exterior but sometimes with Basketweave), plates, and stemmed compotes. The color range includes marigold, amethyst, green, blue, ice blue, purple, white, ice green, aqua opalescent, clambroth, blue opalescent, a rare marigold on custard glass, and a rare vaseline.

Heart Swirl Lamp

I certainly wish I knew more about this attractive lamp base. It has great color and a European look. If anyone knows another name or who the maker is, I'd like to know. Thanks to Tom and Sharon Mordini for sharing it.

Heavy Banded Diamonds

This beautiful Australian pattern is a joy to behold. The diamonds are heavily moulded and stand out below the narrow thread lines, and the iridescence is very rich. It can be found in a berry set, flower set with frog, and a water set. It is available in both marigold and purple.

Heavy Diamond (Imperial)

Heavy Diamond is most often seen in the pedestal-based vase shape, but is also found in a 10" bowl, a creamer and sugar, and a compote. Most pieces are found in marigold, but the compote is known in green and the vase comes in marigold, smoke, clambroth, and green. The sugar and creamer are considered a breakfast set and apparently other table set pieces were not made. The pattern of crisscrossing bars with the sections between puffed out is a good one.

Heavy Grape (Dugan)

Although similar in many ways to the Millersburg Vintage bowls, this Dugan pattern does have several distinct qualities of its own. The most obvious one is, of course, the grape leaf center with grapes around its edge. Also missing are the usual tendrils and small leaflets, and the exterior doesn't carry a hobnail pattern but a typical near-cut design. Thanks to the Remmens for this excellent bowl example.

Heavy Grape (Imperial)

Imperial's strong grape pattern with the #700 Flute exterior can be found in small and large bowls and plates, a handled nappy, and a medium size bowl. Colors include marigold, purple, green, smoke, powder blue, aqua, cobalt blue, white, olive, ice green, vaseline, and the spectacular amber shown in a plate from David DeMoss.

Heavy Hobnail

This rare item was first shown in Bill Edward's *Rarities in Carnival Glass*. At that time, only the white version was known, but since then a spectacular purple example has been seen. These were Fenton Rustic vases that weren't pulled or swung into the vase shape and very few are known.

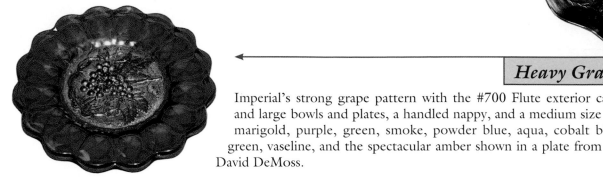

Heavy Iris

Possibly Dugan's most artistic pattern, Heavy Iris is top notch carnival glass. The pitcher is blown with an applied handle and most of the top treatments are ruffled. The few straight tops reported are white, while the ruffled pitchers are known in marigold, white, amethyst, and peach opalescent (one reported). Tumblers are reported in all these colors plus lavender, and a JIP whimsied tumbler is known in white. Heavy Iris has been reproduced by L.G. Wright in water sets and a strange red or blue handled basket was made in the 1980s.

Heavy Pineapple (Fenton)

This pattern can be found in many shapes in satinized crystal, rose satin, and ruby glass, including bowls, compotes, and candlesticks, but carnival pieces are limited to the large bowl. Colors are marigold, cobalt blue, and white with less than a dozen pieces known in all three colors! The exterior only pattern of pineapples, thick trunk-like vines, and leaf-fans is distinctive and unusual. It can be flat or footed.

Heavy Prisms

This beautiful celery vase stands 6" tall and shows the quality English carnival glassmakers attained. Colors reported are marigold, amethyst, and blue. The glass is very thick and heavy, and the lustre top-notch.

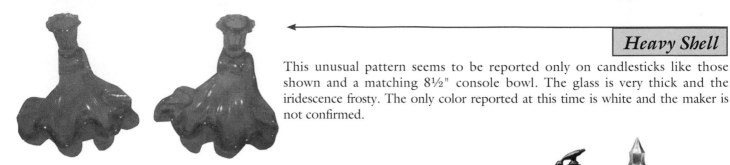

Heavy Shell

This unusual pattern seems to be reported only on candlesticks like those shown and a matching 8½" console bowl. The glass is very thick and the iridescence frosty. The only color reported at this time is white and the maker is not confirmed.

Heavy Vine

This well-made Rindskopf design is found in several shapes including a tumble-up, cologne, perfume, perfume atomizer, ring tree, puff box, pintray, miniature rose bowl, a covered bowl, and a shot glass. Most pieces have rich marigold iridescence. The design is a center band of vine set off from panels that are much like those of Jacobean Ranger.

Heavy Web

Heavy Web is a very interesting Dugan pattern found primarily on large, thick bowls in peach opalescent. It has been found with two distinct exterior patterns — a beautifully realistic grape and leaf design covering most of the surface and an equally attractive morning glory pattern. I've seen various shapes including round, ruffled, square, and elongated ones. A vivid purple or green bowl in this pattern would certainly be a treasure.

Heinz Tomato Juice

This juice glass with white enameled lettering is obviously late carnival glass, made after the 1920s, but nonetheless is an interesting example of iridized advertising. It is shown in a soft pastel marigold. It is the first I've seen but was probably widely available at the time of production.

Heisey #473 (Narrow Flute with Rim)

Called a breakfast set by some collectors, this two-piece grouping consists of an individual creamer and a two-handled tray. Each is marked with the H-in-a-diamond mark. In addition the tray is marked "Pat. 6/20/16." The coloring is a soft pastel like other iridized Heisey, and the lustre strong. The creamer measures 2⅞" tall and 3¾" across while the tray is 8" across. It has been suggested the tray held lump sugar.

Heisey Colonial

Besides a compote, dresser tray, hair receiver, juice tumbler, perfume and cologne bottles, and a puff box, this Heisey pattern is known in this marked vase on a stem. It has the soft, yellowish iridescence often seen with Heisey glass (they did no iridizing but had it done for customers). The vase is marked "SUPERIOR BATH HOUSE." This is one of the bathhouses in the Hot Springs, Arkansas, area.

139

Heisey Crystolite

Crystolite was made in dozens of shapes in crystal (Heisey blank #1503), but in carnival glass only the spittoon is known (Heisey called this a vase shape). Carnival colors are marigold, the zircon blue shown, and a watery lavender. This is a rather late Heisey pattern, made during the Depression.

Heisey Flute

I thought this neat little piece of Heisey glass (it's marked) was a shot glass until I read John Britt's write-up about it being a toothpick holder. In fact it is very much like their Colonial #300 pattern. Of course Heisey had numerous patterns they termed colonial and it is a bit hard to distinguish between them. The Flute toothpick holder has a flat top, eight flute panels, and a 16-pointed star in the base. The color is very rich, something unusual for Heisey.

Heisey Laverne

Made in 1924, this Heisey pattern was advertised as their #1201 and came in colors they called moongleam, flamingo, vaseline, and crystal. Here is a pretty iridized version with typical pale yellow lustre so often found in Heisey carnivalized items. The low footed bowl measures 11" across and has a rim that droops to a nice shape, giving the piece a very attractive look. Like most Heisey iridized items, this one is a very scarce piece and will bring top dollar.

Heisey Puritan (#341)

Since I first showed this very nice compote that was part of a large colonial line in crystal from the Heisey Company, I've seen another marigold example as well as the shorter stemmed compote in a soft yellow iridescence on clear glass. These pieces were both marked with the Heisey trademark. The distinctive layered knob in the center of the stem is the easy way to spot the Puritan pattern. It is known also in amethyst.

Helen's Star

Helen's Star is similar to the Diamantes Star vase as well as other Indian vases. It is 6½" tall with pale iridescence on the part below the ring and clear glass above.

Heron Mug

Like the Fisherman's mug, this pattern came from Dugan, but is harder to find and in my opinion, better designed. The Heron is on one side of the mug only, but does fill more space in a graceful rendering of the bird and its marshy domain. The Heron mug has been reported in marigold, purple, and amethyst only.

Herringbone and Beaded Ovals

This very hard to find compote was listed in Imperial advertising as #B-54½. The pattern was shown on a light shade. The compote has superb marigold color on the bowl, and the stem and base are clear. No other color has been reported and only three or four are known.

Herringbone and Mums

Made by the Jeannette Glass Company in the late 1920s, this rare Depression era tumbler is a close relative to the Iris and Herringbone pattern by the same company. Both are found only in marigold, but the Herringbone and Mums is shorter and has the novel six-sided block base.

Hexagon Square

Here I show a child's breakfast set. The pieces stand 2¼" tall and have a soft lavender iridescence over clear glass. The shape is six-sided, givingthe pattern its name, and the bases of each piece are quite thick and heavy. Probably other colors of flashing were used. These pieces date from the 1920s or later.

Hex Base Candlestick

Nearly every glassmaker had a try at candlesticks shaped like this one, especially in stretch glass. The one shown is reported to be from the Imperial Company and has a very rich dark marigold color. Most of these candlesticks were sold in pairs with a console bowl in a wide range of colors including green, purple, and even red.

Hex Optic

Produced in the late days of carnival glass, the Hex Optic pattern like the Treebark Variant came from the Jeannette Company. The line consisted of water sets, various table pieces including large and small bowls, saucers, and jelly and relish dishes. Sometimes light in iridiza- tion, the mould work is less complicated than early glass, even from the same company.

Hex Panel

After I first showed this pattern, I received information that this is from Jeannette and was a soda tumbler. It stands 7½" tall, has six wide ribs that extend from base to the wide band around the top, and is a strong marigold. Bob Smith reports examples marked with the Jeannette trademark but the example shown has no marking at all. Production is from the late 1920s I believe.

Hickman

Here is the first piece of iridized glass reported in this pattern. The pattern was first made by McKee and Brothers from 1897 to 1904, and then by Federal Glass in 1914. I suspect it was from Federal because it has that soft coloring they produced. Thanks to Mickey Reichel for sharing this find.

Hobnail (Millersburg)

Hobnail pieces run from scarce to rare, depending on shapes and colors. This Millersburg pattern is found on water sets, table sets, a rose bowl, and lady's spittoon. Colors are the standard marigold, amethyst, and green with rare blue examples known in some shapes. Green water sets are rarer than blue ones and there are no reported blue rose bowls or spittoons, with green examples being the rarest color here. The finish is usually a strong radium and the workmanship, like all Millersburg, outstanding.

Hobnail and Cane (Australia)

This wonderful stemmed piece, from Australia's Crown Crystal Company, is found in both a ruffled compote or flattened into a cake stand. The pattern is exterior and features eight panels of hobnail with cane. Colors known are marigold, purple, and the marigold over ice blue glass shown. The pattern is also found as an exterior pattern on the large Emu Variant compotes.

Hobnail Soda Gold

The large spittoon shown is the most often seen shape in this pattern, and there are salt and pepper shakers that are rather rare. The spittoon measures 4" tall and is 7" across the top opening. Colors are usually marigold in varying degrees of quality, but green, amber, and white spittoons are known. The shakers are known only in marigold.

Hobnail Variant

After years of accepting this pattern as a Millersburg product, there now seems to be some controversy with some collectors sure it was made by the Fenton Company. All I can say is my former co-author Bill Edwards was present with two other Millersburg collectors when Frank Fenton took the mould drawing from his folder of Millersburg glass and they all agreed at that time the pattern was from that company. Shapes known are vases, a rose bowl whimsey, and a jardiniere whimsey, both shown elsewhere. Colors are marigold, amethyst, green, and blue. Thanks to Casy Rich for this nice example.

Hobstar (Imperial)

This was Imperial's #282 in their catalog. It was made in many, many shapes in crystal before carnival glass production began in 1911. Carnival shapes are 5" and 10" bowls, a table set, cookie jar with lid, punch bowl and base, punch cup, compote, milk jar with lid, pickle castor (rare), and bride's basket. Colors vary from shape to shape but all are found in marigold, the table set in purple and green, the punch set in green, and one green bowl has been reported but not confirmed.

Hobstar and Arches

Imperial's #3027 pattern has long been known as Hobstar and Arches. It was shown in their 1909 catalog and is actually the same pattern as the Hobstar Flower shown elsewhere in this book. Imperial had a habit of giving similar numbers to different shapes but not giving a single number to some patterns. It is confusing for collectors but I try to give all designations when I can. In addition, a cruet is known with the #302 designation that is the same design. Hobstar and Arches is found on 8½" – 9½" bowls and a fruit bowl with stand. Colors are marigold, purple, green, and smoke.

Hobstar and Cut Triangles

This very unusual pattern is typically English in design with strong contrast between geometrically patterned areas and very plain areas. Rose Presznick lists bowls, a plate, and a rose bowl in this pattern in both green and amethyst, but the only shapes I've seen are bowls, rose bowls, and compotes in marigold or amethyst.

Hobstar and Feather

Hobstar and Feather, one of Millersburg's best conceived patterns, is found in both crystal and carnival glass. Shapes in the latter include a table set (green covered sugar shown), a punch set (with plain interior or with a Fleur-de-lis design), a jelly compote, a bridge set, sauce, giant rose bowl, and many whimsies. Colors are marigold, amethyst, green, and most pieces are rare and desirable. The example shown is a square bowl with a light marigold finish.

Hobstar and Fruit (Westmoreland)

This Westmoreland pattern is known mostly on small shapes from a sauce bowl and can be found in marigold, blue opalescent, peach opalescent, and this rare marigold-over-milk-glass treatment. This shape is called a card tray or a banana bowl. The design is exterior, consisting of eight panels that hold different types of fruits including grapes, strawberries, cherries, and blackberries. Alternating panels contain a hobstar.

Hobstar and Shield

This is another rare pattern found in water pitchers and tumblers. It is from Karhula-Ittala. Besides the handful of marigold pitchers and tumblers, a pitcher is reported in blue, so tumblers in that color probably exist. The design is very balanced and the color is good. The tumbler is slightly shorter than most, standing 2⅝" tall.

Hobstar and Tassels (Imperial)

Once thought to be an English exterior pattern on copies of Scroll Embossed pieces, I now know this was made by Imperial, first in crystal in many shapes and then in carnival. Carnival pieces are primarily bowls, 7" – 9" with either smooth or serrated edges, but there is a smooth edged plate that is 7½" in diameter known in green. The bowls are found with either plain or Scroll Embossed interiors and are found in purple, green, teal (9" bowl), and a recently discovered marigold (shown).

143

Hobstar Band

Here is a bowl shape found in this seldom-discussed pattern. It is also found in water sets with a flat pitcher or pedestal based pitcher and flared or straight tumblers, a two-handled celery vase, spooner, and a variant compote. Colors include marigold, amber, and green. The maker hasn't been confirmed at this time.

Hobstar Diamonds

This very pretty geometric pattern has eight small hobstars around the base, eight larger ones at the top of the design, and long panels of plain diamonds between. It is shown on this rare tumbler. The color is a pretty honey-marigold.

Hobstar Flower (Imperial)

Hobstar Flower was shown in Imperial's 1909 catalog as #302 and #302½. This fine geometric pattern is found in a rare cruet in carnival glass (marigold). The compote is known in marigold, purple, smoke, helios, and the superb emerald green shown. Purple is the easiest color to find with smoke or green rare, and marigold scarce.

Hobstar Panels

Here is a well-conceived geometric design with hobstars, sunbursts, and panels integrated into a very nice whole. The only color I've seen is the deep marigold shown, but certainly there may be others.

Hobstar Reversed

While Davidson isn't known to have made carnival glass, rumors place this pattern (also called Oval Star and Fan) from that company. Colors are mostly marigold but here I show an original pastel flower frog. This piece was found in Scotland and I thank Dorothy Taylor for sharing it.

Hocking Flute

This Hocking Glass tumbler probably dates from the 1920s. The marigold iridescence is very thin and watery. The piece is marked.

144

Hocking Mixing Bowl

Most of these mixing bowls date from Depression glass times. This is the first iridized one I've heard about. It has very strong color and iridescence, indicating it came along at the end of carnival glass production, but certainly not in the time of the Sungold items that are truly Depression glass. It is marked "Hocking" and has a top diameter of 7", I believe. Ads show this same bowl mould used in 1929. Four sizes are known and fit into each other making a "nesting set" for easier storage.

Hoffman House (Imperial)

Apparently Imperial produced a limited amount of these goblets in carnival glass although they are shown in the 1909 crystal catalog and similar ones are known to have been made by several glasshouses in the same treatment. The color is a rich amber and few examples are known. (The owners of the one shown were told by Imperial factory workers only five iridized ones were produced.)

Holiday

Holiday is a Northwood pattern that so far has turned up only on this 11" tray. It is shown here in marigold and has the Northwood mark. It is also known in crystal but seems to have no accompanying pieces.

Hollow Tube Candlesticks

While the design isn't spectacular, these candlesticks from Czechoslovakia do have better-than-average lustre and to add a bit of interest, the boboches were drilled to hold prisms so they become decorative. The maker isn't known to date. I would appreciate any further information readers may offer on these.

Holly (Fenton)

Holly was made in 1911, in bowls, plates, compotes, a hat shape, goblets (from the compote mould), and a rare rose bowl. Colors include marigold, amethyst, green, blue, lime green, lavender, amber, red, white, aqua, celeste blue, amberina, blue opalescent, lime green opalescent, moonstone, vaseline, and clambroth. Thanks to Peter Baerwald.

Holly and Berry

The Holly and Berry pattern was made by the Dugan Company after 1909. It is found on 6½" – 8" bowls and a nappy that is about the same size. Colors are marigold, amethyst, peach opalescent, a rare blue, and the equally rare iridized pink afterglow shown. If you will examine this pattern and the Christmas compote pattern you will see how similar the two are. Thanks to Jerry and Cleo Kudlac for sharing this rare example.

Holly and Poinsettia (Dugan)

While it hasn't been seen in old advertising or company catalogs, most collectors feel this very rare pattern was made at Dugan. It has a design and shape very much like the Christmas compote. Dugan made many dome-based pieces. The only color reported at this time is marigold with a rich finish on all except the base. The holly and poinsettias circle the bowl of the compote from just above the base to the outer rim, filling much of the available space.

Holly Sprig (Millersburg)

This wonderful Millersburg pattern is very realistic with stippled leaves and clusters of berries. It is similar to Holly Whirl but without the extra leaves in the center. It is found mostly on bowls or on bonbons (one has advertising), but here is the very rare compote shape. Colors are clambroth, marigold, amethyst, and green.

Holly Whirl (Millersburg)

If you will compare this pattern to Millersburg's Holly Sprig, you will see what distinguishes one design from the other. Holly Whirl is found on bowls, bonbons, berry sets, and ice cream sets, either with the Flute or the Near Cut Wreath exterior. Colors are the usual marigold, amethyst, and green. Shown is a superb green with blue iridescence.

Holly Wreath Multi-Stars Variant

Here is another variation of the Holly pattern. It is the Multi-Stars variant center design. It can be found on 7" – 8" ruffled bowls or 6" ice cream shaped bowls. Colors are the usual marigold, amethyst, and green, and most have a fine radium finish.

Holly Wreath Variant

Like Millersburg's Grape Wreath pattern, this Holly Wreath has a four feather or feathered leaf center pattern. There are three other center designs. They are Clover and Feather, Multi-Stars, and Stylized Sunburst. Holly Wreath is found on 7" – 8" bowls in marigold, amethyst, and green.

This shade seems to match the one in Hartung's book 10 and according to the information supplied to me by Ron Britt it has the markings "Penna. 701" on the inside of the fitter rim. Since there was already a shade with the Homestead name, I elected to incorporate the additional markings into the name of this nicely done shade. Thanks to Ron for the photo of this piece.

Homestead Shade

There seems to be several painted scenes on these shades: castles, mountains, or winter landscapes. The example shown has a cabin on one side and trees and pasture on the rest. It was named by Marian Hartung. It is 5" tall and has a bell diameter of 4¼". The finish is dull but does show iridescence.

Honeybee Pot

This cute honey pot was shown in a Jeannette catalog as late as 1959. It stands 4¼" tall. Besides the lightly iridized yellowish, it was made in shell pink milk glass as well as clear and amber glass that was not iridized.

Honeycomb (Dugan)

This well-designed novelty rose bowl from the Dugan Glass Company is a very popular item with collectors. The pattern is all exterior and it has no interior pattern. It is found only in marigold or peach opalescent glass. It stands 4½" tall.

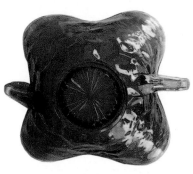

Honeycomb and Clover

This Fenton exterior pattern is found on bowls, a scarce compote, and bonbons. The design has an allover honeycombing with a trail of flowers and vining around the middle. Thanks to Rene Bettis for sharing this bonbon in green with a marigold iridescence.

Honeycomb and Hobstar (Millersburg)

Honeycomb and Hobstar was first an Ohio Flint Glass pattern called Gloria. The moulds were sold at the close of the factory in 1907 and moved from Jefferson Glass to Millersburg in 1909. The vase is the only shape known in carnival glass and it is found in both amethyst and blue. All are rare. The vase stands 8¼" tall. The example shown has been traced back to John Fenton. In addition, crystal examples are known.

Honeycomb Panels

I have been assured this tall tumbler is old, and I must admit it appears so to me. This rather tall purple tumbler has excellent color and iridization. Three rows of honeycombing above a series of eight panels make the design simple yet effective. The maker is unknown at this time. Additional information is appreciated.

Honeycomb Variant

If you compare this pattern to the Fishscales and Beads pattern shown elsewhere in this book you will see the obvious differences. This pattern has a smooth edge and stops about two inches from the very center of the piece, and the design is more of a true honeycomb look with six-sided combs. Notice their combs are pointed and the design goes down into the very bottom of the piece. The only similar feature is that both carry the Leaf Rosette and Beads exterior pattern.

Hoops (Fenton)

In the early 1920s Fenton made a footed pattern they labeled as their #100. It came in three sizes and was found on many colored glass treatments as well as amethyst opalescent, moonstone, jade, orchid, topaz opalescent, and green transparent glass. Here I show a pattern I've named Hoops. It is like #100 but it is on a collar base and is marigold carnival glass. The bowl shown has eight ruffles and is iridized on the inside only. Also seen is a shallow rose bowl shape from the same mould in the same color. The design is a simple one; four concentric rings that circle the exterior of the bowl.

Horn of Plenty

What can I say about this bottle that isn't obvious from the photo? It isn't rare or even good carnival, but it certainly has a place in the history of our glass. The maker and age are unknown at this time.

Horse Chestnut

I'm showing this strictly for identification purposes, although I can't say that these look anything like the chestnuts I've seen out in the woods locally. The ones I am familiar with aren't seen in large clusters and are about the size of hickory nuts and the color of course, is a chestnut brown. This pattern is also known as Leaf and Berry Circle and Berry and Leaf Circle but was changed somewhere along the line, as others have been. This exterior pattern can be found on some Fenton patterns.

Horses' Heads (Fenton)

Horses' Heads Fenton's #1665, is also known as Horse Medallion. It was first made 1912 in collar base bowls, footed bowls, rose bowls, and rare plates. Colors are marigold, green, blue, amethyst, amber, amberina, red, aqua, white, celeste blue, vaseline, and the lime vaseline shown.

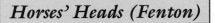

If it weren't for the pretty horseshoe design in the bottom of this bar glass, it would be just another piece of glass. But with the design, it is very collectible, highly sought, and not cheap. Marigold is the only color so far reported.

Hot Springs Vase

This very interesting vase is a beauty. It measures 9⅞" tall and 4½" wide across the top. The color is a pale amber and the iridescence is quite good. It says: "To Lena from Uncle, Hot Spring, Arkansas, Superior Bath House, May 20, 1903." Who says carnival glass was first made in 1907?

Howard Advertising Vase

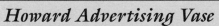

The pattern is called Four Pillars. The vase shown has advertising on the base, which says "Howard Furniture Co., 109 & 11 Nth Howard St." It is 12" tall and has a 4" base diameter. The color is a strong emerald green with good iridescence.

Huaco De Oro Bottle

This bottle is from the same maker as the other Inca style bottles shown elsewhere. It was used for a fermented grape drink. The design shows a sun with a face and the paper label on the base says "Huaco De Oro – Peruano." Thanks to the late Krista Karas for sharing her love for these nice bottles with me.

Hyacinth Gone with the Wind Lamp

This is one of the better carnival glass Gone with the Wind lamps. It stands 22" tall and has a beautiful honey-marigold finish. The metal base designs can vary from lamp to lamp.

Iceburg

If you look closely at the design of this short stemmed bowl, you will see it is exactly the same as the Halloween pattern shown elsewhere. Here we have a color called ice blue with cobalt blue banding on the rim and base. On the bottom is a paper label that reads "MADE IN CZECH SLOVAKIO." Other shapes probably exist.

Ice Crystals

This pattern can be found in a nut cup (shown in Hartung's VIII book), the 7½" plate (shown in the ninth edition), a candlestick, a large bowl, and the covered candy jar here. The roughened surface is produced with an acid solution and is much like the Brocaded pieces from Fostoria. Thanks to Mary P. Hare for sharing this lavender piece (other pieces are known in white).

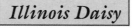

Idyll (Fenton)

Idyll is one of the Fenton Art Glass Company's hidden treasures. This 7" vase is really a variation of their Waterlily and Cattails pattern with an added Butterfly. It is found in chocolate glass as well as the carnival colors of marigold, amethyst (shown), and cobalt blue. All are extremely rare.

Illinois Daisy

How strange this name sounds on a British pattern, but Illinois Daisy was a product of Davidsons of Gateshead. Shapes known are the familiar covered jar and an 8" bowl. The only color I've heard about is marigold, often very weak, but perhaps time will turn up another color.

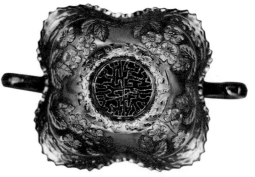

Illinois Soldiers and Sailors

Illinois Soldiers and Sailors is found only on a 7½" plate. It has an exterior pattern called Horse Chestnut (Berry & Leaf Circle or Leaf & Berry Circle) and is known in cobalt blue or marigold carnival glass. While not rare, this plate is very collectible usually bringing good prices and is a desirable find.

Illusion

This is a Fenton pattern with an odd grouping of designs. The center looks like a grid of shapes or even a puzzle, while the middle has four groups of flowers and leaves, and near the outer edge is another ring of the center design. It is found on both marigold and cobalt blue bonbons (some flattened into card tray shapes).

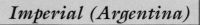

Imperial (Argentina)

This pattern was called Imperial by Cristalerias Piccardo of Argentina. It is shown in a 1934 catalog with a matching stemmed goblet, but I've heard of only the rare pitcher (shown) in carnival glass. The design is a fine one and perhaps the goblets will be found iridized one of these days. Marigold is the only reported color at this time.

Imperial #5

This seldom seen pattern is also called Banded Fleur de Lis. It is found on marigold or amber 7" – 9" bowls as well as on a marigold 6" celery vase. It was first made in crystal in 1905 and then in carnival in 1909. The bowl is dome based and ruffled as shown.

Imperial #30 Cut

In the 1920s, the Imperial Company began a line of glass that had a very stretch look, with additional cuttings. The center-handled plate shown is an example. This piece is in smoke carnival with a heavy stretch finish that has wheel-etched blossoms and tube designs. Shapes were mostly bowls, plates, vases, and novelty pieces, and colors were primarily marigold, clambroth, and smoke.

Imperial #107½

This plain compote is shown in a 1909 Imperial catalog. I'm told that the amber color resembles that of the Hoffman goblet. Until now, amber was the only color seen, but thanks to Allen Bossoli we can now see this in a nice teal.

Imperial #107½ A

Thanks to David Cotton, I now know this pattern is a variation of the #107½ shown above. It differs in that interior fluting has been added. Both patterns are shown in the 1909 Imperial book in goblet shapes but since one was pulled into a compote this one probably was too.

Imperial #203A

This pattern was shown in Imperial's 1909 catalog under #203A (mostly in wines and goblets). Its design is very much like their Swirl Rib design without the swirling, and if you take a close look at the mug shown, you will see its shape is exactly like the Swirl Rib mug. This is the first carnival example I've seen.

Imperial #284

If you compare this Imperial vase to the Jester's Cap vase by Westmoreland, you will see it has eight ribs as opposed to Westmoreland's 12. These vases should not really be called anything but Corinth vases by different makers, but I will bow to earlier naming. This vase was designated as #284 in Imperial ads, and so I've named it.

Imperial #302

Imperial #302 was shown in the 1909 catalog in many shapes in crystal. The carnival version is the oil bottle shown. The pattern has long been confused with Imperial's Crab Claw Variant.

Imperial #393½

Imperial #393½ was shown in the 1909 catalog in crystal and decorated crystal. This water set is apparently not part of either the Chesterfield or Wide Panel lines. This is the first carnival glass example I've heard about. As you can see it is a very dark marigold. Other colors and shapes may exist but I have no knowledge of them at this time.

Imperial #499

Imperial #499 was shown in old Imperial catalogs as part of an ice cream set that consisted of a large bowl and six sherbets. This pretty stemmed sherbet can be found in marigold, clambroth, amberina, and red. It stands 4" tall and the master bowl had a 9" top diameter. Like other Flute or Colonial designs, this pattern is simple, concise, and has nothing that would separate it from many similar patterns.

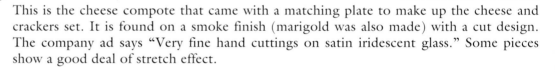

Imperial #641

This is the cheese compote that came with a matching plate to make up the cheese and crackers set. It is found on a smoke finish (marigold was also made) with a cut design. The company ad says "Very fine hand cuttings on satin iridescent glass." Some pieces show a good deal of stretch effect.

Imperial #664 Server

This is another of those center-handled servers that Imperial and others liked to make. The color is called blue ice, but it is actually a smoky blue and very attractive. The finish is heavily stretched with an etched floral design that is very elaborate.

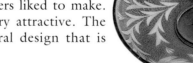

Imperial Basket

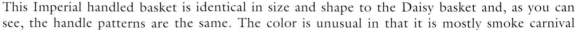

This Imperial handled basket is identical in size and shape to the Daisy basket and, as you can see, the handle patterns are the same. The color is unusual in that it is mostly smoke carnival with just a touch of marigold around the top.

Imperial Flute Vase

While many collectors mistake this vase for the Serrated Flute vase, also from Imperial, this one has the emphasized flute endings of the Flute line. The base diameter is 2⅝" and the example shown stands 8½" tall (these vases range from 6" to 12" tall). Colors are marigold, green, and a superb purple. The top has a sawtooth or serrated top and there are eight flutes around the vase.

Imperial Grape

Imperial's version of the grape pattern is found in many shapes including bowls, plates, a water set, decanter, wine, goblet, water bottle, cup and saucer, punch set, compote, and handled basket. Colors are many. Shown is a very collectible water bottle.

Imperial Grape Variant

I'm still not convinced this is one of the Imperial Grape pattern variants, but I will call it by the name given. The only shape reported is a 7" – 8" deep bowl in marigold. The bowl has a collar base with a well detailed grape leaf. There are six clusters of grapes and leaves around the bowl and below the bowl's rim are the familiar Imperial Grape double rows of arcs. The pattern is all exterior.

Imperial Grape Variant #2

I hate to use all the variants with some of these patterns but this one seems necessary. It is very close to the Imperial Grape Variant. The center leaf and the grapes are different, but the arcs are there. This shallow bowl is 6½" in diameter.

Imperial Grecian

All the Flute, Chesterfield, Colonial, and Wide Panel patterns from Imperial are so similar, but this one seems to fit with none of the others. It is marked with the Imperial Iron Cross trademark and is shown in white carnival glass. The two handles are nearly identical to those on Westmoreland's Prisms piece. Most collectors called these stemmed bonbons but ads list them as preserves or jelly compotes.

Imperial Jewels

Beginning in 1916, the Imperial Glass Company issued a line of art glass that was simple in design, almost severe in its rendering, and consisting mostly of bowls of various sizes and vases like the handled one shown. Colors were a very dark purple, green, blue, and red. Some pieces showed some stretch effect but most did not. Many were marked with Imperial's Iron Cross mark.

Imperial Paperweight

This very rare advertising paperweight is roughly rectangular, 5½" long, 3⅛" wide, and 1" thick. A depressed oval is in the center of the weight, and it is inscribed: "Imperial Glass Company, Bellaire, Ohio, USA," "Imperial Art Glass," "Nucut," "NuArt," and the Iron Cross trademark. These are all trademarks of the company, of course. The glass is a fine amethyst with good, rich lustre.

Imperial Quilted Flute

This is the usual #700 Flute pattern with a diamonding or quilting in the design used as an exterior pattern with Imperial's Heavy Grape. Why the variation, I can't be sure but it is a pleasing pattern change. On emerald green chop plate shown, the design is very evident and adds greatly to the piece.

Imperial Tube Vase

This 5½" tall, emerald green vase was reported by the seller as an experimental piece of Imperial glass. It was purchased from an Imperial factory worker years ago. I can't give any idea as to its age but it looks like much of the glass from Imperial's 1920s Art Glass line.

Imperial Vintage

While this center-handled piece has the same catalog listing (Imperial #473) as the regular Grape pattern, most collectors think of it as a separate design and call it Vintage. It can be found flat as shown, or turned up on the edges. Colors are marigold, clambroth, and smoke (shown), usually with very fine iridescence. It measures 9½" – 11½" across depending on the edging. The forked handle is patterned like tree bark.

Imperial Wide Rays

This square 7" bowl has interior ribbing that is narrower than the Wide Panel ones and wider than the Chesterfield pieces so I've taken the liberty of giving it a name. There are 28 rays on this piece and the base has a many rays design. Other colors known are marigold, clambroth, and white.

Inca Bottle

This unusual bottle stands 9½" tall and can be found with more than one label. The example shown has a paper label saying "HUACO DE ORO PERUANO." Sometimes a second label is found that says "INDUSTRIA PERUANO" around a bird-like figure. Some pieces are reported to have lettering that says "IMITACION MODERNA" (modern imitation) while some say "INDUSTRIA ARGENTINA." It is now believed these bottles were made in both Peru and Argentina and distributed in Bogotá, Columbia. The bottle is sometimes embossed on the base "VINA SANTA JOSEPHA, IND. PERUANA, REG. IND-8067, SEH-2171, IMITACION MODERNA." I am told this bottle held a fermented grape drink, sold in Peru, Argentina, Columbia, and Chile.

Inca Sun Bottle

This bottle is similar to the regular Inca bottle, but shows a rayed face with a necklace. On the base it is lettered "VINA SANTA JOSEPHA – IND. PERUANA, REG. IND. – 8067, SEH 2173, IMITACION MODERNA." There are at least three similar bottles that supposedly held a fermented grape drink sold in Peru, Argentina, Columbia, and Chile. This bottle is considered as variant. Later in this book you will see another variant called Peruvian Pisco Inca Bottle.

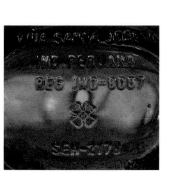

Inca Vase

Like its sister design, the Sea Gulls vase, this is a foreign pattern — probably Scandinavian. The feeling is Art Deco and it is very nicely done. Colors reported are a rich marigold, black amethyst, and a light blue.

Inca Vase Variant

Just what everyone wants, another variant, but I see no way to avoid calling this anything but that. If you'll notice the three paneled sections of the top half of the regular Inca Vase you'll see that there is no pattern inside those sections. In the panels here we see a wavy concentric type design. I've only heard about this variant in marigold so far but feel that other colors may exist, especially light blue.

India Daisy

This oddly shaped 4½" tumbler is from India and is shared by Vikram Bachhawat. The top has the usual frosted coloring while the rest is a strong marigold.

Indiana Flute

Indiana's #165 pattern was shown in the 1914 company catalog. It was primarily a crystal pattern. The 4½" rose bowl on three square feet is the first piece of iridized glass I've heard about. The color is a strong dark marigold.

Indiana Soldiers and Sailors Plate

No question about it, this very rare Fenton plate is a collector's prize with only a few reported to date. All are cobalt blue with a design of the monument that dominates the Circle in downtown Indianapolis. The exterior pattern is a typical Fenton one, Horse Chestnut (or Berry & Leaf Circle or Leaf & Berry Circle, whichever you prefer). The iridization is superb!

Indiana Statehouse

Besides the two versions of the Soldiers and Sailors plates, Fenton also made this very rare plate shown in blue. The size is identical to the other two, and the exterior carries the same exterior design. This was made in marigold also.

Indian Bangles

This very nice water set from India is shared with me by Vikram Bachhawat. The pitcher is 8½" tall and the tumbler stands 4½". The design has mitered ovals, a band of bullets, and the typical Indian diamond links. It is also known as Indian Bracelet Variant.

Indian Bracelet

The Indian Bracelet water set is similar to the Indian Bangles water set except it has two different designs on the top half of each piece. The pattern was given to me by Vikram Bachhawat and hadn't been reported until mid-2001.

Indian Canoe

This small novelty is really very heavy glass for its 6½" length. The color is touched with a bit of amber, but the iridization is quite good. Other measurements are 1½" tall and 2¼" wide. The maker is a mystery.

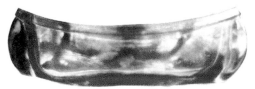

Indian Enameled Blossoms

This 3½" tumbler is from India. It is unusual to find this sort of enamel work on an Indian tumbler. It was furnished by Vikram Bachhawat and I am happy to show it here.

156

Indian Key

The name comes from the band that runs around the tumbler, resembling Greek Key. The color is very good on this example shown. It was furnished by Vikram Bachhawat.

Indian Water Jars

These two water jars are from India and are also called "Kalshi" jars. The example on the left is called Kalshi Flowers and the example on the right is called Kalshi Leaves. These 4" jars were used for water, oil, flowers, foodstuffs, and mostly decoration. Thanks to Vikram Bachhawat and the Ayers family for the photos and the information.

Industria Argentina Star

This pattern, from Cristalerias Papini in Argentina, is found in a bowl, a plate, and the 5½" vase. Only marigold has been reported. The pieces are marked "Industria Argentina." Thanks to Tom and Sharon Mordini for this piece.

Intaglio Daisy (Diamond)

Once believed to be an English pattern, it is now known to be from the Diamond plant. It was shown, along with several of their patterns such as Windflower and Pulled Loop, in one of their ads in a treatment called Afterglow. In carnival glass, Intaglio Daisy is found in marigold and a rare amethyst, shown here. Thanks to W.R. Scholes for sharing this photo.

Intaglio Stars

What a pretty tumbler this is! It stands 4" tall and has twelve ¾" panels around the upper portion and a band of three intaglio stars and sunbursts. The marigold coloring is very rich and has a radium-like finish. It is also known as Inwald's Pinwheel.

157

Intaglio Thistle

I'm not sure if this is from one of the Northwood or Dugan Intaglio lines, but nonetheless it is a very nice pattern. As you can see, it is a full pattern containing a circling group of eight thistles, foliage, and a large button type center. The color is a nice rich marigold. This is the only reported piece to date. Thanks to the Hilkenes for sharing it.

Interior Flute

Here's another of the many Flute patterns so popular in their day. There was probably a matching sugar. I haven't seen any other colors, but they probably exist.

Interior Panels

Here is a familiar treatment, plain on the outside with ribbing, optic, or paneling on the interior. The matching stopper adds a lot to the look. The color is a very rich marigold with purple highlights.

Interior Poinsettia

This Northwood pattern was originally used for opalescent production. At least three pitcher shapes existed. In carnival glass, only the tumbler is found and only in marigold. The pattern is all on the interior and some pieces are trademarked while others are not.

Interior Rays

Besides the covered sugar shown, this U.S. Glass pattern can be found in many shapes including a creamer, covered butter dish, covered jam jar, bowls, and a compote. Colors are often weak marigold. The all-interior design has little going for it except the unusual tongue that rides the top of the handles.

Interior Rib

This very classy 7½" vase is tissue paper thin, and the only design is the inside ribbing that runs the length of the glass. The color is a strong smoke with high lustre, and it is also known in marigold.

Interior Smooth Panel

This tri-cornered spittoon whimsey is the iridized version of a Jefferson Glass pattern found mostly in opalescent glass bowls and plates where it often has a cranberry frit edging. It can be found with a ruffled top or rolled as shown in the example. The 20 ribs are all on the inside, and the base measures 2½". Do not confuse this pattern with Ruffled Rib, which is on the outside.

Interior Swirl and Wide Panel

This squat pitcher is really cute with good color and a lot of character. Other colors and shapes may exist, but I haven't seen them and I don't know who the maker is.

Inverted Coin Dot (Fenton)

What a pleasure it is to show this aqua pitcher from the Pouchers. It is from the Fenton Art Glass Company and is found in marigold and aqua (Mrs. Hartung reported it in amethyst also). In addition, Northwood is credited with a similar tumbler, which has five rows of dots (Fenton's tumbler has six).

Inverted Feather

Inverted Feather is from Cambridge (#2651) and found in crystal as well as carnival glass. Shapes in the latter include a table set, a rare tankard water set, sherbet, wine, covered cracker jar, a milk pitcher, and a beautiful and rare punch set. Marigold is the primary color but green and amethyst items do appear from time to time, as shown with this nice cracker jar supplied by the Remmens.

Inverted Prisms

I've now heard of this pattern in the creamer shown as well as an open sugar and a vase in carnival glass, although it is shown in a Rindskopf catalog in a table set, vases, bowls, biscuit jar, and other shapes not yet reported in iridized glass. The color is a strong marigold.

Inverted Strawberry

Inverted Strawberry is a realistic intaglio Cambridge pattern. Shapes include a berry set, water set, milk pitcher, stemmed celery, sherbet, stemmed creamer and sugar, large and small compotes, powder jar, a rose bowl whimsey, and the beautiful spittoon whimsey shown. Thanks to the Remmens for sharing it.

Inverted Thistle

This pattern was made by Cambridge and can be found in berry sets, a chop plate, pitcher, tumbler, milk pitcher, table set, and the rare 8" compote shown. Colors are marigold, amethyst, and green, but not all shapes are found in all colors. Cambridge called this pattern just "Thistle."

Inwald's Diamond Cut

Many European carnival glass pieces were exported to Australia. This cobalt blue piece matches a 12" marigold piece from Inwald. Although it is similar to an Australian pattern of the same name, Crown Crystal Glass of Australia isn't known to have made blue. The owners of this large oval bowl call it Australian Pineapple because it was found in Australia. Thanks to Joshua Wilson for the photo.

Iris

Along with the plain Buttermilk goblet, this pattern is from Fenton. It is found in both compotes and goblets. Colors seen are marigold, green, amethyst, and a rare white.

Isaac Benesch Bowl

This small bowl pattern has mums and leaves with a lettered ribboning that reads "THE GREAT HOUSE OF ISAAC BENESCH AND SONS, WILKSBARRE, PA., BALTIMORE, MD., ANNAPOLIS, MD." The exterior is wide paneled and there are a few rarities with the Benesch name misspelled. The only color is amethyst, usually with a satin finish.

Isis

This well designed tumbler stands 4¼" tall, has a 3" top diameter, and a 2" base diameter. The color is a strong marigold with even iridescence. The design consists of six convex ribs that extend to two top bands and this is repeated four times around the tumbler. The base is slightly indented. The maker of this design is unknown at this time, but the tumbler appears to be earlier than Depression glass.

Ivy

This was a Cooperative Flint Glass pattern from the 1880s that was later made by Phoenix. The iridized items are found in both the wine and the stemmed claret pieces and have various advertising on them. Marigold appears to be the only color in carnival glass. It is also called Ivy in Snow.

Jack-in-the-Pulpit

Here is Fenton's version of this vase. It's a bit plainer than Northwood's and it isn't nearly as pretty without the footing. It does come in several colors adding a pleasant touch of artistry.

Jack-in-the-Pulpit (Northwood)

Both Dugan and Fenton also made Jack-in-the-Pulpit vases, but the one shown is a Northwood pattern and is so marked. It stands 8¼" tall and has an exterior ribbing. Colors known are marigold, purple, green, aqua opalescent, and white, but others may exist.

Jackman Whiskey

The molds are identical for all three sizes of bottles made by Whithall Tatum Glass Co. of Millville, New Jersey. These were the only three sizes made. The dates of production that are on my bottles are one quart — 1934; one pint — 1936; half pint — 1936. Straight whiskey, 90 proof. From the collection of Clint Arsenault.

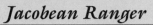

Jacobean Ranger

This Inwald pattern is found in a tumbler, juice glass, shot glass, squat pitcher, creamer, dresser set that includes a powder jar, colognes, perfume, pin tray, atomizer, a large tray, and ring tree. Other shapes are the tumble up set shown. It was later copied by Crystal of Australia as Blocks and Arches and by Cristales Mexicanos as Ranger. This pattern is also called simply Jacobean by some collectors.

Jacob's Ladder Variant (U.S. Glass)

I've heard of this rose bowl shape in the variant and nothing else. Just why more shapes haven't surfaced, I don't know, for the pattern is interesting and well done. The only color is a good marigold.

Jasmine and Butterfly (Engraved)

While the photo of this very scarce pattern came from the McGraths in Australia, this set is from Czechoslovakia and dates from the 1930s. Shown are six tumblers, a matching tray that is 1" deep and 11" wide, and a tumble-up that is 8" tall. Marigold seems to be the only color. The pattern of flower and butterfly is engraved.

Jeannette Colonial

This bowl could have been called Flute or Wide Panel but Colonial was the first terminology used by the glass companies. You will notice the top edging has the same treatment as the Diamond Point Columns bowls from the same company. Marigold seems to be the only color of these bowls.

Jeannette Refrigerator Jar

This is shown in old Jeannette ads in several sizes from this 4½" size to 8½". Similar items were also made by Hazel-Atlas in clear or colored glass but I believe the iridized version is Jeannette's. While it doesn't have much going for it in design or as a collectible, the iridization is quite well done.

Jelly Jar

This falls more into Depression era glass than carnival era glass. Nevertheless, it has some appeal and the complete piece is a nice novelty. The jelly jar stands 2¾" tall and is 3" wide. The pattern is all on the inside, making a jelly mould effect when turned upside down and emptied. Marigold is the only color reported and can be outstanding or just adequate.

Jenkins Lattice

In the late 1920s, the D.C. Jenkins Company iridized some of their earlier crystal lines. One of these was their #336 line called Lattice. I believe the piece shown (a spooner) was from this line. Crystal shapes in Lattice included a water set, table set, berry set, handled nappy, pickle dish, open or covered jelly compotes, and a covered casserole, so other pieces may well show up in carnival.

Jester's Cap (Westmoreland)

Shaped from the Corinth vase from Westmoreland (their #252 pattern made around 1910), this popular vase has been flared at the top with the back pulled up and the front pulled down. Other companies made similar vase shapes but this one is the best known. Colors include marigold, amethyst, teal, white, and peach opalescent. The Westmoreland version always has 12 ribs.

Jeweled Butterflies

This is the first iridized piece I've heard about in this pattern. It was made by the Indiana Glass Co. of Dunkirk, Indiana. This square bowl has eight butterflies on the outer edge with an unusual star of some sort in the center (reminds me of a Ninja weapon you'd see in the movies). It is a pattern that would certainly add to any collection. Thanks to the Hilkenes for sharing it.

First called Victor in 1905 in opalescent glass, Jeweled Heart began its carnival life about 1910. Shapes include a water set, ruffled berry set, medium sized plate, and a small whimsey basket. Colors for the water set are marigold (tumblers also in white), and for the berry set marigold, amethyst, peach opalescent, and white. The plate is known in amethyst and peach opalescent with marigold, and the basket in peach opalescent only.

Jeweled Peacock Tail

This scarce black amethyst vase is now credited to Piccardo of Argentina (according to David and Amy Ayers). It is 7½" tall and seems to have a fine multicolored iridescence. Only three or four are reported at this time.

Jewels (Diamond)

Diamond Glass made a line of products that had a satin finish and this patented candle bowl is one of them. It is similar to their Royal Lustre line. Colors are blue, green, white, and pink (After Glow). Some had a stretch finish, but many did not. Thanks again to Samantha Prince for the nice photo.

Jewels and Drapery

This pattern is normally found only on opalescent glass or in crystal in vases and whimsied bowls from the vase mould. But shown here is a large 16" vase in emerald green glass with a soft radium iridescence. Northwood made this pattern in 1907 in crystal and the following year in opalescent glass, so this piece was obviously made sometime later.

Jockey Club

Apparently Jockey Club was a scent and this piece from Northwood was produced to advertise it. It can be found in bowls, a 6¼" plate, and a handgrip plate. The design shows a horseshoe, a riding crop, and a floral spray. The exterior shows Northwood's Basketweave pattern. Colors are primarily amethyst and a very scarce pale lavender. Thanks to the Remmens for sharing it.

Josef's Plumes

This vase, one of two reported in this pattern so far, belongs to Ken and Pauline Birkett. They say it is from Inwald and only marigold is known in iridized glass so far (crystal was made I'm sure). It is 6" tall and has amazing color.

J.R. Millner Co., Lynchburg, VA

This hard to find tumbler has advertising on the base and is a beautiful honey amber. The lettering says "J.R. Millner Co., Lynchburg, Va." The tumbler pattern is, of course, Cosmos and Cane by U.S. Glass and can be found in white without the advertising as well as marigold. All are fairly scarce, but the advertising example is considered very scarce indeed, except here in Lynchburg where they are a bit easier to locate.

Kaleidoscope

When I first found this bowl I looked for a long while before I located it in a 1915 Butler Brothers ad. The ad didn't give any indication as to maker or a factory name, so I named it. It is a collar-based bowl with a sunburst on the marie. The exterior design seems to be top and bottom sections of paneling, with a centered section of strange geometric figures, almost like calligraphy. Some of these figures are filled with file and some are plain. Marigold is the only color reported at this time. I welcome information from anyone about this pattern. It is also found in crystal bowls and rose bowls.

Kangaroo

This Australian pattern, patented in 1924, is found on large and small bowls in two designs (one is a doe or small kangaroo and the other is a buck or large kangaroo). Both sizes are found in marigold and purple. Shown is a 10" purple bowl featuring the buck kangaroo. Thanks to the McGraths for sharing this information about the difference.

Karen

This is a very well done pattern consisting of an intermittent sawtooth edge, a series of fanned out diamonds and stars circling each piece, and arched filed designs around the base. It is found in berry sets in a rich marigold. I have yet to locate the maker but Argentina can't be ruled out as a possibility. The name and photo came from the owners. Thanks to Karen and Allan Rath for sharing this lovely pattern.

Karve

This 8" vase has an intaglio design of stylized flowers. The color is a soft lilac that has a pink cast. The maker is unknown to me at this time. Thanks to the Ayers Auction Service for sharing this piece.

Kathleen's Flowers

This is another tall tumbler from India. It has a unique flower, stem, and leaves as well as two rings just below the top rim. The color is strong and dark, especially below the rings. It is also known as Fantasy Flowers.

Kedvesh Vase

I have very little knowledge about this vase except to say it is from India, and the name used was given by the owner. The top has the usual milky look associated with Indian glass and the design is more pronounced than on other products from this country, with flowers, beaded peaks, and stretches of leaves.

Keyhole (Dugan)

Keyhole is found alone on opalescent glass, primarily as an exterior pattern on Raindrop bowls, and rarely on carnival bowls without an interior pattern. The colors are marigold, peach opalescent, and amethyst. Thanks to Gerald Welsh for sharing this find.

Keystone Colonial (Westmoreland)

At least three of these compotes have been reported, all with the Keystone trademark containing a "W." They stand 6¼" tall and are very much like the Chippendale pattern compotes credited to Jefferson Glass. The only colors I've seen are marigold and purple.

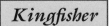

Kingfisher

These bowls from Crystal Glass are found in 9" – 10" sizes as well as 5" sauce sizes. Colors are marigold and purple. The pattern was first made in 1923 (according to a patent application) and is closely related to the Kookaburra pattern.

Kingfisher Variant

This variant is similar to the regular Kingfisher, but has an added wreath of wattle (a bell-like berry on a stem). It too is found in large or small bowls in marigold or black amethyst (a dark purple glass). The area round the bird is stippled and there is a registration number on the right.

King's Crown (U.S. Glass)

This pattern can be found in many shapes in crystal and ruby flashed glass, as well as the carnival example shown. It is a dainty wine goblet in good marigold and is fairly tough to find.

Kitten Paperweight

This slight bit of glass is a rare miniature. Its color, as you can see, is a good even marigold, and the iridization is well applied. In size, it is much like the 3" long Bulldog paperweight.

Kittens

Listed as their #299, Fenton's Kittens pattern was a children's toy glass pattern that has achieved great popularity with collectors. In carnival glass, pieces can be found in marigold, cobalt blue, amethyst, lavender, teal (3½" bowl only), aqua (saucer), and topaz or vaseline (vase shape only). Shapes are cups, saucers, plates, vase, and two sizes of bowls. Bowls may be shaped like banana boats, ruffled, squared, or deep like a cereal bowl. Kittens first appears in Fenton ads in 1918.

Kiwi (Crystal)

Kiwi is one of the rarer Australian glass patterns from Crystal. It was patented in 1926. It is found in a 9" master bowl and the 5" sauce, in marigold and purple. The Kiwi is a native of New Zealand. The bowl shows an adult and chicks with a mountain range in the distance. The exterior has a pattern called Fern and Wattle.

Knights Templar

Knights Templar is found on certain Dandelion mugs. This base pattern is lettered: "PITTSBURGH – MAY 27, 28, 29, 1912." It also has the Knights Templar seal in the center, which reads "ALLEGHANY COMPANY" with a shield that is numbered: "35." Knights Templar mugs were made by the Northwood Company for a special purpose and are known in ice green (shown), ice blue, and marigold (the most common color). All are very collectible.

Knotted Beads (Fenton)

Knotted Beads was made by the Fenton Company (their #509 pattern) in 1915. This vase pattern seems to be a take-off of a couple of other Fenton designs including Long Thumbprint or Diamond Rib that use a series of ovals. Here we have four rows of six ovals filled with connected beading. Colors include marigold, cobalt blue, amber, aqua, vaseline, and red (rare). Sizes range from 7" to 12" in most examples.

166

Kokomo

Most collectors call this pattern Kokomo, although it is also known as Geometric. It can be found on rose bowls or ruffled bowls, all from the same mould, and standing on three squared feet. Marigold seems to be the only color reported and some of the rose bowls have been found with flower frogs in them. Thanks to Samantha Prince for the photo of this nice rose bowl, complete with flower frog.

Kookaburra (Crystal)

Kookaburra was made by Crystal of Australia in 1924. This very nice design is found with an upper edging of flannel flower and wattle and two large groups of waratah flowers. It can be found on large or small bowls in either marigold or purple with an exterior of Fern and Wattle (Wild Fern). The Kookaburra is very well done, sitting on branch, looking to the left.

Kookaburra Float Bowl

In this Australian variant the obvious differences are the fine large waratah flowers around the stippled circle, and, of course, the edging is a bullet rim pattern. It is found in marigold and amethyst, and quite high priced in either color.

Krys-Tol Colonial

This two-piece mayonnaise set (mayonnaise bowl with underplate) was a product of the Jefferson Glass Company. It is marked "Krys-Tol." The color is a soft marigold with a radium finish. Since some items (Millersburg Flute compote) are known to bear this mark and were made at the Millersburg plant after Jefferson bought it, I wonder if this rare item came from there too.

Kulor Vase

This beautiful vase is Eda Glass Works' #2471-73. It is found in 6", 8", and 12" sizes in carnival glass. Colors are marigold, blue, iridized milk glass, and rarely amethyst. The iridescence is very mirror-like on most pieces.

Labelle Rose

Labelle Rose, like the Carnation Wreath pattern shown elsewhere, is more often seen in a goofus glass treatment. It is found in goofus glass in small and large bowls and plates but here is the first piece (5" bowl) reported in carnival glass. The design is all exterior with a large rose on the marie and stems of roses extending up the sides of the bowl.

Laco

This 9¼" tall bottle says "LACO OLIVE OIL." The iridescence is a pale marigold with a yellowish tinge. The owner believes this bottle was from the same maker as the Monkey bottle and Etched Leaves bottle. All have the same coloring and the same opening size and shape. I suspect these may be from South America or Mexico but have no proof at this time.

Lacy Daisy

This vase has two large flowers on either side separated by panels of lovely Spanish Corelli Lace. It is 10" tall. This vase came from Brazil and somewhat resembles the Fircones vase with its scalloped top and deep rich marigold finish. Thanks again to Karen and Allan Rath for sharing the photo, name, and information.

Lacy Dewdrop

This pattern, still a bit of a mystery, was made in crystal as well as milk glass by Co-operative Flint Glass in 1890. But just who made the iridized pieces is not certain. Some collectors credit Phoenix Glass in the 1930s while some believe it may have been Westmoreland. Shapes known in carnival are the covered compote (shown), water sets, covered bowls, a table set, and the goblet shape. All are found on iridized milk glass.

Ladders

Marked with the Iron Cross, this is certainly an Imperial pattern but apparently it hasn't been shown before in any reference. It is a standard 8½" bowl in fine marigold. Thanks to Lance and Pat Hilkene for another first.

Lady's Slipper

Here's another ornamental and appeling novel miniature from U.S. Glass. Very few of these were ever iridized, so all are rare. The Lady's Slipper is 4½" long and 2¾" high and is a good marigold. The entire piece is covered with stippling.

Lake Shore Honey Pot

This neat little honey pot or bottle came as a surprise. It is labeled "Lake Shore Honey" around the top and has honeycombing over most of the surface. Thanks to Don and Barb Chamberlain for sharing this novelty.

Lancaster Compote

This compote was from the Lancaster Glass Company of Lancaster, Ohi o. They called it their White Lustre finish (a clear glass that was enameled white and then iridized and sometimes decorated). The look is sometimes a cream rather than white and most items show some stretch finish. The short stemmed compote shown has a heavy iridescence and a "stepped" interior wide paneling. Production was in the early 1920s.

Late Covered Swan

If you compare this swan, reported only in blue, to the regular Covered Swan, you will see they are not the same. Both are from Sowerby, but many collectors suspect this one came along a few years later. Please note the base is the same as that on the Covered Hen, also from Sowerby. Late Covered Swan has solid glass between the head, neck, and body. Thanks to Alan Sedgwick for this piece.

Late Enameled Bleeding Hearts

Many call this tall tumbler a vase. It has a light airy iridization and delicate white and colored enameled flowers. Like most items with this finish, the Enameled Bleeding Hearts tumbler came along fairly late. It was made in Bavaria.

Late Enameled Grape

This cute goblet has a light airy lustre, but the bold white enameling of leaves and grapes are the real attraction. The goblet, made near the end of carnival glass popularity, stands only 4½" tall and I have seen a very similar tall tumbler called Late Strawberry in the Whitley book. It was made in Bavaria.

Late Enameled Strawberry

Very similar to the Late Strawberry pattern shown in the Whitley book, this lemonade glass has only one roll of glass above the bulging base while the Whitley example has three rolls. The color is light, and the enamel work is all white. It was made in Bavaria.

Late Feather

I know very little about this attractive enameled tumbler. It is from the vast collection of Jim and Peg Perry and I thank them for all the tumblers they shared with me. I'd certainly like to hear any information about this tumbler. It is from Jeannette.

Late Water Lily

For one of the later patterns in carnival glass, this certainly is a good one. The coloring is superior, the shape symmetrical, and the design of cattails and water lilies attractive.

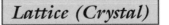

Lattice (Crystal)

Found in several shapes and sizes (all from the same mould), this Australian pattern from Crystal can be found in either purple or marigold. The Lattice pattern is found with Style as its exterior design, and looks much like a Northwood crystal pattern called Cherry and Lattice. The coloring, especially on the purple pieces, is outstanding with a rich rainbow iridescence.

Lattice and Daisy

Dugan's Lattice and Daisy is most often seen on marigold water sets, best was also made on very scarce berry sets. The other colors known are amethyst (rare), cobalt blue, and white (very scarce), but I certainly would not rule out green, especially on the water sets.

Lattice and Grape (Fenton)

Lattice and Grape was originally Fenton's #1563 pattern first made around 1912. This water set design is a good one. (The spittoon whimsey is made from a tumbler.) Colors include marigold, cobalt blue, amethyst, green, white, and peach opalescent according to Fenton records.

Lattice and Leaves

Once thought to be Sowerby, Lattice and Leaves is actually shown in a 1931 Brockwitz catalog as their #1063. This 9½" pedestal-based vase is found in both marigold and blue carnival glass. Only the years ahead will hopefully put all non-American carnival glass in clear perspective.

Lattice and Points

Lattice and Points is distinctive for its latticework as well as the flame design above the base and the cable separating the two. This Dugan pattern is known in marigold, amethyst, and white. Pressed into the bottom is the daisy design often found on the Vining Twigs bowl.

Lattice Heart

Lattice Heart was most recently credited to the Dugan Glass Company by collectors. This pattern is seldom seen and little discussed. It can be found on a deep round bowl as well as flattened out into a near-plate with turned up edges. The iridescence can be on both the exterior and interior, or on the interior only. The glass color is a very dark amethyst. The design is a good one but could have been improved by the addition of an interior pattern. Strangely, many of the Lattice Heart pieces are found in England and Europe.

Laurel and Grape

This very nice stemmed vase is a real mystery. Three are reported, two in peach opalescent glass and one in marigold. The example shown is 7" tall but one sold that was only 5". The design has laurel wreaths filled with a cluster of grapes on opposite sides of the piece. On the balled stem is a rambling vine of leaves and flowers.

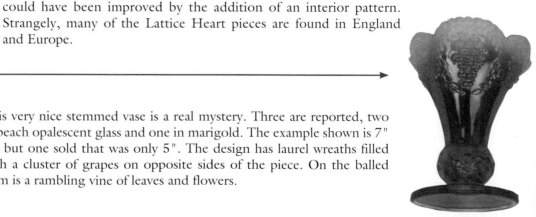

Laurel Band

While the dome-base tumblers are seen frequently in this late pattern, the pitcher shown is a find and seldom makes its way out of collections. The pitcher measures 8" tall and has a 4" dome base while the tumbler stands 4⅞" tall. The only color reported is a strong marigold. It was originally called Austin.

Laurel Leaves

Mrs. Hartung showed this pattern in a round plate, and here is an eight-sided one. The pattern is on the exterior, and while the design will never win any awards, the color is rich and the iridization is good. It is well known in marigold, green, and amethyst.

LBJ Hat

This late carnival ashtray has been called this for the last few years. It has a diameter of 6¼" and stands 3" tall. While not in the class of a Cleveland Memorial ashtray, it is an attractive specimen of iridized glass.

Lea (Sowerby)

This English pattern was made by the Sowerby Company. Most pieces sit on three knobby feet but the pickle dish, which some consider a variant, sits on a flat collar base. Panels filled with ribs border the top and bottom of the piece and the center, divided into panels, is heavily stippled. Colors are marigold and purple and the shapes available are creamers, open sugars, and bowls. There is also a variant, made by the same company shown elsewhere in this edition.

Leaf and Beads

This well-known Northwood pattern was made in opalescent glass around 1906 and then in carnival glass three years later. It has three feet that resemble tree branches. There are several shape variations and some top changes too (most tops are scalloped but some are smooth or even beaded). Shapes include a rose bowl, nut bowl, and a bowl shape. A large number colors can be found.

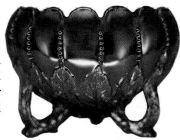

Leaf and Beads Variant

Here is the variant bowl on a dome base, and as you can see, the design is not so strong as the regular Leaf and Beads. These seem to be found mostly in green, as shown, but marigold and amethyst are known. It is marked Northwood. Many collectors consider the shape a nut bowl.

Leaf and Chrysanthemum

Very little is known about this exterior bowl pattern except that it is found on dome-based bowls like the one shown and it may be from Crystal Glass in Australia. I can't confirm this and certainly would appreciate any information readers may offer.

Leaf and Little Flowers

Usually found in one or two shapes (ruffled or round and flared), this mini-compote from Millersburg is a collector's delight. The design has four free-floating blooms, four larger prickly edged leaves, and a center four-petaled blossom. The exterior has wide panels and an octagon-shaped base. Colors are marigold, amethyst, and green, usually with a strong radium finish.

171

Leaf Chain

This pattern is similar to Cherry Chain, but easier to find (both are from Fenton). It is found on 7" or 9" plates and ice cream shaped or ruffled bowls. Colors include marigold, amethyst, green, blue, aqua, clambroth, red, white, vaseline, or lavender. A bowl is occasionally found in ice green and the rare plate shown is emerald green.

Leaf Column

This well-known Northwood vase pattern is a popular one. It was advertised in 1912. Colors include marigold, amethyst, green, white, ice blue, ice green, aqua, teal, and the fantastic cobalt blue example shown. Most of these vases range in size from 9" to 12", but squat examples are known as small as 5" and some are as tall as 13".

Leaf Garden

This Imperial shade has to be one of the best I've seen. The iridescence is outstanding and really stands out on the smoke base glass. If you are a shade collector, this is a must have item. Thanks to Kris and Debra Remmen of Remmen Auction for sharing the name and the great photo.

Leaf Rays

Never a very exciting pattern, this Dugan-Diamond design is limited to one-handled nappies, sometimes spade shaped, sometimes ruffled and fanned out like the pretty amethyst one shown. Colors are marigold, peach opalescent, clear, white, amethyst, and a rare blue. Iridescence is often only so-so but occasionally a superb piece is spotted and it is worth buying.

Leaf Rosette and Beads (Flower and Beads)

Long known in opalescent glass, this Dugan-Diamond pattern was called Leaf Rosette and Beads by Rose Presznick and Flower and Beads by Marion Hartung. The original moulds were a pattern called Blocked Thumbprint and Beads that was combined with an interior called Honeycomb. The floral and leaf sprays were then added to form this pattern. Mostly plates are found in carnival glass with the interior plain. Colors are marigold, peach opalescent, or purple. Thanks to Samantha Prince for the photo.

Leaf Swirl (Westmoreland)

Leaf Swirl is a most attractive pattern shown in old Westmoreland ads, along with other patterns including Pearly Dots and Carolina Dogwood. It can be found in marigold, dark purple, amethyst, lavender, teal, amber, and a scarce marigold over yellow glass. The iridization is on the plain interior of most pieces and on both interior and exterior on a few pieces. This compote is about 5" tall and may be flared and ruffled, or goblet shaped.

Leaf Swirl and Flower

What a beautifully graceful vase this is. It appears to be a Fenton product, stands 8" tall, and has a trail of etched leaves and flowers around the body. I'd guess it was made in marigold and pastels, but can't be sure.

Fenton's Leaf Tiers can be found in berry sets, table sets, water set, a light shade, and a plate. Colors are green, marigold, cobalt blue, and amethyst, but the shade is found in marigold-over-milk-glass. Thanks to Alan Sedgwick for sharing the nice master bowl in blue.

Leafy Triangle

Shown is a 7" bowl that stands 2" tall and has an exterior pattern of flutes that is called Fluted Pillar. Most collectors call this pattern Leafy Triangle but it certainly may have a different name. I strongly suspect this to be European in origin and would welcome any positive proof of the maker from readers. The color is a very rich pumpkin marigold but cobalt blue was probably made as well.

Lea Variant (Sowerby)

Just why Sowerby made this variant of the regular Lea creamer is a mystery but it has several changes from the original. First is the addition of the herringbone sections in each panel. Then the beading along the top has been omitted, and the pouring spout has been left flat on top. Probably the footed sugar has been made to match but I haven't seen it.

Liberty Bell

This Bartlett and Collins cookie jar, while certainly late carnival glass, is well done and a few like the one shown actually have decent iridescence. The lettering (in part) says "Pass and Stow." Coloring is a soft pastel marigold but some I've seen have an almost amberish tint.

Lightning Flower (Northwood)

Since this nappy was first shown, two or three more have surfaced, as have two small bowls in marigold, and the prices have decreased somewhat. The Lightning Flower pattern is the exterior one and inside each piece is a design of Poppies. The color is good but not outstanding on the pieces I've seen, but certainly finding any color other than marigold would drive interest up with this pattern.

Lightolier Lustre and Clear Shade

This very collectible shade is 5½" tall and measures 5" across. The panels are on the interior and the outside is smooth. It was a product of Lightolier Company and has, as you can see, very strong iridization.

Lily of the Valley

Lily of the Valley is undoubtedly one of Fenton's best water pitcher designs. It was made around 1912. Strangely, the tumblers are found in both marigold and cobalt blue while the tankard pitcher is reported only in the latter. And because of its rarity, this pattern always demands a high price. I am told one marigold pitcher once existed but was lost in an earthquake.

Lily Vase

This vase is as scarce as, and very similar to, the Gum Tips vase. It is found in sizes that range from 9" to 13" tall with a base diameter of 4½". Both purple and a rare marigold are known.

Lindal

This neat little vase, standing about 4" – 5" tall, has everything from diamonds to fans to plumes in the design and would certainly add to any collection. I have yet to find the maker, although many similar shapes are shown in various materials from Europe, which were generously supplied to me by Seigmar Geiselberger. I'd like to thank Mike Cain for the name and the photo of this interesting little jewel.

Lined Lattice

This Dugan and then Diamond pattern is called Palisades in opalescent glass. Vases range from 5" to 15" tall. Colors are marigold, amethyst, peach opalescent, white, horehound, and cobalt blue. Thanks to Peter Baerwald for the photo.

Lined Lattice Variant

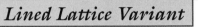

If you will compare the feet of this vase and those of the regular Lined Lattice you will see the variant's are squared and extend out from the vase itself while the other has pointed feet that are joined together. Both examples were made by the Dugan-Diamond Company and one wonders what the variance did to improve the design.

Linn's Mums (Dancing Daisies)

Linn's Mums is named for Linn Lewis and is also called Dancing Daisies by some. This very rare bowl is from Northwood and has the Ruffles and Rings exterior with scrolled feet. The only color reported on the few known bowls is amethyst but there could certainly be other colors I haven't learned about at this time. The design shows nine open flowers with small runners of blossoms and leaves.

Lion

Someone at the Fenton factory had to be an animal lover for more animal patterns were born there than at any other carnival glass factory in America. The Lion pattern is a nice one, rather scarce, and available in bowls and plates. The colors are marigold and blue in the bowls, but rare marigold plates are known.

Little Barrel

Most collectors believe these little containers were made by Imperial as a special order item, probably for someone with a liquid product to sell. They are about 4" tall and can be found in marigold, amber, green, and smoke.

Little Beads (Westmoreland)

With a minimum of pattern and size, this nice stemmed piece still manages to make a statement, especially in color. It measures 2" tall, has a 2½" base, and measures 5½" across. Colors are mostly peach opalescent but aqua, blue opalescent, marigold, and amethyst are known. Little Beads was made by Westmoreland.

Little Daisies

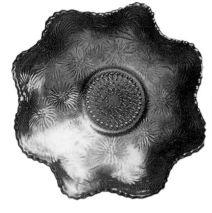

This rare collar-based bowl from Fenton is known in marigold and cobalt blue. The bowls measure 9" – 10", with the daisies bursting like fireworks from a stylized center of beading.

Little Fishes

Production of Fenton's #1607 began in 1914 and continued for several years. Little Fishes can be found in 5½" bowls, 10" footed bowls, and 11" plates. Colors include marigold, green, cobalt blue, aqua, amethyst, vaseline, amber, ice green, and a rare white, but not all sizes or moulds are found in all colors. The pattern closely resembles Fenton's Coral. Photo courtesy of Samantha Prince.

Little Flowers

Here's another pattern once felt to be Millersburg but is now known to be a Fenton product. Little Flowers is found in berry sets and two sizes of rare plates in marigold, green, blue, amethyst, amber, aqua, vaseline, and red. Bowls include square, tri-cornered, or ice cream shapes.

Little Stars (Millersburg)

This Millersburg bowl pattern can be found in 7", 8", 9", and 10" bowls as well as rare 6" sauces. Colors are marigold, amethyst, green, blue, clambroth, and a very rare vaseline.

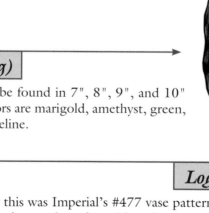

Loganberry (Imperial)

From old company catalogs I know this was Imperial's #477 vase pattern. It stands 10" tall and can be found in marigold, purple, green, amber, and smoke, with teal reported. There are a few with the top whimsied (flared or ball shaped) but these are rare. In addition this vase was reproduced in the 1960s and 1970s in several colors including marigold, smoke, green, and white but they are marked with the IG logo. Photo courtesy of the Remmens.

Log Cabin Syrup

Log Cabin syrup is found in all sorts of containers including metal, glass, and plastic, but this is the first iridized glass container I've heard about. The example pictured has a hole cut in the metal lid for coins. The color is a strong marigold.

Long Buttress

Long Buttress was made in many shapes in crystal and is often mistaken for a similar pattern called Portland. It can be found in iridized glass in tumblers, a water pitcher, and large and small berry bowls. Iridization may range from a good marigold to a frosty clambroth. Long Buttress is a Fostoria pattern and dates from 1904.

Long Hobstar

Imperial was famous for near-cut designs, and Long Hobstar is a prime example of their skills. Shown in a very rare punch bowl and base (no cups known), Long Hobstar can also be found in bowls and a beautiful bride's basket. The colors are marigold, smoke, green, and occasionally purple.

Long Thumbprint (Fenton)

Most knowledgeable collectors now feel this vase pattern is from the Fenton factory but there is a 9" bowl, a compote, a creamer, sugar, and covered butter that probably were made by someone else and these shapes are currently credited to the Dugan-Diamond Company. Vases can be found with plain or patterned maries so this adds to the mystery. Sizes range from 7" to 12" and vase colors are green, amethyst, marigold, peach opalescent, and a reported blue.

Long Thumbprint Hobnail (Fenton)

This is usually considered a variation of Fenton's Knotted Beads vase pattern. It seems to be the Long Thumbprint pattern retooled to hold seven hobnails in each of the ovals, while Knotted Beads has the ovals filled with a series of connected beads. A small difference, but with today's collector, all differences seem important. Colors for the Long Thumbprint Hobnail vase are marigold, amethyst, blue, and green.

Lotus and Grape

Lotus and Grape is from Fenton and is similar to their Water Lily pattern. It is found on bonbons, 7" – 9" flat bowls, 5" and 9" footed bowls, and a 9½" plate (shown). Colors include marigold, green, amethyst, blue, aqua, vaseline, red, red slag, teal (most of the unusual colors are found on the bonbon shape).

Lotus and Grape Variant

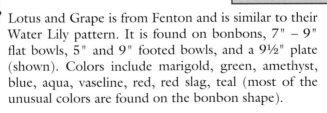

Look at the pattern in its usual form and you will see the lace-like border that edges the lotus sections is not found on the other pieces. This lace-edged variant can be found on small footed bowls, bonbons, and a rare rose bowl in marigold and blue. Just why the Fenton Company would give us two mould variations remains a mystery.

Lotus Bud

Lotus Bud is typical in shape and design of other Indian vases. It has a very nice detailed leaf design with floral sprays above them. The vase is 6" tall and has good marigold color.

Lotus Land

What a privilege to show this very rare bonbon, generous in size (8¼" across) and rich in design. From its stippled center flower to the whimsical outer flowers, the pattern is one you won't soon forget. Amethyst but marigold are known, but very few in either color.

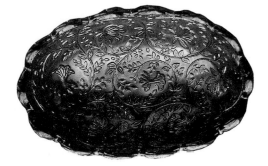

Louisa

This familiar pattern from Westmoreland is found on bowls with three curled feet in various shapes including a deep bowl, ice cream bowl, a nut bowl, and the banana bowl shown. Colors are marigold, amethyst, blue, green, horehound, vaseline, teal, and a rare peach opalescent (shown in the eighth edition). The pattern was later reproduced in the 1950s by Jeannette in pale Depression shades.

Lovely

Found as the interior pattern on some Leaf and Beads pieces, this well-planned design has been credited to the Northwood Company, but shards are reported to have been unearthed at the Dugan factory site. Colors are marigold, amethyst, and green. Because of its scarcity, pieces with this interior always demand a high interest.

Loving Cup

Standing 5¾" tall and measuring 6¼" across the handles, this outstanding piece of glass is known as Fenton's Loving Cup despite carrying the well-known Orange Tree pattern. The interior has a Peacock Tail pattern and there is a scale band above the orange trees as well as scaling on the base. Colors include marigold, amethyst, green, blue, peach opalescent, aqua opalescent, and white. Photo courtesy of Remmen Auction.

Lucile

Originally this was a crystal Indiana Glass pattern called Prosperity. It is also called Ferris Wheel. The carnival water pitchers and tumblers are made by Brockwitz. Pitchers are made in blue and tumblers in blue and marigold. There must have been a marigold pitcher made.

Lucky Bell

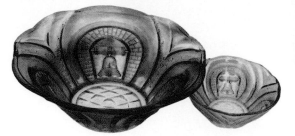

This berry set pattern, which is also known as Bell and Arches, is seldom found or discussed. The large bowls are about 8½" in diameter, the small ones about 4½". The maker isn't known, and marigold is the only reported color.

Lules Argentina

This plate was sold on the internet. It is shown in a Cristalerias Piccardo catalog from Argentina where it was advertised in other shapes as well. It measures 7⅞" across and has a rich marigold iridescence. It is now in West Virginia.

Lustre and Clear

Shown is the handled creamer in this pattern, and I've seen the matching sugar also. Other shapes reported are a berry set, covered butter dish, a water set, and table shakers. Found mostly in marigold, the creamer and sugar are known in purple. The pattern is all interior and the outside plain.

Lustre Flute

Again we have a very familiar pattern to most collectors, but one that is not really too distinguished. I suppose not every pattern should be expected to be spectacular. I've most often seen the hat shape in both green and marigold, but punch sets, berry sets, breakfast sets, bonbons, nappies, and compotes do exist in marigold, green, and purple. The base is many rayed and usually the Northwood trademark is present.

Lustre Match Safe

These match safes or cigarette holders, from Fenton in the 1920s, were made in several colors including marigold, topaz, Florentine green, and Velva Rose (pink). Some have a stretch appearance but the one here is strictly carnival.

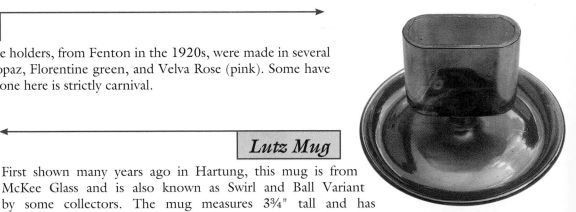

Lutz Mug

First shown many years ago in Hartung, this mug is from McKee Glass and is also known as Swirl and Ball Variant by some collectors. The mug measures 3¾" tall and has a base diameter of 2⅛". The color is a pale marigold that has an amber tint.

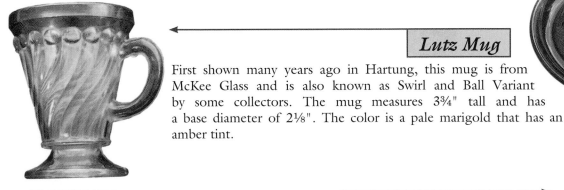

Lustre Rose

Imperial's #489 pattern can be found in a berry set, water set, table set, fernery, fruit bowl, centerpiece bowl, whimsey plate, whimsey vase, novelty bowl, and footed ice cream bowl. Colors are marigold, amber, purple, green, blue, olive green, aqua, clambroth, smoke, white, light blue, lavender, teal, and the rare vaseline shown. Thanks to Wayne Anderson for sharing it.

Maday and Co.

This quite rare advertising bowl is found as the exterior of Fenton's 8½" Wild Blackberry bowl. The only colors known to date are amethyst and green, while the normal bowls are primarily found in green and marigold. The advertising reads "H. Maday and Co. 1910."

Madhu

This Indian tumbler is from Vikram Bachhawat and I believe he named it. It is 4½" tall and has two distinct designs consisting of diamonds and starflowers.

Madonna

Madonna is still another very interesting pattern from India. This one is found on pitchers and tumblers. The design is one of scrolls and leaves with beads that band the pattern above and below.

Mae's Daisies

Mae's Daisies is similar to other Indian tumblers in that it has the spikes rising from the base. This one also has a nice floral spray with two rings below the rim. It stands 5½" tall and is a very dark marigold. It is also known as Grapevine and Flower. Thanks to the Ayers family for the photo.

Mae West (Dugan)

This Dugan-Diamond stretch design is trimmed with a white enamel stripe at top and bottom, giving it the strange name. Mae West was advertised in 1924 in iridescent blue (shown), marigold, white, green, and amethyst. Most sets consisted of two candlesticks and a bowl of various shapes but squat vases and a salver shape are known.

Magnolia Drape

Enameled water sets have a strong following today and this is one of the nicest ones. The pitcher shape is the same as Fenton's #820 but there is a pattern of drapery on the interior. The enameling is a large magnolia with large leaves and foliage. Marigold seems to be the only color in this set but a green one or one in cobalt blue would be a sight to see.

Magnolia Rib

Showing the same enameled flower and leaf design as that of the Magnolia Drape water set (Fenton's #820 pattern), this pattern has interior ribbing that replaces the water set's draping. The top rim is like many Fenton pieces and is a giveaway as to the maker. All pieces in Magnolia Rib are considered scarce. Marigold is the only reported color. Berry sets are also known.

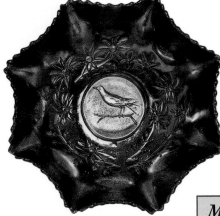

Magpie (Australian)

Magpie had a registration number of 40363 (in 1924) and is found in both large and small bowls in marigold or black amethyst. The bird is probably a New Zealand parson bird rather than a magpie and the wreath around is made of flannel flowers and Wild Fern (Fern and Wattle). The edges of the Magpie pieces may be smooth or serrated.

Maharajah (Jain)

Maharajah is another pattern from India that was found in Australia. Four or five of these shot glasses have been reported. The design is a simple one, two bands of crosshatching at the bottom and below the top, with a large plain center area and the usual plain wide band at the top. Marigold is the only color reported so far but certainly blue is possible.

Maize

This famous Libby Glass pattern can be found in several types of glass including custard. The example shown is clear with pastel blue staining on the husks and a soft iridescence over the rest of the piece. Shapes in the carnival treatment are rare and include the cruet or syrup shown, a celery vase, and a 9" pitcher. All have the blue husks. A rare tumbler also turns up with this treatment.

Majestic

This is a well-designed, very rare tumbler made by the McKee Glass Company. It is 3⅞" tall and has a 24-point star on the base. The design features double fans that enclose a four-section block. Majestic items can also be found in crystal and ruby stained glass.

Malaga

Production must have been late on this Diamond Glass pattern. It is found only in a 9" marigold or amethyst bowl, a rare marigold or amethyst rose bowl, or a 10" marigold chop plate. Its possible that this pattern was a companion to Diamond's Vintage Banded pieces since the grapes and leaves are so similar and the date of production about the same, but I have no proof.

This flower spill vase was from Molineaux, Webb Glass Works of Manchester, England, in 1926. (The company closed in 1927.) It stands 4½" tall and has a series of five ribs that span it in an octagonal ring. The flower frog top is missing. The color is a dark amber with good iridescence. It is considered scarce.

Manhattan

Manhattan was credited to U.S. Glass, although some shapes are shown in a Rindskopf catalog. The iridized pieces known are a decanter, wine glass, and the stemmed vase shown.

Many Diamonds

This may turn out to be a part of the Diamond Stud pattern (from India, I'm told), but until I have more information I'll keep this name. The tumbler in this particular set has a flat, rayed base, and the Diamond Stud tumbler has a recessed base. Even if this turns out to be a variant, it will still have to be determined whether they are from India or Argentina, and I'm told that this set originated in Buenos Aires, Argentina. Photo courtesy of Karen and Allan Rath.

Many Fruits

Many Fruits was made by Dugan about 1911. This very realistic fruit design is found only on punch sets. The base may be round or ruffled with the latter often mistaken for a compote. Colors include marigold, amethyst, cobalt blue, white, and fiery amethyst.

Many Ribs is well known in opalescent glass as a product of the Model Flint Glass Company. But it appears that Northwood had a try at this pattern also, for here is an extremely rare example in aqua opalescent glass. It is the first carnival glass piece reported and really causes more questions than it answers. True, other patterns seem to have been made by both companies in opalescent glass, including Shell and Wreath, but one has to ask why such open theft? At any rate, the Many Ribs vase is a first class rarity in iridized glass, and I thank the Hamlets for sharing it.

Many Stars

Which came first the chicken or the egg? Or in this case, Many Stars or the Bernheimer bowl? For they are the same except for the center design where in the former a large star replaces the advertising. These bowls are generous in size and can be found in amethyst, green, marigold, and blue. The green is often a light, airy shade just a bit darker than an ice green and is very attractive when found with a gold iridescence. Millersburg manufactured this pattern.

181

Many Stars Variant

This is just like the other Many Stars bowl from Millersburg except it has a large six-pointed star in the center rather than the five-pointed one. Colors are marigold, amethyst, green, blue, clambroth, and vaseline. In addition a very rare chop plate is known in marigold.

Maple Leaf

The carnival glass pieces of this Dugan-Diamond pattern date to 1910, but custard items were made earlier and the jelly compote can occasionally be found in opalescent glass. Carnival items include stemmed berry sets, water sets, and table sets. Colors are marigold, amethyst, cobalt blue, and green. The berry sets have an interior pattern of Peacock Tail, obviously borrowed from the Fenton's similar pattern.

Maple Leaf Basket

Like the May Basket and the Prism and Fan Basket, I suspect this pattern also came from the Brockwitz factory in Germany since several very similar baskets appear throughout old catalogs from there. It has the same edge shaping and handle configuration as the other two and the marigold color is identical. However the pattern on the exterior is not found in the two Brockwitz catalogs known, so I can only speculate.

Marianna

This very beautiful vase is marked "MADE IN CZECHOSLOVAKIA" so its origin is known. It is called Marianna by collectors in Europe and England. It was made by Rindskopf.

Marilyn (Millersburg)

Found in both crystal (pitcher) and carnival glass (water sets), this very collectible pattern is one of Millersburg's fine geometric designs. Colors are the usual marigold, amethyst, and a hard-to-find green.

Martec

Martec is another McKee pattern in the Tec series like Aztec. This nice pattern has only been found in the tumbler in carnival glass. It stands 4" tall and is marked "Prescut." The design is geometric with two major hobstar variations.

At a glance this large compote looks so similar to the Marianna pattern that the assumption is they are one and the same, but there are differences upon close inspection. I feel that Rindskopf is the likely maker, but have no proof to date. It is found only in marigold.

Mary Ann

Mary Ann was reportedly named for Thomas E.A. Dugan's sister. This vase was first advertised in 1915 by Diamond. It is found in both opalescent glass and carnival glass (crystal and silver filigree versions are known) and there are two moulds. One has ten scallops on the top and the other eight. In addition a third mould has three handles rather than two and is called a loving cup. It is known in marigold and After Glow (pink) but the two-handled version is also known in amethyst as shown.

Mary Gregory Bottle

Recent information places this decorated bottle as a product of the Hosch Company of Bohemia around 1910. Mary Gregory was a glass decorator and the technique is named for her. The bottle shown is called a barber bottle (some say a cologne). It has a nice marigold finish on the lower half and is clear on the neck.

Massachusetts (U.S. Glass)

While the vase shape shown is the only shape I've heard about in this very attractive pattern, I'd wager it was made in other shapes as well. It is found only in marigold and brings a good price when sold, because it is a scarce and desirable item.

Mayan (Millersburg)

It is a real pleasure to show the only known marigold bowl in this Millersburg pattern. All the rest are green or an off-green that tends toward olive. The design is a simple one, six feathered fans that spread out from a stippled round center with an outer ring of dots. The exterior is a wide panel one. Nearly all of the bowls are ice cream shape (without ruffling) but the marigold example does have eight ruffles. The finish is usually a fine radium one.

May Basket

May Basket is possibly from the Brockwitz factory (although I have no proof), and is also known as Diamond Point and Fleur-de-lis by some collectors. It stands 6" high and has a bowl diameter of 7½". It is found in marigold mostly but has been reported in a smoky hue and may have been produced in cobalt blue as well.

183

Mayflower (Millersburg)

Mayflower is usually found as the exterior of crystal and carnival Grape Leaves bowls, but here is one of two known carnival bowls with Mayflower as the only pattern. Both are marigold and very rare and desirable.

Mayflower Shade

Mayflower was given its name many years ago by Marion Hartung. This shade has a catalog number of 474C and is a variation of the famous 474 pattern by Imperial Glass. It can be found on both electric and gas shades in marigold or the fine helios green as shown. As shades go, this is one of the better ones with a nice design.

Maypole

This bud vase stands 6" tall and is known with both five and six feet. It is found on pastel marigold, marigold, purple, and has been reported in green. The maker seems to be a mystery at least to me. Few of these seem to show up for sale, and collectors snatch them up eagerly.

McKee's #20

This pattern was advertised as McKee's #20 pattern and is known mostly in gilded crystal in table pieces, a punch set (lemonade set), stemmed fruit bowl, salt shaker, and the stemmed dessert shown. It is marked "Pres-Cut."

McKee's Squiggy Vase

This odd looking vase was shown in 1927 McKee catalogs. It was made in crystal and colors and apparently in some iridized pieces. Here is a green example with a watery luster.

Meander (Northwood)

Here's the exterior of the gorgeous Three Fruits Medallion bowl shown elsewhere, and as you can see, the glass is truly black amethyst and has no iridizing on the exterior. The pattern of Meander, however, is a good design.

Melon Rib

Melon Rib can be found on water sets, candy jars, salt and pepper shakers, and a covered powder jar, all in marigold. As you can see, the pitcher is tall, stately, and very pretty.

Melon Rib Genie Vase

This 5" vase is much like the other Melon Rib or rolled vases seen throughout carnival glass. It is often from Europe. This one has great amethyst color with good iridescence and seems a step above most of the rest.

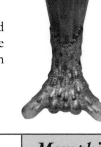

Melting Ice Vase

The owner of a pair of these 8½" vases purchased them in Poland and named them. They have nine upper panels that turn in at the top, while the footed base has the "melting ice" pattern. The maker has not been identified at this time.

Memphis

Memphis is from Northwood (their #19 pattern) and is found in several types of glass. In carnival glass shapes include a berry set, punch set, covered sugar, large compote, a fruit bowl with stand, and the recently discovered salt and pepper shakers shown. Colors are both vivid and pastel.

Metalica

I don't recall ever seeing this unusual covered candy dish before the photo surfaced from Jack Sciara, but it is an item one wouldn't be likely to forget. As you can see, the plain panels are iridized but the rest of the piece has been covered with a metal filagree treatment. Although shaped much like covered dishes from both Fenton and Northwood, it is difficult to imagine who made this oddity.

Metro

It is a real pleasure to show this rare vase pattern. The maker is anyone's guess. The design consists of concave panels, herringbone, diamonds, a diamond section of file, and fans! It somewhat resembles the Spearhead and Rib vase shown elsewhere in this edition and stands some 13" tall. Thanks to Gene and Shirley Metro for this rare vase and I hope they approve of the name.

Mexicali Vase

Shown are a pair of vases that came from Mexico and were shared by Lois Langdon. They are a rich marigold like many pieces from Cristales Mexicanos Glass. They stand 8" tall and have a 3⅜" octagon-shaped pedestal base. The top has a ⅜" band with 24 ribs extending down to another ¼" band, with 24 more ribs then extending down to the bottom banding. I am happy to show these previously unreported vases.

Mexican Bell

Mexican Bell is similar to the Swirled Threads goblet shown elsewhere in this edition. This pretty goblet has a pale green base glass with strong marigold iridescence over the bowl. The glass is rather thin and the stem has a large globe shape separating the bowl from the base.

Meydam (Leerdam)

Meydam was named by Marion Quintin-Baxendale for the chief designer at the Leerdam plant, Floris Meydam. This pattern is very similar to the Greta pattern. Meydam can be found in a creamer, covered butter dish, a short-stemmed cake stand, a stemmed compote from the same mould, and a sugar. The color is a watery marigold that seems to melt into clear in some areas. Shown is the butter dish with the pattern on the lid's interior.

Mikado (Fenton)

Found only on this large compote with Fenton's Cherry on the stem and base, the Mikado pattern is large mum blossoms, rectangles of scrollwork, and a rayed sun center. It is 8" – 9" tall and can be ruffled or round. Iridized colors known are marigold, cobalt blue, amethyst (scarce), green (very scarce), white, and Mandarin red opaque glass that is iridized (both rare).

Mike's Mystery

Mike Smith owns this 8½" bowl and he named it. I feel it is either from Europe or Scandinavia but haven't been able to locate it in the many catalog reprints from either area, so I'm showing it with Mike's name. The bowl is 3½" deep and I'd certainly appreciate any additional information about it.

Milady

Here is, in my opinion, one of the better water sets by the Fenton Company. The pitcher is a tankard size, and the design is paneled with very artistic blossoms and stems with graceful leaves. Colors most seen are marigold and blue, but a scarce green and a rare amethyst do exist.

Millersburg Four Pillars

This vase (shards were found at the Millersburg factory) actually exists in marigold, amethyst, and green. The base of these vases has a rayed design (unlike the Northwood's or Dugan's versions). I am greatly in debt for the photos and information from David Cotton about these rare items.

Millersburg Four Pillars Variant

What a thrill it is to show this very rare Millersburg vase (shards were found at the factory). It is found without the twist and with a rayed base in marigold, green, or amethyst. Thanks again to Dave Cotton for sharing it.

Millersburg Grape

This pattern has been accepted by most collectors as being Millersburg. Actually, one look at the coloring and the radium finish of this green example should convince anyone it is a Millersburg product. It is found in 5½" and 8½" bowls with a wide panel exterior, and either eight ruffles or a three-in-one edge (commonly found only on Millersburg small bowls). Colors are marigold or green but an amethyst wouldn't surprise me. Marigold can be found from time to time but the green is rare (only one example reported).

Miniature Bean Pot

This miniature is only 2½" tall and has a label on the bottom declaring it to be from Czechoslovakia. The coloring is nothing to write home about but it does have a place among all the small iridized collectibles that are popular today.

Miniature Blackberry (Fenton)

This Fenton miniature is scarce in all colors and is highly sought by most serious collectors. It is found in compotes that measure only 4½" across and the rare footed plate whimsey shown. The colors are marigold, amethyst, cobalt blue, green, and white. The rarest colors are white and amethyst, but green is close behind. Marigold is the easiest color to find with blue next.

Miniature Candelabra (Cambridge)

This child's piece was shown in one old Cambridge catalog. It is 4½" tall with three arms for candles. Around the top of the center arm is impressed "Patent Applied For." The design is a simple Colonial or Flute pattern and the color is a very good marigold. This item is quite rare, and virtually all examples are crystal rather than iridized. The non-iridized version is from Westmoreland.

Miniature Child's Shoe

Unlike the slippers known in carnival glass miniatures, the piece shown is like a high baby's shoe. The color is a good strong marigold and the maker is unknown.

Miniature Flower Basket (Westmoreland)

Shown in peach opalescent and blue opalescent, the Westmoreland Miniature Flower Basket can also be found in marigold. Many are found with the original wire clip-on handle. The pattern is one of a single flower, buds, and leaves on two floral sprays. Some pieces are also found with souvenir printing on the inside. This is a desirable little mini-basket for the collector.

187

Miniature Hobnail

Shown is the very rare pitcher and tumblers of this desirable toy collectible. The complete set is known in crystal. The pitcher is 5⅛" tall and the tumblers 2½" tall. The marigold color is quite good on the pieces reported. In addition, a miniature Hobnail cordial set is also known in marigold but I cannot confirm this is the same design or has the same maker as the water set pieces.

Miniature Hobnail

Here is the complete set. It consists of a tray, decanter with stopper, and six cordials. It was made by Brockwitz (their #12150) and is shown in a catalog furnished to me by Bob Smith. The only color I've heard about is marigold.

Miniature Loving Cup

Many collectors have a weakness for miniatures and the one shown here would bring joy to any of them. It stands 3½" tall and measures 3" from handle to handle. The color is strong and the iridescence good.

Miniature Sandal

Miniatures seem to have a fascination all their own and this sandal is no exception. It measures 4½" from heel to toe and is 2⅛" tall at the highest area. The sole is very realistic with a woven design. Purchased in Argentina, there is no way to know the origin or maker. Along with the Lady Slipper and Wooden Shoe miniatures, this is a real find for any collector.

Miniature Wash Bowl and Pitcher

It is hard to imagine so many miniature items were made in iridized glass but here is another one. The pitcher stands 2¾" tall and the bowl has a diameter of 3⅝". The marigold color is quite good. I would appreciate any further information about this set. Thanks to Nigel Gamble for sharing it.

Mini Diamonds

Shown is a small 3½" juice tumbler. The design is a simple one of small diamond gridding covering the piece except for a band of plain glass at the top. The color is a bit pale on this example. It is reported to be from India.

Minuet

Here is another of the late iridized tumblers. It is from a water set that has a brown stenciled decoration. dates to the 1930s or possible 1940s and doesn't create much of a stir but I felt it should be shown.

188

Mirror and Crossbars (Jain)

This beautiful Jain tumbler is 5¼" tall and known by most collectors as lemonade size. It is very similar to other tumblers from Jain in both pattern and size. It has the typical 1" band at the top, the oval plain mirror design, and crosshatching. I wouldn't be surprised to see one of these show up in blue since Jain made several of their tumbler patterns in blue as well as marigold.

Mirrored Lotus

Here is a Fenton pattern that is quite scarce, especially in some colors. Found mostly on 7" ruffled bowls in blue, green, marigold, or white, it is also known on the rare ice-cream shaped 7" bowl in celeste blue, a rare plate in the same color, and a rare white rose bowl.

Mirrored Peacocks (Jain)

Here's another of the tumbler patterns originally felt to be from Czechoslovakia but now known to have been a product of the Jain Glass Works in India. It is slightly taller than most tumblers and of rather thin glass. This very pretty tumbler has really fine iridescence with rich, deep marigold. The stylized Peacock is the national symbol of India.

Mirrored Vees

Although found in Brazil, this 4¼" tumbler is identical in size to the Andean Cherries tumbler listed earlier in this edition. Since the Andean Cherries pattern is shown in a Rindskopf catalog as their #2201, I'm putting this tumbler in that camp as well, unless I find out different. Thanks to the Raths once again for supplying the name and photo.

Misty Morn

This very pretty vase is from the Jain Glass Works and has their typical carnival and frosting combination. The name comes from that used by an auction house. This pattern may well be known by another name to some collectors, but if so I haven't heard it. The design has flowers, leaves, and odd flora edged by banding.

Mitered Block

The very pretty lamp is one of a pair and it has an amethyst font with heavy gold iridescence. The pattern is a series of rectangles running vertically and horizontally in rows. The base is pot metal, as is the center stem. I suspect these lamps are from Europe but have no proof. The age is uncertain.

Mitered Diamonds and Pleats

This design, long felt to be a Sowerby pattern, can be found in a handled sauce and the 8½" bowl (without handles) shown, and Rose Presznick reported a 10" tray. Colors are marigold and a smoky blue.

Mitered Maze

After a two year search for information on this vase (Fenton made a similar design in 1955 but Frank Fenton says they are not the same and they didn't make this vase), I decided to give it a name and show it, hoping someone will know more about it. It stands 12" tall I and has a rich smoke finish toward the bottom that shades to a rich green and finally a purple at the top! The iridescence is fantastic. The base has a pontil mark but no identification.

Mitered Ovals

Besides the People's Vase, this is the most important of Millersburg's rare and desirable vase designs. Here I show marigold, green, and amethyst (only a rare teal is missing). Mitered Ovals is mould blown and stands 10½" tall. The tops are always crimped and then ruffled in this shape.

Moderne

I'd guess this cup and saucer to be fairly late carnival, but it still has good color and a nice lustre. A table set is also known. None are very sought after by collectors but it is worth showing. Thanks to Bill Edwards for naming it.

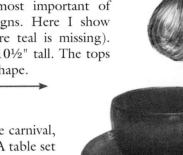

Moller

These beautiful Eda Glass rose bowls (bowls are also reported) are about as pretty as bowls can get. Colors are marigold and blue and the finish is superb. Thanks to the Ayers family for the photos and the information about this and many other patterns.

Monkey Bottle

Very little has been learned about this miniature bottle except it was sold in a Burns Auction in the late 1980s for $200.00. It has fairly good marigold iridescence and would be a jewel in any collection of miniatures or animal pieces. It stands 4¾" tall. Thanks to Nigel Gamble for this item.

Monsoon

Monsoon is one of the more attractive water sets from India. It has rows of file, sections of diamonds, and distinct optical bull's eyes. The pitcher is 8½" tall and the tumbler 4¼". Thanks to Vikram Bachhawat for sharing it.

Moon and Stars Band

Moon and Stars Band is found only in a marigold water set to date. Groups of moons and stars are situated between two ribbed bands circling the mid section on the pitcher and the top section on the tumbler. Both pitcher and tumbler have a paneled section around the bottom portion of each piece. This is also known as Celestial Band. Thanks again to Karen and Allan Rath for the photo.

Moonprint

This pattern was called Globus by the Brockwitz Company in their catalog. Shapes are many in crystal, and in carnival glass include a covered butter dish, open sugar, cordial set with tray, fruit bowl on a stand, squat pitcher, wine, pedestal vase, epergne, covered dish, round bowl, covered cheese dish, squat vase (flat base), and the footed vase shown. In addition a covered jar in peach opalescent has been reported but not confirmed. Thanks to the Remmens for the photo.

Morning Glory (Millersburg)

Morning Glory is perhaps the most regal water set in all of carnival glass. This very rare pattern found only on the tankard pitcher and matching tumblers is a collector's dream. Found in marigold, amethyst, and green, less than a dozen sets in all colors are known. The morning glories wind around the center of the pitcher and tumblers trailing vines and leaves. The glass is sparkling with a radium finish.

Morning Glory Vase (Imperial)

This fine vase can be found in marigold, amber, purple, green, smoke, lavender, olive, clambroth, and the fantastic blue shown in a 13" vase with a 5" base diameter. It can also be found in 2½" and 3⅝" base diameters (a mid-size vase in this color was shown in the ninth edition).

Mountain Lake

Painted shades seem to be plentiful lately. They are showing up in different sizes, shapes, and designs. This particular shade is the larger example, which hangs in the center of a chandelier containing four smaller shades on the outer arms. Most feel that these are Czechoslovakian in origin but this is speculation only. Thanks to Joan Jolliffe for the photo.

Moxie Bottle

I normally avoid the bottle cycle unless they are as attractive as this well-designed scarcity. The color is obviously a very frosty white with heavy lustre, and the design of plain and stippled diamonds is a good one. Moxie was a soft drink that went out of favor in the mid-1920s.

Mt. Gambier Mug

Like the Quorn and the #110 mugs shown elsewhere in this book, I now know these mugs were sold after being etched as souvenirs in South Australia. The mugs can be found etched or plain and no proof that they were made by Crystal has come to light.

Multi Fruits and Flowers

This wonderful Millersburg pattern shows grapes, peaches, pears, cherries, berries, leaves, and blossoms. It is found on punch sets, rare water sets (pitchers in two shapes), and a stemmed sherbet or fruit cup. Colors are the usual marigold, amethyst, and green, but rare punch sets are known in cobalt blue.

191

Multi-Rib Vase

This vase is from Silvestri Mouth Blown Glass in Chicago, and was probably produced for them in Taiwan. It stands 10" tall. The age is very questionable.

Muscadine

Muscadine is almost a twin to the Beaded Panels and Grapes tumbler, except it has a band of geometric squares-within-squares and diamonds-within-diamonds instead of a band of grapes and leaves. The color is marigold, and the tumbler stands 5⅛" tall.

My Lady

Here is a favorite with collectors and a good price is always assured when one of these sell. It is found only in marigold of a good rich quality. The powder jar stands 5½" tall and has a base diameter of 3¼". The figure on the lid is made of solid glass.

Mystic

Bill Edwards named this 7" vase and if anyone knows it by another name, I'd be happy to hear from them. The design of elongated shields separated by a hobstar and file filler is interesting. The very mellow color reminds me of other Cambridge products, and that is just who made it, according to a 1908 advertisement.

Mystic Grape

This 13½" decanter with stopper has to be my favorite, and I'm not really a big fan of decanters. Found in Brazil, this well designed beauty has a variety throughout the pattern such as grapes, leaves, and one peculiar design below the center grape cluster which reminds me of two unstrung tennis rackets or the face of an owl. The back of the decanter has somewhat of a different pattern. The overall shape is most interesting, especially the thin side profile. Only the marigold decanter has been seen to date and I would love to see the rest of the set. Many thanks to Karen and Allan Rath for naming this pattern and sending the nice photo.

Nanna

This very pretty line by Eda Glass Works includes a small oval jardiniere as well as the 6" vase shown. It is shown in a 1929 catalog (furnished to me by Siegmar Geiselberger) and the reported carnival glass colors are marigold or blue.

Napco #2255

Napco #2255 was made by Jeannette Glass and is mostly found in a pink milk glass that was made in the 1950s. The iridized version shown must have come about a bit earlier. Shown is a 6" square compote with lettering on the bottom that says "NAPCO 2255–CLEVELAND, OHIO." I'd certainly appreciate any information about this iridized piece.

192

Napoli

The owner of this liquor set with six different colored glasses was fortunate to find the entire grouping in the original box. The decanter isn't marked but each of the glasses have base markings that say "MADE IN ITALY – 3" and have a star with the lettering "SF" in the center. The pieces show a flower and leaf etching and have gold rims. The age is probably late 1930s.

Nautilus

While the Northwood Company made the custard pieces, the carnival pieces were all made by Dugan, despite some trademarks to the contrary. When Northwood left the Indiana, Pennsylvania, plant and the moulds for Nautilus behind, some were signature cut. The carnival pieces are the small novelty piece shown shaped in two different ways and a very rare large marigold berry bowl. Colors for the small pieces are peach opalescent or purple.

Navajo

The only information I have on this very nice vase is that its marigold in color and 7" tall. Any information would be appreciated. Thanks to the Vandevander's for sharing it.

Near-Cut (Northwood)

This near-cut design, also known as Northwood's #12 pattern, is found in crystal in 34 different shapes and in limited pieces in carnival glass. The pattern dates from 1906. Carnival shapes include a tall water pitcher (found in marigold only), the tumbler shown (known in marigold or amethyst), a goblet in the same colors, and a compote (found in marigold, amethyst, and green). All pieces of iridized glass are quite rare and very collectible. Shown is a tumbler with a radium finish, rare for a Northwood product.

Near-Cut Decanter

This rare Cambridge pattern is a triumph of near-cut design! This 11" beauty is found in a sparkling green, but amethyst or marigold are possibilities. The mould work is some of the best, and the finish is equal to any from the Millersburg plant.

Near Cut Wreath (Millersburg)

This is another of those superior exterior geometric patterns the Millersburg factory did so well. It is found as the exterior on some Holly Sprig and Holly Whirl bowls. The pattern combines several interesting components including ovals, hobstars, file diamonds, and crosshatching. It is another example of great mould work and allover patterning.

Nesting Swan

This pattern has become one of the most sought Millersburg bowl patterns, and it is certainly easy to see why. The graceful swan, nesting on a bed of reeds surrounded by leaves, blossoms, and cattails, is a very interesting design. The detail is quite good, and the color and finish exceptional. The beautiful Diamond and Fan exterior contrasts nicely and echoes the fine workmanship throughout. In addition to green, marigold, and amethyst, Nesting Swan can be found in a beautiful honey-amber shade and a very rare blue.

193

New England Wine Co.

I'm told that this rather large wine bottle has embossing on the bottom reading: "Boston, Mass." I feel certain it once had a paper label on the front where the flat oval area is, and would appreciate any additional information about this bottle. It has been reported in marigold only to date.

New Jersey (U.S. Glass)

It is always a real pleasure to show this honey amber wine in the New Jersey pattern (also known as Loops and Drops) from U.S. Glass. It is the only piece so far reported in this pattern, which was part of the States line and was made in many shapes in crystal as the company's #15070 pattern. More and more U.S. Glass rarities seem to crop up every year, giving the collector a real reason to continue the search.

New Orleans Shrine

This champagne is on clear iridized glass with hand-painted designs. The alligators along the sides are unique in carnival glass, and the crowned and bearded man represents Rex, King of the Mardi Gras. I really can't think of anything more fitting for a piece of carnival glass.

Newport Ship Bottle

This bottle, from the Pouchers, shows a ship on waves, a panel of gothic spires and quatrefoil, and a pedestal of stippling at the base. The color is a greenish with good iridescence.

Niagara Falls Souvenir

Here is yet another of those pitchers Jeannette seemed to turn out from the same mould, some with an internal mould design, others with enameling on the outside. This one has a picture of the falls and says "Souvenir of Niagara Falls." All of these water set pieces were late carnival and probably should be called iridized Depression glass rather than carnival glass.

Nightshade (Czech)

This beautiful bowl or low compote is marked "Made in Czechoslovakia" so its origin is known. The upper part is a beautiful celeste blue and the dome base is black amethyst, all iridized. The effect is stunning and I feel this is one of the prettier pieces of Czech glass. Thanks to Clint and Joanne Andrews for sharing this find.

Night Stars (Millersburg)

Night Stars can mostly be found in the deep bonbon shown, but can also found in a spade-shaped nappy and a shallow two-handled card tray. Colors are mostly green, but marigold, amethyst, and rare vaseline examples are known.

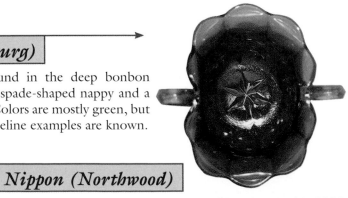

Nippon (Northwood)

Nippon, Northwood's version of the popular Peacock Tail pattern, was first advertised in 1912. It can be found in bowls, either ruffled or with a piecrust edge, and plates. Bowls are known in marigold, amethyst, green, cobalt blue, ice blue, ice green, white, lime green, and lime green opalescent. Plates are reported in marigold, amethyst, green, white, and ice blue. The example shown is a superb electric purple with wild blue and red highlights.

Norris N. Smith

Like many other advertising pieces, this one has the Garden Mums as a floral design, and the lettering says "Norris N. Smith, Real Estate and Insurance, Rome, Ga." The only color known in these pieces is amethyst. The example shown is a shallow ice cream bowl shape, nearly a plate. The iridescence is rich and satiny.

Northern Lights

Northern Lights is from Brockwitz and part of a design line that includes Star and Hobs and the Texas tumbler. Colors are marigold and blue. I thank the Ayers family for the photo and the information.

Northern Star (Fenton)

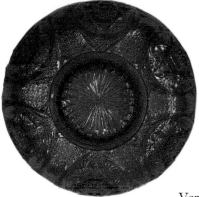

Made in crystal as early as 1909, and then in opalescent glass the following year, Northern Star then became a carnival glass product with the small bowl mould used to form a card tray, a plate, and the bowl shown. Marigold is the only color reported in iridized glass. The bowls are usually ruffled also, but here is a shallow ice cream shape that is rare. It has a 6½" diameter and stands 1½" tall. Just why the larger plates (11½") or the 4" and 7" bowls that were made in opalescent glass were ignored in the iridized glass production is a mystery.

North Star

Very little is known about this pattern except it seems to have been made by the Lancaster Glass Company, starting in 1910 (ads in Butler Brothers show it as late as 1914), in crystal in a table set, water set, and a berry set, as well as novelty bowls. Here is the bowl to a punch set, the first item reported in iridized glass, so obviously such a set was made. I'd certainly like to hear from anyone who has additional information about this pattern. It is also known as Stippled Fans. Thanks to Dave Cotton for this piece.

Northwood #38 Shade

This nice shade is heavily stippled in each panel, which contains a feathery sort of look separated by ribs. The bottom edge has alternating small and large points. Inside the collar lock is embossed: "Northwood #38." The color is between a white and a moonstone. Thanks to Ron Britt for sharing it.

Northwood #569

Primarily a stretch glass pattern from the Northwood Company after 1916, this interior paneled pattern is found on flared vases as well as the hat vase shown. Colors besides the marigold are blue, topaz, white, and Royal purple. The example shown has a touch of stretch finish on the top rim but the rest of the vase is pure carnival glass.

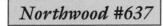

Northwood #637

Shown in a 1920 ad titled Rainbow & Cobweb, this tall cupped compote in a ribbed pattern was numbered 637 while companion pieces carried various other numbers including 631, 644, 638, 646, 643, 301, and 639. Colors seem to be blue, canary, and russet. Some of the blue pieces seem to have a smoky look but the iridescence is strong and ranges in color from a bit of aqua to a strong darker blue. The canary or topaz items are a strong vaseline color and the russet is olive green with touches of bronze.

Northwood #657

Made in two sizes, these russet candlesticks had an accompanying console bowl and were part of the 1920s Rainbow line. Several shapes such as bowls, rose bowls, compotes, candlesticks, and specialty items such as a cheese and cracker set (see Northwood's #699) and covered candy dishes were included. Colors were exotic with names like topaz, blue iris, russet, jade blue, and emerald green. Some items were opaque iridized and others were not. Many had gold decoration. I will try to show a sampling of this vast line.

Northwood #699

Shown is the cheese holder that originally came with a cracker plate. The plate had a lip around the center that held the base of the cheese holder in place. Like other pieces of the Rainbow line, this interesting item came in iridescent blue, topaz, emerald green, russet, and opaque iridized colors that included iridescent ivory and jade blue.

Northwood Wide Flute Vase

I expect some controversy about the name of this pattern, but the owner says it definitely has a different base than the Northwood Flute vase or the Northwood Wide Panel vase. The example shown has ten panels or flutes, is 13" tall, and has a base diameter of 4¾", while the top flares to 7½" with sharp flames. Two purple examples are reported. Thanks to the Hamlets for this fine vase.

Northwood Wide Panel Vase

This seldom-discussed Northwood marked vase is about 18" tall and has an Alaskan (marigold over green) iridescence inside the neck. The base has a 4¾" diameter. Some have suggested this piece was pulled from a punch set base, but I am skeptical. Other colors reported include marigold and vaseline.

Notches

Research has revealed very little about this 8" plate. The only design is the series of ribs that run from the marie to the outer edges on the exterior where the rim of the plate is notched out to eliminate the arc. The color is a rich marigold and the interior of the plate is plain.

Nu-Art Chrysanthemum (Imperial)

This companion to the Nu-Art Homestead plate is a bit harder to find. It is a 10½" chop plate found in marigold, amethyst, amber, smoke, white, green, and cobalt blue. The exterior has a ribbing. The plate was reproduced in the 1960 – 1970 era, and again later by other makers once Imperial closed.

Nu-Art Drape Shade

This very attractive Imperial shade has a design that is all interior. It is 5" tall and has a bell spread of 5½". The color and iridescence is superb and the drapes all have tiny stitching lines, showing fine mould work.

Nu-Art Homestead (Imperial)

This 10" plate is a standout. It is from Imperial (their #525 pattern) and is similar to the Double Dutch pattern. Some are marked "Nu-Art" while others are not. Colors include marigold, green, purple, amber, white, smoke, emerald green, and cobalt blue (ice green has also been reported but not confirmed). This plate has been reproduced in many colors so be cautious when buying.

Nu-Art Paneled Shade (Imperial)

Imperial made many light shades in many patterns and several were signed "Nu-Art." The example shown is one of the engraved examples with grapes and leaves. In shape this shade is nearly identical to the Lustre and Clear Lightolier shade except it has a nearly straight bottom and the Nu-Art shade is slightly scalloped. The color is a very rich marigold. There are 10 panels, all interior.

Nugget Beads

Here is another string of carnival beads, but it is much more impressive than the set shown elsewhere in this book. The stringing includes gold spacers, regular iridized beads, and graduated nugget-shaped chunks. The color is a very rich amethyst.

#110 Mugs

Although I think every pattern should have a name rather than a number, I'm forced to list several in a row, simply because I'm told that they have no names. The mugs shown are the same pattern as the Quorn mug shown elsewhere in this edition, with the exception of the lettering. These three have the following different lettering: "Greetings from Yacha," "Greetings from Moonta," and "Greetings from Mt. Gambier." The color is a very nice marigold. Thanks to Wayne Delahoy for the photo and information.

#195

This nice little sherbet is from Crown Crystal in Australia and can be found in marigold. A simple paneled design, this is a bit scarce to find. Thanks to Wayne Delahoy for the pattern number and photo.

#221

This pattern is from Crown Crystal in Australia. It has been reported in a 5" and 8" size bowl and can be found in marigold. The pattern has an allover coverage of diamond prisms on the exterior, with a rayed base and smooth edge. Although very similar to Cut Prisms shown elsewhere, this pattern has one less row of prisms. Thanks to Wayne Delahoy for providing the pattern number and photo.

#270 (Westmoreland)

This is really a very poor name for this little compote, since it was known to be a part of the #252 line of glass that included the Corinth vases. It dates from 1904 and is found in the typical iridized colors from Westmoreland: amber, peach opalescent, and teal (Westmoreland called this color turquoise). The compote isn't much in demand and never brings a large price.

#321

This rather interesting design from Crown Crystal in Australia is found in an oval bowl shape in marigold. Two rows of prism shaped panels and a serrated top make this a nice item for any collection. Thanks to Wayne Delahoy for the pattern number and photo.

Nutmeg Grater

The covered butter dish (shown), a stemmed creamer and matching open sugar, and a bowl, all in marigold, are the shapes I can confirm. The pattern is from Brockwitz.

Oak Leaf Lustre

This pattern is also known as Acanthus Leaf or Acanto, and is from Cristalerias Piccardo in Argentina. It can be found in a covered butter dish and a cheese dish. Colors reported are marigold and blue. Thanks to Gary Vandevander for the photo.

Octagon

Here is one of carnival's best known geometric patterns. It was made by Imperial and is found in a host of shapes including berry sets, table sets, water sets (two sizes of pitchers), milk pitcher, vase, punch set, stemmed sherbet, handled nappy, compote, toothpick holder, goblet, cordial, wine decanter, stemmed wine, and shakers. Colors include marigold, purple, green, smoke, aqua, clambroth, white, teal, and light blue with marigold overlay, but not all colors are found in all shapes.

Octet

Even if this pattern were not marked, I would attribute it to Northwood because the exterior pattern is the Northwood Vintage found on the Star of David and Bows bowl. Octet is also a dome-footed bowl, usually about 8½" in diameter. It is a simple but effective pattern — one that wouldn't be easily confused with others. The colors are marigold, purple, green, white, and ice green. The purple is the most common.

Ogden Furniture

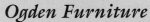

This is another of the many Fenton advertising pieces. It is found in ruffled or ice cream shaped bowls as well as handgrip or flat plates. Only amethyst is reported and the design shows the usual mums, leaves, and tendrils with lettering that says "Ogden Furniture and Carpet Co. — Ogden, Utah."

Ohio Star (Millersburg)

Ohio Star was made in crystal from the beginning of the Millersburg Glass Company in 1909. This very fine pattern can be found in carnival glass in vases, a tall compote shape, whimsied small relish dishes, and a short stemmed compote. All pieces are rare with the vases a bit easier to find than other shapes. At least three swung vases are known and the tall compote may be flattened as one example is. Colors are marigold, purple, green, one white, and two aqua opalescent slag vases. The other shapes are marigold only. Thank to Seeck Auction for the nice photo.

Oklahoma

Thought first to be shown in Imperial crystal catalogs, this tumbler in carnival glass is marked "CM" (Cristalis de Mexico) so it is believed that the moulds were sold to Mexican glassmakers who produced this iridized tumbler. The only reported color is marigold. These tumblers are quite desirable.

Old Dominion

While this is in reality another interior Smooth Rays pattern, it has some distinctions from the others. The rays are centered in the bowl, stopping well short of both the top and bottom. The stem has six panels and a nice swelling just below the bowl. The piece stands 5½" tall. Quality iridescence is on the inside only. In design, this piece looks like many Imperial items, but I haven't a clue who made it.

Old Fashion Set

I am told by the owner of this drink set and matching tray that he purchased them in the 1970s from a well-known East Coast dealer and he has had this set for many years. The purple is just superb as is the iridescence. The design indicates they were probably made in the pre-World War II era, but beyond that there is little evidence to establish a timeframe or a maker.

Old Oaken Bucket

This novelty is 3¼" tall and 2⅞" across the top. It is of a pale marigold with fine iridescence. There are 14 staves around the body, with three rings (the bottom one contains the lettering: "PATENTED"). The glass design shows realistic wood graining. The bucket has a wire handle and a metal lid that says "THE OLD OAKEN BUCKET." All in all, a rare bit of glass for that special place in a collection of novelties.

Olympic Compote

The Millersburg Olympic miniature compote is extremely rare. Its measurements are the same as the Leaf and Little Flowers compote made by the same company, and the exterior and base are identical also. If ever the old adage "great things come in small packages" could apply, certainly it would be to the Olympic compote.

Omera (Imperial)

Omera was shown as Imperial's Special Lot #1933 in an ad for this pattern in Rose Marie (pink), amber, and green Depression glass. This design in carnival glass vases is called Smooth Panels. As you can see this #646B bowl has been shaped into a rose bowl. The color is well done and the iridescence all interior. The bowl sits on a large flat (collar) base that has a 6" diameter. Besides the bowl and vase shapes, a handled celery vase, handled berry, handled compote, and handled celery bowl are known but certainly not all of these were iridized.

Omnibus

This is a well-known U.S. Glass pattern (their #15124) that is called U.S. Hobstar in crystal. The carnival glass pieces are suspected to be from later production by foreign makers. Some collectors believe pieces were made by Brockwitz and there is evidence to believe U.S. Glass shipped items to Mexico and South America. Carnival glass shapes include a water set in marigold and cobalt blue and the mug shaped pitcher in green.

Oneata

Oneata was made by Riverside Glass in 1907, primarily in crystal or gilded crystal. This pattern wasn't known in iridized glass until this shallow ice cream bowl came to light online. The iridescence is thin. This is from the company that gave us the Wild Rose syrup.

Open Edge Basketweave

Open Edge Basketweave is a well-known Fenton pattern that was first made in 1911. It was known as #1092. It can be found in hat shapes, banana bowls, a JIP shape, rare plates, and rare vases. Colors are marigold, blue, green, amethyst, white, pink, smoke, ice blue, ice green, red, aqua, and celeste blue. Shown is a rare pulled vase.

Open Rose (Imperial)

Open Rose is actually part of the Lustre Rose line (#489), and is on found plates and rose bowls with an exterior pattern called Paneled Rose. Shown is a beautiful plate in amethyst. In the ninth edition I showed the rose bowl in purple.

Optic and Buttons

Optic and Buttons was originally listed as Imperial's #582. It can be found in many shapes in crystal, but in carnival glass, it is known in berry sets, a two-handled bowl, water sets, rose bowl, plates in two sizes, cup and saucer, stemmed goblets and wines, and a rare handled open salt on a short stem. Colors are mostly marigold or clambroth but the plates are known in smoke and a rare stemmed compote is found in smoke and a pale lavender.

Optic Flute

This Imperial pattern is seldom mentioned but can be found on berry sets as well as compotes. Colors seen are marigold and smoke, but others may have been made.

Optic Rib

If you compare this water pitcher with Unshod (Fine Rib Variant) shown elsewhere in this edition, you will see they are identical except for the top (Unshod is scalloped, Optic Rib isn't). The example shown is a rich, dark amber, even the handle. The ribs are interior thus the name. I welcome any information on this pattern.

Optic Variant

If you examine Optic Flute, you will recognize the base of this Imperial bowl but will notice the fluting is missing. This pattern has been found on berry sets, but I feel sure other shapes were made. The interior of the 6" bowl shown was highly iridized and had a stretch appearance, and the exterior had only slight lustre.

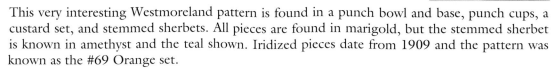

Orange Peel

This very interesting Westmoreland pattern is found in a punch bowl and base, punch cups, a custard set, and stemmed sherbets. All pieces are found in marigold, but the stemmed sherbet is known in amethyst and the teal shown. Iridized pieces date from 1909 and the pattern was known as the #69 Orange set.

Orange Tree

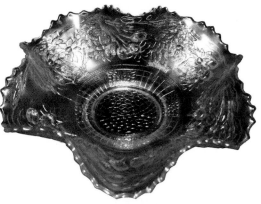

Fenton's Orange Tree can be found in a berry set, table set, water set (all footed), novelty bowls, plates, a rose bowl, goblet, breakfast set, sherbet, large orange bowl, centerpiece bowl, hatpin holder, mug (two sizes), powder jar, punch set, and several whimsies. The many colors range from pastels to dark colors. Shown is the first reported bowl in Ice Blue. Thanks to Mary Sigler for sharing it.

Orange Tree and Scroll

What a beauty this hard-to-find tankard set is. The orange trees are like those on the regular pieces and the Orange Tree Orchard set, but below the trees are panels of scrollwork much like the design on the Milady pattern. Colors reported to date are marigold, blue, and green.

Orange Tree Orchard

This rather scarce Fenton water set has a nicely shaped, bulbous pitcher. Obviously a spin-off pattern of Orange Tree, the design is a series of orange trees separated by fancy scrollwork. It has been reported in marigold, blue, green, amethyst, and white.

Orbit

Orbit is one of the prettiest of all the Indian patterns. This vase stands 9" tall and not only is it found in the usual marigold but also in a very watery blue as shown. The design shows various sizes of large bubbles with rows of beading and ribbing.

Orebro Epergne

For years this was thought to be the Sungold epergne and I apologize for the error. It is actually found in Swedish ads of 1914 and is called Orebro in Europe. It is really the Northern Lights (or Star and Hobs) pattern. The rose bowls are credited to Brockwitz so perhaps the moulds were moved to Sweden from there. Orebro is known in the epergne, a round bowl, and a deep oval bowl.

Oregon

U.S. Glass's #15053 was made at their Bryce Factory in crystal in 1907. Only a few pieces are known in carnival. The pattern is also known as Beaded Loop or Beaded Ovals. Shown is a 3½" tall spittoon whimsey shaped from a celery vase.

Oriental Poppy (Northwood)

Oriental Poppy is one of the stately tankard water sets from the Northwood Company that were produced in 1911. The large blooming poppy design is very realistic. Carnival colors include marigold, amethyst, green, cobalt blue, white, olive green, smoke, ice green, and the ice blue shown.

Oval and Round

This very nice Imperial pattern is mostly found on bowls, but can also be found on rare rose bowls, a bride's basket, and the rare chop plate shown. Colors are primarily marigold, but the berry bowls are known in smoke, the plate in marigold, smoke, and amber, and the berry sets are reported in purple.

Owl Bank

While it isn't in the class of a Peacock bowl, this bank is attractive in its own way, and despite being late carnival, the mould work and color are rather good. It stands nearly 7" tall, has a #4 impressed in the base, and is lettered "Be Wise" along the base.

Pacifica

Made by the U.S. Glass Company, the Pacifica tumbler is quite rare. Originally cataloged as #6425 by the maker, Pacifica has a rather complex pattern of hobstars, file sections, and small daisy-like flowers. The lustre is light, and the color has a bit of amber in the marigold.

Pacific Coast Mail Order House

Shown are two colors in a very Fenton rare advertising item. The exterior is, of course, Grape and Cable. Examples are known in green, marigold, and blue. The bowls are footed.

Paden City #198

This interesting syrup with a liner (underplate) was made by the Paden City Glass Company of Paden City, West Virginia, in the 1920s. It actually has no pattern except for its nice shape and excellent color, a deep marigold that is heavy and rich. The liner or plate has a ring inside to hold the base of the syrup in place and one piece actually fits down into the other.

Painted Pearl

This is another of the large bowls and plates in the Aurora series from Austria. The example shown is iridized moonstone with an enameling of grapes and leaves and is 12" in diameter. Thanks to the Remmens for updating my previous photo.

Palm Beach

Palm Beach, from U.S. Glass, was made in crystal, opalescent glass, and carnival glass. Shapes include a berry set, table set, cider set, rose bowl, plate, whimsey bowls, compotes, and vases, as well as a whimsey banana bowl. Shown is a whimsey vase.

Pandora

This bowl measures 5½" across the top and has the same center design as the Diamond Flower mini-compote shown elsewhere in this book. The color is very strong and the design quite good. It was found by Peter Dahlin in Malaysia. I have no further information about this pattern but assume it too came from Europe. I appreciate any information from readers on this pattern.

Paneled

This is one of two handled sugars from Australia. It is very similar to the Diamond pattern, without the diamonds. The paneling is all exterior with a typical banding at the waist of the piece. Both marigold and amethyst examples are reported.

Paneled Cane

This 8" vase remains pretty much a mystery and I've learned little about it since it was in the Britt collection years ago. It is reported only in marigold and is from Rindskopf.

Paneled Cruet

If you compare this cruet to the two shown under Carnival Cruets you will see that this one has less bulge to the base and the panels are exterior. In addition, there is no ring on the neck so this isn't the design shown by Hartung in her Book #5. Jane Dinkins believes the other two may be from Federal but this one must have a different maker.

Paneled Daisy and Cane

Standing 11" tall to the top of the handle, this very attractive basket has a top opening of 6", is notched at the top edge, and has four panels of cane and four panels of daisies and leaves. The basket is iridized both inside and out and the interior is plain. Marigold is the color on this, the only example of this piece that has been reported.

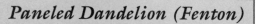

Paneled Dandelion (Fenton)

Advertised by Fenton in 1910, this tankard water set is one of the standouts from this company. Colors include marigold, amethyst, blue, and green. In addition there is a handle variation where the applied handle is over a seam instead of on a panel. A rare vase whimsey is also known.

Paneled Diamond and Bows

For some reason this Fenton vase pattern isn't often found despite not being rare. It ranges in size from the small 6½" version shown to the standard 11" vases. Colors are marigold, blue, green, amethyst, white, and an unusual peach opalescent. The design, a panel of geometric hobstars in diamonds separated by rayed bows, appears on alternating panels (three of six).

Paneled Diamond Point and Fan

Found previously in clear flint glass, this rare bowl is the only example reported in carnival glass. The pattern is all exterior and there is a map of Australia on the base. Production is reported to be from Crown Crystal in 1931. This example came to me from Margaret and John McGrath.

Paneled Fish Palms

The squared shape of this 5½" tall vase from India gives it a very appealing look. Besides the stylized fish on a feathered background and bubbles, the four sides are framed by ribs that run from top to bottom. The color is pale marigold.

Paneled Holly

This exterior Northwood pattern from 1908 or 1909 is primarily found in crystal, emerald green, or opalescent glass, but can occasionally be found in limited pieces of carnival glass. In carnival, a very rare amethyst water pitcher is known and a few table set pieces (creamer, spooner, sugar) are found. In addition a two-handled bonbon dish (from the spooner) is available. Colors are mostly amethyst, but the spooner is found in marigold and the bonbon in marigold and green.

Paneled Palm (U.S. Glass)

This is a very pretty little mug by U.S. Glass. It measures 3⅜" tall, has a 20-point star in the base, and a very good finish. In addition to the mug, a stemmed wine in marigold has been seen, indicating more shapes were iridized. This pattern was U.S. Glass #15095, dating from 1906. It was made in crystal and rose-flashed glass in tumblers, toothpick holder, bowls, wine, cake stand, shakers, and a sauce dish.

Paneled Prism

Rose Presznick called this pattern Block Diamond but it was first shown by Sherman Hand under the name of Paneled Prism. It is a 5½" tall container with lid, which some call a mustard pot but most know as a jam jar. The lid has a cut-out area for a spoon. I strongly suspect this is an English product for it has that look. The color is a good, strong marigold on the jar and lid with only the stubby feet and the lid's finial left in plain glass.

Paneled Rose (Imperial)

Paneled Rose is found only as the exterior pattern on Imperial's Open Rose plates, bowls, and rose bowl. The design consists of large and small panels. The large ones have the Open Rose design repeated, while the smaller ones have a stem of daisy-like flowers and leaves. These panels are separated by a raised vertical line that extends from the collar base to the bordered scalloped edge. I've seen one non-carnival rose bowl that had only this exterior pattern, with the interior plain. It was on an aqua colored glass.

204

Paneled Smocking is credited to U.S. Glass and was made in a basic table service. The only iridized shapes reported are the open sugar shown in the ninth edition and the creamer shown here. Marigold is the only reported color.

Paneled Thistle

This is the first example of a well know pressed glass pattern reported in carnival glass. The compote has a very nice lemon colored iridescence applied over the entire piece. In Crystal, this pattern was made by Higbee in 1910 and later by Dominion of Canada in 1920. Uncertainty remains over which one made this iridized piece, although I lean toward Higbee since other patterns have turned up from that company that were not made in Canada. Thanks to Lance Hilkene for sharing it.

Paneled Tree Trunk

While similar to the Northwood Tree Trunk vase, this scarce and interesting vase has an appeal all its own. The example shown is 7½" tall and has a base diameter of 4⅞". It has eight panels, and the color is a fine amethyst. It is made by Dugan.

Paneled Twigs (Inwald)

Some collectors also call this Inwald pattern Nola. Carnival shapes include a pitcher, tumbler, and a tumble-up set. The color is very rich on most pieces.

Panels and Drapery (Riihimaki)

I located this in a 1939 Riihimaki company catalog. It is listed as their numbers 7201 and 7202, although other shapes are pictured in the same design. Thank to the Hollenbachs for sharing the photo.

Panji Peacock Eye Vase

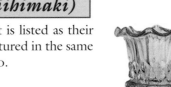

This beautiful vase from India is shaped like many vases from that country. It is found in at least two sizes; the example shown is 8½" tall. The peacock eyes are in the center of the vase with stylized feathering above and below. Thanks to David, Amy, and Camiella Ayers for sharing this and many of the photos in this edition.

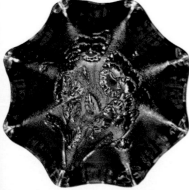

Pansy

The Pansy bowl shown typifies the Imperial quality found in iridized glass. The lustre is outstanding with a gleaming finish. The mould work is superb, enhanced by the very rich gold finish. While the Pansy pattern doesn't bring top dollar, it is a pleasure to own such a beautiful item.

Panther

This interior pattern from the Fenton Art Glass Company is found in large and small berry bowls as well as a centerpiece (ice cream) bowl whimsey. Colors include marigold, amethyst (small bowl), blue, green, aqua, and Nile green (large bowl). The small bowls are also found in red, amberina, clambroth, and lavender, while the centerpiece is found only in blue and marigold. The design is very realistic with two panthers. The exterior is Butterfly and Berry.

Paperchain Candlestick

The photo of this unknown candlestick was supplied by Alan Sedgwick who tells me they show up often in England. The marigold is rich and has a nice darkness to it. Anyone who can tell me more about this pattern is urged to do so. It is shown in an Inwald catalog.

Papini Victoria

Shown in a 1934 Cristalerias Papini (Argentina) catalog, this pattern is known in crystal in large stemmed compotes, bowls, a jelly compote, ice cream bowl, tumbler, banana bowl, handled cup, vase, and the squat pitcher shown. In carnival glass, I've heard of only the pitcher, tumbler, and large stemmed compote, but other shapes may exist. Photo courtesy of Roberto D. Frassinetti of Argentina; information from a Papini catalog.

Park Avenue

Park Avenue was from Federal Glass (#1122) and is found in crystal and gilded glass as well as amber. Shapes include pitchers, tumblers, an ashtray, and bowls.

Parlor Panels (Imperial)

This wonderful vase from Imperial is found in several sizes including squat (4" – 5") and larger (up to 18" tall). Colors are usually very strong and the marigold example shown is no exception.

Parquet

I haven't learned much about this creamer. It isn't from the United States and is probably European. Marigold seems to be the only reported color and the finish is weak. There are four mould lines and the piece measures 3⅝" tall. I am told there is a matching collar based open sugar bowl. Thanks to Wayne Delahoy for the photo.

Passion Flower

A vase very similar to the one shown here is found in a Christalerias Papini catalog, but there are enough differences that I can't place the maker at this time. The coloring is a thin, watery marigold. I'd appreciate any information readers may have about this vase.

Pastel Swan

These very popular master salt holders were made by Northwood, Dugan, and Fenton. They can be found in opalescent glass as well as the iridized versions. The colors are marigold, purple, ice blue, ice green, peach opalescent, celeste blue, amethyst opalescent, and pink. The example shown is a Fenton experimental piece of amber, cobalt, and aqua glass mixed at the end of the day's production.

Patricia

Although similar to Rindskopf's Inverted Prisms, this mustard pot with lid has some differences so I can't confirm it is from that company. At any rate I certainly thank Alan Sedgwick for sharing it and giving it a name.

Patrician

Patrician was named by its owner, Lance Hilkene. In general shape, it resembles Finland's Moth candlestick as well as several from Brockwitz, but I haven't been able to identify the maker.

Peace Lamp

This rarity was named by the owner. It is the only reported example. When assembled it is 16" tall and has an English burner. The design is similar to Riverside's Florentine pattern. I thank Alan Sedgwick for sharing this beautiful lamp with me.

Peach (Northwood)

I am happy to show this spooner in marigold since only it and the tumbler shape have been found in this color at this time. Other shapes include a berry set (cobalt blue or white), table set (white, with the spooner and creamer also known in cobalt blue), and the water set (cobalt blue or white). The white pieces often have a fired-on gilt decoration and some of the blue items are electric in appearance.

Peach and Pear

These large oval bowls were made by Diamond and are usually found in amethyst or marigold. In the ninth edition of this book I showed the first reported cobalt blue bowl, and here is shown the first reported green example. These bowls are usually about 12" in diameter, and I understand they date from about 1925.

Peacock (Millersburg)

Peacock is similar to Millersburg's Peacock and Urn pattern, except it has no bee and no beading on the urn. It is found in large and small berry bowls, large and small ice cream shaped bowls, a small plate, a small proof sauce (missing one of the bird's legs), and whimsey shapes including a banana bowl and a rose bowl shape. Colors are the usual marigold, amethyst, and green on most shapes but the small berry bowl is found in blue and the banana bowl in vaseline. In addition, the large berry bowl is known in a beautiful clambroth, a rare color for Millersburg.

Peacock and Dahlia

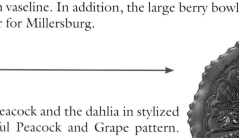

Typically Fenton, this pattern features both a peacock and the dahlia in stylized panels, much like the more plentiful Peacock and Grape pattern. It is found on both bowls (7" – 7½") and plates. Peacock and Dahlia has the Berry and Leaf Circle on the exterior. Colors include marigold, cobalt blue, vaseline, aqua, and white. This was Fenton's #1645 pattern, made in 1912.

Peacock and Grape

Fenton's #1646 pattern from 1911, found in both bowls and plates, is a sister pattern to Peacock and Dahlia. Colors are marigold, blue, green, amethyst, aqua, vaseline, white, red, lavender, and marigold-over-milk-glass. Shown is an odd smoky blue bowl. Thanks to the Remmens for sharing it.

Peacock and Urn (Fenton)

Peacock and Urn was made by Fenton in 1915 in compotes, bowls, and plates. The exterior pattern on the bowls and plates is Bearded Berry and the edges are sawtooth. Colors are many including vivids, pastels, and red. Thanks to Samantha Prince for the lovely 3 in 1 edge bowl photo.

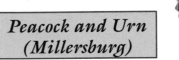

Peacock and Urn (Millersburg)

Millersburg Peacock and Urn differs from the regular Peacock pattern in that it has a bee by the bird's beak. The shapes known are large bowls, small 6½" bowls, a chop plate, and a giant compote in the usual colors of marigold, green, and amethyst.

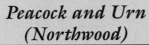

Peacock and Urn (Northwood)

Northwood's version of this pattern can be found on a chop plate (shown in ice green), an ice cream set, a large ruffled bowl, and a small plate. Some pieces are plain and some stippled. Colors include marigold, amethyst, green, blue, white, ice green, ice blue, smoke, lime green, Renninger blue, sapphire blue, and aqua opalescent.

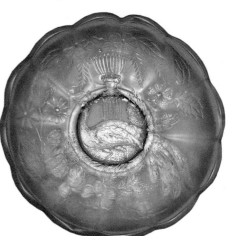

Peacock and Urn Mystery Bowl (Millersburg)

This variation from Millersburg has a larger bee, two rows of beading on the urn, and a "fuller" look to the design. It is found on 8" – 9" bowls that can be ruffled or ice cream shape. The colors are marigold, amethyst, and green.

Peacock and Urn Variant

This variant is found only on the 6" ice cream shaped bowls (so far). This neat little amethyst piece has a bee and the urn has three rows of beads. The exterior has a Flute or Wide Panel design consisting of 12 panels and there is a rayed star base. There are now about eight to ten of these reported but surely more exist.

Peacock at the Fountain

This prolific pattern was made mostly by Northwood. Dugan did make some water sets. It is known on a berry set, water set, table set, punch set, orange bowl, compote, and several whimsey shapes. Colors include marigold, blue, amethyst, green, aqua opalescent, ice blue, ice green, white, lavender, smoke, lime green, horehound, sapphire blue, Renninger blue, iridized custard, and blue opalescent. Shown is the very rare fruit bowl in sapphire. Thanks to the Remmens for sharing it.

Peacock Garden Vase

In addition to the marigold vase previously shown, I'm thrilled to add the rare white (French) opalescent carnival example. There is also a reported white carnival without the opalescence. I believe Northwood made this vase in the 1912 – 1916 era and Fenton began their version in 1933 calling it their #791 and continued it until 1935. Fenton started reproducing the 8" vase in 1971 and in 2006 the 10" mold was found. Both are still being made to this date in many types of glass, both iridized and noniridized. None of the old colors have been reproduced to date, thanks to Fenton.

Peacock Lamp

This beautiful crystal lamp base has an enameled interior and an iridized exterior. Colors are red, marigold, amethyst, smoke, and white, and all are rare. It's 10¼" tall, and sometimes has no hole indicating these were sold as both lamps and vases. Shown is a superb pastel marigold vase, which doesn't have the hole drilled out for lamp production. Thanks to the Remmens for sharing it.

Peacock Proof Sauce (Millsburg)

This unusual Millersburg "mistake" was caused by a mould that wasn't finished, leaving a portion of the bird's legs blank. These sauces are found in both marigold and amethyst and are much prized.

Peacocks (On the Fence)

This is a well-known Northwood pattern made in 1912 in both carnival and opalescent glass. Shapes are bowls or plates that have either a Basketweave or Fine Rib exterior. Colors are many. Pieces may have stippling. Thanks to Peter Baerwald for sharing this emerald green bowl.

Peacock Tail (Fenton)

Peacock Tail was made by Fenton in 1911 (their #409 pattern) in a hat shape, bowls, a bonbon, and 6", 9", and 10½" plates. Colors are marigold, amethyst, green, peach opalescent, amber, and red.

Peacock Tail (Millersburg)

I'm listing this as Millersburg because of several factors. I've compared it to the Millersburg Grape bowl (both 8½" – 9") and other than a different interior pattern both measure the exact same in all areas and were obviously made from the same mould. All of these Peacock Tails have a rayed base with a smooth edge and all have 20 circled loops making up the interior pattern. Fenton examples mostly have 21 loops but some will have 20. Fenton bowls will have a smooth base and either a sawtooth edge or smooth edge. The wide panel exterior of Fenton bowls will arch off near the collar base where this example has a straight line all the way under the collar base. Confusing, but when examined side by side there's no mistaking the difference. Only one green radium example was known until I located a second bowl in Ohio in greenish teal with a satin finish. Also two marigold examples with an odd three in one edge and radium finish have shown up. Both having the "one" part of the three in one edge crimped up (found on no other three in one edge I've seen) instead of down as found in Fenton's three in one and Dugan's three in one edge. I suspect amethyst was made also, but none have been reported to me. Thanks to Casy Rich for the photo.

Peacock Tail and Daisy

I am thrilled to finally show this very scarce Westmoreland bowl pattern. Besides the marigold, there is an amethyst and a blue opal milk glass that isn't iridized, but no other shapes or colors. The pattern is graceful as can be, and the design is very well balanced. It has been reproduced.

209

Peacock Tail Variant

Peacock Tail Variant was made and advertised by Millersburg in 1911. This short-stemmed compote is known in marigold, amethyst, and green. Pieces are nearly always found with a radium finish, and the design is distinctive with a six-petal center, rays of smooth and stippled banding, and rays of feathers.

Peacock Tree

Peacock Tree is also known as Mayuri. This 6" vase is from India and is similar to the Goa type vases. The color is well done. The design shows a peacock on a tree limb with leaves, branches, and blossoms around it. It is quite a nice pattern.

Peacock Variant (Millersburg)

This 7¼" bowl is known as the shotgun bowl by Millersburg collectors. It is normally found with a three-in-one edge, but here we have a very rare marigold six-ruffle example. Colors are marigold, green, amethyst, and blue.

Pearly Dots

This Westmoreland pattern was also known as Coin Dot by many collectors. The Pearly Dots name does separate this pattern from Fenton's Coin Dot pattern. Shapes are bowls, a compote, and a rose bowl. Colors reported are marigold, amethyst, green iridized milk glass, blue iridized milk glass, aqua opalescent, and teal.

Pebble and Fan

Pebble and Fan is now believed to be from Czechoslovakia. This impressive Art Deco stylized vase is over 11" tall and has a base diameter of 4½". It is known in marigold, cobalt blue, vaseline with a marigold iridescence (shown), and a reported amethyst (I haven't seen it yet). Some collectors feel this piece was designed as a lamp base but it is considered a vase by most.

Pebbles

This seldom discussed Fenton pattern is found on small bowls like the one shown or on two-handled bonbons. The exterior has the familiar Honeycomb and Clover pattern. Bowls are known in marigold or green, while the bonbons are found in marigold, amethyst, green, and blue.

Penny and Gentles Plate

At the time of this writing, only this one double-handgrip plate has been reported. It is lettered "Penny and Gentles - Broadway and Morgan." It is high on the list of lettered or advertised rarities and created a stir when it first came to light.

Penny Match Holder

The Penny match holder is now felt to be from the Dugan-Diamond factory. This unique novelty item is found in purple and usually has a fine even iridescence. It measures 3¼" tall and has a base diameter of 3¾". There are six panels around the body that extend from the base to the matchbox holder. The Penny match holder is a scarce and desirable novelty and usually brings a good price at sale. Photo courtesy of Seeck Auction.

Long rated as the top Millersburg rarity, the blue vase shown recently sold for an astronomical sum. The total combined examples reported to date can be counted on both hands with room to spare. All have straight sides except the amethyst ones and they are flared and crimped. Information indicates this vase may have been Millersburg's #70 called a Holland Vase by the factory. The design of children holding hands, dancing on a cobbled street, while elderly gentlemen watch, is a unique one. The vase stands 11½" tall, has a 5½" diameter, and weighs 5 pounds. The colors are marigold, amethyst, green, and blue, all with a vibrant radium finish.

Pepper Plant

This Fenton pattern is very similar to the Holly hat shaped pieces, except this one has berries that have been pulled into peppers and each stem ends in a floral design. These pieces have octagonal bases and at least one amethyst example has advertising on the base that says "GENERAL FURNITURE." Other colors known are green, marigold, and cobalt blue, with a vaseline example reported.

One of Millersburg's premier water sets, the Perfection pattern is just that…perfection. It is found only on the pitcher and tumbler shapes (the bulbous pitcher is 9½" tall, the tumblers 4" tall) in marigold, amethyst, and green. The top of the pitcher may be flared or ruffled. The design is distinct with beaded-edged ovals above veined acanthus leaves.

Persian Garden

This well balanced Dugan and then Diamond pattern is found in large and small bowls, large and small plates, and a fine fruit bowl with separate base. Bowls can be ice cream shape or ruffled and can have either a Pool of Pearls or Big Basketweave exterior. Colors are marigold, amethyst, green, white, blue, lavender, peach opalescent, and the rare pink afterglow. Shown here in a 7" plate. Thanks to the Jerry and Cleo Kudlac for sharing it.

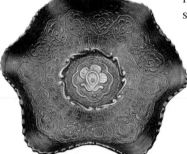

Persian Medallion

Very Oriental in flavor, Persian Medallion is one of those well-known Fenton patterns that was extremely popular when it was made. It is available on bowls of all shapes and sizes, plates both large and small, compotes, rose bowls, even a hair receiver, and a very rare 9½" footed bowl in blue (not to mention interiors on punch sets). Colors are marigold, blue, green, amethyst, white, amber, ice green, black amethyst, clambroth, and red.

Peruvian Pisco Inca Bottle

Here is another variant of the Inca bottles. As you can see, the bottle is round and fat, unlike the other two Inca bottles. It came from Argentina and has labels on the front as well as the back, which read: "HUACO PERUANO" and "PISCO PERUANO ANEJO." This bottle also has embossing on the bottom which reads: "VINA SANT JOSEFA // IND. PERUANA." The color is a nice dark amber and marigold is also known. Many thanks to Adriana Sanchez from Argentina for sharing the photo and information.

This very interesting 10¼" pitcher with a 5" base diameter is from Peru and has a series of stacked rings topped off with a nice enameled decorated section. It has a polished pontil on the bottom and the base color is dark teal, as can be easily seen in the handle. Additional information from anyone would be appreciated. Thanks again to Karen and Allan Rath for sharing the photos from their nice collection.

Petal and Fan

This Dugan pattern is found only in bowls of various sizes with the Jeweled Heart exterior design. The motif itself is simple but attractive — a series of alternating stippled and plain petals on a plain ribbed background with a fan-like design growing from each plain petal. The feeling is almost one of ancient Egypt where such fans were made of feathers. Petal and Fan is available in many colors including peach opalescent.

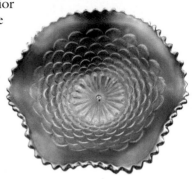

Petaled Flower

Petaled Flower is found on the interior of some Leaf and Beads pieces, just like the Lovely pattern. It shows a plain button center with 23 petals that extend toward the outside of the bowl. This amethyst rose bowl with this interior shows the design quite well. Some pieces are marked and some are not.

Petals (Northwood)

This has always seemed one of Northwood's less sought after patterns. This example shows the interior design well, but remember this is a stemmed compote if you are searching for one. Other colors in this low compote are marigold, amethyst, green, and a rare ice blue. Dugan also made bowls and a banana bowl in a similar pattern in marigold, amethyst, and peach opalescent, but did not copy the low compote shape used by Northwood.

Petals and Prisms

Here is another of those foreign patterns that can be found on several shapes including the collar-based sugar shown. Other shapes known are a stemmed sugar, a creamer, a 9" bowl, and a large (10½") bowl. The stemmed sugar can be upended and used as a base for the larger bowls making a fruit set. The design is all exterior, consisting of incised petals and circles, edged with vertical prism bands.

Peter Rabbit

Fenton's Peter Rabbit is a companion pattern to Coral and to Little Fishes. Bowls and plates come in marigold, amethyst, green, blue, and honey amber.

Pickle Paperweight

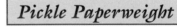

Of all the oddities I've come across in carnival glass, this is probably the oddest of all time. It measures 4½" in length and is hollow. As you can see, it has a superb color and finish. I assume it to be a paperweight for I can think of little else it could be used for. The maker is unknown, and the only color reported is amethyst.

Pillar and Sunburst

Pillar and Sunburst was originally Westmoreland's #25194 patent, and called Elite. The only reported shape in carnival glass until recently was the bowl, but now I've seen two plates in marigold. Colors are marigold and amethyst that tends to have a touch of sienna in the coloring. The pattern is all exterior and the bowls average 8" in diameter.

212

Pillar Flute (Imperial)

Imperial's #682 pattern was made in bowls, a compote (shown), oval pickle dish, square plate, rose bowl, shakers, water set, footed vase, and three-piece console set. Colors are mostly marigold, smoke, and clambroth but here is an amethyst compote. Some pieces have the Iron-Cross trademark. Thanks to Lance Hilkene for the photo.

Pinched Rib

This is actually a variation of Rib and Panel and just why the glassmakers collapsed the sides of these vases remains a mystery to me, but certainly they thought there was a reason, for several sizes exist. Most are found in marigold or peach opalescent glass, and they range in size from 4" tall to over a foot. The one shown has a pretty crimped lip. This one is a Dugan product, but I'm sure other makers had a try at them.

Pinched Swirl (Dugan)

Apparently the earlier production of the art glass lines (Japanese and Venetian) had an influence on this piece of Dugan carnival glass. This rather free-flowing pattern is found in marigold and peach opalescent in the 6½" vase shown, a rose bowl shape, and a rare spittoon whimsey shape. Marigold is scarcer than peach in all shapes in this pattern.

Pineapple (Sowerby)

This Sowerby pattern is also known as Pineapple and Bows or Bows and English Hob. It is found in a creamer, open stemmed sugar, a rose bowl, compote, and large bowl. Colors are marigold, amethyst, and cobalt blue. Thanks to the Ayers family for sharing this piece.

Pineapple and Fan

This pattern has a tray or plate like the Three Diamonds three-piece night set shown elsewhere in this edition. The complete set measures 8" tall. The tray has a diameter of 5⅛" and the tumbler is 3⅝" tall. The bottle alone is 7¼" high. As you can see, the color is very rich marigold. This pattern is also known in wine sets that contain a decanter, tray, and six stemmed wines. I know U.S. Glass made a Pineapple and Fan pattern exactly like this in crystal table pieces but can't be sure if the iridized items are theirs or foreign copies. It is also known in blue.

Pineapple Crown

Pineapple Crown was named by Marian Quintin-Baxendale. The bowl shown has been found in two sizes, the one shown being 8½" x 4" and 2½" tall. It is oval with a light airy color. The mould work is quite good with most of the surface covered with design. The maker is unknown.

Pine Cone

Fenton's Pine Cone is known in 5½" or 7½" bowls and 6 ¼" or 7½" plates. Colors reported are marigold, blue, green, amethyst, lavender (bowl), amber (plate), and teal.

Pinnacle

The owner of this Jain Glass Works tumbler calls it Pyramid but the name used by most collectors is Pinnacle. It is the same size as the Four Suites tumbler, measuring 5½" tall, with a 2¼" base diameter and a 3⅛" top diameter. The design is a typical one for Jain with a band of circles on a squared background and panels of triangles filled with geometric prisms. The rest of the body also has prisms in lines. In addition, there is a vase known in a similar pattern that is called Diamante Stars by some collectors. Pinnacle is found in pale blue with marigold iridescence.

Pin-Ups

This Australian pattern is found on the interior of 8" – 9" marigold and purple (shown) bowls. The exteriors are plain and the only pattern is the series of three pin-like figures grouped together around the bowl.

Pinwheel (Sowerby)

Perhaps the viewer can get a better idea of what this Sowerby pattern looks like with this side-view photo. It is a strong marigold and can be found on bowls or in the rose bowl shape shown. The design is all exterior and is a diamond file pattern that has a mould line about one inch from the base. The base design is a swirl that spins out from the center and seems to collide with the diamond filing.

Pinwheel/Derby (Sowerby)

This pattern is called Derby in Sowerby ads of 1927. It is called Pinwheel in this country despite another Sowerby pattern having that name. It is found in a variety of shapes in crystal. In carnival glass the Derby pattern is found in 6¼" or 8" vases (both shown) in marigold, amethyst, and blue, with black amethyst reported, and a cookie jar, a rose bowl, and a salad bowl. Shown are the rare blue 6½" and 8" vases.

Pipe Holder Ashtray

Thanks to Lance Hilkene, I can now show this novelty that isn't discussed much. It is an ashtray that has a ring to hold the bowl of a pipe. Marigold is the only reported color to date. I have no idea who made it.

Pipe Humidor

Here is a fantastic Millersburg pattern many collectors haven't even seen, because it is just that rare. And what a pity so few of these are around since it is lovely enough to grace any collection. The color and iridescence are exceptional and the design flawless. Imagine how difficult to remove the lid from the mould without damage to the pipe and stem. The humidor is just over 8" tall and measures 5" across the lid. A three-pronged sponge holder is inside the lid, intended of course, to keep the tobacco moist. Around the base is a wreath of acorns and leaves above another leaf-like pattern that runs down the base.

Plaid (Fenton)

Plaid is one of Fenton's more inventive patterns. It seems to gain in popularity each year. Colors include marigold, amethyst, cobalt blue, green, red, and celeste blue in bowl shapes, and marigold, cobalt, and amethyst with red reported in plates. Sometimes the amethyst examples are a light and airy lavender.

Plain and Fancy (Heisey)

While I am reasonably convinced Heisey did not iridize glass, this is their pattern, iridized. The pitcher stands 7¼" tall with a clear applied handle. The tumbler is 4" tall. Both have interior shallow panels and the only decoration is the factory engraving near the top of each piece. The finish, like most pieces of Heisey that have been iridized, is very soft and delicate.

214

Plain Coin Dot (Fenton)

Fenton Coin Dot bowls and rose bowls, for the most part, have stippled dots, but this variant, shown in a 1909 Butler Brothers ad with other Fenton patterns, has plain dots! Yes, I own an amethyst rose bowl with stippling in exactly the same shape with edging of arc and point. They both measure 3½" tall and are 6½" across with a 3¼" marie. The pattern is all interior. Just why the variation, it is hard to say but here it is.

Plain Jane (Imperial)

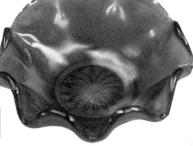

This pattern is just what the name implies. The only design is in the marie where an 18-point star is present. It is found in a handled basket as well as in 5", 7", 9", and 12" bowls. Colors are marigold and smoke in the bowls and the basket can be found in marigold, smoke, aqua, white, and ice green. The rims of the bowls can be serrated or smooth, as shown, and the small 5" bowls have a 16-point star.

Plain Jane Basket

Long credited to the Imperial Company, this large basket, while rather plain, has great appeal. It has been seen in smoke as well as marigold, and measures 9¼" to the top of the handle.

Plain Petals

Here is a pattern seldom discussed, yet it is found as the interior design of some pieces of Leaf and Beads. It is my opinion that Leaf and Beads was made by both Northwood and Dugan, and these pieces with the Plain Petals interior as well as the famous rose bowl are Northwood. The example shown is on a very interesting leaf-shaped nappy.

Plain Pilsner

This stemmed pilsner glass is 6" tall and has a top diameter of 2". It is entirely without pattern but has a nice dark marigold color and the iridescence is very good. Surely it came along late in the carnival timeframe but it is a step above the Depression era glass.

Pleats

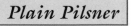

Marion Quintin-Baxendale shows a drawing of this bowl in her *Collecting Carnival Glass* book but I can offer no information about the maker. I believe it is European but have no proof and it may well be known by another name by European collectors. I'd appreciate any information from readers. It is found in shallow bowls and the rose bowl shown.

Plume Panels (Fenton)

While Fenton made this vase about 1912, there was an earlier vase made in opalescent glass that was a near twin called Inverted Chevron. Plume Panel vases can be found in sizes that range from 6" to 12" tall. Colors are marigold, amethyst, green, cobalt blue, white, and red. There are six panels of plumes with plain banding between them.

Plume Panels and Bows

I showed the tumbler in this pattern previously and here we have the pitcher and goblets that made up the stemmed water set. The pattern is from Brockwitz I suspect.

Quill

While both the marigold and purple pieces in this pattern are rare and desirable, the latter is more difficult to find. The pitcher is 10" tall with a base diameter of 4½", and the tumblers are standard size with a slight flare below the ribbon top. The pitcher flares from the neck to the base in a graceful swoop and is very pretty. The Quill pattern came from Dugan who made a similar pattern called Waving Quill in other types of glass.

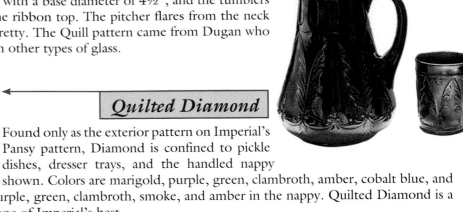

Quilted Diamond

Found only as the exterior pattern on Imperial's Pansy pattern, Diamond is confined to pickle dishes, dresser trays, and the handled nappy shown. Colors are marigold, purple, green, clambroth, amber, cobalt blue, and ice blue in the pickle dish, and marigold, purple, green, clambroth, smoke, and amber in the nappy. Quilted Diamond is a well-conceived, very attractive pattern and one of Imperial's best.

Quilted Rose

I have no idea who made this 5⅛" bowl but suspect that it is European. The color is a soft amberish marigold. Thanks to Wayne Delahoy for the photo.

Quorm Mug

This mug, like the Mt. Gambier mug and the #110 mugs, is lettered "Greetings from Quoran." It is 3⅜" tall. There may be other mugs with different lettering, so be on the lookout. All are from Australia.

Radiance

Radiance was from Riverside Glass (their X-Ray pattern as #462) and was first produced in 1896 in crystal. Several pieces were later made with marigold stain and enameling. Shapes include a table set, water set, toothpick holder, goblet, shakers, berry set, 7" bowl, cruet, open and covered compotes, a jelly compote, tray, vase, water carafe, plate, cake salver, ice cream set, mustard jar, and a breakfast set.

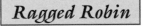

Ragged Robin

Only a bowl shape has been reported in this pattern from the Fenton Company. The design is one of a center flower and a ring of outer flowers. Bowls are about 8" in diameter and have a three-in-one edge. Colors known are marigold, amethyst, blue, green, and white (at least one white bowl surfaced briefly in the early 1980s and company records seem to indicate the existence of this color).

Rainbow (McKee)

Besides the whiskey tumbler shown, there is a champagne tumbler (3⅜" tall) found in iridized glass. It bears an enameled line saying "Souvenir of Columbus, Ohio." Both pieces are from McKee Glass in a soft marigold. The design has four cane panels, ¾" wide, separated by concave flute panels that arch above the top of the cane. All pieces are scarce.

Rainbow (Northwood)

Rainbow is completely plain with iridescence on the inside only. It is similar to the Northwood Raspberry compote or the one with only a Basketweave exterior. The lustre swirls around the glass in layers, just like a rainbow, thus the name.

Rainbow Opaque (Northwood)

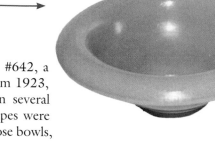

The bowl shown is listed as Northwood's #642, a 7½" bowl with a retourne rim. Dating from 1923, this line of iridized opaque glass came in several bright new colors including ivory, coral, and the jade blue shown. Shapes were candlesticks of all sizes, console bowls, covered candy dishes, compotes, rose bowls, and stemmed bowls.

Raindrops

This Dugan pattern is scarce in any color. It is mostly found in peach opalescent glass. Fine purple items exist as shown, and they are a find. The bowls are on a dome base and the exterior carries a pattern called Keyhole. Bowls can be ruffled or three-in-one edge and are known in round or banana boat shapes.

Rambler Rose

Rambler Rose was made by Diamond after 1914. It is found on pitchers and tumblers only in marigold, amethyst, and cobalt blue, and green has been reported. The pattern looks good on the tumblers but the water pitchers seem to lack any punch and only the cobalt blue ones create any great interest. This pattern has been reproduced, so buy with caution.

Randy

This 13" tall vase has applied glass ribboning called rigoree running up the sides. At this time I can't verify the age or place of origin of this piece but it has the look of fine, old glass from Europe. I'd appreciate any information readers can share about this pattern.

Ranger

Ranger was first made by Imperial in 1909, then by others including Inwald, Christales de Mexico, and even Crystal Glass of Australia. This well-known pattern is found in many shapes in crystal. In carnival glass, there are various size bowls, a table set, water set, sherbet, footed vase, and a two-handled cookie jar (sometimes called a candy jar) labeled as their #711. Colors are marigold and clambroth.

Raspberry

Besides the water set and the milk pitcher (shown) in this Northwood pattern, there is a footed piece, sometimes called an "occasional piece," gravy boat, or creamer. Colors are normally marigold, amethyst, green, blue, or pastels for the pitchers and tumblers. Thanks to the Remmens for the photo.

Rays (Dugan)

The Rays pattern from the Dugan-Diamond Company has several distinctions and this beautifully decorated bride's basket piece shows most of them. First, the rays stop short of the center and are smooth, not stippled as in other companies' patterns. Secondly, most pieces are found on peach opalescent glass, a Dugan-Diamond staple color. Shapes include large and small bowls, a scarce 6¼" plate, and the bride's basket. Pieces may have a plain exterior or have a Jeweled Heart pattern. Other reported colors are marigold, amethyst, and green.

225

Rays and Ribbon

Each of the makers of carnival glass seems to have had a try at a pattern using stippled rays. The Millersburg version is quite distinctive because of the ribbon-like border resembling a fleur-de-lis design. Most of the bowls do not have a radium finish and usually carry the Cactus pattern on the exterior. Occasionally a plate is found in Rays and Ribbons, but one wonders if this were not produced as a shallow bowl. Amethyst is the usual color, followed by green, marigold, and vaseline in that order.

Regal Cane

This allover Brockwitz pattern is known in a water set, tray, cordials, ashtray, and the clock shown. This clock was in Argentina and has a dial face that reads "Tienda, El Gauncho, Mar Del Plata." Obviously the clock was shipped from Germany and the mechanics were added in Argentina. Thanks to the Vandevanders for allowing me to photograph this nice item.

Regal Flower

Ever since I found this vase, then parted with it, I wish I hadn't. The vase stands nearly 14" tall and the color blends from a clear to slightly green base to a very rich marigold at the top. The enameling is very fine, much like several Dugan items that have surfaced in an experimental line that dates from 1905 to 1910. A quick comparison of this enameling and that on the standard pieces in carnival glass reveals striking superiority.

Regal Iris

Credited to the Consolidated Company, this very fine Gone-with-the-Wind lamp is one of the best of this style lamp in carnival glass. It is known in marigold on milk glass, red carnival, and the beautiful caramel color shown. It has been reproduced in aqua opalescent, cranberry, and red, so be aware of what you are buying.

Regal Rose

If you look closely you will see this is Imperial's Ripple vase with enameled roses and leaves. It is purple, stands 9¾" tall, and has a 2¾" base diameter. The vase was purchased in England and is now in Canada. I am indebted to Nigel Gamble for sharing this beauty.

Reindeer

This dome-based tumbler was found in Australia, but is marked "Made in Germany." It is a late glass product. In design, it matches the Bird-in-the-Bush tumbler shown elsewhere. Both photos are from Bob Smith. Reindeer shows a running deer with tall branches of flora and leaves below and at each side of the animal.

Rekord

This beautiful pattern by Eda can be found on the 8" vase shown, as well as a bowl. All pieces found so far are cobalt blue. Thanks to the Remmens for sharing it. The pattern is also known as Diamond Wedges.

Rex

Despite the McKee credit by Marion Hartung, this pattern probably came later than her 1912 date. Only marigold pitchers and tumblers are reported in carnival. I welcome any information about this pattern.

Rex was shown in Eda Glass Works' 1929 catalog. It is shown here courtesy of Siegmar Geiselberger. This vase shape came in at least three sizes and can have a straight top, a rolled and flared top, or just be flared. Colors are cobalt blue, marigold, and an iridized milk glass that is called Pearl.

Rib and Flute

This vase is 12¼" tall and has a 32-rayed base with a diameter of 3⅞". It is named for the two main sections of design. This vase has a Dugan look but I have no evidence it is from that company. I'd appreciate any information readers may have about this pattern.

Rib and Panel

Information on this pattern is very sparse although some feel it is Imperial. I do know it was made in a spittoon whimsey and the vase shape shown. In 1915 Fenton made a similar pattern called Rib Optic but I have no proof it was ever iridized or that this is the same pattern. All pieces reported in Rib and Panel have a pontil mark, all came in marigold but have been rumored in peach opalescent and amethyst.

Ribbed Band and Scales

While I haven't confirmed the origin of this pattern, most examples have been found in Argentina and a pitcher recently surfaced from there as well as the tumbler shown in previous editions. Both are marked on the base "N.C.P." indicating they may well be from Christalerias Papini. I'd appreciate any additional information on this piece.

Ribbed Ellipse (Higbee)

Ribbed Ellipse was made by the J.B. Higbee Company in 1905 in crystal. This pattern was available in an extended table service including a cake plate, tumbler, plate, bowls, a compote, and the mug. Only the mug seems to have shown up in carnival glass. It is of an amber-toned marigold with fine iridescence. Ribbed Ellipse is also known as Admiral by crystal collectors.

Ribbed Panels

In the eighth edition, I showed the single silver-framed pot. Here is the double-frame holder with center lily. All pieces have an inside ribbing and ground bottoms. Vaseline Glass specialist, Dave Peterson informs me that these are almost certainly from the Stourbridge region of England, before or around 1920. Thanks to Dave for his input on this pattern and also to Wayne Delahoy for the photo.

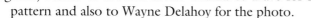

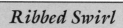

Ribbed Swirl

This very pretty tumbler stands about 3¾" tall and has 24 swirls circling the outside like the stripes on a barber pole. It shows absolutely superb color and iridescence. While this tumbler had been reported in green only, the marigold shown is confirmed at this time.

Ribbed Tornado (Northwood)

Ribbed Tornado is like the regular Tornado vase except for the addition of ribs. This variation is very rare, especially in ice blue. Other colors known in the ribbed version are marigold, amethyst, cobalt blue, and white. Please notice that the base is on this version slightly different from the whimsey in lavender previously shown (see the fifth edition).

Ribbons and Leaves

I've known about this pattern for years, but this is the first example I've been able to show. It is an open sugar made by Sowerby, I believe. It measures 6½" across the handles and 2¼" tall. The ribboning and binding around the rim are unique.

Ribbon Swirl

From Alan Sedgwick, this beautiful stemmed cake plate is probably European (the maker hasn't been reported as far as I know) and Alan believes it may well be from Belgium. The amber color is very rich and dark with superb iridescence.

Ribbon Tie (Fenton)

This Fenton pattern, also called Comet by some collectors, came about in 1911. It is found on large bowls and plates. Colors are the usual marigold, amethyst, green, and blue, but bowls are known in red and smoky blue, and plates are found in black amethyst. Shapes in bowls are generally a three-in-one edge or ice cream shape.

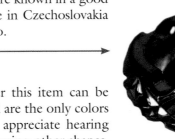

Ribs (Small Basket)

When only the soap dish shape was known this pattern was called Small Basket. Now a complete dresser set consisting of a tumbler, ring tree, puff box, three perfumes, a bud vase, and the soap dish are known in a good marigold. This set was made in Czechoslovakia and has paper labels saying so.

Riihimaki Star

Thanks to catalogs from Siegmar Geiselberger this item can be found as Riihimaki's #5706. Blue and marigold are the only colors I've seen to date but others are possible. I'd appreciate hearing additional information anyone may have concerning other shapes, and do apologize if another name has been established for this pattern. Thanks to Kris and Debra Remmen for the nice photo.

Riihimaki Tumbler

If there are other shapes in this pattern, I'd certainly like to hear about them from anyone. Here is one of the two reported tumbler shapes known in cobalt blue. The pattern was named for the company who made it. And in case there is any doubt about that, it is clearly marked on the base: "Riihimaki." I suspect it was made in marigold as well, but have no proof.

Rindskopf

While the information I was given about this vase being Rindskopf #1716 differs from the example shown in the Rindskopf catalog, it is still believed that this vase came from that maker. I urge anyone with information about this piece to contact me.

Rings

This 1927 Hocking Glass pattern is also known as Banded Rings. It was made mostly in Depression colors. In iridized glass, only the vase shown in previous editions and this covered cookie jar are known.

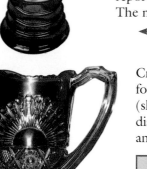

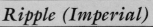

Ripple (Imperial)

This prolific Imperial vase pattern comes in five different moulds in heights from 4½" to 22". Colors range from vivid to pastel. Shown is a dark amber example with stunning iridization.

Rising Comet

This vase is distinguished by the band of threading above the wide paneled base with inverted rays leading to a ring of five-pointed stars above it. It has been reported in three sizes (6", 8", and 10"). Marigold is the only color confirmed. The maker is unknown at this time.

Rising Sun

Credited to U.S. Glass (their #15110 Sunshine pattern), Rising Sun is found in iridized pitchers (pedestal water pitcher), dome-footed juice pitcher (shown), tumbler, juice tumbler, serving tray, covered butter dish, creamer, sugar, and small bowls. Colors are marigold and cobalt blue.

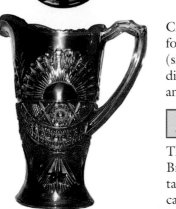

River Glass

This flute or wide panel pattern was shown in a 1910 Butler Brothers catalog. It is mostly found in crystal in berry sets, a table set, water set, oil bottle, and the celery vase (shown). In carnival glass only 2 sizes of bowls and the celery vase have been reported. The name comes from stories about this glass being used on the Ohio River by boats in the early 1900s. Some feel that Millersburg is the maker.

Riverside's Florentine

Riverside Glass's 1906 Floretine pattern (the same pattern as the Wild Rose syrup) is found in crystal, gilded crystal, green, or milk glass as well as iridized items in marigold and green. Shapes in carnival glass include the Wild Rose syrup (shown elsewhere in this book), a water set, a berry set, and a table set. Thanks to the Hilkenes for sharing this 8½" berry bowl.

Roaring Twenties

This powder jar was produced in the 1920s as part of a dresser set. The lid is made of celluloid with a gold decoration. The marigold hexagonal base has iridization that is quite good. It is marked with the Cambridge Glass trademark of a C-inside-a-triangle. Thanks to Roger Bufler for sharing this find.

Robin

Robin was made by Imperial (their #670 pattern) and was reproduced in the 1950s. It is found only in a water set and a mug shape. The mug is known in marigold, smoke, and light green, and here for the first time is an old smoke pitcher and matching tumbler. New items are marked "IG" and are found in strange colors like white, red, pink, and blue. Thanks to Jess Harper for sharing this find.

229

Rococo

Rococo was made by Imperial in 1909 in many shapes in crystal. The carnival version of this #248½ pattern is found in a 9" bowl, a 5" bowl, and a ruffled candy dish from the small bowl, as well as the vase shape shown (also from the small bowl mould). All pieces have a dome base. The colors in iridized glass are marigold, smoke, lavender (vase), and a rare vaseline (candy dish). Carnival pieces date to 1910 or 1911.

Roll

This pattern really has no design other than the rolling shape of the glass itself. It is found in pitchers, tumblers (sometimes with a black banded rim), a cordial set with decanter and six glasses, and salt shakers. The tankard pitcher stands 10" tall and looks as if it may have once had a lid. The tumblers are 4" tall. The colors seen are marigold and clambroth, usually quite good.

Rolled Band

I showed the blue trimmed tumbler in the last edition and here is the complete water set without the blue trim. It comes from Czechoslovakia. Notice the pitcher has a lid.

Rolled Ribs

Rolled Ribs is apparently a part of the New Martinsville line called Muranese. This very beautiful bowl has striking marigold iridescence on the outer half of the rim and then turns to a milky opalescence. Muranese ware came in a host of shapes and finishes. One color is known as New Martinsville Peachblow. Only some of the finishes were iridized. Production was from 1904 to 1907 with the iridized pieces near the end of production.

Rolling Ridges

I've been able to learn virtually nothing about this late carnival glass tumbler. But as you can see it has very good iridescence and deserves to be seen. If anyone can shed some light on this pattern, please let me know. Surely a pitcher was made to match.

Roly-Poly

The covered jar shown stands 7" tall and the name seems appropriate. It is, of course, late carnival glass that shows very little imagination, but the color is fair. There were probably other pieces shaped like this but I don't recall them.

Roman Rosette Goblet

While this pattern is not difficult to find in pressed glass, this is the only reported item in iridized glass to the best of my knowledge. As you can see, it is slightly crooked, but the iridization on the clear glass is unmistakable with beautiful blue and pink coloring. It measures 6" tall and has a base diameter of 2¾".

Rood's Chocolates

Here is one of the few reported examples of this rare plate and it is about as plain as an advertising piece can get. Only the lettering: "Rood's Chocolates – Pueblo" runs through the center of the plate (much like the Broecker's Flour and the Ballard pieces). Nonetheless, it is quite desirable and brings a sizable price when sold.

Rooster Ashtray

I have very little information about this scarce ashtray and certainly welcome any information. Thanks to David and Amy Ayers for sharing the photo.

Rosalind (Millersburg)

This pattern is found on the interior of the famous Dolphin compote, large bowls, medium bowls (rare), small bowls, a 9" plate, a 6" compote, and a tall jelly compote. Colors are marigold, amethyst, green, and an aqua (10" bowl only). Bowls can be ruffled or ice cream shape. Prices are consistent with the compotes and the plate (green or amethyst) in demand. Photo courtesy of Seeck Auction.

Rosalind Variant

While most collectors feel this is a Millersburg variant of the Rosalind pattern, some do not. It is found on a compote that is very similar to Fenton's Peacock Tail compote but there are distinct differences. The Rosalind Variant is found only on green and amethyst so far (I expect a marigold will eventually turn up).

Rose and Fishnet

Like the Primrose and Fishnet vase shown elsewhere, this one was also made by Imperial in crystal, goofus glass, and red carnival. The floral design is on only one side. These vases measure about 6" in height.

Rose Ann Shade

Rose Presznick named this shade and says it can also be found in other treatments including goofus glass. The one shown is a very rich marigold with good iridescence. There are four panels of design around the piece and the bell is slightly curved inward.

Rose Band

This pattern is shown in the 1931 Brockwitz catalog in many shapes in crystal, and is known as Ariadne. It is found in the tumbler shown in marigold. It is a relatively short tumbler measuring 3¾" tall. Surely other pieces were iridized and I suspect blue was possibly made.

Rose Bouquet (Fenton)

This rare Fenton bonbon is similar in design to Northwood's Rose Wreath bonbon (called Basket of Roses), but the Fenton version has a center rose in the design. The exterior is plain like many other patterns in this shape from Fenton. Notice the roses fill each corner, with vining and leaves between. So far it has only been found in white, and reported in marigold.

Rose Column (Millersburg)

This handsome vase Millersburg is a mould blown and stands 10" tall with a 5" diameter. Colors are marigold, amethyst, green, blue (very rare), and aqua that is really more teal. In addition, there is one amethyst example with decorated leaves and flowers. All colors are considered rather rare with the green most often seen.

Rose Garden

Rose Garden was made by both Brockwitz and Eda of Sweden (this pitcher is believed to be from Brockwitz). This is one of the more appreciated patterns that isn't American made. Colors are marigold and cobalt blue and shapes known include a covered butter dish, rose bowls in two sizes, a columnar or round vase, and oval vases that have been traced to Eda.

Rose Garden (Sweden)

This version of the Rose Garden pattern is shown in Eda catalogs. This an oval vase is found in both marigold and cobalt blue in three sizes. It is also called Rosor by European collectors. Only time will tell just which shapes of this pattern can be credited to which maker.

Rose in Swirl

I have no idea of the maker or age of this compote. It looks a bit like late art glass. The design is composed of diagonal swirls with a single rose with a stem going around the vase. The color is marigold. Any information is appreciated. Thanks to Mickey Reichel for sharing the photo.

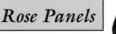

Rose Panels

There seems to be some question among collectors concerning the origin of this pattern (which was once considered to be from Australia). Since the last edition of this book I have received many additional factory catalogs of various glass makers from around the globe and these may provide solid information for future editions. As for now, it will have to remain "maker uncertain."

Rose Pinwheel

This 9" mystery bowl is found in marigold, green, and amethyst shown. The design is much like Imperial's Acanthus, but it has five roses at the edges and a puffed look like the Roses and Greek Key plates shown elsewhere. The maker is unknown at this time.

Rose Powder Jar

This attractive powder jar is very distinctive. It is a rich even marigold with the design highly raised. The maker is unknown at this time. Thanks to Alan Sedgwick for this fine item.

Roses and Fruit

This scarce stemmed bonbon from Millersburg is a collectors' favorite. It measures 5½" from handle to handle and is nearly 4" tall. The interior design is one of a pear, berries, leaves, and gooseberries, with a wreath of roses, stems, and leaves around the outer edges. Colors are marigold, amethyst, green, and a very rare cobalt blue.

Roses and Greek Key

Most collectors call this a "square plate," but whatever you call it, just add rare to the description. The example shown has a smoky-amber color and there is also a marigold example known. They measure about 8½" across or 10" from corner to corner. The design is a beautiful border of puffed roses, with the center holding bands of Greek key design. These bands are also on the exterior where the roses are hollow, much like those on the Rose Show pieces. The maker is unknown at this time.

Roses and Ruffles Lamp (Red)

I'm frankly not too taken with Gone with the Wind lamps, but the beautifully iridized ones are in a class by themselves. The very few known are simply beautiful. The Roses and Ruffles lamp is 22" tall. It has excellent fittings of brass and is quality all the way. The mould work on the glass is quite beautiful and the lustre superior.

Rose Show

What a handsome piece of glass this is! The design is flawless, heavy, and covering every inch of available space. Yet it isn't in the least bit busy looking. One has the distinct feeling he is looking into a reeded basket of fresh-cut roses and can almost smell the perfume. This beautiful pattern, found only on bowls and a plate, was produced in small amounts in marigold, purple, blue, green, white, ice blue, ice green, peach opalescent, amber, aqua opalescent, and a rare ice green opalescent.

Rose Show Variant

One has to wonder why glassmakers went to all the trouble of making variants. Even if they had to replace moulds, one would think they'd simply duplicate the successful one. The variant has a different arrangement of the roses and leaves, and a sawtooth edge. The glass is much thinner, and the pattern is less defined. Perhaps, as some have suggested, they were made for a different market. At any rate, the variant is found on bowls and plates in marigold, cobalt blue, that ever-puzzling color called Renninger blue, and the rare amethyst shown.

Rose Spray (Fenton)

Made in opalescent glass as well as iridized glass, this poorly done Fenton stemmed pattern has a faint design of rose, stem, and leaves along the upper edge of one side of the bowl, near the top. In opalescent glass and custard, this same pattern was used on a mug shape but I haven't seen one of these in carnival glass. Colors for the compote or goblet in iridized glass are white, ice green (florentine), celeste blue, as well as the marigold shown. The compotes measure approximately 4½" tall and the goblet shape is 5".

Rose Sprig Miniature Loving Cup

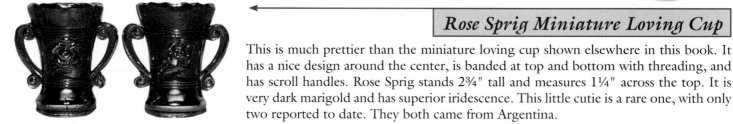

This is much prettier than the miniature loving cup shown elsewhere in this book. It has a nice design around the center, is banded at top and bottom with threading, and has scroll handles. Rose Sprig stands 2¾" tall and measures 1¼" across the top. It is very dark marigold and has superior iridescence. This little cutie is a rare one, with only two reported to date. They both came from Argentina.

Rose Tree

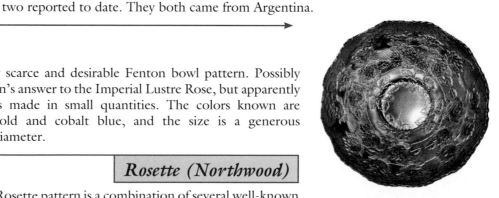

Make no mistake about it, this is a very scarce and desirable Fenton bowl pattern. Possibly Fenton's answer to the Imperial Lustre Rose, but apparently it was made in small quantities. The colors known are marigold and cobalt blue, and the size is a generous 10" diameter.

Rosette (Northwood)

The Rosette pattern is a combination of several well-known designs including Stippled Rays, Prisms, and Beads and Daisies. It is found as the interior pattern of 8" – 9" footed bowls. The exterior pattern is Ruffles and Rings, a pattern first made by Jefferson Glass (Northwood bought the mould). Colors are marigold, amethyst, blue, and green, with blue being quite rare. In addition, I've seen an example on black amethyst glass. Shown is a green example with fine bronze lustre.

Rose Windows (Fostoria)

This is a Fostoria pattern, made in the 1909 – 1922 era of production. The pitcher was made in crystal in gallon, half-gallon, and one-quart sizes. Both the half-gallon pitcher and tumbler were iridized in marigold and a flash-lustered version and the tumbler has been found advertising: "Wm Oberdalhoff – Baltimore, Md." Two of these advertising pieces have been reported.

Round-Up

Round Up was made by Dugan Glass in about 1910. This well-structured pattern is found on a 9" plate and on 8" – 9" ice cream shape, ruffled, or three-in-one bowls. Colors are marigold, amethyst, cobalt blue, white, peach opalescent, and a reddish amethyst called oxblood. The exterior carries the Big Basketweave pattern.

Royal Diamonds

I have no specific information on this tumbler other than to speculate that it is probably European. The tumbler has a plain 1" band at the top followed by a covering of diamonds continuing to the bottom. The color is an average marigold. Thanks to Lance Hilkene for supplying me the name and the photo.

Royal Pineapple

Please compare this attractive 8" vase to the photo of the Thistle vase shown elsewhere in this edition and you will see a remarkable similarity. The Royal Pineapple has a neat crowning edge around the top and while the color isn't great, the iridescence is good. These vases were found in the 1930s – 1940s in crystal also, mostly in florist shops.

Royal Swans (Sowerby)

In the eighth edition of this book I showed the amethyst version of these rare salt dips, and here is the marigold example. It was made by Sowerby (their #1326) in 1882 in Queen's Ware, Malachite, and Blanc de Lait. The only two carnival pieces came along later. The marigold version is in Australia.

Royalty

One might mistake this for the Fashion pattern at first glance, but with a little concentrated study it becomes obvious they aren't the same. Royalty is an Imperial pattern formed from a series of hobstars above a series of diamond panels. It is found on punch sets and two-piece fruit bowls, mostly in marigold, but the fruit bowl set has been found in smoke.

Ruffled Ribs

This piece of glass is a mystery in some ways and some collectors question its origin. The top can be ruffled, square-rolled, tri-cornered with a roll, or candy-ribbon edged. It is mostly found in marigold but can also be found in green, amethyst, and a rare aqua opalescent. The maker is uncertain at this time.

Ruffles and Rings

Originally a Jefferson Glass pattern, this mould was purchased by Northwood and used in carnival as a secondary pattern (Rosette). Jefferson made this pattern in mostly opalescent glass or crystal.

Rustic

Fenton's #517 pattern is found on vases with three base sizes. The pattern has 11" rows of hobs with 21 in each row. Vases can be as short as 9" and as tall as 21". Shown is a huge "plunger base" funeral vase (plunger bases are recessed immediately above the actual base).

Rustic Variant

If you examine the regular Rustic vase (Fenton's #517) and compare it with this, their #507 pattern, you will see this vase has nine rows of hobs while the Rustic has 11. The Rustic Variant is made in the usual colors but here I show a rare peach opalescent example. Do not confuse this with the Hobnail Variant vase shown elsewhere in this edition.

Sacic Ashtray

This small ashtray from Argentina reads "NARANJA SACIC POMELO" which is an advertisement for a fruit drink. The ashtray is of solid glass with a flat base and has three notches around the rim to hold cigarettes. The finish is a deep, dark marigold with good iridescence.

Sacic Bottle

This bottle, similar in shape to the Canada Dry bottle, has "S.A.C.I.C." embossed at the base of the neck and around the bottom outer edge it has "INDUSTRIA ARGENTINA CONTINEDO 260CM3," with the "3" in superscript to represent cubic centimeters. On the bottom you have a triangle with a "7" at the top point, "C" at the left point, and a "R" at the right point, then below the triangle near the outer edge are the numbers, "6283." It is made by Christalerias Rigolleau of Buenos Aires, Argentina. The color is a rich marigold. Thanks to Wayne Delahoy for sharing the information and photo.

Sailboat

Fenton made the Sailboat (#1774) in 5½" bowls, 6¼" plates, a compote, a wine goblet, and the water goblet shown. Colors are marigold, amethyst, cobalt blue, green, amber, vaseline, aqua, red, amberina, and lavender. Not all shapes can be found in all colors, and only the bowl is known in red. The plate is rare in cobalt blue and the water goblet is rare in cobalt blue and the green shown.

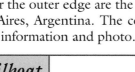

Sailboat Variant

If you compare the Sailboat wine glass in blue here with the regular example shown elsewhere in this book, you will see several differences. The variant has a smooth texture on the swirled base, one tree between the mountains instead of two, a half moon in the sky, and differences in the palm trees, the waves of the lake, and the ship's sails. Finally, on the variant there is no filler pattern just above the stem like the one that circles the regular piece.

Sansara

This tumbler from India somewhat resembles the Shalimar tumbler but with the two primary designs reversed. The top is clear, as are many tumblers from Jain. The base has a wheel design of six segments with a dot in each segment. Thanks to Andres Neveu for this tumbler.

San Telmos

The pattern name is appropriate for this nice ashtray, since it was found in San Telmos, Argentina, at a flea market. The prisms are similar to the Inverted Prisms pattern. I have no information that the two were made at the same company, but doubt it since the latter is documented in Rindskopf catalogs in many shapes. The color is marigold. Thanks to the Hilkenes for naming it and sharing the photo.

Sarita

Tumbler production in India seems overwhelming. Here is another pattern furnished to me by Vikram Bachhawat. It stands 4" tall and features a combination of two designs. It is also known as Anna Eve.

Savanna's Lily Epergne

These single-lily epergnes have matching silver stands and are a very rich marigold with a satin finish, giving them a jewelry store look. They are courtesy of Connie Wilson.

Sawtooth Band

Sawtooth Band is from Heisey and is often called just Band. This pattern is rather plentiful in crystal but carnival pieces are much scarcer. The pitcher is even harder to find than the tumblers. I am grateful to Bernie and Janice Maxfield for sharing the complete set with me.

Sawtoothed Honeycomb

This pattern, first made by Steiner Glass and then Union Stopper in 1906, is well known in crystal and ruby stained crystal, but this is the first piece of carnival glass I've heard about. It is a 7½" pickle dish in a strong marigold. Over the years, the pattern has acquired other names including Chickenwire, Loop Radiant, and Serrated Block.

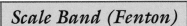

Scale Band (Fenton)

Fenton's #212 pattern was made from 1908 to 1924. It can be found in marigold and cobalt blue water sets (with rare green tumblers); a 6" marigold, red, white, and a rare peach opalescent bowl; a scarce 8" – 10" marigold and cobalt blue bowl; and a dome or collar based marigold, red, white, and vaseline 6½" plate. A rare pitcher in vaseline has been reported, as has a very rare small aqua opalescent bowl but I haven't seen either of these to verify them.

Scales

This Westmoreland pattern is sometimes confused with the Honeycomb as well as Fishscales & Beads pattern by Dugan. Westmoreland pieces are small bowls, 8" – 9" bowls, 6" and 8½" plates, and a banana bowl whimsey that was pulled from the small bowl. Colors are marigold, amethyst, lavender, peach opalescent, marigold on milk glass, teal, blue opalescent, and iridized moonstone.

Scarab Paperweight

I have no information on this very well done paperweight, other than the color is amber. The center scarab is connected by four diamonds, which are then connected to a band encircling the piece. This leaded stained glass style piece is rather large, coming in at somewhere around 5" by 7". I'd appreciate any additional information anyone may have on this item.

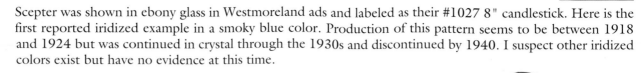

Scepter

Scepter was shown in ebony glass in Westmoreland ads and labeled as their #1027 8" candlestick. Here is the first reported iridized example in a smoky blue color. Production of this pattern seems to be between 1918 and 1924 but was continued in crystal through the 1930s and discontinued by 1940. I suspect other iridized colors exist but have no evidence at this time.

Scotch Thistle

This very pretty compote pattern is rarely discussed by collectors and seldom seems to come up for sale, although price remains low for such a scarce pattern. It was made by the Fenton Art Glass Company in the 1911 – 1912 era, has a plain exterior, and stands approximately 5½" tall. The ruffling is usually very pronounced, as on the scarce green example shown, often making the piece seem almost top heavy. Marigold and cobalt blue are most often seen and the amethyst and green ones are a bit hard to find.

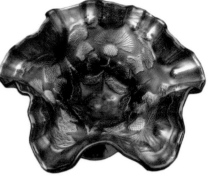

Scottie

Surely there isn't a collector that hasn't seen these covered powder jars in the flea markets with Scotties, poodles, deer, ducks, or rabbits. They are all marigold, and made near the end of the carnival glass heyday. Still the color is usually respectable, and they are cute little critters.

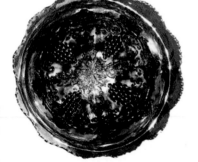

Scroll and Flower Panels

This pattern (#480) from Imperial Glass is rather scarce despite being reproduced in the 1960s. The vase is 10" tall. Colors are marigold and purple as well as the rare smoke example shown. New pieces have the "IG" mark.

Scroll and Grape (Millersburg)

First reported in 1987, this beautiful Millersburg test pattern was found only once, on the interior of an amethyst Multi-Fruits and Flowers punch bowl. The design is one of the best things ever from the Millersburg factory, where a reputation was built on fine design. From the center, four groups of acanthus leaves form a cross and extend outward, and four clusters of grapes fill the spaces between. Around all this, just below the rim of the bowl are scroll and leaves.

Scroll Embossed (Imperial)

Scroll Embossed is found in plates and bowls with three different exterior patterns, three sizes of compotes, a goblet, sherbet, and a nut dish. Colors are many. I am grateful to Alice Widtfeldt for sharing this photo.

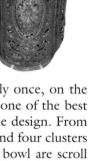

Scroll Embossed Variant (English)

This English pattern, copied from an Imperial pattern, is found on small bowls, plates, handled ashtrays, compotes, as well as on the Diving Dolphin pieces. The exterior design is the giveaway; File on Imperial, a vine-like pattern on the English pieces. Colors are marigold, blue, green, and amethyst.

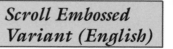

237

Scroll Fluted

What a surprise when I walked into a craft shop in Ripley, Ohio, and found this unlisted item. Scroll Fluted is shown in old Imperial Glass Company ads. Crystal can be found in several shapes but this rose bowl is the only iridized piece reported to date. The design of panels of beveling against plain panels that extend higher at the rim is an unusual one.

Scroll Panel Lamp

This lamp is similar in many ways to the Mitered Block lamp shown elsewhere in this book. It is red carnival and has panels bordered by nice scrolling. It is marked "Falkenstein-9002" inside the metal fittings and stands nearly two feet tall. I strongly suspect this is European and thank the Mel Buels for sharing this nice lamp.

Seacoast Pintray

This beautiful piece is one of two pin tray designs from Millersburg (the other is the Sunflower). It features a lighthouse, seascape, a sailboat, and a large fish. It can be found in marigold, green, amethyst (shown), and even a deep purple.

Seafoam

Seafoam was made in both carnival glass and opalescent glass, along with the crystal and colored line. This is really Dugan's S-Repeat goblet that has been reshaped and renamed. The interior pattern is called Constellation (shown elsewhere in this book). Carnival glass colors are marigold, amethyst, white, peach opalescent, and an unusual yellow glass with marigold lustre.

Seagulls Bowl

If one rarity in this book stands as an example of "scarce but not prized," the Seagulls bowl is that rarity. Certainly there are far fewer of these to be found than many items that bring 10 times the money, but for some strange reason, these cuties are not sought by most collectors. The two bird figures are heavily detailed, as is the bowl pattern. The color, while not outstanding, is good and is iridized both inside and out. The diameter of the bowl is 6½" and the depth is 2⅞". The manufacturer is uncertain but Dugan is certainly a possibility.

Seagulls Vase

This rare vase has been traced to the Eda Glassworks of Sweden, adding to their growing importance as a non-American maker of iridized glass. Colors reported are a rich marigold with a good deal of amber hue and a powder blue.

Seaweed

Seaweed is one of Millersburg's prettier interior patterns. It is found on 5", 6", 7", 8½", and 10½" bowls and on rare 10" plates. Colors are marigold, clambroth, amethyst, green, aqua (rare large bowls), and blue (rare sauces and rare large bowls). Shown is a rare green plate with a superb radium finish.

Seaweed Lamp

The Seaweed lamp is now known to have been a product of Bartlett-Collins in the 1930s used primarily as an export item to South America as early as 1925. It was their #260 item. Most were not iridized but came in crystal, Nu-Rose, or Nu-Green colors. The patent date is recorded as March 17, 1925. Many reproductions have been made over the years and new lamps with this design are in most malls across the country.

Serpentine Rose

The owner of this very unusual bowl called it by this name and since I haven't found it listed by any other, I am continuing with it here. The pattern is a series of rose and twisting vine and leaf patterns, three around the bowl. The feet are spatula and clear while the bowl has a very rich marigold finish with great iridescence.

Serpent Vase

This is actually a variation of the Fish vase. On this one the creature is wrapped counterclockwise. The Serpent vase is 9" and most are marigold on clear glass. Here is shown the first reported marigold on a pastel blue glass. The iridescence is outstanding. This example is marked "AVM." Thanks to the Pouchers for sharing it.

Serrated Flute

This vase is credited to Imperial by most collectors. It has eight exterior wide panels that end in arcs at the top and bottom. The top is serrated or scalloped and the base contains a 24-rayed star. It is found in marigold, helios, smoke, and the clambroth shown (purple is a possibility too). Sizes vary and range from 8" to 13" tall.

Shalimar

Here is another rare tumbler from the Jain Glass Works of India. The example shown was found in Australia. It stands 4¼" tall and has a curved or bowed look that is different from most Indian tumblers. The coloring is typical of Jain glass. Thank to Andres Neveu for sharing this pattern.

Shanghai (Etched)

Since I first showed this tumbler from Dean Hanson, he's come up with two more and they both have a strange etched flower. They match the Etched Vine tumbler in workmanship. These pieces are 3" tall and measure 2½" across the lip. Each has stamped in the base: "SHANGHAI, CHINA" or "MADE IN CHINA" and a small triangle. These were likely made prior to WWII in the 1930s, and are relatives of the Etched Vines, Bamboo Spike, and Snow Chrysanthemum tumblers.

Sharon's Garden

This beautiful bowl was named by Sharon Mordini and it is the only one I've heard about with this enameled flower work. The glass color is peach opalescent with a deep three-in-one edging and the mould pattern has a melon rib-like design.

Sharp Shot Glass

The Sharp shot glass was first shown years ago by Marion Hartung in book #6. It is a very rare item found in a dark smoky finish. It is 2¼" tall with a lip diameter of 2". It has a plain base and there are 14 spearhead panels on the exterior. This fine rarity is now owned by the Whitleys of Texas.

Shasta Daisy

Here is the familiar Zig-Zag water set from Fenton with a painted design that is called Shasta Daisy. It is a fine frosty white and the flowers and leaves are pastel too, showing greens, blues, and reds.

Shasta Daisy with Prism Band

Just like the enameled design on the Shasta Daisy pitcher and tumbler, this one has the well-known Fenton Prism Banding below the tumbler's top. I understand this variation was also made in marigold, ice green, and white, just like the other set.

Shazam

This outstanding design from India is featured on both the pitcher and matching tumblers. A few years ago, I couldn't have imagined the staggering amount of iridized glass from India. Thanks to Vikram Bachhawat for sharing this pattern.

Shell

This is a very simple yet effective pattern. This is especially true on the few plates I've seen. The pattern is a well-balanced one of eight scalloped shells around a star-like pattern. The background may or may not be stippled — I've seen it both ways. The shapes are bowls, plates, and a reported compote I haven't seen. The colors are marigold, green, purple, smoke, and amber.

Shell and Jewel

This easily found Westmoreland pattern was made only in the shapes shown in colors of marigold, amethyst, and green (white has been reported but not confirmed). The pattern is a copy of the Nugget Ware pattern of the Dominion Glass Company of Canada. Shell and Jewel has been reproduced, so buy with caution.

Shell and Sand

This pattern is identical to Imperial's Shell pattern with the exception of the added stippling, which for some reason really sets this pattern off more, in my opinion, than does the stippling on most other patterns. The iridescence on some pieces can be breathtaking. Bowls and plates exist in marigold, amethyst, green, and smoke, and I'm sure other colors are possible.

Shielded Flower

Shielded Flower is thought to be from India. This 6" tumbler has a pale ginger ale color and a very strong design (much different than most Indian tumblers). The pattern has a wide ribbed band with formal drapery at the top, wide panels with flowers, and bordering bands of fine file work. Thanks to the Ayers family for this one.

Ship's Decanter Set

This set was purchased from a family in Czechoslovakia. It came to America in the 1920s and now belongs to the Hilkenes. The ship is 10" long, 4" high at the stern, and 6" tall at the bow. A metal fitting holds the decanter and glasses in place. The glasses are 2" tall, and each is a different color (clear, amethyst, smoke, lavender, pastel marigold, and deep marigold). A rare, rare item indeed.

240

Shirley's Sunburst

I've spent quite some time searching for the origin of this bowl that is in the collection of Shirley Metro and her husband, but haven't learned a thing. It is a deep bowl with a 6½" diameter and a depth of 5". The color is a strong marigold and the pattern is an allover design of cane-filled arcs of scrolling over a sunburst of scrolling. I'd like to hear anything readers have to say about this piece.

Shrike

This pattern is called Thunderbird by Americans and Shrike or Piping Shrike by Australians. It is found in both large and small bowls. The colors are marigold, purple, and the beautiful aqua with marigold iridescence shown.

Shrine Champagne (Rochester)

Despite recent belief that these shrine pieces are from Westmoreland, here is a Rochester goblet that clearly has a U.S. Glass label. I suspect at least all three goblet designs are U.S. Glass.

Shrine Sheath of Wheat Toothpick

This is similar to other Shrine souvenir items, although this one is a stemmed toothpick holder instead of a champagne glass or plate. It has a ruby flashed body with gilding on the wheat and was made for a 1908 convention in St. Paul, Minnesota.

Signature

Here is a pattern that leaves no doubt as to its maker since on the bottom it bears the elusive Jeannette trademark — a J in a square. While previous writers had reported this trademark, it is the first example I've seen. The piece is an open candy dish whose design reminds one of the Imperial Columbia design. While the color doesn't equal earlier carnival glass, it is still a find.

Silver Queen

This Fenton water set is distinguished by its silver bands and white enameled flowers and scrolling. It is found on bulbous or tankard pitchers. The only color reported is marigold and while this isn't the best designed decorated water set, it remains a bit hard to find.

Simple Simon

This variation of the Graceful vase, credited to the Northwood Company, has a different stem and base. This piece is well known to opalescent glass collectors where it is called Simple Simon. Colors are the same as the other, marigold, amethyst, or green.

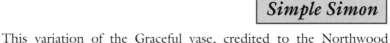

Simplicé

I'm not certain if this item is a marmalade or mustard jar, but either way it certainly is a nice item. From Italy, this lidded piece has an interesting set of wire handles on each side. The color is a nice marigold. Thanks to Wayne Delahoy from Australia for sharing the name and photo.

Simplicity Scroll

This very interesting toothpick holder (match holders are also known) is shown in an old Westmoreland ad along with several Estate pieces and the Miniature Basket with wire bale handle. The toothpick holder is in a smoke over gold finish Westmoreland called their Antique Iridescent. It stands 2⅞" tall and 2⅝" wide. It is lettered.

Singing Birds

This fine Northwood pattern from 1911 is found in a water set, table set, berry set, a mug (plain or stippled), and a rare sherbet. Colors are marigold, amethyst, green, blue, white, ice blue, ice green, horehound, lavender, smoke, olive, and aqua opalescent. The piece shown is a rare electric blue master berry bowl from Peter Baerwald.

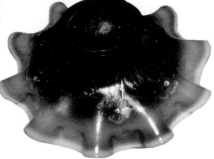

Single Flower (Dugan)

Single Flower is very similar to Dugan's Triplets as well as their Single Flower Framed pattern. This one is also found on 7½" bowls, a basket whimsey, and a rare banana bowl shape. Colors are marigold, amethyst, and peach opalescent as shown. Sometimes these peach pieces have interior enameling, adding to their interest.

Single Flower Framed

Single Flower Framed is much like the Single Flower pattern, but has an odd framing of double wavy lines that encircle the flowers. The pattern is exterior and the colors the usual Dugan ones. Shapes are large and small bowls, and the interior of the one shown has a Fine Rib pattern.

Sitting Bulldog Paperweight

Unlike the other Bulldog paperweight where the dog stands, this one shows a seated dog. The dog shows signs of once being gilded but most of that has worn off. Beneath the gilding is a soft iridescence over the entire piece. I thank Martha Cope for this paperweight. It was made by Westmoreland and has been reproduced.

Six Panel Flute

This is the name given to this pattern at a glass auction and so I've kept it. In design it looks much like a clear glass pattern called Red Flute, and it also resembles Fostoria's Essex pattern. Anyone with additional information is asked to contact me.

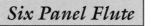

Six Petals

Dugan made Six Petals starting in 1910. It can be found only in purple, green, blue, black amethyst, white, and marigold bowls (plates are rumored but none are confirmed). Thanks to Peter Baerwald for sharing the photo.

Six Ring

I'm sure this tumbler has at least one other name but the one used here is a good description of the design. The pitcher has the same type of rings around it and the only color I've seen is marigold. Notice that the tumbler shades from a very deep marigold at the base to a nearly clear flared top. There are at least two sizes in the tumbler and maybe more. The one shown is 7" tall and 3¼" across at the flared top.

Six-Sided Candlestick

These very well designed candlesticks were first shown in a 1909 Imperial ad in crystal. They have a stylish knob at the top of the stem that holds hobstars and around the base are panels of file and clear panels, giving the piece a real look of class. Colors are marigold, green, purple, smoke, and the amber shown. Purple brings the most money but all are very hard to locate except the marigold. Photo courtesy of Remmen Auction.

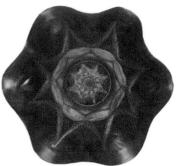

Ski Star

While this Dugan pattern is found occasionally on small bowls in purple, blue, and green, it is on the larger dome-footed bowls in peach opalescent where the pattern shines. These are found in many variations, some crimped with one side turned down, others with both sides pulled up to resemble a banana bowl. The exterior usually carries the Compass pattern, an interesting geometric design, or is plain.

Slewed Horseshoe

Slewed Horseshoe was originally a U.S. Glass pattern (their #15111) and is sometimes called Radiant Daisy or U.S. Peacock. It is usually found in clear glass or colored treatments with gold trim. Here we have an iridized bowl (an iridized slag punch cup is also known) in cobalt blue. Inside the bowl is the mark "ITTALA," indicating it was made in Finland after 1920. Apparently Iittala and the Karhula factory were sister works.

Slick Willie Vase

This advertising piece is about 11½" tall and is marked "Hale Baths – Hot Springs, Ark." The design looks like raindrops running down the surface. Thanks to my former co-author for the interesting name.

Slim Jim Vase

Standing 13" tall, with a base diameter of 2", this vase is almost too slender to hold more than one flower. I haven't been able to track down the production number but suspect it may a Dugan-Diamond product. It is a very soft marigold and looks much like the Slick Willie vase except it has no dribble of glass running down the sides.

Small Basket

Small Basket was made by Sowerby in England. This handled pintray measures a bit less than 6" across from handle to handle and stands 1½" tall. It is eight-sided and ribbed over each section with pie-shaped sections in the bottom that are also ribbed. The color is typical English carnival of a soft marigold.

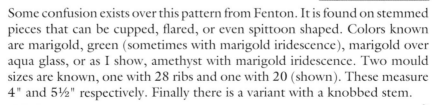

Small Rib

Some confusion exists over this pattern from Fenton. It is found on stemmed pieces that can be cupped, flared, or even spittoon shaped. Colors known are marigold, green (sometimes with marigold iridescence), marigold over aqua glass, or as I show, amethyst with marigold iridescence. Two mould sizes are known, one with 28 ribs and one with 20 (shown). These measure 4" and 5½" respectively. Finally there is a variant with a knobbed stem.

Small Rib Variant

This variant of the Fenton Small Rib pattern has a different stem that has a bulbous finial at the base. I've seen these shaped as ruffled compotes, as cupped and dimpled rose bowls as shown, or even flattened out as a tray. Colors are primarily marigold and green with amber iridization.

Small Thumbprint

Small Thumbprint was made in custard glass accredited to the Tarentum Glass Company. This pattern is known in carnival glass in a mug, toothpick holder, creamer, and sugar. The only pattern is banding of side-by-side ellipses near the bottom of the piece. Each piece has a well-applied marigold lustre and as you can see, each one is stenciled with souvenir lettering. The mug shape is 3" tall, the creamer and sugar 2½" tall.

Smoothie

The owner of this interesting little vase suspects it may be from England, but I have no proof of origin to date. Although it is a simple vase in design, it does carry some pleasing features. The color is a nice deep emerald green with good iridescence. Thanks to Clint Arsenault for sharing it.

Smooth Panels

Smooth Panels is from Imperial and has convex panels rather than concave. Shapes are mostly vases but bowls, rose bowls, and a squat sweet pea vase are known. Colors include marigold, purple, clambroth, smoke, red, teal (shown), marigold over milk glass, and a fabulous smoke over milk glass. Vases range from 4" to 18" tall.

Smooth Rays (Dugan)

Here is the Dugan-Diamond version of this much used pattern and it differs very little from the others except to include the peach opalescent coloring. The bowl shown is tri-cornered. Other colors seem to be marigold, amethyst, and possibly blue. The exterior may contain the Jeweled Heart pattern but not always. Do not confuse this with Dugan's Rays pattern where the design does not come into the center.

Smooth (Imperial) Rays

Nearly identical to the Westmoreland pattern with the same name, Imperial's version came in many more shapes including the bowl shown, large and small plates, goblets in two sizes, stemmed champagne, wine (two sizes), a cordial, a water set, and a custard cup. Colors are primarily marigold and clambroth on all shapes but I show a rare amber 9" flared bowl. In addition to the above, there is a salad set consisting of a 12" plate, a 10" round bowl, an 8" plate, and a stemmed sherbet.

Smooth Rays (Northwood)

Smooth Rays is found in large two-handled bonbons as well as a 6" plate, a compote, and large and small bowls. Colors are mostly marigold, amethyst, and Alaskan (marigold-over-green), but the bonbon is known in cobalt blue, and here is the only reported cobalt blue bowl courtesy of Peter Baerwald.

Smooth Rays (Westmoreland)

Smooth Rays was first made in 1910 as part of Westmoreland's Special Iridescent Line that featured Daisy Wreath, Pearly Dots, Scales, and Carolina Dogwood. It is found in marigold, amethyst, green, marigold-on-milk glass, and iridized blue milk glass as shown. In addition, examples have been reported in teal and amber. Shapes are compotes and bowls.

244

Snow Fancy (Imperial)

Although it was long felt to be a product of McKee, I now know this pattern was made by Imperial. In carnival glass only a creamer, spooner, and small berry bowls have been reported, but I am happy to show the first master berry bowl in marigold. It is one of two from New Zealand. The small bowls are known in marigold, purple, green, and white, while the table set pieces are reported only in marigold. The large berry bowl measures 8¼" across the top and is unruffled. The photo is shared by Peter Dahlin, and I am in his debt for this rare find.

Snowflake (Cambridge)

Snowflake was advertised as Cambridge's #2635 pattern and it also known as Fernland by some collectors. It is well known in crystal in many shapes, but here is the piece in carnival glass. The iridescence is a soft marigold with good pink, blue, and green highlights. It is real privilege to show this tankard water pitcher. Two more are known.

Soda Gold

Imperial's Soda Gold is often confused with Tree of Life and Crackle. It differs from both in that the veins are much more pronounced and are highly raised from the stippled surface. It is found only on short candlesticks, a chop plate, a rare 9" bowl, and beautiful water sets in marigold or smoke.

Soda Gold Spears

This allover design is easy on the eye and has a good background to hold iridescence well. It is similar to the Tree of Life and Crackle patterns. The bowl shown is the 8" size, but 5" bowls and plates are known in both marigold and clambroth.

Songbird (Jain)

While the owner of this fine Jain tumbler calls it Bird of Paradise, I am told by Bob Smith it was previously named Songbird by John McGrath. The design is a good one showing a long-tailed bird on each side of the glass with various leaves and flowers. One-half inch from the plain top is a one-half inch band of lattice.

Soutache (Dugan)

Known in both bowls and plates, this rare Dugan pattern is a real treat to see. Resting on a dome base, Soutache seems to be found only in peach opalescent. The plate is known in a round shape but here is an unusual example. The edges have been shaped to follow the design! In addition, a lamp with matching shade has been reported but I haven't seen it.

Sowerby Flower Frog

Alan Sedgwick provided this photo of a nicely done footed flower from Sowerby and it bears the registration number 706202, indicating it was produced in 1924. He suggests it may have been copied by Crown Crystal of Australia at a later date.

Sowerby Swan

Sowerby Swan is found in iridized glass (as well other treatments), according to Sheilagh Murray in her book *The Peacock and the Lions*. The color is a pinkish-amethyst sometimes found on the Diving Dolphins pieces.

Sowerby Wide Panel

While there isn't much special about this bowl, a wide panel exterior with a many rayed star base, it does have very good color and finish and the scalloping around the rim adds a touch of class. It is English and made by Sowerby.

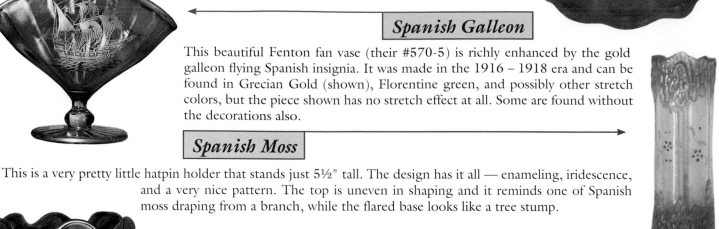

Spanish Galleon

This beautiful Fenton fan vase (their #570-5) is richly enhanced by the gold galleon flying Spanish insignia. It was made in the 1916 – 1918 era and can be found in Grecian Gold (shown), Florentine green, and possibly other stretch colors, but the piece shown has no stretch effect at all. Some are found without the decorations also.

Spanish Moss

This is a very pretty little hatpin holder that stands just 5½" tall. The design has it all — enameling, iridescence, and a very nice pattern. The top is uneven in shaping and it reminds one of Spanish moss draping from a branch, while the flared base looks like a tree stump.

Spearhead and Rib (Fenton)

At last I am able to show this pattern in a vase that hasn't been pulled so much the design is distorted. Here is the 7" example of Fenton's #916, so often mistaken as another Fine Rib vase. As you can see the ribbed sections are broken in two places and the spearheads are actually columns of diamonds. Colors known to date are marigold, amethyst, green, and cobalt blue but perhaps a rare red or white one will eventually show up. Sizes are 8" – 17". Thanks to Samantha Prince for the photo.

Spearhead and Rib Variant

Unlike the regular Spearhead and Rib pattern where the ribs are "broken," this one has no breaks and the ribs run from top to bottom. The color is cobalt blue and it was made by Fenton. I thank Roger Lane for sharing this with me.

Spector's Department Store

The familiar Fenton design called Heart and Vine is used here as an advertising piece on a 9" plate. The added lettering says "Compliments of Spector's Department Store." The only color is marigold.

Spice Grater (India)

Spice Grater is one of the many fine patterns made in India. The water set shown is typical of their designs. The pitcher is 8" tall and tumblers are 4½". I thank Vikram Bachhawat for sharing so many previously unseen Indian patterns.

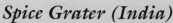

Spice Grater Variant

This variant from India has a slightly different shape from their regular Spice Grater pattern, and has added rings below the rims of the tumbler and the matching pitcher.

Spicer Beehive

The Spicer Beehive was made by the Spicer Studios, 532 E. Market Street, Akron, Ohio, in the 1920s. This interesting piece was advertised by the maker in rainbow iridized shades of amber, blue, amethyst, and a color they called rainbow (this may be the smoky shade shown). The piece held honey and has a spoon opening.

Spider Web

Besides the 4" tall vase shown in green, an 8" bulbous vase is also known in pale amber. The design is often confused by beginning collectors with both Crackle and Soda Gold patterns. There is another bud vase known with both Spider Web and Tree Bark. The maker hasn't been confirmed at this time. Anyone with confirmation of the maker of any of these vases is urged to contact me.

Spiked Grape and Vine (Jain)

Of all the Jain glass tumblers, this is one of the nicer examples. The grapes and the spiked ribs at the base seem to be a perfect complement to each other. The color is a strong marigold and the tumbler is marked "Jain" on the base. It is also known as Grapevine and Spikes.

Spiral Candle

These heavy, practical candlesticks were sold in pairs and were made in green, smoke, and marigold. They measure 8¼" from the base to the top and, as far as I know, did not have a console bowl to match. The smoke color is particularly beautiful with many fiery highlights. It is Jeannette's #30 pattern.

Spiraled Diamond Point

After years of seeing the drawing of this rare vase in the Hartung books, it is a real privilege to show it. This vase is 6" tall, with a 2⅝" base diameter, and fans to 2¾" at the top. The pattern of twisting bands of file and a series of fans at the top is very nice. The iridescence is all interior. There is a small flange inside the lip as if a lid was intended.

Spiralex

This vase is Dugan's #1028 pattern. It is similar to the #1016 vase that is known as Wide Rib. Spiralex is found on 8" – 13" sizes primarily in marigold, peach opalescent, amethyst, white, and rarely cobalt blue. Please note that the ribs usually twist to the left as on the vase shown.

Spirals and Spines (Northwood)

For all who doubt rare, unreported patterns are still out there, please examine this Northwood vase that collectors hadn't seen until it came out for sale in 1996. It is now in the possession of a California collector and I am pleased to be able to show it here. It is marked "Northwood," of average height, and in white carnival. The spiral design is similar to the Ribbed Tornado vase and the three ribs or spines have rolls or bumps from top to bottom. The vase was bought at a carnival auction where the brochure stated, "you buy it, you name it." The current owner bought it and named it, so I'm honoring this name and really appreciate the photo.

Split Diamond

This very well done geometric pattern is hard to mistake for any other. The two prominent wedges of filed diamond are split down the center. Shapes reported are a covered butter dish, an open sugar (bowl shape) sometimes called a sauce, a stemmed open sugar, a jam pot (sometimes called a covered sugar), and the creamer shown. Most pieces are found in marigold but an amethyst bowl shape does exist so other shapes were probably made in this color also.

247

Springtime

Due to either short runs of this pattern or extreme loss, Springtime is one of the scarcer patterns from the Northwood Company. It is found in berry sets, water sets, and table sets in marigold, amethyst, or green. It was made around 1910 or 1911 and the base to the butter dish is the same as that of the Singing Birds and Peacock at the Fountain sets. Pieces of Springtime are usually marked and green is the most difficult color to find.

Spry Measuring Cup

From Gary Vandevander, this well iridized measuring cup is marked "Spry" on the bottom, has a clear handle, and lettered measurements on the side. It is the first I've seen.

Spun Flowers

This 10" plate has a ground base and a very pretty etched pattern around the rim. It is white carnival with a bit of a stretch look. I feel sure it was made by the Imperial Glass Company of Bellaire, Ohio. Surely it came in several shapes besides the plate.

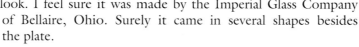

Spun Threads

This very fragile hat vase has five rows of cobalt threading around the top and the base is the platform type. The color is a good marigold. The owners feel this vase may be from Czechoslovakia and they may be correct, but I have no information that confirms this. Anyone with knowledge of this piece is urged to contact me.

Square Diamond (Column Flower)

This was first a product of Brockwitz in the 1920s and was shown in their catalogs (thanks to Siegmar Geiselberger for his many catalogs). It was then made by Riihimaki in the 1930s as I first reported. It stands about 8½" tall and can be found in both marigold and blue carnival glass. The pattern is intricate and stunning. Thanks to Seeck Auction for sharing it.

S-Repeat

S-Repeat was made in crystal, decorated crystal, and gilt glass prior to being made in carnival glass. It is found on only a small range of shapes in iridized glass. Besides the punch set shown, there is a rare toothpick that has been widely reproduced and a handful of marigold tumblers that some believe are questionable. At any rate, in carnival glass, Dugan's S-Repeat is a very scarce item. Thanks to the Remmens for sharing the photo.

Ssss's

How original can you be with a name like this? I have no idea of the maker or the age of this interesting vase but it does have a certain appeal to it, if you like the snake look. I can't say what this piece was used for other than the fact that it resembles a water bottle to some degree. It has a ground base and the color is a very nice emerald green with decent iridescence. Thanks to Clint Arsenault for sharing the name and the photo.

Stag and Holly (Fenton)

Stag and Holly, from Fenton in 1912, is found in small spatula-footed bowls, large scroll-footed bowls, two sizes of plates, and a large rose bowl. Colors include marigold, amethyst, blue, green, vaseline, aqua, red, amber, and the rare sapphire blue shown. Plates and the rose bowl are mostly found in marigold and amethyst. Photo courtesy of Remmen Auction.

The owner of this berry set says it is thin as tissue paper. It stands on three legs and has good iridescence. The defining feature is, of course, the stained rim on each piece and is much like other items found from Czechoslovakia in that respect. The marigold color is fine and even, making this set unique. There is also a dressing table set known.

Standard

This very attractive tubular vase is in two parts and stands 5¼" tall. The top flares to almost 3", matching the bottom diameter of the metal stand. Possibly a Dugan product, I suspect it may have been made in colors other than the very strong marigold shown.

Star

While there may not be a great deal of inventiveness to this English pattern, it certainly serves a useful purpose and does it with a good deal of attractiveness. The clear center shows off the star on the base quite well, and the two tiny rows of rope edging add a bit of interest. Marigold is the only color I've heard about.

Star and Drape (Crystal)

What a joy it is to finally show this very fine pitcher from the Australian glassmaker, Crystal Glass Company, Limited. It is found only in marigold and no matching tumblers are known. The design is all intaglio with a series of rayed stars, incised drapery, and scored panels at the base. The pitcher holds one pint. As you can see, the iridescence is quite good. Thanks to the McGraths for sharing this beauty.

Star and Fan Cordial Set

The shapes in this cordial set are a tray, a decanter with stopper, and stemmed cordial glasses. Some collectors feel this is a pattern from Europe but most of the recent examples are coming from South America. It is much like the same shapes in the Zipper Stitch pattern. Colors are marigold and the beautiful aqua set shown (missing four cordials).

Star and File

This is Imperial's #612. It was made in crystal as well as carnival glass where shapes include a celery vase, 6" – 9" bowls, footed juice glass, ice tea tumbler, water set, milk pitcher, goblet, table set, custard cup, cordial, sherbet, compote, small plate, bonbon, and a deep nut bowl. Colors include marigold (all pieces), purple, amber, smoke, ice green, and helios green. In addition, a compote and a bowl are known in clambroth so other shapes may have been made in this color. All colors besides marigold are a bit scarce in this pattern.

This Brockwitz pattern has some variations (Northern Lights, Texas Tumbler). Besides the beautiful rose bowl I've shown before (two sizes) and an epergne, there is the beautiful jardiniere shape shown here. Colors are marigold and blue. I thank the Ayers family for sharing this fine photo.

Starburst (Riihimaki)

Shapes in this Riihimaki pattern include several sizes and shapes of vases, a rose bowl, the tumbler, and the spittoon whimsey in amber. Most pieces are found in blue or marigold, but Riihimaki did make several items in amber so be aware of the possibility.

Starburst and Diamonds

This 10½" pedestal vase from the Riihimaki Glass Works of Finland is known in marigold and blue carnival glass as well as crystal. It is a very interesting item with a design that is similar to other European designs.

Starburst and File

This is the exterior of the Four Leaf Clover bowl, and as you can see, it closely resembles Sowerby File shown elsewhere in this edition. The color is quite good and the mould work well done.

Starburst Lustre

While this bowl's exterior has no pressed design, the pattern of spray used in iridizing it gives it a very pretty pattern called Starburst Lustre, similar to the Rainbow treatment also used by Northwood. It can be found on bowls and compotes as well as with a few true patterns (see Stippled Mum).

Starburst Perfume

The only thing I know about this pattern is that the name appears in the Hartung series of books. The design consists of alternating panels of vertical ribs followed by horizontal ribs (resembling a flight of stairs). The stopper is fabulous but the pattern is only on one side of it. This is the only shape I've seen and the color is a rich marigold. If anyone can give any additional information I would appreciate it. Thanks to Remmen Auction for the photo.

Star Cut

The owner calls this a ship's decanter (there are matching tumblers). It stands 8" tall including the clear stopper. The pattern shows two rows of eight-pointed stars, cut into the glass. The neck has a 1" wide banding of gilt. Star Cut may be European but this one is in Australia.

Stardust

This name was given to this pattern by Marion Quinton-Baxendale and she shows a small marigold bowl in her book. Here we have a superb 7¾" cobalt blue vase. The base carries a sunken 10-pointed star. The owner bought this vase in Finland so I believe it may be a Riihimaki pattern. Anyone with additional information is urged to contact me.

Starfish

This Dugan pattern is not discussed much. It is found on a stemmed two-handled bonbon and a scarcer compote shape. Colors are marigold, amethyst, and peach opalescent (shown), and production dates from the 1910 – 1912 time period. I once heard rumors of a cobalt blue example but haven't confirmed it.

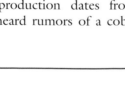

Starflower (Fenton)

Starflower is found only on the pitcher. This appealing design is usually seen in cobalt blue but very scarce marigold and white examples do exist. Production records say this design began around 1911. It somewhat resembles the Milady pattern, also from Fenton.

Starflower and Ribs

Glass from India often had this frosted work with just touches of iridescence. This water set is no exception. If you compare this pitcher and that of Star Flower and Rolls, you will see the designs are the same but the mould work is different.

Starflower and Rolls

This is one of the many frosted patterns from India. This one has the standard starflower, but the base of the pitcher and the matching tumbler has four rolls.

Star Goblet

A goblet is the only reported shape in this simple pattern. The milk goblet shows just how beautiful the iridescence is. The only designs are the incised, four-pointed stars that circle the goblet's bowl.

Starlyte Shade

Imperial made several very attractive light shades, and this is certainly one of them. The Starlyte shade stands 4" tall and has a bell diameter of 8". The pattern is a series of panels containing graduated hobstars on a stippled background. Colors are a rich marigold and clambroth, but smoke and green are also possibilities.

Star Medallion

Star Medallion is a much overlooked but well designed near-cut Imperial pattern. It was very popular for it is found in many shapes, including bowls, a table set, a handled celery, a 9" plate, milk pitcher, punch cup, tumbler, goblet, and a very beautiful compote. Colors are marigold, smoke, and occasionally helios green.

Star Medallion and Fan

To date, I've had only this bowl (8" diameter, 3½" deep) reported in marigold as shown. It doesn't seem to be in the European catalogs I've reviewed nor in the ones from South America, so I can't pin down the maker at this time. It has the look of Scandinavian glass as far as the pattern is concerned so I'll just keep searching for a maker. Thanks to Roger Lane for sharing it.

Star of David

This very scarce Imperial bowl has the Arcs exterior and the Star of David in the center of the interior. The 8" – 9" bowls are found in marigold, purple, green, and a rare smoke. An electric purple with rich highlights is shown.

Star of David and Bows

This very attractive dome-footed bowl shows Northwood's version of this pattern. (Imperial also produced a Star of David bowl.) It is a tribute to the Jewish religion. The star is interlaced and is beaded while a graceful border of flowers, tendrils, and bows edge the stippled center. The exterior is the Vintage pattern, and the colors are marigold, green, and amethyst. Thanks to Samantha Prince for the photo.

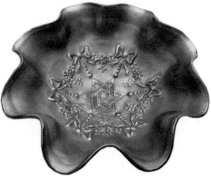

251

Star Paperweight

This very rare paperweight measures 5½" in diameter and dates from 1915. This is also found in clear glass. Marigold iridized ones are a carnival collector's dream. The beads are raised while the leaves and berries on the points are intaglio. The example shown has a rural scene in the bubbled center and the iridescence covers the top and the bottom of the piece.

Starred Scroll

This pattern from the early 1900s is also known as Crescent and Fan. Primarily found in crystal, this is the first reported iridized piece. It is a hair receiver. I welcome any information about the pattern or its maker. Thanks to Mickey Reichel for sharing the photo.

Star Rosette

Found in tumblers like the one shown and a stoppered decanter, this very well done pattern is easy to spot. The tumblers are small, standing 3⅜" tall. Their base has a 16-point star, and there are four elongated ovals around the tumblers, each containing a 16-point star. The color and iridescence are outstanding, the pieces are rare, and the maker is unknown.

Stars Over India

Only the banding of this tumbler is similar to the regular Moon and Stars pattern. Here we have a band of crosshatch with stars and a full moon. The rest of the tumbler has a pattern of stacked squares that form pyramids at the base and rows of diamonds that have antennae-like scrolls above and below. The color is very good with strong iridescence from top to bottom.

Star Spray

This 7½" Imperial bowl can be found in crystal as well as marigold and smoke iridized glass. The pattern is all exterior and intaglio. It was also made in a 7" plate. The pattern is rare in vaseline. This pattern is also shown in a Crown Crystal catalog.

The States

The States was usually a U.S. Glass crystal pattern. The only four pieces known in carnival glass were found in South America, prompting questions about their origin. Only the covered butter dish, the oval bowl, the sugar shaker (clambroth), and a large three handled nappy (green) have been reported, but other iridized pieces may well be out there.

Stippled Diamonds

I've now seen this rare Millersburg pattern not only on the spade-shaped nappy in green and vaseline but also on an equally rare card tray with two handles (shaped from a bonbon). In June 2007 I saw the second green nappy to be reported and the new owners from Indiana were very happy to have it.

Stippled Diamond Swag

For years the only stemmed piece known was the open sugar (at one time thought to be a compote), but here is the matching creamer. These are from Josef Rindskopf and are shown in catalog pages Siegmar Geiselberger was kind enough to furnish.

Stippled Estate (Albany)

Before Dugan-Diamond acquired the moulds for this pattern, it was produced in Albany, Indiana, by the Model Flint Glass Company (1900 – 1902), in 2½", 3½", and 5½" sizes in amber (shown), amethyst, green, blue, and speckled glass. In addition, Model Flint production included a toothpick holder in this pattern. The Model Flint piece shown is 5½" tall and is mould blown.

Stippled Estate (Dugan)

Stippled Estate is found only on this small bud vase in both carnival glass and opalescent glass. This is a difficult pattern to find in either treatment. Opalescent glass colors are white, blue, and green. Carnival glass colors are the peach opalescent shown, a pastel green, and a rumored celeste blue. Production began in 1905 and iridized pieces are advertised in blue, green, and amethyst as part of their Venetian assortment, but no amethyst ones have been reported to date.

Stippled Flower

This Dugan pattern is really just the much used rayed or ribbed look with a stippled, six-petal flower in the center. It is seen most often in peach opalescent glass. The bowl shown is about 8" in diameter and has a collar base.

Stippled Mum (Northwood)

I have a special fondness for this pattern, as an amethyst example was my first piece of carnival glass over two decades ago and I still have it tucked away in a special place. Most who see this pattern call it Stippled Rays but it certainly isn't. The mum is only in the center of the bowl and it is completely stippled. The bottom center is marked "Northwood" and the rest of the bowl has an iridizing treatment called Starburst Lustre, a Northwood treatment that seems to be used by no one else.

Stippled Petals

This Dugan pattern from 1910 is found mostly in peach opalescent, but amethyst and marigold were also made. Shapes are mostly dome-based bowls, handled baskets, banana bowls, and compotes from the bowl mould. Here is a fantastic piece that was never crimped.

Stippled Rambler Rose

Most trails seem to lead to the Dugan Company with this seldom-discussed pattern, but I have no proof they made it. The shape shown is the only one I've seen, and the colors are marigold and blue only.

Stippled Rays (Fenton)

Just about every company had their version of this pattern, but the Fenton is the most often seen. It was made in bonbons, large and small bowls, compotes, a creamer, sugar, and a 7" plate. Colors include marigold, amethyst, blue, green, red, white, amberina, celeste blue, red slag, aqua, and lime green.

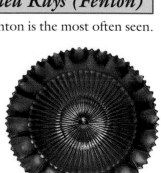

Stippled Rays (Northwood)

This Northwood version differs from the other makers' examples of this pattern in that it stops far short of the outer edges. It is marked inside the center. Shapes include a ruffled bowl, a piecrust edge bowl (shown), with compotes and bonbons reported. Colors are marigold, amethyst, green, cobalt blue, lavender, aqua, white, and black amethyst, with ice blue reported. Production dates from 1909, continuing for 36 months.

Stippled Rays Breakfast Set

Some of the pieces of this breakfast set have plain interiors but some have the stippled rays on both the interior and exterior. The sugar has two handles and no lid. There is also a whimsey sugar known that is flared out. Colors are marigold, purple, green, cobalt blue, amber, smoke, and vaseline. While some collectors once thought this to be from Imperial, it is now considered a Fenton product, mostly due to the colors it has been found in.

Stippled Strawberry

Stippled Strawberry is a companion pattern to the Cherry Smash pattern shown earlier. They were both made by U.S. Glass in 1928. This one is found in pink and green Depression colors of as well as iridized marigold. Shapes in carnival include a stemmed dessert, tumblers, and the water pitcher shown, but since a berry set, table set, compote, olive dish, plates, and a pickle dish are known in Depression colors, these too may show up iridized.

Stjarna

This Eda (Sweden) covered candy jar (bonbonniere) is a very scarce item. It dates in carnival glass from the 1920s and is found in either marigold or blue as shown. I thank Ayers Auction Service for sharing it.

Stork ABC Plate

Made and advertised in crystal, pink, green, and frosted green glass by the Belmont Glass Company of Bellaire, Ohio, in the 1880s, this well-known child's plate may have found its way to another factory for the carnival treatment. The latest speculation centers on U.S. Glass. It is found only in a pale marigold carnival. The plate measures 7½" across, and has a flat base and a raised rim with a stork in the center, ringed by numbers and then the alphabet.

Stork and Rushes

Made by Diamond, Stork and Rushes is found in a wide variety of shapes including berry sets, water sets, punch sets, a hat whimsey, basket whimsey (from a tumbler), and a well-known mug. Colors are primarily marigold and purple, but blue exists and the mug has been reported in a pastel blue. Tumblers come in two variations. One has two rows of beading, the other two rows of lattice at top and bottom. I know of no pitcher to match the lattice one, but mugs are found with this same treatment.

Stork Vase

The Stork vase is much like the Swirl vase in concept. It was made by Jenkins and is usually found in a pale marigold glass. The stork is on one side only with stippling covering the other side. It stands 7½" tall.

Strawberry (Dugan)

This stately epergne (10" tall, 9¼" diameter) is now recognized as a Dugan-Diamond pattern. The design is interior on the dome-based bowl with four groups of strawberries and leaves. On the tall lily is a pattern of quilted diamonds and a lower section of hobbed paneling. This epergne is reported only in amethyst carnival glass and is very desirable.

Strawberry (Fenton)

This little bonbon shape has been seen in all sorts of glass including crystal, custard, milk glass, and carnival glass. Carnival colors range from marigold, cobalt, amethyst, and green to the rare red amberina shown and a good rich all red. The design qualities aren't all that good, but the iridescence is usually adequate and on the whole, the Fenton bonbon comes off nicely.

Strawberry (Northwood)

This is a popular and well-known Northwood pattern was made in 1910. It can be found in bowls, plates, and handgrip plates, in many colors. Both ribbed and basketweave exteriors are known. Pieces can be stippled, and edges on bowls may be ruffled or piecrust finished. Thanks to Kris and Debra Remmen for the photo.

Strawberry Intaglio

This Northwood pattern from 1908 is like its sister patterns, Cherry Intaglio and Apple and Pear Intaglio. They are all exterior designs, cut in rather than raised. Strawberry Intaglio is found in large or small shallow bowls on very thick glass. Some even bear the Northwood mark. The iridescence is all on the exterior.

Strawberry Scroll

This is one of Fenton's best water sets. It rivals the Lily of the Valley pattern for design perfection. The pitcher is a pinched waist shape with a band of scrolling above the pinch. The rest of the design features vines, leaves, and strawberries above and below the band. Colors reported are blue or marigold.

Strawberry with Checkerboard (Jenkins)

For years I've mistakenly thought this design was Stippled Strawberry. It wasn't until studying a pattern glass book that I was aware this was actually a Jenkins Glass pattern called Strawberry with Checkerboard, dating from 1920. It was made in table set pieces mainly in crystal, but here we have a spooner shape that was iridized. I'm sorry for my mistake but I'm happy to correct it now.

Strawberry Wreath (Millersburg)

Like its close relatives, Grape and Blackberry Wreaths, this beautiful pattern is the culmination of the design. Its detailing is much finer than either of the other patterns, and the glass is exceptional. The color is a true grape purple and the iridescence is a light even gold. Like other Millersburg patterns, the shapes vary, but the deep tri-cornered bowl with candy-ribbon edge is my favorite. A rare compote exists in the usual colors. Many thanks to the John and Rae Ann Calai for the photo of this square bowl in green.

Streamline

I was told by Wayne Delahoy this pattern was made by Crown Crystal of Australia and by appearance it must have come along late in their production. I know of the creamer and covered sugar in iridized glass and both are shown here, but certainly other shapes may exist.

Stream of Hearts

The same heart shape employed by Fenton on the Heart and Vine and Heart and Trees designs is found here on the scale fillers that form a peacock's tail. Usually found on the compote shape, often with Persian Medallion as an exterior companion, Stream of Hearts is available on a 10" footed bowl also. Colors are marigold, blue, and white.

Stretch

Since this very collectible glass was made with nearly the same process as carnival glass, I like to show at least one example labeled as such. Stretch glass is usually found with little or no pattern and often has an onion skin look with some stretch effect to the glass. This is achieved by shaping the glass after the iridizing salt spray has been applied whereas in carnival glass, the reverse is true. Shown is a very rare iridized punch bowl in red.

Stretched Diamonds and Dots

Very little information seems to be available about this tumbler. It is 4½" tall, comes from a two-part mould, and has an unusual star design in the base. The pattern of diamonds filled with large buttons above stretched diamonds is very attractive, despite the color being rather light.

Strutting Peacock

Strutting Peacock was made by the Westmoreland Company and reproduced in the '70s. The only shapes reported are the covered creamer and sugar that make up a breakfast set and a green or black amethyst rose bowl whimsey pulled from the sugar base. Regular pieces are found in amethyst. The design is very close to a sister one called Shell and Jewel. Thanks to the Remmens I am happy to show a nice photo of both pieces with their lids.

Studs

Studs was made by Jeannette Glass in 1921. It is called Holiday Buttons & Bows by Depression glass collectors. In iridized glass, marigold is the only reported color. Shapes include a handled cake plate, bowls on short stubby feet, and the 11" x 9" oval platter shown. The pattern is all exterior. I want to thank Jill Evans for sharing this platter.

Style (Australian)

Style is seen in both marigold and purple in 7" – 8" bowls. The beautiful example shown measures 7" and has superb iridization. Bowls can be ruffled or plain in shape, have either a plain interior or the Lattice design, and are all from the same mould.

Stylized Flower Center

Fenton's Stylized Flower Center is found on some Orange Tree bowls and plates as a specialized design. It is sometimes called a Tree Trunk center. Thanks to Peter Baerwald for sharing this fantastic electric blue plate.

Sunbeam Whiskey Glass (McKee)

This whiskey glass was made by McKee Glass Company. It stands 2⅞" tall, with a top opening of 2¼", and has a 1¾" base with a 12-point star. The geometric design is a good one with diamond sections of fine file, hobstars, and blazes. The color is a rich and mellow marigold.

Sunflower

Sunflower must have been a very popular pattern in its day, for numerous examples have survived to the present time. It's quite easy to see why it was in demand. It's a pretty, well-designed Northwood pattern that holds iridescence beautifully. The bowl is footed and carries the very pleasing Meander pattern on the exterior. It is also found, rarely, on a plate. The colors are marigold, green, amethyst, and a rare teal blue.

Sunflower and Diamond

This vase was in a 1931 Brockwitz catalog and also appeared in Eda catalogs from Sweden, so one can assume it was part of the monumental pattern swapping that went on in Europe. It can be found in 6", 8", and 9" sizes. The 6" vase isn't reported in carnival glass. Here is the 8" size in a rare cobalt blue. Both sizes are also known in marigold.

Sunflower Pintray

Like its companion piece, the Seacoast pintray, this Millersburg item joins the list of a select few. It is 5¼" long and 4½" wide and rests on a collar base. The most unique feature is, of course, the open handle. The colors are marigold, purple, amethyst, and a rich green.

Sungold Flora

Sungold Flora was shown in Brockwitz's 1931 catalog in the bowl shown and an epergne with one center lily (their #10800). It is also known as Sungold Floral by some collectors. The bowl is 7¾" – 9" in diameter and the pattern is all exterior with very good iridescence. Marigold is the only color reported at this time.

Sunk Daisy

Collectors consider this fine design to be from Riihimaki Glass in Finland and Eda Glass in Sweden. If so, it is an exact copy of the old Cambridge Glass Company pattern #2760. Actually several patterns seem to have found their way from Cambridge to European makers, so its not surprising. The piece shown is considered a footed rose bowl with the intaglio design deep and beautiful. The color is a striking cobalt blue but marigold exists.

Sunken Hollyhock

Sunken Hollyhock is probably found more readily than the other Gone with the Wind lamps. It can be found in marigold (often with a caramel coloring) and a very rare red. The lamp stands an impressive 25" tall and is certainly a showstopper.

Sun Punch

This and the Universal bottle were made by the Hemingray Glass Company in 1931 and shown in their company literature. This unusually shaped soft drink bottle is 8" tall. The surface is stippled and a diagonal band says "Sun Punch." There are rayed suns above lines of zig-zagging. The shape of three balls, one on top of the other is unique and adds even more whimsey.

Superb Drape

This rare vase has been reported in green (one known), aqua opalescent (two known), and marigold (one known). In addition to the carnival examples known, one crystal example has turned up. They measure ½" tall with a 7" top opening. The maker hasn't been confirmed but some feel it is Northwood because of the aqua opalescent color. The pattern is dramatic with drapes that start at the neck and go all the way to the collar base.

Superstar

This is really part of Brockwitz's Zurich line that is known as Curved Star, but most collectors call this jardiniere shape by the Superstar name. It is shown in a 1928 Brockwitz catalog (furnished to me by Siegmar Geiselberger who writes a wonderful glass newsletter) and can be found in marigold and blue carnival glass.

Svea

Svea is another pattern from Eda of Sweden. It was also made by Karhula in Finland a few years later. It is known in a wide range of shapes in crystal. The Eda catalog showing this pattern dates from 1929. Iridized pieces include a pin tray, pickle tray, a bowl, rose bowl, and a vase. Colors reported are marigold and blue, but here is shown a previously unreported lavender bowl with marigold iridescence, as well as a cobalt blue rose bowl. Both measure 5½" in diameter.

Svea Variant

I don't know if this is actually a variant of the Svea pattern from Eda of Sweden, or possibly a Rindskopf product (a very similar tumbler is shown in that catalog as their #1578), so both are possibilities. Whoever made it, this very lovely vase has a certain attractiveness to it. With its ruffled top, this half plain and half

diamond pattern would make a nice addition to any vase collection. It can be found in a small 4½" size as well as a 6 – 7" size and I'm told there is another size but haven't seen it. I'd appreciate hearing from anyone with additional information. Thanks to the Mordinis for the name and photo.

Swan

This Australian pattern, patented in 1924, can be found in large and small bowls in marigold or purple. It can be found with two different floral interior designs and usually has Fern and Wattle on the exterior. The bird is the black swan, a native of Australia.

Swans and Flowers

Here is another tumbler pattern marked "Jain," from India. The design is etched with swans on one side and flowers on the other. In addition etched initials are present and seem to be U.M.M. Thanks to Lance and Pat Hilkene for sharing this find.

Sweetheart

Sweetheart was Cambridge's #2631 pattern called Marjorie. The very rare cookie jar and the very rare tumbler (shown) are found iridized. The covered cookie jar is known in green, amethyst, and a marigold reported, while the tumbler is known only in marigold.

Swirl (Imperial)

This 7" vase is shown in old Imperial catalogs. I've heard of it in marigold, smoke, green, and white (unconfirmed). The design is nothing outstanding, but the useful shape and the iridescence are adequate.

Swirl (Northwood)

Just why the Northwood Company made so many Swirl water sets in at least four different shapes is certainly a mystery, but they did. Three are tankards and the fourth a standard size pitcher shaped much like the Raspberry pitcher. Colors are marigold, amethyst, green, and Alaskan treatment. Only the tumbler has been reported in amethyst so far but I'm sure a pitcher is out there.

Swirled Gum Tip Variant

Most of these vases come in black amethyst. This one has a twist; the veins are swirled. They were made by Crown Crystal in Australia. The example shown has remarkable iridescence.

Swirled Morning Glory (Imperial)

These are like the regular Morning Glory vases from Imperial, but they have been swirled and are a bit harder to find. They can be found in flared shapes or in the jack-in-the-pulpit shape shown here. Colors to date include marigold, purple, and smoke.

Swirled Rib

Swirled Rib was shown by Marion Hartung in her tenth book (page 112). This pitcher is also called Interior Swirl by some collectors. The pitcher is shown in a 1909 Northwood ad in Butler Brothers catalog. The pitcher is reported in marigold only but the tumbler is also reported in amethyst and green.

Swirled Threads

What a very pretty piece of glass this stemmed goblet is. The color is dark and rich, and the stem ending in a ball shape gives it a nice touch. The threadings are all interior. I'd guess it came from Europe but can't be sure, and it certainly looks to be late carnival to me. I'd appreciate any information on this piece.

Swirled Threads and Optic

The owner of this miniature vase (6" tall with a 1" lip diameter) declares it to be a kissing cousin to the Swirled Threads pattern, but here we have an added optic pattern on the inside of the piece. The color is a good marigold with very nice iridescence. The glass appears to be on the thin side and is probably another European product from the 1920s and 1930s, or possibly later. Additional information is appreciated.

Swirl Hobnail (Millersburg)

It is a real privilege to show the ultra rare green spittoon in this marvelous Millersburg pattern. It is one of three reported in this color (one is badly damaged). The Swirl Hobnail pattern was made in rose bowls, spittoons, and vases all from the same mould. Colors are marigold, amethyst, and green but the vase is known in a rare blue. The pattern of swirling threading around and between the hobs is similar to Northwood's Tree Trunk design where the lines are broken and not continuous.

Swirl Variant #2 (Northwood)

This was shown in a 1909 Northwood ad that featured three of the four shapes in a Swirl pattern (two styles of tankards and this one). The ad calls them a "Golden Iridescent Lemonade Assortment" and each has an applied handle.

Sword and Circle

Sword and Circle was apparently from Hocking Glass in the 1920s (according to Phillip Hopper) and originally called High Point. This pattern is found in crystal as well as both marigold and red iridized. Tumblers are found in several sizes.

Sydney

While this Fostoria pattern is known in other shapes in crystal, the tumbler and smaller champagne glass are the only shapes reported in carnival glass. The color is an amber-like marigold that is well iridized. The tumbler is nearly 4" tall and the champagne measures 3¼".

Syrup Set

If you look closely at this set and compare it with the Heisey #473 set shown elsewhere in this book you will see that the handles are different as well as the rays on the bottom of the handled saucer. I believe this set was made by Fostoria, although Paden City isn't out of the question, but have no proof at this time. The color is a good marigold. These sets may be a creamer and sugar holder but the owner calls this a syrup set, so it was named that.

Taffeta Lustre Candlesticks

These very scarce Fostoria candlesticks were manufactured in 1916 or 1917 (according to an old Fostoria catalog) in amber, blue, green, crystal, and orchid. They were part of a flower set which included a centerpiece bowl, 11" in diameter. The candlesticks themselves came in 2", 4", 6", 9", and 12" sizes. These shown still have the original paper labels on the bottom. When held to the light, the ultraviolet color is fantastic, and the iridescence is heavy and rich. Fostoria made very small amounts of iridized glass, and these examples of their Taffeta Lustre line are quite difficult to find.

Tall Hat

Like the pastel hat pieces, this taller version is usually found in pastel blue with a pink top. However, I've also seen marigold examples of this same piece. The example shown is a little over 7" and the lip is turned down on three sides and up on the back side almost like a jack-in-the-pulpit vase. These are possibly from the Aramas line.

Tarentum's Virginia

Virginia is also called Many Crystals by some pressed glass collectors. This pattern hasn't been known to carnival collectors, but here it is! It was first made by the Tarentum Glass Company and then U.S. Glass. This spooner shape must be from the latter's production.

Target Vase

This well-known vase was made by Dugan and then Diamond. It is found in sizes ranging from the 5" squat vase shown to vases as tall as 15". Colors range from the usual marigold, amethyst, peach opalescent, cobalt blue, and white to unusual ones such as vaseline, lime green, vaseline opalescent, green, smoky blue, and a very scarce lavender.

Tassels

This wonderful lamp shade comes from Alan and Loraine Pickup, and it is a real pleasure to show it. It is marigold-over-moonstone and is 4½" tall with a 5" flare. The pattern has 12 draped tassels with a band of dots and dashes at the bottom. The maker is unknown at this time.

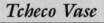

Tcheco Vase

The name for this thin vase on fine amethyst glass comes from the paper label on the base, which reads: "Tcheco Slovachia," indicating the origin as Czechoslovakia. The design is a simple series of nine stacked rings below a flared rim. The iridescence is outstanding with gold and green highlights. Anyone knowing more about this piece is urged to contact me.

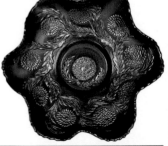

Ten Mums

This is Fenton's #1075 pattern found on water sets, large bowls (three-in-one or ruffled), and rare plates. Colors are marigold, amethyst, cobalt blue, green, and white, with rare peach opalescent reported. The mould work is very good, especially on the bowls and plates, and the water pitcher is a tall graceful one.

Tennessee Star

Similar but different is the way one collector described this vase pattern by Riihimaki. These vases may be found in marigold, amber, and blue (shown), and I understand the tops may be found in different shapes. I am grateful to the Ayers family for sharing the photo.

Ten Pointed Star (Higbee)

Standing 3¼" tall, this rare Higbee mug is a real beauty. The pattern is shown in crystal in other shapes including a pitcher but the iridized mug is a real find. The pattern, while busy, is very balanced, covering the available space in fine order and the lustre is quite good. The base measures 2⅝" across and the top opening 2⅞". The handle is deeply notched on both sides.

Texas (U.S. Glass)

This U. S. Glass States pattern is also called Texas Loop or Loop with Stippled Panels. It is found mostly in crystal and was first made in 1900. I've heard of soft marigold items in this pattern that were iridized by Robert Hanson, but the breakfast set shown here (3" tall) is on a lavender colored glass and has all the attributes of old carnival glass. Texas was pattern #15067.

Texas Tumbler

This well-known Brockwitz piece is not really a tumbler but more like a vase or celery holder. It is found in either blue or marigold carnival glass. The pattern is really a part of a line that includes Star and Hobs and Northern Lights variations. I certainly thank the Ayers family for the photo and the information they've shared.

Thin and Wide Rib (Northwood)

Thin and Wide Rib is often confused with Northwood's Thin Rib, although this one has alternating wide and thin ribs. It is found in several sizes in marigold, amethyst, green, cobalt blue, olive green, white, ice blue, ice green, vaseline, aqua, teal, smoke, sapphire, and the rare ice lavender shown. Thanks to Connie Wilson for sharing this beautiful pastel with me.

Thin Rib (Fenton)

Most collectors lump this pattern into the Fine Rib pattern from the same company but it really is quite different. A close look discloses that the ribs are farther apart and are not arranged in groups that end in an arc. Thin Rib's design ends at both top and bottom in a point and are all the same length. It is found on candlesticks and vases. Colors are marigold, amethyst, green, cobalt blue, and the rare red shown, one of only two reported in this color. Thanks to Quindy Robertson for photo.

Thin Rib (Northwood)

Here is an exterior pattern everyone must know because it is found on some of Northwood's best known bowl patterns, including Good Luck and Strawberry. It is simple enough, but held to the light, it adds greatly to the design.

Thin Rib and Drape

There seems to be some mystery about these small 4" – 7" vases. Many collectors consider this just another small Imperial pattern, but on close examination, you'll learn the base is the same pattern as the English Hobstar and Cut Triangles pattern, and word from England is that this is a Sowerby vase. Colors are marigold, purple, green, and cobalt blue. And since green isn't found on many English items (Diving Dolphins is known in green), we may have a vase that was made by Imperial and copied by Sowerby.

Thistle (English)

What a pretty little vase this is. This 6" soft amber Thistle vase is a well designed bit of color for vase lovers. The maker is English.

Thistle (Fenton)

Fenton's Thistle is one of three thistle patterns from this company. It is found on 8" – 9" bowls, a 9" plate, and on a bowl with advertising on the base. Bowls are found in marigold, amethyst, green, blue, aqua, vaseline, and horehound, while the plate is known in only the first three colors.

Thistle and Lotus

Fenton's Thistle and Lotus seems to be a very neglected pattern. It is actually rather scarce. It is found on small 6¼" – 7" bowls with either a ruffled edge or in an ice cream shape. Colors are limited to marigold, green, and cobalt blue with marigold more easily found. The exterior is the familiar Berry and Leaf Circle pattern.

Thistle and Thorn

Credited to the Sowerby Glass Company by many collectors, this pattern has a British look about the design. It is found in the creamer (shown), a footed sugar, an 8½" footed plate (pulled from the large sugar piece), and a sugar that has been turned up and is called a nut bowl. The only color I've seen is marigold with a good deep color and a strong iridescence.

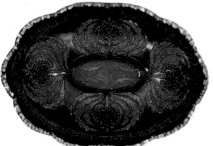

Thistle Banana Boat

This beautiful Fenton banana boat is another of the underrated patterns in carnival glass. The four-footed banana boat is massive in concept and bold in design with the Thistle on the interior and Cattail and Water Lily outside. It is usually found in marigold, amethyst, green, and cobalt blue. The iridescence is quite heavy, usually with much gold.

Threaded Butterflies

It is a distinct pleasure to be able to show this rare, rare U. S. Glass plate. The exterior is the familiar Colorado pattern, not known before in carnival glass and the color is a beautiful aqua. I am very grateful to Maxine Burkhardt for allowing me to photograph this back in 1997 (no others have shown up since).

Threaded Petals

Shown is a small bowl, 5¾" wide and 2½" deep. It has the horizontal mould seam so often found on Sowerby products so I suspect it was from that company. The design is a simple one of threading and a six-petal flower extending from a small starred center. Thanks to the Hilkenes for this one.

Threaded Six Panel

Shown is a bud vase that is 7¾" tall. It has six panels and a banded top with threading and the base has a whirling star with a 16-point inner star. The maker is unknown, at least to me, but I feel it is possibly a product of this country. Thanks to Nigel Gamble for this one.

Threaded Wide Panel

Threaded Wide Panel is found in goblets and covered candy compotes in red, green, amethyst, white, celeste blue, and pink iridescent. The name is derived from the threading that runs around the rim. Both shapes are made in two sizes and shown in a recent Dugan-Diamond book.

Threaded Wide Panel Variant

This variant is apparently from Dugan like the Threaded Wide Panel. The goblet has a soda gold type decoration around the top band. The color is a rich cobalt blue.

Three Diamonds

This interesting pattern is from Argentina (Papini). It is found on a three-piece night set (the underplate is missing from this set). The only color reported is marigold and the complete set consists of a water bottle, tumbler, and an underplate.

Three Footer

Three Footer is another pattern credited to Eda. This interesting bowl was shared by the Ayers family. It is known in marigold, blue (shown), and an unusual lavender.

Three Fruits

Northwood's Three Fruits is a cousin to the Fruits and Flowers design. Several mold variations are known. The plate shown has weak stippling (maybe from a worn mold) and you will notice that on the center group of cherries, the middle leaf is pointing to the right of the two apples/plums (whatever they may be), as opposed to some which point to the middle of the apples. These are found with a combination of designs: stippled and banded with the middle leaf pointing one way or another, no stippling and no bands with the middle leaf pointing to either direction. Either way, other than stippling or certain back patterns, it won't make much, if any difference in pricing. It can be found in bowls of all sizes and plates. Colors include both brights and pastels, and bowls can be flat or footed. Thanks to Samantha Prince for sharing the photo.

Three Fruits Banded

I'm showing this as a different pattern name strictly for illustration purposes. Banded versions will price about the same as non-banded, however stippled pieces and pieces with certain back patterns seem to bring more. If you'll notice, this bowl has banding circling the entire bowl just beyond the outer edge of the pattern. The center leaf design has the middle leaf pointing between the two apples. Some of these have the middle leaf pointing to the right, between the two apples and the group of cherries. Some are stippled and some are not. If you compare this to the regular Three Fruits pattern you can see the difference. Thanks to the Remmens for the nice photo.

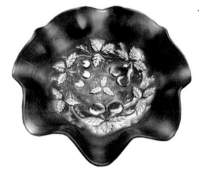

Three Fruits Medallion

One of the variations of the regular Three Fruits pattern from Northwood, this one has a medallion of three leaves in the center, hence the name. It can be found on either spatula footed or collar based bowls with the exterior having either the Basketweave or Meander patterns. Colors include marigold, green, amethyst, black amethyst, cobalt blue, horehound, pearl, aqua opalescent, ice green opalescent, ice blue opalescent, sapphire, and the odd clear example with amethyst swirls throughout (shown).

Three Fruits Variant

Whether it is a Fenton pattern or Dugan/Diamond, this design is very different from the Northwood Three Fruits. It is found mostly on plates (bowls exist and one was shown in the eighth edition of this book). Colors are marigold, blue, green, and amethyst and pieces were reproduced for L. G. Wright in amethyst.

Three-In-One

Imperial Glass's premier crystal pattern from 1904 is known in carnival glass in bowls, small plates (6" – 7"), a rose bowl, and a toothpick holder that has been widely reproduced. Colors known are marigold, purple, and smoke on bowls, marigold and vaseline on plates, marigold on the sauce bowl or the rose bowl, and green on the toothpick holder. Here is shown a beautiful purple bowl that is deep and round, without ruffles.

Three Monkeys Bottle

I'm not sure how many of these are around, but not many I'd guess. The one shown is the reported example in all the previous pattern books, so it may have only a few brothers. The Three Monkeys bottle is of clear glass with good iridescence, stands 8" tall, and bears the words "Patent Pending – 8 oz." on the base. It is a rare find for bottle lovers.

Three Rivers Variant

Similar to both Canadian and Cape Cod patterns in crystal, this variant of a seldom discussed pattern called Little Rivers was a surprise to find in iridized glass. I have no idea of its age at this time. It may be a copy of the original that dates to the 1870s in clear glass. At any rate, the piece shown is a pickle jar with metal lid and fitted holder. The iridescence is a pale marigold.

This is one of Imperial's better vase patterns (there is a Two Row Variant). It stands about 8" tall and is known in marigold, purple, and smoke carnival glass. The color is superb on all the examples I've seen and the rarity of this piece is underrated. The marigold is rarer than the purple but the smoke is rarer than either.

Thumbprint and Oval

This beautiful piece shows one of Imperial's best small vase designs. It stands only 5½" tall, and can be found in marigold and the rich purple shown. The pattern is simple, yet strong.

Tiered Panels

This unusual cup sits on a dome base that swells into the bowl and then swells again. The interior has smooth paneling on each section and the outside is perfectly plain. The color is a good marigold with strong iridescence. I suspect this may be an Imperial design but have no proof. The shape resembles Fenton's Scale Band pitcher however, so anyone having additional information is asked to contact me.

Tiered Thumbprint

Here is a pattern with thin iridization but a very nice pattern that fills the glass much like Moonprint. Tiered Thumbprint may well be a British pattern but I can't be sure. It has been seen in two sizes of bowls also and certainly other shapes may exist.

Tiers

This 7½" bowl is a very interesting piece of glass because it has the following lettering just inside the rim: "Pat. 4 – 4 – 22 #60746." I have no idea who made this pattern but the glass is quite thick and heavy, and the iridescence is quite good. The design consists of a series of wide bands that are in tiers, hence the name. It has been reported in a tumbler also.

Tiger Lily

Imperial's #484 pattern on this intaglio water set is so well designed that it was later copied in Finland. Colors are usually marigold, purple, green, olive, and aqua, but tumblers are found also in cobalt blue, violet, amber, and clambroth. In January 2008 a rare green hat shaped whimsey made from the tumbler showed up.

265

Tiger Lily (Finland)

This pattern is also called Tiger Lily Variant by some collectors. It was copied by Riihimaki from the well-known Imperial pattern and is shown in Riihimaki catalogs after 1936. This version can be found in a milk pitcher, a water pitcher, and a tumbler with straight or flared tops. Colors are marigold and a spectacular blue.

Tiny Bubbles

This 8½" tall vase that was found in Sweden has an allover design of bubbles in rows. The color is a green glass with a marigold iridization. Thanks Kristina, for sharing it with me, and I welcome additional information about it.

Tiny Daisy

Here is a marigold covered dish from Sowerby. This pattern was previously reported in a vaseline creamer. These are the only pieces I've heard about and I welcome any additional information.

Tiny Hat

Miniatures seem to have an attraction all their own and this rare hat shape is no exception. Fewer than half a dozen of these are known in various shapes. The one shown is the smallest, measuring 1¾" tall, 2½" wide, and 3" long. The color looks like a strong purple but the glass is actually dark cobalt blue. Westmoreland is mentioned as a possible maker but I have no confirmation at this time.

Tiny Hobnail Lamp

Although late in carnival glass history only a few of these miniature oil lamps have been reported. The base is 3" high and has a diameter of 2¼". The shade, which matches, is clear. I haven't a notion as to the maker, but the lamps are scarce and cute as can be.

Tobacco Leaf

Like the other Shrine champagnes shown elsewhere in this edition, this piece was produced as a souvenir for a convention. Here is the 1909 Louisville piece with a tobacco leaf base, swords on either side, with Louisville and a horseshoe on one side and Pittsburgh, Pa., and a Syria seal on the other.

Tokio was shown in an Eda (Sweden) catalog. This very attractive vase is 7½" tall and is shown in cobalt blue. The pattern is also known in a bowl shape in the same color (marigold and pearl carnival were also made). Production, I am told, dates from the late 1920s or early 1930s.

Toltec

Part of McKee's "tec" series, Toltec is mostly found in crystal in many shapes. The only shapes reported in carnival glass are a covered butter and the tankard pitcher shown. I want to thank Ronald and Carolyn Chesney as well as John H. Nielsen for the photo of this rare item.

Tomahawk

Tomahawk was made by Cambridge Glass and reproduced by Degenhart. This 7½" long novelty piece is mainly found in cobalt blue but at least two rare amethyst examples are known and here is one of them. New pieces are found in aqua and vaseline as well as non-iridized pieces.

Tomato Band

Tomato Band was made in Czechoslovakia as shown on the paper label on the bottom of the decanter. This liquor set consists of a tray, decanter, and liquor glasses, all with gold trim. The tray does not have the tomato banding of red enameling but the other pieces do. The glass is thin and fragile and the iridescence is good. Each glass is about half the size of a shot glass in capacity.

Top Hat Vase

Oddly named by Mrs. Hartung, this vase is 9½" tall and has a 2½" base diameter. It is shown in marigold but is known in pastel blue, lavender, clambroth, rose, and clear also. On the example shown is a paper label that says "Berlin, N.H." I believe this pattern was made by the Dunbar Glass Company in the 1930s, the same firm that produced the Aramis pattern.

Torchiere Candlestick

These are rather short and have a flat base with a rolled stem that flares into a wax catcher before narrowing to the candle cup. I'd appreciate any information readers can share on these candlesticks. It is Duncan-Miller's #28 pattern.

Tornado

This very well designed 6" vase is found both plain and ribbed. In addition, there is a variant shown below, as well as a flared whimsey, shown in previous editions. Colors are marigold, amethyst, green, cobalt, white, ice blue, and the rare whimsey is in lavender. The Tornado vase is a collectors' favorite, one that usually sells for top dollar and always brings excitement to any collection.

Tornado Variant

This extremely rare variant is one inch taller that the regular Tornado vase. The base closely resembles that of Northwood's Corn vase, and the top is tightly crimped. The only color reported is a deep rich marigold, iridized both inside and out.

Towers

Shown is the small flared vase shape in this pattern, long suspected to be from the Sowerby Company of England. The color is a good strong marigold and while I feel other shapes and possibly other colors may exist, they haven't been reported.

Town Pump

This Northwood creation is one of the better recognized novelties in carnival glass. It was made in 1912 (a similar pump with trough was made in opalescent glass in the 1890s). The very collectible Town Pump is 6½" tall, has a flat collar base, and is decorated with ivy. Colors are purple (most easily found), marigold (somewhat rare), and green (very rare). Perfect examples are few due to the protrusions, which are easily damaged.

Tracery (Millersburg)

The exterior of this large 7½" bonbon is plain, certainly not typical for a Millersburg design. It is found in the oval shape as shown, or sometimes squared. Tracery has been seen in amethyst as shown and green. Surely a marigold was made, so be on the lookout.

Trailing Flowers (Crystal)

Trailing Flowers was shown in a Crown Crystal catalog of 1929 as their #2520. This scarce and attractive interior pattern shows small branches that trail flowers just as the name implies. The shape of the bowl's edge is just like the Fenton Holly bowls. The example shown measures 7" in diameter. It is seen in marigold only and has an exterior pattern called Crown of Diamonds.

Despite being late carnival glass, some of these pieces are quite well done and the pitcher (no lid) shown illustrates that. Shapes known are pitchers, tumblers, a plate, pickle jar, console bowl, candy jar, candlesticks, and a lidded pitcher. Colors are mostly marigold, but both amber and aqua have been reported in the water pitcher. This was Jeannette's Finlandia pattern. It is also known as Crepe.

Tree Bark Variant

This is now known to be a Jeannette pattern. Shapes are a water set, planter, candleholder, vase, and various bowl shapes like the one shown which has a ringed base. All these pieces are, of course, late carnival and should be bought as such with prices paid accordingly. Still the color and workmanship is quite good and superior to most iridized Depression glass products.

While not the most well designed pattern, it does have its place. It is often confused with Crackle, which has stippling; Tree of Life doesn't. Shapes known are water sets, plates, perfume bottles, a vase whimsey, bowls, a handled basket, and a plate. Shown is the standard tumbler in rich marigold and a very rare juice tumbler in softer pastel marigold.

Tree Trunk (Northwood)

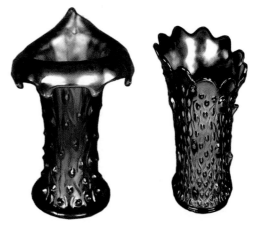

Because of the availability of sizes and colors, this vase was either very popular or a much loved design of the company. Found in at least five sizes and several design variations, whole collections could be made from this pattern and prices and desirability are both high. Vases are termed as squat, standard, mid-sized funeral, large funeral, and elephant's foot. Colors are marigold, amethyst, green, cobalt blue, ice blue, ice green, white, teal, aqua opalescent, lime green, marigold in custard (shown), and a very rare iridized blue slag treatment. Heights range from 5" on the squat vases to a huge 22" on the large funeral size. Nearly every vase has the trademark. Shown are the rare elephant's foot funeral vase in amethyst and the very rare J.I.P. (jack-in-the-pulpit) shape in marigold.

Tree Trunk Variant (Northwood)

The distinguishing characteristic of this vase is the band above the collar base. This base is sometimes called the "plunger base." It is found in marigold, amethyst, blue, and green. Midsize vases have a base diameter of 3¾" to 4¾", and the funeral vase has a base diameter of 5¼". Note the difference in the base of this variant and the elephant's foot funeral vase's base shown in the regular Tree Trunk photo.

Trefoil Fine Cut (Millersburg)

What a joy it is to show this Millersburg rarity! Usually found as the exterior pattern of Many Stars bowls in carnival glass, this rarity when found alone, either in crystal or on this marigold chop plate, is a showstopper. This single example was once owned by Jerry and Carol Curtis but was sold at auction in Oct. 2007. It is a privilege to show it here. The interior is unpatterned. Thanks to Dave Doty and the Britts for the superb photo.

Trevor's Tesselated Rose

This unusual light fixture is from Alan Sedgwick who apparently found it in England where he lives. I can't identify a maker, but being a utilitarian item, it was probably made in some quantity. It was named by Alan.

Triands

This pattern was called Niobe in Brockwitz's 1929 and 1931 catalogs. Catalog drawings show bowls, a table set, compote, rectangular tray, breakfast creamer and sugar on a tray, a covered compote, a vase, a large stemmed fruit bowl, a large plate, and the celery vase shown. Marigold seems to be the only reported color in carnival glass.

Tribal Vase

The Tribal vase is from India and much like GOA and the CB vase. This one has more design variations including arabesques, a flower, diagonal lines, and even beaded circles. The vase is almost hourglass in its shape.

Triple Alliance

Triple Alliance is Brockwitz's #8379. This biscuit jar shown here with the proper lid is 6½" tall and has a 4" base. It can be found in a beautiful blue as well as the marigold shown.

Triplets

Please compare this Dugan bowl pattern with its sister pattern called Daisy Dear and you will see very little imagination was used to distinguish one pattern from the other. Triplets has true leaves on the stems while Daisy Dear's are more fern-like and the flowers on the former are pointed while Daisy Dear's have rounded petals. Found mostly on marigold and weak amethyst, Triplets can occasionally be seen on green also and I suspect a peach opalescent may turn up one day.

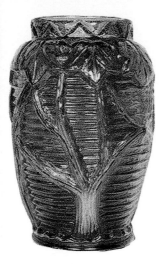

This impressive 9" vase is a real beauty with a very unusual design of branches and leaves over rings. At the top is a collar that has zig-zagging. A rich marigold with amberish hue is shown.

Trout and Fly

Trout and Fly is one of Millersburg's best-known patterns and very similar in design to the scarcer Big Fish pattern. The Trout and Fly has a different arrangement of floral spray and of course there is the fly just beyond the mouth of the fish. It is found on bowls that are ruffled, three-in-one edge, ice cream shape, square, or tri-cornered, and a very rare plate shape. Colors are marigold, amethyst, green, lavender, and a rare horehound (ruffled bowl).

Trumpet

I haven't found the maker of these nice candlesticks yet but do suspect Dugan. The color is a nice ice green with good iridescence and I feel that other colors such as ice blue and white may exist also. Thanks to Tom Mordini for the name and photo.

Tsunami

Margaret Yvonne Iley shares this impressive 10" bowl (4" deep) and that's about all the information I have. It is probably European or Scandinavian, but the edge treatment is very unusual. I certainly welcome any information on this piece.

Tulip (Millersburg)

This beautiful and rare compote is exactly like the Flowering Vine one shown elsewhere except it has no interior design. It stands about 9" tall, and the bowl measures roughly 6" across. The only colors I've seen are marigold and amethyst, but green was more than likely made. In addition to this size, a 7" variant is known in amethyst.

Tulip and Cane (Imperial)

This very pretty pattern, also known as Imperial's #9, can be found in many shapes in crystal, dating from 1909. But in carnival glass, only a small dome-based bowl, an 8 ounce goblet, a 3 ounce wine, a 1¼ ounce wine, a 4 ounce stemmed claret, and the rare nappy (shown) are known. All pieces are known in marigold, but the bowl can be found in smoke as well, and I suspect it was made in clambroth too. The goblet is also known in smoke and was reproduced in a strange blue carnival in 1970. Thanks to Christine and Dennis Golden for the photo.

Tulip Scroll (Millersburg)

Only a few of these attractive Millersburg vases seem to show up from time to time, mostly in amethyst, but once in a while in green or the quite rare marigold. I've seen them as tall as 11", but most are about 7" and less stretched out. They are always quickly snatched up and are a popular vase pattern.

Tuscan Column

This interesting mini-vase whimsey is green carnival with a stretch finish. It stands 3" tall and has a porcelain floral applied top. The maker isn't known to me at this time but in shape it much resembles a Jefferson Glass opalescent pattern called Jefferson Spool. I'd like to hear from anyone with information about this piece.

Twelve Rings

Much like the Tiered Thumbprint candlestick, this one has a series of overlying rings from top to bottom. The color is a bit weak but the iridescence is adequate. I suspect this is another European pattern but can't be sure. It is 9" tall with a 4½" base diameter. It is Jeannette's #23 pattern.

Twigs

Twigs was made by Diamond and found in opalescent glass as well as carnival. This could be called "the Beauty Bud Vase with arms." They range in size from 3½" to 12" tall, depending on how much they were pulled. Colors are marigold and purple. Beware: It is suspected that old white opalescent examples have been newly iridized and sold as old peach opalescent versions.

Twin Golden Thistle

Like the other "golden" patterns, this one may be from Karhula of Finland. The oval tray shown measures 10¼" in length and has twice as many thistles and leaves as the regular Golden Thistle. All of these pieces seem to have enchanted collectors and are eagerly sought.

Twins

Like Imperial's Fashion pattern, Twins is another geometric design manufactured in large quantities in berry sets, a rare bride's basket, and the familiar fruit bowl and stand. Pieces have been found in a good rich marigold and a very beautiful smoke, and the berry set has been found in green, as shown. Needless to say, a purple fruit bowl and stand would be a treasure!

This interesting candlestick stands 8½" tall and has a base diameter of 4¼". Only the base and the candle bell are iridized in a rich marigold while the twists are clear and uniridized. Please note the base is the same as Imperial's Premium candlesticks. I am not certain the maker of this at this time and welcome any information. Tiffin is the suspected maker. Thanks to Nigel Gamble for sharing it.

Twisted Optic

Imperial's Twisted Optic is called Swirled Rib by some collectors. It is found in candlesticks, a mug, cup, saucer, center-handled server, creamer, sugar with a lid, bowls (6" – 9"), a covered jar, a 6" plate, a sherbet, a stemmed candy dish, and the huge 14½" plate shown. Colors are primarily marigold but clambroth and smoke do exist. Many of the smoke items show a stretch finish.

Twisted Rib (Dugan)

Dugan's Twisted Rib is pulled or twisted from the #1016 Wide Rib vase. This vase is most often seen in peach opalescent but can be found in marigold, amethyst, green, and cobalt blue. The large ball at the top of each rib distinguishes this vase from the similar Spiralex vase, also by Dugan-Diamond. In addition, Twisted Rib vases usually twist to the right while Spiralex mostly twists to the left.

Two Flowers (Fenton)

Two Flowers is found on several sizes of footed bowls that may have either scrolled feet or spatula feet, on footed plates in two sizes, footed rose bowls in two sizes, and in collar based bowls. Colors are marigold, amethyst, green, cobalt blue, and a rare white. The pattern uses several Fenton fillers: scale band, water plants, and leaves.

Two Fruits

Two Fruits is Fenton's #1695, first made in 1912 and later in 1930 in pink glass. The early carnival pieces are found in round shapes as well as scarce ruffled or square pieces. Colors are marigold, blue, amethyst, scarce green, the rare marigold-over-vaseline shown, and a reported white.

Two-Handled Swirl

Like the regular Two-Handled vase (see Handled Vase), this one with the swirl interior is from Imperial. It is shown in a fan shape but was also made in a JIP shape, a flared top, or a rolled top. Colors are marigold or smoke and each are a bit hard to find.

Universal Home Bottle

This bottle was made by the Hemingray Glass Company in 1931 and illustrated in a brochure. Hemingray made primarily bottles and glass lamp chimney parts. Factories were located in Muncie, Indiana, and Covington, Kentucky, and the Universal Home bottle was made for the Queen City Bottling Company of Cincinnati, Ohio. Thanks, Bob Stahr, for all your research on this company and for sharing this item.

Unpinched Rib

If you will look at the Pinched Rib pattern elsewhere in this edition, you will see this is the same vase without the pinching that is the norm. The example shown is in a dark amber or horehound color with satin iridescence. Thanks to Yvan Beaudry for this unusual item.

Unshod

Often called Fine Rib Variant, this water set is more commonly called Unshod by most collectors. Marigold seems to be the only color reported and the iridescence is about average on most pieces. Unlike the Rex pattern, which has a vine pattern running the length of the handle, Unshod is plain and has more panels than the Rex pattern.

Urn Vase

This unusually shaped vase has been seen in white as well as marigold carnival glass. It stands 9" tall and has a finely grained stippling over the surface. It is made by Tiffin and marked with the ◈ trademark.

U.S. #310 (U.S. Glass)

U.S. #310 was actually a stretch glass pattern from U.S. Glass. It was made in a host of shapes including a tall pedestal vase, hat vase, mayonnaise set, cheese and cracker set, covered candy jar, 12½" footed plate, 10" server with center handle, 8½" plate, flat and footed bowls in several sizes, and 6" and 7½" compotes. Colors are blue, pink, green, olive, and topaz. The piece shown is a 9½" footed bowl with flared rim in blue.

U.S. Glass #15021

U.S. Glass #15021 was found in opalescent glass as well as carnival glass and shown in Butler Brothers ads. The vase shown is nearly 22" tall and is a strong marigold with an amber tint. There are 12 panels that run from top to the collar base of this piece. It resembles both the Slick Willie and Slim Jim vases but is not the same.

U.S. Regal

U.S. Regal was shown in U.S. Glass catalog reprints and was likely exported. It can be found in stemmed cups, stemmed sherbets, and a jardiniere shaped bowl. To date this has only been reported in marigold.

This nice advertising piece has "Lewis 66 Rye, UTAH LIQUOR CO, Phones 478, 228 S. Main St." combined in between the two mums. This piece is of average desirability among advertising collectors and prices are normally affordable. It can be found on plates, one side up bowls, and two sides up (banana) bowls. It is know in amethyst only. Thanks to the Remmens once again for the nice photo.

Valentine

Valentine was originally advertised in crystal as Northwood's #14 pattern where it was available in many shapes. In carnival glass only the berry set pieces are known. The design is all exterior. Certainly an interior companion would boost the interest, but Valentine really deserves more attention than it gets. Marigold is the only reported color.

Venetian

Venetian was made by Millersburg. The original mould came from Ohio Flint Glass where the pattern was called Kenneth. This rare pattern is found in many shapes in crystal, but in carnival glass only the giant vase (rose bowl) and a table set are known. After Millersburg closed, the mould moved to Cambridge and became a lamp base.

Vera

Vera is now credited to Eda Glass Works. This very well done vase is shown in black amethyst with awesome iridescence. It stands about 7" tall and is also reported in marigold. Thanks to David and Amy Ayers for sharing this information with me.

Victorian (Dugan)

This massive, well-balanced bowl pattern is found on shapes that measure from 10" to 11½", depending on shape. Most pieces are found in amethyst (shown) but can also be found in a rare peach opalescent bowl (only a very few are reported to date). The design is much like a quilt with the Wedding Ring pattern. Bowls are found in ruffled or low ice cream shapes. Photo courtesy of Samantha Prince.

Victorian Hand Vase

If you will compare this hand vase with the regular one from Jain Glass Works of India, you will see many differences, so I believe the Victorian Hand vase is not from that firm. Shown is a beautiful lavender example. Please note the beading on the vase and the floral wreath on the wrist, making it far different from the Jain vases. I'd appreciate any information on this vase.

Victorian Trumpet Vase

Only three of these stately vases (also known as Enameled Pansy), have been reported. All have rich marigold leaf bases and lightly iridized tops with delicate enameling. The maker is unknown at this time. Thanks to Mickey Reichel for sharing the photo.

Vineland

These candleholders are very stocky looking and should hold tall candles easily without tipping over. I'm assigning them to Dugan unless I hear different. I suspect colors other than the Ice Blue exist but they've not been brought to my attention to date. Thanks to Samantha Prince for the nice photo.

Vineyard (Dugan)

Made in several shapes in earlier types of glass (probably by Northwood), this pattern in iridized glass was a Dugan product produced about 1910. Pitchers and tumblers are found in marigold as well as amethyst, but the pitcher is also known in peach opalescent as shown.

Vineyard Harvest (Australian Grape)

Because the first tumblers in this pattern were found in Australia, they were named Australian Grape, but since then and especially since Robert Smith made his Jain Glass Works discovery, I know this was a pattern from India. This tumbler stands 5½" tall and has a lip diameter of 3⅝". The color is marigold but it may have been made in blue also.

Vining Daisies

This very nice decanter was found in Argentina, so I suspect it came from there despite not being in my catalogs from that country. I welcome any information from readers.

Vining Leaf

There are two variations of the pattern — one with small berries along portions of the stylized leaves. The examples shown, a rather small bud vase and an ample lady's spittoon, give us this pattern nicely. Please note the frosted effect around the leaves.

This bowl is credited to Dugan and Diamond Glass companies. The bowl is known in marigold, amethyst, white, and clambroth, while the plate shape is found in white and is rather rare. The bowls measure approximately 6½" in diameter and the plate 7½".

Vinlov

Vinlov was Eda's #2502 pattern made in the mid-1920s. This beautiful jardiniere shape, roughly 10" – 11" in length, can be found in purple or marigold.

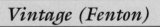

Vintage (Fenton)

Primarily a pattern of bowls and plates, this well-known Fenton design is also found on a one-lily epergne (two sizes), a fernery on feet, a wine glass, bonbon, compote, and several whimsey shapes. Bowls are found in a sauce, a medium bowl (7" – 8"), a large bowl (9" – 10"), 6" (rare), 7" – 8", 9" plates, and 10" chop plate. Colors include marigold, amethyst, purple, green, blue, celeste blue, red, lime green, aqua opalescent, and amberina. Of course not all shapes are found in all these colors. Some pieces are also called Vintage Leaf (has center leaf) but I've grouped all the Vintage patterns together.

Vintage (Millersburg)

This Millersburg pattern is a real favorite. It is found in a 6" sauce and a 9" – 10" larger bowl. It has the Vintage pattern (three large bunches of grapes and a wreath of leaves) on the inside and a hobnail exterior. Colors are the usual Millersburg ones of marigold, amethyst, and green, but blue examples are known. All pieces are rare in this pattern.

Vintage (Northwood)

Northwood purchased this mould from Jefferson Glass in 1907. Northwood then used it for opalescent production and in 1910 added it to their carnival line as an exterior pattern. The Vintage bowl is dome based. It can also be found in carnival glass without an interior pattern like the green example with an Alaskan treatment shown.

Vintage Banded

Although documented in both pitchers and tumblers, the mug shape is the most often seen. Colors are mostly marigold but the mug is known in smoke and here is a rare, rare amethyst one. Made by Diamond, production was probably rather late as the mug was advertised in 1922 in Butler Brothers. Additionally, I've heard of mugs in a light green glass with marigold iridescence but haven't seen one yet. Beware, as I am told that L. G. Wright reproduced the water set.

Violet Baskets

Here are two of the dainty little baskets designed to hold small bouquets like violets. One has its own glass handle, while the other fits into a handled sleeve. The File pattern in the glass is much like that on some Stork and Rushes pieces, and I suspect both of these baskets come from the Dugan company.

Virginia (Banded Portland)

Virginia was U.S. Glass's #15071, part of the States series, made in 1901 in crystal in a toothpick holder, shakers, cruet, vase, compote, wine, water bottle, jam jar, relish, candlesticks, tumbler, cologne, tray, and the puff box shown. Only the salt shakers, the puff box, the toothpick holder, and two rare tumblers have been seen in carnival glass to date. The tumblers are found in a soft finish called Maiden's Blush.

Virginia Blackberry

Found many years ago, this child's pitcher is the lone carnival example reported to date. It is 4½" tall. The pattern is known in a child's water set in crystal. The mould pattern without the berries is called Galloway, a U.S. Glass pattern, but many collectors believe this pitcher is European. If anyone can supply a new photo of this piece I'd love to have one.

Vogue (Fostoria)

With a plain narrow band around the top, alternating concave panels in two sizes, and handles that are "hipped" or lowered from the top, this is a real beauty. The Vogue toothpick holder stands 2⅛" tall and has a top diameter of 1¾". The base is about 1½" wide and has a 14-point star. Rare and desirable, this piece is shown in Weatherman's *Fostoria – Its First Fifty Years*.

Votive Light

From the Cristales Mexicanos factory in Mexico and marked with the M-inside-a-C mark, this votive is a rare and desirable item. It stands 4¼" tall, has a raised cross on one side and the Bleeding Heart of Jesus on the other. Marigold is the only reported color, usually quite strong with fine iridescence.

Waffle

While there are many similar designs with a waffle-type pattern, this one seems to be the same as a crystal pattern once made by Bryce Brothers, Pittsburgh. This company joined U.S. Glass in 1891 and five years later moved to Mt. Pleasant, Pennsylvania, where they remained in business until 1952. I feel there must have been at least a creamer made in carnival glass to go with this nice open sugar and perhaps other shapes as well.

Waffle Block

Waffle Block was made by the Imperial Company (their #698) in more than a dozen shapes in carnival glass including bowls, a 6" plate, a 10" vase, a rose bowl, water set, sugar, creamer, parfait, punch set, handled basket, shakers, and a whimsey spittoon. In addition there is a variant tumbler. Colors include marigold, clambroth, or teal but not all colors are found on all shapes. The handled basket seems to be the only piece reported in purple.

Waffle Block and Hobstar (Imperial)

Obviously a product of Imperial, this 13" basket resembles several others from that company in shape and size and is a cousin of the well-known Waffle Block basket. The major difference is the addition of a banding of hobstars at top, bottom, and down each side below the handles. Marigold is the only color reported to date, but a clambroth, smoke, or even a helios green wouldn't shock me as possibilities, nor would aqua since the first Imperial "Whirling Star" punch top was recently found in that color.

Wagon Wheel

Besides this attractive covered candy bowl that stands 5" tall and has a brown enameling cut-back design, I've seen a taller version that has green enameling, so other shapes and colors may well exist. I still haven't learned the maker but I lean strongly toward Czechoslovakia. Any information from readers would be appreciated.

Washboard

Despite being a late pattern with the crystal items made well into the 1970s, the carnival pieces are not plentiful. I've previously shown a tumbler, a creamer, and a punch cup, but here is the scarce covered butter dish and it is the most appealing of all the shapes. The tumbler measures 4⅞" tall and the creamer 5¼".

Water Lily

Similar in design to Fenton's Lotus and Grape pattern, this naturalistic pattern actually has sections of lotus and poinsettia blossoms. It is found on both flat or footed berry sets and a bonbon shape. Colors are marigold, amethyst, green, blue, teal, vaseline, red, lime green opalescent, amber, amber slag, and aqua, but certainly not all sizes or shapes are found in all these colors.

Water Lily and Cattails (Fenton)

This pattern is most often seen as the exterior pattern on the Thistle banana boat by Fenton. Shown is the very scarce to rare, large berry bowl in green. Although they don't often come up for sale, the price hasn't risen, as you would think, likely due to it being an exterior pattern, which is less desirable. It can also be found on a water set and small berry bowls in marigold.

Water Lily and Cattails (Northwood)

This is Northwood's design found only on water sets primarily in marigold. Here is the only reported cobalt blue pitcher and it is a real beauty (cobalt tumblers also exist). Please note that the pitcher's shape is quite different than Fenton's, but I believe the Northwood version followed soon on the heels of Fenton's in 1908.

Water Lily and Dragonfly (Crystal)

I'm told this bowl didn't come with a flower frog as I previously showed it so I stand corrected. This bowl comes with a plain exterior or may have the Broken Chain (S-Band) exterior pattern. Colors are marigold and purple, and the design of a center water lily, two side lilies, and four dragonflies is a good one.

Water Lily Variant

This Fenton Water Lily pattern has a true water lily in the center of the bowl, while the other has a stylized flower that covers the entire center. Oddly, more of these variants are found than the other. Thanks to the Remmens for sharing it.

Webbed Clematis

Here is the vase shown in earlier books but this example has an added goofus paint treatment. It stands 12½" tall and is on a soft marigold carnival treatment but can also be found in black amethyst in the vase as well as a rare lamp made from the vase. The maker is unknown at this time.

Weeping Cherry

Weeping Cherry was made by the Diamond Glass Company in the 1920s, and is found on flat or dome based bowls. The design resembles the Dugan Cherry made by Diamond's predecessor at the factory. Colors are marigold mostly, but cobalt blue and amethyst are known, and white and peach opalescent have been reported for years but not confirmed.

Western Daisy

I'm very thankful to Jackie Peay for this photo, which finally allows me to show this hard-to-find pattern. As you can see, the pattern is all exterior, which is not pleasing to some collectors, but the design is nice nonetheless. This Dugan pattern can be found in peach opalescent and the green shown, which is the first example in that color I've heard of to date.

Western Thistle

This nicely done Riihimaki Glass pattern is known in a water set, a vase, and a berry bowl. Here are two tumblers, and as you can see, they have slightly different shapes and they are of different heights. Colors for this pattern are marigold and cobalt blue.

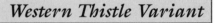

Western Thistle Variant

Western Thistle Variant is from Riihimaki and is just like the regular Western Thistle except without the diamond banding. This pattern is found on a compote, bowls in two sizes, a vase, and this beautiful chop plate shown. Colors known are marigold, pink, blue, smoky blue, and amber.

Westmoreland #750 Basket

This pattern is much like their #752 basket, but it has no oval medallion on the sides. These baskets date from the 1920s in carnival glass but were made in crystal, decorated crystal, and a range of colors (sometimes with black trim). Westmoreland literature says these baskets were made in 3", 4", 6", 7", and 8" sizes but I'm not sure how many were iridized. The examples shown measure 7" and 11½" from bottom to the top of the handle, so Westmoreland measurements must be only for the body of the baskets.

Westmoreland #1700

Introduced in 1912 in crystal, this pattern originally had 22 shapes. It was continued as late as 1932 in an expanded list. In many ways, it is similar to #1776 line, also known as Keystone Colonial. Shown is a two-handled open sugar on a stem in a pretty marigold carnival. It is the only piece I've seen to date in this pattern that was iridized. If you will compare this piece with the Chippendale Kry-stol pieces shown elsewhere in this edition you will see they are quite similar.

Westmoreland #1776

This piece is similar in design and size to the Keystone Colonial handled compote. With the rolled rim it is called a sweetmeat by the company. It was made in the 1910 – 1912 era and is found on purple carnival glass with a mirror-like thin iridization.

Westmoreland Colonial Lily Vase

Made by Westmoreland (1912 – 1940), this vase is primarily found in crystal or colored glass (ruby stained versions were reproduced in the 70s), but here is the first iridized example that I've heard of. The finish is a mirror-like radium with good color (which makes the age very questionable to me). The vase stands 6" tall. A 9" was made in other treatments.

Wheat

Besides the rare stemmed sherbet and the rare sweetmeat featured in previous books, I am happy to feature the only other shape reported, a covered bowl. The design is from the Northwood Company. To date, two sweetmeats are known (green and amethyst), one sherbet (amethyst), and one bowl (amethyst). The design is good and one has to wonder why more pieces aren't found.

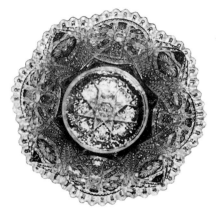

Wheels

Wheels is credited to the Imperial Glass Company and was only reported on large, 8" – 9" bowls in marigold carnival and crystal, but now I am happy to show the first reported 5" bowl in clambroth. The pattern is all exterior with a collar base. The clambroth iridescence is on both the interior and the exterior, making photographing quite difficult. All carnival pieces in Wheels are rare and very collectible.

Whirling Hobstar (U.S. Glass)

Here is a child's punch bowl, base, and cups that were made by the U.S. Glass Company. The pattern was also known as Radiant Daisy or Slewed Horseshoe and was later produced by Iittala-Karhula Glass of Finland. Known primarily in crystal or ruby stained glass, a few items must have been iridized.

Whirling Leaves (Millersburg)

Found on 9" – 10" bowls that may be round, ice cream shape, tri-cornered, ruffled, or square, this Millersburg pattern always has an exterior pattern called Fine Cut Ovals. The colors found are marigold, amethyst, green, and a rare blue. The square or tri-cornered shapes are the rarest and the example shown has gold edge gilding and is the first of this treatment reported, making it even rarer.

Whirling Star (Imperial)

Whirling Star was originally Imperial's #555, made mostly in crystal. It is perhaps best known for the reissues in the 1960s. Few iridized pieces are really old. Shapes known in old carnival glass are the punch bowl and base, punch cups, 9" – 11" ruffled bowls, and a stemmed compote. Colors are mostly marigold, but the compote is reported in green, and thanks to Rick Kojis this nice aqua punch bowl top can now be shown as the first piece reported in that color. Avoid all smoke pieces, because all are new. Also, be aware that the old punch bowls and bases were also turned into lamps with the base being the lamp's body and the bowl turned upside down to serve as the shade.

Whirlsaway (Jain)

Here is another of the unusual tumblers traced to the Jain Glass Works of India. It was named by its owner, Robert Smith, and comes in two sizes as well as two shapes. The example shown is tall and flared and the other is shorter with a bulging middle and a flaring collar base. Both show excellent marigold iridescence.

Whirlwind

I haven't been able to locate this bowl in any reference, but believe it may be an unlisted Westmoreland pattern. The pattern and iridescence are very much like finishes from that company. Only the interior is iridized with a thin glossy finish with some opalescence on the edges. Thanks to Charles Knucha for sharing it with me and I welcome any information about this pattern.

White Oak

For years this wonderful tumbler (there is no matching pitcher reported) has been a mystery. Many believe it was made by Dugan and many others believe it was made by Millersburg. It is rare and desirable regardless.

Wickerwork (English)

Besides the bowl and base I've shown in marigold, this shallow bowl is known in amethyst, as shown. This is Sowerby's #1102 pattern that was made over a number of years in various glass treatments.

Wide Panel (Fenton)

Primarily used as an exterior pattern by the Fenton Company, Wide Panel was also a vase pattern, shown in a 1920 Butler Brothers catalog. The vase was made in marigold, green, cobalt blue, amethyst, and red. The bowl shown exhibits the Fenton Wide Panel as it is usually seen, on the exterior of bowls.

Wide Panel (Imperial)

Constituting several pattern numbers from Imperial (#645, 647, 6569), this Wide Panel pattern is found in 9" bowls, 8" and 10" plates (the salad set), and a huge 12" centerpiece bowl with a 14" underplate. Colors are marigold, clambroth, teal, red, white, and celeste blue, as well as smoke, and pink for the salad set pieces, and marigold, clambroth, and smoke for the centerpiece bowl and plate. Here is the centerpiece set in clambroth.

Wide Panel and Diamond

I've heard of this 7" vase (the base measures 3½" with a 3¾" top) in black amethyst as well as the marigold example shown. It has a three-part mould and a 20-rayed base. The shape seems to mimic vases from Brockwitz but I have no proof of the maker at this time.

Wide Panel Cherry

Wide Panel Cherry is now known to be a Jenkins product and was made around the same time as their Cherry Smash and Stippled Strawberry patterns shown elsewhere. This piece is lidded and is found in marigold as shown, or on white carnival (a most unusual color for a piece from Jenkins).

Wide Panel Epergne

This standout four-lily epergne is really part of Northwood's Wide Panel line that also includes vases, bowls, and plates. Colors are marigold, amethyst, green, cobalt blue, white, ice blue, ice green, and aqua opalescent. It was made from 1909 to 1913.

Wide Panel Shade

Shown is one of the most beautiful light shades I've run across. The emerald green color is spectacular as is the iridescence. The owner says she was told it came from the Northwood Company which certainly is possible, since they made many fine shades, both marked and unmarked.

Wide Panel Variant

Rather plain for a Northwood product, this water set relies on symmetry and grace for its charm. It can be found in marigold and white as well as enameled in both colors and a beautiful Persian blue.

Wide Rib (Dugan)

Dugan-Diamond's #1016 vase pattern resembles others from Northwood and Imperial. The distinguishing feature is the knob-like tips at the top of each rib. The vases can be shaped in several ways and often form a twisted ribbing. Colors are marigold, amethyst, green, cobalt blue, peach opalescent (most often seen), and white.

Wide Rib (Northwood)

This is one of Northwood's better known vase shapes. It is available in a wide range of colors: marigold, amethyst, purple, green, cobalt blue, olive green, white, ice blue, ice green, teal, smoke, sapphire, aqua opalescent, and the vaseline shown. Sizes include standard, mid-size funeral, and large funeral. Most vases are ruffled and flared but some are a JIP shape. Wide Rib vases are found as short as 5" and as tall as 22".

Wide Swirl

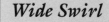

Hartung calls this just Swirl in her tenth book but since I already have a pattern with that name, I've added the wide to point out the differences. Shown is the 7½" milk pitcher in marigold. This one is very different from the Imperial or Northwood Swirl patterns. The maker is unknown, at least to me.

Wigwam (Heisey)

The Heisey Wigwam tumbler stands 3¾" tall with a top diameter of 2¾" and a base measuring 2⅜". The base has a 20-point star that is a bit depressed and is ground. Rare in any treatment, Wigwam can be found in ruby stained glass as well as the beautiful example shown with great color and iridescence.

Wild Berry (Westmoreland)

This small powder box with lid is from Westmoreland. It stands 2½" tall and has a base diameter of 2¾". It is mostly found in marigold but here is a variant in blue opalescent.

Wild Berry Variant

This variant is like the regular Wild Berry covered jar except it has no band of Greek Key design around the top. Only two or three examples are known. The lid says "Souvenir Moorefield, S.D." Thanks the Hamlets for sharing it.

Wild Blackberry

Although very much like the other Fenton Blackberry patterns in design, this is strictly a bowl pattern. It is easily identified by the four center leaves and the wheat-like fronds around the outer edges. Colors are marigold, blue, green, and amethyst. The exterior has the Wide Panel pattern.

Wildflower (Millersburg)

This rare and desirable jelly compote has the cloverleaf base and a fine design of flowers and vines inside. Shapes can be deep and straight, ruffled, or flared as shown. Colors are marigold, green, amethyst, and vaseline with marigold iridescence.

Wildflower (Northwood)

This very fine pattern can be found only as an exterior pattern on the compote. It can be accompanied by a plain interior or the pretty Blossomtime one. The stem is unusual in that it is shaped like a large screw. Colors are marigold, amethyst, green, and blue.

Wild Grape

Wild Grape is often mistaken for the Vintage exterior bowl Northwood purchased from Jefferson Glass. This one has the same dome base but a different grape and wreath pattern altogether. It is closer to Palm Beach in structure and I feel this is probably a Dugan product. So far it is reported only in marigold.

Wild Loganberry (Dewberry)

Here's a pattern that has been around the bases, first from Co-operative Flint Glass, then briefly made by Kemple Glass, and then by Phoenix. The iridized pieces now seem to be credited to Phoenix. All carnival pieces reported are on iridized milk glass. Shapes include a pitcher, covered compote, creamer, sugar, an open compote, and a wine goblet.

Wild Rose (Northwood)

This well-known pattern, found in both collar based bowls and footed bowls like the example shown, was made in marigold, amethyst, green, cobalt blue, and ice blue. Some bowls are shaped into rose bowls or nut bowls simply by turning up or in the open-edge top. The interior of the Wild Rose pieces may be plain, have a standard stippled ray pattern, or oddly, have this variant shown of a stippled ray pattern, where the plain rays are flat and go all the way to the edge while the stippled ones end in an arc. There have been a handful of examples reported in this variant. Most are marked.

Wild Rose Lamp

Found in three sizes (5", 5½", 6" base diameters), this rare and desirable lamp was first made by Riverside as part of their Lucille line. Millersburg bought the moulds when the Riverside factory closed and produced this lamp in marigold, amethyst, and green carnival glass. A variation exists that has medallions on the underside of the base with cameos of ladies said to be the wives of Riverside's owners; it is called the Ladies' Medallion lamp.

Wild Rose Shade

Rose Presznick called this shade Wild Rose, and I will honor that name despite so many other patterns with the same name. The shade is a strong marigold and it has a series of stippled panels, separated by beading with each panel holding a spray of leaves, stems, and a flower that forms the outer edge of the shade.

Wild Rose Syrup

This Riverside Glass pattern was originally called Florentine. It is found in decorated crystal, emerald green, milk glass, light green iridescent, and marigold iridescent glass (it is not known if the carnival pieces were iridized by Riverside since they closed in 1907). The syrup stands 6½" tall.

Wild Rose Wreath (Miniature Intaglio)

The Butler Brothers ad showing this rare and desirable U.S. Glass miniature calls it a "stemmed almond," so you assume it was intended as a nut cup. It stands 2½" tall and is usually about 3" across the top. The design is intaglio, and the only color reported is marigold.

Wild Strawberry

One might think of this as the "grown-up" version of the regular Northwood Strawberry, since it is much the same. The primary difference is the addition of the blossoms to the pattern and, of course, the size of the bowl itself, which is about 1½" larger in diameter.

Wills's Gold Flake

This handy little ashtray, which reminds me of a pet food dish, comes with gold lettering on both sides reading: "Wills's Gold Flake." It has a convenient cigarette or cigar holder in the center. It has only been found in marigold to date, which is the case with most ashtrays, with exception of those from South America. Thanks again to Clint Arsenault for sharing it with me.

Windflower

Made by Diamond Glass in 1914 or 1915 and produced for several years, this pattern is found in bowls (6-ruffled, 8-ruffled, 10-ruffled, ice cream shape, and deep round), plates, and a one handled deep nappy shape. Bowls are found in marigold, pastel marigold, amber, cobalt blue, pale lavender, vaseline, smoke, smoky blue, horehound, pink, and black amethyst; plates are found in marigold, amethyst, and cobalt blue; and the nappies are reported in marigold, amethyst, blue, lavender, ice green, ice blue, and a very rare peach opalescent.

Windflower Nappy

Besides the bowls and plates shown elsewhere in this Diamond pattern, this unusual nappy exists and seems to give novice collectors trouble in identifying it. With the nappy there are two rows of floral design (only one on the bowls and plates) and two bands of notching. Colors for the nappy are marigold, amethyst, cobalt blue (rare), ice green (shown), and ice blue. The latter colors usually have a stretch effect on the edges, much like the usual stretch glass of the era.

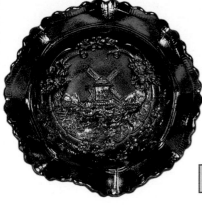

Windmill

This Imperial pattern is well known to collectors and was reproduced in the 1960s. It is found on a water set, milk pitcher, large and small bowls, dresser tray, pickle tray, and footed fruit bowl. Colors include marigold, purple, helios green, emerald green, smoke, aqua, teal, lavender, olive green, amber, cobalt blue, and marigold on milk glass.

Windsor Flower Arranger

Although named by Rose Presznick after she purchased one in Windsor, Ontario, this flower arranger actually was made in Czechoslovakia. The glass is very thin and the piece measures about 5" tall.

Wine and Roses

This is Fenton's #922 pattern from 1915. It is found in a marigold or blue cider pitcher, marigold, blue, aqua, or vaseline goblet, and a margiold compote (whimsied from the goblet). All colors other than marigold are rare.

Wishbone

Not to be confused with the Windsor flower arranger, this one has an open top and none of the points touch, which isn't true with the Windsor. I am told that Imperial is the maker but will hold off labeling it so until this is confirmed. The only colors reported to me are marigold, smoke, and the iridized pink example shown. Anyone with information on this is urged to contact me.

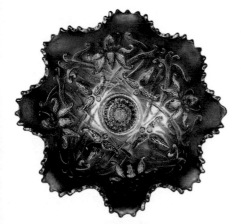

Wishbone (Northwood)

Wishbone is found in collar base bowls, footed bowls, a tumbler, pitcher, chop plate, and a one-lily epergne. The exteriors can be Basketweave or plain. Colors include marigold, blue, amethyst, green, white, ice blue, ice green, lavender, horehound, smoke, lime green, sapphire blue, clambroth, pearlized custard, and aqua opalescent. Shown is an electric purple ruffled bowl.

Wishbone and Spades

Dugan's Wishbone and Spades from 1911 can be found in large and small bowls, a 10" ice cream bowl, tri-cornered and banana bowls, and both small and large plates. Colors are mostly peach opalescent or amethyst. An 11" chop plate from Alice Widfeldt is shown in electric amethyst.

Wisteria

What a beautiful pattern this is, a first cousin to the Grape Arbor pattern in carnival and the Lattice and Cherry in other types of glass. Wisteria is found only on water set pieces, with both pitchers and tumblers found in white and ice blue, and only tumblers found in ice green. There is a very rare whimsey vase made from the pitcher in green also (one known).

Wooden Shoe

While it is difficult to tell from her drawing, I believe this is a pattern Marion Hartung calls Wooden Shoe in Book X. As you can see the iridescence is very thin and soft. Thanks to the Hollenbachs for sharing it with me.

Woodlands Vase

This very scarce vase stands only 5½" tall and is known in marigold as well as smoke. The design is simple and well balanced and both colors are very cherished by collectors.

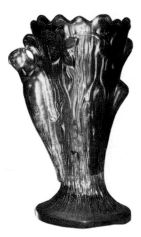

Woodpecker and Ivy Vase

What a treat it is to show this rare vase, believed to be from the Millersburg Glass Company (shards have been retrieved from that plant site). Reported to date are one marigold (shown), one vaseline, and one green example, and I understand the green one was broken. The design shows a tree stump with flowers around the top and a woodpecker on the side pecking at a knobby limb. This is a rare and imaginative item that has to be a top vase shape.

Woodpecker Vase

The Woodpecker vase is 8¼" long and measures 1⅝" across the top. The only color I've run into is marigold, usually of good color. Perhaps this is strictly a Diamond pattern. If so, it would explain the lack of other colors or shapes. These vases were usually hung in doorways or used as auto vases and were quite popular in their day.

World Bank

First shown in Presznick's third book in 1965, this attractive late carnival bank isn't often seen on the market. It measures 4½" tall and has a diameter of 4".

Wreathed Cherry (Dugan)

Wreathed Cherry is a pattern from Dugan and then Diamond. It is found on an oval berry or banana set, a table set, and a water set. An amethyst toothpick holder has long been rumored but these are reproductions like all colors in this shape in carnival glass. Colors known are marigold, amethyst, cobalt blue, oxblood, white, and peach opalescent. Only the berry set has been reported in the latter color at this time.

Wreath of Roses (Dugan/Diamond)

There has never been much interest in the shapes (all from the same mould) of this small piece. This Dugan/Diamond pattern should not be confused with the Fenton pattern of the same name. It can be found mostly in rose bowls but can also be found in a nut bowl, a tricornered whimsey, or a rare spittoon whimsey. Colors are marigold and amethyst but the spittoon is known in lavender.

Wreath of Roses (Fenton)

This well-known Fenton Art Glass pattern from 1912 is found on compotes, bonbons (stemmed or with a collar base), and majestic punch sets as shown. These punch bowls may have either the Vintage pattern or Persian Medallion pattern as an interior design. Colors are marigold, green, blue, amethyst, or white.

Wreath of Roses Variant

All of us dislike the variant tacked on to glass names, but sometimes it just can't be helped. This compote's interior is very different from the regular designs from both Fenton and Dugan/Diamond. Here we have four skimpy roses and leaves in a design that looks almost unfinished. Colors are marigold, amethyst, blue, and green.

Zig Zag (Fenton)

I suspect the same mould shape was used for this nicely done Fenton water set and the Fluffy Peacock pattern. The Zig-Zag was brought along in the enameled carnival period and can be found in marigold, blue, green, amethyst, ice green, and white. The floral work may vary slightly from piece to piece.

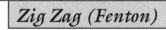

Zig Zag (Millersburg)

This lovely Millersburg bowl pattern is an improved version of a stippled ray theme but with a twist, resulting in a beautiful sunburst effect. This, coupled with a curious star and fan design on the exterior base, creates a unique and intriguing pattern. It can be found in large bowls in a variety of shapes and in rare small bowls (shown) in ruffled, square, and tricornered shapes. Colors on large bowls are marigold, amethyst, green, and occasionally clambroth. Small bowls have only been reported in marigold, but other colors are surely a possibility.

Zig Zag (Northwood)

This Northwood product is exactly like the water set of the same name attributed to the Fenton Company. The tumblers are signed "Harry," "H. Northwood," or "Harry Northwood" (three are blue and three fiery amethyst). The pitcher has the following inscription on the base: "NOT TO BE SOLD...HARRY NORTHWOOD...COBALT OXIDE CHLORIDE K2 CO CO 32 4hdD CO 304...SAMPLE #7." Speculation is that Frank Fenton brought this design from the Northwood plant when he worked there. I know Zig Zag from Fenton dates to 1912 and was their #1015. Apparently Northwood made nothing except the sample!

Zippered Heart (Imperial)

Found in many shapes in crystal, this Imperial pattern was offered in carnival glass about 1911, and was their #292 pattern. In carnival, the shapes are large and small bowls, a 5" vase, a 5" rose bowl, a giant rose bowl, and a large vase called a queen's vase. Colors are mostly marigold or purple, but the queen's vase and large rose bowl are known in green. This is one of Imperial's better patterns and only a few pieces in carnival are available.

Zipper Loop

This is one of Imperial's well-known carnival oil lamps. It was reproduced in the 1950s. This piece is found in both marigold and smoke (shown). It is found in a small hand lamp and three sizes of stemmed lamps.

Zipper Stitch

Besides the cordial tray, there is also a decanter and stemmed cordial glasses that make up the set. The tray has a 9" diameter and turns up a slightly on the outer edges, while the decanter is 10¼" tall. Marigold is the only reported color. Most of these are coming from Argentina and I suspect they were made there originally.

Zipper Variant

Over the years I've learned very little about this pattern. It is shown mostly in a covered sugar or a 10" bowl. I've seen the sugar in an opaque blue milk glass as well as the marigold carnival pieces, a crystal piece, and the marigold over lavender glass shown. Most pieces have a late look but some are heavily iridized.

Hatpins

Thanks to those who helped, namely Rick McDaniel, Jim and Peg Perry, Richard Cinclair, Jim and Jan Seeck, Kris and Debra Remmen, and anyone I may have overlooked for sharing their hatpins. The Isabelle hatpin shown is especially nice and the lettering on it is a bit different: "GES. GESCHUZT F. SCH."

I still feel these hatpins come from the 1920s and from the Gablonz area of what was formerly Czechoslovakia. As I said, those marked "Geschutzt" mean they are patented. I welcome anyone else who has unusual hatpins or designs not shown here to contact me for future inclusion.

Banded Criss-Cross

I understand this hatpin is a bit on the scarce side, but in design, it doesn't cause much excitement. The pattern is a series of plain panels that have thinner bars that cross over them with the entire piece bordered with rings. The example shown is blue.

Bars and Beads

Reported only on amethyst glass, this hatpin seems to rely on the simplicity of its design: rows of beading separated by bands of plain ribbon.

Basket Flower

The name says it all. A simple Basketweave center with a circled flowered boarder. This particular example has a nice blue iridescence over amethyst glass. It is very affordable hatpin for the collector.

Beaded Ball Bat

I guess the name for this beaded hatpin comes from its shape and it does look something like a ball bat. The beads are purple and not too exciting as most hatpins go.

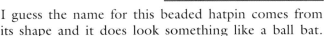

Beaded Oval

Here is another beaded hatpin named for its shape and while it is collectible, it really doesn't cause the excitement hatpins with well-done designs do. It is purple.

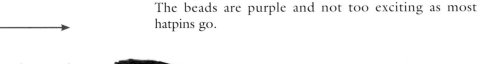

Beaded Parasol

I suppose the shape of the beading does resemble a parasol if you have a good imagination. At any rate, it is another hatpin with purple beading that isn't too imaginative.

Beaded Tears

This very well-done hatpin has a ribbon of beading that swirls around three teardrops, hence the name. The color is a strong amethyst.

Bee on Honeycomb

One of my favorite hatpins. I love honey and just looking at this hatpin I can almost taste that sweet nectar from the honeycomb. Found in marigold, blue, and the amber shown, this is a must for hatpin collectors. Non-iridized examples also exist.

293

Belle

This is a scarce hatpin that has brought high prices but seems to have peaked and now sells for a bit less. The purple color is outstanding and the design very interesting.

Big Butterfly

Early on these were called Scarab by collectors but since then other true scarab hatpins have come to light. It is a very nicely done hatpin but rather common and the price usually reflects this.

Blister Beetle

What a fierce looking creature this one is with its entire body and even the head covered in tiny indentations. It is shown in blue and is a real beauty.

Bordered Cosmos

This interesting hatpin is dark and has a border of spearheads while the center is filled with a flower that has seven petals and a geometric look to its design.

Border Path

Rather a plain looking hatpin, this one still brings fair prices. It is purple and is sometimes called Triangles or Garden Path. Most I've seen are very well iridized and show well.

Butlers Mirror

This simple design has a nice dental type boarder on the very edge. Found in amethyst, you should find one of these with little trouble.

Cameo

Much like the Cameo pendant shown elsewhere, this one has a nicely iridized glass cameo, framed in an intricate metal holder. Since most collectors believe the hatpins in carnival glass were made in Czechoslovakia, this one is probably no exception.

Checkers

Similar to the Border Path hatpin without the edge pattern, this is scarce, and despite its plain appearance is a good one to own. The color is purple.

Chrismas Star

Simple in conception, this hatpin does make a major statement in design alone. It is very similar to the Star Prism hatpin shown elsewhere in this book without the bordering.

Cockatoo

While this is a beautiful hatpin, I can't find any relationship to a cockatoo except for the small arc of feathers that grow from the head. The rest of the bird looks like a quail but maybe I'm just seeing things.

Concentric Circles

If you stare at this hatpin too long you may become hypnotized, both by its simplistic beauty and the effects of the circles. It is found only in lavender to date.

Coolie Hat

The name is derived from the shape and when looked at from the side it does resemble one. Only purple seems to be reported and prices are not high for this one.

Coqui

Coqui means "frog" in French. This hatpin is a real winner, with a design so well done it looks as if it could leap off the glass. It is right up there with Flying Bat in design, and the iridescence is outstanding.

Diamond Sphere

The name pretty well tells the story on this one. It brings a very respectable price. Purple is the only color I've heard about.

Dimples and Brilliants

This rather common hatpin has a bordering band of rhinestones around the outside while the inside is just as described, dimpled. The color is a strong purple.

Dinner Ring

This hatpin, also called Bubble Wrap by the owner, is a very rich amethyst with fine iridization, filled with blues and golds. Only two or three of these have been reported so far.

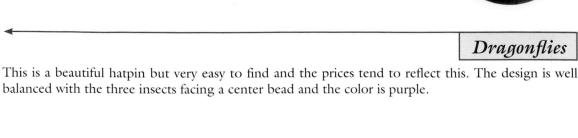

Doves

I know very little about this hatpin but the design looks quite good with two doves facing each other and flora on the outer edges. I'd be happy to learn of any other color or if there is another name for this one.

Dragonflies

This is a beautiful hatpin but very easy to find and the prices tend to reflect this. The design is well balanced with the three insects facing a center bead and the color is purple.

Faceted Dome

Similar in design to other hatpins, this one has a dome of prisms and a thin border band. It is available but not plentiful.

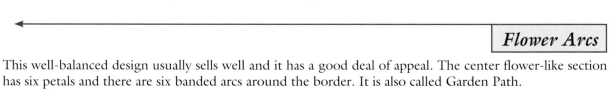

Flower Arcs

This well-balanced design usually sells well and it has a good deal of appeal. The center flower-like section has six petals and there are six banded arcs around the border. It is also called Garden Path.

Flying Bat

This very distinctive hatpin is high in appeal and design and deserves its lofty place in collectors' opinions. It shows a bat with wings spread and five stars.

Gazebo

Gazebo is brilliantly iridized and very pretty in its design. It has a look of embroidery about it with stitches quite visible. It is similar to Double Crown but much nicer.

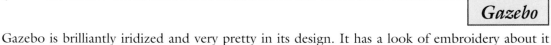

Geisha Girl

Figural hatpins with people seem to be a bit scarcer than most and this is a very good one that makes us wish there were more.

I think this must be a very popular hat-pin because the design is so good. It is found in several colors including blue, green, lavender, and amber, and all are top-notch, especially the amber one.

Hearts and Cross

I understand this hatpin is also called Four of Hearts, which seems to be a good name. The pattern has a cross of sorts with scoring and four triangle sections each containing a heart. It is in the medium price range.

Horsefly

This large rectangular hatpin has to be a favorite with collectors. It is marked "Geschutzt" on the back, which means patented, and is part of the line of pins found as samples of Albert Lorsch & Company, Inc., of New York.

Indian Blanket

Very aptly named, this beautiful green hatpin has a fine central band with a triangle-in-a-V pattern and edging of notched panels. It was probably made in other colors.

Iridized Star

This hatpin sports a six-pointed star with rays in between which extend to the outer edge. Not an easy one to find, this nice hatpin has only been reported in green so far.

Isabelle

The owner says this is the proper name for this hatpin. Its value is high, considering what it previously sold for. The color is a strong amethyst with much blue in the iridescence and the design is very balanced.

Japanese Garden

Bordered with dots on stitchery and cubes, this hatpin has a center square of stitched flowers on panels of stitchery, all making this piece very interesting as well as precise and crisp.

King Spider

Animal hatpins are very popular, but personally this one gives me the creeps. I don't like spiders ever since one bit me! This particular one looks as if it could do you some serious damage, especially to your wallet, as it is quite pricey. It is found in amethyst.

Knotty Tree Bark

Here are three colors in this rather plain hatpin but the green and blue are the only hatpins reported on slag glass that has been iridized. In addition there is a lavender example on standard glass.

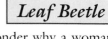

Leaf Beetle

Insects were a very popular subject for hatpins, but one has to wonder why a woman would choose such a thing to put on her hat. At any rate, this is a good one, shown in green.

Marquisite Flower

The owner of this very well-done hatpin named it so I've used his name. The design features flowers that overlap and cover the surface.

Moire Beetle

This is also known as Moire Scarab or Taffeta. This last name is the best because the design of this hatpin looks exactly like that fabric. Priced at the low end of the hatpin list.

Nasty Bug

The name says it all! But beyond that, the hatpin is very well done and does have its own appeal, especially to collectors. The iridescence is very good too.

Oval Prisms

Another prism hatpin with a different shape, this is similar to the Oval Sphere hatpin and has about the same value. It has appeal but not in the class of the Flying Bat or Horned Owl hatpins.

Owl

This is one of the more recognizable hatpins. There are several varieties of owls. The example shown is found in marigold, lavender, and ice green. Some have metal decoration and there are two sizes reported.

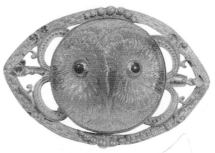

The Peacock pin is apparently a very popular design as it is in other pieces of carnival glass. It can be found in amethyst, blue, ice blue, and green as well as uniridized enameled examples, which have the blue dots on the peacock's tail.

Penstar

Although not too high end, this is a very classy looking hatpin. It is found in amethyst only.

Pine Sawyer

This bug is a stranger, at least to me, but the design of this hatpin leaves no doubt as to its appearance. It could well be called nasty bug two! The coloring on this one is green.

Pith Helmet

Shown here in amethyst and brown iridized, this hatpin is also known in ice blue, as well as non-iridized glass in black amethyst. The pattern is aptly named.

Propeller Variant

Similar to the regular Propeller pin, this one has a different design on the four blades and even different filler between the blades. The color is a good amethyst with fine iridescence.

Rooster

This must have been a popular hatpin because it is found in many colors including green, ice blue, celeste blue, red, sapphire, lavender, teal, blue, white, amber, and painted. But with all these choices, it still brings modest prices.

Royal Scarab

There are so many versions of scarab hatpins that I've renamed this one to distinguish it from others. This example is a rare red carnival on a gilt roping, holding a pearl in its pinchers. Its eyes are garnets.

Scarab Shell

Found in purple, green (shown), or blue, this hatpin is another fine example of the insect world. It usually sells for an above average price, especially the blue ones.

Shell

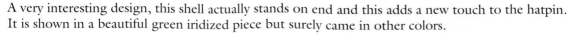

A very interesting design, this shell actually stands on end and this adds a new touch to the hatpin. It is shown in a beautiful green iridized piece but surely came in other colors.

Shining Peaks & Valleys

Sometimes the names given to these hatpins are almost as interesting as the designs themselves. Here is a beautiful blue pin with ridges that are faceted with a buttoned center.

Six Plums

Probably the easiest of all hatpins to find, this one still has a nice design that is distinctive in its own right. times only the fruit is iridized. This hatpin is also called Cattails by some collectors.

Snake Head

This small but interesting hatpin is in the shape of a snake's head and can be found in amethyst. This is the first example I've seen of this one. Thanks to Seeck Auction for the photo.

Spring Buds

Appropriately named, this rare smoke colored hatpin shows flower buds just about to open with the beginning of leaves just creeping out at the edges.

Star Prism

With a border of prisms and a center star of prisms, this piece has all the facets of a diamond. The color is a dark purple but the iridescence is a good blue.

Stork

Shown here in blue with pink iridescence, this hatpin is also known in powder blue. It is an expensive hatpin, bringing a very high price at auction and obviously a collectors' favorite.

Strawberry

This is a rare and desirable hatpin found in green (most seen color) as well as amber. The design is very appealing and the flowing berries and stems cover most of the space available.

Shown in green, this beetle is just as ugly as most and naturally has to be a collectors' favorite. The design is much like the old carved scarabs in jewelry and is very well done.

Sunflower

This one has a charm all its own. It is white carnival, with a stippled background and 12 petals on the flower. It probably came in purple also and for the collector of hatpins would be a real find.

Tiny Triangle-back Beetle

This is similar to the regular Triangle-back Beetle pattern, except this one is smaller. It is shown in black amethyst with superb iridescence and it almost leaps out at you.

Top of the Morn

Also called Pheasant by some collectors, this hatpin is a good one, often with brilliant coloring that just jumps out at you. It is a well known item.

Triad

Always a favorite and easy to find, this amethyst hatpin is certainly worth owning.

Triangle-back Beetle

Shown in both black amethyst and with green iridization, this beetle hatpin is very attractive (as beetles go). The surface is mostly plain and it holds the lustre quite well.

Tufted Throw Pillow

This is a fairly easy-to-find hatpin, but one that most hatpin collectors want to own. It usually sells for a reasonable price and most beginning collectors own one of these.

Turban

Like other geometric hatpins, this one relies on a quilted center with sweeps of four folded sections to imitate the look of fabric. It is reasonably priced.

Twin Gators

Although personally I think these are lizards, or what I call "Skinks," make no mistake about it, this is a very well designed and expensive hatpin. It is sound in amethyst only to date.

Two Flowers

What would carnival glass be without flowers and beads? Here you get a combination of both in a very tastefully done setting. It is found in amethyst.

Two Flowers Variant

One of several designs that have this name, I've taken the liberty of giving it a variant title in order to show some separation. It is shown in a brilliant blue and is well done.

Veiling

Often called Veiling and Beads, this hatpin is one of the better designs that sell for little money. The design is a finely stippled background with a net-like crosshatching over the entire piece.

Vintage Cluster

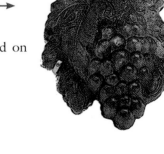

Some collectors are suckers for grapes and I'm one of them. This design is really enhanced on smoke carnival and it really has a great look. It is a superb hatpin.

Waves

While it has been seen in purple, green, and blue, this rather plain hatpin is mostly found in the chocolate color shown. Popular with collectors, prices are reasonably strong, especially in green and blue. This pattern is also know as Chocolate Waves.

Whirling Cobblestone

Similar to another hatpin called Spiral Dance, this one relies on facets and a swirled grooving to give it a pattern. It is pretty but not in the class of some of the beetles, grapes, or birds on other hatpins.

Introduction

Writing a price guide for carnival glass is a difficult task because it not only must take into account patterns, colors, and shapes, but also the quality of the iridescence. Beginning collectors sometimes fail to understand that a price guide cannot easily reflect individual sales. At the same time, advanced collectors have complicated the mix by concocting new colors or shades of colors that affect prices (see section "The Basics of Carnival Glass Collecting" in the front of this book for further guidance).

In this guide some prices have risen, many greatly. Some prices have remained nearly constant also, and some prices have fallen (I've tried to cushion and slowly adjust some of these toward current market value to protect collectors, but not everyone will be satisfied I'm sure). Most prices listed are based on research of auction sales (internet included), shop taggings, private sales where information was forthcoming, and a certain amount of speculation on items such as newly listed patterns which haven't established a current market value, or one of a kind items which rarely come up for sale but certainly appreciate in value over the years.

Please remember no two pieces in the same color, pattern, shape, and size can be expected to bring identical prices, due to variations, in iridescence, interest generated by a particular auction, and a host of other variables (see section "Grading Carnival Glass" for additional pricing factors). Please keep in mind that prices from older editions of this book cannot reflect today's market value and should be used only by well seasoned collectors. This is evident by a drastic decline in prices noted in this book (as well as the 10th edition) of most all glass coming from India (Jain, etc.) as the market was flooded with those pieces around 2005 – 2006, which caused this downward spiral in value.

This guide is only a general listing of, for the most part, average prices gathered in the year prior to publication. Use it *only* as a guide.

Color Code

A — Amethyst or Purple
AB — Amberina
ALS — Alaskan (Marigold Over Green)
AM — Amber
AMG — Amber Milk Glass
AO — Aqua Opalescent
AP — Apricot
AQ — Aqua
AS — Amethyst Swirl
AT – O — Amethyst Opalescent
B — Blue
BA — Black Amethyst
BLK — Black Glass
BO — Blue Opalescent
CeB — Celeste Blue
CHP — Champagne
CL — Clear
CLB — Colonial Blue
CM — Clambroth
CRAN — Cranberry Flash
CRN — Cranberry
CT — Citrene
EB — Electric Blue
EmG — Emerald Green
G — Green

GO — Green Opalescent
GW — Gold Wash
HA — Honey Amber
HO — Horehound
IB — Ice Blue
IC — Iridized Custard
ICG — Iridized Chocolate Glass
IG — Ice Green
IGO — Ice Green Opalescent
IL — Ice Lavender
IM — Iridized Moonstone
IMG — Iridized Milk Glass
LG — Lime Green
LO — Lime Opalescent
LV — Lavender
LVO — Lavender Opalescent
M — Marigold
MMG — Marigold Milk Glass
MUC — Mustard Custard
NG — Nile Green
OB — Opaque Blue
OG — Olive Green
PaS — Pastel
PB — Powder Blue
PeB — Persian Blue
PHO — Pastel Horehound

PK — Pink
PKA — Pink Afterglow
PL — Pearl Opalescent
PM — Pastel Marigold
PO — Peach Opalescent
R — Red
RA — Reverse Amberina
ReB — Renniger Blue
RG — Russet Green (olive)
RS — Red Slag
SA — Sapphire Blue
SM — Smoke
SMG — Smoke Milk Glass
SO — Smokey Olive
TG — Tangerine
TL — Teal
V — Vaseline
VI — Violet
VO — Vaseline Opalescent
W — White
WO — White Opalescent
WS — Wisteria
Y — Yellow
ZB — Zircon Blue

303

Pattern Name	M	A	G	B	PO	AO	IB	IG	W	Red	Other
ABALONE											
Shade, very scarce									200		
ABSENTEE DRAGON (FENTON)											
Plate, rare	3800										
ABSENTEE FERN (FENTON)											
Pitcher, rare	3000										
*Variant of Butterfly & Fern without Fern)											
ABSENTEE MINIATURE BLACKBERRY VARIANT											
Compote, small, stemmed	60	85	95	90							
*Variant of Miniature Blackberry with plain interior											
ACANTHUS (IMPERIAL)											
Bowl, 8" – 9½"	60	225	100	275							140 AQ
Plate, 10"	165										350 SM
ACORN											
Vase, handled, rare	2800	3300	4000								6500 V
ACORN (FENTON)											
Bowl, 6¼" – 7½"	35	325	145	45	175	550			450	450	250 AM
Plate, 8½", rare	1350	2000		1900					2000		2000 BA
ACORN (MILLERSBURG)											
Compote, rare	2000	2700	4000								6800 V
ACORN BURRS (NORTHWOOD)											
Bowl, flat, 5"	30	40	50								
Bowl, flat, 10"	90	250	175								
Covered Butter	225	300	800								
Covered sugar	135	235	275								
Creamer or Spooner	95	115	225								
Punch Bowl and Base	1000	1600	2300	37000		39000	7900	15500	6000		
Punch Cup	45	75	85	100		1800	90	110	95		
Pitcher	550	575	800								
Tumbler	60	85	95						500		225 WS
Whimsey Vase, rare	3000	3600									
ACORN AND FILE											
Footed Compote, rare	1100	1400	1400								1500 V
ADAM'S RIB (DUGAN/DIAMOND)											
Candleholders, pair, pressed or blown	95							145			125 CeB
Covered Candy	90							135			110 CeB
Fan Vase	45							85			175 CeB
Pitcher	160							400			425 CeB
Tumbler	40							150			425 CeB
ADVERTISING ASHTRAY											
Various Designs	60+										
AFRICAN SHIELD (ENGLISH)											
Toothpick Holder (or bud holder)	175										
AGE HERALD (FENTON)											
Bowl, 9", scarce		1300									
Plate, 10", scarce		3300									
ALLAN'S RINGS											
Cracker Jar	75										
ALTERNATING DIMPLES											
Vase, enameled, 8 sided	70										
AMAN (INDIA)											
Pitcher	365										
Tumbler	150										
AMARYLLIS (DUGAN)											
Compote, deep round	450			1000							
Compote, tricorner	300	400									
Plate Whimsey, very scarce	475	650							600		
AMERICAN (FOSTORIA)											
Rose Bowl, rare	400										
Tumbler, rare	125		140								
Vase, very rare	300										
AMERICUS											
Tumbler, very scarce	75										
AMV											
Hand Vase	225										
ANDEAN CHERRIES											
Tumbler, rare	200										
ANEMONE (NORTHWOOD)											
Pitcher	225										
Tumbler	25										
ANGELA											
Perfume	50										
ANGOORI											
Tumbler	175										
APOTHECARY JAR											
Small size	60										
APPLE AND PEAR INTAGLIO (NORTHWOOD)											
Bowl, 5"	60										
Bowl, 10"	115										

Pattern Name	M	A	G	B	PO	AO	IB	IG	W	Red	Other
APPLE BLOSSOM (DIAMOND)											
Bowl, 6" – 7½"	25	55	200	150	100				65		45 PK
Rose Bowl	125										
APPLE BLOSSOM (ENAMELED)											
(NORTHWOOD)											
Pitcher				475							
Tumbler				90							
APPLE BLOSSOM TWIGS (DUGAN)											
Banana Bowl		350			300						
Bowl, 8" – 9"	40	175		200	375				125		400 SM
Plate, 8½"	200	325		350	400		2500		225		400 LV
Plate (smooth edge)		365			400						
APPLE PANELS (ENGLISH)											
Creamer	35										
Sugar (open)	35										
APPLE TREE (FENTON)											
Pitcher	300			1100					1200		
Tumbler	30			75					185		1000 MMG
Pitcher, Vase Whimsey, rare	7500			9000							
APRIL SHOWERS (FENTON)											
Vase	30	70	125	60					150	2400	1400 AT – O
A-Q											
Perfume, 4", rare		150									
ARAMIS & VARIANT											
(DUNBAR GLASS CORP)											
Hat Whimsey	75										
Pitcher, late (either shape)	60										
Tumbler, late (either shape)	10										
Vase Whimsey from pitcher	100										
ARCADIA BASKET											
Plate, 8"	50										
ARCADIA LACE											
Rose Bowl	155										
ARCHED FLEUR-DE-LIS (HIGBEE)											
Mug, rare	250										
ARCHED FLUTE (FENTON)											
Toothpick Holder		150 WS		125 CeB				125			100 V
ARCHED PANELS											
Pitcher	185										
Tumbler	70										95 PB
ARCHES AND SAND											
Tumbler	200										
ARCS (IMPERIAL)											
Bowls, 8½"	30	60	50						175		35 CM
Compote	65	90									
ARGENTINA BLOSSOM											
Ink Well, very rare											2700 AM
ARGENTINA RIBBED BARREL											
Tumbler	125										
ARGENTINE											
Honey Jar w/lid	250										
ASTERS											
Bowl	60			100							
Compote	90										
Rose Bowl	200										
Vase	225										
ASTRAL											
Shade	55										
ATLANTIC CITY ELKS BELL											
See Elks (Fenton)											
ATHENIA											
Toothpick Holder	450										
AUCKLAND											
Vase, 7¼"	225										
AUGUST FLOWERS											
Shade	40										
AURORA DAISIES											
Bowl, Enameled											750 IM
AURORA PEARLS											
Bowl, 2 sizes, decorated		700		750						825	1350 IM
Bowl In Brides Basket											1750 IM
AURORA PRIMROSE SCROLL											
Bowl, enameled				850							
AURORA RUBINA VERDE											
Bowl, enameled & gilded											800
AUSTRAL											
Jug 7¼"											125 AM
AUSTRALIAN DAISY (JAIN)											
Tumbler, very scarce	175										
AUSTRALIAN DAISY & SHIELD											
(INDIA)											
Pitcher	325										

Pattern Name	M	A	G	B	PO	AO	IB	IG	W	Red	Other
Tumbler	175										
AUSTRALIAN FILE BAND											
Exterior pattern only											
AUSTRALIAN HOLLY											
Bowl, footed 7½"	275										
AUSTRALIAN KOOKABURRA											
Bowl, 9", lettered, very rare	1500										
AUTUMN ACORNS (FENTON)											
Bowl, 8½"	60	95	110	100						800	125 LG
Plate, 9" – 9½", scarce		1200	1550	1350							
AZTEC (McKEE)											
Pitcher, rare	1300										
Tumbler, very scarce	650										
Creamer	250										250 CM
Sugar	250										250 CM
Rose Bowl											400 CM
AZTEC HEADDRESS											
Vase, 10", very scarce	325										
BABY BATHTUB (U. S. GLASS)											
Miniature piece	225										
BABY'S BOUQUET											
Child's Plate, scarce	115										
BAKER'S ROSETTE											
Ornament	75	90									
BALL AND SWIRL											
Mug	120										
BALLARD – MERCED, CA (NORTHWOOD)											
Bowl	750										
Plate	1900										
BALLOONS (IMPERIAL)											
Cake Plate	85										110 SM
Compote	65										90 SM
Perfume Atomizer	60										90 SM
Vase, 3 sizes	75										100 SM
Vase, blank	65										
BAMBI											
Powder Jar w/lid	25										
BAMBOO BIRD											
Jar, complete	800										
BAMBOO SPIKE (CHINA)											
Tumbler	75										
BAND (DUGAN)											
Violet Hat	25	40		75							
BANDED DIAMOND AND FAN (ENGLISH)											
Compote, 6"	100										
Toothpick Holder	80										
BANDED DIAMONDS (CRYSTAL)											
Bowl 5"	50	75									
Bowl 9"	100	125									
Flower Set, 2 pieces	150	195									
Pitcher, very scarce	900	1250									
Tumbler, very scarce	250	400									
BANDED DIAMONDS AND BARS											
Decanter, complete	200										
Plate	200										
Tumbler, 2¼"	475										
Tumbler, 4"	450										
BANDED DRAPE (FENTON)											
Pitcher	200		500	400					750		
Tumbler	40		75	50					95		
BANDED FLUTE											
Compote, 4½", scarce	60										
BANDED GRAPE (FENTON)											
Mini Creamer	75										
BANDED GRAPE & LEAF (JAIN)											
Pitcher, rare	650										
Tumbler, rare	100										
BANDED KNIFE AND FORK											
Shot Glass	75										
BANDED LAUREL WREATH											
Juice Tumbler, footed	25										
BANDED MOON & STARS (JAIN)											
Tumbler, rare	225										
BANDED MOON & STARS VARIANT (JAIN)											
Tumbler, rare	275										
BANDED NECK											
Vase	50										
BANDED PANELS (CRYSTAL)											
Open Sugar	45	60									

Pattern Name	M	A	G	B	PO	AO	IB	IG	W	Red	Other
BANDED PORTLAND (U.S. GLASS)											
Puff Jar	125										
Toothpick	150										
Tumbler	150										
BANDED RIB											
Pitcher	125										
Tumbler, 2 sizes	40										
BANDED RIB NECK VASE (CZECH)											
Vase w/black band	75										
BANDED ROSE											
Vase, small	175										
BAND OF ROSES											
Pitcher	250										
Tumbler	150										
Tray	75										
Tumble-up, 2 pieces	200										
BAND OF STARS											
Decanter	175										
Wine, stemmed	35										
BARBELLA (NORTHWOOD)											
Bowl	50										70 V
Plate	70										85 TL
Tumbler											225 V
BARBER BOTTLE (CAMBRIDGE)											
Complete	575	750	750								
BARBER BOTTLE (CZECH)											
Cordial Bottle	60										
Stemmed Cordial	40										
Tray	50										
BAROQUE											
Tumbler, very rare	500										
BARREL											
Tumbler, scarce											150 V
BASKET OF ROSES (NORTHWOOD)											
Bonbon, scarce	325	550		480							300 V
stippled, add 25%											
BASKETWEAVE (NORTHWOOD)											
Compote	60	75	95	120							
BASKETWEAVE AND CABLE (WESTMORELAND)											
Creamer w/lid	50	75	100						175		
Sugar w/lid	50	75	100						175		
Syrup Whimsey	180										
BASKETWEAVE/VINTAGE VARIATION											
See Vintage (Northwood)											
BAVARIAN BERRY											
Enameled Pitcher	240										
BAVARIAN BERRY BEADED ACANTHUS (IMPERIAL)											
Milk Pitcher	300		375								175 SM
BEADED BAND AND OCTAGON											
Kerosene Lamp	250										
BEADED BASKET (DUGAN)											
Basket, flared	50	325	375	350					225		350 AQ
Basket, straight sided, rare	85	350							325		450 AQ
BEADED BLOCK											
Milk Pitcher											75 CM
BEADED BULL'S EYE (IMPERIAL)											
Vase, 8" – 14"	65	235	200								240 AM
Vase, squat, 5½" – 7½"	85	300	185								
Vase, mold proof, scarce	125										
BEADED CABLE (NORTHWOOD)											
Candy Dish	50	70	80	185		200	135	160	200		8000 IC
Rose Bowl	75	125	250	295	10000	350	400	750	275		10500 V
Ribbed interior, add 25%											
BEADED DAISY PANELS (GERMAN)											
Compote, scarce	125										
BEADED FLORAL BAND											
Tumbler	25										
BEADED HEARTS (NORTHWOOD)											
Bowl	50	85	90								
BEADED LOOP (OREGON)											
Vase Whimsey	100										
BEADED MIRRORS (JAIN)											
Tumbler, rare	200										
BEADED MIRRORS VARIANT (JAIN)											
Tumbler, rare	250										
BEADED MIRRORS WITH ETCHED FLOWERS (JAIN)											
Tumbler	150										

Pattern Name	M	A	G	B	PO	AO	IB	IG	W	Red	Other
BEADED PANELS (DUGAN)											
Compote	60	225		350	95						
BEADED PANELS (IMPERIAL)											
Bowl, 5"	25										
Bowl 8"	45										
Powder Jar w/lid	50										
BEADED PANELS & GRAPES (JAIN)											
Tumbler	275										
BEADED SHELL (DUGAN)											
Bowl, footed 5"	35	40									
Bowl, footed 9"	75	95									
Covered Butter	130	150									
Covered Sugar	90	110									
Creamer or Spooner	75	90									
Mug	145	80		175							175 LV
Mug Whimsey		450							700		
Pitcher	500	650									
Tumbler	60	70		180							
BEADED SPEARS (JAIN)											
Pitcher, rare	490	560									
Tumbler, rare	190	200									
BEADED SPEARS VARIANT (JAIN)											
Tumbler	225			300							
BEADED STAR MEDALLION											
Shade, either	75										
BEADED STARS (FENTON)											
Banana Boat	25										
Bowl	20										
Plate, 9"	65										
Rose Bowl	50										
BEADED SWAG MEDALLION											
Vase, 5½", scarce	350										
BEADED SWIRL (ENGLISH)											
Compote	50			60							
Covered Butter	70			85							
Milk Pitcher	75			90							
Sugar	50			55							
BEADED TEARDROPS (FOSTORIA)											
Vase, 6"	150										
BEADS (NORTHWOOD)											
Bowl, 8½"	45	60	70								
BEADS AND BARS (U.S. GLASS)											
Rose Bowl, rare	350										300 CM
Spooner, rare	125										
BEARDED BERRY (FENTON)											
Exterior pattern only											
BEAUTY BUD VASE (DIAMOND)											
Tall Vase, no twigs	20	75									
BEE											
Ornament	275										
BEETLE ASHTRAY (ARGENTINA)											
One size, rare	650			500							850 AM
BELLAIRE SOUVENIR (IMPERIAL)											
Bowl, scarce	125										
BELL FLOWER (FUCHSIA)											
Compote, handled, rare	2200			2000							
BELL FLOWER VASE											
Vase, very rare				1200							900 BA
BELLS AND BEADS (DUGAN)											
Bowl, 7½"	45	90	115	120	90						
Compote	70	75									
Gravy Boat, handled	55	70			140						
Hat Shape	40	60									
Nappy	60	95			100						
Plate, 8"		170									
BELTED RIB											
Vase, 8"	95										
BENZER											
Car Vase	90									125		
BERNHEIMER (MILLERSBURG)											
Bowl, 8¾", scarce				2500							
BERRY BASKET											
One size	50										
Matching Shakers, pair	75										
BERRY LEAF											
Mustard w/lid	700										
BERTHA (BROCKWITZ)											
Bowls	45 – 95										
Butter, covered	200										
Creamer	35										
Sugar, open	30										

Pattern Name	M	A	G	B	PO	AO	IB	IG	W	Red	Other
BIG BASKETWEAVE (DUGAN)											
Basket, small	25	60									
Basket, large	75	145									
Vase, squat, 4" – 7"	125	200			300				150		250 HO
*(4" is also base for Persian Garde											
punch bowl)											
Vase, 8" – 14"	75	200		300	425		600		100		450 LV
BIG CHIEF											
One shape		95									
BIG FISH (MILLERSBURG)											
Bowl, 8½"	600	625	750								6250 V
Bowl, tricornered	5000	9000	13,000								2000 V
Bowl, square, rare	1000	1800	2000								5800 V
Bowl, square (fish turned left,											
very rare)		2800									
Banana Bowl, rare		1900	1900								
Rose Bowl, very rare		10000									11000 V
BIG THISTLE (MILLERSBURG)											
Punch Bowl & Base, very rare		15000									
BIRD AND STRAWBERRY											
Tumbler, very scarce	150										
BIRD EPERGNE (CZECH)											
Epergne	150										
BIRD GALAXY											
Vase, 10¼", very rare			4200						3800		4000 IMG
BIRD-IN-THE-BUSH (GERMANY)											
Tumbler	250										
BIRD OF PARADISE											
(NORTHWOOD)											
Bowl, advertising		400									
Plate, advertising		450									
BIRDS AND CHERRIES (FENTON)											
Bonbon	40	125	80	65							
Bowl, 9½", rare	200	325		375							
Bowl, 10" ICS, rare				1800							
Compote	45	60	85	60							
Plate, 10", rare	2000	16000		3000							
BIRD WITH GRAPES (COCKATOO)											
Wall Vase	125										
BISHOP'S MITRE (FINLAND)											
Vase 8"	150			200							
BLACK BAND (CZECH)											
Vase	75										
BLACKBERRY (AKA: BLACKBERRY											
OPEN EDGE BASKET) (FENTON)											
Hat shape	35	150	165	50					135	400	85 LG
Plate, rare	1350			1800							
Spittoon Whimsey, rare	3200			3600							
Vase Whimsey, rare	925			1700					800	3000	
BLACKBERRY (NORTHWOOD)											
Compote, either exterior pattern	85	100	150	325					150		
BLACKBERRY BANDED (FENTON)											
Hat Shape	35	75	55	45	135				200		125 IM
BLACKBERRY BARK											
Vase, rare		12000									
BLACKBERRY BLOCK (FENTON)											
Pitcher	400	1250	1400	1250							6500 V
Tumbler	65	80	95	75							350 V
BLACKBERRY BRAMBLE (FENTON)											
Compote	40	50	70	55							
BLACKBERRY/DAISY & PLUME											
(NORTHWOOD)											
Candy Dish, 3 footed, Berry interior	90	200	165	1500			750	900	500		900 LG
Rose Bowl, 3 footed, Berry interior	100	185	175	900		9000	1300	1150	550		1000 AM
BLACKBERRY INTAGLIO											
Plate, 6"	165										
BLACKBERRY RAYS (NORTHWOOD)											
Compote	425	450	500								
BLACKBERRY SPRAY (FENTON)											
Bonbon	35	45	50	45							400 AB
Compote	40	50	55	50							
Hat Shape	45	100	200	40		800				400	135 AQ
Absentee Variant, J.I.P.								55	45		
BLACKBERRY SPRAY VARIANT											
(FENTON)											
Hat Shape	65									450	125 AQ
BLACKBERRY WREATH											
(MILLERSBURG)											
Bowl, 5½"	175	125	95								125 CM
Bowl, sauce, decorated, rare	500										
Bowl, 7" – 9"	75	125	110	1300							
Bowl, 10"	95	300	325	1650							

309

Pattern Name	M	A	G	B	PO	AO	IB	IG	W	Red	Other
Plate, 6", rare	1400	1200	2800								
Plate, 8", rare			4200								
Plate, 10", very rare	7000	7500									
Spittoon Whimsey, rare			8000								
BLACK BOTTOM (FENTON)											
Candy w/lid, either size	50										
Candy w/lid, decorated, very scarce	90										
BLAZING CORNUCOPIA											
(U.S. GLASS)											
Spooner, very scarce	150										
BLOCK BAND DIAMOND											
(U.S. GLASS)											
Berry Bowl, small	75										
Berry Bowl, large	125										
Butter	300										
Creamer	90										
Spooner	90										
Sugar w/lid	115										
Syrup, decorated, rare	250										
Tumbler	150										
*All pieces scarce to rare and have enameled decoration.											
BLOCKS AND ARCHES (CRYSTAL)											
Creamer	40										
Pitcher, rare	100	140									
Tumbler, rare	75	90									
BLOSSOM (INDIANA GLASS)											
Covered Jar	100										
BLOSSOM & SHELL											
(NORTHWOOD)											
Bowl, 9"	50	65	70								90 ALS
BLOSSOM AND SPEARS											
Plate, 8"	50										
BLOSSOMS & BAND											
Bowl, 5"	20	30									
Bowl, 10"	30	40									
Wall Vase, complete	45										
BLOSSOMTIME (NORTHWOOD)											
Compote	275	325	425								
BLOWN CANDLESTICKS											
One size, pair	90										
BLUEBELL BAND & RIBS											
(ARGENTINA)											
Pitcher, very scarce				500							
BLUEBERRY (FENTON)											
Pitcher, scarce	500			2000							
Tumbler, scarce	45		150	100						200	
BLUE RING (CZECH)											
Decanter	200										
Shot Glass, each	35										
BLUM DEPARTMENT STORE											
Tumbler, rare	300										
BOGGY BAYOU (FENTON)											
Vase, 6" – 11"	40	125	150	135							800 LGO
Vase, 12" – 15"	60	145	160	150							
BOND (BROCKWITZ)											
Vase	145			225							
BOOKER											
Cider Pitcher	500										
Mug	100										
BOOT											
One shape	150										
BO PEEP (WESTMORELAND)											
ABC Plate, scarce	550										
Mug, scarce	160										
BORDER PLANTS (DUGAN)											
Bowl, flat, 8½"		125			180						
Bowl, footed 8½"	175	475			250						
Handgrip Plate	350	495			350						
Rose Bowl, scarce		700			525						
BOTTLE ASHTRAY											
Whimsey, one shape	100										
BOUQUET (FENTON)											
Pitcher	285			485							
Tumbler	30			100							
BOUQUET TOOTHPICK HOLDER											
One size	75										
BOUTONNIERE (MILLERSBURG)											
Compote	100	135	150								
BOW AND KNOT											
Perfume	45										
BOXED STAR											
One Shape, rare										110	

Pattern Name	M	A	G	B	PO	AO	IB	IG	W	Red	Other
BRAND FURNITURE (FENTON)											
Open edge basket, advertising	90										
BRAZIERS CANDIES (FENTON)											
Bowl		675									
Plate, handgrip		1000									
BREAKFAST SET (INDIANA)											
Creamer or Sugar, each	50										
BRIAR PATCH											
Hat shape	40	50									
BRIDE'S BOUQUET (JAIN)											
Tumbler, scarce	250										
BRIDE'S VASE											
Vase, in metal stand	25			30							25 CL
BRIDE'S WALL VASE											
Vase in holder	50										75 SM
BRIDLE ROSETTE											
One shape	85										
BRILLIANT MEDALLIONS (INWALD)											
Bowl, 5"	95										
BRITT (KARHULA)											
Pitcher, very rare				5000							
Tumbler, very rare	400			600							
BROCADED ACORNS (FOSTORIA)											
Bowl w/handle							115				
Cake Tray, center handled							200				
Candleholder, each							85				65 LV
Compote							165				
Covered Box							185				
Ice Bucket							255				325 LV
Pitcher, rare							1700				
Tray							135				
Tumbler							65				
Vase							200				
BROCADED BASE											
Vase	65										
BROCADED DAFFODILS (FOSTORIA)											
Bonbon							100	90			
Cake Plate, handled							125	85			
Cake Tray							150				
Flower Set							225				
Vase							200				
BROCADED DAISIES (FOSTORIA)											
Bonbon								70			
Bowl								100			
Tray								210			
Vase								275			
Wine Goblet								200			
BROCADED PALMS (FOSTORIA)											
Bonbon								55			
Bread Tray								185			
Cake Plate								150			
Covered Box								225			
Dome Bowl								85			
Footed Center Bowl								225			
Ice Bucket								250			
Planter w/frog								500			
Rose Bowl								175			
Vase								225			
BROCADED POPPIES (FOSTORIA)											
Bonbon								75			
Bowl								100			
Cake Tray								150			125 PK
Vase								285			
BROCADED ROSES (FOSTORIA)											
Bonbon								75			
Cake Plate w/center handle								200			
Covered Box								185			
Dome Bowl								100			
Ice Bucket								295			
Large Footed Bowl								210			
Rose Bowl								145			
Tray								175			
Wine Goblet								200			
Vase								300			
BROCADED SUMMER GARDENS											
Bonbon									75		
Cake Plate w/center handle									85		
Compote									100		
Covered Box									100		
Covered Sectional Dish									125		

Pattern Name	M	A	G	B	PO	AO	IB	IG	W	Red	Other
Ice Bucket									145		
Large Footed Bowl									75		
Plate									65		
Rose Bowl									80		
Sweetmeat w/lid									125		
Tumbler									125		
Tray									75		
Vase									50		
Wine Goblet									40		
BROCKWITZ HENS											
Hen w/lid, small	225										
Hen w/lid, large	300										
BROEKER'S FLOUR (NORTHWOOD)											
Plate, advertising		3000									
BROKEN ARCHES (IMPERIAL)											
Bowl, 8½" – 10"	45	50	75								
Punch Bowl & Base, round top	400	1100									
Punch Cup	20	45									
Punch Bowl & Base, ruffled top and ringed interior pattern, rare		2000									
BROKEN CHAIN AKA: S-BAND (CRYSTAL)											
Bowl	90	150									
BROKEN BRANCH (FOSTORIA)											
Vase	165										
BROOKLYN											
Bottle w/stopper	75	95									
BROOKLYN BRIDGE (DIAMOND)											
Bowl, scarce	325										
Bowl, unlettered, rare	4700										
BUBBLE BERRY											
Shade											75 CRAN
BUBBLES											
Lamp Chimney											50 HO
BUBBLE WAVES											
Compote, rare				150							
BUCKINGHAM (U.S. GLASS)											
Open sugar	165										
BUD VASE WHIMSEY (FENTON)											
Vase, 2 or 4 sides up	50			100							125 CeB
BUDDHA											
6" size, sitting, rare	2000			2300					2000		
10" size, sitting, rare			2500								
BUDDHA VARIANT											
Large size, reclining position, rare	2200										
BULLDOG											
Paperweight	1250										
BULL RUSH & ORCHIDS											
Bowl, 8" – 9"	90										
Plate	250										
BULL'S EYE (U.S. GLASS)											
Oil Lamp	210										
BULL'S EYE AND BEADS (FENTON)											
Vase, 14" – 18"	125			150							
BULL'S EYE & DIAMONDS											
Mug	150										
BULL'S EYE AND LEAVES (NORTHWOOD)											
Bowl, 8½"	40	55	50								
BULL'S EYE AND LOOP (MILLERSBURG)											
Vase, 7" – 11", rare	600	500	400								
BULL'S EYE AND SPEARHEAD											
Wine	90										
BUNNY											
Bank	30										
BUSHEL BASKET (NORTHWOOD)											
One shape, footed	100	90	300	125		375	350	275	200		350 HO
BUSHEL BASKET VARIANT (NORTHWOOD)											
Basket, smooth handle, very scarce	450	350	600								
BUTTERFLIES (FENTON)											
Bonbon	60	70	75	65							
Bonbon, advertising (Horlacher)		125									
Card Tray	55			60							
BUTTERFLY (JEANNETTE)											
Pintray	10										15 TL
Party Set (complete in Box)	75										95 TL
BUTTERFLY (FENTON)											
Ornament, rare	1800	2000	2200	2400			1600	1700	1200		1350 AQ
BUTTERFLY (NORTHWOOD)											
Bonbon, regular	50	75	125	325							

Pattern Name	M	A	G	B	PO	AO	IB	IG	W	Red	Other
Bonbon, threaded exterior	700	400	1100	625			3250				
BUTTERFLY (U.S. GLASS)											
Tumbler, very rare	6500		10000								
BUTTERFLY AND BERRY (FENTON)											
Bowl, footed, 5"	25	85	110	125					95	1000	
Bowl, footed, 10"	85	225	200	135					725		
Bowl, 5" tricorner whimsey, very rare				3500							
Bowl Whimsey (Fernery)	600	500		800							
Centerpiece Bowl, rare				1400							
Covered Butter	130	240	300	225							
Creamer or Spooner	40	150	200	85							
Covered Sugar	70	160	200	150							
Hatpin Holder, scarce	1900			2100							
Hatpin Holder Whimsey, rare	2300										
Nut Bowl Whimsey		700									
Plate, 6", footed, very rare	1000										
Plate, footed, whimsey				1500							
Pitcher	300	500	750	500					1500		
Tumbler	30	65	125	85							325 V
Spittoon Whimsey, 2 types		3000		3000							
Vase, 6½" – 9"	35	85	300	100					150	850	500 AQ
BUTTERFLY AND CORN											
Vase, very rare	6500	15000	16000								9000 V
BUTTERFLY AND FERN (FENTON)											
Pitcher	325	400	650	425							
Tumbler	45	55	85	65							
Variant Pitcher (no ferns), rare	3000										
BUTTERFLY & FLANNEL FLOWER											
Compote, ruffled	150										
Compote, round	100										
BUTTERFLY & PLUME											
Tumbler				125							
BUTTERFLY & SINGLE FLOWER											
Oil Lamp											425PK
BUTTERFLY AND TULIP (DUGAN)											
Bowl, footed, 10½", scarce	350	2500			13500						
Bowl, Whimsey, rare	600	2700									
BUTTERFLY BOWER (CRYSTAL)											
Bowl, 9"	115	150									
Cake Plate, stemmed		200									
Compote	225	325									
BUTTERFLY BUSH (CRYSTAL)											
Cake Plate, 10", rare	450										
Compote, large	220	300									
BUTTERFLY BUSH & CHRISTMAS BELLS											
Compote	220	245									
BUTTERFLY BUSH AND FLANNEL FLOWER (CRYSTAL)											
Compote, ruffled	175										
BUTTERFLY BUSH AND WARATAH (CRYSTAL)											
Compote	200	400									
BUTTERFLY LAMP											
Oil Lamp	1500										
BUTTERFLY ORNAMENT											
See Butterfly (Fenton)											
BUTTERMILK GOBLET (FENTON)											
Goblet	50	75	85							125	
BUTTONS & DAISY (IMPERIAL)											
Hat (old only)											70 CM
Slipper (old only)											80 CM
BUTTONS & STARS (NORWAY)											
Sugar Basket	70										
BUTTRESS (U.S. GLASS)											
Pitcher, rare	450										
Tumbler, rare	250										
BUZZ SAW											
Shade	40										
BUZZ SAW (CAMBRIDGE)											
Cruet, 4", scarce			575								
Cruet, 4", with metal tag lettered;			1000								
B.P.O.E. #1, rare	425		400								
Cruet, 6", scarce											
BUZZ SAW (EUROPEAN)											
Pitcher	100										
BUZZ SAW & FILE											
Goblet	175										
Pitcher	350										
Tumbler, juice	150										
Tumbler, lemonade	175										
BUZZ SAW & FILE FRAMED											
Bowl, 5½"	100										

Pattern Name	M	A	G	B	PO	AO	IB	IG	W	Red	Other
BUZZ SAW SHADE											
Lamp Shade, scarce	75										
CACTUS (MILLERSBURG)											
Exterior only											
CALCUTTA DIAMONDS (INDIA)											
Pitcher	325										
Tumbler	125										
CALCUTTA ROSE (INDIA)											
Tumbler	135										
CAMBRIDGE #2351											
Bowl, 9", rare			350								
Punch Bowl w/base, very rare	1500										
Punch Cup, scarce		65	65								
Vase, 4", rare	500										
CAMBRIDGE #2660/108											
Cologne Bottle, very scarce	1300		800								
CAMBRIDGE #2760 (VARIANT											
OF SUNK DAISY)											
Shakers, each	100										
CAMBRIDGE COLONIAL #2750											
Cruet, rare	450										
CAMBRIDGE HOBSTAR											
(CAMBRIDGE)											
Napkin Ring	165										
CAMEO (FENTON)											
Vase, 11" – 17", scarce											250 CeB
CAMEO MEDALLION BASKET											
(WESTMORELAND)											
Basket, 3 sizes	35 – 75										
CAMEO PENDANT											
Cameo piece		250									
CAMIELLA LOOP											
Vase, 5¾"	150										
CAMPBELL & BEASLEY											
(MILLERSBURG)											
Plate, advertising, handgrip		1400									
CANADA DRY											
Bottle, 2 sizes	25								45		
Tumbler Whimsey, cut from bottle	45										
*Double price for unopened bottle											
with all labels.											
CANARY TREE (JAIN)											
Tumbler	235										
CAN-CAN											
Candy Tray	155										
CANDLE DRIP VASE											
Vase, 5", rare	300										
CANDLE LAMP (FOSTORIA)											
One size	110										
CANDLE VASE											
One size	55										
CANDLE VASE VARIANT (DUGAN)											
Vase, 12"											75 CeB
CANE (EUROPEAN)											
Tankard	170										
CANE (IMPERIAL)											
Bowls, various	15 – 35										45 SM
Goblet	45										
Pickle Dish	25										
CANE AND DAISY CUT (JENKINS)											
Basket, handled, rare	220										250 SM
Vase	150										
CANE AND PANELS											
Tumbler	200										
Tumble- up	350										
CANE AND SCROLL (SEA THISTLE)											
(ENGLISH)											
Creamer or Sugar	45										
Rose Bowl	125			75							
CANE AND WEDGE (FINLAND)											
Vase, 4⅞"											250 AM
CANE OPEN EDGE BASKET											
(IMPERIAL)											
Basket, squat, very rare											500 MMG
CANE PANELS											
Vase	85										
CANNONBALL VARIANT											
Pitcher	240			285					400		
Tumbler	40			50					75		
CANOE (U.S. GLASS)											
One size	150										
CAPITOL (WESTMORELAND)											
Bowl, footed, small		70		70							

Pattern Name	M	A	G	B	PO	AO	IB	IG	W	Red	Other
Mug, small	140										
CAPTIVE ROSE (FENTON)											
Bonbon	45	80	125	105							
Bowl, 8½" – 10"	50	110	70	80							250 BA
Compote	70	80	100	95					100		125 PB
Plate, 9"	500	850	950	875							
CARNATION (NEW MARTINSVILLE)											
Punch Cup	50										
CARNATION WREATH											
Bowl, 9½", scarce	125										
CARNIVAL BEADS											
Various strands	30+										
CARNIVAL BELL											
One size	425										
CARNIVAL CRUETS											
Cruets, various designs	50 – 75										
CAROLINA DOGWOOD (WESTMORELAND)											
Bowl, 8½"	80	110				450					150 MMG
Plate, rare											300 BO
CAROLINE (DUGAN)											
Bowl, 7" – 10"	70	275			100						
Banana Bowl					125						
Basket, scarce					250						600 LVO
CARRIE (ANCHOR-HOCKING)											
One size	60										
CARTWHEEL, #411 (HEISEY)											
Bonbon	60										
Compote	50										
Goblet	75										
CAR VASE											
Automobile vase	45										
CASTLE											
Shade	50										
CAT FACE (ARGENTINA)											
Ashtray Novelty	250										
CATHEDRAL ARCHES											
Punch Bowl, 1 piece	400										
CATHEDRAL WINDOWS (INDIA)											
Pitcher	175										
Tumbler	60										
CB VASE (INDIA)											
Vase, 6"	125										
CB VASE VARIANT (INDIA)											
Vase	125										
CELEBRATION (JAIN)											
Tumbler	125										
CELESTIAL BAND											
Tumbler, 3¼", very scarce	150										
CENTRAL SHOE STORE (FENTON)											
Bowl, 6" – 7"		1000									
Plate, scarce		2500									
Plate, handgrip		1200									
CHAIN AND STAR (FOSTORIA)											
Covered Butter, rare	1500										
Creamer or Sugar	175										
Tumbler, rare	900										
CHANNELED FLUTE (NORTHWOOD)											
Vase, 10" – 16"	65	90	100								150 ALS
CHARIOT											
Compote, large	100										
Creamer, stemmed/opened	70										
Sugar	65										
CHARLIE (SWEDEN)											
Bowl	100			200							
Rose Bowl	250			375							
CHARLOTTE (BROCKWITZ)											
Compote, large	325			450							
CHARLOTTE'S WEB											
Mirror	275										200 PK
CHATELAINE (IMPERIAL)											
Pitcher, very scarce		3000									
Tumbler, very scarce		300									
CHATHAM (U.S. GLASS)											
Candlesticks, pair	90										
Compote	75										
CHECKERBOARD (WESTMORELAND)											
Cruet, rare											750 CM
Goblet, rare	350	250									
Punch Cup, scarce	80										

Pattern Name	M	A	G	B	PO	AO	IB	IG	W	Red	Other
Pitcher, rare		3000									
Tumbler, rare	675	400									
Wine, rare	300										
Vase, scarce		2400									
CHECKERBOARD BOUQUET											
Plate, 8"	80										
CHECKERBOARD PANELS											
(ENGLISH)											
Bowl	70										
CHECKERS											
Ashtray	40										
Bowl, 4"	25										
Bowl, 9"	35										
Butter, 2 sizes	200										
Plate, 7"	75										
Rose Bowl	85										
CHEROKEE											
Tumbler				65							
CHERRIES AND DAISES (FENTON)											
Banana Boat	800			1000							
CHERRIES AND LITTLE FLOWERS											
(FENTON)											
Pitcher	175	265		325							
Tumbler	25	35		40							
CHERRY (DUGAN)											
Banana Bowl		300			250						
Bowl, flat, 5" – 7"	30	60			50				125		
Bowl, flat, 8" – 10"	100	300			250				525		
Bowl, footed, 8½"	75	375		600	225						
Bowl Proof Whimsey				500							
Chop Plate, 11", very rare		4000									
Plate, 6"		300			250						
CHERRY (FENTON)											
(See Mikado Compote)											
CHERRY (MILLERSBURG)											
(AKA: HANGING CHERRIES)											
Banana Compote, rare		4000									
Bowl, 5½"	75	125	90	1800							
Bowl, 7"	100	125	165	2600							
Bowl, 9", scarce	150	250	250								
Bowl, 10"	175	300	340	2800							375 AQ
Bowl, 5", Hobnail exterior, rare			1000	1800							
Bowl, 9", Hobnail exterior, rare	1650	2500		3350							
Bowl, 9" – 10", plain back, rare		475									
Compote, large, rare	1250	2800	1650	4500							5000 V
Compote Whimsey, either shape, rare		5000									
Covered Butter	250	375	450								
Covered Sugar	170	300	325								
Creamer	75	175	250								275 TL
Milk Pitcher, rare	1600	900	1100	7000							
Pitcher, very scarce	1800	1400	2000	8000							
Tumbler, 2 variations	135	175	200								
Tumbler, goofus, experimental			500								
Spooner	100	175	200								
Plate, 6", rare	3400										
Plate, 7½", rare	825	3000	4300								
Plate, 10", rare	2500	3500	3700								
Powder Jar, very rare	4600		3800								5000 MMG
CHERRY AND CABLE											
(NORTHWOOD)											
Bowl, 5", scarce	75										
Bowl, 9", scarce	110										
Butter, scarce	400										
Pitcher, scarce	1200										
Tumbler, scarce	150										
Sugar, Creamer											
Spooner, each, scarce	175			350							
CHERRY AND CABLE INTAGLIO											
(NORTHWOOD)											
Bowl, 5"	50										
Bowl, 10"	75										
CHERRY BLOSSOMS											
Pitcher				150							
Tumbler				40							
CHERRY CHAIN (FENTON)											
Bonbon	50	60	65	60							
Bowl, small 4½" – 5"	25	60	75	50							45 CM
Bowl, 9" – 10"	70	350	300	85					100	6500	150 V
Plate, 6"	115	900	1350	175					250		1700 EmG
Chop Plate, rare	2100								1300		
CHERRY CHAIN VARIANT (FENTON)											
Bowl, 7" – 9"	55	135	300	135						7000	

316

Pattern Name	M	A	G	B	PO	AO	IB	IG	W	Red	Other
Plate, 9½"	225	600	850	225							
CHERRY CIRCLES (FENTON)											
Bonbon	45	125	200	95						4000	225 PB
CHERRY SMASH (CHERRYBERRY)											
(U.S. GLASS)											
Bowl, 8"	55										
Butter	160										
Compote, 3¾", scarce	75										
Pitcher, very scarce	225										
Tumbler	150										
CHERRY VARIANT (MILLERSBURG)											
Plate, 11", rare		7000									
Bowl, 10", very scarce		900	1100								
CHERUB											
Lamp, rare											150 CL
CHERUBS											
Mini Toothpick Holder	200										
CHESTERFIELD (IMPERIAL)											
Candy w/lid, tall	65									300	90 SM
Champagne, 5½"	35									175	50 SM
Candlesticks, pair	60										105 SM
Compote, 6½"	35										40 CM
Compote, 11½"	75								95	400	125 SM
Creamer or Sugar	45									175	
Lemonade Pitcher	150								300	8000	
Lemonade Tumbler	35								145	1500	
Punch Bowl & Base	500										
Punch Cup	50										
Rose Bowl	45										60 SM
Lemonade Mug, handled	50								110		40 CM
Sherbet, 2 sizes	25									80	50 TL
Table Salt	85										60 CM
Toothpick, handled	250										
(add 25% for Iron Cross)											
CHEVRONS											
Vase, very scarce	325										
CHIPPENDALE KRYSTOL											
(JEFFERSON)											
Bonbon, small, stemmed	35										
Bonbon, large, stemmed	60										
CHIPPENDALE SOUVENIR											
Creamer or Sugar	65	85									
CHRISTMAS COMPOTE (DUGAN)											
Large Compote, scarce	5700	4500									
CHRYSANTHEMUM (FENTON)											
Bowl, flat, 9"	65	95	200	100					500	5500	250 TL
Bowl, footed, 10"	50	80	225	225						3500	325 V
Plate, very rare	2000										
CHRYSANTHEMUM DRAPE											
Oil Lamp											900 MMG
CHRYSANTHEMUM DRAPE											
VARIANT											
Oil Lamp									950		
CIRCLED ROSE											
Plate, 7"	95										
CIRCLED STAR AND VINES (JAIN)											
Tumbler	150										
CIRCLE SCROLL (DUGAN)											
Bowl, 5"	40	45									
Bowl, 10"	65	80									
Butter or Sugar	375	425									
Compote, scarce		225									
Creamer or Spooner	95	175									
Hat Shape, scarce	60	95									
Pitcher, rare	1600	2200									
Tumbler, very scarce	350	425									
Vase Whimsey, scarce	135	265									300 BA
CLASSIC ARTS											
Powder Jar	400										
Rose Bowl	450										
Vase, 7½", very scarce	425										
CLEOPATRA											
Bottle	110										
CLEVELAND MEMORIAL											
(MILLERSBURG)											
Ashtray, rare	15000	7000									
COBBLESTONE (IMPERIAL)											
Bowl, 8½"	135	300	125	500							550 LV
Plate, rare		1300									
COIN DOT (FENTON)											
Bowl, 6" – 10"	30	50	50	45	150					1000	100 LV
Plate, 9", rare	200			260							

Pattern Name	M	A	G	B	PO	AO	IB	IG	W	Red	Other
Rose Bowl	100	150	175	140						1450	
COIN DOT VARIANT (FENTON)											
Bowl	35	45	55	50							
COIN SPOT (DUGAN)											
Compote	45	80	70	100	175	375		350			
Goblet, rare								500			
COLOGNE BOTTLE (CAMBRIDGE)											
One size, rare	600		850								
COLONIAL (IMPERIAL)											
Child's Mug, handled	65										
Lemonade Goblet	40										
Open Creamer or Sugar	30										
COLONIAL DECANTER											
Decanter w/stopper	250										
COLONIAL LADY (IMPERIAL)											
Vase, scarce	1000	750									
COLONIAL LOOP											
Wine	150										
COLONIAL TULIP (NORTHWOOD)											
Compote, plain			65								
Compote, rayed interior			80								85 TL
COLORADO (U.S. GLASS)											
*Exterior pattern only											
COLUMBIA (IMPERIAL)											
Cake plate, scarce	125										75 CM
Compote	60	300	225								85 SM
Rose Bowl, rare	200										
Vase	45	125	165								110 SM
COLUMBIA VARIANT (IMPERIAL)											
Compote, scarce	75										
COLUMBUS											
Plate, 8"	45										
COLUMNS AND RINGS											
Hat Whimsey	65										
COMPASS (DUGAN)											
(Exterior only)											
COMPOTE VASE (FENTON)											
Stemmed Whimsey	50	65	70	75							
COMPOTE VASE VARIANT (FENTON)											
Compote, stemmed		75									
CONCAVE COLUMNS											
Vase, very rare						3500					
CONCAVE DIAMOND (NORTHWOOD)											
Coaster, not iridized											65 CeB
Pickle Caster, complete	750										175 V
Pitcher w/lid			450RG								300 CeB
Tumbler			400RG								60 CeB
Tumble-up, complete, rare			115 OG								155 RG
Vase											200 CeB
CONCAVE DIAMOND (FENTON)											
Vase											125 V
CONCAVE FLUTE (WESTMORELAND)											
Banana Bowl	65	85									100 AM
Bowl	45	55	65								75 TL
Plate, 8½" – 9", rare		135									
Rose Bowl	60	95	100								
Vase	40	65	65								90 IM
CONCORD (FENTON)											
Bowl, 9"	225	275	550	300							400 AM
Plate 10", rare	1900	2400	4900								3500 AM
CONE AND TIE (IMPERIAL)											
Tumbler, very rare		3500									
CONNIE (NORTHWOOD)											
Pitcher									750		
Tumbler									150		
CONSOLIDATED SHADE											
Shade, 16", rare											500 MMG
CONSTELLATION (DUGAN)											
Compote	85	450			400				100		425 LV
CONTINENTAL BOTTLE											
2 sizes	40										
COOLEEMEE, NC (FENTON)											
Plate, advertising, rare (J. N. Ledford)	9000										
CORAL (FENTON)											
Bowl, 9"	325		225	500					400		
Plate, 9½", rare	1350										
CORINTH (DUGAN)											
Banana Boat	55	75			150						

Pattern Name	M	A	G	B	PO	AO	IB	IG	W	Red	Other
Bowl, 9"	40	50			125						
Plate, 8½", rare					225						
Vase	30	40			150						200 AM
CORINTH (WESTMORELAND)											
Bowl	40	60									75 TL
Lamp, scarce		250									
Vase	30	50	75		150	550BO					150 AM
CORN BOTTLE (IMPERIAL)											
One size, scarce	375		350								465 SM
CORN CRUET											
One size, rare									1100		
CORNFLOWERS											
Bowl, footed	125										
CORNING INSULATOR (CORNING)											
Insulator, Various shapes	35+										
CORNUCOPIA (JEANNETTE)											
Vase	40										
CORN VASE (NORTHWOOD)											
Regular Mold	1000	750	1000	2300		3250	2500	425	400		400 LG
Pulled Husk Variant, rare		16500	13000								
CORONATION (ENGLISH)											
Vase, 5" (Victoria Crown design)	250										
CORONET											
Tumbler	30										
COSMOS (MILLERSBURG)											
Bowl, ice cream shaped	1650		85								
Bowl, 6 ruffles, scarce			125								
Bowl, 8 ruffles, very scarce			200								
Plate, rare			525								
COSMOS (NORTHWOOD)											
Pitcher	265										
Tumbler	30										
COSMOS AND CANE (U.S. GLASS)											
Basket, 2 handled, rare											1000 HA
Bowl, 5" – 7"	40								145		50 HA
Bowl, 10"	75								235		95 HA
Breakfast Set, 2 pieces									475		165 HA
Butter, covered	175								300		400 HA
Chop Plate, rare	1200								1350		1300 HA
Compote, stemmed, tall	400								350		
Compote Whimsey	450								400		
Creamer or Spooner	65								200		75 HA
Flat Tray, rare									275		
Pitcher, rare	850								1950		1250 HA
Tumbler	75								150		95 HA
Tumbler, advertising, J.R. Millner, very scarce											250 HA
Rose Bowl, large	350	1200									1800 HA
Rose Bowl Whimsey	650	1500									
Spittoon Whimsey, rare									3000		4750 HA
Sugar w/lid	100								165		
Stemmed Dessert									150		
Whimsey, Volcano shape	550								500		
COSMOS AND HOBSTAR											
Bowl (on metal stand)	450										
COSMOS VARIANT											
Bowl, 9" – 10"	40	65		75					125	775	950 AB
Plate, 10", rare	190	250			400				425		
COUNTRY KITCHEN (MILLERSBURG)											
Bowl, 5", very scarce	90										
Bowl, 8", very scarce	175										
Bowl, 10", very scarce	295										
Bowl, square, rare	500										
Covered Butter, rare	650	900									
Creamer or Spooner	300	350	750								
Spittoon Whimsey, rare		4650									
Sugar w/lid	325	400	800								
Vase Whimsey, 2 sizes, rare	850	1350									2000 V
COURTESY											
Bowl, 3¼"	25	55									
COURTHOUSE (MILLERSBURG)											
Bowl, lettered, scarce		875									3500 LV
Bowl, unlettered, rare		4500									
COVERED FROG (COOPERATIVE FLINT)											
One size	375	450	500	275				325			
COVERED HEN (ENGLISH)											
One size	350			500							
COVERED LITTLE HEN											
Miniature, 3½", rare											90 CM
COVERED MALLARD (U.S. GLASS)											
One Shape											450 CM

319

Pattern Name	M	A	G	B	PO	AO	IB	IG	W	Red	Other
COVERED SWAN (ENGLISH)											
One size	325	425		525							
CRAB CLAW/BLAZE (IMPERIAL)											
Bowl, 5"	25	35	40								65 SM
Bowl, 8" – 10"	50	125	95								75 SM
CRAB CLAW VARIANT (IMPERIAL)											
Pitcher	275										
Tumbler	35										
CRACKLE (IMPERIAL)											
Bowl, 5"	15	20	20								
Bowl, 9"	25	30	30								
Candy Jar w/lid	30										
Candlestick, 3½"	25										
Candlestick, 7"	30										
Plate, 6" – 8"	25										
Punch Bowl and Base	55										
Punch Cup	10										
Pitcher, dome base	90										
Tumbler, dome base	20										
Salt Shaker											60 AQ
Sherbet	20										
Spittoon, large	50										
Wall Vase	40										
Window Planter, rare	110										
CRACKLE (JEANNETTE)											
Auto Vase	25										
Bowl, 8"	25										
CR ASHTRAY (ARGENTINA)											
Ashtray	175		450	350							400 AM
CREOLE											
Rose Bowl, stemmed	750										
CROSSHATCH (SOWERBY)											
Creamer	75										
Sugar, open	75										
CROWN OF DIAMONDS (CRYSTAL)											
*Exterior of Trailing Flowers											
CROWN OF INDIA (JAIN)											
Tumbler	250										
CRUCIFIX (IMPERIAL)											
Candlestick, each, rare	600										
CRYSTAL DIAMONDS (CRYSTAL)											
Bowl	65										
CUBA (McKEE)											
Goblet, rare	50										
CURTAIN OPTIC (FENTON)											
Pitcher											450 V
Tumbler											150 V
Tumble- up, complete											350 V
CURVED STAR/ CATHEDRAL											
Bowl, 3½"	25										
Bowl, 10"	50										
Bowl, square, 7¾"	175										
Butterdish, 2 sizes	275										
Chalice, 7"	100			200							
Compote, 2 sizes	60										
Creamer, footed	60										
Epergne, rare	675										
Flower Holder	135										
Pitcher, rare				3200							
Rose Bowl, scarce	200			400							
Vase, 9½", rare	325	475		875							
CUT ARCHES (ENGLISH)											
Banana Bowl	80										
CUT ARCS (FENTON)											
Bowl, 7½" – 10"	50		120								250 V
Compote	55	60		55							
Vase Whimsey (from bowl)	40	50	150	50					75		
CUT COSMOS											
Tumbler, rare	225										
CUT CRYSTAL (U.S. GLASS)											
Compote, 5½"	110										
Water Bottle	185										
CUT DAHLIA (JENKINS)											
Flower Basket	185										
CUT DIAMOND DECANTER											
Decanter with clear stopper	100										
CUT FLOWERS (JENKINS)											
Vase, 10"	125										140 SM
CUT GRECIAN GOLD (FENTON)											
Lamp Font	100										
CUT OVALS (FENTON)											
Bowl, 7" – 10"	60									350	75 SM
Candlesticks, each	135									800	210 SM

320

Pattern Name	M	A	G	B	PO	AO	IB	IG	W	Red	Other
CUT OVALS (RIIHIMAKI)											
Butter											300 AM
CUT PRISMS (RINDSKOPF)											
Bowl, 6¼", scarce	60										
CUT SPRAYS (IMPERIAL)											
Vase, 10½"	45										175 IM
CZECH FLOWER											
Cruet	200										
CZECH INTERIOR COIN DOT											
Vase, 12"											65 PB
CZECH INTERIOR SWIRL											
Lemonade Pitcher	175										
Lemonade Tumbler	25										
CZECHOSLOVAKIAN											
Liquor Set, complete	350										
Pitcher	350										
Tumbler	100										
(All pieces have black enameling)											
CZECH SWIRLS											
Tumbler w/enameling	90										
DAGNY (SWEDEN)											
Vase	300			350							
DAHLIA (DUGAN)											
Bowl, footed, 5"	40	65							95		
Bowl, footed, 10"	95	225							225		
Butter	120	155							350		
Creamer or Spooner	75	90							125		
Sugar	90	100							200		
Pitcher, rare (old only)	500	725							800		
Tumbler, rare (old only)	90	185							175		
DAHLIA (FENTON)											
Twist Epergne, one lily	325								325		
DAHLIA											
Button		20									
DAHLIA (JENKINS)											
Compote, very scarce	150										
Vase, 10", rare	200										
DAHLIA AND DRAPE (FENTON)											
Tumble-up, complete	150										
DAINTY BUD VASE											
One size	55										
DAINTY FLOWER											
Vase, 5", with enameled design		75								125	
DAISIES & DIAMONDS											
Bowl, 9"	90										
DAISY (FENTON)											
Bonbon, scarce	125			200							
DAISY AND CANE (TARTAN)											
Bowl, footed	50										
Bowl, oval 12"	90										
Decanter, rare	100										
Epergne	175										
Pitcher											
Salver	80										
Spittoon, rare	1400			1275							
Vase, scarce	175										
Wine, very scarce	125										
DAISY AND DIAMOND POINT											
Bowl, rare	150										
DAISY AND DRAPE (NORTHWOOD)											
Vase	575	600	3200	900		700	2200	3500	210		700 LV
DAISY AND LITTLE FLOWERS (NORTHWOOD)											
Pitcher				300							
Tumbler				40							
DAISY AND PLUME (DUGAN)											
Candy Dish, 3 footed	65	140			200						325 LG
Bowl, footed, 8" – 9", Cherry interior, rare		600									
DAISY AND PLUME (NORTHWOOD)											
Candy Dish, 3 footed	50	135	75				600	800	350		650 LG
Compote, stemmed, plain interior	45	75	60								300 AM
Compote, tricorner top, very scarce			150								
Rose Bowl, stemmed	40	90	110	375							225 AM
Rose Bowl, 3 footed	70	130	110	425		6000	1200	1000	750		1250 AQ
*Some have Northwoods Fern interior											
DAISY AND PLUME BANDED (NORTHWOOD)											
Compote or Rose bowl, stemmed	85	100									125 PHO
DAISY AND SCROLL											
Decanter w/stopper	250										
Wine	75										

Pattern Name	M	A	G	B	PO	AO	IB	IG	W	Red	Other
DAISY BASKET (IMPERIAL)											
One size	65										
DAISY BLOCK (ENGLISH)											
Rowboat, scarce	225	325									
DAISY CHAIN											
Shade	50										
DAISY CUT BELL (FENTON)											
One size, scarce	350										
DAISY DEAR (DUGAN)											
Bowl	20	45			60				85		100 AQ
Whimsey, J.I.P., scarce	65										
Whimsey Plate, rare					275						
DAISY DRAPE (INDIA)											
Vase	225										
DAISY DRAPES											
Vase, 6¼"	60										
DAISY IN OVAL PANELS (U.S. GLASS)											
Creamer or Sugar	55										
DAISY MAY											
* Exterior pattern only											
DAISY ROSE (LADY FINGERS)											
Vase, 8"	175										
DAISY SPRAY											
Vase	65										
DAISY SQUARES											
Celery Vase Whimsey	600										
Compote, various shapes, rare	575										900 LG
Goblet, rare	600	750									750 V
Rose Bowl, scarce	475		600					625			
DAISY WEB (DUGAN)											
Hat, very scarce	300	675		750							
DAISY WREATH (WESTMORELAND)											
Bowl, 8" – 10"	175	250		200	300						225 BO
Vase, very rare	500										
DANCE OF THE VEILS (FENTON)											
Vase, rare	12000										
DANDELION (NORTHWOOD)											
Mug	125	200	550	325		750					750 BO
Mug (Knight Templar), rare	300						650	800			
Pitcher	475	650	1200				7000	30000	7500		
Tumbler	45	70	105				135	300	125		245 LV
Vase Whimsey, rare		850									
DART											
Oil Lamp, rare	500										
DAVANN											
Vase, 8" – 9", scarce	175										
DAVENPORT											
Lemonade Tumbler	35										
DAVISONS SOCIETY CHOCOLATES											
Plate, handgrip		1000									
DECO											
Vase, scarce	275										
DECO LILY											
Bulbous Vase	400										
DECORAMA											
Pitcher	550										
Tumbler	175										
DEEP GRAPE (MILLERSBURG)											
Compote, rare	1800	2200	2000	7000							
Compote, ruffled top, rare		2500									
Rosebowl, stemmed, rare			8000								
DELORES											
Perfume	60										
DELTA BASE (IMPERIAL)											
Candlesticks, pair	150										
DESERT GODDESS											
Epergne			475								500 AM
DE SVENSKA											
Vase 11½"				200							
DeVILBISS											
Atomizer, complete	100										
Perfumer	65										
DEWHIRST BERRY BAND											
Carafe, 7"	175										
Compote	85										
DIAGONAL BAND											
Tankard, scarce	675	550									
DIAGONAL RIDGE											
Pitcher	50										

Pattern Name	M	A	G	B	PO	AO	IB	IG	W	Red	Other
Tumbler	10										
DIAMANTES STAR (JAIN)											
Vase	100										
DIAMOND (CRYSTAL)											
Creamer	60	80									
Sugar, open	70	85									
DIAMOND AND BOWS (DIAMOND & GRAPES)											
Tumbler	200										
DIAMOND AND DAISY CUT (U.S. GLASS)											
Pitcher, rare	400			450							
Tumbler, 4", very scarce	65			95							
Tumbler, 5", rare	150										
Vase, square, 10"	225										
DIAMOND AND DAISY CUT VARIANT (JENKINS)											
Punch Bowl w/Base, rare	625										
DIAMOND AND FAN											
Compote					100						
Cordial Set, 7 pieces	350										
DIAMOND AND FAN (MILLERSBURG) Exterior only											
DIAMOND & FILE (FENTON)											
Bowl, 7" – 9"	45										
Plate, 2 sides up 9½", scarce	150										
DIAMOND AND RIB (FENTON)											
Jardinere Whimsey	1400	1600	2000	1600							
Vase, 7" – 12"	20	60	60	100					155		75 SM
Vase, Funeral, 17" – 22"	2300	1650	1650	1900					800		
Vase Whimsey, spittoon shape			1800								
DIAMOND AND SUNBURST (IMPERIAL)											
Decanter w/Stopper	125	325									
Oil Cruet, rare			900								
Wine	55	60									
DIAMOND ARCHES											
Bowl	85										
DIAMOND BAND (CRYSTAL)											
Float Set, scarce	400	550									
Open Sugar	45	60									
DIAMOND BAND AND FAN (ENGLISH)											
Cordial set, complete, rare	900										
DIAMOND BLOCK SHADE (IMPERIAL)											
Light Shade	65										
DIAMOND CANE											
Sugar Box	165										
DIAMOND CATTAILS (INDIA)											
Tumbler	100										
DIAMOND CHAIN											
Bowl, 6¼"	60										
DIAMOND CHECKERBOARD											
Bowl, 5"	25										
Bowl, 9"	40										
Butter	90										
Cracker Jar	85										
Tumbler	100										
DIAMOND COLLAR (INDIANA GLASS)											
Bowl	65										
DIAMOND CUT											
Banana Bowl	90	115									
Bowl, 10"	90	150									
Compote	75										
Rose Bowl, 9½", rare	175	425									
DIAMOND CUT SHIELDS											
Pitcher	475										
Tumbler	125										
DIAMOND DAISY											
Plate, 8"	95										
DIAMOND FLOWER											
Compote, miniature	85										
DIAMOND FOUNTAIN (HIGBEE)											
Bowl, scarce	100										
Cruet, very Scarce	425										
Plate, handgrip, rare	250										
DIAMOND HEART											
Vase, 5½"	70										

Pattern Name	M	A	G	B	PO	AO	IB	IG	W	Red	Other
DIAMOND HONEYCOMB											
Sugar, w/lid	85			200							
DIAMOND LACE (IMPERIAL)											
Bowl, 5"	25	30	50								
Bowl, 10" – 11"	65	110	250								
Bowl, 10" ICS, scarce											110 CM
Pitcher		375									
Tumbler	190	50							250		
Rosebowl Whimsey, very rare	2000										
DIAMOND OVALS (ENGLISH)											
Bottle & Stopper	100										
Compote (open sugar)	40										
Creamer	40										
Plate, stemmed	150										
DIAMOND PANELS & RIBS (INDIA)											
Tumbler	175										
DIAMOND PINWHEEL (ENGLISH)											
Bowl, 10⁷/₈"	60										
Butter	90										
Compote	45										
DIAMOND POINT (NORTHWOOD)											
Vase, 7" – 14"	30	85	110	250		1300	800	425			300 SA
Vase w/original label		2500									
DIAMOND POINT COLUMNS (FENTON)											
Banana Bowl, scarce	80										
Bowl, 5"	25										
Bowl, 7½"	35										
Plate, 7", scarce	55										
Vase	40	100	75	90							125 V
DIAMOND POINT COLUMNS (LATE)											
Bowl, 5"	20										
Bowl, 9"	30										
Compote	35										
Butter	40										
Creamer, Spooner, or Sugar	30										
Powder Jar w/lid	40										
Milk Pitcher	50										
DIAMOND POINTS (NORTHWOOD)											
Basket, rare	1400	2100		2500					2800		
DIAMOND POINTS VARIANT (FOSTORIA)											
Rose Bowl, rare	1200										
DIAMOND PRISMS											
Basket	75										
Compote	55										
DIAMOND RAIN											
Tumbler, scarce	150										
DIAMOND RING (IMPERIAL)											
Bowl, 5"	25	30									30 SM
Bowl, 9"	40	50									55 SM
Fruit Bowl, 9½"	65	90									65 SM
Rose Bowl, scarce	250	425									325 SM
DIAMONDS (MILLERSBURG)											
Pitcher	275	385	425								525 TL
Tumbler	65	90	80								175 TL
Punch Bowl & Base, rare	3200	5500	4000								
Pitcher (no spout), rare		600	600								
Spittoon Whimsey, very rare	4500										
DIAMOND SHIELD											
Compote	150										
DIAMOND SPARKLER (U.S. GLASS)											
Vase, very rare	250										
DIAMOND'S ROYAL LUSTRE											
Candlesticks, pair	80	125		175				125		300	
Console Bowl	55	70		85				60		135	
DIAMOND'S SODA GOLD											
Exterior pattern only											
DIAMOND STAR											
Mug, 2 sizes	125										
Vase, 8"	80										
DIAMOND STORM											
Tumbler, scarce	125										
DIAMOND STUD (INDIA)											
Pitcher	325										
Tumbler	150										
DIAMOND STUDS											
Spittoon Whimsey, rare			350								
DIAMOND THUMBPRINT											
Mini Oil Lamp, 6½"	250										

Pattern Name	M	A	G	B	PO	AO	IB	IG	W	Red	Other
DIAMOND TOP (ENGLISH)											
Creamer	40										
Spooner	40										
DIAMOND VANE (ENGLISH)											
Creamer, 4"	35										
DIAMOND WEDGE											
Tumbler	125										
DIAMOND WHEEL											
Exterior pattern only											
DIANA, THE HUNTRESS											
Bowl, 8"	350										
DIANTHUS (FENTON)											
Pitcher								475	500		
Tumbler								60	65		
DIMPLES (INDIA)											
Vase	75										
DINOSAUR (RINDSKOPF)											
Bowl, 8" – 9"	2500										
DIPLOMAT (FENTON)											
Tumbler, rare	165										
DIVING DOLPHINS (ENGLISH)											
Bowl, footed, 7"	225	275	425	325							
Rose Bowl, scarce	325	475									
Whimsey Bowl, rare											600 AQ
DOG											
Ashtray	90										
DOG & DEER											
Decanter, enameled	250										
Shot Glass, enameled	75										
DOGWOOD SPRAYS (DUGAN)											
Bowl, 9"	150	250		350	225						325 BO
Compote	175	225			250						
DOLPHINS (MILLERSBURG)											
Compote, rare		2300	4000	5700							
DORIA											
Gravy Boat w/underplate	200										
DOROTHY											
Perfume	50										
DORSEY AND FUNKENSTEIN (FENTON)											
Bowl, advertising, very scarce		1100									
Plate, advertising, very scarce		2600									
DOT											
Vase, 5¼", rare		350									
DOTTED DAISIES											
Plate, 8"	90										
DOTTED DIAMONDS & DAISIES											
Pitcher	175										
Tumbler	55										
DOUBLE BANDED FLUTE											
Vase, 9"	125										
DOUBLE DAISY (FENTON)											
Pitcher, bulbous	200										
Pitcher, tankard	250		385								
Tumbler	30		40								
DOUBLE DIAMOND (BROCKWITZ)											
Perfume	145										
Tumbler	125										
Tumble-up	175										
DOUBLE DIAMONDS											
Cologne	90										
Pin Tray	60										
Puff Box	50										
Perfume	80										
Ring Tree	85										
Tumble-up	110										
DOUBLE DOLPHIN (FENTON)											
Bowl, flat, 8" – 10"											65 CeB
Bowl, footed, 9" – 11"											115 CeB
Cake Plate, center handled											85 CeB
Candlesticks, pair											90 CeB
Compote											70 CeB
Covered Candy, stemmed											80 CeB
Fan Vase											90 CeB
DOUBLE DUTCH (IMPERIAL)											
Bowl, footed, 9"	50	180	75								85 SM
DOUBLE LOOP (NORTHWOOD)											
Creamer	175	200	250	425		600					
Sugar	55	100	150	100		300					
DOUBLE SCROLL (IMPERIAL)											
Bowl, console	50									250	425 V
Candlesticks, pair	75									400	275 V

Pattern Name	M	A	G	B	PO	AO	IB	IG	W	Red	Other
DOUBLE STAR (CAMBRIDGE)											
Bowl, 9", rare			400								
Pitcher, scarce	600	700	450								
Tumbler, scarce	275	225	65								
Spittoon Whimsey, rare			3900								
DOUBLE STEM ROSE (DUGAN)											
Bowl, dome base, 8½"	45	200		195	175			1750			600 CeB
Plate, footed, scarce	200	350			285				165		
DOUBLE STIPPLED RAYS											
Bowl											85 AM
DOUGHNUT BRIDLE ROSETTE											
One size		95									
DOZEN ROSES, A (IMPERIAL)											
Bowl, footed, 8" – 10", scarce	500	900	1400								
DRAGON AND LOTUS (FENTON)											
Banana Bowl, very rare	1800										
Bowl, flat, 9"	55	155	190	100	700	2850				2250	150 AM
Bowl, footed, 9"	90	195	175	150	250					2200	185 SM
Nut Bowl, scarce				425							
Plate, 9½"	2000	2500		2500	2900				7000		
DRAGON & BERRY (STRAWBERRY)											
Bowl, flat, 9", scarce	500	3500	2400	1800							
Bowl, footed, 9", scarce	400		1700	1100							
Plate (Absentee Dragon), rare	3800										
DRAGONFLY LAMP											
Oil Lamp, rare								1900	1400		1800 PK
DRAGON'S TONGUE (FENTON)											
Bowl, 11", scarce	1200										
Shade	225										150 MMG
DRAGON VASE											
Vase, with Dragons, very rare				1200							1200 BA
DRAGONFLY											
Shade											65 AM
DRAPE AND TASSEL											
Shade	45										
DRAPED ARCS (BROCKWITZ)											
Bowl					125						
DRAPERY (NORTHWOOD)											
Candy Dish	80	135	375	165			125	225	135		300 V
Rose Bowl	265	200		300		375	500	800	775		3000 ReB
Vase	90	250	325	350		550	325	225	175		1500 SA
DRAPERY BRACELET (INDIA)											
Pitcher	200										
Tumbler	75										
DRAPERY ROSE (INDIA)											
Vase	65										
DRAPERY VARIANT (FENTON)											
Pitcher, rare	525										
Tumbler, scarce	200										
DRAPERY VARIANT (FINLAND)											
Pitcher	600										
Tumbler	200										
Shot Glass	225										
DRAPERY VARIANT (NORTHWOOD)											
Vase, scarce	85	200	550	175							350 LV
DREIBUS PARFAIT SWEETS (NORTHWOOD)											
Plate, 2 or 4 sides up		850									
Plate, flat, rare		1100									
DRESSER BOTTLE SET											
Complete, 5 bottles w/holder	250										
DUCKIE											
Powder Jar w/lid	20										
DUGAN-DIAMOND'S RAINBOW											
Candy Jar, footed w/lid	55		75	85							
DUGAN'S #1013R (DUGAN)											
Vase 8" – 13"	50	75		85							
DUGAN'S FLUTE											
Vase, 7" – 13"	45	60									
DUGAN'S FRIT											
Vase, pinched				175							
DUGAN'S HYACINTH											
Vase	75			175							
Vase Whimsey, pinched 3 sides	95	225		300							350 CeB
DUGAN'S MANY RIBS (DUGAN)											
Hat Shape	30	40		75	95						
Vase	60	80		75	125						
DUGAN'S PLAIN JANE											
Interior pattern on some Leaf Rosette and Beads bowls and plates											

Pattern Name	M	A	G	B	PO	AO	IB	IG	W	Red	Other
DUGAN'S STIPPLED RAYS											
Bowl	35	45	50								
Hat	25	35	45								
DUGAN'S TRUMPET											
Vase 14" – 16", very scarce	60										300 CeB
DUGAN'S TWIST											
Bowl		75									
DUGAN'S VENETIAN											
Rose Bowl		125		200							225 LV
DUGAN'S VENETIAN HONEYCOMB											
Either shape		90		110							
DUGAN'S VINTAGE VARIANT											
Bowl, footed, 8½"	85	175	250	200							900 CeB
Plate	300	575									
DUNCAN (NATIONAL GLASS)											
Cruet	600										
DURAND ADVERTISMENT (FENTON)											
Orange Bowl, footed (Grape & Cable w/advertising, very scarce)				1600							
DUTCH MILL											
Ashtray	65										
Plate, 8"	50										
DUTCH PLATE											
One size, 8"	45										
DUTCH TWINS											
Ashtray	50										
EAGLE FURNITURE COMPANY (NORTHWOOD)											
Plate, advertising		1200									
E.A. HUDSON FURNITURE (NORTHWOOD)											
Bowl, rare, advertising		1500									
Plate, flat, advertising		1700									
Plate, handgrip, advertising		1300									
EARLY AMERICAN (DUNCAN & MILLER)											
Plate	75										
EASTERN STAR (IMPERIAL)											
(Exterior on some scroll embossed compotes)											
EBON											
Vase		110BA									
EGG AND DART											
Candlesticks, pair	90										
EGYPTIAN LUSTRE (DUGAN)											
Bowl		75 BA									
Plate		85 BA									
Vase		100BA									
EGYPTIAN QUEEN'S VASE											
Vase, 7"	425										
ELEGANCE											
Bowl, 8¼", rare	2800						3000				
Plate, rare							3400				
ELEGANCE											
Pitcher, enameled, rare	800										
Tumbler, enameled, rare	350										
ELEKTRA											
Butter	150										
Compote, 4½"	50	60		65							
Creamer	70										
Sugar, open	65										
ELEPHANT											
Paperweight	1250										
ELEPHANT'S FOOT VASE											
See Tree Trunk (Northwood)											
ELEPHANT VASE (JAIN)											
Vase, 3 sizes	110										
ELEPHANT VASE VARIANT											
Vase	125										
ELKS (DUGAN)											
Nappy, very rare		7000									
ELKS (FENTON)											
Detroit Bowl, very scarce	9000	800	1100	1000							
Parkersburg Plate, rare			2000	2500							
Atlantic City Plate, rare			18000	1800							
Atlantic City Bowl, scarce				1300							
1911 Atlantic City Bell, rare				2200							
1912 Portland Bell, very rare				23000							
1914 Parkersburg Bell, rare				2500							
ELKS (MILLERSBURG)											
Bowl, rare		2500									
Paperweight, rare		2500	4000								

Pattern Name	M	A	G	B	PO	AO	IB	IG	W	Red	Other
ELYSIAN											
Vase, 9½"	350										
EMBROIDERED FLOWER & URN (JAIN)											
Tumbler	90										
EMBROIDERED FLOWERS (JAIN)											
Tumbler	150										
EMBROIDERED MUMS (NORTHWOOD)											
Bowl, 9"	300	350		850		11,000	800	950			250 LV
Plate				8000			1300	1700	2100		
Stemmed Bonbon									1000		
EMBROIDERED PANELS (JAIN)											
Spittoon (lamp base)	125										
Tumbler	75										
EMMA'S VASE											
Vase	400										
EMU (CRYSTAL)											
Bowl, 5", rare	150	175									
Bowl, 10", rare	900										1400 AM
Compote Variant, rare	700	850									
ENAMELED BLOSSOM SPRAY (DUGAN)											
Bowl, decorated				100							
Plate, decorated				120							
Handgrip Plate, decorated				145							
ENAMELED CHERRIES (or GRAPES) (NORTHWOOD)											
Pitcher				400							
Tumbler				50							
ENAMELED CHRYSANTHEMUM											
Pitcher	140			195							
Tumbler	25			40							
ENAMELED CHRYSANTHEMUM WITH PRISM BAND											
Pitcher	165	225	225	200				265	200		
Tumbler	30	45	45	35				50	40		
ENAMELED COLUMBINE (FENTON)											
Pitcher	250	325	350	450							
Tumbler	30	40	55	60							
ENAMELED CORAL											
Pitcher	200										
ENAMELED CROCUS											
Pitcher	125			175					165		
Tumbler	20			35					30		
ENAMELED CROCUS VARIANT											
Pitcher	130			185					175		
Tumbler	25			40					35		
ENAMELED CROCUS W/PRISM BAND											
Pitcher	145			200					180		
Tumbler	30			45					35		
ENAMELED DIAMOND POINT											
Bottle	100										
ENAMELED DOGWOOD											
Pitcher	400										
Tumbler	50										
ENAMELED DOUBLE DAISY											
Pitcher	130			165					170		
Tumbler	20			30					30		
ENAMELED FLORAL SPRAY											
Pitcher											500 CL
Tumbler											90 CL
ENAMELED FORGET-ME-NOT (FENTON)											
Pitcher	400		600	450							
Tumbler	45		75	60							
ENAMELED FREESIA											
Pitcher	125			190							
Tumbler	25			30							
ENAMELED GOOSEBERRY (NORTHWOOD)											
Tumbler				80							
ENAMELED GRAPE BAND											
Tumbler	50										
ENAMELED HONEYSUCKLE											
Tumbler	250										
ENAMELED IRIS (FENTON)											
Pitcher	550	700	1000	650							
Tumbler	40	50	65	55							
ENAMELED LILY OF THE VALLEY											
See Stippled Flower (Dugan)											

Pattern Name	M	A	G	B	PO	AO	IB	IG	W	Red	Other
ENAMELED LOTUS (FENTON)											
Pitcher	225		325					450			
ENAMELED PANEL											
Goblet	190										
ENAMELED PERIWINKLE											
Pitcher	150										
Tumbler	25										
ENAMELED PHLOX											
Pitcher		275									
Tumbler		40									
ENAMELED PRISM BAND											
Pitcher	200	350	375	300				450	365		
Tumbler	45	55	65	55				85	55		
ENAMELED PUNTY BAND											
Tumbler, rare	325										
ENAMELED ROSE OF PARADISE											
Tumbler			200								
ENAMELED STIPPLED PETALS											
See Stippled Petals (Dugan)											
ENAMELED STORK (GERMAN)											
Pitcher	175										
Tumbler	50										
ENAMELED SWALLOW											
Tankard Pitcher, with lid	225										
Tumbler	50										
ENAMELED WINDFLOWER											
Tumbler	75										
ENCORE											
Bottle (late)	10										
ENCRUSTED VINE											
Tumbler	25										
ENGLISH BUTTON BAND (ENGLISH)											
Creamer	45										
Sugar	45										
ENGLISH FLUTE & FILE (SOWERBY)											
Compote	70										120 LV
Creamer or Sugar	45										70 LV
ENGLISH HOB AND BUTTON (ENGLISH)											
Bowl, 7" – 10"	60	80	95	70							
Epergne (metal base)	125			145							
ENGLISH HOBSTAR											
Oval Bowl, 6", in holder	150										
ENGRAVED CORNFLOWER (FENTON)											
Pitcher, scarce	450										
Tumbler, scarce	75										
ENGRAVED DAISY											
Tumbler, scarce	40										
ENGRAVED DAISY & SPEARS											
Goblet, 4½"	75										
ENGRAVED FLORAL (FENTON)											
Tumbler			95								
ENGRAVED GRAPES (FENTON)											
Candy Jar w/lid	85										
Juice Glass	30										
Pitcher, squat	120										
Pitcher, tall	145										
Tumbler	30										
Tumble-up	150										
Vase	65										
ENGRAVED ZINNIA (FENTON)											
Tumbler	50										
ESBERARD-RIO											
Plate, rare	250										
ESTATE (WESTMORELAND)											
Bud Vase, 6"	50										75 SM
Creamer or Sugar	55				75	210 BO					110 AQ
Mug, rare	75										
Perfume, very scarce											400 SM
ETCHED BUTTERFLY (IMPERIAL)											
Vase	135										
ETCHED DECO (STANDARD)											
Bowl, 3 footed, 7"	35										
Creamer	45										
Hat shape	45										
Nappy, handled	40										
Plate, 3 footed, 8"	50										
Plate, pedestal footed, 8"	60										
Variant Plate (no etching)	55										

Pattern Name	M	A	G	B	PO	AO	IB	IG	W	Red	Other
ETCHED GARDEN MUMS											
Bowl		250									
ETCHED LEAVES											
Oil Bottle, 6⅞"	80										
ETCHED VINE											
Tumbler	40										
ETCHED VINE & FLOWERS (INDIA)											
Pitcher	425										
Tumbler	135										
EURO											
Vase w/brass top	45										
EURO DIAMONDS											
Berry Bowl, small			15								
Berry Bowl, large			45								
EUROPA											
Vase, 9¾"	40										
EUROPEAN POPPY											
Butter											165 AM
EUROPEAN VINTAGE GRAPE											
Bowl, 8", rare	400										
EVELYN (FOSTORIA)											
Bowl (1940s)			1000								
EXCHANGE BANK (FENTON)											
Bowl, advertising		800									
Plate, advertising, 6"		1700									
Plate, advertising, handgrip		1600									
EXOTIC LUSTRE											
Lemonade Tumbler, scarce	50										
EYE CUP											
One size	90										
FAMOUS											
Puff Box	75										
FAN (DUGAN)											
Bowl, Sauce, 5"	40	55			100						
Gravy Boat, footed	65	180			150						
FANCIFUL (DUGAN)											
Bowl, 8½"	125	350		550	275				110		350 LV
Plate, 9"	200	625		775	550				225		950 LV
FANCY (NORTHWOOD)											
Interior on some Fine Cut & Roses pieces											
FANCY CORN HUSK VASE (DUGAN)											
Fancy Husk, rare	1300										
FANCY CUT (ENGLISH)											
Miniature Pitcher, rare	225										
Miniature Tumbler, scarce	60										
FANCY FLOWERS (IMPERIAL)											
Compote	120		175								
FAN MONTAGE											
Biscuit Jar w/lid, rare	225										
FANS											
Cracker Jar (metal lid)	175										
Pitcher	300										
Tumbler	125										
FAN STAR (MILLERSBURG)											
(Exterior only)											
FAN-TAIL (FENTON)											
Bowl, footed, 9"	100		275	250					325		
Bowl, shallow ICS shape, very scarce	200		400	325							
Plate, footed, rare	5600			6000							
FAR EASTERN											
Jar	135										
FARMYARD (DUGAN)											
Bowl, 10", scarce		7500	11000		13000						
Bowl, 10", square, very scarce		8250	12500								
Plate, 10½", very rare		18000									
FASHION (IMPERIAL)											
Bowl, 9"	40		90								55 SM
Bride's Basket	125										150 CM
Butter	75	200									
Compote	600										525 SM
Creamer or Sugar	25	145									100 SM
Punch Bowl w/base	175	1800									4000 SM
Punch Cup	10	40									60 SM
Pitcher	150	900									550 SM
Tumbler	20	300									85 SM
Rose Bowl, very rare	225	900	375								
FEATHER AND HEART (MILLERSBURG)											
Pitcher, scarce	425	650	1000								14500 V

330

Pattern Name	M	A	G	B	PO	AO	IB	IG	W	Red	Other
Tumbler, scarce	60	100	200								
Hair Receiver Whimsey, very rare	2000										
Spittoon Whimsey, very rare	7000										
FEATHER COLUMNS (INDIA)											
Tumbler	175										
FEATHERED ARROW											
Bowl, 8½" – 9½"	65										70 CM
Rose Bowl, rare	200										
FEATHERED FLOWERS											
(Exterior only)											
FEATHERED RAYS (FENTON)											
Bowl, rare			450								
FEATHERED SERPENT (FENTON)											
Bowl, 5"	30	40	45	40							
Bowl, 10"	90	75	90	65							
Bowl, 6", tricorner	70	110	130								
Spittoon Whimsey, rare		6000	7500								
FEATHERS (NORTHWOOD)											
Vase, 7" – 14"	45	85	75				200		400		
FEATHER STITCH (FENTON)											
Bowl, 8½" – 10"	80	125	175	125						7500	275 AQ
Plate (low bowl), scarce	950										
FEATHER SWIRL (U.S. GLASS)											
Butter	165										
Vase	65										
FELDMAN BROS (FENTON)											
Open Edge Basket	65										
FENTON FLUTE											
Vase	25	55	65	50					90	300	100 V
FENTONIA (FENTON)											
Bowl, footed, 5"	30	70	70	60							
Bowl, footed, 9½"	100	125	125	110							
Butter	115			185							
Creamer, Sugar, or Spooner	75			90							
Fruit Bowl, 10"	85			100							
Pitcher	400			625							
Tumbler	50			75							
Vase Whimsey, rare	325			450							
FENTONIA FRUIT (FENTON)											
Bowl, footed, 6"	60			120							
Bowl, footed, 10"	125			175							
Butter, very rare				1000							
Pitcher, rare	600			1200							
Tumbler, rare	200			475							
FENTON LEMON WEDGE SERVER											
One size	45							100	75		125 AM
FENTON'S #3											
Creamer	45										
Sugar, open	45										
FENTON'S #9											
Candy Jar w/lid	35										70 V
FENTON'S #232											
Candlesticks, each	40										110 CeB
FENTON'S #260											
Compote, 7"	40										75 CeB
FENTON'S #314											
Candlesticks, pair											200 WS
FENTON'S #568											
Candy Compote w/lid											125 IG
FENTON'S #574											
Vase/Compote, 6" & 12"	25 – 40		35 – 55								60 V
FENTON'S #631											
Plate, 9"											60 CeB
FENTON'S #643											
Compote	50										70 CeB
Covered Candy	70										95 CeB
Plate, 7"	35							40			
Salver	65							75			
FENTON'S #649											
Candlesticks											160 V
FENTON'S #736 ELITE											
Candy Jar	75										90 CeB
Compote	65										75 CeB
Rose Bowl, very scarce	175									300	225 CeB
FENTON'S #847											
Bowl									65		
Candy Jar											125 AQ
Fan Vase									85		
FENTON'S #888											
Vase	55			70							
FENTON'S #1502											
Bonbon											125 AQ

Pattern Name	M	A	G	B	PO	AO	IB	IG	W	Red	Other
Bowl											90 AQ
Compote											110 AQ
FENTON'S CHERRIES (FENTON)											
Banana Boat, very rare	3000			2750							
FENTON'S CORNUCOPIA											
Candlesticks, pair	75						195	100	85		
FENTON'S FLOWERS (FENTON)											
Nut Bowl	35	135	150	500					165		
Rose Bowl	45	125	150	100	1300				175	2200	300 V
Rose Bowl Variant, smooth top, rare				600							
FENTON SMOOTH RAYS											
Bowl, 5" – 6"	25	35	40	45				55			
Bowl, tricorner, 6½"	30	45	50	55				70			
Bowl, square, 9", scarce	70		90								
FERN (FENTON)											
Bowl, 7" – 9", rare				1100							
FERN (NORTHWOOD)											
Compote	100	90	135				1400				
*(Daisy & Plume exterior)											
FERN & WATTLE (CRYSTAL)											
*Exterior pattern only											
FERN BRAND CHOCOLATES (NORTHWOOD)											
Plate		1300									
FERN PANELS (FENTON)											
Hat	45		60	50						425	
FESTIVAL MOON (JAPAN) AKA: ID KA CHAND											
Tumbler, rare	150										
FIELD FLOWER (IMPERIAL)											
Milk Pitcher, rare	180	200	220								225 AM
Pitcher, scarce	165	550	450	2000							325 TL
Tumbler, scarce	35	60	70	350						1500	125 VI
FIELD THISTLE, (U.S. GLASS)											
Bowl, 6" – 10"	50					250					
Butter, rare	125										
Breakfast Set, 2 piece, rare						325					
Compote	150										
Plate, 6", rare	200										
Plate, 9", rare	300										
Pitcher, scarce	175										
Tumbler, scarce	45										
Sugar, Creamer, or Spooner, rare	100										
Vase, 2 sizes	250 – 500										
FILE (IMPERIAL & ENGLISH)											
Bowl, 5"	30	40									
Bowl, 7" – 10"	45	50									60 CM
Compote	40	50									60 CM
Creamer or Spooner	85										
Juice Tumbler, rare	300										
Lemonade Tumbler (Variant), rare	1000										
Pitcher, rare	300	500									
Tumbler, scarce	100										
Sugar	125										
Vase Whimsey, from sugar, scarce	350										
FILE (SOWERBY)											
Handled Sweetmeat Bowl	175										
FILE AND FAN											
Bowl, footed, 6"	40				160						
Compote	100					200					175 MMG
FILE & SHELL (SOWERBY)											
Candle Lamp, 9¼"	350										
FILED RIB (FEDERAL)											
Bowl, 8½" – 9"	35										
Bowl, 5"	15										
Plate, 10¾"	65										
FILED STEM											
Vase	75										
FILIGREE (DUGAN)											
Vase, rare		4500									
FINE BLOCK (IMPERIAL)											
Shade			50								
FINE CUT AND ROSES (NORTHWOOD)											
Candy Dish, footed	45	55	70	200		350	325	400	125		
Rose Bowl, footed	125	95	175	400		1000	365		200		175 LV
Candy Dish Variant, footed, (no collar base), scarce			100								
Rose Bowl Variant, footed, rare		200	300								500 LV
(Add 25% for Fancy interior)											
FINE CUT AND STAR											
Banana Boat, 5"	150										

Pattern Name	M	A	G	B	PO	AO	IB	IG	W	Red	Other
FINE CUT FLOWERS & VARIANT											
(FENTON)											
Compote	65		125								
Goblet	75		125								
FINE CUT HEART											
(MILLERSBURG)											
(Exterior pattern only)											
FINE CUT OVALS (MILLERSBURG)											
(Exterior pattern only)											
FINE CUT RINGS (ENGLISH)											
Bowl, oval	140										
Bowl, round	135										
Butter	170										
Celery	160										
Creamer	145										
Jam Jar w/lid	165										
Stemmed Cake Stand	175										
Stemmed Sugar	145										
Vase	150										
FINE CUT RINGS VARIANT											
(ENGLISH)											
Cake Stand, footed	200										
Celery Vase	150										
FINE PRISMS & DIAMONDS											
(ENGLISH)											
Vase, 7" – 14"											90 AM
FINE RIB (DUGAN)											
Vase, 8" – 15"	60	70	90		125						
FINE RIB (FENTON)											
Vase, 2⅝", base	20	80	90	40	150	450				450	250 SA
Vase, 2⅞", base	35	90	95	125							
FINE RIB (NORTHWOOD)											
Vase, 7" – 14"	25	65	45	165		500	180	195	100		225 AQ
FINE RIB SHADE (ELECTRIC)											
One shape	70										
FIRCONE (FRANCE)											
Vase, 11¾", very scarce	1000										
FIR CONES (FINLAND)											
Pitcher				600							
Tumbler				350							
FIREFLY (MOTH) – (FINLAND)											
Candlesticks, pair	90										
FIRESTONE TIRE											
Ashtray, advertising, various	100			375							150 AM
FISH BOTTLE											
Novelty Bottle	175										
FISH BOWL											
Bowl, 7½", very scarce	375										
FISHERMAN'S MUG (DUGAN)											
One size	200	125		650	1100						250 HO
FISHNET (DUGAN)											
Epergne		300			350						
FISHSCALES AND BEADS (DUGAN)											
Bowl, 6" – 8"	35	100		300	80				90		
Bride's Basket, complete					150						
Plate, 7"	80	350			75				100		
Plate, souvenir of Sturgis, Michigan									375		
FISH VASE (JAIN)											
2 sizes, very scarce	100										
FIVE HEARTS (DUGAN)											
Bowl, dome base, 8¼"	125	275			300						
Bowl, flared, very rare	650										
Rose Bowl, rare	1300										
FIVE LILY EPERGNE											
Complete, metal fittings	175	250									
FIVE PANEL											
Candy Jar, stemmed	70										
FIVE PETALS											
Compote, rare	65										90 AM
Bowl, rare		60									
FLANNEL FLOWER (CRYSTAL)											
Cake Stand	140	195									
Compote, large	120	155									
FLARED PANEL											
Shade					75						
FLARED WIDE PANEL											
Atomizer, 3½"	90										
FLASHED DIAMONDS											
Shakers, pair	50										
Vase Whimsey, from creamer	75										
FLASHING STARS											
Tumbler, rare		325		275							

Pattern Name	M	A	G	B	PO	AO	IB	IG	W	Red	Other
Pitcher, rare		950									
FLEUR-DE-LIS (INWALD)											
Bowl, 8", rare	350										
Chop Plate, 12", rare	700										
Plate, 6¼", rare	425										
Rose Bowl, rare	525										
Vase, rare	650										
FLEUR-DE-LIS & VARIANT (MILLERSBURG)											
Bowl, flat, 9" – 10"	225	550	250								6500 V
Bowl, footed, 9" – 10"	225	325	325								
Bowl, footed, square, very rare											5000 V
Bowl, tricornered, scarce	400	650	475								
Compote, very rare			5000								
Rose Bowl, either base, rare		2700									
FLEUR-DE-LIS MINIATURE LAMP											
Miniature Lamp, "Gone with the Wind"	Shade								50		
FLOATING HEN											
Candy, footed w/lid	400										
FLORA (ENGLISH)											
Float Bowl				200							
Vase	100			125							
FLORABELLE											
Pitcher								500			
Tumbler								175			
FLORAL ACCENT											
Cup & Saucer, mini	125										
FLORAL FAN											
Etched Vase	50										
FLORAL AND GRAPE (DUGAN)											
Hat Whimsey	40										
J.I.P. Whimsey, scarce											100 PHO
Pitcher	145	300		350					325		
Tumbler	20	50		35					55		
FLORAL & GRAPE VARIANT (FENTON)											
Pitcher, 2 variations	195	285	300	300				600			
Tumbler	30	35	100	30							
Pitcher Whimsey Vase, from Pitcher, very rare				4500							
FLORAL & MELON RIB											
Ale Decanter	600										
Ale Glasses	175										
FLORAL AND OPTIC (IMPERIAL)											
Bowl, footed, 8" – 10"	35			150MMG						350	140 SM
Cake Plate, footed	60			180MMG						550	170 SM
Rose Bowl, footed	75			200MMG							200 AQ
FLORAL AND SCROLL											
Shade, various shapes	45										
FLORAL AND WHEAT (DUGAN)											
Bonbon, stemmed, 2 shapes	40	125		250	75				125		
FLORAL BUTTERFLIES (FENTON)											
Vase, etched	135										
FLORAL OVAL (HIGBEE)											
Bowl, 7"	50										
Creamer	60										
Goblet	75										
Plate, 7", rare	90										
FLORAL SUNBURST (SWEDEN)											
Bowl	95			175							
Rose Bowl	225			325							
Vase, flared top	650			1100							
Vase, tricorner or turned in top	950			1500							
FLORENTINE (FENTON AND NORTHWOOD)											
Candlesticks, large, pair	125		160RG	700				125		1100	
Candlesticks, small, pair	75		120	450						900	110 CeB
FLORENTINE (IMPERIAL)											
Hat Vase											65 CM
FLOWER AND DIAMON											
See Dahlia (Jenkins)											
FLOWER BASKET											
One size	50										
FLOWER BLOCK											
Various sizes	20+										
FLOWERING DILL (FENTON)											
Hat	25	60	65	50						475	125 IM
FLOWERING VINE (MILLERSBURG)											
Compote, tall, very rare		8500	9500								
FLOWER MEDALLION (INDIANA GLASS)											
Tumbler, rare	400										

Pattern Name	M	A	G	B	PO	AO	IB	IG	W	Red	Other
FLOWER POT (FENTON)											
One size, complete	60			75							
FLOWERS & BEADS (DUGAN)											
Bowl, 6" – 7"	30	60			75						
Plate, 6 sided, 7½"	75	110			125						
FLOWERS AND FRAMES (DUGAN)											
Bowl, 8" – 10"	60	425			200						
FLOWERS AND SPADES (DUGAN)											
Bowl, 5", scarce		75			65						
Bowl, 9½", rare		350			450						
FLOWER WEB (INDIA)											
Tumbler	100										
FLUFFY PEACOCK (FENTON)											
Pitcher	325	700	750	575							
Tumbler	40	70	110	75							
FLUTE (ENGLISH)											
Sherbet, marked "English"	50										
FLUTE (MILLERSBURG)											
Compote, 6" (marked "Krystol"), rare	500	600									
Vase, rare	450	600	800	3000							
FLUTE (NORTHWOOD)											
Bowl, 5"	25	30									
Bowl, 9"	45	55									
Bowl, 3 in 1 edge, rare			150								
Butter	135		185								
Celery Vase	75										
Creamer or Sugar	75		95								
Individual Salt, footed	35										50 V
Master Salt, footed	75										150 V
Plate, very scarce	300										
Ringtree, rare	175										
Rose Bowl, rare	300										
Sherbet	35	50	45								80 TL
Pitcher, rare	400	700	600								
Tumbler, 3 varieties	50		300								
FLUTE #700 (IMPERIAL)											
Bowl, 5"	30	70									
Bowl, 10"		225									
Celery Vase, rare	275	400									
Chop Plate, 11", rare	350										
Covered Butter	180	240	210								
Creamer or Sugar	90	100	100								
Cruet	90										
Custard Bowl, 11"		300	400								
Fruit Bowl & Base, scarce	300	700	500								900 V
Cup	25	40	40								65 V
Nappy, one handled	60	135									
Pitcher	300	600	500	600							
Tumbler	45	175	150	200						350	300 V
Toothpick, regular	65	110	140	500							300 V
Toothpick, handled	250										
FLUTE #3939 (IMPERIAL)											
Bowl, 5½", rare	60	75	75								
Bowl, 10", rare	80	150	150								
Bowl, Fruit, 11", rare	95	175	175								
Punch Bowl w/base, scarce	300	500	500								
Punch Cup, scarce	35	50	50								
FLUTE AND CANE (IMPERIAL)											
Bowl, 7½" – 10"	30 – 35										
Champagne, rare	125										
Compote, large	60										
Milk Pitcher	150										
Pickle Dish	25										
Punch Cup	25										
Pitcher, stemmed, rare	350										400 PM
Tumbler, rare	400										
Wine	60										
FLUTE AND HONEYCOMB (IMPERIAL)											
Bowl, 5", scarce	65	95									60 CM
Bowl, 8½", rare	150										
FLUTED PILLARS											
See Leafy Triangles											
FLUTED RIB											
Jelly Jar	50										
FLUTED SCROLLS (DUGAN)											
Rose Bowl, footed, very rare	800	2000									
FLUTE FLOWER ARRANGER											
Bowl, scarce	60										
Flower Arranger, pulled from bowl, scarce	75										

335

Pattern Name	M	A	G	B	PO	AO	IB	IG	W	Red	Other
FLUTE VARIANT (NORTHWOOD)											
Bowl, 8"	75		90								
FOLDING FAN (DUGAN)											
Compote	65	75			125						
FOOTED DRAPE (WESTMORELAND)											
Vase	75								50		
FOOTED PRISM PANELS (ENGLISH)											
Vase	85		120	100							
FOOTED SHELL (WESTMORELAND)											
Small, 3"	45	55	60	60	100MO						75 AM
Large, 5"	40	50	500 GO	55							70 AM
FORGET-ME-NOT (FENTON)											
***BANDED DRAPE STYLE**											
Pitcher	200		350								
Tumbler	35		60								
FORKS											
Cracker Jar, very scarce	1750		600								
FORMAL (DUGAN)											
Hatpin Holder, very scarce	900	1100									
Vase, J.I.P., very scarce	600	900									
FORUM (FINLAND)											
Candle Sticks, pair											250 PK
FOSTORIA FLEMISH											
Vase, 8¾"											145 AM
FOSTORIA #600 (FOSTORIA)											
Napkin Ring	75										
FOSTORIA #1231 (FOSTORIA)											
Rose Bowl											145 CM
FOSTORIA #1299 (FOSTORIA)											
Tumbler	150										
FOUNTAIN (ENGLISH)											
Epergne, silver fittings, various	250										
Lamp, complete, scarce	300										
FOUR FLOWERS (DUGAN)											
Banana Bowl, scarce		400			350						
Bowl, 5", 7"	35	45			90						
Bowl, 8" – 10"	150	400	500		285						600 V
Plate, 6½"	150	375			175						
Plate, 9" – 10½"	350	2500	375		650						
Rose Bowl, rare	500	900									
Whimsey Bowl					400						
FOUR FLOWERS VARIANT (EUROPEAN)											
Bowl, footed, 8½"		80	125								
Bowl, 9" – 11"	70	75	100		200						225 AM
Bowl on metal base, rare		350LV			300						350 TL
Plate, 10½", rare		450	375								425 TL
FOUR GARLANDS											
Vase, 7½"	225										
FOUR LEAF CLOVER (SOWERBY)											
Bowl, handled, 5"	90										
FOUR PILLARS (NORTHWOOD & DUGAN)											
Vase	50	60	100			200	225	250			250 SA
FOUR PILLARS WITH DRAPE											
Vase, very scarce	100		325	425							575 SA
FOUR SUITS (JAIN)											
Tumbler	100										
474 (IMPERIAL)											
Bowl, 8" – 9"	45		85								
Compote, 7", rare	125	275									
Cordial, rare	90	210									
Goblet	50	90	65								
Punch Bowl & Base	200	2350	700								1650 AQ
Punch Cup	15	40	30								135 EmG
Milk Pitcher, scarce	225	825	375								600 LV
Pitcher, standard, scarce	175	3300	500								600 PK
Pitcher, large, rare	350	5000									
Tumbler, scarce	30	100	70	350							275 VI
Wine	100										
Vase, 7", rare	375									3200	
Vase, 10", rare	500										
Vase, 14", rare	700		1100								
474 VARIANT (SWEDEN)											
Compote, 7"			125								
49'ER											
Atomizer	90										
Decanter w/stopper	125										
Perfume, 3 sizes	80										
Pin Box	60										
Pin Tray, 2 sizes	50										
Powder Box	70										
Pitcher, squat	175										

Pattern Name	M	A	G	B	PO	AO	IB	IG	W	Red	Other
Tumbler	75										
Ring Tray	70										
Wine	80										
49'ER VARIANT (INWALD)											
Decanter, scarce	175										
Tumblers, 3 sizes, scarce	40 – 125										
Tray, scarce	95										
FOXHUNT											
Decanter	275										
Shot Glass	75										
FRANKLIN FLUTE (U.S. GLASS)											
Hat Whimsey, from tumbler	95										
FREEFOLD (IMPERIAL)											
Vase, 7" – 14"	30	55	45						70		115 SM
FREESIA (FENTON)											
Pitcher	225										
Tumbler	35										
FRENCH GRAPE											
Bowl, 4"	180										
FRENCH KNOTS (FENTON)											
Hat	30	40	40	45							
FRIT PINCHED VASE (DUGAN)											
Vase					150						
FROLICKING BEARS (U.S. GLASS)											
Pitcher, very rare			45000								
Tumbler, very rare			13500								
FRONDS AND ARCHES											
Bowl, 4½", rare	100										
FROSTED BLOCK (IMPERIAL)											
Bowl, 6½" – 7½"	20										35 CM
Bowl, 9"	30										40 CM
Bowl, square, scarce	35										55 CM
Celery Tray	35										
Compote	40										75 CM
Covered Butter	65										
Creamer or Sugar	30										35 CM
Milk Pitcher, rare	90										
Nut Bowl Whimsey											55 CM
Pickle Dish, handled, rare	70										65 CM
Plate, 7½"	40										65 CM
Plate, 9"	45										150 CM
Rose Bowl	80										100 CM
Vase, 6"	35										100 SM
(Add 10% if marked, "Made In USA")											
FROSTED BUTTONS (FENTON)											
Bowl, footed, 10"											175 PM
FROSTED INDIAN (JAIN)											
Vase	150										
FROSTED LOTUS (INDIA)											
Vase	75										
FROSTED OXFORD											
Bobeche, each	60										
FROSTED RIBBON											
Pitcher	85										
Tumbler	30										
FROSTY											
Bottle	25										
FRUIT & BERRIES (JENKINS)											
Bean Pot, covered, rare	400			425							
FRUIT BAND											
Decanter	250			350							
Glass	75			90							
FRUIT BASKET (MILLERSBURG)											
Compote, handled, rare		1600									
FRUIT BONBONNIERE											
Bonbonniere w/lid, 5½", very scarce	550										
FRUIT JAR (BALL)											
One size	50										
FRUIT SALAD											
Punch bowl & base, rare	600	700			3900	6000					
Punch Cup, rare	30	40			60						
FRUITS AND FLOWERS (NORTHWOOD)											
Bonbon	65	110	225	175		950	400	675	235		125 VI
Bowl, 7"	30	65	135	145				325			400 AQ
Bowl, 9" – 10½"	65	125	125	250				900	1500		
Plate, 7"	95	125	190	300							
Plate, handgrip, 7", scarce	100	150	200								
Plate, 9½"	115	235									
*Add 25% for Stippled											

Pattern Name	M	A	G	B	PO	AO	IB	IG	W	Red	Other
FRUITS & FLOWERS VARIANT											
Bowl, 7" – 8", very scarce	125		225								
FRUITS & FLUTES											
Bowl	125										
GAELIC (INDIANA GLASS)											
Butter	165										
Creamer or Spooner	60										
Sugar w/lid	85										
GALLOWAY (U.S. GLASS)											
Creamer, rare	125										
GANADOR (PAPINI)											
Pitcher	350										
Tumbler	100										
Vase	145										
GANGES GARDEN (INDIA)											
Tumbler	100										
GARDEN ARBOR (INDIA)											
Tumbler	100										
GARDEN MUMS (FENTON)											
Bowl, 5" – 6", scarce		300									
Bowl, 5", deep round, rare		375									
Plate, regular or handgrip, 7"		450									250 LV
GARDEN PATH (DUGAN)											
Bowl, 6" – 7"	35	110			150		1500		100		
Bowl, 8" – 9½", ruffled	75	600			350				350		
Bowl, 10", ICS, scarce	450	1200			950				1000		
Compote, rare	225	400							500		
Plate, 6", rare	425	650			525				425		
Chop Plate, rare	4500	5000			7500						
Rose Bowl, rare	200										
GARDEN PATH VARIANT (DUGAN)											
Bowl, 5¾" – 6½"	40	125			160		1300				
Bowl, 8" – 10", deep round	75	425			300				350		
Chop Plate, rare	4500	5250			7250						
Chop Plate, Soda Gold exterior		6750			7500						
Rose Bowl, rare	200										
GARLAND (FENTON)											
Rose Bowl, footed	45	350	400	90							425 AM
GARLAND & BOWS (RIIHIMAKE)											
Bowls, various	40 – 75										
Compote	190										
Covered Butter	225										
Creamer	70										
Open Sugar	75										
Salver, low ruffled	225										
GAY 90'S (MILLERSBURG)											
Pitcher, rare		8500	9500								
Tumbler, rare	1000	1150	1450								
GEM DANDY											
Butter Churn (age?)	500										
GEO. W. GETZ PIANOS (FENTON)											
Bowl, scarce		1200									
Plate, scarce		1850									
GEORGE (BROCKWITZ)											
Bowl, 4 sizes	50+										
Compote, 3 sizes	75+										
Covered Butter	125										
Creamer	65										
Salver	70										
GEORGETTE (INDIA)											
Tumbler	85										
GEORGIA BELLE (DUGAN)											
Card Tray, footed, rare	75	80	95		175						
Compote, footed	65	75	85		140						
GERMAN STEINS											
Various sizes	175+										
GEVURTZ BROTHERS (FENTON)											
Bowl, advertising, scarce		800									
Plate, advertising, rare		2000									
Plate, handgrip, scarce		1400									
GIANT LILY (CZECH)											
Vase	250										
GIBSON GIRL											
Toothpick Holder	60										
GLOBE											
Vase, 9½"	25										
GOA (JAIN)											
Vase, 6½"	85										
GOD AND HOME (DUGAN)											
Pitcher, rare				2200							
Tumbler, rare				175							

Pattern Name	M	A	G	B	PO	AO	IB	IG	W	Red	Other
GODDESS (JAIN)											
Vase, 8½", rare	200										
GODDESS OF ATHENA											
Epergne, rare			2000								2000 AM
GODDESS OF HARVEST (FENTON)											
Bowl, 9½", very rare	13000	30000		25000							
Plate, very rare		35000									
GOLDEN BIRD											
Nappy, footed, w/handle	300										
GOLDEN CUPID											
Bowl, 5", rare	225										
GOLDEN FLOWERS											
Vase, 7½"	95										
GOLDEN GRAPES (DUGAN)											
Bowl, 7"	30	40	50								50 CM
Rose Bowl, collar base	90										
GOLDEN HARE (INDIA)											
Pitcher	225										
GOLDEN HARVEST											
Decanter w/stopper	145	250									
Wine	25	35									
GOLDEN HONEYCOMB											
Bowls, various	20 – 35										
Compote	35										
Creamer	25										
Plate	25										
Sugar	40										
GOLDEN OXEN (JEANNETTE)											
Mug	20										
GOLDEN PANSIES											
Tray, 10" x 5½"	350										
GOLDEN PINEAPPLE & BLACKBERRIES											
Bowl, 9"	400										
Plate, 10"	500										
GOLDEN PRESS											
Wine Bottle	45										
GOLDEN THISTLE											
Tray, 5", rare	350										
GOLDEN WEDDING											
Bottle, 4 sizes	20 – 75										
GOLD FISH											
Bowl	125										
GOOD LUCK (NORTHWOOD)											
Bowl, 8½"	250	350	400	425	3000	2650		14,000			1350 SA
Bowl, decorated, very rare				3200							
Proof Bowl, rare	600										
Plate, 9"	450	600	900	1950			9500	20000	11000		1050 HO
(Stippled add 25%)											
GOOD LUCK VARIANT (NORTHWOOD)											
Bowl, 8½", rare	300	425	450								600 LV
Bowl, prototype, 8½", very rare	3250										
Plate, rare	350	375	400								
GOODYEAR											
Ashtray in tire	225										
GOOSEBERRY SPRAY (U.S. GLASS) (PALM BEACH EXTERIOR)											
Bowl, 5", scarce	75	110									225 HA
Bowl, 5½", tricorner, rare	150								375		225 HA
Bowl, 10", scarce	65	95							200		165 HA
Compote, rare		225							300		
Rose Bowl, 4½", rare	125										325 HA
GOTHIC ARCHES (IMPERIAL)											
Vase, 9" – 17", rare	125										400 SM
GRACE											
Bowl				225							
GRACEFUL (NORTHWOOD)											
Vase	45	85	120	150					200		
GRACEFUL VARIANT (NORTHWOOD)											
Vase (different base)	55	110	145								
GRACEFUL WATER SET											
Pitcher, rare				1500							1700 AM
Tumbler, scarce	450			325							700 AM
GRAND THISTLE (FINLAND)											
Pitcher, rare				700							750 AM
Tumbler, rare				120							350 AM
GRANKVIST (EDA)											
Bowl	165			235							
Rose Bowl	250			375							

Pattern Name	M	A	G	B	PO	AO	IB	IG	W	Red	Other
GRAPE & CABLE (FENTON)											
Bowl, ball footed, 7" – 8½"	75	90	85	110							130 V
Bowl, flat, 7" – 8"	35	60	80	70		850				750	145 V
Bowl, spatula footed, 7" – 8"	65	90	95	125							
Bride's Basket, handled, very rare		2000		2600							
Centerpiece Bowl, w/Persian Medallion interior, very rare			1500								
Orange Bowl, footed	110	225	250	175							
Orange Bowl, advertising, Pacific Coast mail order, rare	2400		3500	2800							
Orange Bowl w/Persian Medallion interior, scarce	225	350	600	425				3500			
Plate, spatula footed, 9"	80	125	175	185						1475	
Spittoon Whimsey, rare	1200										
GRAPE & CABLE (NORTHWOOD)											
Bowl, ruffled, 5½"	25	35	50	75					95		55 LV
Bowl, ruffled, 8" – 9"	45	55	70	95		2750	1000	3000	1000		1500 EmG
Bowl, ruffled, 10" – 11½"	100	140	160	250					525		200 LG
Bowl, spatula footed, 8" – 9"	60	75	100	275				900			
Ice Cream Bowl, 5" – 6"	50	75	175	125				325	100		70 LV
Ice Cream Bowl, 11"	200	450	1250	625				1600	325		350 LV
Banana Boat, footed	175	225	350	425			600	500	400		400 PL
Bonbon	65	65	175	160					275		385 PL
Breakfast Set, 2 pieces	150	225	250								
Orange Bowl, footed	175	250	350	450				950	725		4000 MUC
Orange Bowl (blackberry interior) rare		2200		3000							
Centerpiece Bowl, footed	250	350	900	450			1250	750	550		1500 LG
Candlesticks, each	150	200	250								
Candlelamp, complete	750	800	900								
Compote, covered	2000	350									
Compote, open	300	500	1000								
Cologne w/stopper	160	325	325				550		650		
Cologne Vase Whimsey, very rare		7000									
Cup & Saucer, rare	400	450									
Dresser Tray	165	275	300				900		1000		
Fernery, scarce	1000	1300	1600				1800	3500	1000		700 IC
Hatpin Holder	200	300	350	1200		13500	2300	1450	2500		600 EmG
Hatpin Whimsey Vase, rare		4300	5200								
Nappy (From Punch Cup)	50	75	75	100			625				
Oil Lamp Whimsey		3500									
Powder Jar w/lid	135	175	250	475		4000	700	1650	1750		550 LV
Pin Tray	125	250	300				700		800		400 IC
Plate, spatula footed, 9"	65	100	125	550				500			
Plate, flat, 7" – 7½"	800	175	225								275 HO
Plate, flat, 8" – 9"	165	225	275	750			2800				2700 SA
Plate, handgrip	150	200	225								400 HO
Plate, 2 sides up	150	175	350								
Plate, advertising			575								
Punch Bowl & Base, small	300	600	700	1500		120,000	9000	8000	4500		
Punch Bowl & Base, mid-size	375	750	800	1800			20,000	13,000	3500		
Punch Bowl & Base, banquet	2000	2200	3100	4300			45,000	16,000	6000		
Punch Cup, 2 sizes	25	30	40	60		1200	100	125	70		
Shade	175	200									
Spittoon, from powder jar, very rare	5000	6500	6000								
Sweetmeat w/lid	2800	200		3000							
Sweetmeat Whimsey Compote	400	300									
*(Stippled pieces, add 25%)											
*(Pie crust edge bowls & plates, add 10%)											
GRAPE & CABLE BANDED (NORTHWOOD)											
Banana Bowl	275			600							650 ReB
Dresser Tray	135										
Hatpin Holder	250	450		700							
Orange Bowl	425			650							3000 IC
GRAPE & CABLE VARIANT (NORTHWOOD)											
Bowl, 6" – 8"	65	75	90	145		3900	900				325 EmG
Plate, 7½" – 9", scarce	135	250	650	550							1200 EmG
Plate, handgrip, scarce	165	190	245	500							325 LV
Plate, 2 sides up, 6" – 7½", scarce	125	200									
(Stippled pieces, add 25%)											
GRAPE & CABLE WITH THUMBPRINT (NORTHWOOD)											
Berry Bowl, 5½"	20	40	50	125				100			
Berry Bowl, 9" – 10"	90	145	175					375			
Butter	150	225	225				2300				
Cracker Jar	300	450		600		15000		2500	1200		
Creamer	65	80	95				550				
Decanter w/stopper	600	700									
Hat Whimsey, from tumbler	75	125	125								150 AM

340

Pattern Name	M	A	G	B	PO	AO	IB	IG	W	Red	Other
Pitcher, regular	200	275	325					8000			800 SM
Pitcher, tankard	475	800	2500					6500			1000 LV
Sherbet	35	45	60								
Tumbler, regular	25	35	45					500			
Tumbler, tankard	50	60	75					525			
Tobacco Jar (humidor)	300	475		650							600 SM
Shot Glass	115	195									
Spittoon, from humidor, very rare	7500										
Spooner	60	70	85				625				
Sugar	70	95	140				900				
*Stippled pieces add 25%											
GRAPE AND CHERRY (ENGLISH)											
Bowl, 8½", rare	100			200							
GRAPE & GOTHIC ARCHES (NORTHWOOD)											
Bowl, 5"	15	40	40	50							225 AQ
Bowl, 10"	70	95	100	200							150 PL
Butter	100	150	150	150							425 PL
Creamer or Spooner	40	85	85	70							125 PL
Sugar w/lid	75	100	100	125							125 PL
Pitcher	300	395	425	475							750 PL
Tumbler	30	80	110	75							175 PL
GRAPE ARBOR (DUGAN) (FEATHER SCROLL EXTERIOR)											
Bowl, footed, 9½" – 11"	150	300		500	1200				150		
GRAPE ARBOR (NORTHWOOD)											
Hat	60	100		145			225	325	110		
Pitcher	325	625		14000			1300	10000	425		
Tumbler	45	100		400			160	325	70		140 LV
Tumbler (etched)		450		575					75		
GRAPE BASKET											
See Imperial Grape											
GRAPE DELIGHT (DUGAN)											
Nut Bowl, footed, 6"	50	120		80					95		
Rose Bowl, footed, 6"	65	125		100					65		
GRAPE FRIEZE (NORTHWOOD)											
Bowl, 10½", rare											800 IC
GRAPE LEAVES (MILLERSBURG)											
Bowl, 9", very scarce	600	800	900								3000 V
Bowl, 7" – 8", square, very rare		3200	5000								
Bowl, 7" – 8", tricorner, very rare			4200								
GRAPE LEAVES (NORTHWOOD)											
Bowl, 8½", ruffled or 3 in 1 edge	45	95	85	150			1400				225 AM
Bride's Basket, complete		300									
GRAPES OF RATH											
Vase, 6⅝", very scarce	225										
GRAPE SPITTOON											
Spittoon, one shape, rare	1500										
GRAPE VARIANT											
See Imperial Grape Variant											
GRAPEVINE & SPIKES (JAIN)											
Tumbler	100										
GRAPEVINE LATTICE (DUGAN)											
Bowl, 6" – 7"	30	65							50		75 LV
Hat Shape, J.I.P.	75	150									
Plate, 6½" – 7½"	145	200		325					150		375 LV
Pitcher, rare	325	850		1200					950		
Tumbler, rare	50	75		165					150		
GRAPE WREATH (MILLERSBURG)											
Bowl, 5"	95	120	165								
Bowl, 7½" – 9"	100	125	150	800							
Bowl, ice cream shape, 10"	400	275	300								
Spittoon Whimsey, rare	3500		4000								
GRAPE WREATH CLOVER AND FEATHER VARIANT											
See Grape Wreath/Multistar Variant											
GRAPE WREATH/MULTI-STAR VARIANT (MILLERSBURG)											
Bowl, 5"	50	60	70								
Bowl, 7½"	70	80	90								
Bowl, 9"	90	90	90								
Bowl, ice cream, 10"	150	175	175								
GRAPE WREATH VARIANT (MILLERSBURG)											
Bowl, 5"	40	65	70								
Bowl, 7½"	50	75	80								
Bowl, 9"	55	90	100								
Bowl, ice cream shape, 10"	125	150	150								
GRECIAN DAISY											
Pitcher, scarce	400										
Tumbler, scarce	60										
GRECIAN URN											
Perfume, 6"	50										

341

Pattern Name	M	A	G	B	PO	AO	IB	IG	W	Red	Other
GREEK KEY (NORTHWOOD)											
Bowl, 7" – 8½", collar base	150	200	225	400				2700			
Plate, 9", scarce (basketweave back)	1250	700	850	2000							
Plate, 9", rare w/rib back	3850										
Pitcher, rare	750	900	1800								
Tumbler, rare	110	225	235								
GREEK KEY AND SCALES											
(NORTHWOOD)											
Bowl, footed	75	100	100								
GREENGARD FURNITURE											
(MILLERSBURG)											
Bowl, advertising, very rare		1900									
Plate, handgrip, rare		2200									
GROUND CHERRIES											
Pitcher				125							
Tumbler				50							
GUEST SET (FENTON)											
Pitcher & Tumble-up, complete	200										
GUM TIPS (CRYSTAL)											
Vase (8 ribs), very scarce		375									400 BA
GUM TIPS VASE (CRYSTAL)											
Vase (10 ribs), very scarce		400									450 BA
HAIR RECEIVER											
Complete	75										
HALLOWEEN											
Pitcher, 2 sizes	375										
Tumbler, 2 sizes	50										
Spittoon	600										
HAMBURG (SWEDEN)											
Jardiniere			225								
HAMILTON SOUVENIR											
Vase, 6¼"	70										
HAMMERED BELL											
CHANDELIER											
Complete, 5 shades									600		
Shade, each									75		
HANDLED TUMBLER											
One size	75	125									
HANDLED VASE (IMPERIAL)											
3 shapes	45										90 SM
Candle Bowl, scarce	110	500									
HAND VASE (JAIN)											
One shape, 5½" – 8"	75	200								1450	
HARVARD YARD											
Decanter w/Stopper, 11½"	250										
HARVEST FLOWER (DIAMOND)											
Pitcher, rare	2800										
Tumbler, very scarce, rare	200	900	1100								
HARVEST POPPY											
Compote, scarce	320	450	400	450							500 AM
HATCHET (U.S. GLASS)											
One Shape	175										
HATPINS (VARIOUS MAKERS),											
(ALL PATTERNS LISTED BELOW)											
Banded Basketweave		90									
Banded Berry Cluster											135 LV
Banded Criss Cross		85									
Banded Flower											100 LV
Bars & Beads		120									
Basket Flower		75									
Beaded Ball Bat		45									
Beaded Fringe		175									
Beaded Oval		75									
Beaded Parasol		75									
Beaded Pinwheel		400									
Beaded Tears		225									
Bee on Flower		600									
Bee on Honeycomb											135 AM
Beetle		115									
Belle		225									
Big Butterfly		80									
Bird of Paradise		1100									
Blister Beetle				1500							
Bordered Cosmos		125									125 BA
Border Path		37									
Bubbles		200									
Bullet		125									
Bumblebee (Dragonfly)		60									
Butlers Mirror		50									
Butterfly		100									
Button and Fan		60									
Cameo		200									

Pattern Name	M	A	G	B	PO	AO	IB	IG	W	Red	Other
Cane		200									
Checkers		200									
Cherries		115									
Christmas Star		300									
Circled Basketweave		145									
Cockatoo		800									
Concentric Circles											200 LV
Coolie Hat		45									
Coqui		1800									
Corona		165									
Daisy & Button		100									
Diamond Spearhead	145	300									
Diamond Sphere		375									
Diamond & Oval		300									
Dimples		135									
Dimples & Brilliance		225									
Dinner Ring		250									
Dogwood		200									
Dots and Curves		50									
Double Crown		55									
Doves		350									
Dragonflies		65									
Elegance		120									
Elegance Variant		160									
Embroidered Circles		150									
Faceted Butterfly		150									
Faceted Dome		85									
Faceted Ovals		75									
Faceted Spearhead		150									
Faceted Dome		175									
Fancy Beetle		400									
Ferris Wheel		400									
Floral Spray		165									65 AM
Flower Arcs		85									
Flower Petals		325									
Flying Bat	100	135	200								200 BA
Four Hearts (Hearts & Cross)		300									
Fringed Beads		250									
Fuchsia Basket		2100	2250								
Gazebo		700									
Geisha Girl		800									
Grape		750	800	800							300 LV
Greek Key Variant		75									
Hearts & Cross (Four Hearts)		65									
Honeycomb Ornament		80		125							
Horsefly		250									
Indian Blanket			300								
Iridized Star			225								
Isabelle		1800									
Japanese Garden		600									
Jute Braid		225									
King Spider		700									
Knotty Tree Bark			900	900							900 LV
Large Beetle		800									
Laurel Jewel		325									
Leaf Beetle			1200								
Leaf & Veil		400									
Long Prisms		75									
Looped Buckle		200									
Lots of Diamonds		150									
Marquisite Flower (Anemone Cushion)		250									
Marvelous		550									
Moire Beetle		40									
Nasty Bug		1800									
Nautical											250 CM
Orchid (Flower & Jewel)		700									
Oval Prisms		75									
Oval Sphere		75									
Owl, 2 sizes	2000		1000								900 LV
Owl, horned		1400									
Paisley		50									
Peacock		2000	2000	3000			2000				
Penstar		175									
Piazza		350									
Pine Sawyer			800								
Pith Helmet		500						600			500 Brown
Prisms		75									
Propeller		600									
Propeller Variant		625									
Rectangular Diamonds		175									
Ribbon Triangle		475									

Pattern Name	M	A	G	B	PO	AO	IB	IG	W	Red	Other
Rooster		150	100	65			110			115	60 AQ
Royal Scarab										350	
Salamanders		75									
Scarab		100									150 AM
Scarab Shell		450	500								1050 LV
Shell			600								
Shining Peaks & Valleys		700									
Six Plums		55									
Snake Head		300									
Spider	250										125 AM
Spinner											225 MMG
Spiral Dance		80									
Spring Buds											500 SM
Star Center		100									
Star Prism		400									
Star & Flower				1100							
Star & Diamond Point		75									
Star & Nearcut		60									
Star & Rosette		75									
Star & Scroll		85									
Star of David & Baguetted		500									
Stork				2800							
Strawberry			1000								1100 AM
Stubby Beetle			700								
Stylized Scarab		175	200								
Sunflower									75		
Suns Up		200									220 LV
Swirley Taffeta		175									
Throw Pillow		75									
Tiny Triangle-Back Beetle											700 BA
Top of the Morn		200									
Top of the Walk		200									
Triad		60									
Triangle-back Beetle		500	700								
Triplets		55									
True Scarab				825							
Tufted Throw Pillow		45									
Turban		85									
Twin Gators		1300									
Two Flowers		150									
Two Flowers Variant				250							
Ugly Bug		1600									
Umbrella Prisms, small		50									
Umbrella Prisms, large		75									
Veiling		50									
Vintage Cluster											350 SM
Waves		100	125	160							225 ICG
Wavy Satin		95									
Whirling Cobblestones		400									
Zig Zag											125 AM
HATTIE (IMPERIAL)											
Bowl	60	295	135	725							150 SM
Plate, very scarce	2000	2800	600								3500 AM
Rose Bowl	600	3000									1500 AM
HAVELLI (INDIA)											
Tumbler	100										
HAWAIIAN LEI (HIGBEE)											
Sugar	75										
Creamer	75										
HAWAIIAN MOON											
Pitcher	200										250 CRAN
Tumbler	75										90 CRAN
HAZEL											
Vase, scarce	225										
HEADDRESS											
Bowl, 7" – 10"	175			225							
Compote	80			125							
HEADDRESS VARIANT (COSMOS & CANE EXTERIOR)											
Bowl, 7" – 10"	125		200	175					195		145 HA
HEART & HORSESHOE (FENTON)											
Bowl, 8½"	2500										
Plate, 9", rare	4000							18000			
HEART & TREES (FENTON)											
Bowl, 8¼"	350		700								
HEART & VINE (FENTON)											
Bowl, 8½"	60	75	95	85							125 LV
Plate, 9", very scarce		400	625	900							
Plate, advertising (Spectors), rare	1600										
HEART & VINE VARIANT (FENTON)											
Plate, 9", scarce	800			1000							

Pattern Name	M	A	G	B	PO	AO	IB	IG	W	Red	Other
HEART BAND											
One shape (Salt)	45										
HEART BAND SOUVENIR (McKEE)											
Mug, small	55		100								125 AQ
Mug, large	70		125								150 AQ
Tumbler, mini or shot glass	35		70								
Tumbler, rare	250		325								450 LV
HEARTS & FLOWERS (NORTHWOOD)											
Banana Bowl Whimsey, very rare		850									
Bowl, 8½", ruffled	325	425	1800	850	6500	600	800		300		2300 EmG
Bowl, 8½", pie crust edge	550	625	1300	2800	6500		625	1600	450		
Compote	200	350	1500	325		600	700	850	175		600 LV
Plate, 9", scarce	1100	1500	2000	6500			1900	2800	3200		3500 LG
HEART SWIRL											
Lamp	450										
HEAVY BANDED DIAMONDS (CRYSTAL)											
Bowl, 5"	50	75									
Bowl, 9"	100	125									
Flower set, 2 piece	150	195									
Pitcher, very scarce	900	1250									
Tumbler, very scarce	250	400									
HEAVY DIAMOND											
Nappy	40										
HEAVY DIAMOND (IMPERIAL)											
Bowl, 10"	45										
Compote	45		55								
Creamer	30										
Sugar	35										
Vase	50		65								85 SM
HEAVY DRAPE (FOSTORIA)											
Vase, 7½"	90										
HEAVY GRAPE (DUGAN)											
Bowl, 5", scarce	125	175			225						
Bowl, 10", scarce	700	550			435						
HEAVY GRAPE (IMPERIAL)											
Bowl, 5" – 6"	25	40	30	500							70 AM
Bowl, 7" – 8"	35	55	45								125 SM
Bowl, 9" – 10"	100	250	165	800							300 AM
Fruit Bowl w/base	275										400 AM
Nappy	45	55	50								75 OG
Plate, 6"	300										
Plate, 8"	65	200	200								225 SM
Plate, 11"	225	850	300						450		400 AM
Punch Bowl w/base	350	950	525								1000 AM
Punch Cup	55	100	75								85 AM
HEAVY HEART (HIGBEE)											
Tumbler	150										
HEAVY HOBNAIL (FENTON)											
Vase, rare		600							475		
HEAVY HOBS											
Lamp (amber base glass)					300						
HEAVY IRIS (DUGAN)											
Pitcher	250	1000			2500				1100		
Tumbler	60	105							175		125 HO
Tumbler Whimsey	350								400		
HEAVY PINEAPPLE (FENTON)											
Bowl, flat or footed, 10"	1000			1500					2000		1600 AM
HEAVY PRISMS (ENGLISH)											
Celery Vase, 6"	85	115		100							
HEAVY SHELL											
Bowl, 8¼"									150		
Candleholder, each									100		
HEAVY VINE											
Atomizer	85										
Cologne	90										
Lamp	250										
Powder Box	75										
Tumbler	150										
Tumble-up	200										
Shot Glass	80										
HEAVY WEB (DUGAN)											
Bowl, 10", very scarce					700						
Plate, 11", rare					3500						
HEINZ											
Bottle											60 CM
HEINZ TOMATO JUICE											
Juice Glass	75										
HEISEY #357											
Tumbler, scarce	85										
Water Bottle	190										
HEISY #473 (NARROW FLUTE W/ RIM) See Heisey Set											

Pattern Name	M	A	G	B	PO	AO	IB	IG	W	Red	Other
HEISEY CARTWHEEL											
Compote											85 PM
HEISEY COLONIAL											
Compote	80										150 Y
Dresser Tray	100										
Hair Receiver	135										
Juice Tumbler	65										
Perfume (Cologne)	90										
Puff Box	120										
Vase	75										
HEISEY CRYSTOLITE											
Spittoon	325										250 ZB
HEISEY FLORAL SPRAY											
Stemmed Candy w/lid, 11"							100				
HEISEY FLUTE											
Punch Cup	35										
Toothpick Holder	150										
HEISEY LAVERNE											
Bowl, footed, 11", rare	300										
HEISEY OLD WILLIAMSBURG											
Candlestick w/prisms	350										
HEISEY PURITAN (#341)											
Compote	75	200									150 V
Compote, tricorner whimsey	125										
HEISEY SET											
Creamer and Tray	150										
HELEN'S STAR (INDIA)											
Vase	190										
HERON (DUGAN)											
Mug, rare	1500	125									
HERRINGBONE & BEADED OVALS											
Compote, rare	200										
HERRINGBONE & MUMS (JEANNETTE)											
Tumbler, very rare	400										
HEXAGON & CANE (IMPERIAL)											
Covered Sugar	90										
HEXAGON SQUARE											
Child's Breakfast Set (complete)											60 LV
HEX BASE											
Candlesticks, pair	75	125	110								175 SM
HEX OPTIC (HONEYCOMB) (JEANNETTE – DEPRESSION ERA)											
Bonbon	20										
Bowl, 5"	10										
Compote	25										
Creamer or Sugar	20										
Lamp, oil	100										
Lamp Shade	80										
Plate, 7"	25										
Pitcher	125										
Tumbler	25										
HEX PANEL (Jeannette)											
Parfait or Soda	60										
HICKMAN											
Banana Bowl Whimsey, very rare	150										
Caster Set, 4 piece	325										450 PM
Rose Bowl	200										
HOBNAIL (FENTON)											
Vase, 5" – 11"									100		
HOBNAIL (MILLERSBURG)											
Butter, rare	450	325	650	1000							
Creamer or Spooner, rare	275	375	450	625							
Sugar w/lid, rare	350	500	575	750							
Hat Whimsey, rare	1700										
Pitcher, rare	3000	2500	4000	5000							
Tumbler, rare	1700	750	1500	1100							
Rose Bowl, scarce	225	350	1300								
Spittoon, scarce	700	625	1800								
HOBNAIL & CANE (CRYSTAL)											
Compote	85	165					225				
Salver	100	190					250				
HOBNAIL PANELS (McKEE)											
Vase, 8¼"											70 CM
HOBNAIL SODA GOLD											
Spittoon, large	65		100								125 AM
HOBNAIL VARIANT (MILLERSBURG)											
Jardinere, rare		950		1500							
Rose Bowl, rare	800										
Vase Whimsey, rare	600	700	800								
Salver	100	190					250				

346

Pattern Name	M	A	G	B	PO	AO	IB	IG	W	Red	Other
HOBSTAR (IMPERIAL)											
Bowl, Berry, 5"	25										15 CM
Bowl, Berry, 10"	40										30 CM
Bowls, various shapes, 6" – 12"	30										40 CM
Bride's Basket, complete	75										
Butter	80	195	185								90 CM
Cookie Jar w/lid	65		100								
Creamer or Spooner	45	85	75								50 CM
Fruit Bowl w/base	100	250	150								
Pickle Castor, complete	750										
Sugar w/lid	65	100	90								60 CM
Vase, flared	350	200									
HOBSTAR AND ARCHES (IMPERIAL)											
Bowl, 5", very scarce	30	55	40								60 SM
Bowl, 9", very scarce	65	100	75								60 SM
Fruit Bowl w/base	125	300	225								
HOBSTAR & CUT TRIANGLES (ENGLISH)											
Bowl	30	40	60								
Plate	70	100	110								
Rose Bowl	45	55	70								
HOBSTAR AND FEATHER (MILLERSBURG)											
Bowl, round or square, 5", rare		450	1400								
Bowl, 6" – 9", square, rare	500										
Bowl, diamond, 5", rare	550										
Bowl, heart, 5", rare	700										
Butter, rare	1500	1800	1900								
Card Tray Whimsey, very rare									750		
Compote, 6", rare	1500										
Compote Whimsey (from rose bowl), rare		7000	8000								
Creamer, rare	750	900	1100								
Dessert, stemmed, rare	650	700									
Punch Bowl & Base (flared), rare											
Punch Bowl & Base (tulip), rare											
*On Punch Bowl & Base; add 25% for Fleur-De-Lis interior											
Punch Cup, scarce	60	75	85	1300							
Punch Bowl Whimsey, rare			7200								
Rose Bowl, giant, rare	9000	3000	2700								
Spittoon Whimsey, very rare		6500									
Spooner, rare		1000	1300								4000 V
Stemmed Whimsey Tray, footed, 4½", very rare	800										
Sugar, w/lid, rare		950	1250								4250 V
Tricorner Whimsey, very rare									750		
Vase Whimsey, rare		12000	8000								
HOBSTAR AND FILE											
Pitcher, rare	1700										
Tumbler, rare	200										
HOBSTAR AND FRUIT (WESTMORELAND)											
Bowl, 6", rare					115	300					350 MMG
Plate, 10½", rare							385				
HOBSTAR & SHIELD (EUROPEAN)											
Pitcher	325										
Tumbler	125										
HOBSTAR AND TASSELS (IMPERIAL)											
Bowl, 6", deep round, rare	125	175	225								
Bowl, 7" – 8", scarce	150	200									350 TL
Plate, 7½", rare			900*								
HOBSTAR & WAFFLE BLOCK (IMPERIAL)											
Basket	100										
HOBSTAR BAND											
Bowl, 8" – 10", rare	75										
Butter, scarce	200	275									
Celery, scarce	70		275								
Compote, scarce	90										
Pitcher, 2 shapes, scarce	250										
Tumbler, 2 shapes	35										
Sugar w/lid	115										
Spooner	85										
HOBSTAR DIAMONDS											
Tumbler, very rare	500										
HOBSTAR FLOWER (IMPERIAL)											
Compote, very scarce	60	110	110								200 SM
Cruet, rare	400										
HOBSTAR PANELS (ENGLISH)											
Creamer	45										
Sugar, stemmed	45										

Pattern Name	M	A	G	B	PO	AO	IB	IG	W	Red	Other
HOBSTAR REVERSED (ENGLISH)											
Butter	55	75		70							
Frog & Holder	85										
Rose Bowl	60	95									
Spooner	45										
HOCKING FLUTE											
Tumbler	100										
HOCKING MIXING BOWL											
4 sizes, (nesting set)	30+										
HOFFMAN HOUSE (IMPERIAL)											
Goblet, very scarce										350	150 AM
HOLIDAY											
Bottle											75 PM
HOLIDAY (NORTHWOOD)											
Tray, 11", scarce	225										
HOLLOW TUBE CANDLESTICKS											
Candleholder with Prisms, each	35										
HOLLY (FENTON)											
Bowl, 8" – 10"	45	75	85	70					125	900	155 AM
Bowl, deep, 7½"	60			90						1200	150 BA
Compote, 5"	25	100	125	45					750	800	110 PB
Goblet	30	110	200	80						750	100 TL
Hat	20			55		900				300	125 IM
Plate, 9"	300	550	675	425		19000			225	4000	175 CM
Rose Bowl, very scarce	250			325							650 V
HOLLY & BERRY (DUGAN)											
Bowl, 6" – 7½"	55	110			90						
Nappy	70	125		325	90						225 PKA
HOLLY & POINSETTIA (DUGAN)											
Compote, very rare	5000										
HOLLY SPRIG (MILLERSBURG)											
Bonbon, 2 shapes,	50	75	80								100 LV
Bowl, 5½" deep sauce, rare	325	225	300								
Bowl, 5½" – 6", ice cream or 3 in 1 shape, very scarce	325	350	375								
Bowl, 5½" – 6", ruffled or candy ribbon edge, scarce	250	225	300								
Bowl, 7" – 8", ruffled, deep, ice cream shape or candy ribbon edge	250	275	325								
Bowl, 7" – 8", tricorner	275	300	325								
Bowl, 7" – 8", square, scarce	325	350	400								
Bowl, round or ruffled, 9" – 10"	120	175	225								75 CM
Bowl, tricorner, 9" – 10"	325	400	500								
Compote, rare	900	1250	2100								1500 V
Nappy, tricornered	80	95	100								1600 V
Rose Bowl Whimsey, rare	500										2800 V
HOLLY WHIRL (MILLERSBURG)											
Bonbon, 2 shapes,	60	80	85								
Bonbon (Isaac Benesch)	140										
Bowl, 9" – 10", round or ruffled	125	185	235								
Bowl, large, tricorner	350	425	525								
Nappy, tricornered	85	95	110								
HOLLY WREATH (MILLERSBURG)											
Bowl, 6", CRE, very scarce	225	350	375								
Bowl, 7½" – 9", ruffled or 3 in 1	175	325	350								
Bowl, 8" – 9", ice cream shape (All have 4 Feather center)	200	350	375								
HOLLY WREATH VARIANTS (MILLERSBURG)											
Bowl, 6", CRE, very scarce	225	350	375								
Bowl, 7½" – 9", ruffled or 3 in 1	175	325	350								
Bowl, 8" – 9", ice cream shape (*These have multi-star, clover or sunburst centers)	200	350	375								
HOLM SPRAY											
Atomizer, 3"	65										
HOMESTEAD											
Shade	65										
HOMESTEAD PENNA. 701											
Shade										100	
HONEYBEE (JEANNETTE)											
Honey Pot w/lid				180							85 TL
HONEYCOMB (DUGAN)											
Rose Bowl	75			125							
Rose Bowl (Pontil Base)	150										
HONEYCOMB & CLOVER (FENTON)											
Bonbon	30	50	50	40							90 V
Compote	35	50	60	50							
Spooner, rare	100										200 AM
HONEYCOMB & HOBSTAR (MILLERSBURG)											
Vase, 8¼", rare		7300		8200							

Pattern Name	M	A	G	B	PO	AO	IB	IG	W	Red	Other
HONEYCOMB PANELS											
Tumbler		175									
HONEYCOMB VARIANT											
(DUGAN)											
Banana Bowl, scarce				90							
Bowl, 6" – 7½"	35	55		65							
Plate, 7" – 7½"	45	95		75							
HOOPS											
Bowl, 8", scarce	50										
Rose Bowl, low 6½"	75										
HORN OF PLENTY											
Bottle	50										
HORSE CHESTNUT (FENTON)											
Exterior pattern only											
HORSES' HEAD (FENTON)											
(HORSE MEDALLION)											
Bowl, flat, 7½"	200	500	275	220						1250	850 AB
Bowl, footed, 7" – 8"	100	225	325	225						1600	350 TL
Nut Bowl, scarce	80	250		300						1300	500 V
Plate, 6½" – 8½"	300	3250	4000	850							1500 PB
Rose Bowl, footed	165		1300	350						6000	725 V
HORSE RADISH											
Jar w/lid	55										
HORSESHOE											
Shot Glass	35										
HOT SPRINGS SOUVENIR											
Vase, 9⅞", rare	100										
HOURGLASS											
Bud Vase	45										
HOWARD ADVERTISING											
(FOUR PILLARS) (NORTHWOOD)											
Vase			125								
HUACO DE ORO											
Bottle	175										
HUMPTY-DUMPTY											
Mustard Jar	75										
HYACINTH											
GONE WITH THE WIND											
Lamp, rare											4000 CA
ICEBURG (CZECH)											
Bowl					95						
ICE CRYSTALS											
Bowl, footed									85		
Candlesticks, pair									160		
Plate									150		
Salt, footed									65		
IDYLL (FENTON)											
Vase, very rare	650	800		900							
ILLINOIS DAISY (ENGLISH)											
Bowl, 8"	40										
Cookie Jar w/lid	60										
ILLINOIS SOLDIERS AND SAILORS											
See Soldiers and Sailors (Fenton)											
ILLUSION (FENTON)											
Bonbon	45			75							
IMPERIAL (ARGENTINA)											
Pitcher, very scarce	400										
IMPERIAL #5											
Bowl, 8"		50									65 AM
Vase, 6", rare		175									
IMPERIAL #30 CUT											
Fruit Bowl, 9", handled	75										125 SM
Tray, 10", handled	65										100 SM
IMPERIAL 107½											
Compote or Goblet	65										80 TL
IMPERIAL #107½ A											
Compote or Goblet	65										90 AM
IMPERIAL 203A											
Mug	65										
IMPERIAL #284											
Vase, 6" – 14"	100	225	160								
IMPERIAL #302											
Cruet w/stopper, scarce	400										
IMPERIAL # 393½											
Pitcher	250										
Tumbler	65										
IMPERIAL #499											
Sherbet	15		30							95	
IMPERIAL #537											
Compote	175										
IMPERIAL #641											
Cheese Compote	25										40 SM
Cheese Plate	50										100 SM

Pattern Name	M	A	G	B	PO	AO	IB	IG	W	Red	Other
IMPERIAL #664											
Tray, center handle											65 SM
IMPERIAL BASKET											
One shape, rare	150										175 SM
IMPERIAL DAISY											
Shade	45										
IMPERIAL FLUTE VASE											
Vase w/serrated top	40	80	65	500							
IMPERIAL GRAPE											
Basket, handled	55		85	225							75 SM
Bowl, 5"	15	40	30								75 OG
Bowl, 8" – 9", low ruffled	60	260	65	2300	1600						
Bowl, 10" – 11", flared	65	375	75								200 SM
Bowl, 10" – 12", ruffled	65	175	100	900							225 SM
Bowl, ice cream shape, scarce	200	400									
Compote	150	190	75								200 AQ
Cup and Saucer	75	175	95								
Decanter w/stopper	95	325	125								300 SM
Goblet	30	100	45								75 AM
Nappy	25		40								35 SM
Milk Pitcher	225	350	200								225 SM
Plate, 6½"	125	295	100	3500							250 LV
Plate, 9"	100	2500	100								1100 AM
Pitcher	100	500	150								325 SM
Tumbler	20	55	90								75 SM
Tumbler, varient	30	55	35								225 W
Punch Bowl & Base	150	450	275								375 SM
Punch Cup	20	45	30								35 SM
Rose Bowl, rare	450	900	300								650 AM
Shade	85										
Spittoon Whimsey, rare	2200		2750								
Water Bottle, scarce	200	185	150								175 LV
Wine	25	75	35								95 SM
IMPERIAL GRAPE VARIANT											
Bowl, 8", scarce	65										
IMPERIAL GRAPE VARIANT #2											
Shallow Bowl, 6½", very scarce	80										
IMPERIAL GRECIAN											
Compote, handled	65										
IMPERIAL JEWELS											
Bowl, 4" – 6"		45	35	55					100		
Bowl, 7" – 10"		60	45	70					150		
Creamer or Sugar									200		70 CeB
Hat shape		70							225		100 CeB
Plate, 7"		75	60	80					225		
Vase, 5" – 12"	100	100	80	110					250		
IMPERIAL PAPERWEIGHT											
Advertising weight, very rare		1200									
IMPERIAL QUILTED FLUTE											
*Exterior pattern only of Heavy Grape											
IMPERIAL TUBE VASE											
Vase 5½"											75 EmG
IMPERIAL VINTAGE											
Tray, center handled	35										60 SM
IMPERIAL WIDE RAYS											
Bowl, 9"	30								35		35 CM
Bowl, square, 8", scarce	40								45		40 CM
INCA BOTTLE (ARGENTINA)											
Bottle, scarce	175										
INCA SUN BOTTLE (ARGENTINA)											
Bottle, scarce	200										
INCA VASE											
Vase, very scarce	1900			3000							2350 BA
INCA VASE VARIANT											
Vase, very scarce	1800										
INDIA DAISY (INDIA)											
Tumbler	100										
INDIANA FLUTE											
Compote	70										
Rose Bowl, 4½" – 5", very scarce	100										
INDIANA GOBLET (INDIANA GLASS)											
One shape, rare											800 AM
INDIANA SOLDIERS AND SAILORS PLATE See Soldiers and Sailors (Fenton)											
INDIANA STATEHOUSE (FENTON)											
Plate, rare	16000			7500							
INDIAN BANGLES (INDIA)											
Pitcher	150										
Tumbler	75										

Pattern Name	M	A	G	B	PO	AO	IB	IG	W	Red	Other
INDIAN BRACELET (INDIA)											
Pitcher	125										
Tumbler	65										
INDIAN CANOE											
Novelty Boat shape	100										
INDIAN ENAMELED BLOSSOMS (INDIA)											
Tumbler	75										
INDIAN KEY (INDIA)											
Tumbler	90										
INDIAN WATER JARS (KALSHI FLOWERS) (INDIAN)											
Jar	125										
INDUSTRIA ARGENTINA STAR											
Bowl	85										
Plate	150										
Vase	200										
INSULATOR (VARIOUS MAKERS)											
Various sizes	15+										
INTAGLIO DAISY (DIAMOND)											
Bowl, 4½"	30	90									
Bowl, 7½"	50	150									
INTAGLIO FEATHERS											
Cup	25										
INTAGLIO OVALS (U.S. GLASS)											
Bowl, 7"											75 PM
Plate, 7½"											100 PM
INTAGLIO STARS											
Tumbler, rare	600										
INTAGLIO THISTLE											
Bowl, scarce	125										
INTERIOR FLUTE											
Creamer	50										
Sugar	60										
INTERIOR PANELS											
Decanter	65										
Mug	75										
INTERIOR POINSETTIA (NORTHWOOD)											
Tumbler, rare	400										
INTERIOR RAYS (U.S. GLASS) (Depression Era)											
Many shapes & sizes from $5.00 – 50.00											
INTERIOR RIB											
Vase	50										50 SM
INTERIOR SMOOTH PANEL (JEFFERSON)											
Spittoon, rare						1500					
INTERIOR SWIRL											
Tumbler	50		70								
Spittoon					140						
Vase, footed, 9"	40										
INTERIOR SWIRL AND WIDE PANEL											
Squat Pitcher	75										
INVERTED COIN DOT (FENTON)											
Pitcher, rare	100										
Tumbler, scarce	25										
INVERTED COIN DOT (NORTHWOOD)											
Tumbler, very rare	300										
INVERTED FEATHER (CAMBRIDGE)											
Bonbon Whimsey (from Cracker Jar), very rare			2700								
Compote	75										
Covered Butter, rare	450	500									
Cracker Jar w/lid		750	300								
Creamer, Sugar, or Spooner, rare	400	450									
Cup, rare	75										
Parfait	60										
Punch Bowl w/base, rare	3000		4600								
Pitcher, tall, rare	4500	6500									
Pitcher, squat, rare	1600										
Tumbler, rare	450	575	675								
Wine, rare	375										
INVERTED PRISMS (ENGLISH)											
Creamer	70										
Sugar, open	60										
INVERTED STRAWBERRY (CAMBRIDGE)											
Bonbon, stemmed w/handle, rare			900								

Pattern Name	M	A	G	B	PO	AO	IB	IG	W	Red	Other
Bonbon Whimsey from spooner, 2 handled, rare			1700								
Bowl, 5"	40	115	75								
Bowl, 7"		235		125							
Bowl, 7½" square, rare				450							
Bowl, 9" – 10½"	145	235	275	375							
Candlesticks, pair, scarce	425	475	950								
Celery, very scarce		600	900	1000							
Compote, small, very scarce	400			900							
Compote, large, very scarce	225	325	450	1300							
Compote Whimsey, rare	1500										
Covered Butter	850	1100									
Creamer, Sugar, or Spooner, each, rare	375	225	325	425							
Hat Whimsey, rare				950							
Ladies Spittoon, rare	900	1350	1800								
Milk Pitcher, rare		5000									
Powder Jar, very scarce	200		325								
Pitcher, rare	2200	2400	2000								
Rose Bowl, 8", rare	550	850									
Tumbler, rare	135	165	200	500							
Table Set, 2 pieces (stemmed), rare		1300									
INVERTED THISTLE (CAMBRIDGE)											
Bowl, 5", rare		150	150								
Bowl, 9", rare		325	325								
Bowl, Whimsey, footed, rare			600								
Butter, rare	500	600	700								
Chop Plate, rare		2700									
Compote, 8", rare			2000								
Covered Box, rare				400							
Creamer, Sugar, or Spooner, rare	350	400	500								
Milk Pitcher, rare		2700	2900								
Pitcher, rare	3000	1800									
Tumbler, rare	350	350									
Spittoon, rare		4000									
INWALD'S DIAMOND CUT											
Bowl (Jardinere)				400							
Vase	475										
INWALD'S PINWHEEL											
Vase, 5"	150										
IOWA											
Small Mug, rare	100										
IRIS (FENTON)											
Buttermilk Goblet	25	65	65	125							80 AM
Compote	50	60	60	90					235		
ISAAC BENESCH (MILLERSBURG)											
Bowl, advertising, 6½"		425									
misspelled version, rare		1000									
ISIS											
Tumbler, rare	150										
IVY											
Stemmed Claret	85										
Stemmed Wine	75										
I.W. HARPER											
Decanter w/stopper	85										
JACK-IN-THE-PULPIT											
Vase	45	75		80	125						
JACK-IN-THE-PULPIT (NORTHWOOD)											
Vase	50	175	200	275		375			100		
Vase, advertising, very rare						600			150		
JACKMAN											
Whiskey Bottle	50										
JACOBEAN (INWALD)											
Decanter	200										
Tumbler, 3 sizes	40 – 125										
Tray	95										
JACOBEAN RANGER (CZECH & ENGLISH)											
Bowls, various shapes	60+										
Decanter w/stopper	200										
Juice Tumbler	125										
Miniature Tumbler	150										
Pitcher	325										
Tumbler	90										
Wine	40										
JACOB'S LADDER											
Perfume	60										
JACOB'S LADDER VARIANT (U.S. GLASS)											
Rose Bowl	85										

Pattern Name	M	A	G	B	PO	AO	IB	IG	W	Red	Other
JASMINE & BUTTERFLY (CZECH)											
Decanter	100										
Guest Set, complete	200										
Tumbler	25										
JEANNETTE COLONIAL											
Rose Bowl, 5½"	30										
JEANNETTE REFRIGERATOR JAR											
Jar, covered	50										
JELLY JAR											
Complete	65										
JENKINS LATTICE (#336)											
Spooner	75										
JESTER'S CAP (DUGAN/DIAMOND)											
Vase	45	75			100						200 CeB
JESTER'S CAP (NORTHWOOD)											
Vase	85	175	175	225							250 TL
JESTER'S CAP (WESTMORELAND)											
Vase	75	100	100		200	300BO					150 TL
JEWEL BOX											
Ink Well	150		200								
JEWELED BUTTERFLIES (INDIANA)											
Bowl, square, rare	225										
JEWELED HEART (DUGAN)											
Basket Whimsey, rare					450						
Bowl, 5"		40			65				65		
Bowl, 10"		95			135				250		
Plate, 6"	150	175			200						
Pitcher, rare	900										
Tumbler, rare	100								575		
JEWELED PEACOCK TAIL											
Vase, 8", rare		375									
JEWELED SUNFLOWER											
Vase, scarce	155										
JEWELS (DUGAN)											
Bowl, various sizes		50	150	175						200	80 CeB
Candle Bowl	85							175			
Candlesticks, pair	100	150	175	200						275	150 CeB
Vase	75	150	150	175						200	200 AM
JEWELS & DRAPERY (NORTHWOOD)											
Vase, rare			325								
JOCKEY CLUB (NORTHWOOD)											
Bowl, very scarce		1500									
Plate, flat or handgrip, scarce		1800									
JOSEF'S PLUMES											
Pitcher	725										
Vase, 6"	325										
J. R. MILNER, CO., LYNCHBURG, VA See Cosmos and Cane (U.S. Glass)											
KALEIDOSCOPE											
Bowl, 8" – 9", scarce	65										
KANGAROO (AUSTRALIAN)											
Bowl, 5"	100	180									
Bowl, 9½"	300	500									
KAREN											
Bowl, small, rare	90										
Bowl, large, rare	275										
KARVE (FINLAND)											
Vase, 7"											200 LV
KATHLEEN'S FLOWERS (INDIA) AKA: FANTASY FLOWERS											
Tumbler	100										
KEDVESH (INDIA)											
Vase	85										
KEYHOLE (DUGAN)											
Bowl, 9½", very scarce	300	375			350						
*Also exterior of Raindrops bowl											
KEYSTONE COLONIAL (WESTMORELAND)											
Compote, 6¼", scarce	300	300									
KINGFISHER AND VARIANT (AUSTRALIAN)											
Bowl, 5"	95	185									
Bowl, 9½"	225	325									
Jardiniere, from large bowl, very rare		800									
KING'S CROWN (U.S. GLASS)											
Stemmed Wine	30										
KITTEN											
Miniature paperweight, rare	250										
KITTENS											
Bottle											65 PM
KITTENS (FENTON)											
Bowl, 2 sides up, scarce	100	400		250							250 LV

353

Pattern Name	M	A	G	B	PO	AO	IB	IG	W	Red	Other
Bowl, 4 sides up, scarce	100			300							350 AQ
Cereal Bowl, scarce	150	250		350							375 LV
Cup, scarce	125			400							
Plate, 4½", scarce	125	300		325							650 V
Ruffled Bowl, scarce	100			350							285 AQ
Saucer, scarce	125			325							250 PB
Spooner or Toothpick Holder	100			225							500 V
Spittoon Whimsey, very rare	4500			7000							
Vase, 3", scarce	100			235							
KIWI & VARIANT (AUSTRALIAN)											
Bowl, 5", rare	250	200									
Bowl, 10", rare	350	1000									
KNIGHT'S TEMPLAR											
See Dandelion (Northwood)											
KNOTTED BEADS (FENTON)											
Vase, 4" – 12"	25	65	60	80						725	250 AM
KOKOMO (ENGLISH)											
Bowl, 8"	55										
Rose Bowl, footed	75										
KOOKABURRA (AUSTRALIAN)											
Bowl, 5"	175	225									165 BA
Bowl, 9"	425	1300									
Bowl, 9", lettered, very rare	1500										
KOOKABURRA FLOAT BOWL											
Bowl, 10" – 11", round or ruffled, rare	900	2300									
KRYS-TOL COLONIAL (JEFFERSON)											
Mayonnaise set, 2 pieces	125										
KULOR (SWEDEN)											
Vase, 6" – 8", very scarce	1100	4000		2000							3000 TL
LABELLE ROSE											
Bowl, 5", rare	200										
LACO											
Oil Bottle, 9¼"	80										
LACEY DAISY											
Vase, 10", very scarce	250										
LACY DEWDROP (WESTMORELAND)											
*All pieces, scarce, rare											
Banana Boat											350 IM
Bowl, covered											300 IM
Cake Plate											200 IM
Compote, covered											450 IM
Goblet											225 IM
Pitcher											650 IM
Tumbler											175 IM
Sugar											175 IM
(Note: all items listed are in Pearl Carnival)											
LADDERS (IMPERIAL)											
Bowl, 8", very scarce	100										
LADY'S SLIPPER											
One shape, rare	250										
LAKE SHORE HONEY											
Honey Jar, one size	200										
LANCASTER COMPOTE											
Compote										150	
LANGERKRANS (SWEDEN)											
Candy w/lid, 5"	125										
LARGE KANGAROO (AUSTRALIAN)											
Bowl, 5"	60	75									
Bowl, 10"	300	450									
LATE COVERED SWAN											
One shape w/lid				550							
LATE ENAMELED BLEEDING HEARTS											
Tumbler	175										
LATE ENAMELED GRAPE											
Goblet	100										
LATE ENAMELED STRAWBERRY											
Lemonade Tumbler	75										
LATE FEATHER											
Pitcher	55										
Tumbler	15										
LATE STRAWBERRY											
Pitcher	225										
Tumbler	75										
LATE WATER LILY											
Pitcher	50										
Tumbler	20										
LATTICE (CRYSTAL)											
Bowl, 7" – 8"	100	145									

Pattern Name	M	A	G	B	PO	AO	IB	IG	W	Red	Other
LATTICE (DUGAN)											
Bowls, various sizes	60	70									85 LV
LATTICE & DAISY (DUGAN)											
Bowl, 5"	30								100		
Bowl, 9"	65										
Pitcher	175	1200		1600							
Tumbler	20	90		80					200		
LATTICE & GRAPE (FENTON)											
Pitcher	225			450	2200			1600			
Tumbler	30			45	500				145		100 PB
Spittoon Whimsey, rare	3500										
LATTICE & LEAVES											
Vase, 9½"	275			300							
LATTICE & POINTS (DUGAN)											
Vase	40	95		225	175				100		
LATTICE & PRISMS											
Cologne w/stopper	65										
LATTICE & SPRAYS											
Vase, 10½"	50										
LATTICE HEART											
Bowl, 6½" – 7½"		175									200 BA
Plate, 7" – 8"		300									325 BA
LAUREL											
Shade	40										
LAUREL & GRAPE											
Vase, 6"					120						
LAUREL BAND											
Pitcher	95										
Tumbler	40										
LAUREL LEAVES (IMPERIAL)											
Compote	65										
Plate	40	55									65 SM
LAUREL WREATH											
Compote, 5"	65										
LAVERNE											
Perfume	40										
LBJ HAT											
Ashtray	25										
LEA (SOWERBY)											
Bowl, footed	40										
Creamer or Sugar, footed	45	50									
Pickle Dish, handled	45										
LEAF & BEADS (NORTHWOOD)											
Bowl, dome footed	50	80	70								
Candy Dish, 3 footed	40	100	85	325		700					
Nut Bowl, footed, scarce	110	125	85	300		1750			325		1500 SM
Plate Whimsey, rare	150		200								
Rose Bowl, footed	135	150	165	225		350	1100	1450	500		1700 GO
Rose Bowl, sawtooth edge, very scarce	300	425		535							
Rose Bowl, smooth edge, very scarce	285	400									1400 IC
(Add 25% for patterned interior)											
LEAF & CHRYSANTHEMUM											
Bowl	115										
LEAF & LITTLE FLOWERS (MILLERSBURG)											
Compote, miniature, rare	325	500	525								
LEAF CHAIN (FENTON)											
Bowl, 7" – 9"	30	125	100	85		2500		2600	85	1100	225 LV
Plate, 7½"	70		325	150				4100			135 CM
Plate, 9¼"	360	2500	300	875					200		5100 Y
LEAF COLUMN (NORTHWOOD)											
Shade											100 AM
Vase	75	115	250	950			1400	450	325		255 HO
LEAF GARDEN (IMPERIAL)											
Shade, very scarce											300 SM
LEAF RAYS (DUGAN)											
Nappy, spade shape	30	40		375	45			225	85		100 LV
Nappy, ruffled, scarce	65	125			90				90		125 LV
(Add 10% for Daisy May exterior)											
LEAF ROSETTES & BEADS (DUGAN) *SAME AS FLOWERS & BEADS											
Bowl, 6" – 7"	30	60			75						
Plate, 7", hex shape	75	110			125						
LEAF SWIRL (WESTMORELAND)											
Compote	50	70		80 TL							145 Y
Goblet shape	60	80		95 TL							160 Y
LEAF SWIRL & FLOWER (FENTON)											
Vase	50								65		
LEAF TIERS (FENTON)											
Banana Bowl Whimsey	200										

Pattern Name	M	A	G	B	PO	AO	IB	IG	W	Red	Other
Bowl, footed, 5"	30										
Bowl, footed, 10"	60			2000							
Butter, footed	175										
Creamer, Spooner, footed	75										
Plate Whimsey, from Spooner	450										
Sugar, footed	90										
Pitcher, footed, rare	525			725							
Tumbler, footed, rare	125			165							
LEAFY TRIANGLE											
Bowl, 7"	55										
LEA VARIANT (SOWERBY)											
Creamer, footed	50										
LIBERTY BELL											
Bank	20										
Cookie Jar w/lid	40										
LIGHTNING FLOWER (NORTHWOOD)											
Bowl, 5", rare	100										
Nappy, rare	125										
Nappy Variant (Proof-Absentee design in Flowers and Leaves), very rare	350										
LIGHTOLIER LUSTRE & CLEAR											
Shade	45										
LILY OF THE VALLEY (FENTON)											
Pitcher, rare				7000							
Tumbler, rare	525			225							
LILY VASE (AUSTRALIAN)											
Vase, 9" – 13"											800 BA
LINDAL											
Vase, 4" – 5", miniature	200										
LINED LATTICE (DUGAN)											
Vase, squat, 5" – 7"	150	200		425	100				125		325 HO
Vase, 8" – 12"	80	100		350	175				125		275 HO
LINED LATTICE VARIANT (DUGAN)											
Vase, 9" – 16"	75	125			250						150 BA
LINCOLN DRAPE											
Mini Lamp, rare	1000										
LINN'S MUMS (NORTHWOOD)											
Bowl, footed, very rare		1800									
LION (FENTON)											
Bowl, 7", scarce	115			300							250 PB
Plate, 7½", rare	1300										
LITTLE BARREL (IMPERIAL)											
One shape	150		200								200 SM
LITTLE BEADS											
Bowl, 8"	20				45						
Compote, small	30	40			65	85					70 AQ
LITTLE DAISIES (FENTON)											
Bowl, 8" – 9½", rare	1200			1400							
LITTLE DAISY											
Lamp, complete, 8"											500 AM
LITTLE DARLING											
Bottle	50										
LITTLE FISHES (FENTON)											
Bowl, flat or footed, 5½"	95	145		150					350		200 AQ
Bowl, flat or footed, 10"	175	425		425				8000	1500		
Plate, 10½", rare	5000										
LITTLE FLOWERS (FENTON)											
Bowl, 5½"	25	40	85	65							75 AQ
Bowl, 6", ice cream shape	40	50	95	75							
Bowl, 5½" square, rare	150										
Bowl, 6", tricorner	125	175									
Bowl, 9½"	70	175	165	145							1000 AB
Bowl, 10", ice cream shape, very scarce		175		250						4300	
Plate, 7", rare	165										250 PB
Plate, 10", rare	2500										
LITTLE JEWEL											
Finger Lamp, rare	650										
LITTLE MERMAID											
One shape											100 AM
LITTLE STARS (MILLERSBURG)											
Bowl, 6", ice cream shape, rare		700	825	2500							
Bowl, 7" – 7½", scarce	125	150	300	3000							125 CM
Bowl, 8" – 9", scarce	350	450	450								400 CM
Bowl, 10½", rare	600	700	800	4200							
Plate, 7½", rare	1150	1400	1600								
LITTLE SWAN											
Miniature, 3"											75 AM
LOGANBERRY (IMPERIAL)											
Whimsey Vase, scarce		2500									

Pattern Name	M	A	G	B	PO	AO	IB	IG	W	Red	Other
Vase, scarce	325	2200	550								775 AM
LOG CABIN SYRUP											
Cabin shaped syrup, rare	325										
LOG PAPERWEIGHT											
Novelty, 3" x 1¼", rare	150										
LONG BUTTRESS											
Pitcher	400										
Tumbler	250										
Toothpick	200										
LONG HOBSTAR (IMPERIAL)											
Bowl, 8½"	45										
Bowl, 10½"	60										
Compote	65										
Punch Bowl w/base	125										150 CM
LONG HORN											
Wine	60										
LONG LEAF (DUGAN)											
Bowl, footed					175						
LONG THUMBPRINT (FENTON)											
Vase, 7" – 11"	30	35	45	100							
Vase, Whimsey	75										
LONG THUMBPRINT HOBNAIL (FENTON)											
Vase, 7" – 11"	50	65	75	130							
LONG THUMBPRINT VARIANT											
Bowl, 8¾"	30	40									
Butter	75										
Compote	30	40	40								
Creamer or Sugar, each	40										50 SM
LOTUS (FENTON)											
Pitcher	400										
Tumbler	35										
LOTUS & GRAPE (FENTON)											
Absentee Bowl, rare				1900							
Bonbon	40	110	150	85						1200	225 V
Bowl, flat, 7" – 8½"	65	70	165	125							375 PeB
Plate, 9½", rare	7000	2200	1800	1400							
LOTUS & GRAPE VARIANT (FENTON)											
Bonbon, footed, scarce	45	110	150	100							
Bowl, footed, 6"	40	75	90	80							
Rose Bowl, footed, rare	425			500							
LOTUS BUD (INDIA)											
Vase	80										
LOTUS LAND (NORTHWOOD)											
Bonbon, rare	1500	750									
LOUISA (JEANNETTE)											
* Floragold Depression name, many shapes & sizes, prices from $10.00 – 650.00, late 1950s											
LOUISA (WESTMORELAND)											
Bowl, footed		95	75		135						65 AQ
Candy Dish, footed	50	85	65								70 AQ
Mini-Banana Boat (old only)	45	70									
Nut Bowl, scarce		250									
Plate, footed, 8", rare	100	165			350						125 AQ
Rose Bowl	50	70	65	175							75 TL
LOVEBIRDS											
Bottle w/stopper	575										
LOVE BIRDS (CONSOLIDATED)											
Vase, very rare									450	600	375 SM
LOVELY (NORTHWOOD)											
Bowl, footed		900	1100								
LOVING CUP (FENTON)											
Loving Cup, scarce	225	700	400	325	7000	15000			550		
*Part of the Orange Tree line											
LUCILE											
Pitcher, rare	1200			1000							
Tumbler, rare	450			250							
LUCKY BANK											
One shape	35										
LUCKY BELL											
Bowl, 4", rare	65										
Bowl, 8¾", rare	135										
LULES ARGENTINA											
Plate	225										
LUSTRE											
Tumbler	45										
LUSTRE & CLEAR (FENTON)											
Fan Vase	40		60	55				90			
LUSTRE & CLEAR (IMPERIAL)											
Bowl, 5"	20										
Bowl, 10"	25										
Butter Dish	65										

Pattern Name	M	A	G	B	PO	AO	IB	IG	W	Red	Other
Console Set, 3 pieces	60									375	
Creamer or Sugar	25	65	150								30 CM
Pitcher	145										
Tumbler	40										
Rose Bowl	75										
Shakers, pair	75										
LUSTRE FLUTE (NORTHWOOD)											
Bonbon		50	50								
Bowl, 5½"	25	30	30								
Bowl, 8"	50	65	65								
Compote		55	50								
Creamer or Sugar	40	55	55								
Hat	25	30	30								
Nappy (from punch cup)	50	75	70								
Punch Cup	20	25	20								
Sherbet	35										
LUSTRE MATCH SAFE (FENTON)											
Match Safe	70										
LUSTRE ROSE (IMPERIAL)											
Bowl, Fruit, footed, 11" – 12"	40	750	125							2000	1500 V
Bowl, Berry, footed, 5"	20	55	30	125							20 CM
Bowl, Berry, footed, 8" – 10"	35	225	50								40 CM
Bowl, Centerpiece, footed	100	425	200								250 SM
Butter	70	250	70								225 AM
Creamer, Sugar, or Spooner	35	150	40								100 PB
Fernery	40	200	120	75							125 PB
Milk Pitcher	100										125 CM
Plate Whimsey, footed	250										200 CM
Pitcher	125	600	225								350 AM
Tumbler	20	100	40								140 CM
Tumbler Whimsey, rare											525 AM
LUTZ (McKEE)											
Mug, footed	100										
MADAY & CO.											
See Blackberry (Fenton)											
MADHU (INDIA)											
Tumbler	125										
MADONNA (INDIA)											
Pitcher	225										
Tumbler	95										
MAE'S DAISIES (GRAPEVINE & FLOWER) (INDIA)											
Tumbler	100										
MAE WEST (DUGAN)											
Candlesticks, each											150 CeB
MAGNOLIA DRAPE (FENTON)											
Pitcher	200										
Tumbler	35										
MAGNOLIA RIB (FENTON)											
Berry Bowl, small	20										
Berry Bowl, large	55										
Butter	125										
Creamer or Spooner	60										
Sugar w/lid	75										
MAGPIE & VARIANT (AUSTRALIAN)											
Bowl, 5"	95	200									
Bowl, 8" – 10"	250	475									
MAHARAJAH (JAIN)											
Shot Glass, rare	100										
MAIZE (LIBBEY)											
Syrup (cruet), rare											235 CL
Vase celery, rare											185 CL
MAJESTIC (McKEE)											
Tumbler, rare	500										
MALAGA (DIAMOND)											
Bowl, 9", scarce	75	150									
Plate, 10", rare		500									400 AM
Rose Bowl, rare	125	400									
MALLARD DUCK											
One Shape											550 CRAN
MANCHESTER											
Flower holder w/frog											100 AM
MANHATTAN (U.S. GLASS)											
Decanter	250										
Wine	40										
Vase, rare	350										
MANY DIAMONDS											
Ice Bucket	225										
Tumbler	60										
MANY FRUITS (DUGAN)											
Punch Bowl w/base	400	700		2500					1400		
Punch Cup	25	30	40	125					70		

Pattern Name	M	A	G	B	PO	AO	IB	IG	W	Red	Other
MANY PRISMS											
Perfume w/stopper	75										
MANY RIBS											
(MODEL FLINT-NORTHWOOD)											
Vase, 8", very rare						3000					
MANY STARS & VARIANT											
(MILLERSBURG)											
Bowl, ruffled, 9", scarce	375	500	550	3000							3000 V
Bowl, ICS, 9½", rare	475	1100	1100	4250							
Bowl, tricornered, rare		2500									
Chop Plate, very rare	5000										
MAPLE LEAF (DUGAN)											
Bowl, stemmed, 4½"	30	35	50	40							
Bowl, stemmed, 9"	60	100		100							
Butter	125	150		150							
Creamer or Spooner	45	55		70							
Sugar	70	80		90							
Pitcher	175	300		350							
Tumbler	25	40		55							300 PB
MAPLE LEAF BASKET											
Basket, handled, large	65										
MARGUERITE											
Vase, 10"	110										
MARIANNA (CZECH)											
Vase	260										
MARIE (FENTON)											
(Rustic vase interior base pattern)											
MARILYN (MILLERSBURG)											
Pitcher, rare	950	1350	2000								
Tumbler, rare	135	225	350								
MARTEC (McKEE)											
Tumbler, rare	500										
MARTHA											
Compote, 7½"	160										
MARY ANN (DUGAN)											
Vase, 2 varieties, 7"	100	375									
Loving Cup, 3 handled, rare	550										1000 PkA
MARY GREGORY											
Cologne Bottle, rare	175										
MASSACHUSETTS (U.S. GLASS)											
Mug, rare	150										
Tumbler, very scarce	200										
Vase, very scarce	175										
MAYAN (MILLERSBURG)											
Bowl, 8½" – 10"	3500		150								
*(Common in green, all others, rare)											
MAY BASKET											
Basket, 7½"	40		95								
Bowl, 9", rare			160								
MAYFLOWER (IMPERIAL)											
Light shade	45		70								
MAYFLOWER (MILLERSBURG)											
Bowl, 9" – 9½", very rare	3000										
(Exterior of Grape Leaves Bowls)											
MAYPOLE											
Vase, 6¼"	45	105	60								
McKEE'S #20											
Sherbet	35										
McKEE'S SQUIGGY											
Vase	90		125								
MEANDER (NORTHWOOD)											
(Exterior only)											
MELON RIB											
Candy Jar w/lid	30										
Decanter	90										
Powder Jar w/lid	35										
Pitcher	60										
Tumbler	20										
Shakers, pair	35										
MELON RIB GENIE											
Vase, 5"		150									
MELTING ICE											
Vase, 8½", scarce		200									
MEMPHIS (NORTHWOOD)											
Berry Bowl, 5"	35	45									
Berry Bowl, 10" – 12"	125	350				5100					
Fruit Bowl w/base	325	400	800	2400			4000	6000	1200		2600 LG
Punch Bowl w/base	450	625	2300				4500	15000	2100		65 LG
Punch Cup	25	40	50				85	95			
Shakers, each, rare			200								
METALICA											
Covered Candy w/ metal filagree work	50										

359

Pattern Name	M	A	G	B	PO	AO	IB	IG	W	Red	Other
METRO											
Vase, 9" – 14", rare	275										
MEXICALI VASE											
Vase, footed, 8"	90										
MEXICAN BELL											
Goblet, flashed	40										
MEYDAM (LEERDAM)											
Butter	135										
Cake Stand	95										
Compote	75										
MIKADO (FENTON)											
Compote, large	200	850	1750	600					1000	9000	600 PB
MIKE'S MYSTERY											
Bowl, 8½"	135										
MILADY (FENTON)											
Pitcher	650	2500	2900	1200							
Tumbler	85	100	325	125							
MILLER FURNITURE (FENTON)											
Open Edge Basket, advertising	50		125								
MILLERSBURG FOUR PILLARS											
Vase, star base, rare	300	250	350								
MILLERSBURG FOUR PILLARS VARIANT											
Vase, swirled, plain base, rare		500									
MILLERSBURG GRAPE											
Bowl, 5"	40										
Bowl, 8½"	90		900								
MINIATURE BATHTUB											
One shape	150										
MINIATURE BEAN POT (CZECH)											
One shape, 2½"	80										
MINIATURE BELL											
Paperweight, 2½"	60										
MINIATURE BLACKBERRY (FENTON)											
Compote, small	80	125	200	75					525		
Compote, Absentee Variant	60	85	95	90							
Stemmed Plate, very scarce				450					450		
MINIATURE CANDELABRA (CAMBRIDGE)											
One size	500										
MINIATURE CHILD'S SHOE											
One shape	325										
MINIATURE COW											
One size	700										
MINIATURE FLOWER BASKET (WESTMORELAND)											
Basket				150							300 BO
MINIATURE HOBNAIL											
Pitcher, 6", rare	250										
Tumbler, 2½"	50										
MINIATURE HOBNAIL (EUROPEAN)											
Cordial Set, rare	1250										
Nut Cup, stemmed, rare	400								550		
(Also known as Wild Rose Wreath)											
MINIATURE LOVING CUP											
One size	75										
MINIATURE ROSE BOWL											
One shape, 4"	30										
MINIATURE SANDAL											
One shape	500										
MINIATURE SHELL											
Candleholder, each											75 CL
MINIATURE URN											
One shape	40										
MINIATURE WASH BOWL & PITCHER											
Bowl, 3⅝"	55										
Pitcher, 2¾"	70										
MINI DIAMONDS (INDIA)											
Juice Tumbler	100										
MINNESOTA (U.S. GLASS)											
Mug	100										
Toothpick Holder	60										
MINUET (LATE)											
Pitcher	75										
Tumbler	20										
MIRROR & CROSSBAR (JAIN)											
Tumbler, rare	225										
MIRRORED LOTUS (FENTON)											
Bowl, 7" – 8½"	75			165				2500			3000 CeB

Pattern Name	M	A	G	B	PO	AO	IB	IG	W	Red	Other
Plate, 7½", rare	500			650							4900 CeB
Rose Bowl, rare	325			500					600		
MIRRORED PEACOCKS (JAIN)											
Tumbler, rare	225										
MIRRORED VEES (RINDSKOPF)											
Tumbler, very scarce	175										
MISTY MORN (JAIN)											
Vase	150										
MITERED BLOCK (EUROPEAN)											
Lamp, scarce	195										
MITERED DIAMOND & PLEATS (ENGLISH)											
Bowl, 4½"	25			30							
Bowl, shallow, 8½"	40			45							
Rose Bowl Whimsey	95										
MITERED MAZE											
Vase, 12"										300	200 SM
MITERED OVALS (MILLERSBURG)											
Vase, rare	9000	10000	8000								
MODERNE											
Cup or Saucer	15										
MOLLER (EDA)											
Bowl	210			325							
Rose Bowl	350			500							
MONKEY BOTTLE											
Bottle, 4¾"	250										
MONSOON (INDIA)											
Pitcher	250										
Tumbler	80										
MOON & STAR (WESTMORELAND)											
Compote (Pearl Carnival)											385 IC
MOON & STARS BAND											
Pitcher	450										
Tumbler	100										
MOONGLEAM (HEISEY)											
Pitcher w/lid, rare			400								
Tumbler, rare			30								
MOONPRINT (BROCKWITZ)											
Banana Boat, rare	135										
Bowl, 8½"	45										
Bowl, 14"	80										
Butter	100										
Candlesticks, each, rare	90										
Cheese Keeper, rare	175										
Compote	55										
Cordial	35										
Creamer	40										
Decanter w/stopper	250										
Jar w/lid	65										
Pitcher, squat, scarce	225										
Sugar, stemmed	50										
Tray	75										
Vase, very scarce	400										
MORNING GLORY (IMPERIAL)											
Vase, squat, 4" – 7"	65	135	120								125 SM
Vase, standard, 8" – 15"	55	225	125								145 SM
Vase, funeral, 13" – 22"	575	900	450	10000							250 SM
MORNING GLORY (MILLERSBURG)											
Pitcher, rare	18000	19000	21000								
Tumbler, rare	1000	2500	4000								
MOUNTAIN LAKE											
Lamp Shade	85										
MOXIE											
Bottle, rare									90		
MT. GAMBIER (CRYSTAL)											
Mug	100										
Mug, Quorum	125										
MULTI-FRUITS & FLOWERS (MILLERSBURG)											
Dessert, stemmed, rare		900	900								
Punch Bowl w/base, fared, rare	1800	2100	3900	25000							
Punch Bowl w/base, tulip top, rare	3800	4300	4900	55000							
Punch Cup, rare	60	85	100	900							
Pitcher (either base), rare	11,000	8000	9000								
Tumbler, rare	900	1000	1200								
MULTI-RIB											
Vase, 10"	85										
MUSCADINE (JAIN)											
Tumbler, rare	225										
MUSCADINE VARIANT (JAIN)											
Tumbler	250										

Pattern Name	M	A	G	B	PO	AO	IB	IG	W	Red	Other
MY LADY											
Powder Jar w/lid	125										
MYSTERY											
Perfume	50										
MYSTERY GRAPE											
Bowl			175								
MYSTIC (CAMBRIDGE)											
Vase, footed, rare	175										
MYSTIC GRAPE											
Decanter w/stopper, 10½", rare	475										
NANNA (EDA)											
Jardiniere	325			500							
Vase	350			575							
NAPCO #2255 (JEANNETTE)											
Compote	75										
NAPOLEON											
Bottle											85 CL
NAPOLI (ITALY)											
Decanter	75										
Wine	20			25			25				25 V
NAUTILUS											
(DUGAN – NORTHWOOD)											
Creamer or Sugar, scarce		190			200						
(lettered add 25%)											
Giant Compote, rare	3000										
Vase Whimsey, rare	300	400									
NARCISSUS & RIBBON											
(FENTON)											
Wine Bottle w/stopper, rare	1200										
NAVAJO											
Vase, 7", very scarce	165										
NEAR-CUT (CAMBRIDGE)											
Decanter w/stopper, rare	2100		3000								
NEAR-CUT (NORTHWOOD)											
Compote	100	150	200								
Goblet, rare	175	125									
Pitcher, rare	3500										
Tumbler, rare	300	1200									
NEAR-CUT SOUVENIR											
(CAMBRIDGE)											
Mug, rare	200										
Tumbler, rare	275										
NEAR CUT WREATH											
(MILLERSBURG)											
(Exterior only)											
NELL (HIGBEE)											
Mug	75										
NESTING SWAN (MILLERSBURG)											
Bowl, round or ruffled											
10", scarce	250	375	375	3100							700 HA
Bowl, square, rare			1500								
Bowl, tricornered, rare	550	1150	1300	3700							750 CM
Plate, 10", very rare			3500								
Proof Bowl, rare		2500	3200								
Rose Bowl, rare	4000										
Spittoon Whimsey, very rare		5000	5000								
NEW ENGLAND WINE CO.											
Bottle, scarce	85										
NEW JERSEY (U.S. GLASS)											
Wine											100 HA
NEW ORLEANS SHRINE											
(U.S. GLASS)											
Champagne											150 CL
NEWPORT SHIP BOTTLE											
Bottle, one size			135								
NIAGARA FALLS (JEANNETTE)											
Milk Pitcher	35										
Pitcher	50										
Tumbler, 3 sizes	15										
NIGHTSHADE (CZECH)											
Bowl, dome base											165 CeB
NIGHT STARS (MILLERSBURG)											
Bonbon, rare	700	850	1400								1700 OG
Card Tray, rare	800	900	1200								
Nappy, tricornered, very rare	1500	1200	1800								
NIPPON (NORTHWOOD)											
Bowl, 8½"	150	450	600	500		21000	400	700	375		2000 HO
Plate, 9", scarce	800	925	1200				9000		1100		
NOLA (SCANDINAVIAN)											
Pitcher, squat	300										
Tumbler, 2 shapes	100										
Atomizer	125										
Perfume	80										

Pattern Name	M	A	G	B	PO	AO	IB	IG	W	Red	Other
Basket, handled	65										
Tumble-up	250										
Ring Tray	50										
Powderbox w/lid, 2 sizes	75										
NORRIS N. SMITH (FENTON)											
Bowl, advertising, scarce		900									
Plate, advertising, 5¾", scarce		1800									
NORTHERN LIGHTS (BROCKWITZ)											
Bowl, 2 sizes	100–150			175–225							
Rose Bowl, 2 sizes	225–275			300–400							
NORTHERN STAR (FENTON)											
Bowl, 6"	30										
Bowl, 5" ICS, scarce	75										
Bowl, tricorner	40										
Card Tray, 6"	40										
Plate, 6½", rare	100										
NORTH STAR (LANCASTER)											
Punch Bowl, 15", top only	300										
*(No base has been found to date)											
NORTHWOOD #38 SHADE											
Lamp Shade									125		
NORTHWOOD #569											
Vase, various shapes	40	55		65							75 V
NORTHWOOD #637											
Compote (either shape)											125 CeB
NORTHWOOD #657											
Candlesticks, 2 sizes			100	135							150 V
NORTHWOOD #699											
Cheese Dish											100 V
Underplate											75 V
NORTHWOOD WIDE FLUTE											
Vase, mid-size funeral, 8"–15"	125	400	200	1000							150 ALS
NORTHWOOD WIDE PANEL											
Vase	80										335 V
NOTCHES											
Plate, 8"	50										
NU-ART CHRYSANTHEMUM (IMPERIAL)											
Plate, rare	900	3100	9250	12000					1700		25000 EG
*Signed pieces, add 50%											
NU-ART DRAPE (IMPERIAL)											
Shade	60										
NU-ART HOMESTEAD (IMPERIAL)											
Plate, scarce	650	2000	7000	10000							1400 LV
*Signed pieces, add 50%											
NU-ART PANELLED SHADE (IMPERIAL)											
Shade, plain	50										
Shade, engraved	75										
NUGGET BEADS											
Beads		125									
#110											
Mugs, various lettering	100										
#195 (CROWN CRYSTAL)											
Sherbet	65										
#221 (CROWN CRYSTAL)											
Bowl, 5"	65										
Bowl, 8½"	100										
#270 (WESTMORELAND)											
Compote	50	90	140RG		100MMG	150BO					150 AQ
#321 (CROWN CRYSTAL)											
Oval Bowl	125										
#600 (FOSTORIA)											
Toothpick Holder	50										
#2176 (SOWERBY)											
Lemon Squeezer	60										
NUTMEG GRATER											
Butter	125										
Creamer	55										
Sugar, open	55										
OAK LEAF LUSTRE (ARGENTINA)											
Butter	215										
Cheese Dish w/cover	140										
OCTAGON (IMPERIAL)											
Bowl, 4½"	20	40	35								
Bowl, 8½"	50	150	70								
Bowl, Fruit, 10"–12"	75	250	150								
Butter	200	500	375								325 PB
Compote, 2 sizes	85	325									
Cordial	250										325 AQ
Creamer or Spooner	50	175	100								

Pattern Name	M	A	G	B	PO	AO	IB	IG	W	Red	Other
Decanter, complete	110	500	750								
Goblet	50										100 AM
Handled Nappy, very scarce	200										
Milk Pitcher, scarce	100	350	250								150 CM
Pitcher, 2 sizes	225	650	400								500 SM
Tumbler	30										75 SM
Tumbler, variant	40	100	80								325 AQ
Rose Bowl, very rare	400										
Shakers, pair (old only)	325	525									
Sugar	60	225	100								
Toothpick Holder, rare	125	475									
Wine	65	100	150								200 PB
Vase, rare	100	200	150								75 CM
OCTET (NORTHWOOD)											
Bowl, 8½", scarce	100	135	170					325			
OGDEN FURNITURE (FENTON)											
Bowl, scarce		1350									
Plate, scarce		1000									
Plate, handgrip, scarce		1100									
O'HARA (LOOP)											
Goblet	25										
Pitcher	120										
OHIO STAR (MILLERSBURG)											
Compote, tall, rare	1300										
Cloverleaf Shape Dish, very rare	3000										
Vase, very scarce	3000	2500	2800			25000			5000		
Vase Whimsey (stretched), very rare		12000	14000								
OKLAHOMA (MEXICAN)											
Decanter	850										
Tumbler, rare	500										
OLD DOMINION											
Compote, 5⅜", scarce	40										
OLD FASHION											
Tray w/6 Tumblers, complete	150										
OLD OAKEN BUCKET											
Novelty, complete w/lid	200										
OLYMPIC (MILLERSBURG)											
Compote, small, very rare		4800	5300								
OLYMPUS (NORTHWOOD)											
Bowl, very rare				12000							
Shade	125										
OMERA (IMPERIAL)											
Bowl, 6"	25										25 CM
Bowl, 8"	35										30 CM
Bowl, 10"	45								75		40 CM
Celery, handled	40										35 CM
Nappy	35										35 CM
Plate, 8"	50									160	200 AM
Rose Bowl	75										60 CM
(Iron Cross add 25%)											
OMNIBUS											
Pitcher, very rare	700										
Tumbler, rare	200		400	550							
Pitcher Whimsey (no spout)			1200								
ONEATA *AKA: CHIMO (RIVERSIDE)											
Bowl, 9", rare	150										
OPEN EDGE BASKETWEAVE (FENTON)											
Bowl, small, either shape	30	150	150	50					160	325	150 SM
Bowl, large, either shape	75	175	175	70			300	375	190		450 CeB
Bowl, square, scarce	50	160	250	80						600	115 AQ
Bowl, tricorner, very scarce				200							
Hat, J.I.P. shape	25	125	180	40					125	375	225 AQ
Plate, rare	900			1400			1900		625		
Vase Whimsey, rare	800		1200							3000	
OPEN FLOWER (DUGAN)											
Bowl, flat or footed, 7"	35	45	50		85						
OPEN ROSE (IMPERIAL)											
Bowl, flat, 5½"	15	50	25	80							60 AQ
Bowl, flat, 9"	40	125	60	300							225 SM
Bowl, fruit, 10" – 12"	50	425	150							2200	200 SM
Plate, 9"	100	1800	525								225 AM
Rose Bowl	65	500	125								155 AM
OPTIC (IMPERIAL)											
Bowl, 6"	25	50									30 SM
Bowl, 9"	35	75									40 SM
Rose Bowl	80										100 SM
OPTIC & BUTTONS (IMPERIAL)											
Bowls, 5" – 8"	30										40 CM
Bowl, handled, 12"	45										50 CM
Cup & Saucer, rare	300										250 CM

Pattern Name	M	A	G	B	PO	AO	IB	IG	W	Red	Other
Goblet	60										90 LV
Plate, 10½"	70										75 CM
Pitcher, small, rare	185										200 CM
Tumbler, 2 shapes	50										40 CM
Rose Bowl	90										75 CM
Salt Cup, rare	200										
OPTIC BLOCK											
Plate	60										
OPTIC FLUTE (IMPERIAL)											
Bowl, 5"	20										35 SM
Bowl, 10"	35										50 SM
Compote	50										60 CM
Plate, 8", rare											200 CM
Spittoon Whimsey, scarce	225										
OPTIC RIB											
Water Pitcher											65 AM
OPTIC VARIANT											
Bowl, 6"		90									
OPTIC 66 (FOSTORIA)											
Goblet	50										
ORANGE PEEL (WESTMORELAND)											
Custard Cup, scarce	25										
Dessert, stemmed, scarce	45	70	80RG								70 TL
Punch Bowl w/base	200	250									250 TL
Punch Cup	10	40									35 TL
ORANGE TREE (FENTON)											
Bowl, footed, 5½"	40		50	45					100		
Bowl, footed, 9" – 11"	100		175	125			7400		200		4000 CeB
Bowl, flat, 8" – 9"	40	250	300	100			3000			2600	1500 IM
Breakfast Set, 2 pieces	150	125	230	200					250		
Butter	325			300					365		
Centerpiece Bowl, footed, 12", rare (from orange bowl)	900	4000	4500	1500							
Compote, regular size, banded	25		75	85							
Compote, small, without band			195								250 AM
Creamer or Spooner	45			65					125		
Creamer Whimsey from Cup									195		
Cruet or Syrup Whimsey from mug, very rare				5000							
Hatpin Holder	350	750	2000	325					700		3000 ICG
Hatpin Holder Whimsey, rare				2600							
Ice Cream/Sherbet – short stemmed	25			35							
Loving Cup, scarce	225	700	400	325	7000	15000			550		
Mug, 2 sizes	35	150	475	65						475	275 TL
Orange Bowl, footed, large	100	1600	1000	225							
Punch Bowl w/base	200		650	325	1000 MO				550		
Punch Cup	20		50	35					50		
Powder Jar w/lid	95	250	500	135		5500		3500	200		450 PB
Plate, 8" – 9½"	325	3000	4000	1100		17000			275		200 CM
Pitcher, 2 designs	300			850							18000 LO
Tumbler	40			75					110		
Rose Bowl (See Fenton's Flowers)											
Spittoon Whimsey, very rare	5500										
Sugar	60			70					125		
Wine, 2 sizes	25		275	30					60	AQ	125 V
Vase Whimsey, very rare				2300							
(Add 10% to bowls & plates, for Stylized Flower center design)											
ORANGE TREE & SCROLL (FENTON)											
Pitcher	475			900							
Tumbler	50			75							
ORANGE TREE ORCHARD (FENTON)											
Pitcher	400			600					425		
Tumbler	35			85					125		
Whimsey, handled, from pitcher, rare	7000										
ORBIT (INDIA)											
Vase, 9"	80			325							
ORCHID											
Pitcher									400		
Tumbler									65		
ORCHID VARIENT											
Pitcher	275										
Tumbler	40										
OREBRO (SWEDEN)											
Epergne, metal base	350										
Bowl, oval	80			185							
Bowl, round	65			125							
OREGON											
See Beaded Loop											

Pattern Name	M	A	G	B	PO	AO	IB	IG	W	Red	Other
ORIENTAL POPPY (NORTHWOOD)											
Pitcher	400	900	1400	4500			3600	4300	1000		16000 SA
Pitcher, ribbed interior, rare	525										
Tumbler	40	90	95	200			175	250	165		
OSTRICH (CRYSTAL)											
Cake Stand, rare	325	450									
Compote, large, rare	265	385									
OVAL & ROUND (IMPERIAL)											
Bowl, small	15	60	40								45 AM
Bowl, large	30	90	65								70 AM
Plate, 10", scarce	75	75	85								400 AM
Rose Bowl	125										
OWL BANK											
One size	50										
OWL BOTTLE											
One shape											65 CL
OXFORD											
Mustard Pot w/lid	75										
PACIFICA (U.S. GLASS)											
Tumbler	400										
PACIFIC COAST MAIL ORDER HOUSE See Grape and Cable (Fenton)											
PADEN CITY #198											
Syrup w/liner, rare	350*										
PAINTED CASTLE											
Shade	65										
PAINTED PANSY											
Fan Vase	50										
PAINTED PEARL											
Bowl											275 IM
PALACE GATES (JAIN)											
Tumbler	125										
PALM BEACH (U.S. GLASS)											
Banana Bowl	100	175									175 HA
Bowl, 5" – 6"	100								95		90 HA
Bowl, 9"	55								120		40 HA
Butter	135								275		150 HA
Creamer or Spooner	75								125		75 HA
Plate, 9", rare	225	275							250		
Pitcher, scarce	325								600		500 HA
Tumbler, scarce	150								140		100 HA
Rose Bowl Whimsey, rare	350										150 LG
Sugar, covered	95										125 LG
Vase Whimsey, rare	785	500							900		
PALM LEAF											
Plate, handgrip, 6"	225										
PANAMA (U.S. GLASS)											
Goblet, rare	150										
Rose Bowl	575										
Spittoon	750										
PANDORA											
Bowl, 5½"	60										
PANELED (AUSTRALIAN)											
Creamer	50	70									
Sugar, open	60	75									
PANELED CANE											
Vase, 8"	250										
PANELED CRUET											
One size	95										
PANELED DAISY & CANE											
Basket, rare	700										
PANELED DANDELION (FENTON)											
Candlelamp Whimsey, rare			3200								
Pitcher	285	400	575	525							
Tumbler	30	50	70	55							
Vase Whimsey, rare				16500							
PANELED DIAMOND & BOWS (FENTON)											
Vase, 5" – 12"	75	125	160	95						700	175 V
PANELED DIAMOND POINT AND FAN											
Bowl, 9¾"	1500										
PANELED FISH PALMS (INDIA)											
Vase, 5½"	150										
PANELED HOLLY (NORTHWOOD)											
Bonbon, footed	60	90	75								
Bowl		75	70								
Creamer or Sugar	65										
Pitcher, very rare		22000									
Spooner	55										
PANELED PALM (U.S. GLASS)											
Mug, rare	100										
Wine, rare	150										

Pattern Name	M	A	G	B	PO	AO	IB	IG	W	Red	Other
PANELED PRISM											
Jam Jar w/lid	55										
PANELED ROSE (IMPERIAL)											
*Exterior only of Open Rose											
PANELED SMOCKING											
Creamer	55										
Sugar	50										
PANELED SWIRL											
Rose Bowl	65										
PANELED THISTLE (HIGBEE)											
Compote, rare	200										
Tumbler, very scarce	100										
PANELED TREE TRUNK (DUGAN)											
Vase, 7" – 12", rare		5250									
PANELED TWIGS											
Tumbler	200										
PANELS & BALL (FENTON) (ALSO CALLED PERSIAN PEARL)											
Bowl, 11", scarce	60								175		
PANELS & BEADS											
Shade											55 VO
PANELS & DRAPERY (RIIHIMAKI)											
Bowl	70										
PANJI PEACOCK EYE (INDIA)											
Vase, 8½"	100										
PANSY (IMPERIAL)											
Bowl, 8¼"	45	165	95	350							240 SM
Creamer or Sugar	25	60	50								125 SM
Dresser Tray	50	175	65								100 AM
Nappy (old only)	20	75	30	1300							85 LV
Pickle Dish, oval	30	80	40	275	425						70 SM
Plate, ruffled, scarce	100	325	200								125 SM
PANTHER (FENTON)											
Bowl, footed, 5"	25	225	350	115						850	350 AQ
Bowl, footed, 10"	225	500	485	400							800 AQ
Whimsey, footed, 5", scarce	200		500	375							200 CM
Whimsey, footed, 10", scarce	400			700							
(Note: Whimsey pieces rest on collar – base, feet are not touching)											
PAPERCHAIN											
Candlesticks, pair	80										
PAPERWEIGHT											
Flower-shaped, rare											200 PM
PAPINI VICTORIA (ARGENTINA)											
Compote	250										
Pitcher	375										
Tumbler	75										
PARADISE SODA (FENTON)											
Plate, advertising, scarce		650									
PARK AVENUE (FEDERAL)											
Pitcher, very scarce	100										
Tumbler, 5 sizes	5 – 20										
PARLOR											
Ashtray				95							
PARLOR PANELS (IMPERIAL)											
Vase, 4" – 14"	110	325	110	900							475 AM
PARQUET											
Creamer	70										
Sugar	80										
PASSION FLOWER											
Vase	125										
PASTEL HAT											
Various shapes & sizes	25+										25+ PB
PASTEL SWAN (DUGAN, FENTON & NORTHWOOD)											
One size, regular shape	185	225	200	200	325		125	65	375		195 TL
Whimsey (head down touching neck), rare											1200 TL
PATRICIA (EUROPEAN)											
Mustard Pot w/lid	120										
PATRICIAN											
Candlesticks, pair	400										
PEACE											
Oil Lamp, 16", very rare		8500									
PEACH (NORTHWOOD)											
Bowl, 5"									50		
Bowl, 9"									150		
Butter									275		
Creamer, Sugar, or Spooner, each	400								150		
Pitcher				1300					950		
Tumbler	2000			150					175		

Pattern Name	M	A	G	B	PO	AO	IB	IG	W	Red	Other
PEACH & PEAR (DUGAN)											
Banana Bowl	90	150		600							
PEACH BLOSSOM											
Bowl, 7½"	60	75									
PEACHES											
Wine Bottle	45										
PEACOCK (MILLERSBURG)											
Banana Bowl, rare		3500									10000 V
Bowl, 5"	250	185	250	2500							
Bowl, square, sauce, rare	1000	1200									
Bowl, 9"	325	475	550								650 CM
Bowl, variant, 6", rare		175									
Bowl, shotgun, 7½", rare	500	500	450								
Bowl, square, 9", rare				2500							
Bowl, tricorner, very rare		4500									
Ice Cream Bowl, 5"	225	300	400								
Ice Cream Bowl, 10", scarce	3300	2400	3000								
Plate, 6", rare	1000	1350									
Proof Whimsey, rare	300	325	350								
Rose Bowl Whimsey, rare		4600									
Spittoon Whimsey, rare	6000	7500									10500 V
PEACOCK & DAHLIA (FENTON)											
Bowl, 7½"	45	300	150	125							160 AQ
Plate, 8½", rare	450			600							
PEACOCK & GRAPE (FENTON)											
Bowl, flat, 8" – 9"	60	175	200	300						1100	175 V
Bowl, footed, 8" – 9"	65	175	150	100						950	325 V
Plate, flat, 9" – 9½"	650	800	2700	1300							275 TL
Plate, footed, 9"	300		425	475							300 LV
Nut Bowl, footed, scarce	55			125							
PEACOCK & URN (FENTON)											
Bowl, 8½"	125	225	300	225					165	6000	1400 PeB
Compote	35	175	200	75					200		550 OG
Goblet, scarce	65	325	350	200					125		
Plate, 9", scarce	750	1800	900	1600					400		
PEACOCK & URN (NORTHWOOD)											
Bowl, small, ruffled	75	100									
Bowl, large, ruffled	375	525	900								
Bowl, Ice Cream, 6"	125	100	675	115		2300	250	400	165		1300 ReB
Bowl, Ice Cream, 10"	550	600	2600	1200		31000	1050	1650	475		23000 SA
Plate, 6", rare	550	800		1300							
Plate, 11", rare	2200	2000						12000	13000		
(Add 25% for stippled)											
PEACOCK & URN & VARIANTS (MILLERSBURG)											
Banana Bowl, rare											11000 V
Bowl, ruffled, 6"	200	250	250								
Bowl, 9½"	350	400	425	2500							
Bowl, Ice Cream, 6", rare	300	150	300	800							
Bowl, Ice Cream, 10", rare	400	800	1200	4000							
Bowl, 3 in 1, 10", rare				5000							
Compote, large, rare	1400	1600	2200								
Plate, 6", very rare	2300										
Plate, 10½", rare	3000										
Mystery Bowl, variant, 8½", rare	400	500	550	1850							
PEACOCK AT THE FOUNTAIN (DUGAN)											
Pitcher				525							
Tumbler		90		50							
PEACOCK AT THE FOUNTAIN (NORTHWOOD)											
Bowl, 5"	45	60	95	75			75	110	100		
Bowl, 9"	150	125	350	300			650	1250	300		
Butter	250	350	600	300			1200		625		
Compote, scarce	650	750	1800	975		3250	1500	1250	400		
Creamer or spooner	135	120	300	200			250	300	150		
Creamer Whimsey, from punch cup, very rare				1200							
Orange Bowl, footed	275	900	3500	1200		12000					8000 SA
Punch Bowl w/base	500	1000		1000		36000	7500	8000			5500 LG
Punch Cup	30	50		60		1800	100	300	75		
Punch Cup Whimsey, rare		2000									
Pitcher	325	500	3500	475			2500		725		
Tumbler	35	55	300	45			145		200		800 PL
Spittoon Whimsey, rare		15000	17000								
Sugar	125	200	400	275			500		225		
PEACOCK GARDEN (NORTHWOOD)											
Vase, 8", very rare	16000										5000 WO
PEACOCK HEAD											
Tumbler, rare	150										

368

Pattern Name	M	A	G	B	PO	AO	IB	IG	W	Red	Other
PEACOCK LAMP											
Carnival Base	800	450	500						500	900	
PEACOCKS (ON FENCE) (NORTHWOOD)											
Bowl, 8¾"	300	500	1300	600		1300	1400	1600	700		3000 EmG
Plate, 9"	500	775	1400	1500			1600	500	425		4500 CM
(Add 25% for stippled pieces)											
(Add 10% for PCE bowls)											
PEACOCK TAIL (FENTON)											
Bonbon, handled, stemmed or flat	60	75	90	65							
Bowl, 5" – 7", various shapes	40	50	60	55	400					2500	
Bowl, 8" – 10", scarce	85	125	135	170							
Chop Plate, 11", rare	2200										
Compote	35	45	60	50					55		
Creamer, rare			375								
Hat	30	40	55	50							
Hat, advertising	50		100								
Plate, 6" – 7"	900	800	900	1000							
Plate, 9"	900			600							
Spittoon Whimsey, very rare				4500							
Sugar, rare		325									
PEACOCK TAIL (MILLERSBURG)											
Bowl, 9", rare			200								
PEACOCK TAIL & DAISY (WESTMORELAND)											
Bowl, rare	1500	1900			2200 BO						
PEACOCK TAIL VARIANT (MILLERSBURG)											
Compote, scarce	70	150	175								
PEACOCK TREE *AKA: MAYURI (INDIA)											
Vase, 6"	80										
PEACOCK VARIANT (MILLERSBURG)											
See Peacock (Millersburg)											
PEARL & JEWELS (FENTON)											
Basket, 4"									200		
PEARL LADY (NORTHWOOD)											
Shade											90 IM
PEARL #37 (NORTHWOOD)											
Shade					100						
PEARLY DOTS (WESTMORELAND)											
Bowl	40	60	70					250			40 TL
Compote	60				150						350 BO
Rose Bowl	40	75	60								300 TL
PEBBLE & FAN (CZECH)											
Vase, 11¼", rare	325			750							700 AM
PEBBLES (FENTON)											
Bowl, sauce	15		30								
Bonbon	25	45	65	50							
PENNY & GENTLES											
Advertising Bowl, 6", rare		3000*									
PENNY MATCH HOLDER (DUGAN)											
Match Holder, rare		1200									
PEOPLE'S VASE (MILLERSBURG)											
Vase, large, either shape, very rare	75,000	65,000	85,000	100,000							
PEPPER PLANT (FENTON)											
Hat shape	40	85	100	60						725	
Advertising, General Furniture, rare		300									125 V
PERFECTION (MILLERSBURG)											
Pitcher, rare	5000	5500	6000								
Tumbler, rare	800	600	400								
PERIWINKLE (NORTHWOOD)											
Pitcher, 2 styles	450										
Tumbler, 2 styles	55										
PERSIAN GARDEN (DUGAN)											
Bowl, Berry, 5"	50	60			80				60		
Bowl, Berry, 10"	235	325	1350		350				200		
Bowl, Ice Cream, 6"	70	125			100				75		
Bowl, Ice Cream, 11"	300	800			450				250		
Fruit Bowl w/base	675	650		4500	500				400		
Plate, 6", scarce	100	700		900	325				350		700 LV
Plate, Chop, 13", scarce		12000			6000				3000		2000 LV
Punch Bowl & Base, rare	1200	1650									
*(Add 25% for Pool of Pearls exterior)											
PERSIAN MEDALLION (FENTON)											
Bonbon	70	110	170	125						650	200 V
Bowl, 5"	40	60	45	50						1000	110 AQ
Bowl, 8½" – 9"	70	155	175	175						2800	1200 AM
Bowl, 9½" footed plain exterior, very rare				2150							
Bowl, 10"	80	275	425	550							

369

Pattern Name	M	A	G	B	PO	AO	IB	IG	W	Red	Other
Bowl, footed, small, w/Grape & Cable exterior, scarce	125										
Bowl, footed, large, w/Grape & Cable exterior, scarce	225	350	600	425				3500			
Compote, small	85	250	425	225					400		
Compote, large	90	375	325	100					225		200 CM
Fruit Bowl	150	300	325	225							
Hair Receiver	70	95		85					125		
Orange Bowl, footed	275	425	325	350							
Plate, 6"	160	300	450	350							235 BA
Plate, 7"	100	400	400	375							300 BA
Plate, 9½"	2000	3000	3500	800					2700		
Plate, 9¼", 2 sides up, very rare	2300*										
Plate, 10¾", chop plate, scarce				350							
Punch Bowl w/base	300	500	625	800							
Punch Cup	25	40	50	50							
Rose Bowl	75	325	300	400					210		
Spittoon Whimsey, very rare			7500								
*Small plates w/Orange Tree exterior, add 25%											
PERUVIAN PISCO INCA BOTTLE											
Figural bottle, scarce											300 AM
PERUVIAN RINGS (ARGENTINA)											
Pitcher											500 TL
Tumbler											85 TL
PETAL & FAN (DUGAN)											
Bowl, 5½" – 6"	40	80			125				95		
Bowl, mold proof, very scarce		125									
Bowl, 8" – 9"	85	250			150				225		
Bowl, 10" – 11"	140	325			250				300		
Plate, ruffled, 6"		550									
PETALED FLOWER											
*(Interior of Leaf & Beads)											
PETALS (DUGAN)											
Banana Bowl		90			100						
Bowl, 8¼"	40	50			80						
PETALS (NORTHWOOD)											
Compote	50	65	150	1100			925				
PETALS & PRISMS (ENGLISH)											
Bowl, 9"	60										
Fruit Bowl, 2 pieces	90										
Open Sugar	65										
Sugar, footed, 5"	70										
PETER RABBIT (FENTON)											
Bowl, 8½", very scarce	1250		2300	2000							
Plate, 9½", rare	4000		6300	6000							2200 AM
PHLOX (NORTHWOOD)											
Pitcher	400										
Tumbler	55										
PICKLE											
Paperweight, 4½"		75									
PIGEON											
Paperweight	200										
PILLAR & DRAPE											
Shade					75 MO				90	625	
PILLAR & SUNBURST (WESTMORELAND)											
Bowl, 7½" – 8"	45	50			100						80 AM
Plate, 8", very rare	500										
PILLAR FLUTE (IMPERIAL)											
Celery Vase	60										85 SM
Compote	50	90									225 BA
Creamer or Sugar	35										40 SM
Pickle Dish	30										35 CM
Rose Bowl	65										80 SM
PINCHED RIB											
Vase	85			180							
PINCHED SWIRL (DUGAN)											
Rose Bowl	100				135						
Spittoon Whimsey	150				200						
Vase	60				80						
PINEAPPLE (ENGLISH)											
Bowl, 4"	40										
Bowl, 7"	60	70		70							
Butter	85										
Compote	50	70		60							
Creamer	75	100									100 AQ
Rose Bowl	250										
Sugar, stemmed or flat	75										
PINEAPPLE & FAN											
Tumble-up Set, 3 pieces	450			600							
Wine Set, complete, 8 pieces	575										

Pattern Name	M	A	G	B	PO	AO	IB	IG	W	Red	Other
PINEAPPLE CROWN											
Oval Bowl, 8"	60										
PINE CONE (FENTON)											
Bowl, 6"	45	80	150	65					265		200 SA
Bowl, ICS, 6½", scarce	75	100	185	85							
Plate, 6¼"	135	325	375	250							
Plate, 6¼", 12 sided, smooth edge				350							
Plate, 7½"	450	550		375							1000 AM
PINNACLE (JAIN)											
Tumbler	125										
Vase	100			500							
PIN-UPS (AUSTRALIAN)											
Bowl, 4" – 6", rare	95	175									
Bowl, 7" – 8¼", rare	200	450									
PINWHEEL (ENGLISH)											
Bowl, 6", scarce	75										
Rose Bowl, 5½", rare	250										
PINWHEEL/DERBY (ENGLISH)											
Bowl, 8", rare	125										
Vase, 6½", rare	350	450									
Vase, 8", rare	200	375		450							
PIPE CANDY CONTAINER											
One shape									200		
PIPE HOLDER ASHTRAY											
Ashtray	225										
PIPE HUMIDOR (MILLERSBURG)											
Tobacco Jar w/lid, very rare	15000	14000	12000								
PIPE MATCH HOLDER											
One shape	100										
PLAID (FENTON)											
Bowl, 8¾"	200	350	425	350						2300	425 LV
Plate, 9", rare	400	900		575						8000	
PLAIN & FANCY (HEISEY)											
Pitcher, very scarce	450										
Tumbler, very scarce	125										
PLAIN COIN DOT (FENTON)											
Rose Bowl	65										
PLAIN JANE											
Paperweight	90										
PLAIN JANE (IMPERIAL)											
Basket	30	125						200			65 SM
Bowl, 4"	15	50	35								25 SM
Bowl, 4", smooth edge	25										55 PB
Bowl, 8" – 9"	40	70	45								65 SM
Bowl, 10" – 12"	60	100	70								100 SM
Rose Bowl, small	45										75 SM
PLAIN PETALS (NORTHWOOD)											
Nappy, scarce		85	90								
(Interior of Leaf & Beads nappy)											
PLAIN PILSNER											
Stemmed Glass, 6"	25										
PLAIN RAYS											
Bowl, 9"	40	45	50	65							
Compote	45	55	60	70							
PLEATS											
Bowl	55										
Rose Bowl	95										
PLEATS & HEARTS											
Shade											90 PM
PLUME PANELS (FENTON)											
Vase, 7" – 12"	30	100	225	165						1300	500 V
Vase, JIP, rare										1400	
PLUME PANELS & BOWS											
Tumbler, scarce	150										
PLUMS & CHERRIES (NORTHWOOD)											
Spooner, rare				1800							
Sugar, rare				1800							
Tumbler, very rare	2500			4000							
PLUTEC (McKEE)											
Vase	200										
POINSETTIA (IMPERIAL)											
Milk Pitcher	95	2500	500								300 SM
POINSETTIA (NORTHWOOD)											
Bowl, 8½" – 9½"	300	325	8000	450		11000	1500		8500		500 SM
POLO											
Ashtray	85										
POMONE (CRISTALERIAS PICCARDO)											
Candy Dish, covered											250 AM
POMPEIAN (DUGAN)											
Hyacinth Vase	70				175				250		
Vase Whimsey, pinched 3 sides	110	225			300						

371

Pattern Name	M	A	G	B	PO	AO	IB	IG	W	Red	Other
POND LILY (FENTON)											
Bonbon	55	125	125	60					150		600 PeB
PONY (DUGAN)											
Bowl, 8½"	90	250						1100			1400 AQ
Plate (age questionable), 9", rare	450	700									
POODLE											
Powder Jar w/lid	20										
POOL OF PEARLS											
(Exterior only)											
POPPY (MILLERSBURG)											
Compote, scarce	575	725	750								
Salver, rare	2000	1700	1600								
POPPY (NORTHWOOD)											
Pickle Dish, oval	125	250	325	350		2000	600		325		700 AQ
Tray, oval, rare		325		450							
POPPY & FISH NET (IMPERIAL)											
Vase, 6", rare										750	
POPPY SCROLL (NORTHWOOD)											
Bowl, 11", rare	1800						3600				
(AKA Oriental Poppy)											
POPPY SCROLL VARIANT (NORTHWOOD)											
Compote, 7½"											150 V
POPPY SHOW (NORTHWOOD)											
Bowl, 8½"	425	550	2200	2200		20000	1400	1200	400		1000 LG
Plate, 9", scarce	850	1400	3500	3600		26000	1650	2200	575		
POPPY SHOW VASE (IMPERIAL)											
Hurricane Whimsey		2500							2500		
Lamp Whimsey	1400	1400									
Vase, 12", old only	700	3500	1100								1300 SM
POPPY WREATH											
(Amaryllis Exterior)											
POPPY VARIANT (NORTHWOOD)											
Bowl, 7" – 8"	40	60	70	175	350	595					85 ALS
POPPY VARIANT BASE											
Bowl, 7" – 8", very scarce	60	75	95								
PORTLAND (U.S. GLASS)											
Bowl, 5"	95										
Bowl, 8"	170										
Toothpick Holder	140										
Wine	165										
PORTLAND ELKS BELL (FENTON)											
See Elks (Fenton)											
PORTLY (FENTON)											
Candlesticks, pair									85		
POST LANTERN											
Shade											95 AM
POTPOURRI (MILLERSBURG)											
Milk Pitcher, rare	2500	4500									
POWDER HORN (CAMBRIDGE)											
Candy Holder	200										
PRAYER RUG (FENTON)											
Bonbon, scarce											1500 IC
Creamer, very rare											3300 IC
Plate, 7", very rare											7000 IC
PREMIUM (IMPERIAL)											
Candlesticks, pair	45	175								425	175 SM
PREMIUM SWIRL (IMPERIAL)											
Candlesticks, pair	50										200 SM
PRESCUT (McKEE)											
Vase											150 CM
PRESSED HEXAGON (McKEE)											
Covered Butter	150										
Creamer, Sugar, or Spooner, each	85										
PRETTY PANELS (FENTON)											
Pitcher w/lid									500		
Tumbler, handled	60							90			
PRETTY PANELS (NORTHWOOD)											
Pitcher	125		150								
Tumbler	60		70								
PRIMROSE (MILLERSBURG)											
Bowl, ruffled, 8¾"	100	225	200	4500							175 CM
Bowl, ICS, scarce	135	250	225								
Bowl, Goofus exterior, rare		900									
PRIMROSE & FISHNET (IMPERIAL)											
Vase, 6", rare										750	
PRIMROSE & RIBBON											
Lightshade	90										
PRIMROSE PANELS (IMPERIAL)											
Shade	60										
PRINCELY PLUMES											
Caster, 3¼"		475									

Pattern Name	M	A	G	B	PO	AO	IB	IG	W	Red	Other
PRINCESS (U.S. GLASS)											
Lamp, complete, rare		950									
PRINCESS FEATHER (WESTMORELAND)											
Compote	85										
PRINCETON (CZECH)											
Vase, 10½", rare	750										
PRISCILLA											
Spooner	75										
PRISM											
Shakers, pair	60										
Tray, 3"	50										
PRISM & CANE (ENGLISH)											
Bowl, 5", rare	45	65									
PRISM & DAISY BAND (IMPERIAL)											
Bowl, 5"	15										
Bowl, 8"	25										
Compote	35										
Creamer or Sugar, each	30										
Vase	25										
PRISM & FAN (DAVISON)											
Basket, handled	150										
PRISM & PLEATS											
Bowl, 8½"	45										
Rose Bowl	70										
PRISM & STAR											
Shot Glass, 2¼"	75										
PRISM BAND (FENTON)											
Pitcher	200			300				450			
Tumbler	30			45				100			
PRISM COLUMNS											
Bowl, Low, 7¾"	55										
Rose Bowl	75										
PRISM PANELS											
Bowl, 8"–9"	60										
PRISMS (WESTMORELAND)											
Compote, 5", scarce	50	90	100								150 TL
Nappy, one handle, rare			375								
PRISM WITH BLOCK (WESTMORELAND)											
Creamer	95										
PRIYA (INDIA)											
Tumbler	135										
PROPELLER (IMPERIAL)											
Bowl, 9½", rare	175										
Compote	50		85								80 SM
Vase, stemmed, rare	90										
PROUD PUSS (CAMBRIDGE)											
Bottle	85										
PROVENCE											
*AKA BARS & CROSS BOX											
Pitcher, rare	800										
Tumbler	150										
PULLED LOOP (DUGAN)											
Vase, squat, 5"–7"	80	175			300				385		750 CeB
Vase, 8"–16"	40	75	300	175	250						950 CeB
PUMP, HOBNAIL (NORTHWOOD)											
One shape (age questionable)			850								
PUPPY											
Mini Candy Holder	100										
PURITAN (McKEE)											
Bowl, 4", rare				250							
Plate, 6", rare	150										
PUZZLE (DUGAN)											
Bonbon or Compote	40	85	150	130	85				125		165 LV
PUZZLE PIECE											
One shape				100							
QUARTER BLOCK											
Butter	125										
Creamer or Sugar, each	60										
QUATREFOIL BAND											
Shot Glass, enameled	45										
QUEEN'S JEWEL											
Goblet	55										
QUEEN'S LAMP											
Lamp, complete, rare			3000								
QUESTION MARKS (DUGAN)											
Bonbon	25	40		225	50			300	60		80 LV
Cake Plate, stemmed, rare	155	250							200		
Compote	40	70			125				75		70 BA
(Add 50% for Exterior pattern)											

Pattern Name	M	A	G	B	PO	AO	IB	IG	W	Red	Other
QUILL (DUGAN)											
Pitcher, rare	900	2000									
Tumbler, rare	200	250									
QUINCY JEWELRY (FENTON)											
Hat, scarce			225								
QUILTED DIAMOND (IMPERIAL)											
Exterior pattern to some Imperial											
Pansy pieces are priced under Pansy											
QUILTED ROSE											
Bowl	150										
QUORN MUG											
Mug w/lettering	100										
RABBIT BANK											
Small	90										
Large	100										
RADIANCE											
Bowl, 5"	25										
Bowl, 8"	85										
Butter	150										
Compote, open	150										
Compote, covered	175										
Creamer or Spooner	100										
Jelly Compote	125										
Mustard Jar, covered	175										
Goblet	125										
Shakers, each	55										
Sugar	125										
Syrup	325										
Toothpick Holder	85										
Pitcher	225										
Tumbler	70										
RAGGED ROBIN (FENTON)											
Bowl, 8¾", scarce	85	150	150	125							
RAINBOW (McKEE)											
Whiskey Glass, scarce	125										
RAINBOW (NORTHWOOD)											
Bowl, 8"	45	65	75								125 LV
Compote	45	65	80								
Plate, 9", scarce		100	150								
Plate, handgrip, 9", scarce		150	175								
RAINBOW OPAQUE (NORTHWOOD)											
Bowls, various											30 – 75 OB
RAINDROPS (DUGAN)											
Banana Bowl, 9¾"		185			250						
Bowl, 9"	65	150			200						
Nut Bowl Whimsey					275						
RAMBLER ROSE (DUGAN)											
Pitcher	160	250		400							
Tumbler	30	50		65							
RANDY											
Vase, 13"			600								
RANGER (ENGLISH)											
Toothpick Holder	100										
Vase, 10"	65										
RANGER (EUROPEAN)											
Tumbler	100										
RANGER (IMPERIAL)											
Bowl, round, 4½" – 8"	25										
Bowl, flared, 6¼" – 10"	40										60 CM
Breakfast Set, 2 pieces	90										
Cracker Jar	80										
Nappy	45										
Pitcher	450										
Tumbler	150										
Sherbet, footed	55										
Vase, 8"	95										145 CM
RANGER (MEXICAN)											
Butter	150										
Creamer	40										
Decanter w/stopper, scarce	225										
Milk Pitcher	150										
Perfume, 5¼"	150										
Shot Glass, rare	450										
Sugar	75										
RASPBERRY (NORTHWOOD)											
Gravy Boat, footed	85	135	200	300							400 TL
Milk Pitcher	175	275	325				2200	2400	1000		3550 LG
Pitcher	200	325	400	10000			1250	5000	850		
Tumbler	75	60	100	950			250	375			85 HO
RATH'S RINGS											
Cracker Jar	125										

Pattern Name	M	A	G	B	PO	AO	IB	IG	W	Red	Other
RAYS (DUGAN)											
Bowl, 5"	40	50	50		70						
Bowl, 9"	55	90	90		125						
Plate, 6¼", very scarce		190									
RAYS & RIBBONS (MILLERSBURG)											
Banana Bowl, rare		1400	1250								
Bowl, round or ruffled, 8½" – 9½"	175	225	225	3600							
Bowl, tricornered	210	275	325								
Bowl, square, scarce	325	600	600								
Chop Plate, rare (1 known, weak iridescence)		1000									14000 V
Rose Bowl, rare	900										
RED PANELS (IMPERIAL)											
Shade										225	
REGAL (NORTHWOOD)											
Bowl, sauce, 4½", rare					250						
REGAL											
Jardinere	275										
REGAL CANE											
Cordial	200										
Decanter w/stopper	600										
Goblet	200										
Pitcher	650										
Tray	300										
Tumbler, very rare	1500										
REGAL FLOWER (DUGAN/DIAMOND)											
Vase, decorated, 14", rare	350										
REGAL IRIS (CONSOLIDATED)											
Gone with the Wind Lamp, rare	2500									12000	
REGAL ROSE (IMPERIAL)											
Vase, rare		300									
REGAL SWIRL											
Candlestick, each	75										
REINDEER (GERMANY)											
Tumbler	300										
REKORD (EDA)											
Bowl, scarce			225								
Vase, rare			425								
REX											
Buttermilk Pitcher	75										
Pitcher	50										
Tumbler	10										
REX (EDA)											
Vase	275			550							475 MMG
RIB & FLUTE											
Vase, 12¼", very scarce	125										
RIB & PANEL											
Spittoon Whimsey	200										
Vase	125	300		300	400						
RIBBED BAND & SCALES											
Pitcher	200										
Tumbler	65										
RIBBED BEADED SPEARS (JAIN)											
Tumbler	100										
RIBBED ELLIPSE (HIGBEE)											
Mug, rare											150 HA
Tumbler	250										
RIBBED PANELS											
Mustard Pot	350										
Shot Glass	225										
Toothpick Holder	300										
RIBBED SWIRL											
Pitcher	125		225								
Tumbler	60		80								
RIBBED TORNADO (NORTHWOOD)											
See Tornado (Northwood)											
RIBBON & BLOCK											
Lamp, compote	600										
RIBBON & FERN											
Atomizer, 7"	90										
RIBBONS & LEAVES (ENGLISH)											
Sugar, open	55										
RIBBON SWIRL											
Cake Stand, very scarce											425 AM
RIBBON TIE (FENTON)											
Bowl, 8¼"	110	275	300	145						5600	
Plate, 9½", low ruffled		250		325						7500	
RIBS (SMALL BASKET) (CZECHOSLOVAKIA)											
Bud Vase	60										
Perfume	110										

Pattern Name	M	A	G	B	PO	AO	IB	IG	W	Red	Other
Pinbox	75										
Puff Box	95										
Ringtree	60										
Soap Dish	60										
Tumbler	85										
RIIHIMAKI											
Tumbler				225							
RIIHIMAKI STAR											
Ashtray, very scarce	150			275							
RINDSKÖPF											
Vase, 5¾"	150										
RINGS (HOCKING)											
Vase, 8"	25										
RIPPLE (IMPERIAL)											
Vase, squat, 4" – 7"	150	175	100								150 SM
Vase, standard, 7" – 12"	40	145	110	600					200	1500	145 TL
Vase, mid-size, 12" – 15"	200	275	200								265 SM
Vase, funeral, 15" – 21"	175	450	400								500 TL
RISING COMET (AKA COMET)											
Vase, 6" – 10"	150 – 400										
RISING SUN (U.S. GLASS)											
Bowl, small sauce	35										
Butter Dish	400										
Creamer	75										
Juice Tumbler, rare	150										
Pitcher, 2 shapes, very scarce	325			1400							
Pitcher, squat, rare	600										
Tumbler, scarce	135			350							
Sugar	95										
Tray, rare	300			500							
RIVER GLASS		300									
Bowl, 8" – 9"	65										
Celery Vase	85										
RIVERSIDE'S FLORENTINE											
Bowl, small	20										
Bowl, large	55										
ROARING TWENTIES (CAMBRIDGE)											
Powder Jar	180										
ROBIN (IMPERIAL)											
Mug, old only	60										150 SM
Pitcher, old only, scarce	150										650 SM
Tumbler, old only, scarce	35										75 SM
ROCK CRYSTAL (McKEE)											
Punch Bowl w/base, rare		800									
Punch Cup, rare		75									
ROCOCO (IMPERIAL)											
Bowl, 5", footed	40										225 LV
Bowl, 9", footed, rare	175										
Vase, 5½"	125										200 SM
ROLL											
Cordial Set, complete (Decanter, Stopper & 6 Glasses)	350										
Pitcher, rare											300 CL
Tumbler, scarce	40										
Shakers, each, rare	45										
ROLLED BAND (CZECH)											
Pitcher	125										
Tumbler	30										
ROLLED RIBS (NEW MARTINSVILLE)											
Bowl, 8" – 10"											200 MMG
ROLLING RIDGES											
Tumbler	25										
ROLY-POLY											
Jar w/lid	30										
ROMAN ROSETTE (U.S. GLASS)											
Goblet, 6", rare											110 CL
ROOD'S CHOCOLATES (FENTON)											
Plate, advertising		3600									
ROOSTER											
Novelty Ashtray, rare	325										
ROSALIND (MILLERSBURG)											
Bowl, 5", rare	1300	300	550								
Bowl, 10", scarce	200	250	275								600 AQ
Compote (variant), 6", rare		675	575								
Compote ruffled, 8", rare	2500										
Compote, jelly, 9", rare	4000	3800	4000	15000							
Chop Plate, 11", very rare	10000										
Plate, 9", very rare		2400	3000								
ROSE											
Bottle										125	

Pattern Name	M	A	G	B	PO	AO	IB	IG	W	Red	Other
ROSE AND FISHNET											
Vase, very scarce										750	
ROSE ANN											
Shade	40										
ROSE BAND											
Tumbler, rare	700										
ROSE BOUQUET											
Bonbon, rare				900					400		
ROSE COLUMN (MILLERSBURG)											
Vase, rare	5500	5500	3800	10000							6000 TL
Vase, experimental, very rare		21000									
ROSE GARDEN (SWEDEN & GERMAN)											
Bowl, 6", scarce	105	175		140							
Bowl, 8¼"	150	350		225							
Butter, rare	450			600							
Pitcher, rare	1150			1700							
Rose Bowl, small, very scarce	1600										
Rose Bowl, large, very scarce				1600							
Vase, round, rare	500			900							
Vase, small, scarce	800			1500							
Vase, medium, scarce	1100			2000							
Vase, large, scarce	1300			4000							
ROSE IN SWIRL											
Vase	75										
ROSE PANELS											
Compote, large	175										
ROSE PINWHEEL											
Bowl, rare	1600	1900	2000								
ROSE POWDER JAR											
Jar w/lid	100										
ROSES & FRUIT (MILLERSBURG)											
Bonbon, footed, rare	600	800	800	3000							
ROSES & GREEK KEY											
Plate, square, very rare	17000										8000 AM
ROSES & RUFFLES (CONSOLIDATED GLASS)											
Lamp, Gone with the Wind, rare	2900								10000		
ROSE SHOW (NORTHWOOD)											
Bowl, 8¾"	375	650	1600	725		1800	1000	1700			900 AQ
Plate, 9½"	725	1200	2500	950		10000	2000	2900	525		8000 IGO
ROSE SHOW VARIANT (NORTHWOOD)											
Bowl, 8¾"	900			1300							1200 ReB
Plate, 9"	1550			1400							2400 ReB
ROSE SPRAY (FENTON)											
Compote	50						145	145	125		
ROSE SPRIG											
Mini Loving Cup	195										
ROSETIME											
Vase, 7½"	100										
ROSE TREE (FENTON)											
Bowl, 10", very rare	2000			3300							
ROSETTE (NORTHWOOD)											
Bowl, footed, 7" – 9"	60	100	165								
ROSE WINDOWS											
Pitcher, very rare	900										
Tumbler, rare	200										
Tumbler, advertising, very rare	550										
ROUND-UP (DUGAN)											
Bowl, 8¾"	150	400		300	250				195		600 LV
Plate, 9"	250	525		475	600				350		
ROYAL DIAMONDS											
Tumbler, rare	150										
ROYAL GARLAND (JAIN)											
Tumbler	125										
ROYAL PINEAPPLE											
Vase	80										
ROYAL SWANS (SOWERBY)											
Vase, rare	1500	2000									
ROYALTY (IMPERIAL)											
Fruit Bowl w/stand	100										100 SM
Punch Bowl w/base	150										
Punch Cup	35										
RUFFLED RIBS											
Spittoon, either top shape	65	80	70			800					
RUFFLES & RINGS (NORTHWOOD)											
Bowl, 8½", scarce (exterior pattern)	125	150			500						

Pattern Name	M	A	G	B	PO	AO	IB	IG	W	Red	Other
RUFFLES & RINGS WITH DAISY BAND (NORTHWOOD)											
Bowl, footed, 8½", rare					1100 MO						
RUSTIC (FENTON)											
Vase, squat, 6" – 7½" (3"+base)	50	80	85	80							
Vase, standard, 8" – 13" (3"+base)	35	70	65	65	1400				125	3500	1200 LO
Vase, mid-size, 11" – 17" (4"+base)	75	145	135	125					200		
Vase, funeral, 16" – 23" (5"+base)	1900	2000	2300	1800					950		15000 EmG
				2500							
Whimsey, pinched jardiniere, very rare											
Vase, oddity, with penny in base		1000									
Vase Whimsey, spittoon shape, very rare		7500									
Variant Vase *(10% more than above prices of regular vases)											
*Add $1,000 for funeral size with banded (Plunger) base.											
SACIC ASHTRAY (ARGENTINA)											
Ashtray	95										
SACIC BOTTLE (ARGENTINA)											
Soda Bottle, very scarce	75										
SAILBOAT (FENTON)											
Bowl, 6"	40	75	125	70						600	275 V
Compote	65			195							
Goblet	225	400	500	100							190 PB
Plate, 6"	350			850						1000	250 LV
Wine	35			80							350 V
Wine (Variant), scarce	55			125							
SAILING SHIP (BELMONT)											
Plate, 8"	25										
SAINT (ENGLISH)											
Candlesticks, each	300										
SALT CUP (VARIOUS MAKERS)											
One shape, average	50	60	90								85 V
SANSARA (JAIN)											
Tumbler	100										
SAN TELMOS											
Ashtray	75										
SARITA *AKA: ANNA EVE (INDIA)											
Tumbler	125										
SATIN SWIRL											
Atomizer											75 CL
SAVANNA'S LILY											
Single lily on metal stand	275										
SAWTOOTH BAND											
Tumbler, rare	250										
Pitcher	375										
SAWTOOTHED HONEYCOMB (UNION GLASS)											
Pickle Dish, 7½"	85										
SAWTOOTH PRISMS											
Jelly Jar, 3 sizes	60										
SCALE BAND (FENTON)											
Bowl, 6"	25			100					90	325	
Bowl, 8½" – 10", very scarce	100			400							350 V
Plate, flat, 6½"	50									425	
Plate, dome base, 7"	80									600	
Pitcher	150		800	550							350 V
Tumbler	40		225	300							
SCALES (WESTMORELAND)											
Banana Bowl, 6" & 9"					75 – 125						
Bonbon	40	50			100	200 BO					75 TL
Bowl, deep, 5"		40									
Bowl, 7" – 10"					90 IM	225 BO					100 PeB
Plate, 6"	45	65									65 TL
Plate, 9"		100				250 BO					200 MMG
SCARAB PAPERWEIGHT											
Paperweight, large, 6" – 7"		475									
SCEPTER											
Candleholder, pair, scarce	95										125 SM
SCOTCH THISTLE (FENTON)											
Compote	50	80	90	75							
SCOTTIE											
Paperweight, rare	200										
Powder Jar w/lid	20										
SCROLL (WESTMORELAND)											
Pin Tray	75										
SCROLL & FLOWER PANELS (IMPERIAL)											
Vase, 10", old only	600	2350									2000 SM
SCROLL & GRAPE (MILLERSBURG)											
Punch Bowl w/base, very rare (Multi-Fruits and Flowers Exterior)		5000									

Pattern Name	M	A	G	B	PO	AO	IB	IG	W	Red	Other
SCROLL EMBOSSED (IMPERIAL)											
Bowl, 4" – 7"	40	65	185								100 SM
Bowl, 8" – 9"	50	135								1300	425 TL
Bowl Whimsey		175									
Compote, goblet shaped whimsey		400	225								
Compote, miniature	140	375									265 LV
Compote, small	40	115	55	750							150 AM
Compote, large, either exterior	45	125	85								165 AM
Dessert, stemmed	65	110	90								
Nut Bowl, scarce		175									
Plate, 9"	100	375	125								290 LV
(Add 10% for File exterior & 50% for Hobstar and Tassels exterior)											
SCROLL EMBOSSED VARIANT (ENGLISH)											
Ashtray, handled, 5"	45	60									
Plate, 7"	165										
SCROLL FLUTED (IMPERIAL)											
Rose Bowl, very rare	325										
SCROLL PANEL											
Lamp										475	
SEACOAST (MILLERSBURG)											
Pintray, very scarce	1000	800	800								900 CM
SEAFOAM (DUGAN)											
(Exterior only)											
SEAGULLS (CZECH)											
Vase, very rare	1800										2500 V
SEAGULLS (DUGAN)											
Bowl, 6½", scarce	110										
SEAWEED											
Lamp, 2 sizes	250										
Lamp Variant, 8½", rare					400						
SEAWEED (MILLERSBURG)											
Bowl, 5" – 6½", rare	850	1000	2000	2800							
Bowl, 9", scarce	275	525	400	2000							
Bowl, 10½", ruffled or 3 in 1, scarce	400	600	450								1750 AQ
Bowl, 6", ICS, very rare				2000							
Bowl, Ice Cream, 10½", rare	500	1600	1900	5500							
Plate, 10", rare	1800	2500	3350								
SERPENT (JAIN)											
Vase, scarce	400										
SERPENTINE ROSE (ENGLISH)											
Rose Bowl, footed	90										
SERRATED FLUTE											
Vase, 8" – 13", scarce	30	100	75								40 CM
SERRATED RIBS											
Shakers, each	60										
SHALIMAR (JAIN)											
Tumbler	100										
SHANGHI (CHINA)											
Tumbler, 2 kinds	50										
SHARON'S GARDEN											
Bowl					350						
SHARP											
Shot Glass	50										
SHASTA DAISY											
Pitcher	250							425	375		
Tumbler	35							55	40		
SHASTA DAISY W/PRISM BAND											
Tumbler	45							75	65		
SHAZAM (INDIA)											
Pitcher	250										
Tumbler	75										
SHELL											
Shade									75		
SHELL (IMPERIAL)											
Bowl, 7" – 9"	45	150	75								125 SM
Plate, 8½"	375	1000	600								500 SM
SHELL & BALLS											
Perfume, 2½"	65										
SHELL & JEWEL (WESTMORELAND)											
Creamer w/lid	55	65	60						90		
Sugar w/lid	55	65	60						90		
Sugar Whimsey (age ?)			200								
SHELL & SAND (IMPERIAL)											
Bowl, 7" – 9"	125	250	100								225 SM
Plate, 9"	800	1500	275								900 SM
SHERATON (U.S. GLASS)											
Butter											130 PM
Creamer or Spooner											75 PM
Sugar											90 PM

Pattern Name	M	A	G	B	PO	AO	IB	IG	W	Red	Other
Pitcher											170 PM
Tumbler											50 PM
SHIELDED FLOWER											
Tumbler	150										
SHIP & STARS											
Plate, 8"	25										
SHIP'S DECANTER											
Decanter Set, complete	2000										
SHIRLEY'S SUNBURST											
Bowl, 6½", rare	250										
SHOVEL											
Mini Novelty	250										
SHRIKE (AUSTRALIAN)											
Bowl, 5"	165	180									
Bowl, 9½"	350	600									1200 AQ
Whimsey Bowl, square, very rare		750									
SHRINE (U.S. GLASS)											
Champagne											100 CL
SHRINE SHEATH OF WHEAT											
Toothpick, St. Paul, Minnesota											125 CL
SIGNATURE (JEANNETTE)											
Open Candy	35										
Parfait, tall	25										
Sherbet	15										
SIGNET (ENGLISH)											
Sugar w/lid, 6½"	75										
SILVER & GOLD											
Pitcher	150										
Tumbler	50										
SILVER QUEEN (FENTON)											
Pitcher	250										
Tumbler	60										
SIMPLE SIMON (NORTHWOOD)											
Vase	60	75	90								
SIMPLICÉ (ITALY)											
Lidded Jar with wire handles	90										
SIMPLICITY SCROLL (WESTMORELAND)											
Match Holder											375 SM
Toothpick Holder											300 SM
SINGING BIRDS (NORTHWOOD)											
Bowl, 5"	30	35	45	300							
Bowl, 10"	75	275	295	5500							
Butter	185	325	425								
Creamer	75	85	125								
Mug	65	100	200	190		1200	435		600		200 LV
Mug, stippled	150	400	400	525							
Mug Whimsey, w/spout, very rare	750										
Pitcher	350	500	1100								
Tumbler	45	70	90								
Sherbet, rare	400										
Spooner	75	125	150								
Sugar	175	250	300								
SINGLE FLOWER (DUGAN)											
Banana Bowl, 9½", rare					375						
Basket Whimsey, handled, rare	225				350						
Bowl, 8"	35	45	125		140						
Bowl, 9" (Lily of the Valley decoration)					100						
Hat	30	45	65								
SINGLE FLOWER FRAMED (DUGAN)											
Bowl, 5"	40	65			85						
Bowl, 8¾"	65	150	125		130						
Plate		300			250						
SITTING BULLDOG PAPERWEIGHT											
One shape	350										
SIX PANEL FLUTE											
Tumbler	20										
SIX PETALS (DUGAN)											
Bowl, 8½"	40	125	75	125	75				85		400 BA
Hat	45	70	85		100						150 BA
SIX RING											
Tumbler, 3 sizes	30 – 40										
SIX-SIDED (IMPERIAL)											
Candlestick, each	225	750	300								250 SM
SIX-SIDED BLOCK											
Creamer, child's											55 LV
Sugar, child's											95 LV
SKATER'S SHOE (U.S. GLASS)											
One shape	120										
SKI STAR (DUGAN)											
Banana Bowl		175			225						

Pattern Name	M	A	G	B	PO	AO	IB	IG	W	Red	Other
Basket, handled, rare					500						
Bowl, 5"	40	65	75	100	85						
Bowl, 8" – 10"	60	250		250	200						
Plate, 6"					275						
Plate, handgrip, 8" – 10"					295						
Rose Bowl, rare					700						
SLEWED HORSESHOE											
Bowl, 8" – 9"				165							
Punch Cup											75 G. Slag
SLICK WILLIE (HALE BATHS)											
Vase, 13"	125										
SLIM JIM											
Vase, 13"	45										
SMALL BASKET											
One shape	50										
SMALL BLACKBERRY (NORTHWOOD)											
Compote	55	65	75								
SMALL PALMS											
Shade	45										
SMALL RIB											
Compote	40	45	50								60 AM
Rose Bowl, stemmed	50	65	80								75 AM
SMALL RIB & VARIANT (FENTON)											
Card Tray whimsey	40	60									
Compote, 4½"	30	50	50	55							
Compote, 5½"	35	55	55	60							
Spittoon Whimsey, stemmed, rare	100	150	150	170							200 AM
SMALL THUMBPRINT											
Creamer or Sugar	60										
Mug, scarce	100										
Toothpick Holder	70										
SMOOTHIE											
Vase			75								
SMOOTH PANELS (IMPERIAL)											
Bowl, 6½"	30										35 SM
Rose Bowl, scarce	50										75 SM
Sweet Pea Vase, scarce	75								100		60 CM
Vase, squat, 4" – 7"	50									250	300 MMG
Vase, standard, 8" – 14"	40	150	175		200					325	250 MMG
Vase, funeral, 15" – 18"	125									800	350 TL
SMOOTH RAYS (DUGAN)											
Bowl	45	75			100						
SMOOTH RAYS (FENTON)											
Spittoon Whimsey, rare	450										
SMOOTH RAYS (IMPERIAL)											
Bowl, 9" – 10"	25										20 SM
Champagne	40										40 SM
Custard Cup	15										15 SM
Goblet, 2 sizes	30										30 SM
Plate, 8"	35										40 SM
Plate, 12"	50										55 SM
Pitcher	65										75 SM
Rose Bowl	80										
Tumbler	20										25 SM
Wine, 2 sizes	35										40 SM
SMOOTH RAYS (NORTHWOOD)											
Bonbon	35	45	55								60 ALS
Bowl, 6" – 7"	30	40	45	750		1500					
Compote	40	45	55								
SMOOTH RAYS (WESTMORELAND)											
Bowl, flat, 6" – 9"	40	55	50		75	125 BO					75 TL
Bowl, dome base, 5" – 7½"			60		85	125 BO					75 TL
Compote	35	45	55								75 AM
Plate, 7" – 9"	75	100	110								150 AM
Rose Bowl	40	70									85 AM
SNOW FANCY (IMPERIAL)											
Bowl, 5"			60								
Bowl, 8½", very scarce	235										
Creamer or Spooner	50										
SNOWFLAKE (CAMBRIDGE)											
Tankard, very rare	2000										
SODA GOLD (IMPERIAL)											
Bowl, 9"	45										55 SM
Candlestick, 3½", each	55										60 SM
Chop Plate, scarce	125										
Pitcher	200										350 SM
Tumbler	50										200 SM
Shakers, scarce	125										140 SM
SODA GOLD SPEARS (DUGAN)											
Bowl, 4½"	30										30 CL
Bowl, 8½"	40										40 CL
Plate, 9"	75										150 CL

Pattern Name	M	A	G	B	PO	AO	IB	IG	W	Red	Other
SOLDIERS & SAILORS (FENTON)											
Plate (Illinois), scarce	2300	2850		2100							
Bowl (Indiana), very rare				15000							
Plate (Indiana), very rare				30000							
SONGBIRD (JAIN)											
Tumbler, very scarce	125										
SOUTACHE (DUGAN)											
Bowl, 10", scarce					200						
Plate, 10½", rare					350						
Lamp, complete, scarce	350										
SOUTHERN IVY											
Wine, 2 sizes	45										
SOUVENIR BANDED											
Mug	85										
SOUVENIR BELL											
One shape, lettering	180										
SOUVENIR MINIATURE											
One shape, lettering	50										
SOUVENIR MUG (McKEE)											
Any lettering	65										
SOUVENIR PIN TRAY (U.S. GLASS)											
One size (same as Portland pattern)											75 PM
SOUVENIR VASE (U.S. GLASS)											
Vase, 6½", rare	100	135			150	400					
SOWERBY DRAPE											
Vase											225 BA
SOWERBY FLOWER BLOCK (ENGLISH)											
Flower Frog	60										
SOWERBY FROG											
Flower Frog, footed, scarce	125			200							225 BA
SOWERBY SWAN (ENGLISH)											
Swan		350									
SOWERBY WIDE PANEL (SOWERBY)											
Bowl	45	75 BA									
SPANISH GALLEON (FENTON #570 – 5)											
Fan Vase	95										
SPANISH MOSS											
Hatpin Holder, 5½", rare	165										
Hatpin Holder, 8½", rare	235										
SPEARHEAD & RIB (FENTON'S #916)											
Vase, 8" – 15"	70	135	140	95							
SPEARHEAD & RIB VARIANT (FENTON)											
Vase				175							
SPECTOR'S DEPARTMENT STORE											
See Heart and Vine (Fenton)											
SPHINX											
Paperweight, rare											600 AM
SPICE GRATER (INDIA)											
Pitcher	175										
Tumbler	75										
SPICE GRATER VARIANT (INDIA)											
Pitcher	200										
Tumbler	75										
SPICER BEEHIVE (SPICER STUDIOS)											
Honey Pot w/catch plate		95									110 AM
SPIDERWEB (NORTHWOOD)											
Candy Dish, covered											40 SM
SPIDER WEB (NORTHWOOD – DUGAN)											
Vase, 2 shapes	55		75								80 SM
SPIDER WEB & TREEBARK (DUGAN)											
Vase, 6"	65										
SPIKED GRAPE & VINE (JAIN)											
Tumbler	75										
SPIRAL (IMPERIAL)											
Candlesticks, pair	165	185	195								175 SM
SPIRALED DIAMOND POINT											
Vase, 6"	140										
SPIRALEX (DUGAN)											
Vase, 8" – 13"	35	75		150	75				85		
SPIRALS & SPINES (NORTHWOOD)											
Vase, very rare									1750		
SPLIT DIAMOND (ENGLISH)											
Bowl, 8", scarce	40										
Bowl, 5", scarce	25										

Pattern Name	M	A	G	B	PO	AO	IB	IG	W	Red	Other
Butter, very scarce	85										
Compote	55										
Creamer, small	25										
Sugar, open, scarce	30										
SPRING BASKET (IMPERIAL)											
Basket, handled, 5"	50										
SPRINGTIME (NORTHWOOD)											
Bowl, 5"	40	60	80								
Bowl, 9"	80	200	250								
Butter	250	400	475								
Creamer or Spooner	375	350	400								
Sugar	300	400	425								
Pitcher, rare	600	700	1100								
Tumbler, rare	130	145	120								
SPRY MEASURING CUP											
Measuring Cup	125										
SPUN FLOWERS											
Plate, 10", very scarce									75		
SPUN THREADS											
Hat Whimsey	55										
SQUARE DAISY & BUTTON (IMPERIAL)											
Toothpick Holder, rare											125 SM
SQUARE DIAMOND											
Vase, rare	900			750							
SSSS'S											
Vase			125								
S-REPEAT (DUGAN)											
Creamer, small		75									
Creamer Whimsey (from punch cup)		100									
Punch Bowl w/base, rare		4800									
Punch Cup, rare		100									
Sugar, rare (variant, light iridescence)		250									
Toothpick Holder, old only, rare		90									
Tumbler	475	125									
STAG & HOLLY (FENTON)											
Bowl, ball footed, 9" – 13"	185	350	1000	400							1750 SA
Bowl, spatula footed, 8" – 10"	100	175	225	165						1600	275 AQ
Rose Bowl, footed, scarce	225		4600	3400							
Plate, 9", scarce	750	2500	4600	3100							
Plate, 13", scarce	1000										
STAINED RIM (CZECH)											
Berry Bowl, footed, small	20										
Berry Bowl, footed, large	70										
STANDARD											
Vase, 5½"	50										
STAR											
Paperweight, rare	1500										
STAR											
Buttermilk Goblet	25										
Variant w/Draped interior	30										
STAR (ENGLISH)											
Bowl, 8"	50										
STAR & DRAPE (CRYSTAL)											
Pitcher	165										
STAR & FAN CORDIAL SET											
Cordial Set (decanter, 4" stemmed cordials and tray)	625										900 AQ
STAR & FILE (IMPERIAL)											
Bonbon	35										
Bowl, 7" – 9½"	30										40 CM
Bowl, handled	35										
Bowl, square	45										
Celery Vase, handled	50										50 CM
Champagne	35										
Compote	40										35 CM
Cordial	30										
Creamer or Sugar	30										45 CM
Custard Cup	30										
Decanter w/stopper	100										
Goblet	30										
Ice Tea Tumbler	70										
Juice Tumbler	50										
Juice Glass, stemmed, rare	650										
Lemonade Tumbler, rare	800										
Nut Bowl	45										70 CM
Pickle Dish	40										
Plate, 6"	60										
Pitcher	300										
Tumbler, rare	200										300 SM
Rose Bowl	75	175	125								150 AM

Pattern Name	M	A	G	B	PO	AO	IB	IG	W	Red	Other
Sherbet	30										
Spooner	30										
Stemmed Ice Cream	60										50 CM
Wine	65							250			
STAR & HOBS											
(NORTHERN LIGHTS)											
Rose Bowl, 7", rare	300			375							
Rose Bowl, 9", rare	250			350							
STARBURST (FINLAND)											
Creamer	35			55							
Rose Bowl	75			90							
Spittoon	600			900							2000 AM
Tumbler	150			325							
Vases, various shapes and sizes	375			600							500 AM
STARBURST & DIAMONDS											
(FINLAND)											
Vase, 10½", scarce	350										
STARBURST & FILE (SOWERBY)											
Sauce, 4 handles	95										
STARBURST LUSTRE											
(NORTHWOOD)											
Bowl	45	50	60								
Compote	55	65	80								
STARBURST PERFUME											
Perfume w/stopper	150										
STAR CENTER											
Bowl, 8½"	30	40									30 CM
Plate, 9"	60	80									80 CM
STAR CUT											
Decanter	100										
Tumbler	25										
STARDUST (FINLAND)											
Vase, 7¾"	85			145							
STARFISH (DUGAN)											
Bonbon, handled, scarce		200			165				325		
Compote	45	185	75		125						
STARFLOWER											
Pitcher, rare	6000		15000	3500					18000		
STARFLOWER & RIBS (INDIA)											
Pitcher	175										
Tumbler	75										
STARFLOWER & ROLLS (INDIA)											
Pitcher	175										
Tumbler	75										
STARLYTE (IMPERIAL)											
Shade	100										
STAR MEDALLION (IMPERIAL)											
Bowl, 5" – 5½", dome footed	25								50		30 CM
Bowl, 7" – 9"	30										40 SM
Bowl, square, 7"	40										45 SM
Butter	100										
Celery Tray	60										50 CM
Compote	45										
Creamer, Spooner, or Sugar, each	60										
Custard Cup	20										
Goblet	45										60 SM
Handled Celery	80										65 SM
Ice Cream, stemmed, small	35										
Milk Pitcher	80		95								80 SM
Tumbler, 2 sizes	30		50								50 CM
Pickle Dish	40										
Plate, 5"	50										35 CM
Plate, 10"	70										85 CM
Vase, 6"	40										45 CM
STAR OF DAVID (IMPERIAL)											
Bowl, 8¾"	225	250	200							3000	100 SM
Bowl, round, 7½", rare	300										
STAR OF DAVID & BOWS											
(NORTHWOOD)											
Bowl, 8½"	50	175	125								200 AM
STARRED SCROLL											
Hair Receiver	225										
STAR ROSETTE											
Decanter, very scarce	350										
Tumbler, very scarce	150										
STARS & BARS											
Rose Bowl	130										
STARS & BARS (CAMBRIDGE)											
Wine, rare	150										
STARS & STRIPES (OLD GLORY)											
Plate, 7½", rare	150										
STARS OVER INDIA (JAIN)											
Tumbler	100										

384

Pattern Name	M	A	G	B	PO	AO	IB	IG	W	Red	Other
STAR SPRAY (IMPERIAL)											
Bowl, 7"	35										40 SM
Bride's Basket, complete, rare	90										125 SM
Plate, 7½", scarce	75										95 SM
STATES, THE (U.S. GLASS)											
Bowl, 8", rare	175										
Butter, very rare	600										
Nappy, 3 handled, very rare			1200								
Shaker, very rare	500										
STERLING FURNITURE (FENTON)											
Bowl, advertising, rare		1000									
Plate, advertising, rare		1475									
Plate, advertising, handgrip		1800									
STIPPLED ACORNS (JEANNETTE)											
Covered Candy, footed	25	35		55							
STIPPLED CHERRY											
Tumbler	100										
STIPPLED DIAMONDS (MILLERSBURG)											
Card Tray Whimsey, 2 handled, very rare	2500	2400									
Nappy, handled, very rare		2200	2300								2600 V
STIPPLED DIAMOND SWAG (ENGLISH)											
Compote	45		65	60							
STIPPLED ESTATE (ALBANY)											
Vase, 2½" – 5½"			60 – 90	70 – 100							95 – 120 AM
STIPPLED ESTATE (DUGAN)											
Bud Vase	150				200			225			
STIPPLED ESTATE (WESTMORELAND)											
Vase, 3"	125				150						
STIPPLED FLOWER (DUGAN)											
Bowl, 8½" (Add 25% for Lily of the Valley decoration)					85						
STIPPLED MUM (NORTHWOOD)											
Bowl, 9", scarce	65	90	100	200							
STIPPLED PETALS (DUGAN)											
Bowl, 9"		60			80						
Bowl, enameled decoration					175						
Handled Basket		150			170						
STIPPLED RAMBLER ROSE (DUGAN)											
Nut Bowl, footed	75				90						
STIPPLED RAYS (FENTON)											
Bonbon	30	40	50	45						350	
Bowl, 5" – 10"	35	45	55	50						350	115 AM
Bowl, square, ruffled, 8"	50	55	60								
Compote	30	40	45	40							300 CeB
Creamer or Sugar, each	25	75	75	55					75	450	
Plate, 7"	55	125	125	100						600	
Rose Bowl, very scarce	75	160	110								
STIPPLED RAYS (NORTHWOOD)											
Bonbon	35	40	45	90							
Bowl, 8" – 10"	40	55	60	170					125		225 AQ
Bowl, 11", very scarce		100									
Compote	50	60	65								
Rose Bowl, very rare		950									
STIPPLED RAYS BREAKFAST SET											
Creamer, stemmed	30	85	70	50						300	85 SM
Sugar, stemmed	30	85	70	50						300	85 SM
Whimsey Sugar, rare	75	150	130	110						600	225 V
STIPPLED SALT CUP											
One size	45										
STIPPLED STRAWBERRY (U.S. GLASS)											
Pitcher, rare	350										
Sherbet, stemmed	60										
Tumbler	95										
STJARNA (SWEDEN)											
Candy w/Lid	225										
STORK (JENKINS)											
Vase	60								90		
STORK ABC											
Child's Plate, 7½"	75										
STORK & RUSHES DUGAN)											
Basket, handled	125										
Bowl, 5"	30	30									
Bowl, 10"	40	50									
Butter, rare	150	175									
Creamer or Spooner, rare	80	90									
Hat	25	75		30							
Mug	25	175		1000							650 AQ

Pattern Name	M	A	G	B	PO	AO	IB	IG	W	Red	Other
Punch Bowl w/base, rare	200	300		350							
Punch Cup	20	30		35							
Pitcher	250	225		500							
Tumbler	30	60		75							
Sugar, rare	90	120									
STRAWBERRY (DUGAN)											
Epergne, rare		900									
STRAWBERRY (FENTON)											
Bonbon	50	75	90	140						450	375 LO
STRAWBERRY (NORTHWOOD)											
Bowl, 8" – 10" (Stippled add 25%)	145	150	200	325	2750	25,000		2000			450 LG
Plate, handgrip, 7"	175	265	300								
Plate, 9"	250	325	285		4250						500 LV
Plate, stippled, 9"	2100	1050	1100	5000			23000	15500			
STRAWBERRY INTAGLIO (NORTHWOOD)											
Bowl, 5½"	30										
Bowl, 9½"	65										
STRAWBERRY POINT											
Tumbler	150										
STRAWBERRY SCROLL (FENTON)											
Pitcher, rare	3500			3000							
Tumbler, rare	160			135							
STRAWBERRY SPRAY											
Brooch				175							
STRAWBERRY W/ CHECKERBOARD (JENKINS)											
Butter	85										
Creamer or Sugar	35										
Spooner	45										
STRAWBERRY WREATH (MILLERSBURG)											
Banana Boat Whimsey, rare		2000	2000								2600 V
Bowl, 6½" – 7½"	75	150	200								1800 V
Bowl, 6½" – 7½", square			250								
Bowl, 6½" – 7½", very scarce	150	200	250								
Bowl, 8" – 10", scarce	185	275	300								1500 V
Bowl, 9", square	325	400	425								
Bowl, tricornered, 9½"	450	650	750								
Compote, scarce	350	300	400								2100 V
Gravy Boat Whimsey, rare											3000 V
STREAMLINE (CRYSTAL)											
Creamer	60										
Sugar w/lid	80										
STREAM OF HEARTS (FENTON)											
Compote, rare	150										
Goblet, rare	225										
STRETCH											
Punch Bowl & Base										3500	
STRETCHED DIAMOND (NORTHWOOD)											
Tumbler, rare	175										
STRETCHED DIAMONDS & DOTS											
Tumbler	175										
STRING OF BEADS											
One shape	35		40								
STRUTTING PEACOCK (WESTMORELAND)											
Creamer or Sugar w/lid		100	100								
Rose Bowl Whimsey			150								175 BA
STUDS (JEANNETTE) (Depression Era – Holiday Buttons & Bows) (Many shapes & sizes from $5.00 – 145.00)											
STYLE (CRYSTAL)											
Bowl, 8"	100	145									
STYLIZED FLOWER CENTER (FENTON) (Center design on some Orange Tree bowls & plates)											
SUMMER DAYS (DUGAN)											
Vase, 6"	50	90		125							
(Note: This is actually the base for the Stork and Rushes punch set)											
SUNBEAM (McKEE)											
Whiskey, scarce	125										
SUNFLOWER (MILLERSBURG)											
Pin Tray, scarce	800	600	625								
SUNFLOWER (NORTHWOOD)											
Bowl, 8½"	95	175	165	700		13000	1750				800 ReB
Plate, rare	600	1250									
SUNFLOWER & DIAMOND											
Vase, 2 sizes	300			500							

386

Pattern Name	M	A	G	B	PO	AO	IB	IG	W	Red	Other
SUNGOLD											
Epergne											450 AM
SUNGOLD FLORA (BROCKWITZ)											
Bowl, 9", rare	175										
SUNK DAISY *AKA AMERIKA											
Bowl	225	375		275							
Rose Bowl, 3 sizes, rare	350	150		500							
SUNK DIAMOND BAND											
(U.S. GLASS)											
Pitcher, rare	150								250		
Tumbler, rare	50								75		
SUNKEN DAISY (ENGLISH)											
Sugar	30			40							
SUNKEN HOLLYHOCK											
Lamp, "Gone with the Wind," rare	4000									12000	
SUN PUNCH											
Bottle	30								35		
SUNRAY											
Compote		45			60						
SUNRAY (FENTON)											
Compote (Iridized Milk Glass)					110 MO						
SUPERB DRAPE (NORTHWOOD)											
Vase, very rare	2500		3500			5000					
SUPERSTAR (BROCKWITZ)											
Jardiniere				295							
SVEA (AKA SWEDEN)											
Bowls, various	75 – 100			100 – 145							
Plate, 6"				275							
Rose Bowl, small, 5½"	100			175							
Rose Bowl, large, 8"	175	325		300							
Trays, various	45 – 85			60 – 110							
Vase, 9", scarce	110			225							
Vase, 4", rare				350							
SVEA VARIANT											
Vase, various sizes, very scarce				200 – 375							
SWAN (AUSTRALIAN)											
Bowl, 5"	150	170									
Bowl, 9"	225	400									
SWANS & FLOWERS (JAIN)											
Tumbler, rare	175										
SWEETHEART (CAMBRIDGE)											
Cookie Jar w/lid, rare	1550		1100								
Tumbler, rare	650										
SWIRL (IMPERIAL)											
Bowl	40										
Candlestick, each	35										
Mug, rare	90										
Plate	80										
Vase	40										
SWIRL & VARIANTS (NORTHWOOD)											
Pitcher	225		700								
Tumbler	75		125								
Whimsey Pitcher, no handle	300										
SWIRLED GUM TIP VARIANT											
Vase											500 BA
SWIRLED MORNING GLORY											
(IMPERIAL)											
Vase	40	75									90 SM
SWIRLED RIB (NORTHWOOD)											
Pitcher	165										
Tumbler	70	75									
SWIRLED THREADS											
Goblet	95										
SWIRLED THREADS & OPTIC											
Vase, 6"	80										
SWIRL HOBNAIL (MILLERSBURG)											
Rose Bowl, scarce	300	1000									
Spittoon, scarce	500	750	4000								
Vase, 7" – 14", scarce	250	275	700	5800							
SWIRL VARIANT (IMPERIAL)											
Bowl, 7" – 8"	30										
Cake Plate											85 CL
Dessert, stemmed	30										
Epergne			200		50						
Juice Glass	40										
Pitcher, 7½"	100										
Plate, 6" – 8¼"	50		60		65						75 CL
Vase, 6½"	35		45		200				70		
SWORD & CIRCLE											
Tumbler, rare	150									600	
Juice Tumbler, rare	225										
SYDNEY (FOSTORIA)											
Tumbler, rare	700										

Pattern Name	M	A	G	B	PO	AO	IB	IG	W	Red	Other
SYRUP SET											
2 piece set	135										
TAFFETA LUSTRE (FOSTORIA)											
Candlesticks, pair, very scarce		300	350	400							450 AM
Compote, rare											325 BA
Console Bowl, 11", rare		150	150	175							200 AM
(Add 25% for old paper labels attached)											
Perfume w/stopper	100	150									175 LV
TALL HAT											
Various sizes, 4" – 10"	40										50 PK
TARENTUM'S VIRGINIA											
Spooner, rare	250										
TARGET (DUGAN)											
Vase, 5" – 7"	40	250		225	140				150		225 LV
Vase, 8" – 13"	25	175	425	175	65						400 V
TASSELS											
Shade											100 IM
TCHECO (CZECH)											
Vase, 9"		65									
TEN MUMS (FENTON)											
Bowl, footed, 9", scarce	450	650									
Bowl, flat, 8" – 10"	300	275	300	375							
Plate, 10", rare				1900							
Pitcher, rare	500			800					3000		
Tumbler, rare	75			100					300		
TENNESSEE STAR (RIIHIMAKI)											
Vase	425			500							600 AM
Vase Whimsey, small				700							
TEN POINTED STAR (HIGBEE)											
Mug	250										
TEXAS (U.S. GLASS)											
Breakfast Creamer or Sugar, each											75 LV
TEXAS HEADDRESS (WESTMORELAND)											
Punch Cup	45										
TEXAS TUMBLER (BROCKWITZ)											
Giant Tumbler (Vase)	625			500							
THIN & WIDE RIB (NORTHWOOD)											
Vase, ruffled	35	60	60	125			275	300			600 IL
Vase, J.I.P. shape	85	175	175	240							250 TL
THIN RIB (FENTON)											
Candlesticks, pair	80									450	
Vase, 7" – 17"	35	60	60	70						2800	150 AM
THIN RIB (NORTHWOOD)											
(Exterior pattern only)											
THIN RIB & DRAPE											
Vase, 4" – 11"	125	225	200	900							
THISTLE											
Shade	60										
THISTLE (ENGLISH)											
Vase, 6"	105										
THISTLE (FENTON)											
Bowl, 8" – 10"	45	60	70	90							290 AQ
Bowl, advertising (Horlacher)		250	225								
Plate, 9", very scarce	5000	4100	3750								
THISTLE & LOTUS (FENTON)											
Bowl, 7"	55		75	70							
THISTLE & THORN (ENGLISH)											
Bowl, footed, 6"	50										
Creamer or Sugar, each	60										
Nut Bowl	75										
Plate/Low Bowl, footed, 8½"	100										
THISTLE BANANA BOAT (FENTON)											
Banana Boat, footed, scarce	150	325	450	300							
THREAD & CANE (CRYSTAL)											
Compote	90	150									
Salver	110	175									
THREADED BUTTERFLIES (U.S. GLASS)											
Plate, footed, very rare											6500 AQ
THREADED PETALS (SOWERBY)											
Bowl, 6", rare	200										
THREADED SIX PANEL											
Bud Vase, 7¾"	75										
THREADED WIDE PANEL											
Candy w/lid, 2 sizes	75							125		275	
Goblet	50			125				85		165	
THREADED WIDE PANEL VARIANT											
Goblet shape, very scarce				225							
THREADS (CRYSTAL)											
Compote	75	145									
THREE DIAMONDS											
Tumble-up, 3 pieces	175										

Pattern Name	M	A	G	B	PO	AO	IB	IG	W	Red	Other
Vase, 6"–10"	45	50	60	75	75						60 CM
THREE FLOWERS (IMPERIAL)											
Tray, center handled, 12"	60										70 SM
THREE FOOTER (EDA)											
Bowl, footed, 8"	175			300							450 LV
THREE FRUITS (NORTHWOOD)											
Bowl, 9"	100	225	300			1700	1150	1350			1000 LGO
Bowl, 9", stippled	225	325	650	500		1550	3900	2600			5200 SA
Bowl, 8", stippled, proof, very rare											700 IC
Plate, 9"	300	400	400	850		2900	9000	11500			450 LV
Plate, 9", stippled	400	650	2500	800		7000	6000	8500			8000 HO
THREE FRUITS BANDED											
*Photo for illustration only. Prices same as regular Three Fruits pattern.											
THREE FRUITS MEDALLION (NORTHWOOD)											
Bowl, spatula footed or dome base, 8"–9½" *Stippled add 25%	100	150	185	500		1300	900	375	475		55 ICO
THREE FRUITS VARIANT											
Bowl, 8"–9"	100	200	250								
Plate, 12 sided	135	200	200	225							
THREE-IN-ONE (IMPERIAL)											
Banana Bowl Whimsey, scarce	100										
Bowl, 4½"	20	40	30								30 SM
Bowl, 8¾"	30	60	40								75 AM
Plate, 6½"	75										95 SM
Rose Bowl, rare	125										
Toothpick Holder, rare (variant)	75										
Tricornered Whimsey, rare	250										
THREE MONKEYS											
Bottle, rare											90 CL
THREE RIVERS											
Pickle Castor (age?)	225										
THREE ROLL											
Tumble-up, complete	90										
THREE ROW (IMPERIAL)											
Vase, rare	2400	2900									4500 SM
THUMBPRINT & OVAL (IMPERIAL)											
Vase, 5½", rare	400	1700									
THUMBPRINT & SPEARS											
Creamer	50		60								
TIERED PANELS											
Cup, scarce	30										
TIERED THUMBPRINT											
Bowls, 2 sizes	45										
Candlesticks, pair	120										
TIERS											
Bowl, 9"	40										
Tumbler	60										
TIGER LILY (FINLAND)											
Pitcher, rare				950							
Tumbler, rare				450							
TIGER LILY (IMPERIAL)											
Hat, whimsey			500								
Pitcher	140	550	300								400 TL
Tumbler	25	145	50	225							100 OG
TINY BERRY											
Tumbler, 2¼"				45							
TINY BUBBLES											
Vase, 8½"			225								
TINY DAISY (SOWERBY)											
Butter	245										
Creamer											125 V
TINY HAT											
Hat Shape, 1¾"				75							
TINY HOBNAIL											
Lamp	110										
TINY THUMBPRINT											
Creamer, lettered	25										
TOBACCO LEAF (U.S. GLASS)											
Champagne											100 CL
TOKIO (EDA)											
Bowl				225							
Vase, 7½"				350							
TOLTEC (McKEE)											
Butter (ruby iridized), rare		375									
Pitcher, tankard, very rare	2600										
TOMAHAWK (CAMBRIDGE)											
One size, rare				3000							
TOMATO BAND (CZECH)											
Liquor Set, complete	175										
TOP HAT											
Vase, 9½"	35								50		

Pattern Name	M	A	G	B	PO	AO	IB	IG	W	Red	Other
TORCHIERE											
Candlesticks, pair	75										
TORNADO (NORTHWOOD)											
Vase, plain, 2 sizes	400	425	550	1200					1000		550 HO
Vase, ribbed, 2 sizes	450	500		2000			7250		1250		
Vase Whimsey, very scarce											2200 WS
Vase Whimsey Rose bowl, very rare		3500									
Vase, ruffled, very rare		1400									
TORNADO VARIANT (NORTHWOOD)											
Vase, rare	1700										
TOWERS (ENGLISH)											
Hat Vase	65										
TOWN PUMP (NORTHWOOD)											
One shape, rare	2250	900	3500								
TOY PUNCH SET (CAMBRIDGE)											
Bowl only, footed	100										
TRACERY (MILLERSBURG)											
Bonbon, rare		1300	1100								
TRAILING FLOWERS (CRYSTAL)											
Bowl, 7"	175										
TREE BARK (IMPERIAL)											
Bowl, 7½"	15										
Candlesticks, 4½", pair	40										
Candlesticks, 7", pair	55										
Candy Jar w/lid	35										
Console Bowl	35										
Pickle Jar, 7½"	55										
Pitcher, open top	50										100 AM
Pitcher w/lid	75										
Plate, 8"	50										
Sauce Bowl, 4"	15										
Tumbler, 2 sizes	25										
Vase	30										
TREE BARK VARIANT											
Candleholder on stand	75										
Juice	20										
Planter	60										
Pitcher	60										
Tumbler	20										
TREE OF LIFE											
Bowl, 5½"	25										
Basket, handled	25										
Perfumer w/lid	35										
Plate, 7½"	35										
Pitcher	60										
Tumbler	30										
Tumbler, Juice, rare	75										
Rose Bowl, 2 sizes	40										
Vase Whimsey, from pitcher											150 CL
TREE TRUNK (NORTHWOOD)											
Jardinere Whimsey, rare		4000									
Vase, squat, 5" – 8"	60	165	200	800			1000	600			
Vase, standard, 8" – 12"	75	100	125	250		1200	550	400	200		400 SA
Vase, mid-size, 12" – 15"	325	350	325	625		3000	1600	1400	1300		3600 LG
Vase, funeral, 12" – 22"	4000	5000	5500	5000			26000	28500	3000		
Vase, J.I.P., very rare	3500	9500									
(Add 25% for Elephant foot or Plunger base)											
TREFOIL FINE CUT (MILLERSBURG)											
Plate, 11½", very rare	8000										
TREVOR'S TESSELATED ROSE											
Light Fixture	225										
TRIANDS (ENGLISH)											
Butter	65										
Celery Vase	55										
Compote, small scarce	75										
Creamer, Sugar, or Spooner	50										
TRIBAL (INDIA)											
Vase	175										
TRIPLE ALLIANCE (BROCKWITZ)											
Biscuit Jar	200			350							
TRIPLETS (DUGAN)											
Bowl, 6" – 8"	25	30	65	75							125 V
Hat	30	40	70								
TROPICANA											
Vase, rare	1600										
TROUT & FLY (MILLERSBURG)											
Bowl, 8¾" (various shapes)	400	550	700								700 LV
Plate, 9", rare		9000	14000								6000 LV
TRUMPET (DUGAN)											
Candlesticks, each								65			

Pattern Name	M	A	G	B	PO	AO	IB	IG	W	Red	Other
TSUNAMI (EUROPEAN)											
Bowl, 10"	110										
TULIP (MILLERSBURG)											
Compote, 9", rare	1600	1500	1800								
TULIP & CANE (IMPERIAL)											
Bowl	35										
Claret Goblet, rare	175										
Goblet, 8 oz., rare	100										
Jelly Compote, ruffled, 5", rare	150										
Nappy, handled, very rare	200										
Wine, 2 sizes, rare	85										
TULIP & CORD (FINLAND)											
Mug, handled	125										
TULIP PANELS											
Ginger Jar	125										
TULIP SCROLL (MILLERSBURG)											
Vase, 6" – 12", rare	550	750	850								
TUMBLE-UP (FENTON-IMPERIAL)											
Plain, complete	85					375					
Handled, complete, rare	295										320 V
TUSCAN COLUMN											
Vase Whimsey, 3"			125								
TWELVE RINGS											
Candlesticks, each	45										
TWIGS (DUGAN)											
Tall Vase	30	70									
Squat Vase, very scarce	300	1100				2300					
TWIN GOLDEN THISTLE											
Tray, 10½" x 6"	275										
TWINS (IMPERIAL)											
Bowl, 5"	15		30								20 CM
Bowl, 9"	35		50								40 CM
Fruit Bowl w/base	80										
TWIST											
Candlesticks, pair	125										
TWISTED OPTIC (IMPERIAL)											
(Depression Era — many shapes & sizes from $5.00 – 75.00)											
TWISTED RIB (DUGAN)											
Vase, various sizes	35	75		150	75				85		
TWISTER (JAIN)											
Tumbler	100										
TWITCH (BARTLETT-COLLINS)											
Creamer	30										
Cup	30										
Sherbet	45										
TWO FLOWERS (FENTON)											
Bowl, footed, 6" – 7"	25	60	65	55							
Bowl, footed, 8" – 10"	75	325	250	225						5500	1650 SM
Bowl, spatula footed, 8"	90	110	140	110						1800	135 V
Bowl, 8" – 9", flat, rare	150										
Plate, footed, 9"	700		675	650							
Plate, 13", rare	2200									7000	
Rose Bowl, rare	125	150	450	175					375	4500	500 SM
Rose Bowl, giant, rare	250			800							
TWO FORTY NINE											
Candleholders, pair										700	
TWO FRUITS (FENTON)											
Bonbon, flat, either shape, scarce	65	125	200	100					140		300 V
TWO HANDLED SWIRL (IMPERIAL)											
Vase	50										75 SM
TWO ROW (IMPERIAL)											
Vase Rare		1150									
UNIVERSAL HOME BOTTLE											
One Shape	125										
UNPINCHED RIB											
Vase	85										225 AM
UNSHOD											
Pitcher	85										
URN											
Vase, 9"	25										
U.S. #310 (U.S. GLASS)											
Bowl, 10"								75			
Candy w/lid								90			
Cheese Set								90			
Compote								65			
Mayonnaise Set								95			
Plate								60			
Vase								85			
U.S. DIAMOND BLOCK											
Compote, rare	65			90							
Shakers, pair, scarce	80										

Pattern Name	M	A	G	B	PO	AO	IB	IG	W	Red	Other
U.S. GLASS #15021											
Vase, 22"	125										
U.S. REGAL											
Bowl, very scarce	150										
Cup, stemmed, with handle	100										
Sherbet, stemmed, with handle	125										
UTAH LIQUOR (FENTON)											
Bowl, advertising, scarce		850									
Plate, advertising, scarce		1350									
Plate, advertising, handgrip, scarce		1600									
UTILITY											
Lamp, 8", complete	90										
VALENTINE											
Ring Tray	80										
VALENTINE (NORTHWOOD)											
Bowl, 5", scarce	100	225									
Bowl, 10", scarce	400										
VENETIAN											
Bowl, 10½", rare	500										
Butter, rare	950										
Creamer, rare	500										
Sugar, rare	625										
Vase (lamp base), 9¼", rare	1000		1400								
VERA											
Vase	125	325		325							
VICTORIAN (DUGAN)											
Bowl, 10" – 12", rare		350			2500						
Bowl, ICS, rare		1000									
VICTORIAN HAND VASE											
Fancy Vase											275 LV
VICTORIAN TRUMPET VASE											
Vase, various painted designs, rare	700										
VINELAND											
Candlesticks, each						70					
VINEYARD (DUGAN)											
Pitcher	120	350			1300						
Tumbler	20	50							250		
VINEYARD & FISHNET (IMPERIAL)											
Vase, rare										675	
VINEYARD HARVEST (JAIN)											
Tumbler, rare	175										
VINING DAISIES (ARGENTINA)											
Decanter	150										
VINING LEAF & VARIANTS (ENGLISH)											
Rose Bowl, rare	250										
Spittoon, rare	350										
Vase, rare	225		350								
VINING TWIGS (DUGAN)											
Bowl, 7½"	35	45	50								
Hat	40	50							65		
Plate, 7", rare									425		300 LV
VINLOV (SWEDEN)											
Banana Boat	175	325									
VINTAGE (FENTON)											
Bonbon	35	50	70	60							
Bowl, 4½"	20	35	40	40							55 PB
Bowl, 6", tricorner	30	60	80	70							
Bowl, 6½" – 7"	30	40	45	45	475					3900	100 V
Bowl, 8" – 9"	40	45	50	50	3700					2000	750 PeB
Bowl, 10"	45	60	90	110						5000	130 V
Compote	40	50	55	60							
Epergne, one lily, 2 sizes	125	165	145	145							
Fernery, 2 variations	55	100	135	115						550	625 AM
Plate, 6" – 8"	200	300	325	275							
Plate, 9", very scarce	3900	4000	4000								
Punch Bowl w/base (Wreath of Roses exterior)	300	450	500	450							
Punch Cup	25	35	40	35							
Rose Bowl	95			125							
Spittoon Whimsey	6500										
Vase, Whimsey from epergne Base, very rare	1400										
Whimsey Fernery		425									
Whimsey, from Punch Bowl, very rare		1500									
VINTAGE (MILLERSBURG)											
Bowl, 5", rare	800		1100	2500							
Bowl, 9", rare	700	950	825	400							
VINTAGE (NORTHWOOD)											
Bowl, 8" – 9"	60	75	90								100 BA
VINTAGE (U.S. GLASS)											
Wine	40	50									

Pattern Name	M	A	G	B	PO	AO	IB	IG	W	Red	Other
VINTAGE BANDED (DUGAN)											
Mug	20	600									500 SM
Pitcher	325	800									
Tumbler, rare	300										
VIOLET BASKETS											
Basket, either type	40	50		95							
VIRGINIA (BANDED PORTLAND)											
See Banded Portland (U. S. Glass)											
VIRGINIA BLACKBERRY											
(U.S. GLASS)											
Pitcher, small, rare				950							
(Note: Tiny Berry Mini Tumbler											
may match this)											
VOGUE (FOSTORIA)											
Toothpick Holder, scarce	250										
VOLTEC (McKEE)											
Covered Butter		150									
VOTIVE LIGHT (MEXICAN)											
Candle Vase, 4½', rare	450										
WAFFLE											
Open Sugar or Creamer	65										
WAFFLE BLOCK (IMPERIAL)											
Basket, handled, 10"	50										175 TL
Bowl, 7" – 9"	30										
Bowl, 8", square	45										
Bowl, 11½"	55										65 CM
Butter	100										
Creamer	60										
Nappy	40										65 CM
Parfait Glass, stemmed	30										35 CM
Pitcher	125										150 CM
Punch Bowl & Base	110										165 CM
Tumbler, scarce	275										350 CM
Tumbler, variant, rare											500 CM
Plate, 6"	30										40 CM
Plate, 10" – 12", any shape	90										150 CM
Punch Bowl	175										250 TL
Punch Cup	20										35 TL
Rose Bowl	75										
Shakers, pair	75										
Sherbet											35 CM
Spittoon, scarce	75										85 CM
Sugar	60										
Vase, 8" – 11"	40										55 CM
WAFFLE BLOCK & HOBSTAR											
(IMPERIAL)											
Basket, handled	250										265 SM
WAFFLE WEAVE											
Inkwell	95										
WAGON WHEEL											
Candy w/lid, enameled	45										
WAR DANCE (ENGLISH)											
Compote, 5"	120										
WASHBOARD											
Butter	70										
Creamer, 5½"	45										
Punch Cup	15										
Tumbler	85										
WATER LILY (FENTON)											
Bonbon	40										
Bowl, footed, 5"	50		200	115						1100	155 V
Bowl, footed, 10"	90	140	400	225						3500	200 BA
Chop Plate, 11", very rare	4500										
*Add 10% for variant with lily center											
WATER LILY & CATTAILS											
(FENTON)											
Bonbon	60	85		90							
Berry Bowl, small	35	50		50							
Berry Bowl, large	50			180							
Bowl, 6", tricorner	35										
Bowl, 10½", rare			300								
Butter	175										
Creamer or Spooner	75										
Sugar	100										
Pitcher	340			5500							
Tumbler	60										
Spittoon Whimsey, rare	2500										
Vase Whimsey or Jardiniere	275										
WATER LILY & CATTAILS											
(NORTHWOOD)											
Pitcher	400			6000							
Tumbler	75	250		700							
Tumbler, (etched name)				1700							

Pattern Name	M	A	G	B	PO	AO	IB	IG	W	Red	Other
WATER LILY & DRAGONFLY (AUSTRALIAN)											
Float Bowl, 10½", complete	150	185									
WEBBED CLEMATIS											
Lamp											800 BA
Vase, 12½"	250										500 BA
WEEPING CHERRY (DUGAN)											
Bowl, footed	90	130		275							
Bowl, flat	75	110									
WESTERN DAISY											
Bowl, rare			450		325						
WESTERN THISTLE											
Cider Pitcher				350							
Tumbler, rare	340			250							225 AM
Tumbler Whimsey, rare	300										
Vase, rare	325										
WESTERN THISTLE VARIANT											
Berry Bowl, small	35										
Berry Bowl, large	70										
Compote, small	100										
Vase	250										
WESTMORELAND #750 BASKET											
Basket, small	25										
Basket, large	45										
WESTMORELAND #1700											
Lily Vase, 6" – 9"		125–175									
Sugar, open, handled											75 AM
WESTMORELAND #1776											
Compote, tall stemmed		95									
WESTMORELAND COLONIAL LILY VASE											
Vase, 6" (age questionable)		125									
WHEAT (NORTHWOOD)											
Bowl, w/lid, very rare		8000									
Sherbet, very rare		6000									
Sweetmeat w/lid, very rare		8000	9500								
WHEAT SHEAF (CAMBRIDGE)											
Decanter, very rare		4000									
WHEELS (IMPERIAL)											
Bowl, 8" – 9"	50										
Bowl, 5½"	20										30 CM
WHIRLING HOBSTAR											
Cup	40										
Pitcher	200										
Child's Punch Bowl & Base	125										
WHIRLING LEAVES (MILLERSBURG)											
Bowl, 9" – 11", round ruffled or 3 in 1 edge	135	250	250	4750							2600 V
Bowl, square, very scarce	400	500	600								
Bowl, 10", tricornered	385	425	475								3500 V
WHIRLING STAR (IMPERIAL)											
Bowl, 9" – 11"	40										
Compote	55		85								
Punch Bowl w/base	125										400 AQ
Punch Cup	10										25 AQ
WHIRLSAWAY (JAIN)											
Tumbler, 2 sizes, 2 shapes	275										
WHIRLWIND											
Bowl				125							
WHITE ELEPHANT											
Ornament, rare									350		
WHITE OAK											
Tumbler, rare	275										
WICKERWORK (ENGLISH)											
Bowl, w/base, complete	250	400									
WIDE PANEL (FENTON)											
Covered Candy Dish	40	65									100 CeB
Lemonade Glass, handled	30								70		
Vase, 7" – 9"	30	40	50	60						400	
WIDE PANEL (IMPERIAL)											
Bowl, 7" – 10"	40	100								250	125 MMG
Bowl, square, 6", scarce	50										45 CM
Bowl, master, 11" – 12"	65										175 AM
Bowl, console, 13"+, rare										900	
Plate, 6"	25										25 CM
Plate, 8"	50									200	250 SM
Plate, 10" – 11"	75								75	400	75 CM
Rose Bowl, 6½" – 8"									75		
Rose Bowl, giant, scarce	150										175 SM
Underplate, 14" – 15"	85									750	150 SM
Spittoon Whimsey, large, rare	550										

Pattern Name	M	A	G	B	PO	AO	IB	IG	W	Red	Other
Spittoon Whimsey, medium, rare	400										
Spittoon Whimsey, small, rare	250										
WIDE PANEL (NORTHWOOD)											
Bowl, 8" – 9", very scarce	50		75								
Compote (#645)	40										85 V
Console Set (bowl & 2 candlesticks)	75										175 V
Covered Candy Dish	45					100					
Epergne, 4 lily, scarce	900	1300	1250	1900		26000	13500	14000	2800		
WIDE PANEL (U.S. GLASS)											
Salt	50										
WIDE PANEL (WESTMORELAND)											
Bowl, 7½"											60 TL
Bowl, 8¼"											75 TL
WIDE PANEL & DIAMOND											
Vase, 6¼"	150										200 BA
WIDE PANEL BOUQUET											
Basket, 3½"	75										
WIDE PANEL CHERRY											
Pitcher w/lid, rare	1200								195		
WIDE PANEL SHADE											
Lightshade	95		175								
WIDE PANEL VARIANT (NORTHWOOD)											
Pitcher, tankard	200	275	300								
WIDE RIB (DUGAN)											
Vase, squat, 4" – 6"	30	100			65						
Vase, standard, 7" – 12"	25	75		150	50						165 AQ
Spittoon Whimsey from vase, 5½", rare					125						
WIDE RIB (NORTHWOOD)											
Jardinere Whimsey, 4", rare		800	700								
Vase, squat, 5" – 7"	50	60	65	125					120		300 LG
Vase, standard, 8" – 14"	40	50	50	110		1300					425 V
Vase, funeral, 15" – 22"	300	350	375	725							1000 SA
(J.I.P. add 25%)											
WIDE SWIRL											
Milk Pitcher	100*										
WIGWAM (HEISEY)											
Tumbler, rare	150										
WILD BERRY											
Powder Jar w/lid	450										
Powder Jar Variant, w/lid											425 BO
WILD BLACKBERRY (FENTON)											
Bowl, 8½", scarce	100	150	175	300							
Bowl, advertising (Maday), rare		600	1100								
Plate, very rare		8500									
WILD FERN (AUSTRALIAN)											
Compote	200	275									
WILDFLOWER (MILLERSBURG)											
Compote, jelly, rare	1300	1700									
Compote, ruffled, rare	900	1300	1800								
WILDFLOWER (NORTHWOOD)											
Compote (plain interior)	250	300	300	425							
WILD GRAPE											
Bowl, 8¾", very scarce	125										
WILD LOGANBERRY (PHOENIX)											
Cider Pitcher, rare											520 IM
Compote, covered, rare											295 IM
Creamer, rare											150 IM
Goblet					150						
Sugar, rare											100 IM
Wine	145										
(*Also known as Dewberry)											
WILD ROSE											
Syrup, rare	600										
WILD ROSE (NORTHWOOD)											
Bowl, footed, open edge, 6"	75	120	100	300		8000					300 HO
WILD ROSE (MILLERSBURG)											
Lamp, small, rare	1000	1200	1850								
Lamp, medium, rare	1200	1500	2200								
Medallion Lamp, rare	2400	2400	2400								
Lamp, marked "Riverside," very rare			3000								
WILD ROSE SHADE											
Lampshade	95										
WILD ROSE WREATH (MINIATURE INTAGLIO)											
Nut Cup, stemmed, rare	400								550		
WILD STRAWBERRY (NORTHWOOD)											
Bowl, 6", rare	75	150	250				225	275	125		
Bowl, 9" – 10½"	95	125	300				1100	1650	400		1650 LG

Pattern Name	M	A	G	B	PO	AO	IB	IG	W	Red	Other
Plate, 7" – 9", handgrip, scarce	200	225	225								
WILLS'S GOLD FLAKE											
Ashtray	75										
WINDFLOWER (DUGAN)											
Bowl, 8½"	30	75		125							800 V
Nappy, handled	45	95		250	200			200			
Plate, 9"	125	300		325							
Plate, decorated, very rare	425										
WINDMILL (IMPERIAL)											
Bowl, 5"	20	25	25								125 VI
Bowl, 9"	35	175	40								200 V
Bowl, footed, 9"	30	70	55								90 SM
Fruit Bowl, 10½"	40		40								
Milk Pitcher	80	475	140								275 SM
Pitcher	170	350	175								200 PB
Tumbler	50	150	45								175 AM
Pickle Dish	30	200	85								75 CM
Tray, flat	30	250	85								75 CM
WINDMILL & CHECKERBOARD											
Dutch Plate, 8", late	15										
WINDSOR FLOWER ARRANGER (CZECH)											
Flower Arranger, rare	100						125				95 PK
WINE & ROSES (FENTON)											
Cider Pitcher, scarce	450										
Compote, ruffled, rare	150										
Wine Goblet	90			100		600					145 AQ
WINGED HEAVY SHELL											
Vase, 3½"									95		
WINKEN											
Lamp	125										
WINTERLILY (DUGAN)											
Vase, footed, 5½", very rare	850										
WISE OWL											
Bank	30										
WISHBONE											
Flower Arranger	75										90 PK
WISHBONE (NORTHWOOD)											
Bowl, flat, 8" – 10"	150	500	900	1650			925		400		575 EmG
Bowl, footed, 7½" – 9"	150	175	250	1150		5000	1500	1500	400		475 HO
Epergne, rare	350	650	850				3800	5000	1700		3000 LG
Plate, footed, 9", rare	2000	400	1000								
Plate, flat, 10", rare	4000	2500	3500								
Pitcher, rare	800	1100	900								
Tumbler, scarce	100	125	125								2200 PL
WISHBONE & SPADES (DUGAN)											
Bowl, 5"		225			190						
Bowl, 10"		400			325						
Bowl, tricorner or banana shape					375						
Plate, 6", rare		600		2000	300						
Plate, 10½", rare		2000			1800						
WISTERIA (NORTHWOOD)											
Bank Whimsey, rare									3500		
Pitcher, rare							13000		4700		
Tumbler, rare							600	525	450		
Vase Whimsey, very rare			22000								
WITCHES POT											
One shape, souvenir	300										
WOODEN SHOE											
One shape, rare	175										
WOODLANDS VASE											
Vase, 5", rare	235										
WOODPECKER (DUGAN)											
Wall Vase	165										120 V
WOODPECKER & IVY											
Vase, very rare	4500		6000								7500 V
WORLD BANK											
Bank, 4½"	100										
WREATHED BLEEDING HEARTS (DUGAN)											
Vase, 5¼"	125										
WREATHED CHERRY (DUGAN)											
Bowl, oval, 5"	25	40		125	100				60		65 BA
Bowl, oval, 10½" – 12"	90	140		300	400				175		150 BA
Butter	125	275							225		
Creamer or Spooner	65	80							80		
Pitcher	400	550							650		
Tumbler	90	100							100		
Sugar	70	110							110		
Toothpick, old only		175									
WREATHED MEDALLION											
Oil Lamp	150										

Pattern Name	M	A	G	B	PO	AO	IB	IG	W	Red	Other
WREATH OF ROSES (DUGAN)											
Nut Bowl	70										
Rose Bowl Whimsey, scarce	125	150									
Tricorner Whimsey	65	90									
Spittoon Whimsey, very rare	1800										3200 LV
WREATH OF ROSES (FENTON)											
Bonbon	40	100	80	125							
Bonbon, stemmed	40	75	70	100					225		
Compote	45	55	50	50							
Punch Bowl w/base	400	575	700	900	2200						
Punch Bowl w/base, square top, very rare		2300									
Punch Cup	20	30	40	40	320						
WREATH OF ROSES VARIANT											
Compote	55	65	65	60							
ZIG ZAG (FENTON)											
Pitcher, decorated	425			450				600			
Tumbler, decorated	50			80				75			
ZIG ZAG (MILLERSBURG)											
Bowl, 5½" – 6½", ruffled, rare	325										
Bowl, square, 6", very rare	600										
Bowl, tricornered, 6½", very rare	700										
Bowl, round or ruffled, 9½"	125	225	325								
Bowl, 10", ice cream shape	400	550	1200								
Bowl, square, 8½" – 9½"	550	800	950								500 CM
Bowl, tricornered, 10"	500	750	900								
Card Tray, rare			1100								
ZIG ZAG (NORTHWOOD)											
Pitcher, very rare *		5000		800							
Tumbler, very rare *		500									
*Experimental samples											
ZIPPERED HEART (IMPERIAL)											
Bowl, 5"	40	65									
Bowl, 9"	85	110									
Queens Vase, rare	4200	4800	5500								
Rose Bowl, 5", very rare	1200										
Giant Rose Bowl, very rare			5000								
ZIPPER LOOP (IMPERIAL)											
Hand Lamp, 2 types, rare	825										1500 SM
Small Lamp, 7", rare	500										800 SM
Medium Lamp, 8", rare	550	~									600 SM
Large Lamp, 10", rare	450										500 SM
ZIPPER STITCH (CZECH)											
Bowl, 10", oval	125										
Cordial Set (tray, decanter & 4 cordials), complete	1400										
ZIPPER VARIANT											
Bowl, oval, 10"	60										
Sugar w/lid	35										50 LV
ZIP ZIP (ENGLISH)											
Flower Frog holder	60										

more great TITLES from collector books

DOLLS

6315	**American Character Dolls**, Izen	$24.95
7346	**Barbie Doll** Around the World, 1964 – 2007, Augustyniak	$29.95
2079	**Barbie Doll** Fashion, Volume I, Eames	$24.95
6319	**Barbie Doll** Fashion, Volume III, Eames	$29.95
7621	Collectible African American Dolls, Ellis	$29.95
6546	Collector's Ency. of **Barbie** Doll Exclusives & More, 3rd Ed., Augustyniak	$29.95
6920	Collector's Encyclopedia of American **Composition Dolls**, Volume I, Mertz	$29.95
6451	Collector's Encyclopedia of American **Composition Dolls**, Volume II, Mertz	$29.95
6636	Collector's Encyclopedia of **Madame Alexander Dolls**, Crowsey	$24.95
6456	Collector's Guide to **Dolls of the 1960s and 1970s**, Volume II, Sabulis	$24.95
6944	The Complete Guide to **Shirley Temple** Dolls and Collectibles, Bervaldi-Camaratta	$29.95
7028	**Doll Values**, Antique to Modern, 9th Edition, Edward	$14.95
7634	Madame Alexander 2008 Collector's Dolls Price Guide #33, Crowsey	$14.95
6467	**Paper Dolls** of the 1960s, 1970s, and 1980s, Nichols	$24.95
6642	20th Century **Paper Dolls**, Young	$19.95

TOYS

6938	Everett Grist's Big Book of **Marbles**, 3rd Edition	$24.95
7523	**Breyer Animal** Collector's Gde., 5th Ed., Browell/Korber-Weimer/Kesicki	$24.95
7527	Collecting Disneyana, Longest	$29.95
7356	Collector's Guide to Housekeeping Toys, Wright	$16.95
7528	Collector's Toy Yearbook, 100 Years of Great Toys, Longest	$29.95
7355	**Hot Wheels**, The Ultimate Redline Guide Companion, Clark/Wicker	$29.95
7635	**Matchbox Toys**, 1947 to 2007, 5th Edition, Johnson	$24.95
7539	**Schroeder's Collectible Toys**, Antique to Modern Price Guide, 11th Ed.	$19.95
6650	**Toy Car** Collector's Guide, 2nd Edition, Johnson	$24.95

JEWELRY, WATCHES & PURSES

4704	Antique & Collectible **Buttons**, Wisniewski	$19.95
4850	Collectible **Costume Jewelry**, Simonds	$24.95
5675	Collectible **Silver Jewelry**, Rezazadeh	$24.95
6468	Collector's Ency. of Pocket & Pendant **Watches**, 1500 – 1950, Bell	$24.95
6554	**Coro Jewelry**, Brown	$29.95
7529	**Costume Jewelry** 101, 2nd Edition, Carroll	$24.95
7025	**Costume Jewelry** 202, Carroll	$24.95
4940	**Costume Jewelry**, A Practical Handbook & Value Guide, Rezazadeh	$24.95
5812	Fifty Years of Collectible **Fashion Jewelry**, 1925 – 1975, Baker	$24.95
6833	**Handkerchiefs**: A Collector's Guide, Volume II, Guarnaccia/Guggenheim	$24.95
6464	Inside the **Jewelry** Box, Pitman	$24.95
7358	Inside the **Jewelry** Box, Volume 2, Pitman	$24.95
5695	**Ladies' Vintage Accessories**, Johnson	$24.95
1181	100 Years of Collectible **Jewelry**, 1850 – 1950, Baker	$9.95
6645	100 Years of **Purses**, 1880s to 1980s, Aikins	$24.95
7626	Pictorial Guide to Costume Jewelry, Bloom	$29.95
6942	**Rhinestone Jewelry**: Figurals, Animals, and Whimsicals, Brown	$24.95

ARTIFACTS, GUNS, KNIVES, & TOOLS

6039	Signed Beauties of **Costume Jewelry**, Brown	$24.95
6341	Signed Beauties of **Costume Jewelry**, Volume II, Brown	$24.95
7625	20th Century **Costume Jewelry**, 2nd Edition, Aikins	$24.95
5620	Unsigned Beauties of **Costume Jewelry**, Brown	$24.95
1868	Antique **Tools**, Our American Heritage, McNerney	$9.95
6822	**Antler, Bone & Shell** Artifacts, Hothem	$24.95
1426	**Arrowheads & Projectile Points**, Hothem	$7.95
6231	**Indian Artifacts** of the Midwest, Book V, Hothem	$24.95
7037	**Modern Guns**, Identification & Values, 16th Ed., Quertermous	$16.95
7034	**Ornamental Indian Artifacts**, Hothem	$34.95
6567	**Paleo-Indian Artifacts**, Hothem	$29.95
6569	**Remington Knives**, Past & Present, Stewart/Ritchie	$16.95
7366	Standard Guide to **Razors**, 3rd Edition, Stewart/Ritchie	$12.95
7035	Standard **Knife** Collector's Guide, 5th Edition, Ritchie/Stewart	$16.95

PAPER COLLECTIBLES & BOOKS

6623	Collecting **American Paintings**, James	$29.95
7039	Collecting **Playing Cards**, Pickvet	$24.95
6826	Collecting Vintage **Children's Greeting Cards**, McPherson	$24.95
6553	Collector's Guide to **Cookbooks**, Daniels	$24.95
1441	Collector's Guide to **Post Cards**, Wood	$9.95
7622	Encyclopedia of Collectible Children's Books, Jones	$29.95
7636	The Golden Age of Postcards, Early 1900s, Penniston	$24.95
6936	**Leather Bound Books**, Boutiette	$24.95
7036	**Old Magazine Advertisements**, 1890 – 1950, Clear	$24.95
6940	**Old Magazines**, 2nd Edition, Clear	$19.95
3973	**Sheet Music** Reference & Price Guide, 2nd Ed., Pafik/Guiheen	$19.95
6837	Vintage **Postcards** for the Holidays, 2nd Edition, Reed	$24.95

GLASSWARE

7362	American Pattern Glass Table Sets, Florence/Cornelius/Jones	$24.95
6930	Anchor Hocking's **Fire-King** & More, 3rd Ed., Florence	$24.95
7524	Coll. **Glassware from the 40s, 50s & 60s**, 9th Edition, Florence	$19.95
6921	Collector's Encyclopedia of **American Art Glass**, 2nd Edition, Shuman	$29.95
7526	Collector's Encyclopedia of **Depression Glass**, 18th Ed., Florence	$19.95
3905	Collector's Encyclopedia of **Milk Glass**, Newbound	$24.95
7026	Colors in **Cambridge Glass** II, Natl. Cambridge Collectors, Inc.	$29.95
7029	**Elegant Glassware** of the Depression Era, 12th Edition, Florence	$24.95
6334	Encyclopedia of **Paden City Glass**, Domitz	$29.95
3981	Evers' Standard **Cut Glass** Value Guide	$12.95
6126	**Fenton Art Glass**, 1907 – 1939, 2nd Ed., Whitmyer	$29.95
6628	**Fenton Glass** Made for Other Companies, Domitz	$29.95
7030	**Fenton Glass** Made for Other Companies, Volume II, Domitz	$29.95
6462	Florences' **Glass Kitchen Shakers**, 1930 – 1950s	$19.95

5042	Florences' **Glassware Pattern Identification** Guide, Vol. I	$18.95
5615	Florences' **Glassware Pattern Identification** Guide, Vol. II	$19.95
6643	Florences' **Glassware Pattern Identification** Guide, Vol. IV	$19.95
6641	Florences' **Ovenware** from the 1920s to the Present	$24.95
7630	**Fostoria Stemware**, The Crystal for America, 2nd Edition, Long/Seate	$29.95
6226	**Fostoria** Value Guide, Long/Seate	$19.95
6127	The **Glass Candlestick** Book, Volume 1, Akro Agate to Fenton, Felt/Stoer	$24.95
6228	The **Glass Candlestick** Book, Volume 2, Fostoria to Jefferson, Felt/Stoer	$24.95
6461	The **Glass Candlestick** Book, Volume 3, Kanawha to Wright, Felt/Stoer	$29.95
6648	Glass **Toothpick Holders**, 2nd Edition, Bredehoft/Sanford	$29.95
5827	**Kitchen Glassware** of the Depression Years, 6th Edition, Florence	$24.95
7534	**Lancaster Glass** Company, 1908–1937, Zastowney	$29.95
7359	**L.E. Smith Glass** Company, Felt	$29.95
6133	**Mt. Washington Art Glass**, Sisk	$49.95
7027	Pocket Guide to **Depression Glass** & More, 15th Edition, Florence	$12.95
7623	Standard Encyclopedia of **Carnival Glass**, 11th Ed., Carwile	$29.95
7624	Standard **Carnival Glass** Price Guide, 16th Ed., Carwile	$9.95
6566	Standard Encyclopedia of **Opalescent Glass**, 5th Ed., Edwards/Carwile	$29.95
7364	Standard Encyclopedia of **Pressed Glass**, 5th Ed., Edwards/Carwile	$29.95
6476	**Westmoreland Glass**, The Popular Years, 1940–1985, Kovar	$29.95

POTTERY

6922	**American Art Pottery**, 2nd Edition, Sigafoose	$24.95
6326	Collectible **Cups & Saucers**, Book III, Harran	$24.95
6331	Collecting **Head Vases**, Barron	$24.95
6943	Collecting **Royal Copley**, Devine	$19.95
6621	Collector's Encyclopedia of **American Dinnerware**, 2nd Ed., Cunningham	$29.95
5034	Collector's Encyclopedia of **California Pottery**, 2nd Ed., Chipman	$24.95
6629	Collector's Encyclopedia of **Fiesta**, 10th Ed., Huxford	$24.95
1276	Collector's Encyclopedia of **Hull Pottery**, Roberts	$19.95
5609	Collector's Encyclopedia of **Limoges Porcelain**, 3rd Ed., Gaston	$29.95
6637	Collector's Encyclopedia of **Made in Japan Ceramics**, First Ed., White	$24.95
5841	Collector's Encyclopedia of **Roseville Pottery**, Vol. 1, Huxford/Nickel	$24.95
5842	Collector's Encyclopedia of **Roseville Pottery**, Vol. 2, Huxford/Nickel.	$24.95
6646	Collector's Ency. of **Stangl Artware, Lamps, and Birds**, 2nd Ed., Runge	$29.95
6634	Collector's Ultimate Ency. of **Hull Pottery**, Volume 1, Roberts	$29.95
6829	The Complete Guide to **Corning Ware & Visions Cookware**, Coroneos	$19.95
7530	Decorative **Plates**, Harran	$29.95
7638	Encyclopedia of Universal Potteries, Chorey	$29.95
7628	English China Patterns & Pieces, Gaston	$29.95
5918	Florences' Big Book of **Salt & Pepper Shakers**	$24.95
6320	Gaston's **Blue Willow**, 3rd Edition	$19.95
6630	Gaston's **Flow Blue China**, The Comprehensive Guide	$29.95
7021	Hansons' American **Art Pottery** Collection	$29.95
7032	**Head Vases**, 2nd Edition, Cole	$24.95
2379	Lehner's Ency. of **U.S. Marks** on Pottery, Porcelain & China	$24.95
4722	**McCoy Pottery** Collector's Reference & Value Guide, Hanson/Nissen	$19.95

5913	**McCoy Pottery**, Volume III, Hanson/Nissen	$24.95
6835	**Meissen** Porcelain, Harran	$29.95
7536	The Official **Precious Moments**® Collector's Guide to **Figurines**, 3rd Ed., Bomm	$19.95
6335	Pictorial Guide to **Pottery & Porcelain Marks**, Lage	$29.95
1440	**Red Wing Stoneware**, DePasquale/Peck/Peterson	$9.95
6838	**R.S. Prussia** & More, McCaslin	$29.95
7637	**RumRill Pottery**, The Ohio Years, 1938–1942, Fisher	$29.95
6945	**TV Lamps** to Light the World, Shuman	$29.95
7043	**Uhl Pottery**, 2nd Edition, Feldmeyer/Holtzman	$16.95
6828	The Ultimate Collector's Encyclopedia of **Cookie Jars**, Roerig	$29.95
6640	Van Patten's ABC's of Collecting **Nippon Porcelain**	$29.95

OTHER COLLECTIBLES

7627	Antique and Collectible Dictionary, Reed	$24.95
6446	Antique & Contemporary **Advertising Memorabilia**, 2nd Edition, Summers	$29.95
6935	Antique **Golf Collectibles**, Georgiady	$29.95
1880	Antique **Iron**, McNerney	$9.95
7024	B.J. Summers' Guide to **Coca-Cola**, 6th Edition	$29.95
1128	**Bottle** Pricing Guide, 3rd Ed., Cleveland	$7.95
7532	Bud Hastin's **Avon** Collector's Encyclopedia, 18th Edition	$29.95
6924	Captain John's **Fishing Tackle** Price Guide, 2nd Edition, Kolbeck	$24.95
6342	Collectible **Soda Pop** Memorabilia, Summers	$24.95
6625	Collector's Encyclopedia of **Bookends**, Kuritzky/De Costa	$29.95
7365	Collector's Guide to Antique **Radios**, 7th Edition, Slusser/Radio Daze	$24.95
7023	The Complete Guide to Vintage **Children's Records**, Muldavin	$24.95
6928	Early **American Furniture**, Obbard	$19.95
7042	The Ency. of Early American & Antique **Sewing Machines**, 3rd Ed., Bays	$29.95
7031	**Fishing Lure** Collectibles, An Ency. of the Early Years, Murphy/Edmisten	$29.95
7629	**Flea Market Trader**, 17th Edition	$15.95
6458	**Fountain Pens**, Past & Present, 2nd Edition, Erano	$24.95
7631	**Garage Sale** & Flea Market Annual, 16th Edition	$19.95
3906	**Heywood-Wakefield** Modern Furniture, Rouland	$18.95
7033	Hot **Kitchen & Home** Collectibles of the 30s, 40s, and 50s, Zweig	$24.95
7038	The Marketplace Guide to **Oak Furniture**, 2nd Edition, Blundell	$29.95
6939	Modern Collectible **Tins**, 2nd Edition, McPherson	$24.95
6564	Modern **Fishing Lure** Collectibles, Volume 3, Lewis	$24.95
6832	Modern **Fishing Lure** Collectibles, Volume 4, Lewis	$24.95
7349	Modern **Fishing Lure** Collectibles, Volume 5, Lewis	$29.95
6322	Pictorial Guide to **Christmas Ornaments** & Collectibles, Johnson	$29.95
6842	Raycrafts' **Americana** Price Guide & DVD	$19.95
6923	Raycrafts' **Auction Field Guide**, Volume One, Price Guide & DVD	$19.95
7538	**Schroeder's Antiques** Price Guide, 26th Edition	$17.95
6038	**Sewing Tools** & Trinkets, Volume 2, Thompson	$24.95
5007	**Silverplated Flatware**, Revised 4th Edition, Hagan	$18.95
7367	**Star Wars** Super Collector's Wish Book, 4th Edition, Carlton	$29.95
7537	Summers' Pocket Guide to **Coca-Cola**, 6th Edition	$14.95
6841	**Vintage Fabrics**, Gridley/Kiplinger/McClure	$19.95

This is only a partial listing of the books on antiques that are available from Collector Books. All books are well illustrated and contain current values. Most of these books are available from your local bookseller, antique dealer, or public library. If you are unable to locate certain titles in your area, you may order by mail from COLLECTOR BOOKS, P.O. Box 3009, Paducah, KY 42002-3009. Customers with Visa, MasterCard, or Discover may place orders by fax, by phone, or online. Add $5.00 postage for the first book ordered and 60¢ for each additional book. Include item number, title, and price when ordering. Allow 14 to 21 days for delivery.

News for Collectors   Request a Catalog   Meet the Authors   Find Newest Releases   Calendar of Events   Special Sale Items

www.collectorbooks.com